COMMODORE
THE FINAL YEARS

Brian Bagnall
Variant Press

Variant Press
112-1000 Wilkes Avenue
Winnipeg, Manitoba
R3P 2S3

Edited by Nick Lines

Designed by Hayden Sundmark

Manufactured in Canada

Commodore is a trademark of Polabe Holding N.V.
Commodore Microcomputers and Commodore Magazine are copyrights
of Cloanto Corporation
Neither Polabe Holding N.V. nor Cloanto Corporation sponsor,
authorize, or endorse this book.

Library and Archives Canada Cataloguing in Publication

Title: Commodore : the final years / Brian Bagnall.
Other titles: Commodore (2019) | Final years
Names: Bagnall, Brian, 1972- author.
Description: Includes bibliographical references and index.
Identifiers: Canadiana 20190056320 | ISBN 9780994031037 (hardcover)
Subjects: LCSH: Commodore computers—History. | LCSH: Commodore Interna-
tional—History.
Classification: LCC QA76.8.C63 B34 2019 | DDC 004.165—dc23

Acknowledgments

It's been a long journey to tell the story of Commodore and it could not have been done without the help of some incredible people. I'd first like to thank the Kickstarter backers for supporting this endeavor. Your generosity and enthusiasm has fueled this project from the start.

Thank you to Christian Bartsch of *The Software Preservation Society* and Christian Euler for making available the incredible materials that gave this book some much needed accuracy. They supplied the next best thing to a time machine. Thanks also to Archive.org for allowing access to their massive collection of computer magazines.

Thanks to all the former Commodore employees who trusted me enough to sit down and record their history: Ron Nicholson, Bob Welland, Hedley Davis, Jeff Porter, Ed Hepler, Glenn Keller, David Pleasance, Colin Proudfoot, Guy Wright, Eric Cotton, Andy Finkel, Jeff Bruette, David Baraff, Greg Berlin, Bryce Nesbitt, Don Reisinger, Mike Sinz, Gerard Bucas, Joe Augenbraun, Eric Lavitsky, Don Gilbreath, Brian Dougherty, Carl Sassenrath, RJ Mical, Dale Luck, Dave Haynie, Paul Lassa, Bil Herd, and Thomas Rattigan.

And those who recorded their history in photographs: Bill Koester, Bob Welland, Dale Luck, David Pleasance, Eric Cotton, Gerard Bucas, Dave Haynie, John Schilling, Steve Tibbett, Terry Ryan, and Sandy Fisher.

A big thank you to the editor of this book, Nick Lines. Nick has made this book more "literary" than it would have otherwise and it took a lot of cutting, shuffling, and correcting to get it this far. Thanks for sticking with it despite having a tough year in 2018.

And special thanks to to the reviewers who took the time to comb through every page of this book looking for errors. All of you have a unique skill of being able to find needles in haystacks that everyone else overlooked. Jared Brookes (the "Comma King"), Dave Farquhar, Jarno Mielikainen, Zed Beeblebrox, Nate Lawson, Balazs Szaszak, Christopher Chapman, and Benjamin Nice. Your suggestions have made this book better than ever.

Table of Contents

Introduction

"Obituaries customarily focus on the deceased's accomplishments, not the unpleasant details of the demise. That's especially true when the demise hints strongly of self-neglect tantamount to suicide, and nobody can find a note that offers some final explanation. There will be no such note from Commodore, and it would take a book to explain why this once-great computer company lies cold on its deathbed. But Commodore deserves a eulogy, because its role as an industry pioneer has been largely forgotten or ignored by revisionist historians who claim that everything started with Apple or IBM."

"But Commodore's high point was the Amiga 1000 (1985). The Amiga was so far ahead of its time that almost nobody—including Commodore's marketing department—could fully articulate what it was all about. Today, it's obvious the Amiga was the first multimedia computer, but in those days it was derided as a game machine because few people grasped the importance of advanced graphics, sound, and video. Nine years later, vendors are still struggling to make systems that work like 1985 Amigas."

"Even more amazing was the Amiga's operating system, which was designed by Carl Sassenrath. From the outset, it had preemptive multitasking, messaging, scripting, a GUI, and multitasking command-line consoles. Today's Windows and Mac users are still waiting for some of those features. On top of that, it ran on a $1200 machine with only 256 KB of RAM."

"We may never see another breakthrough computer like the Amiga. I value my software investment as much as anyone, but I realize it comes at a price. Technology that breaks clean with the past is increasingly rare, and rogue companies like Commodore that thrived in the frontier days just don't seem to fit anymore."

– Tom Halfhill, Byte Magazine, August 1994 (condensed)

CHAPTER 1

Amiga 500 to the Rescue 1987

Prolog

Commodore had industry-wide success after it released the low-cost C64 in 1982, but after that, it flailed around looking for a new product to continue its legacy. The company eventually landed on the Amiga computer and attempted to evolve into a high-end computer company similar to Apple.

In 1985, the company hired a new CEO and president, Thomas Rattigan, who attempted to steer the company back to its retail roots. He settled on developing the Amiga 500 at the low-end and the Amiga 2000 at the high-end.

Rattigan received his baptism into Commodore during a phase in which it had little money, and he was forced to be frugal, much as his predecessor, Jack Tramiel, had been. He also witnessed the failed Amiga 1000 launch, giving him a unique education. And then, just prior to the launch of the A500 and A2000, chairman Irving Gould terminated Rattigan's contract with the company.

As would be shown, Thomas Rattigan was the high water mark for company leadership. The succession of presidents that came and went after Rattigan became steadily worse. Each time Gould reshuffled the deck, he dealt himself diminishing cards with which to play his hand. "It had one real chance to go further after that, with Tom Rattigan at the helm, but unfortunately the company wasn't big enough for him and the Chairman, Irving Gould. After that, it was downhill," observes marketing director Paul Higginbottom.[1]

---

[1] Personal interview conducted by Rick Melick March 18, 1997.

After Rattigan's departure and closing down the original Amiga company in Los Gatos, the first task for the year was to introduce the Amiga 500 computer to the public. If everything went well, the A500 could push the company into a golden era.

Easter Egg

In early 1987, the Amiga software team was nearing completion of AmigaOS 1.2. The new system, which would be released along with the A500 and A2000 computers, was a much more complete operating system compared to the previous two releases. But it also contained a nefarious message.

Director of software RJ Mical recalls, "In the end, we were feeling that we had done this beautiful work of art, and then Commodore, for their lack of experience or their lack of knowledge about the computer industry, let us down."

When working on Workbench 1.2, an Amiga engineer inserted a message expressing his feelings towards Commodore. "This happened when I was director of the whole effort," explains Mical. "One day, one of the guys showed me with great delight what they had put in there. It was this thing where you had to press a certain number of keys on the keyboard and it would bring up this message that said, 'We made the Amiga, they fucked it up.' I saw that and I made a sort of nervous chuckle."

Mical knew the parting shot at Commodore could not remain. "I said, 'This is cute but we can't really put this in the machine. That's just not acceptable.' They said, 'Aw, come on!' I said, 'No way, man. We're just not putting this in the machine. You've got to take it out.'"

Mical double-checked before signing off on the code. "The final release of the OS was done, and with great fear I did the keystrokes to make sure that it wasn't there," he recalls. "When you put in that keystroke, a line of text came up, but it said, 'The Amiga, born a champion.'"

Unknown to Mical, the offending text remained. "They didn't take it out," he says. "All they did was bury it one level deeper and encrypt it." Now it remained to be seen if anyone would discover the secret.

With the Amiga team's impending departure, Commodore engineers now had to take responsibility for further AmigaOS development. This was difficult but not futile because the programmers had already developed parts of the AmigaOS; generally low-level support modules such as printer drivers. The team included former VIC Commandos Andy Finkel and Eric Cotton, as well as programmers Benny Prudin and Judy Braddock. They had learned C-language and the AmigaOS library.

A formal transition period began in January 1987 to hand over development to Commodore, and the transition completed when Amiga, Inc. closed its doors on March 31, 1987. Andy Finkel had learned the most in that time and was put in charge of the group. "Once I had gone out to California and worked with the Amiga guys, I sort of got sucked into the Amiga culture and thought like they did," he says.

Despite his mixed feelings, RJ Mical felt he was leaving the Amiga legacy in good hands. "There were a number of Commodore engineers that were brilliant people who were a real treat to work with," he says. "Not all of them were brilliant; some of them were real clunkers but you could say that about the original Amiga guys. There were a whole bunch of them, but Andy Finkel and Dave Haynie were guys that really stood out as the heroes."

Soon after the old team departed, Finkel and his team began work on the new version of the Amiga software, AmigaOS 1.3. The software transition did not go as smoothly as hoped, and Finkel soon realized Commodore needed to pull in key Amiga developers from the original software team.

In May, a few months after the Los Gatos closing, Commodore reopened an office at 16795 Lark Avenue, a five minute walk north of the old Amiga premises. The building rented out to at least eight different companies. Here, in suite 106, Bart Whitebook and Dale Luck, along with his garbage bag full of popcorn, continued developing AmigaOS. Caryn Mical (née Havis), now married to RJ Mical and on maternity leave, would also consult for Commodore on third party software development.

GRR

Commodore pinned all its hopes on the success of the A500 in 1987. The hands-on engineer of this cost-reduced marvel was George Robbins, better known as Grr. "George used his initials when he signed things and so we called him Grr (growling noise) a lot," recalls his coworker Bil Herd.

Born in 1954 in the town of Wilmington, Delaware, Robbins grew up with a brother and three sisters. He had a natural affinity for technology from an early age, reading through electronics catalogs in the second grade. He was also obsessed with trains and restored a railway handcar in the family garage to working condition.

As a teenager in the early 1970s Robbins frequently hung out with other kids his age at a drop-in center named Brown House in Claymont, Delaware, helping to setup and run the electronics inside. He also worked at a non-profit music venue called the Side Door Coffee House. Robbins graduated a year after everyone else his age because he was forced to repeat the second grade. He also did not quite graduate from Concord High School because he missed a partial credit by failing gym class.

After high school, Robbins attempted to attend the University of Delaware. He and his best friend Ray Leonard moved into a dorm room on campus together, but then Robbins found out his university application was rejected because of the missing gym credit. However, he was more interested in using computers than attending classes, and he clandestinely lived in Leonard's dorm room just so he could sneak into the data center after hours. This lasted several months until, during Thanksgiving when all the students were gone, campus security finally nabbed him.

These youthful experiences left Robbins with a skepticism of authority. It also left him with a lifelong appreciation of computer games following his early exposure to mainframe classics like *Colossal Cave Adventure* and *Zork*. From there he worked a variety of jobs, including inventory manager aboard an oil tanker and computer administration jobs before he ended up at Commodore as a consultant.

"George Robbins was one of the best engineers of all the systems engineers there," says his coworker Hedley Davis. "He had a lot of depth and a lot of knowledge. He was totally out of control in terms of being a brilliant engineer."

Robbins was unique, even among the unusual band of Commodore engineers. "George was a nonconformist in many ways," recalls Bob Welland. "He lived in a decommissioned railway station and drove a truck without registration. He's kind of a libertarian and so he didn't have tags and I don't think he had insurance."

The railway station was an apt home for the man who had once loved trains as a boy. Sitting next to the railway tracks just south of Lincoln University, the station used to see throngs of students disembark each semester. Located at the corner of Elkdale Road and Walnut Street in lower Oxford Township, it was a 30 mile drive from the West Chester headquarters.

The proximity of Robbins' home to the university was no accident. At the time, universities were among the only institutions connected to the Internet and Robbins wanted in badly. He hatched a plan to sneak onto the campus, much as he had earlier in his life at the University of Delaware. In the evening, he wandered a short distance down the road onto campus where he could use the university computers to connect to the Internet and access his favorite newsgroups.

Robbins also attended computer shows such as the Trenton Computer Festival in New Jersey, a one hour drive from Commodore's headquarters. There, he met Eric Lavitsky, who ran the Jersey Amiga User Group (JAUG). "George would come up to the Trenton Computer Festival which I frequented," says Lavitsky. "Our user group would always have a table."

Robbins attended the festival for the notable keynote speakers, such as Adam Osborne, Gary Kildall, and Bill Gates. But it also hosted a flea market filled with equipment that, even in 1986, was considered obsolete. "People would go out and have these big swap tables out in the parking lot," recalls Lavitsky. "People would bring mini-computers and disk packs and teletypes and any possible piece of hardware junk that you could name. You could sell them or barter for them or whatever."

Robbins soon began a collection of old mainframe servers which he hooked up and operated out of his spacious railroad station. In effect, he was collecting retro computers in the days before eBay and long before it became a popular hobby. "George was just the penultimate geek," says Lavitsky. "He was a real old-school hacker, a great guy."

Speeding to and from work every day in his green van without proper vehicle registration was bound to attract the notice of the law. "They pulled him over once and told him he had to get tags and insurance," says Welland. Robbins ignored the warning and continued driving, only to run afoul of the police again. This resulted in him losing his licence and a more severe warning. "They pulled him over again and said next time we pull you over, you're going to jail."

Robbins was in a dilemma, wanting to avoid incarceration while maintaining his libertarian principles. Most people would probably register the vehicle at this point, but Robbins was determined not to compromise. "George's solution was to ride his bike to work," says Welland. "This seems like a reasonable solution until you know that George lived 33 miles from work. George was also not in the greatest of shape and rather overweight at the time. So he started riding his bicycle."

The daily 66 mile rides soon sapped him of his energy. "It became kind of impractical for him to ride his bike to work and then ride home," says Welland. "So, his solution was to ride to work and sleep at work for a few days and then ride home."

Robbins parked his old run-down green van behind Commodore's FCC radio emissions testing shed, where he would sometimes sleep at night. There he would curl up with a sci-fi book from staples such as Robert A. Heinlein, Orson Scott Card, and Frank Herbert, to less known fare from C. J. Cherryh, Poul William Anderson, and Alfred Bester.

These overnight stays soon benefited Commodore because Robbins put in long hours on different projects, and after hours spent even more time administering the VAX computers.

A500 Production

The eccentric George Robbins seemed like an odd fit for someone who would create a neatly designed motherboard. "There are a thousand details associated with a printed circuit board, like EMI protection and what bypass capacitors you should have, how you should lay out the board," explains Bob Welland. "He owned all the issues around the peripherals that were hanging off the side, access to them, the side bus, memory expansion. George was one of the most meticulous designers I have ever met; which was the opposite of George in life, who was a rather messy, complicated, and very easy to get along with fellow."

Once George Robbins completed his final motherboard design, he added the words, "B52/Rock Lobster" onto the PCB surface as an homage to the music that fueled the development team. This was partly inspired by the B52 nickname given to it by the senior management. "The younger engineers took that and ran with that name to give PCBs a code name like Rock Lobster. So it worked for both generations," says his manager Jeff Porter.

By March 1987 George Robbins, Jeff Porter and Gerard Bucas (VP of engineering) were ready to take the Amiga 500 to production. The Amiga 1000 had been expensively manufactured in a Sanyo VCR factory, but now it was time to switch back to manufacturing the A500 at Commodore's Braunschweig and Hong Kong facilities.

Most of the chips within the A500 would be manufactured by Commodore's secret weapon, Commodore Semiconductor Group (CSG), known internally by its historical name, MOS Technology. Other companies attempting to analyze Commodore's profit margins wildly overestimated the costs due to CSG's efficiency. "Apple did not make chips and really did not have a good handle on chip economics," says Bob Welland. "As such, they thought that the margins on the A500 were very thin. They had estimated that the A500 chipset would cost something like $140 [to manufacture] when the true cost was closer to $20."[2]

CSG was able to produce Agnus, Denise, and Paula for $5.49, $5.19, and $7.91 respectively. Curiously, Gerard Bucas did not trust CSG to produce

---

2   Welland observed this firsthand when he later worked at Apple.

the Gary chip on time. "MOS Technology, I would say, eventually became a millstone around Commodore's neck," he says. "Jeff Porter and I, but especially me, decided, 'Listen, I'm not going to do the gate array with them. I don't believe they can meet the timeline and I don't believe they can make it in volume at the right price.'"

This was not politically popular at Commodore, but Bucas felt it was the correct move. "We designed it, but the manufacturing of that, we actually outsourced to someone else," he says. "We outsourced the chip to VLSI Technology, which was a third-party chip company."

It was up to Bucas to negotiate with suppliers and make sure Commodore received the best prices. A few years ago, the 68000 sold for $15 in quantity. Now Bucas negotiated it down to $5 per unit. "I was personally responsible for every component that was more than fifty cents," he says. "Jeff Porter's nickname for me was 'the Dutch trader'. It was fun. At Commodore, we had a cost structure which was second to none in the sense that we got the best pricing from everybody. We were obviously, at that stage, a key player with Japanese manufacturers and suppliers. People that made floppy drives were all in Japan: Mitsumi and Panasonic and a number of others."

Given the time constraints and pressure of producing a new system, mistakes were bound to occur. One error came from the Hitachi-manufactured masked ROM chips that contained the Kickstart code. "We needed to send them a master to make the masks from," says Bob Welland. "The master came in the form of a bunch of 512K EPROMs that we programmed from a master file. I'll blame Jeff Porter and myself for the following, subtle error. We programmed the EPROMs using a device called a Data I/O programmer."

As a result of their inexperience with the programmer, the pair inadvertently left out the last byte in the ROM. "This turned out to be a rather confusing source of bugs in the final masked ROM," says Welland. It proved to be costly, since the whole batch of chips could not be used.

During the initial pilot production run, Porter set up an assembly line at West Chester to work out the manufacturing process. With stopwatch in hand, he honed the process until Amiga 500s came off the line in rapid succession.

He also carried the process over to the manufacture of PCBs. "One of the things that I did really well with the Amiga 500 board is I figured out the speed of all the equipment in the factory in Hong Kong," he says. "I needed to know how long it's going to take for the machines to stuff the boards with all the components and I made sure that the component mixture was not going to be a bottleneck on the number of machines that they had."

Due to the elimination of bottlenecks, Commodore was able to produce over 2000 "Rock Lobster" motherboards per day. "The guys in the factory in Hong Kong thought the A500 just flew through their production line because it was never a bottleneck," says Porter. "As soon as it was done in that machine, the next machine was ready for it and it was ready to go. It was just incredibly streamlined."

In the end, despite the problems, hundreds of A500s began pouring off the assembly lines in April, followed by thousands in May. "You got a real sense of the machine that was Commodore; its ability to make millions and millions of things and deliver them to places," says Welland. "Amiga was fortunate in the sense that the 'Commodore machine' existed and was able to produce as many of the Amigas as it did."

The results of the West Chester engineers amazed some members of the original Amiga team. "They really knew how to cost-reduce things," says Glenn Keller. "They really knew a lot of stuff that the people in Amiga didn't know, in terms of really getting something into the marketplace. Occasionally, you hear a bunch of disparaging [remarks] about Commodore, but generally, it's not about the engineers."

The Five Finger Trick

In late June 1987, word began spreading of a "Five Finger Trick" with the new AmigaOS Workbench 1.2. "Because they made it harder to get to, it took one of the fans something like two weeks to find it," says RJ Mical. The secret spread to Bulletin Board Systems (BBS), online services, and Usenet.

The programmers had gone to extraordinary lengths to hide their secret message. "You had to do this keystroke where it took eight fingers and both thumbs to press all of the keys that you needed to get the first message to come up that said, 'We made the Amiga,'" explains Mical. "Then, while you had that message up and while you continued to hold all of those keys down, if you could somehow get the floppy disk inserted into the machine (for instance, if you leaned over and shoved it in with your nose) then … the other message would show up."

Word first got back to Commodore a little past midnight the next day as George Robbins was browsing through the Amiga Lounge messages on an online service called BIX (operated by *Byte Magazine*). John Foust of *Amazing Computing* magazine posted the steps to the trick for all to see only half hour earlier. Robbins immediately implored him to remove the post for fear that management could see it and be disinclined to work with the Amiga team ever again. He told Foust, "Please withdraw amiga/lounge 1452 before we lose the option of working with the remaining interested Amiga personnel. Management would not be amused to have this brought to their attention."

Robbins also revealed part of the reason for the Los Gatos closure was due to the persistent, negative attitude shown by the Amiga engineers towards Commodore. "The attitude reflected by the 'We created it, they fucked it up' kind of thinking goes a long way to explain why Amiga no longer exists as a working entity. While there is some truth to this concept, it is only fair to point out that they created it, we paid for it and brought it to market…"

Robbins notified Jeff Porter, and the discovery immediately caused havoc within Commodore. "The machine was already being sold, and it was on the shelves in the UK when this broke," says RJ Mical.

Thankfully, the message did not affect sales of the A500. Commodore UK sold a moderate 40,000 Amiga 500s over the first full year of sales. "In relation to the A500 secret message, I can assure you we never took any stock off shelves or reacted in any adverse way," says UK sales manager David Pleasance. "Even then the Amiga community throughout Europe were a robust lot, and everybody just laughed about it. It was very much seen as quite a trendy thing to know about and tell your mates about. It added to the allure and mystique of Amiga."

Mical was livid at the repercussions of the prank. "The cute joke by one of the engineers hurt us. I know who and I won't tell you his name, but I shake my fist at him even now as I speak."

Some scars have remained for both development teams, even decades later. "What I don't understand is that after we won the race, for lack of a better description of what happened, why the animosity continued," says Bob Welland. "The Amiga 500 was a very successful machine and the people working on the hardware that followed on the A2000; there was a lot of passion there to try to build up the lineup and make a whole range of machines, but I never felt like that was appreciated that much, which makes me a little sad because I think that's a source of some misunderstanding between the groups."

CHAPTER 2

Marketing Miracle 1987

Commodore slowly rolled out the A500 release in mid-1987, but the real marketing and advertising effort towards the system would occur in the latter part of the year. Only then would CEO Irving Gould know if the new product was the smash success his company needed.

COMDEX Atlanta

Both Commodore and Apple had skipped the Fall COMDEX six months earlier. Now they returned for the Spring COMDEX in Atlanta, at the Georgia World Congress Center. This year, the show was pushed back to June 1, 1987, an aggressive move by the organizers to force computer makers to choose between COMDEX and CES Chicago, which was held at the same time.

Curiously, Commodore chose to launch the A500 at COMDEX, even though the new system was clearly a mass-market computer. It was a strange move. How could Commodore sign up large retail stores without attending CES? In contrast, Atari—under Tramiel and his mantra of "computers for the masses, not the classes"—chose CES to launch his Atari ST computers, along with dozens of video games.

Embarrassingly, CES had more vendors showcasing C64 software than any previous year. As the C64 continued to dominate, it appeared as though Commodore forgot to market its own machines.

Commodore UK's David Pleasance recalls the transition away from CES. "In 1984, the first year I went, we had a reasonable sized stand there, but after that we just kind of trailed away," he says. "I think either they didn't want to spend the money or they weren't committed."

Irving Gould hosted a pre-show breakfast for COMDEX attendees, hoping to reassure investors that the recent shakeup in management was a positive change for the company. His stated goal: to bring North American sales up to the level Commodore enjoyed in Europe. According to *Amiga World*, "Gould justified his new, more active role in the company by saying that now when things go wrong, he'll only have to look in the mirror to find the culprit."[1]

Although Commodore did not display the C64 at COMDEX, Gould announced the company had sold over 7 million C64 computers and over one million C128s to date.[2] Most of the games software that year at CES was aimed at the C64, although games for IBM clones were expected to catch up by December, due to the cheap prices and new graphics cards.

Gould also met with over 200 Commodore dealers, promising he would finally do some advertising for the Amiga. He also brought with him Commodore's new general manager of North America, Alfred Duncan, who replaced the recently ousted Nigel Shepherd.

The show marked the official release of the Sidecar, the IBM PC emulator for the Amiga 1000 announced so long ago. Demo versions of the units had been available to Amiga dealers as early as 1986, but the product had entered limbo as engineers worked out the bugs.[3] In December 1986, the hardware finally passed FCC regulations and production began in January 1987.

Unfortunately, the software still had several known bugs. Dealers began selling the units in February using pre-production software, with the promise of a disk upgrade later in the year.

Although Commodore previously announced it would market the Sidecar for "significantly below $1000" it was now put on sale for a suggested retail price of $999. The Sidecar began appearing en masse in retail stores later in June.

In one of its legendary marketing fiascos, the important device appeared just in time for Commodore to phase out the A1000, on which it was dependent. Magazines speculated that, with Commodore moving onto the Amiga 2000, they did not want to sell too many Sidecars. The belated release was primarily meant to avoid false advertising lawsuits.

---

1   *Amiga World*, September/October 1987, p. 10. "Amiga at COMDEX…"

2   *Compute!* magazine, August 1987, page 14. "CES and COMDEX: A Tale Of Two Cities"

3   *Compute!* magazine, March 1987, page 87. "The Sidecar Arrives"

Since the Amiga 500 included an internal disk drive, Commodore could not rely on selling high volumes of external disk drives, as it had done with the C64's 1541 drive. Hence much of the slack was taken up by monitors and printers. Many of these Amiga accessories came from Commodore's "Dutch trader" Gerard Bucas. "In Commodore Japan Limited there were a bunch of people that would go out and buy stuff," says Hedley Davis. "In fact, Jeff Porter coined the term 'the printer of the month club'. Commodore Japan would say, 'Here's your new printer, you're doing these now.' We in engineering had never seen these things before."

A parallel situation existed for monitors too. "With the monitor of the month club, monitors would just show up," says Davis. "Somehow there was this whole portion of the company that would cause all these ancillary support products to suddenly appear."

"Philips, which is a Dutch company, was one of the largest suppliers of computer monitors," says Gerard Bucas. "In fact they had a factory in Taiwan where I went many times. We were the largest customer, so we had a lot of clout from a purchasing point of view."

The new Amiga 500 and 2000 computers generated the most attention at Commodore's COMDEX booth. Thomas Rattigan had previously set the price of the Amiga 500 at $649 and the Amiga 2000 at $1,495. Since then, the prices had jumped to $699 and $1,995. Though this was a long way from the original $500 price target, it was common in the industry to release a product at a higher price while production ramped up. Once demand was satisfied by production the price could come down, much as it had for the C64.

At the same show, Apple displayed the Apple IIGS, which sold for $2500. The comparisons between the Amiga 500 and the IIGS made the Amiga an easy sell. Due to the strength of the product, Commodore would have a hard time mishandling the Amiga marketing effort this time.

US Marketing of A500

After the June 1987 COMDEX show, Commodore released the Amiga 500 to dealers, hoping to repeat the success of the C64. It was up to Irving Gould to carry out the product launch. Jeff Porter, who conceived of the Amiga 500, did not have much confidence in the marketing strategy.

Although the Amiga 1000 marketing was, by all accounts, a resounding failure, Frank Leonardi remained in charge as Commodore's VP of marketing. Leonardi came from Apple and was part of Gould's earlier plan to remake Commodore into a business computer company.

Gould and his executives still wanted to be like Apple, rather than revelling in Commodore's natural strengths. As a result, it seemed like Commodore was abandoning the low-cost home computer market it had once dominated. Alarmingly, important US software developers such as Activision and Electronic Arts were giving up on the Amiga computer by mid-1987, a trend that had to be reversed.

The release of the A500 in the US was a key moment, one that had to be handled correctly if Commodore was to attain the same level of success it previously enjoyed with the C64. "I was probably one of the few engineers that really had a sense of the market timing and things like that," says Porter. "So I'm talking to Frank [Leonardi] about the Amiga 500. And I said, 'Frank, you know we've got to sell this to Sears and Kmart and Toys "R" Us—all the consumer electronics guys that we sold the C64 to. We can make these suckers for $200, sell them for $400, and retail at $500. It's a magic price point. We'll blow their socks off.'"

Leonardi, whose Apple background gave him no experience with mass market retailers, saw things differently. "He basically said, 'Jeff, Jeff, Jeff, Jeff, Jeff, Jeff. No, no, no, no. We're not doing that.'"

Instead, he was going to debut the Amiga 500 the same way he had debuted the Macintosh at Apple. Years earlier, Steve Jobs' vision was to make a computer appliance that could be purchased from a retail store. Leonardi told Porter, "What are we going to do? I had this same conversation with Steve when I was at Apple. He wanted to put the original Macintosh into retail. And we didn't do that and look at where he is today. We put it in the business computer stores and he's done very well. So trust me Jeff, I did okay by Steve, I'll do okay by you."

The explanation did not sound right to Porter. "I said, 'With all due respect, it's a game machine. They're going to buy the Amiga to play the awesome games. You don't go to a computer center to buy a fricking game machine. You go to Toys "R" Us.'"

Rather than marketing it the Commodore way, which had yielded incredible results for customers and investors alike in the past, Leonardi was trying to emulate the competition. "They came from Apple, they know what they're doing," says Porter sarcastically. "They didn't hire a bunch of consumer electronics guys. They hired a bunch of Apple guys that are putting them in the same channel that they're familiar with, next to the Macintosh."

Even though Jeff Porter had engineered the A500 to be a C64 successor, it seemed like Leonardi still viewed the product as a high-end product to be marketed in the same channels as the Macintosh.

Kmart had been a major reason for the success of the Commodore 64. Now, when it needed Kmart more than ever, that relationship was being tested. "They got real ballsy and rejected some of [Kmart's] return policies," says Dave Haynie. "Kmart had the same kind of policy that Walmart has now: 'We can return this item any time we want in any condition and you have to take it back'. Commodore said no. That's when they were going into Sears only and not Kmart."

Would Commodore US have done better if it had emulated the C64 release? Although this is a difficult question to answer definitively, we can look to how other regions marketed the Amiga. Jim Dionne, the General Manager of Commodore Canada, introduced the Amiga 500 in Kmart stores during the latter half of 1987. He even sold the machine into Canadian Tire retail stores. This resulted in proportionally higher sales for the Amiga 500 north of the border.

In contrast, US sales of the A500 ended up being less than half of what Europe was able to achieve. "I don't think more than 30 percent of the sales were in the US," says Gerard Bucas. "The problem with specialty stores was they were typically mom and pop shops but they weren't growing Commodore's sales. Bottom line is, the US was a problem for them."

Bucas had originally asked Jeff Porter for a cost of $200 for the A500, which he anticipated entering mass market retailers like Kmart. This scenario relied on a 2.5 markup ratio from landed cost to consumer price. However, Porter had originally given his absolute lowest estimate of $221.66 to build each Amiga, and after cost increases for FCC certification, the A500 came in at $230 per unit. This meant mass-market retailers could buy for $460 and sell it for around $575.

However, once Leonardi targeted specialty retailers, those numbers changed. Computer stores provided support to customers and sold in lower volumes, therefore they required a higher profit margin. They would buy A500s for $460, but then needed to sell for around $690 to remain profitable. This is how Leonardi and Nigel Shepherd previously arrived at a launch price of $699 for the Amiga 500.

The elevated price of the Amiga 500 had a negative effect. "Mass marketers looked at it and said, 'You're out of your fricking mind,'" says former Amiga marketing executive Don Reisinger. "The A500 was still way more expensive at retail than what they wanted." Unless Commodore could drop the price of the Amiga 500 even further, as it had when it dropped the C64's price from $600 to $300, the Amiga would never equal the success of the C64.

With Commodore US failing to occupy shelf space in the mass-market chains, others moved in. "Because they didn't put the A500 in that consumer electronics channel, that shelf space magically freed up for Nintendo and Sega," says Jeff Porter. "Hence the rise of the gaming consoles."

The weak marketing by Commodore at the time was par for the course. "Commodore [US] was always doing shit like that," says *Amiga World* editor Guy Wright. "They couldn't sell a cure for cancer if they had one."

Commodore attempted one nod to recapture the C64 success with the Amiga 500 by developing C64 emulation on the Amiga, a strategy similar to the IBM PC emulation they developed with the Sidecar. After Gerard Bucas ruled out a hardware C64 emulator due to costs, the company found a third party software developer creating a product called GO64. The application used software only to emulate the C64, along with a serial adapter to emulate the C64's serial bus. This allowed users to plug in a 1541 disk drive or even C64 printers.

Commodore hoped to release an Amiga bundle containing GO64, but by the end of June the GO64 software was still not ready. What had initially looked promising became bogged down with compatibility issues and general slow performance on the standard 68000 processor. As it turned out, C64 emulation in software would not be viable until faster 68000 processors emerged.

A500 Advertising

If there was one area the former Apple executives who now ran marketing excelled at, it was advertising. They developed two infomercials to promote the Amiga, which they distributed to dealers on videotape. With excellent production qualities, the 15 minute videos powerfully displayed the features of the Amiga 500, A2000 and even the remarkable diversity of software that existed by 1987.

Commodore also planned an advertising blitz for the A500 from September through December. Short 30 second advertising spots would appear on TV every week until the first week of December.

Print ads appeared in local newspapers and *USA Today*, along with general magazines like *People*, *Newsweek*, *Sports Illustrated*, *Life*, and *Omni*. These ads also appeared in special interest magazines *Consumer's Digest*, *Commodore*, *Compute!*, *Compute!'s Gazette*, and *High Fidelity*. Most importantly, ads targeted at dealers appeared in trade publications such as *COMDEX Show Daily*, *Computer Software News*, *Computer Dealer*, *Computer Reseller News*, *Computer Systems News*, *PC Week*, and *Infoworld*.

Frank Leonardi also purchased advertising on five outdoor billboards, as well as inflight television ads on Southwest Airlines in California.

Under Tramiel, Commodore devoted approximately 5% of product revenue towards advertising, even releasing television ads. Without mass retail shelf space, however, that level of advertising made little sense.

In the end, the Amiga 500 sold modestly well in the US, rather than ushering in another revolution in computing as the C64 had at the old Commodore. Porter lays the blame on one factor. "They did not put the A500 in the consumer electronics channels. Major fatal flaw. Oh my God."

European Marketing of A500

Although Commodore US's Frank Leonardi did not use mass-market retail distributors to sell the Amiga, other Commodore subsidiaries embraced retail. "In the rest of the world they did, which is why ninety percent of Commodore's revenue in the end came from the rest of the world," says Jeff Porter.

While the US was mishandling its launch of the A500, the European operations received shipments in equal numbers to the US. "When the guys from Germany and the UK saw the Amiga 500, I didn't have to say anything," says Porter. "They said, 'I know how to sell a computer that looks like that. I've been selling 10 million of them, and they used to be called Commodore 64s.'"

Commodore's US operations thought there must be something special about the European market, but in truth, it all had to do with how the products were marketed. "There's always a story behind all these things," says Commodore UK's David Pleasance. Commodore Europe's success in marketing stemmed not just with the comparatively more sophisticated handling of dealer relationships, but also more thought was put into how to package the computers.

In many ways, the success in Europe might be in part due to the focus that was placed on marketing. After all, in the UK they did not have to design or manufacture anything. Hence all they had left to focus on was marketing. That laser focus meant they had a clear measure of success and failure.

Commodore UK's sales and marketing director was David Pleasance. A highschool graduate, Pleasance moved to Australia at the age of 17. There he became obsessed with flamenco guitar. For a while he taught flamenco dance and played in restaurants on the side. Eventually he married and took a job at his father's TV repair shop. This led to work at Provident Financial group, Charge Card Services, 3M, and Pioneer Electronics. By 1983, he had a deep background in retail sales and marketing.

He joined Commodore UK in 1983, where he handled the VIC-20 and C64 accounts. Born in 1948, he was 39 years old at the time of the Amiga 500's launch. "I was there 12 years, and I loved every second of it," he says. "It was the best 12 years of my life."

In June 1987, just as the Amiga 500 was set to launch, Commodore UK received a new managing director named Steve Franklin. He would remain the top boss in the UK for the next five years. At the time, Commodore UK's business division was struggling to survive amid the onslaught of IBM PC clones. "He came from Canon," says Pleasance. "The first thing he did when he joined Commodore is he sacked everyone in the sales division. He kept one guy in the education division and the A1000 marketing manager. He didn't speak one word to me before sacking everyone." Franklin replaced the sales division with his own team from his previous company, Granada.

Pleasance was able to hold onto his job because he was part of the more successful retail sales division. "He told me, 'Seems like I'm stuck with you.' Then he reeled off integrity, honesty, and other values he expected. I told him I agreed with all that."

Pleasance used the opportunity to sell him on an idea he had for marketing the Amiga 500. "I said, 'One more thing, hear me out. We don't sell computers. We sell dreams.' Steve wondered what I was going on about and pointed to the Amiga 500 and said, 'It's a piece of plastic. What do you mean?'"

Pleasance was talking about bundles. Commodore had previously sold the C64 bundled with a tape drive and occasionally a joystick or educational title. But he wanted to try something different. "I wanted to put some bundles together with an emphasis on software. Coincidentally, there is an Amiga in the box, but it's all about the dream of what's inside. That's when we started the bundles."

Pleasance wanted to pack the Transformer emulator software into one of the bundles, the software that would allow an Amiga to run MS-DOS software. Unfortunately the software was still in a rough state, and Commodore did not own the rights to the code, meaning they could not rework it themselves. The plan for the IBM-PC bundle was scratched.

Pleasance assembled a bundle containing the A500 system, the A520 TV modulator, a mouse, 1 MB memory, plus four software titles: *Starglider, De-*

luxe Paint, Goldrunner, and *Defender of the Crown.* This sold for £499 (about $800 US in 1987).

One nice side-effect of bundles was that it gave Commodore a degree of control over the user's first experience with the Amiga, rather than letting users potentially stumble into off-putting software titles in the store.

The allure of high quality software in the bundles helped solidify the Amiga's image as a high quality, low-cost home computer. "When you create a market, and we certainly did create a market, you identify your target audience and do everything you can in order to attract the target audience," says Pleasance. "Then, once you've got the market wanting your product, it's not so difficult to get the distribution channels. Everybody wants a piece of the pie if it's successful."

Pleasance also packaged bundles for the C64, allowing the UK to avoid the excessively low prices the C64 sold for in the US. "We put together a whole bundle of the best software in there that made it a more attractive proposition to everybody and allowed us to keep the price at a reasonable level," he says. "Whereas in the states they sold the 64 on its own."

He also put together a GEOS bundle with the new 1541-II disk drive—the drive that was redesigned by Commodore Taiwan engineer H. P. Shen. He was able to shave off over $10 per unit by using an external power supply, along with a sleeker C64c case styling.

Commodore UK had deftly managed its relationships with retail distributors over the years. Conversely, one of the biggest problems in the US happened when Kmart dropped the price so low that it crowded out Commodore's other retailers. Then when Kmart dropped Commodore in favor of Nintendo, it was Commodore left in the lurch.

But that scenario never played out in the UK (the NES never became very popular in Europe), despite similarities in both countries. Manufacturers in the US are only allowed to suggest a retail price, but there are anti-collusion laws that prohibit manufacturers from enforcing a price. This is how Kmart went rogue on Commodore US. In the UK, however, if a dealer tried to lower the price too much, they would find the product was suddenly in short supply from Commodore when they called up for more stock.

Pleasance also devised strategies to lure computer sellers to favor the Amiga over its rival, the Atari ST. "We had basically two sets of customers," says Pleasance. "We had the national retail chains like Dixons, Comet, and Currys, and then we also had all the independent dealers who we didn't sell to directly. We sold to them via distributors and we usually had about four distributors because you don't want to put all your eggs in one basket."

The independent dealers did not care if they sold an Amiga or an Atari ST, it was all just profit. To sway them to the Amiga, Pleasance worked with the distributors using co-op incentives. "I said, 'Right, what I'm going to do is give you back two percent of your turnover, but you've got to match it with two percent of your own money. I want to put together a program which incentivizes all your independent dealers to sell Commodore products.' So what we did was, every product we had in our range, we awarded them a certain number of points. Then we said, 'Right, if your dealers can achieve this number of points then we will take them on a trip of a lifetime, all expenses paid. But that has to come out of the two percent I give you and the two percent you match it with.'"

The first trip was planned for both Mexico City and Acapulco. Pleasance took a trip to both places ahead of time to plan the activities. "It had to be me of course. I mean, it was rotten job," he laughs. "We picked the very best hotel we could in Mexico City, and then we checked out all the restaurants that we're going to take them, all the things we're going to do with them and then the same thing in Acapulco. When we did this very first trip, all I can tell you is everybody just absolutely loved it. As soon as they got back, they spread the word amongst all their mates.'"

Once the word spread, independent distributors were only interested in selling the Amiga and often tried to divert customer interest away from the Atari ST. "They were all working their socks off and that's how we killed the Atari ST off," says Pleasance. "They don't care because they're going to get the same money for an ST as they get for the Amiga; but if they sell an Amiga, they get a chance to go on this bloody wonderful trip. It's a no-brainer really."

Pleasance also used the trips in order to motivate his sales force. "The first trip was about 45 dealers plus about 5 or 6 people from within Commodore," he says. "We would incentivize all of our staff. Every year we had a big annual get-together for all the staff to thank them for the previous year and the next year we chose a person of the year and they would go on one of the trips as a reward."

In the end, Steve Franklin was happy he did not replace Pleasance and the two became close friends. However, much later Franklin's words to Pleasance about "integrity" and "honesty" would ring hollow, causing the fallout of their friendship under uncomfortable circumstances.

Success!

The A500 would eventually prove to be the most successful computer in the Amiga line, far surpassing sales of any other model. "I was happy that it was doing really well," says Bob Welland. "It was really fun to ship it. It was really fun that it sold a lot. It didn't surprise me that it would sell better than the A1000, simply because of the cost difference and also just the ease with which Commodore could make it."

It was also a turning point in the holy wars against Jack Tramiel and Atari. "[The Atari ST] was really attractive to a lot of people," says RJ Mical. "The religious wars flared over which machine was better, and I'm sure you could find any number of former Atari ST believers who strongly disagree with me that the Amiga was the superior machine. History agrees [the Atari ST] was the inferior machine."

The Amiga turned out to be the weapon Jeff Porter hoped it would be. "The A500 pretty much killed the Atari ST or put a significant dent in its armor," he says. However, Porter thinks he could have added one more feature to the A500 that the ST possessed. "In retrospect maybe I should have put a couple of 15 cent MIDI connectors on the Amiga 500 to finish the deal. But I figured I could just make a cable that had that from the serial port anyway."

The results of the A500 launch were almost immediate on Commodore's bottom line. The July to September quarter yielded revenues of $173.9 million, a 70% increase over the same period a year earlier. Irving Gould commented, "The results of this quarter reflect better margins stemming from a shift in product mix toward the Amiga product line, where unit volumes have increased dramatically over the year-ago period. This is attributable to the successful introduction of the Commodore Amiga 500 and the Commodore Amiga 2000 during the June quarter."

As the Amiga 500 started selling, Mical began to realize it was closer to Amiga's original vision. "I warmed up to the idea because it was continuing the original philosophy that we had with the Amiga, which was to get good computing horsepower into the hands of the masses," he says. "It helped the machine be a lot more popular than it would have been otherwise."

CHAPTER 3

A2000-CR and Unix 1987

Commodore had tried to create a Unix based computer called the C900 and then abandoned it in 1984 when the company finances became too stressed. But many engineers within the company continued to believe that Unix was the only operating system worth caring about and that Commodore should support it. One such engineer, Bob Welland, began pursuing that goal aggressively once his duties on the Amiga 500 ended. This would eventually lead the engineers to consider using Unix on the upcoming Amiga 2000-CR.

Unix Resurrection

One of the strangest detours that remained largely hidden from the public was the push for a Unix-based computer, even after the cancellation of the C900. "They made a lot of mistakes spending money on things that ended up being dead ends," says Dale Luck. "They should have spent money on things that were actually going to be the future of the company, and the future of the company was the Amiga."

This obsession was driven by Gerard Bucas along with engineers Bob Welland and George Robbins, who saw the A500 as the ultimate in low-cost Unix platforms. According to coworker Bil Herd, "One of [Robbins'] taglines we fondly remember was, 'Little Unix boxes that take over the world.'"

Given his history on the C900 project, Welland considered the AmigaOS inferior and felt Unix was the only OS with a bright future. "I like the Amiga hardware and because of my bias about Unix, the AmigaOS just wasn't that important to me," says Welland. "I don't mean to say that there was anything wrong with what they were doing, it was fine. It's just that in a certain market Unix was the de facto thing, and you weren't going to convince a bunch of people to switch from Sun to Commodore by trying to tell them that the AmigaOS was the greatest thing since sliced bread."

Amiga 500 project lead Jeff Porter was also a supporter, having previously worked at Bell Labs, where Unix originated. Now that Gerard Bucas was VP of engineering, he had more power to make it happen, even after the C900 cancellation. "It's funny because Gerard Bucas, the head of engineering at the time, had a really soft spot in his heart for the C900 and so it kind of died a strange death," says Welland.

Bucas saw the possibility of putting the Unix operating system on an Amiga computer, something he often discussed with Bob Welland. The C900 Unix box was dead. Long live Unix!

In 1986, Welland made one more attempt at a Unix machine, this time running on the Amiga's Motorola 68000 processor. "I still thought the idea of the C900 product was a good idea and I wanted to make a 68000-like workstation machine," he says. "I remember writing a proposal to Gerard. And all of that was because I thought it would be fun to have a Unix machine."

When it became clear that Commodore did not have the resources to fund a completely different piece of hardware, the topic turned to using the Amiga as a platform for Unix. "I had come from a Unix background and I still thought the Amiga would make a great Unix machine," says Welland.

Rather than pushing for an Amiga-PC hybrid that the German engineers favored, Welland pushed for a Unix-Amiga hybrid. He explains, "For me, I was always looking for the higher end machines in terms of who those customers were, but at the same time wanting to make one that was inexpensive. That was, from a hardware perspective, always my motivation. The whole time I was at Commodore, I was trying to make something with Unix in it."

With Gerard Bucas in charge of Commodore's engineering group, including Germany, he was in a prime position to support Unix. The proposal was also enthusiastically supported by Clive Smith, General Manager of the Commodore Product and Market Development Group, whose strategy focused on cheaper products than the competition could offer.

Although the Amiga used the same processor shared by most Unix machines at the time, it lacked a memory management unit (MMU), something Amiga founder Jay Miner earlier declined to include. MMUs arbitrate access to memory, and amongst other things can isolate one program's memory from another, ensuring one program going astray can't crash the whole machine, or access data it shouldn't access. "If you don't need a memory management unit, you don't need one, so why build one? But if you want to do something that's multitasking, that does context switching, and memory protection and virtual memory then you have to have that hardware," explains Welland. "So there was this effort to try to get Unix running on the Amiga, and the main problem with that is you can't do Unix without memory management hardware."

In September 1986, Bucas hired two of the lead programmers of Coherent Unix, Johann George and Randall Howard. "I started working on getting Unix running on the Amiga. And that's when Johann George joined that effort," says Welland. "He had gone to University of Waterloo when he was 13. He is a spectacularly bright guy as well as a really nice guy. "

Welland recruited a former C900 software developer to the cause as well. "I was designing memory management units for that effort," says Welland. "One of the guys who had worked on the C900, Rico Tudor (who I had worked with at [Coherent publisher] Mark Williams) and I started trying to get Unix running on the Amiga. We made a series of memory management units, the first one being an exclusive-or gate (XOR). The first version of it was literally a single gate. It was the world's simplest memory management unit for the Amiga. We actually got Unix running in that situation. and then I did a prototype segmenting MMU for it and he got Unix running really very fast on that. And this was Rico Tudor's brilliance actually."

When Tudor and Welland completed their demo version of Unix in the middle of March, 1987, Gerard Bucas was keen to produce an A500 MMU card. But it was not to be. "The only problem was that if you wanted to context switch between two user processes, you had to actually physically copy the user process to the bottom of memory and copy the one that was running up to somewhere else," explains Welland. "The context switching was very slow because it involves an entire process memory copy. But that said, Rico was able to get Unix running and context switch it a couple times a second."

The team continued developing a better MMU. "There was a sequence of those designs that were trying to lead up to making a Unix machine out of the Amiga hardware," says Welland. "And I made a segmenting memory management unit, something very similar to what the PDP-11 would do. At the same time we were doing an MMU cache chip that Commodore was going to make."

Commodore's engineers were impressed with Welland's work. "Bob Welland was designing stuff that was actually very sophisticated," recalls Dave Haynie. "He was trying to get Commodore to leapfrog some of the problems we had with Motorola. They may have actually done a prototype of it, but that was one of the things that was never finished."

Eventually, Welland began looking at building a Unix machine from the recently completed A2000-CR/B2000, a cost-reduced Amiga with a Motorola processor and expansion ports, created by Dave Haynie.

Dave Haynie

Dave Haynie came from a family steeped in engineering. "My dad was an electrical engineer at Bell Laboratories," he says. "He was an analog guy from back when analog was important. For at least four months, he was the main guy in charge of all of their fiber optics before he realized it was too much for one department and they split it up into three separate projects."

Haynie was raised in a picturesque East Coast town. "I was born in Summit, New Jersey in 1961," he says. Through the years, his interests varied from black & white photography, electronic music, and finally computers. He also became a lifelong fan of New Jersey born musician Bruce Springsteen.

Haynie had exposure to technology at an early age because of his father. "I taught myself to program when I was 12 and was writing code for years before I had any formal education in it," he recalls. "The first thing I programmed was for taxes."

Haynie gained programming experience on an HP 9100A, a calculator so large it even had a monitor. "My dad brought home a huge Hewlett-Packard programmable calculator; one of those desktop things with a CRT (Cathode Ray Tube) and it had magnetic cards," he says. "I was goofing around on it and basically learned how to read the machine code that was stored on the cards."

While still a child, Haynie learned programming on a timesharing system. "I kept asking him to bring [the calculator] back, and he said, 'I can't really do that because we only have one.' So he brought home a terminal," he recalls, referring to the Texas Instruments Silent 700 portable terminal. "I had this TI terminal every weekend and a roll of thermal paper, and I would do whatever I could do on their timeshare system, since nobody used it on the weekends."

A 1972 era timesharing system running on a Control Data Corporation mainframe was on the other end of his terminal. "I taught myself BASIC and Fortran by taking apart programs that happened to be on the CDC Cyber 72. That lasted a couple of years."

The Commodore PET was Haynie's first exposure to a personal computer. "My best friend got a PET in 1977 when you could go to the island of Manhattan, and there was one store that had PETs," he recalls. "It was actually just one room in an office building. PETs were on one side and 4K Apple IIs were on the other side."

Haynie was the only teenager in his group with programming experience. He soon created a few games for his friends. "I got my first computer in 1979, but that was after years of wanting one that I couldn't afford," he says. "I ended up getting an Exidy Sorcerer. Exidy at the time was a big video game company out on the west coast and they came out with this computer which was technically cool but had no [software development] whatsoever."

The young programmer also wrote software for the Sorcerer and sold four titles to Creative Computing Software, which distributed them on cassette tape for $7.95 each. The Sorcerer market numbered only about 5,000 machines, and Haynie sold about 500 copies of his software.

In 1979, Haynie entered college. "I studied electrical engineering and mathematics/computer science at Carnegie Mellon in Pittsburgh," he recalls. "I taught myself all the computer science stuff." In his last semester, he took courses in compiler design and robotics.

During summer vacations, Haynie worked for Bell Laboratories. He seemed destined to follow in his father's footsteps after graduation in 1983, but it was the year of the AT&T breakup and the company was in a hiring freeze.

Instead, Haynie went to work for General Electric in Philadelphia. The Space Shuttle work at GE lured him in, but he soon learned 99% of the work was in nuclear weapons. "I was at General Electric for four months and I didn't like it," he says. "I decided I was leaving General Electric and I went to this headhunter and sent out one resume." A week later, he was working for Commodore as one of the C128 Animals.

A2000-CR US Launch

In August 1987, following on the heels of the Amiga 500, the A2000 revision B was ready for launch in the US and a relaunch in Europe.

Haynie had successfully knocked $65 off the cost of the motherboard alone, which could translate to a savings of $200 at retail. He named his motherboard The Boss, in homage to fellow New Jersey native Bruce

Springsteen, whose music fueled his late night engineering. Unfortunately "The Boss" was never made public because the two-layer motherboard was so packed that there was not enough free real estate to stencil the name.

This time, the Gary chip would be manufactured by CSG rather than Toshiba, further adding to the savings. Although the price of the A2000-CR was initially hinted at $1495, it was increased to $2000 prior to launch. Paul Higginbottom in sales began using the phrase, "It's 2000 for a 2000."

Dave Haynie sensed the backlash from the Amiga engineers against the A2000, but overall felt they approved. "After years and years, I don't think anybody thought I was part of the evil empire just because I built the Amiga 2000, which wasn't the shape that the Los Gatos people wanted of course," he says.

Glenn Keller later felt empathy for the task given to the Commodore engineers. "Engineers have a lot of not-invented-here," he laughs. "Their bosses had them take on this brand new thing, designed completely by another group of people, somewhere else. And they took it on as their own and improved it."

This time, Frank Leonardi's Apple marketing background proved helpful for the launch of the Amiga 2000. He felt comfortable pushing the computer into specialty computer stores, although Commodore's dealer network was still without access to the big name computer stores like ComputerLand.

Dealers received videotapes with a 10 minute video, showcasing the Amiga 2000's multimedia and multitasking capabilities. These video demonstrations played on a loop, acting as automatic salesmen to attract customers. "The Amiga 500 and the B2000, Dave Haynie and Greg Berlin's version of the Amiga 2000, really were what saved Commodore in the short term," says Eric Lavitsky. "They ended up being a huge success in Europe and other parts of the world."

The launch of the A2000 resulted in the discontinuation of the Amiga 1000 in 1987. And in one more example of poor market timing, Commodore finally released the A1300 Genlock just as it discontinued the Amiga 1000.

During the same August 1987 launch date, Commodore also released the A2088XT Bridgeboard for the Amiga 2000, codenamed Janus. The reason for the product's existence, to provide a back catalog of software, was diminished now that the Amiga had better software available.

The Bridgeboard was also expensive. At $699, which included a 5¼ inch diskette drive, it was no bargain. As *Amiga World* noted, a complete IBM PC clone cost $700, including a monitor and two floppy drives.[1] Despite these problems, Commodore would continue to pursue myriad updated Bridge-boards for the near future.

A2620 Accelerator Card

Throughout 1987, Bob Welland continued working on his personal vision of a low-cost Unix machine. "The thing that was beautiful about Commodore was the amount of freedom you had and the lack of bureaucracy," he says. "I got to work on six chips when I was there as someone who, when I showed up there when I was 23, had never designed a chip before. I can't imagine another company that would let me do that."

The core requirement of running Unix on the Amiga was an MMU. "I had been trying to do a memory management unit for the 68000 on my quest to get Unix on the Amiga," says Welland. "Because with the way the A2000 works, you couldn't run Unix. It can't be done."

Welland's custom MMU was placed on an accelerator card, along with a Motorola 68020, which plugged into the processor slot on an A2000. Because the 68020 ran at 14.3 MHZ, double the clock speed of the 68000, it benefited the ordinary AmigaOS as well. This version of the accelerator card was publicly acknowledged by Clive Smith as early as December 1986. "I was doing all of that because I thought it would be fun to have a Unix machine, but it benefited the Amiga in a larger sense," says Welland.

When Motorola released the 68851 MMU, Welland's in-house designs were shelved. "That was a little disappointing for me because I was working on a chipset myself but that's when we just decided, why don't we make a board with that on it."

Instead, Welland started over again and designed a proper accelerator card using three of Motorola's chips in combination: a 14.3 MHz 68020 CPU, a 68851 MMU, a 68881 floating point unit (FPU), and 2 MB of fast 32-bit memory. The FPU chip increased the speed of calculations based on float-ing point numbers. "It had a floating point unit suddenly and it had a more sophisticated memory management unit," recalls Welland. "I don't think Commodore could have made that chip. It was just a beefier processor."

Welland would continue working on the accelerator card into 1988, with assistance from Dave Haynie, all the while knowing that, when completed, he would have everything he needed to finally create a Unix-based computer for the masses.

---

1 *Amiga World*. February 1988. p. 24.

CHAPTER 4

Quest for High Resolution 1987

While the engineers were working on a Unix system for Commodore, some of those same engineers were struggling with a different problem. After the release of the Amiga 500 and new Amiga 2000, it was clear Commodore was still struggling to develop the next step in Amiga graphics technology. Throughout 1987, Commodore's engineers proposed several solutions to keep the Amiga at the cutting edge. But with so many voices, the one thing the plans lacked was a clear, decisive plan for the future.

The Portable Amiga

After the launch of the Amiga 1000, Dale Luck became interested in finding different uses for the Amiga technology and wanted to explore the portable computer market. Unfortunately, LCD screens at the time were not capable of displaying color and weren't able to take advantage of the Denise chip's capabilities.

At the same time, Hedley Davis had just finished the 1351 mouse and was looking for a new project. Davis suggested using the chassis from an old SX-64 portable computer to create something new. "This project was done after hours entirely on the sly, although Commodore did pay for the board fabrication and some machining," says Davis. "We had the freedom to pursue projects not directly related to the company's planned business. In that way, we were ahead of Google and their vaunted '20% time' perk. Nothing was formal, we just sometimes did stuff like this."

In late 1986, Davis began to construct a prototype which he called the SX-52, in homage to the B-52 motherboard. "It has a custom A500-based main board crammed into an SX-64 case which had most of its guts reamed out," explains Davis. "An off-the-shelf power supply was added, the cartridge port was sealed off, the floppies were mounted with bailing wire and duct tape. The keyboard was literally an A1000 keyboard Dremeled and cut apart and rewired with lots of little wires and crammed into the SX-64 keyboard case."

The small CRT color display was less than either engineer hoped for and Davis reworked it into a different configuration he called the SX-500. "Five boards were built, three units were assembled," says Davis. "We did some with the SX-64's video display which was NTSC (National Television System Committee), however, the color mask on the CRT was so coarse that you could barely read any text. We also did a couple of monochrome units which were very readable."

Davis even went as far as researching production problems for the machine. "When we did the SX-500, we did examine issues associated with trying to productize it," he says. "I remember sending faxes to CJL [Commodore Japan Limited] asking about tooling and stuff."

In the back rooms at the January 1987 CES show, Davis showed off three portable SX-500 computers. The computers received little interest because the Osborne style of portability was seen as outdated by 1987. "It went absolutely nowhere," says Davis.

Jeff Porter thought the SX-500 was a nice demo—a concept to bring to shows to illustrate the portability of Amiga technology, but he doubted the marketplace would accept it. By January 17, 1987, Porter informed Davis that it was not worth spending time on in the future and began looking for another project for the young engineer.

Porter offered Davis a number of projects, such as modems or printers. He also offered a new project for a better Amiga monitor proposed by Commodore's Chief Operating Officer, Henri Rubin. A few days later, Gerard Bucas offered Davis a project to create a full C64 hardware emulator for the Amiga. Davis felt he should get up to speed on the Amiga technology, since it seemed to be the company's future, so he opted to create a new Amiga monitor.

Hedley

Hedley Davis first developed an interest in electronics in junior high school. "I went to a dance in seventh grade. They had a deejay there. He was flashing these lights along with the music and from my perspective he really sucked," he recalls. "Here is a professional guy doing this lighting and it's just terrible. I could do that better than him. So I kind of developed this lighting hobby."

His hobby soon led him to interesting challenges with electronics. "I started building all these custom lights in my basement with black lights and strobe lights and these things with paint cans with holes punched in them and projectors and incense burning to be sort of a pseudo smoke machine."

These experiments continued through high school and led him to study at the University of Delaware in 1976. "I went to study electrical engineering because I could not build dimmers or could not control lighting the way I wanted to. So electrical engineering was a means to an end."

During college he developed a minor addiction to a seminal pinball game that helped develop his love of microprocessors. "I have to admit, I played pinball a lot on a 1980 *Firepower* machine, which was also a microprocessor-based machine. It was one of the first talking ones, one of the first ones with multi-ball play," he recalls. "It was a very exciting time. Microprocessors were a brand new thing."

After graduating with a Bachelor of Electrical Engineering in 1981, he worked at the Pennsylvania Scale Company with Bil Herd. However, on the side he indulged his love of stage lighting. "There was another company in Lititz, Pennsylvania called Tait Towers Lighting and these guys built huge rotating stages for bands like Yes," explains Davis. "They're one of the hugest stage companies in the US. They build everything twice as good for three times the price. They're hugely profitable.

"I was really into a band called Yes. While I was working at Pennsylvania Scale company, I would go over to this staging company and I would just sweep the floors or stand there filing welds. Eventually they had me get equipment out on the road; a couple of custom lighting widgets and junk like that. It was a lot of fun."

While moonlighting at Tait Towers, something happened that would dramatically change the quality of his future contributions to Commodore. "A staging guy turned me onto a book called *Lateral Thinking*," recalls Davis, referring to the book by Edward De Bono. "The thesis of the book was, if you want to figure out how to solve a problem in a really great way, you sit down and you solve the problem. And then you set your solution aside and you solve the problem again, without using any aspects of the original solution. That forces you to pick up the thing and try to look at it from the side or look at it from underneath to try to get a different perspective on it."

Davis was hired by Commodore in 1984 and was one of the "animals" in Bil Herd's group, making a minor contribution to the C128. He also developed a reputation for the biting sarcasm that he used to poke fun at the engineers around him. Davis speaks at a frantic pace; about double the speed of most Commodore engineers, which gives the impression that his brain must consume a few more calories than the rest of us.

One of Davis' early projects was the 1351 mouse for the C64, which was a resounding technical success. He was about to start rising up the ranks among Commodore's engineers.

The A2024 Hedley Hi-Res

As good as the Amiga video output was in its time, it was not perfect. This is because at higher vertical resolutions the Denise chip produced interlaced video, meaning it drew every second line onto an NTSC monitor during one pass and the other half on the next pass. While the lower resolutions looked okay at 30 frames per second (25 in PAL), at higher resolutions the interlaced video was only 15 frames per second (12.5 in PAL). This resulted in an image that flickered. Business users found it difficult to work in high resolutions for long periods of time.

According to Dale Luck, the Amiga color graphics limited its acceptance in business. "The graphics weren't designed to do spreadsheets," he says. "One of the problems that it had for being a business computer was that the resolution of the display wasn't as good as the Mac, although the Mac was only black and white. So the text was a little big and clunky. The Amiga had a lot more colors than the IBM PC, but it had this interlaced display which didn't do very well for productivity software. It was targeted towards more the video market."

The Macintosh display had a solid appearance with its non-interlaced video, even though it had a lower resolution—512x342 pixels, compared to the Amiga's 640x400. Henri Rubin, the instigator of the new project, wanted to go after the Macintosh by adding non-interlaced monochrome video for the Amiga. "Management's directive was to produce a high-resolution, monochrome business computer," says developer Bryce Nesbitt. "This is what we were supposed to work on."

Rubin wanted his engineers to build a flat paperwhite monochrome monitor, similar to the Macintosh, for the Amiga 500. He proposed using a scan converter chip from NEC that would take the 640x200 video signal from the Denise chip and output 640x400 non-interlaced by combining the two alternating lines onto one frame.

Hedley Davis took on this challenge. He was already known for coming up with creative solutions to difficult problems, and he ended up exceeding the specs Rubin had asked for by a long shot. Davis' plan called for the Amiga to effectively draw four 640x400 screens and stitch them together into one larger 1280x800 screen. His proposed solution would buffer the results in memory, and then output the data to the monitor. By using only 4 colors, it would use less video data.

Davis wrote up a proposal and presented it to Rubin. "I can remember sitting in Henri Rubin's office explaining how we could do this," he recalls. "He had Bob Welland there and Bob had everybody's respect as being a super smart guy. I explained to Henri in great detail about how we can do this. 'It's all digital. It'll work and it's going to be awesome.'"

The plan was simple. "It gathered up 8 individual frames and combined them together," recalls Welland. "The video update rate was something like 60/8, so it would be 12 frames a second, but he refreshed the monitor at 60 Hz so it looked good."

Rubin had little computer experience and no way to tell if the scheme was possible. "So he looks over at Bob and says, 'Bob, is that possible? Does this even make sense?' And Bob said, 'It's an insanely good idea.' That's when I got the go-ahead."

Davis now had to figure out how to build his prototype scan converter. "From my perspective, that was primarily a digital problem," he says. "I really didn't know that much about monitors, but I knew that you had H-sync and V-sync. But I didn't know what the right timings to use were. So I randomly went off and figured out how to build a frame buffer display device that put out hi-res video."

Davis had to produce circuitry to stitch together the four images into one. Using Programmable Array Logic (PAL) chips once again (as he had with his 1351 mouse), he created the circuitry inside his prototype. The circuitry de-interlaced the images by storing up two interlaced images and combining them into one image. It also had modes for NTSC (1008x800) and PAL (Phase Alternating Line) monitors (1008x1024). And it supported the conventional Amiga graphics modes, albeit with 8 and 16 grayscale colors.

By February 1987 he had a working prototype built from an old monochrome Sun workstation monitor. The other engineers were impressed and dubbed it the Hedley Hi-Res. The resulting monitor would be highly proprietary to the Amiga computer and would not work with PCs or Macs. "It was just weird, it didn't line up with anybody's standards," says Davis,

Davis had his prototype monitor, but now he needed to get it working with the Amiga operating system. That same month, he flew to Los Gatos. "The only person that could write the software for it was the guy who knew the Amiga graphics best, and that was a guy named Dale Luck," recalls Davis. "They sent me out to Commodore West in Los Gatos, California, which they were in the middle of shutting down. I was to transfer the hardware design to Dale and let him start bringing this thing up."

It looked like the West Chester-Los Gatos rivalry was about to flare up when Davis, a comparatively high-strung east coast guy, showed up at the more relaxed Amiga offices. "I'm there at the appointed time and nobody's there. I'm waiting around and I'm pissed. Then this guy rides up on this Harley and pops off his helmet with a big smile on his face and puts out his hand. I've just loved the man ever since," he laughs. "I don't know why."[1]

Luck escorted Davis into the almost deserted offices. "I go in this huge building with all these computers and there's like four guys working in it because all the others have been laid off," says Davis.

The casual atmosphere of the Los Gatos offices was even further ingrained on Davis when he saw Luck's desk. "Dale takes me to his workplace and he's got his chair sitting there, and his Sun with a big monitor. Next to his chair is this giant garbage bag and around this chair is all this popcorn in this ring. It looked like a planet surrounded by asteroids. It was the popcorn that missed his mouth! Because he would reach into this bag and throw popcorn in his face. Some would land on the ground and it was a perfect circle around his chair."

Working with the California engineers was a culture shock for Davis, who was used to the brutal honesty of the east coast. "I was definitely a rude east coast guy in the true sense of the word," he says. "So I got to California and started doing the same stuff, and it's like, 'No, no, no. You can't say that's stupid. You can't say that'll never work.' You have to kind of rephrase that like, 'Have you considered this?' or 'What about that aspect?' Dance around the bush and let the engineer figure out, oh yeah, that was dumb. Because otherwise you were being rude I guess. The political correctness was a huge factor."

Davis returned east and left the hardware in Dale Luck's capable hands. The goal was to have the prototype monitor ready to display at the upcoming COMDEX show, which was scheduled for June 1987. Davis and Luck would continue to evolve the display adapter in the months leading up to COMDEX, communicating via email.

---

1   In 2007, Hedley Davis was the sole West Chester engineer invited to attend Dale Luck's wedding.

Hi-Res Chipset Handoff

Jay Miner, Dave Needle, Mark Shieu, and Glenn Keller had begun designing a new higher-resolution Amiga chipset in late 1985, which was intended for the Ranger computer. Although Ranger had been cancelled in mid-1986, the chipset development continued. By January 1987, (with Dave Needle gone since mid-1986) the chip designs were nearing completion.

Miner's team produced two new chips for Denise and Agnus, while ignoring upgrades to Paula. The chipset was meant to compete with the high resolution, monochrome displays of the Atari ST, Macintosh, and Sun systems. Of these, the impressive high-resolution monochrome display of the Atari ST was foremost in the minds of the Amiga engineers. The mode was used mainly for Atari ST productivity software.

Prior designs of Agnus relied on PAL and NTSC versions in two different chips, but the new version, dubbed Fatter Agnus, could handle both standards in one chip. PAL or NTSC were selected via a system configuration setting in software. (Denise had always been compatible with either PAL or NTSC.) The Fatter Agnus chip would also receive a minor enhancement allowing 1 MB of chip memory instead of the original 512 KB.

A new version of Denise, dubbed Hires Denise, had several modes. The hi-res mode could, much like the original Denise, display 640 by 400 interlaced with 16 colors. A new mode, Super Hi-Res, could display 640 by 400 non-interlaced in four colors; another mode called Ultra-Hi-Res could display 1024 by 1024 in monochrome.

Shortly after CES ended in January 1987, Miner did the "tape out" and passed the chip designs over to Commodore's Large Scale Integration (LSI) group. There, the West Chester engineers began planning to layout and manufacture the new hi-res Amiga chipset developed by the Los Gatos chip designers.

On February 4, 1987, LSI head Ted Lenthe produced a development schedule with prototype samples expected in May and the first 1000 production units in July. He assigned Hi-Res Denise the chip number 8369. Commodore engineer Bob Raible would perform the layout for Hi-Res Denise, with assistance from Amiga engineers Glenn Keller and Mark Shieu.

Engineer Victor Andrade became lead designer on another chip, dubbed Hi-Res Fat Agnus, which received chip number 8372. A new chip designer named Bill Gardei would provide simulation and testing support.

Andrade and Raible would need to make a few tweaks on the Los Gatos design in order to ensure plug-in compatibility. The West Chester engineers wanted the new chips to be pin compatible with the A500 and A2000-

CR boards to make future improvements of the systems easy, although the AmigaOS software would need to be upgraded to work with the chips.

Later in February, George Robbins couldn't hold back his enthusiasm and announced to the Usenet newsgroups, "We're working on a higher resolution version of the Amiga chips. Of course there are only so many hardware people and lots of things to do."

Due to the tweaks, LSI head Ted Lenthe's original schedule would prove to be wildly optimistic because of the complexity of the Amiga chipset. Working samples of the chipset would not emerge until well after the summer. Meanwhile, other developments in the computer world would cause the designers to rethink the chipset.

Chipset Crisis

Commodore's LSI group labored through 1987 to complete the Hi-Res chipset, Denise and Agnus. The team ended up blowing past the original schedule, which called for samples in May and the first 1000 production chips in July 1987. In fact, the first samples arrived in August, and by September they were still working out bugs. George Robbins had been put in charge of overseeing the new chipset, along with the LSI engineers. Robbins felt they had done a good job taking over from the Amiga designers, especially in light of integrating new features, such as something called "high speed shifting logic".

By early September the West Chester engineers collectively faced an existential crisis with regards to the goals of the Hi-Res chipset. By mid-1987, they began to notice that the IBM PC and Macintosh were catching up to the Amiga. "You had VGA by then, which was really slow but it gave a lot more colors," says Dave Haynie. "You had the Mac II, which also had a slow 256-color card."

The Macintosh II allowed 16 colors at 640 by 480, or 256 colors at 512 by 384, from a color palette of 16.7 million colors. The original Amiga chipset could display 640 by 400 interlaced video for NTSC, or 640 by 512 for PAL, with up to 16 colors from a color palette of 4096 colors.

In the IBM world, VGA multisync monitors were quickly becoming a standard. Although the specs sounded similar, IBM and Mac could display non-interlaced video, while the interlaced Amiga video appeared to flicker at higher resolutions. The gap was narrowing and Commodore needed to upgrade the Amiga to compete. Even Bob Welland admitted that, of the competing systems, his preference would be the Mac II.

It began to dawn on the engineers that the monochrome hi-res Denise chip developed by the Los Gatos engineers was not worth developing anymore. The Hi-Res chip design had begun when Unix workstations, Mac, and IBM all had few or no colors, and that meant the system was a business machine. By 1987, not even the business world wanted monochrome anymore. The playfield had changed too much.

Bob Welland and George Robbins looked at all this and began to consider two new goals for the chipset. First, they wanted a quick modification to the hi-res Denise chip to allow 640 x 480 non-interlaced with color. And second, they wanted to output the video signal to multisync VGA monitors.

Bob Welland, who was grudgingly working on his accelerator board for the Amiga 2000, came into his own on the chipset discussions. "Bob didn't really want to be at that level," says Dave Haynie. "He didn't want to be in charge of a system. He wanted to be the 'new idea' kind of guy working with the chip people."

In early September, the discussions about what to do with the Hi-Res chipset began to boil over. Ted Lenthe, head of the LSI group, felt the original Amiga team had missed the mark with the hi-res Denise and Agnus because they were only marginally compatible with the existing Amiga chipset due to VRAM (Video RAM), and it lacked color. He wanted a new design for a 640 by 400 Denise with 8 colors, non-interlaced of course.

He also wanted Bob Welland, once he completed his accelerator board, to begin a next generation architecture separate from the Amiga family that included advanced functions such as 3D hardware acceleration.

This view contrasted with Bob Welland and George Robbins, who wanted the designers to add four color registers to the existing mono 8369 Denise in order to produce a color Denise (plus four additional color registers to handle color in the sprites). Robbins in particular believed there was little risk to continuing development on the Hi-Res chipset, considering there were no immediate computer systems in design to take advantage of them, and nothing would be released until late 1988.

When Gerard Bucas arrived back from vacation on September 2, he was surprised to find his engineers in such a state of disagreement. Late in the day he asked his engineers how hard it would be to add those four color registers. After 6:00 pm, when most employees had long departed for home, Welland, Robbins, and even Dale Luck weighed in on behalf of the plan to modify the existing chipset.

Welland felt four colors and the superior Multisync monitor display would give the Amiga a sizable advantage over the Atari ST's grayscale hi-res display. His main concern was how well the display would look running Unix and the X Window System GUI (Graphical User Interface). Dale Luck, signing into the VAX system remotely from the West Coast, agreed with Welland, although he admitted he'd like to see Commodore get more ambitious with the modifications and add more than just four color registers.

Around 9:00 pm, Bucas gave the team the go ahead with the plan to add registers to the Hi-Res chipset, against Lenthe's wishes, with the stipulation that he wanted the chips ready for production no later than December 1987, giving the team less than four months. Robbins, buoyed by the decision, began planning a meeting with Glenn Keller, Neil Kaitin, Jay Miner, Bart Whitebook and Dale Luck on the West Coast to determine a wishlist of features to add.

Unfortunately the decision had been made without the input of an important voice, Ted Lenthe. Lenthe had been struggling with the Hi-Res chipset all year and was finally coming close to delivering working samples. He had gone home, eaten supper, unwound in front of the TV, and then decided to call in remotely to the VAX system to check his email before going to bed.

When he began reading the emails he became increasingly alarmed. Perhaps due to his years of experience in the LSI department, Lenthe sensed danger with the current plan to modify the existing chipset. Normally reserved and measured, Lenthe decried, "Bullshit!! Let's have a meeting and discuss how much longer we want to piss around with the existing hi-res Denise vs. designing the video controller we really want. At this rate, we'll still be tweaking Denise in the year 2010! I'd like to get all the parties (including you) in one room tomorrow, before you go away and sort this out!"

His passionate plea was backed up 10 minutes later by Hedley Davis, who had been quietly sitting on the sidelines of the debate. Davis already had a Hi-Res monitor in the works, which granted him a unique perspective on the situation. He felt adding two more colors to Hires Denise would hurt system response just for "a small check-mark on a feature list." He also believed a narrow subset of Amiga software would work with the new 640 by 400 four color mode, making it irrelevant to most users, while slowing the A500 down even further.

Davis, like Lenthe, favored a complete redesign over modifying the existing chipset. "This whole DeniseHR thing is a design which makes many unfavorable trade-offs and promises to come back and bite us many times over. The software incompatibility alone is a major drawback. I know that people who live in glass houses shouldn't throw stones, but DeniseHR is a kludge, and an ugly one at that. We should be spending our resources working on the next generation machine instead of piddling around with small incremental changes that are very expensive in terms of chip people, software people, and systems designers."

The engineers, including Andy Finkel, continued making arguments until well past one o'clock in the morning. Welland continued pressing for quick changes to the Hi-Res chipset, followed by a longer-term strategy for the next chips. He dismissed Davis' comments, saying, "I don't think that anyone is thinking about abandoning the whole effort or making it into something it is not. Because of this, I feel compelled to ignore Hedley's letter. It goes outside the bounds of the discussion."

Dale Luck preferred attempting 16-bit color first, followed by a 24-bit color next generation chipset. He felt Commodore needed to work with the Amiga chipset to extend the life at least 5 years before moving to a new chipset. And lastly, Luck had explosive comments regarding implementing the 68020 chip in a system. "Christ, I cannot believe this is not done yet. I thought I had a difficult hardware group to manage out here," he said. "How long does the marketplace have to wait before Commodore opens their eyes. I mean, we could blow the doors off the Mac II and we screw around with these plug in boards."

The next day, Gerard Bucas called together a meeting between members of the LSI team (Ted Lenthe, Bob Raible, and Victor Andrade) and the system engineers (Jeff Porter, George Robbins, and Bob Welland), along with Hedley Davis from system software and Andy Finkel from the Amiga software group. The LSI group had spent the past year getting the monochrome hi-res Denise to work and did not want to invest an extensive amount of work into the chip when, in their minds, it was obvious something new was needed.

The arguments they made won over Gerard Bucas, and the team accepted that a 12-bit color table and 8 color registers would be too complex to work into the current chip. However, Bob Welland compromised and presented a case for a simpler scheme to allow a 6-bit color palette (64 colors) and only 4 additional color registers. At the end of the meeting, the engineers agreed to implement his new scheme, subject to more analysis.

A few days later, on September 7, Hedley Davis proposed an alternative plan. Instead of putting the color function in a chip, he proposed a 640 by 400 31 KHz scan converter card. The solution would not rely on VGA multisync monitors, but instead would output through the RGB (Red Green Blue color model) port to existing Amiga monitors. The device cost $31.50

in parts for the A2000 board and $40.50 for the A500 board. It would be 100% software compatible and, in Davis' view, better than Hi-Res Denise in all respects, except price. Davis presented the idea to Henri Rubin, who gave the puzzling, non-committal reply that, "This stuff may end up being very important."

The LSI engineers and system engineers developed a more concrete plan through their regular weekly meetings. Their first decision was to complete the design for Monochrome Hi-Res Denise 8369R1, and have it releasable, but not go into production for any system. It would instead be a useful test platform to work out bugs in the chip.

The new chip, tentatively called Color Hi-Res Denise 8373, began to take shape. The team expected to have full tapeout in two months, meaning samples could arrive as early as December.

At the Commodore Show, held at the Disneyland Hotel the weekend of October 3, 1987, both Dale Luck and RJ Mical attended. There, the two Amiga engineers spilled the beans on Commodore's future chip plans to the press. When Jeff Porter found out, he begged Commodore support manager Gail Wellington to put a gag order out on the two. Porter now had people walking up to him at trade shows asking when the new chips Jay Miner was working on would be ready.

By November 23, the logic design for the new Color Hi-Res Denise was complete, and layout work began. It looked like the engineers might have samples before the Christmas shutdown of CSG. Ted Lenthe planned to work out the color bugs in the first version of 8373, followed by another revision to perfect the color output. He wanted this version ready by the March 1, 1988 Hanover show. That was Phase I. Phase II would then incorporate the changes required for genlock. These features were especially important because genlock was the only major feature not available in other competing chipsets on the market.

The LSI designers walked a tightrope, attempting to improve on the existing architecture while maintaining backward compatibility. Because the Agnus and Denise chipsets were very integrated with each other and the RAM, each piece was very dependent on the others. This made it difficult for the LSI designers to evolve the chipset without breaking basic functionality.

Although they couldn't know it at the time, the decision they made regarding the high-resolution chipset would mark an important turning point for Commodore, one that would determine whether the Amiga's technological lead over the competition would remain.

Fat Paula Upgrade

One afterthought from the chip discussions had to do with improving the Paula chip. Since the early eighties, floppy disk technology continued improving, with finer, more powerful magnetic heads to store more data, faster motors to read data more quickly, and improvements in the quality of floppy disk magnetic media.

The original Mac used GCR (Group Coded Recording) of single density (SD) floppy disks to store 400 KB. Amiga, on the other hand, had chosen Modified Frequency Modulation (MFM) as had the IBM PC. The Amiga 1000 used double density disks to store 880 KB. Although the competing computers used the same physical disks, they were unable to read data from each others' disks once formatted.

Early in 1987, 1.44 MB high density (HD) disks began appearing on the market for the IBM PC. In order to take advantage of these new developments, the engineers would need to improve the Paula chip, which controlled IO functions. George Robbins began talking with engineers to implement SCSI (which would allow faster 2MB/s transfer speeds) into a "Fat Paula" chip.

These ideas did not go anywhere all year until September, when the discussions around the chipset reopened. Ted Lenthe asked for an improved Paula with 2 MB/s support, along with possible networking and serial bus support. He also asked for a sound input channel in Paula which would allow a microphone to record sound digitally to the Amiga. And he wanted sound improvements to Paula, allowing four additional audio channels with 44.1 Khz "CD grade" audio quality.

In order to begin Fat Paula, the team would need to input the old Paula schematics into the Mentor system before they could begin making changes to the chip. However, clearly the Paula improvements were on the back burner and seen as less important than the graphics chip changes.

A2024 monitor for COMDEX

By August 1987, Hedley Davis' high resolution monitor was given full authorization by Henri Rubin to go forward as an official Commodore product. Up until then it had been something Davis and Dale Luck worked on in the background. The two now planned to debut a prototype monitor at the upcoming COMDEX in November.

Davis was somewhat disappointed that Luck, with his relaxed Californian ways, had not progressed more with his AmigaOS modifications. However,

Luck promised he would have the alpha release done by the time COM-DEX arrived.

Luck's changes were a first step towards making the AmigaOS less dependent on specific video hardware. While he worked on that, Davis delivered his PAL equations to CSG, who would soon begin producing his gate array chip for the monitor.

With the software and chip production in other hands, Davis focused on working with a third-party supplier of monitors. He was in talks with an American company with offices in Taiwan named ADI Corporation. "I didn't actually do monitor design, nor did Commodore do monitor design," explains Davis. "We had a Taiwanese company build that product for us. All I did was some digital stuff and some emitter-coupled logic (ECL). The way it was instantiated was a stand-alone monitor with a card built into the bottom."

The end result was, once the AmigaOS modifications were complete, the A2024 could plug into an A500 or A2000's RGB video connector port and work flawlessly, without the need for an additional video card.

Before the show, Davis scrambled to get his "Hedley Hi-Res" monitor working in time. He had just received the first gate array chip from CSG. "He hooks it up and there's no signal at all," recalls Bob Welland.

Davis went to work trying to diagnose the bug. "In those days, you would take the chip to a microprobe station, which is basically a very nice microscope with the ability to move very precisely in X and Y, and actually put probes on the chip itself," explains Welland. "What he found was that he had inverted the horizontal sync signal. So nothing came out because basically it just showed black."

Unable to wait weeks for a new chip revision, Davis tried to fix the problem with microsurgery. "He had to cut a trace on the chip and actually jumper around this inversion," explains Welland. "And then the chip worked!"

Through the summer and fall, Luck had made modifications to the hardware at Davis' direction. "We were making changes to it and enhancements and tweaking it," explains Davis. "It had all these PALs on it, so I would have to send them instructions to say, 'Okay make a new PAL. Here's the code for that new PAL. Cut this wire. Jumper this wire,' so that he could modify his board out there to make the same one I was doing."

Davis had an acerbic wit and couldn't help himself. "Being the snotty smart assed motherfucker I was, I would always say, 'And watch out for the pointy end of the soldering iron. It gets really hot.' This is nothing but a hardware guy poking fun at the software guy."

His jibes came back to haunt him when Davis had some last-minute fixes to make. "We're there on the display floor and it's the night before the show and something's wrong with the display model," Davis recalls. "It's like holy crap! I'm sitting there in the booth, I've got the thing taken apart and I realized I've got to do some soldering. So I whip out the portable soldering iron, which is this cheap-ass Radio Shack soldering pencil and I don't have a proper desk to work on, so it's just kind of hanging over the display case and I'm looking at the monitor and I see what I have to solder. I reached down to grab it and I reached down too low and I grabbed a soldering iron at the hot end."

Davis yelled out in pain, attracting the attention of other engineers. "And damn if Luck wasn't standing right there. He says, 'Dude, watch out for the pointy end, it gets hot.' He got his revenge."

At the November 1987 COMDEX, Davis and Luck debuted the A2024 monitor to the masses. To demonstrate the utility of the higher resolutions, a desktop publishing application called *City Desk* was also shown working at the highest resolution. Although it was never intended to become a mass market device that would sell in the millions, the attendees immediately recognized it, along with the Amiga, as a workstation level solution for a bargain price.

At the same show, a preview of a new product called the Video Toaster, consisting of a genlock and software suite, made its debut. "We were trying to pitch the Amiga as the premier video editing platform in the industry," says RJ Mical. "Commodore saw the wisdom in using that as one of the main selling points of the machine."

In an attempt to improve the Amiga graphics capabilities, Commodore now had multiple projects in the works by multiple engineers. The engineers had yet to agree on the specs for the current evolution of the chipset, however. With the situation still murky, the project continued to grind along, but it became less likely that Commodore would be able to debut a new Amiga with the improved chipset at the upcoming CeBit in March.

Management Moves 1987

The previous year, Chief Operating Officer Henri Rubin had played a crucial role in undermining Thomas Rattigan, leading to the latter's eventual dismissal from Commodore.[1] Now, Rubin became focused on fixing the various criticisms with the Amiga. He and his team also had to come together with a set of goals for the next computer systems Commodore would release, and there was a lot of uncertainty about what those computers should look like.

Henri Rubin

Henri Rubin (along with Gerard Bucas, Clive Smith, and Unix programmer Johann George) hailed from South Africa. He had solid engineering credentials going back to the 1950s. "He was kind of a strange duck but Irving liked him, and he was an engineer's engineer," says Jeff Porter. "Henri had lots of colloquialisms; strange South African expressions of speech."

While working for South African company C. J. Fuchs Electrical Industries, Rubin had pioneered the Residual-current device (RCD), a safety device similar to the ground fault interrupter (GFI) that prevented workers from the dangers of electrocution. "He was the alleged inventor of the ground fault interrupter when he worked for Westinghouse in Johannesburg, South Africa," says Commodore engineer Bill Gardei. "Miners were too often getting electrocuted by pumps used to pull water out of the mines." RCD and GFI later came into wide use among businesses and homes.

---

1   As covered in *Commodore: The Amiga Years* ISBN 9780994031020.

Rubin's RCD invention was later manufactured by another South African company, co-founded by Carl J. Fuchs, called F.W.J. Electrical Industries. Although RCD would become a popular world-changing invention, it would take more than that to earn Rubin a position at Commodore.

Rubin later worked for an electrical appliances company named Tedelex Electrics Ltd., with Rubin as executive chairman. As it turns out, Commodore was a trading partner with Tedelex. "He was the Commodore distributor for South Africa," says Porter. This gave him an outsider's perspective on the types of computers dealers wanted from Commodore.

The engineers weren't sure what to make of Rubin. Opinions ranged from "delightfully eccentric" to "doddering old man". Rubin also had the power to get things done, due to his connection with Irving Gould. The system engineers relied on other departments (LSI, Design Engineering, or even Documentation). Oftentimes engineers would ask for a resource, such as a new case design, and the results came slowly. Now they could use Rubin to produce immediate results. Porter soon realized Rubin would work out well for him and for his engineers.

System Plans for 1988

After George Robbins completed the Amiga 500 and accompanying A520 video adapter, it was time to move on to the next project. With the prototype hi-res Agnus and Denise chips expected soon, Jeff Porter began discussing the next iteration of the A500 with Robbins. It was a given the new A500 would use the hi-res chips, but the two also decided to use the Motorola 68020 processor, which would give faster performance. The engineers also wanted 1 megabyte of expensive VRAM in the system.

Porter dubbed the new computer the Super A500. The total cost of goods came in at $399, meaning it would sell to dealers for $799 and retail to consumers for a whopping $1000. This was a far cry from the $500 goal the team originally had with the B52. Why was it so expensive? Commodore would have to spend $77 for the 68020 chip plus $100 for VRAM on top of the basic $230 cost of the original A500 (minus redundant costs for memory and processor). It was questionable whether or not the Super A500 would appeal to the existing base of A500 users.

Porter expected to see a prototype Super A500 in January 1988. Robbins went to work designing the system while awaiting the prototype hi-res Amiga chipset.

Commodore had released the A2000-CR in the same case Commodore Germany had used for the A2500 (later renamed A2000). Porter wanted something sleeker and cost reduced for the Amiga 2000. "We needed something that could satisfy the business marketplace, and I didn't want it being so big fat and ugly," he explains.

Porter assigned mechanical designer Herb Mosteller to work on a new case which he dubbed the A2001. He planned to place the new cost-reduced A2000 motherboard in the new case.

After Dave Haynie completed the A2000-CR project, it was time for him to get to work on the next iteration of Commodore's high-end line of Amigas. The new project, which the engineers dubbed the A3000, would also reside in the new A2001 case. And much like the Super A500, it would use the hi-res Amiga chipset, a Motorola 68020 chip running at 14.2 MHz (double the clock speed of the A2000), high density floppy disks storing up to 1760 KB, 2 MB of VRAM, and a SCSI interface. The computer would also use Bob Welland's MMU card.

The systems were conceived mainly by the engineers, without input from Commodore's marketing executives, such as Clive Smith or Frank Leonardi. "In the Amiga days, marketing didn't know what they wanted so we had to tell them," says Dave Haynie.

In addition, Haynie would design a new 32-bit Zorro expansion bus. Porter expected to show the new A3000 at the March 1988 Hanover Fair. "We made a more compact desktop factor that had a riser board and side-mounted plugin cards," says Porter. It also would ship with a built-in SCSI hard drive, something that was becoming a requirement by the end of the decade in most computers.

Back in October 1986, Porter had hired an engineer named Jeff Frank to "Commodore-ize" a PC by putting an IBM-PC clone in a keyboard case. Frank completed his radically cost reduced, slotless PC-1 by late 1987. But instead of the "computer in a keyboard" concept, Frank designed a small box with a detachable keyboard. The "PC-Eins" as it was also known was released exclusively in Europe. As Commodore found out, most PC users felt slots were important in the PC world, and the computer sold poorly despite the low price.

On August 6, Porter officially drew up plans for the entire engineering group, which consisted of 18 engineers plus Bart Whitebook of the Amiga group, and some contractors like Dale Luck and Johan George. Now that many smaller projects for the 8-bit lines were completed, such as the

1541-II floppy drive, 1581 disk drive, 1764 RAM expansion, and the new Commodore manufactured version of the 1670 modem, it was time to find new assignments.

Porter devised a new cost-reduced 1571-II disk drive for the C128. He also wanted a genlock for the Amiga 500, which he dubbed the A530. Porter himself would design a new Amiga 1200-baud modem called the 1680, plus a 2400-baud Amiga modem called the 1690. He also resurrected a personal project of his own called Answermate, a Fax/Modem device for the A500, A1000, and A2000.

Porter assigned an Amiga laser printer and a new scanner project to Greg Berlin. He assigned a new AT emulator board for the A2000 to Germany's Wilfried Rusniok. Both Jeff Frank and Ian Kirschemann would work on a new cost-reduced version of the hit PC-10, along with the PC-40 using an Intel 80286 microprocessor and the PC-60 using Intel's 80386 microprocessor. Kirschemann would also work on (but not complete) a genlock card for the PC-40, similar to the Amiga genlock.

Commodore engineer Jeff Boyer would create a hard disk controller board for the Amiga 500, along with a new DMAC (Direct Memory Access Controller) chip to handle a SCSI drive.

Bob Welland had the most diffuse jobs. He would continue working on his 68020 accelerator board for the Amiga 2000, in order to get Unix running on the system. But more importantly, Welland would begin defining the next quantum leap in display chips—the very thing the original Amiga engineers wanted. "We were hoping they would also continue advanced development of graphics," recalls Dale Luck.

Porter specifically wanted 1000 by 800 resolution with 8 bit planes and 16 million colors—something to exceed the current competition. Of importance would be keeping the new video technology compatible with existing commercial Amiga software.

All of these plans would be discussed at Commodore's worldwide engineering meeting, scheduled for September 22, 1987 at the Embassy Suites hotel in New York. The meeting was called by Henri Rubin, and those invited included the main West Chester engineers, along with engineers from Germany and Japan.

Clive Smith Leaves

Commodore's General Manager of the Commodore Product and Market Development Group, Clive Smith, had played a key role in acquiring the Amiga and extending C64 sales by putting together a package that included the GEOS graphical operating system. His efforts helped to grow C64 revenue, allowing Commodore to emerge from a tough financial period, and into the era when revenue from Amiga 500 and Amiga 2000 sales could sustain the company. Then Thomas Rattigan's departure in 1987 caused a management shakeup that could either help or hurt Smith's standing within the company.

Henri Rubin had been with Commodore for over a year and had slowly assumed the product development role. And with that, Clive Smith's position was gradually becoming more irrelevant as the engineers took over. In fact, many within the company, including Jeff Porter, considered Smith to be a loose cannon, someone who challenged their supremacy over Commodore's future products.

And there was more. Gould was increasingly unhappy with the costs incurred by the Quantum Link deal made by Smith.[2] "Commodore lost money doing that," says former marketing executive Kit Spencer. "That was one of the things that he didn't do too well on."

Former Commodore software developer Neil Harris agrees it was a bad deal. "Frankly, from a basic business agreement, Commodore got took on that agreement with Quantum Link," he says. "I don't know what they were thinking at the time but it was just a strange deal."

The problem was that profits from the deal were too far off in the future. "If Commodore had held onto its ownership stake in Quantum Link, it would have made a whole bunch of money," says Finkel. Smith would only be proven to be correct over a decade later when the investment in Quantum Link (then AOL) went stratospheric.

Even with the soured deal, Smith had a lot to be proud of as one of the key supporters of Commodore's mass-market products. The deal for Q-Link had not been great, but the Q-Link service was well regarded in the Commodore community, along with the fantastical *Habitat* MMO game. And Smith had shepherded in GEOS, the 1351 mouse, the C64c, and the 1764 RAM expander for Commodore 64 users.

On June 26, Brian Dougherty and the guys from Berkeley came to Commodore and gave an executive presentation on what was next for GEOS. Then in August, Jeff Porter had presented Commodore's product plans for fiscal year 1988. Smith realized there was little room left for a mass-market-oriented executive like himself and he began looking for an exit from

---

2   The deal with Quantum Link is detailed in *Commodore: The Amiga Years* ISBN 9780994031020.

Commodore. That exit turned out to be Berkeley. "Clive ended up ultimately leaving Commodore and joined our board," says Brian Dougherty.

On August 28, 1987, Smith resigned from Commodore but continued consulting occasionally for the company. With Smith gone, the C64 mantle now fell to a handful of engineers who still had faith in the C64 legacy—including Jeff Porter.

Porter and Rubin met with the worldwide engineering team (including the West Chester engineers) on September 22, 1987. Their goal was to begin moving these plans forward because they needed those products ready for the upcoming CeBIT, as well as for smaller UK and US trade shows in the first half of 1988.

Max Toy

Ever since he had terminated Thomas Rattigan's contract, Irving Gould himself had occupied the position of CEO and President of Commodore International. However, running the day-to-day operations of the company was not something he was naturally suited for, especially considering he hardly spent any time at Commodore's headquarters, much less the United States. He needed someone with a key set of skills.

Commodore's failure to push the Amiga 500 into mass-market retail stores in the US was poorly received by investors, and it affected the company's stock price. By October 1987, the share price had slid from over $12 while Rattigan was in charge to under $8.50. It was obvious the market was not confident in Irving Gould's leadership.

Gould's constant jetting around the globe meant Commodore needed a competent president to run the day-to-day operations at West Chester. More importantly, Gould needed someone who could recapture the US market.

After Thomas Rattigan's right hand man, Nigel Shepherd, departed, it took seven months to find his replacement. In October 1987, Gould named Max E. Toy as president and Chief Operating Officer of Commodore Business Machines in North America. Toy came to Commodore with more computer industry experience than any executive before him. He started at IBM where he worked in a variety of sales and marketing positions, then he moved to the highly successful Compaq Corporation, where he was vice president of sales. More recently, he was an executive who helped turn around ITT Corporation by increasing its distribution channels.

Gould instructed Toy to lead "the company towards our goal of recapturing our market share in the United States." His tenure would depend on the success or failure of this goal.

Industry observers liked the 42-year old president's straightforward, honest approach. Most importantly, Toy was a true believer in the Amiga. His previous experience meant he knew where the Amiga stood compared to the other PC clone computers.

Commodore employees were generally favorable towards Toy. "He gave good talk and he sounded like he had some plans on what he was going to do," says Dave Haynie.

With Commodore fighting the image as a maker of toy computers, it would be ironic if an executive named Max Toy could bring it back to relevance in the North American market.

Black Monday

Within weeks of hiring Max Toy, things got even worse for the company and for the world at large. Irving Gould had already watched Commodore's stock price fall on the New York Stock Exchange since Rattigan's unfortunate departure, but on October 19, 1987 the damage escalated. "It's a day I'll never forget," says Don Gilbreath, who had a desk in the same office as Gould. "I remember getting off the train and the market was already down. I remember looking at the CBU stock on the ticker on the street and I calculated that Irving's fortune was crushed. The company's stock was something like two dollars or less. And I'm thinking, I'm going to an office where a guy from the twenty first floor just lost $600 million dollars in value."

However, when Gilbreath reached his office he was surprised by Gould's demeanor. "I get up there and he's in a good mood! You know why? Well it turns out he was in the soap business."

Gould owned a chain of laundromats across the country, which helped diversify his holdings, and investments in cleaning products were having a good day. "The tech industry was crushed but he was ok in soap," says Gilbreath. It was enough of a silver lining to keep Gould sane. "He could have jumped off of a building. A lot of guys did that day."

The stock market crash, which would become known as Black Monday, was one of the biggest single-day drops on the stock market. It was an ominous sign for Gould's first year as CEO.

The Next Wave

The Amiga was a more complicated machine than previous efforts, and it required full teams dedicated to the operating system, hardware design, and chip design. With so many new projects planned, it would be impossible to contemplate them at Commodore's current staff levels. A hiring freeze had been in effect in the company, but in late 1987 it was finally lifted. Commodore began hiring engineers from colleges, injecting new life-blood into the company.

Many of those applying for positions soon realized they were entering a different kind of organization when they laid eyes on George Robbins. "I had the office right next to his, and I was interviewing this candidate and the guy is in a suit and everything," recalls Bob Welland. "[Robbins] was sitting in his office picking his toes with a giant buck knife. And he's like, 'Who is that guy?' And I said, 'Oh, that's George. He's a consultant.' And he couldn't understand that. 'He's a consultant?!' He's sitting there in this funny way George existed. He was his own person and he wasn't embarrassed by the person he was."

In addition to the main projects Commodore was working on, Henri Rubin added hardware devices such as networking cards and hard drives. He hired an engineer named Joe Augenbraun to work on these. "Apparently before me they had done some big layoffs and they were lean for a while, and I was first hire after they started hiring again," he says. "I was low man on the totem pole, so they put me on all the projects that no one wanted to be on; things that weren't fun or interesting. But I was happy to do the stuff that wasn't fun and interesting."

His first project was to come up with a proper network card for the Amiga computers. "I became the networking guy," he says. "To me it was interesting to learn how networking worked. I was just integrating existing chips and the chipsets weren't very well integrated at the time. It's putting chips that were meant to be for a PC onto an Amiga."

Augenbraun also worked on an Amiga hard drive adapter. "I figured out how to interface an ATA Drive to an Amiga," he says. "It's not the Dave Haynie rockstar A3000 stuff, but I was happy to do it."

Rubin also hired a talented chip designer into the Commodore's LSI group named James Redfield. He would lead the upcoming high-end version of the Amiga chipset, along with George Robbins.

Dragging On

Engineering had made plans during the summer of 1987, but almost no one was able to begin new projects, even late in the year, because they were still occupied with finishing off old projects. Dave Haynie, who was supposed to be working on the new Amiga 3000 computer, instead helped Bob Welland, who was having difficulty completing the accelerator board for the A2000. All Haynie had to show for his A3000 was a wishlist of features he hoped to include.

Finally, in late November, Jeff Porter was forced to take action to motivate the engineers. He wrote to them, "Guys, we really do need to get our projects under control again. We've got some that are dragging on almost a year now! This, of course, puts us all in a very embarrassing position."

The sudden urgency was spurred on by the unlikeliest candidate at Commodore, Henri Rubin. As Porter explained, "It's gotten so bad that even Henri has noticed." As it turned out, Rubin had just got back from the annual board meeting in New York and felt acute pressure from CEO Gould to finish off some long-promised projects.

Engineering usually had relaxed timelines and goals, but now Porter asked his engineers to provide him with detailed bi-weekly progress reports and schedules for each project. He hoped this would keep his engineers focused and more accountable on their assigned projects.

Porter also reduced his project list, including the proposed AnswerMate device and a PC-80 clone.

The A3000 hinged on the engineers creating a new chipset for the machine, but the engineers arguments continued since September with no one able to agree on a spec for the new chipset. At the time, Porter told Bucas and Rubin, "Can you say 'can of worms'? ... Welland and Hedley will still be arguing by February about the next video chips."

The problem was, there were at least three different proposals for a hi-res chipset by three different engineers. Bob Welland wanted to begin fresh with a new architecture. Hedley Davis wanted to revise the existing Agnus/Denise architecture. Similarly, George Robbins wanted to revise the Agnus/Denise architecture based on a 32-bit architecture. No one could agree.

With this situation, it looked like the next generation chipset had every possibility of being bogged down for months. Porter had previously hoped to show a prototype of an Amiga 3000 at the Hanover show in March 1988, but now it looked like that timeline was overly optimistic.

Meanwhile, it seemed most engineers and all management had given up on 8-bit computers and the Commodore 64 legacy. But in the semiconductor design group, a young engineer named Bill Gardei was figuring out how to advance the 6502 chip at the core of the 8-bit computers, which CSG had not significantly improved since 1976.

C65
1985-1987

Commodore's rabid legion of C64 fans had patiently awaited a true sequel and had finally gotten one in 1985 in the form of the C128. However, the original C64 continued to outpace sales of the C128 and many users wanted better graphics and sound, a faster CPU, and an improved C64 mode that could run existing C64 software. Within Commodore, most engineers and managers were done with the C64 line and ready to move on with Amiga products only. But certain engineers were not yet ready to say good-bye to the C64 lineage.

4502 CMOS Chip

Back in 1985, the 6502 chip was ten years old but still in popular use throughout the computer industry. Atari used the 6502 in many of its color arcade games such as *Crystal Castles* (1983) and *Return of the Jedi* (1984), not to mention its home computers and video game consoles. Atari, who bought its chips from Commodore Semiconductor Group (CSG), would continue developing new products with the help of its sworn rival until the late 1980s.

In the same year, Commodore wanted to manufacture 6502 chips using the more efficient CMOS process. "CMOS was relatively new to us at that time," says chip designer Bill Gardei. "All prior parts were NMOS, and prior to that PMOS with its painful power supply requirements."

Engineers hoped to use CMOS chips in future products, such as portable LCD computers and helper chips in other systems. "Commodore needed a new 8-bit CMOS core to embed in other chip projects and for standalone applications like the Amiga's RS-232 expansion board," says Gardei.

Commodore had purchased the rights from the Western Design Center (WDC) to produce Bill Mensch's 65C02 for half price and had plans to use the chips in the LCD computer. However, there were restrictions. "We had the Western Design Center's database for the 65SC02, but it had with it stipulations that it could not be sold as a stand-alone part," says Gardei. If CSG wanted to sell the CMOS chips to Atari or other customers, it would have to design its own.

Gardei also wanted the ability to customize the chips. "Western Design Center did not have what we wanted," he says. "We wanted flexibility and the capability of doing anything we wanted with our own core."

Commodore's Large Scale Integration department, headed by Bob Olah, began preliminary investigations in July 1985 into a CMOS 6502 chip which his design engineer Ted Lenthe called the 55C02. (He eventually shortened the name to 5502.) The LSI group would design the chip using 3 micron CMOS. Lenthe gave no schedule for the project, due to the recent cancellation of the LCD computer, and by December 1985 Commodore scrapped the project.

It seemed like the project was dead, until a new recruit decided to take it on himself. Bill Gardei had worked for the LSI group since the beginning of the year. "I was interviewed and hired by Bob Olah in February of 1985," he says.

On his own, he decided to resurrect the 5502 project, this time using 2 micron CMOS. He dubbed the new chip the 4502. "All new CMOS custom chips were given the series number of 4000 and up, so 4502 was the obvious choice," he says. "The 4502 core development started in late 1985. The original designers were myself and Charles Hauck."

Their design would use the same instruction set as the 6502, but they would improve the efficiency of many of those functions. "It was patterned after the legendary 6502 microprocessor," he says. One major difference was that Gardei hoped his chips could run at clock speeds of 7 MHz (compared to 1 MHz for the 6510 in the C64).

Gardei would design the 4502 chip using microcode, which is similar to creating a chip by programming it with a computer language. "He wrote a 6502 in Verilog," says Hedley Davis, referring to the language used to design the chip.

"Every CPU is internally microcoded," explains Gardei. "The original 6502 (and earlier 6501) were also microcoded, even though their layouts were done with Rubylith."

If all went well, two years later Commodore would have the CMOS chips. With 16-bit chips like the 68000 already in popular use, it was a calculated risk that the chip would still be relevant at the end of the long design process.

4502 Design Done

In 1987, just before the completion of the 4502 project, Bill Gardei's co-designer, Charles Hauck, decided to leave Commodore. "Charles left to go work for Kendall Square Research, a supercomputer company in the Boston area, before the 4502 was finished," says Gardei. "I was left to complete the job."

Thankfully Gardei was capable enough on his own. Among Commodore's engineers, he was particularly noted for his intelligence. "What can I say, Bill is super smart," says Hedley Davis. "A very, very smart guy."

Gardei was not content to just copy the 6502 and make a CMOS version. Rather, he had upgraded it. "The 4502 was an improved 6502 core, which had some or all of the GTE extensions, and some extensions that Hedley Davis came up with," says Dave Haynie.

The GTE extensions consisted of additional opcodes. "The extensions were new opcodes that the original 6502 and 6510 did not have," says Gardei. "Adding instructions to a CPU makes it more flexible and more powerful."

By early August 1987, the design was complete, and Gardei handed it off to other engineers within Commodore's LSI group. For the next several months, they would create a chip layout and finally manufacture samples of the chip.

Commodore Semiconductor head Bob Olah had left Commodore in April 1986 and was replaced by veteran Commodore LSI engineer Ted Lenthe. Lenthe assigned Gardei to several of the ongoing Amiga chip projects while his CMOS 4502 entered the preproduction phase. "I was finding and solving problems with the Amiga chipset," says Gardei. But Commodore had no immediate plans for his 4502. After two years in development, he did not want to see his chip placed on the back shelf. "I had already developed the 4502 core, which could run up to 40% faster than the 6502 at the same clock speed," he says. "Now I needed an application for it."

The most obvious project was a new C64. GEOS creator Brian Dougherty feels it made sense for Commodore to continue the C64 legacy, even by 1987. "With the C64, Commodore eventually needed a technical successor," he says. "I think the problem was they didn't manage the transition. As good as the Commodore 64 was, it eventually was going to get eclipsed by more sophisticated technology."

However, few of Gardei's fellow engineers were interested in developing new 8-bit machines. "Commodore was pretty much giving up on its low-end computer line," says Gardei. "They were the ultimate low- cost computer machines but it looked like the C64 and C128 were going to be the last of their breed."

Ignoring the 65816

Although Brian Dougherty thought it was time for a true C64 successor, he felt it would have made more sense to use a 16-bit chip. "They needed to move to a 16- and 32-bit processor platform. That was their vision with the Amiga, but they just never executed right on that."

Gardei did not seriously consider using a 16-bit chip, such as the successor to the 6502, the 65816 (by Western Design Center), because it would have defeated the purpose of making a low-cost machine. "We could have built our own 16-bit variant," says Gardei. "But every time you double the bus width, you increase system cost. We decided instead to increase cycle efficiency and be able to run at a clock five times faster than WDC."

Gardei assumed the 8-bit C64 success was based on price. He believed a $600 16-bit C64 would fail because it could only succeed if it was cheap, like the current C64c model. However, there may have been early adopters prepared to pay a premium for a 16-bit successor. And with time, the price would fall.

In any event, Gardei was hooked on his 8-bit 4502 chip. "Given the problems we had working with the 65SC02, we didn't want to work with Western Design Center or their part, the 65816," says Gardei. "Fred [Bowen] didn't like it. Neither did I."

That feeling was shared among Commodore's engineers. "Which 16-bit chip are you going to use, the Mensch chip? The 65816 was kind of a weird chip," says Dave Haynie. "I suggested using it one time and I don't think Fred liked it at all."

Andy Finkel at least considered going to WDC. "That might have been interesting. It may have been time to stop trying to do it all and maybe use somebody else's chip."

However, the limited support for the 65816 was a deciding factor against it. "That was at a time when one guy could design a chip completely, like Bill [Mensch] did," says Finkel. "It was kind of at its end because they were just getting more and more complicated. The size of the dies and the number of interconnects were getting enormous. I think Bill did that chip by hand on drafting tables," he laughs. "That was the end of the era and it wasn't going to get a lot of support. Whereas a chip like the 68000 family was going to be a family and get a lot more continued support and continued development work."

It was a rare occurrence; the 65816 was good enough for Apple (in the Apple IIGS) and Nintendo (in the Super Nintendo), but it wasn't good enough for Commodore. Given that the C64 was released in 1982, it seemed like a faster 8-bit system would have been well received in 1984, but now it was almost 1988 and a system using the chip would not be ready for at least another year.

In the end, price was the main factor that pushed the engineers away from the 65816. "The other problem was that they were very expensive," adds Haynie. "They cost quite a bit more than the 68000 and there was some question about whether there was any quantity available. The other simple reason is that Commodore had finally built their own CMOS 6502 compatible, so why not use it?"

Conceiving the Next C64

Over the past two years, the idea to create a sequel to the C64 had slowly taken shape in Bill Gardei's mind as he designed the 4502 chip. He called his sequel the C65. "The C65 was my idea," he says. "I saw what other companies like Nintendo were doing and said, 'We can do that better and cheaper.' If their graphics and computer capabilities could be brought up to current standards, the interest in these machines would continue."

Gardei hoped to remedy the criticisms of the C128, which lacked a worthy successor to the VIC-II chip. The C128 also failed to improve on the C64 by not bringing more memory or faster chip speeds to bear on the C64 software library. Bill Gardei sought to change all that. "Reviving the sagging low-end line by adding 256 colors, a faster clock, and the new CPU looked like the way to do it," he says.

Gardei began writing a proposal to take the C64's many custom chips and "glue logic" (found in TTL circuits) and put them on, as he called them, "two giant Gonzo chips". The result would vastly reduce the number of components in the new computer to only 8 IC's and a few other components.

The power supply would cost only $3 due to the reduced energy requirements of CMOS chips. He also proposed using the motherboard as the keyboard PCB to reduce the keyboard cost to $6.13. Finally, the C65 would omit outdated cassette support altogether.

His two "Gonzo" chips, the 4510 and a proposed new video chip called the 4567, would cost $4 and $5 respectively. The 64 KB of DRAM would cost $4.76. And because of the few components required, the tiny 3 x 5 inch PCB would cost a paltry $2.00.

At the time, the C64c's bill of materials (BOM) came to $52.19. Gardei estimated the BOM for his mostly backward compatible C64 descendent was $39.25. This would make the final retail price in the neighborhood of $100, the same price as a stock NES game console. "He was the perfect guy to work on the C65 because he loved little minimalist architecture with chips doing as much as you possibly can in this very low-end platform," recalls Paul Lassa, who would later join the project.

On October 14, 1987, Gardei sent his proposal to his boss, Ted Lenthe. "It wasn't hard to get Ted interested," he says. "We already had a track record of success with the 4502." Lenthe was receptive, but he wanted more details on backward compatibility with serial devices, such as the 1541 drive and printers, as well as memory expansions.

There were a few anachronistic features in the C65 proposal. Back in 1982, the C64 came with 64 KB of memory. Five years later, Gardei was proposing a computer with the same memory. Gardei explains his decision as, "Cost, cost, and cost. C65 was supposed to be super affordable to the low-end user. The bill of materials came to $39 US in models without disk drives."

His plan was to sneak the product into consumers' hands at an ultra low cost and then offer a separate memory upgrade, much like the Amiga 500 had. "I personally wanted a 1 MB memory stick in it, or at least a slot for it," he says.

Commodore's LSI group would now attempt to create new graphics and microprocessor chips in CMOS to complement the 4502. "Ted authorized work on the C65 chipset," says Gardei.

Although Ted Lenthe gave the project an official go ahead, it did not appear on any official project schedule yet. In fact, it would remain under wraps until it was more developed and Lenthe could build up support from management. Not even Gerard Bucas or Henri Rubin would be aware of it until later.

For the first time in years, a new Commodore computer would emerge from the semiconductor group, rather than the system engineering group. A similar thing had happened in the early 1980s when three chip guys, Al Charpentier, Robert Yannes, and their boss Charles Winterble, had proposed the VIC-20 and C64 computers. Those engineers had developed their system in secret, away from the system engineering group, who at the time were focused on higher end, expensive machines. History was about to repeat itself.

The C64's popularity crested in 1987, so an improved C64 had the potential to become very relevant if Commodore could release it a year later. In fact, 1988 would be an optimal year to introduce an improved C64. But could the C65 survive its own development cycle?

Bill Gardei

The father of the C65 was born April 3, 1954. During his teenage years, he became interested in electronics. His hobbies included amateur radio, model trains and eventually computers. Bill Gardei even helped a famed microcomputer pioneer. "I worked for Don Lancaster in my high school years, who wrote magazine articles for *Popular Electronics* and *Radio-Electronics* magazines, doing product photography and PCB layout," he says.

The experience helped inform his decision to attend university. "I studied electrical engineering at Arizona State University just before the microprocessor was available to the individual. Beyond that, all my computer engineering skills were obtained either on the job or from personal studies."

After graduation, he worked for a number of semiconductor companies, such as GTE, where he helped Bill Mensch of the Western Design Center fabricate his 16-bit 6502 chips. "The WDC chips, including the 65SC02, 65SC802, and 65SC816, were fabbed by GTE Microcircuits in Tempe, Arizona, on 52nd Street at the base of Tempe Butte," says Gardei. "I worked in that fab and was test engineer on all three products and helped Bill Mensch with the initial debug of the 65SC02."

Bill Mensch was also the original creator of the aforementioned extended GTE opcodes. "The GTE extensions were the Western Design Center extensions. And some of them I recommended to Bill Mensch when he designed the 65SC02," says Gardei.

Shortly thereafter, in February of 1985, Commodore's Bob Olah hired him into CSG.

Among the engineers at Commodore during this time period, there are only two who are consistently mentioned for their exceptional intelligence. This is saying something in a place that was already stacked with highly intelligent engineers. The first was Bob Welland, the amiable and gentlemanly co-creator of the Amiga 500. The second was Bill Gardei. Not one engineer could talk about him without mentioning his extreme intelligence.

However, he was also uncompromising, a quality that rankled some. This led to difficult collaborations on projects. "He was one of the chip designers and not a real friendly guy," recalls Dave Haynie. "People didn't like to work with him."

VIC-III

Once his boss, Ted Lenthe, approved of a new set of chips, the 33-year-old Gardei began work on a true successor to the legendary VIC-II chip, with backward compatibility and improved graphics modes. By early November 1987 he had mostly figured out the required video timing for his new 4567 chip.

To prove the design, he produced a simulation of a CMOS version of the 6567 VIC-II chip. "I showed him working SILOS simulations of the 4567 video chip and we all decided this would not be hard to do," he says ominously.

The VIC-III was perhaps the most important aspect of the new system. In fact, it was exactly what Bil Herd would have wanted to create the C128. With it, the C128 would have made a more powerful impact and perhaps spurred on new game development, making the C128 a mega-hit rather than a modest success it became.

The VIC-III would retain backward compatibility with its predecessor chip, unlike the VIC-II, which did not support the VIC video chip modes found in the VIC-20. This would give the VIC-III backward compatibility with C64 software, while adding new graphical modes.

At this early stage, Gardei's plan for the VIC-III was fairly modest. It would support 80-column character mode, just like the C128 had before it, but in one integrated video chip. In bitmap mode, it would produce a 320x200 screen resolution with 64 colors and 640x200 with 16 colors. The latter would of course produce elongated pixels on the screen that would appear strange, however, by doubling the video memory and buffering screens on alternating cycles, the chip could produce interlaced video at 640x400.

One feature the VIC-III did not improve on was the hardware sprites. It would merely support 8 sprites at a resolution of 24 x 21 pixels (or 12 x 21 multicolor); exactly the same as the VIC-II.

Once again, Gardei would design the 4567 using the Verilog language. "That was his model for the C65 and he did the major chips in Verilog," says Hedley Davis.

4502 Samples

While Gardei worked on his 4567 chip, CSG was simultaneously preparing the 4502 chip for production. On the week of November 23, it was ready. The new CMOS 4502 was housed in the same packaging as the old 6502 and totally compatible. "When the 4502 came out of the wafer fab and the first chip was packaged, Ron Wantuck, one of our test engineers, dropped it into a KIM-1 board, powered it up, and hit the reset button," says Gardei. "The display immediately came on. We looked around to see what we did wrong because at that time, chips just didn't work on the first revision. This one did. We noticed the board was now running at one-third its normal supply current."

"I have to give him credit," says Hedley Davis. "The shit he built worked. That's the bottom line, right? Sometimes you have these guys and they iterate on the design and they iterate again and again, and every time you get it back it's broken. Bill's shit basically seemed to work."

It was a gratifying result after years of effort. The engineers then upped the ante. "We pulled it out of the socket and put it into a Commodore VIC-20," says Gardei. "The computer immediately came up with the traditional 'bytes free ready.' It ran the operating system and played the games, but since it was cycle optimized, it was much faster than the original CPU at the same clock speed, so it was hard to win any of the games. Lunar Lander was now a real challenge."

The increased speed made the music sound like a sped-up record player. "As Ron said, 'The music was the goofiest music you ever heard.' With the CPU running up to 40% faster than the original, to me it sounded like merry-go-round music," says Gardei.

Now, if Commodore wanted to use a CMOS version of the 6502, it would no longer have to license Bill Mensch's 65C02. And CSG could offer the 4502 to other companies. But the 4502 would not go into volume production until there was a demand for it.

On December 4, 1987, the 4502 chip was added to CSG's product sheet. Although Gardei aimed for 7 MHz, production chips typically ran at 3.58 MHz. Marketing renamed the 4502 the 65CE02, and it would soon find its way into some Amiga 2000 boards.

But with the 8-bit market fading by 1987, it was questionable if any customers would have a use for the new processor. The 6502 was still relevant in 1987, getting design-wins in new products such as the NEC PC Engine/TurboGrafx-16 video game console, released in October 1987. But were new 8-bit projects being started by engineers in 1987?

4510 Design Begins

While the 4502 chip was compatible with the KIM-1 and VIC-20, it was not compatible with the C64. For that, Commodore would need a CMOS version of the 6510 chip found in the C64.

To create the new chip Gardei needed for his C65, Commodore would cram into the new chip, dubbed the 4510, all of the extra I/O logic in the 6510. Additionally, it would contain functions found in supporting chips in the C64, such as the 6526 CIA chip, which contained the timer and additional I/O pins.

The new "Gonzo" chip would contain the 4502 microprocessor, four 16-bit interval timers, two 24-hour time of day clocks (each with a programmable alarm), serial I/O, a memory map function to access up to 1 megabyte of memory, 30 individually programmable I/O lines and other features.

Commodore LSI's Victor Andrade would design the 4510 CMOS chip around Gardei's 4502 core. The 4510 CPU was planned to be capable of clock speeds up to 7 megahertz, although with the 40% increase in opcode efficiency, it would be equivalent to a 10 megahertz 6510.

Although the rest of the company outside of CSG was unaware of the new project, those within it, including layout technicians such as Sandy Roshong, were aware that something was coming together. Word eventually spread to C128 designer Bil Herd about the new project.

Herd's life was in a downward spiral in 1987, largely due to difficulties battling alcoholism. The startup he had left Commodore to join had since crashed, leaving him out of work. In late 1986 he had attempted to rejoin Commodore but had been rejected. Then on December 9, 1987, when word reached him about a new 8-bit project, he decided to try one more time.

Herd snuck into Commodore to visit a former coworker and used her terminal to send a message to Jeff Porter. He was fully aware of Gerard Bucas' decision not to hire him earlier, but he pleaded his case and laid out his skills point by point in a two page message. "I feel that due to my organizational capabilities and design skills I could once again be an asset to the CBM design team, especially in light of the fire drill atmosphere that pervades Commodore," he wrote.

The C65 project could have used an engineer like Bil Herd who was experienced with system development, highly skilled at fixing bugs, and able to finish projects on schedule. Unfortunately, Bucas was still concerned about his ability to work with Commodore's management team and denied him the position. As the history of the C65 project would show, Herd was exactly the type of engineer the project would have needed to succeed.[1]

C64D

At the same time as Bill Gardei's C64 sequel started, another C64 sequel began in a totally different group. The computer, dubbed the C64D, was an idea going back to May 1986 when Thomas Rattigan, Nigel Sheppard, and Clive Smith were still at the company. The plan called for the C64 to include a built-in floppy disk drive with faster disk access speeds. With the completion of the 1581 3.5 inch disk drive in late 1987, work could now go forward on the system.

The goal of the project was to keep the C64 current with escalating trends in game development. Many recent C64 games required multiple disks. For example, *Ultima IV* occupied four sides of a floppy disk, each storing up to 170K. The next game in the series would occupy eight disks. Something had to be done to save users from endless disk flipping. Commodore's new 1581 3.5 inch drive could store 800K, drastically cutting back on the number of game disks.

Commodore also wanted to spur sales of the 1581 drive, which had a low adoption rate among C64 users. Commodore's marketing had a golden opportunity: European users had been using tape cassettes for a long time, but were slowly becoming interested in diskettes. The European market could have skipped over the 1541 drive and gone straight to the 1581. This in turn could spur game development on 3.5 inch disks that could in turn pull the North American market over to the 1581 drive.

By making the 3.5 inch drive the new standard, once game publishers moved to the new format, existing C64 owners might just purchase the new 1581 drives by the millions. On the flip side, new customers who bought the C64D might also buy the 1541 drive in order to play the old library of titles. Thus, the new system could spur even more sales of Commodore's peripherals.

But that sort of marketing play would have required knowledgeable executives such as Nigel Shepherd, and he was gone. The current management lacked the knowledge to execute such a plan. It was another missed opportunity.

---

1   Bil Herd went on to work at a variety of jobs, including ambulance paramedic at the Cooper Trauma Center in New Jersey.

On November 9, 1987 Gerard Bucas put together a meeting with system programmer Fred Bowen and two Japanese engineers, Takashi Tokuda (an old timer of Commodore Japan going back to the calculator days) and Y. Maruta, a manager in the purchasing department.

The team decided the C64D should be 100% compatible with previous C64 software titles. It would use the same C64c motherboard in a new case, hurriedly designed by Herb Mosteller of Commodore Japan, that would include the 3.5 inch floppy drive. The computer would have two modes. The primary mode allowed access to the 3.5 inch drive and included changes to the system ROM code made by Bowen. To fit the new code, support for the cassette would be removed. If any incompatibilities were found, the user could boot into a pure C64 mode.

The 3.5 inch drive alone cost $26.78. With other parts, the bill of materials came to $120.82, including labor, duty and shipping. This was a lot compared to the C64, which cost Commodore around $50 to manufacture. At retail it would cost customers around $300, three times the proposed retail price of the C65.

Bowen would lead the project and expected to be able to demonstrate a prototype by December 1987. Pre-production units would be completed in March 1988, and at least 5000 units could be built by June 1988. Now the race was on to see if Commodore would succeed in releasing a new and improved low-cost computer to carry on the C64 legacy.

Amiga Unix
1988

Two of the biggest Unix supporters within Commodore were Bob Welland and his boss, VP of engineering Gerard Bucas. But was a Unix machine too much for Commodore to handle? This almost appeared to be a moot point as two of the biggest Unix supporters were about to leave for greener pastures.

Tech Pow-Wow

To prepare the worldwide sales force for the upcoming CeBIT trade show, Henri Rubin and Irving Gould arranged for a meeting with Commodore's sales force on January 12, 1988. It was a commendable move to reach out to their sales people in other territories to discuss product strategy, the type of thing that once happened under Jack Tramiel.

During the gathering, which Jeff Porter called a "tech pow-wow", the engineering group received feedback from the different sales divisions, which were in touch with their respective customer base. Rubin and Porter described the upcoming products, many of which had evolved since earlier discussions in 1987.

The German Braunschweig engineers would create a new line of PCs using the latest chipsets from Intel. In tandem with these, Braunschweig would develop a next generation bridgeboard card for the Amiga 2000, starting with the A2286 which was based on the Intel 286 processor.

Previously, Jeff Porter had proposed a more expensive Super Amiga 500. He believed Commodore had a gap in its product line between the A500 and the A2000. Specifically, he wanted Commodore to have a line of products ranging from low-end to high-end, delineated by multiples of two: $250, $500, $1000, and $2000. Since discontinuing the A1000, the company lacked a product at the $1000 range.

At the meeting the engineers fleshed out ideas for the Super A500, but also decided to rename it the A800 to indicate it had superior abilities to the A500. George Robbins would be tasked with creating a formal spec for the new system.

The team also needed a low-end system to replace the ailing C64. Rubin commissioned a study by the LSI group to see if they could find a silicon solution to produce a cost-reduced A500. Unfortunately, the LSI engineers concluded that there was a limit to how cheap they could offer Amiga technology. It would make more sense to concentrate on the higher-end machines.

The Amiga 500 would receive virtually no new improvements during 1988, although that was unlikely to hinder sales of the mass-market machine. A sequel to the Amiga 500 would be developed by George Robbins and released in 1989.

The foundation of the Amiga plans was an upgrade to the Amiga chipset. These plans had been mired for months by disagreements within the engineering team. As a result, Rubin did not believe Commodore would be able to keep up with the rapid PC release cycle and felt it would be at least 1989 before the engineers could release a completely new computer. But in order to keep the high-end Amiga line current, Commodore would produce upgrade cards for the Amiga 2000's video and processor slots, namely the A2620 accelerator card.

The company would release a "new" machine in 1988 that was merely the old A2000 with different adapter cards and faceplates. Named the Amiga 2500AT, it would contain an A2286 bridgeboard, the A2620 accelerator card, and a 40 MB hard drive with the A2090 card.

Rubin planned to release a brand new, high-end Amiga in 1989 with the moderately improved chipset and a Motorola 68030 CPU. He even dubbed this the Amiga 3000 very early.

Finally, Rubin wanted a machine to continue the legacy of the Commodore 64. Something truly inexpensive that would compete with Nintendo and allow Commodore shelf space in mass-market retailers and even toy stores across the US and Europe. The present plans called for the C64D, but Jeff Porter also revealed the C65 to Rubin.

And incredibly, Commodore still had designs on the Unix workstation marketplace, even though it was unlikely marketing would be able to handle the product. This was being driven by Commodore's engineering group rather than by management. Called the Amiga 2500UX, it would contain an A2620 accelerator card, a hard drive, and a Unix 5.3 compatible operating system developed by software engineer Johann George. Commodore also expected its future Unix customers to favor the A2024 "Hedley High Res" monitor.

And if one workstation wasn't enough, Commodore Braunschweig began working on the Transputer project. This accelerator card would turn an Amiga 2000 into a high performance workstation based on a parallel processor developed by Tim King, the engineer who supplied TRIPOS for Amiga.

It was a diverse plan, yet it also meant Commodore was developing a lot of products, which would one day require vast resources to produce and market properly. On top of that, Commodore already produced, supported, and marketed the C64, C128, A500, and A2000. In many ways, it looked like Commodore was repeating the errors that led it to the financial problems it had only recently escaped. Would Irving Gould, Henri Rubin, or Max Toy identify the problem and change course before that happened?

Less than a month after the meeting, on February 9, 1988, George Robbins produced his spec for the proposed Amiga 800. As Robbins described it, "The A800 is intended as a high performance, moderate cost partner to the low-end A500 personal computer system. The general goal is to produce a system which extracts as much of the potential of the 68020 processor as possible, while keeping a base retail price in the $1000-$1500 range."

The Motorola 68020, running at 14 MHz, would double the speed of the A800 compared to the A500. It would also use the upcoming HiRes chipset, much like the planned A3000. It was undecided whether it should go into an A500 style keyboard-case, or a box with a detachable keyboard. Aside from Robbins, several engineers, including Jeff Boyer and Jeff Porter supported the system, believing it could fill a valuable role in the Amiga lineup.

Bob Welland Leaves

In early 1988, Amiga 500 co-designer Bob Welland started to feel like it was time for him to go. "I felt like they've gotten the Amiga on solid ground from an economic standpoint," he recalls. "But the dreams that I had that came from the C900 effort weren't going to get fulfilled by just pursuing the Amiga vision as it existed at that time."

Welland's dream of a low-cost Unix machine had constantly eluded him. His C900 had been cancelled and his MMU projects ultimately went nowhere. "The last thing I worked on was the 68020 card," he says, referring to the A2620. Still, he made one last attempt to persuade Commodore to take Unix seriously. "I tried to get Gerard Bucas to build a Unix machine before I left. There's a proposal I wrote to Gerard saying we should try to make an inexpensive Unix workstation. And in my fantasy of fantasies we'd actually do our own RISC processor. Gerard said okay, but I didn't really believe that Commodore as a whole was committed to it. That was one of the main reasons I left."

Welland also felt it was always a struggle at Commodore, with his blitter and MMU efforts having failed largely due to his inexperience. "You were hustling a lot," he says. "There was no one to mentor you. You just had to figure it out. So I made tons of mistakes myself. Commodore was seat of the pants. You were doing something that you were passionate about and you were hoping it was going to be the right thing to do, but there wasn't a ton of clear direction from the higher-ups in the company."

On January 28, 1988, Welland accepted an offer from Apple and informed Gerard Bucas of his intention to leave Commodore. His departure would leave a big hole in Commodore's ranks, as they were losing, arguably, their most visionary engineer. Welland possessed a clear understanding of which technologies would be important over the next two to five years, an important trait for keeping ahead of competitors. Jeff Porter had been relying on Welland to come up with the specs for the next few generations of Amiga chipsets. He would have been the perfect engineer to advance the Amiga technology while Commodore bounced back financially with the Amiga 500 and Amiga 2000 successes.

On February 21, Welland spent the day saying goodbye to colleagues and snapping photos with them. He left Pennsylvania to join Apple in Cupertino, where he would work on RISC chips and help pioneer the Newton PDA.

His departure also left the Amiga 2000 accelerator board in limbo. "Halfway through the project, he left to go work at Apple[1] so I finished up the A2620 and then I did the A2630," says Dave Haynie. Haynie worked feverishly to have the complicated product ready in time to demonstrate at the upcoming CeBIT show in March 1988.

---

1   According to Haynie, "He was one of the guys on the Newton. He apparently came up with the concept for their operating system."

Gerard Bucas Leaves

Bob Welland wasn't the only Commodore employee who wanted out. As a result of Henri Rubin's ascension, Commodore's rebellious "Dutch Trader" decided to call it quits when he felt his leadership role within the company deteriorating. What happened to cause him to leave? "Henri Rubin happened," laughs Bucas. "By the time I left, Henri Rubin had been there roughly 18 months."

After the success of the A500, Bucas had a reasonable expectation that his ideas for product development would be more respected. But he saw how things would go at the aforementioned January 12 "Pow-Wow". With Rubin in charge of product decisions, it looked like Bucas would be relegated to just running engineering, getting no credit for product successes, restricted in his financial decisions, yet receiving all the blame when projects were late.

Later that month, Bucas learned of a potential exit from Commodore from one of his employees. "There was another engineer at Commodore, Jeff Boyer," says Bucas. "He designed the SCSI controllers for Commodore and he was part of the C900 team."

After the death of the C900, Boyer moved into designing Amiga controller boards for storage devices. The Amiga lacked a hard disk controller at that point and it was up to Boyer to design one. "Before I left, he was working on the Amiga architecture because after the C900 died, suddenly it was, 'Okay, let's now try and do a hard disk controller for the Amiga product line,' which only had floppies at that stage," says Bucas.

Boyer began to think of how much more money he could make designing the same hardware outside of Commodore. "We were working late, probably nine o'clock in the night," recalls Bucas. "He and I were talking and he effectively said, 'Listen, we really should be doing this hard disk controller, start our own company and basically we can do a much better job than we can do here at Commodore.' I said, 'Yeah, not a bad idea.' We threw the idea around a bit."

Bucas soon decided to launch himself into the unknown with Boyer and they came up with the name Great Valley Products for the new company. "Jeff Boyer is smart. He's wicked smart," says coworker Bryce Nesbitt. "He went off with Gerard and ran Great Valley Products. They were sort of a spinoff of Commodore, but not quite. But they definitely got a lot of the spinoff of engineers."

Commodore's financial results for 1987 arrived in early February, and Bucas anticipated a healthy payout from the bonus plan conceived by Thomas

Rattigan before he departed. For the previous quarter ending December 31, Commodore had generated a profit of $27.7 million with revenues of $281.7 million. The previous year, the holiday quarter generated $270.1 million in revenues (but still down from the 1985 high of $339.2 million).[2]

On Friday, February 26, 1988 (less than a week after Bob Welland departed), Gerard Bucas left Commodore. He timed his departure perfectly and received the seed money for GVP from Commodore. "The first time I got a reasonable bonus there was in 1988," he says. "I got the bonus for '87 which was a substantial amount and I looked at it and left within one week after I got that bonus. Rubin was very pissed off because I just waited for my bonus, literally a couple of days later said, 'Thank you very much,' and resigned."

Bucas received a 60% share in his new startup to Boyer's 40%. Although Bucas fully committed to the new venture, Jeff Boyer wanted to hedge his bet. "He was not prepared to leave," says Bucas. "He had a son, a family and he was not prepared to take the chance and leave to start something new."

Boyer was critically important to Bucas' plan, so he offered him flexibility. "I said, 'OK, good. Alright, I'll do it, but you need to be my design engineer.' He said, 'Sure I'll do it part time, in evenings.' So I left. I basically put in $50,000 and he worked day and night after Commodore hours and designed the ultimate next-generation SCSI controller while he was still working at Commodore."

For the next year, Boyer continued working for Commodore while moonlighting for an upstart competitor on the side. During this time, he successfully developed many of GVP's initial line of products, while Bucas figured out manufacturing and distribution. For the next few years, Commodore management would be confused as to whether GVP was an ally of Commodore who they should help or a competitor to its own products (and engineers).

Promoted Without Being Promoted

Following Gerard Bucas' departure, Henri Rubin took over as VP of engineering, with Jeff Porter handling the day-to-day affairs until a replacement was found. Rubin was known for being slow to reach decisions, or not making any decisions, and generally being ineffectual. As such, he never really

---

2   *Compute!'s Gazette*, March 1988, p. 6. "Editor's Notes"

got around to finding a replacement, and a new status quo took shape.

Jeff Porter had learned a lot under his successful collaboration with Gerard Bucas and was now prepared to fill that role. "Since Gerard left, there was no one left to run engineering, so I ran engineering," says Porter. "I was kind of promoted without being promoted."

The man who had hit a home run with the Amiga 500 would now be determining which projects to undertake and would be overseeing their development. Although Porter inherited Bucas' daily tasks, it was all unofficial. "Jeff Porter was director of new product development during the golden years of the Commodore Amiga," says Dave Haynie.

Porter was an undeniable supporter of the Amiga. "Jeff Porter always had some sort of Amiga on his desk," recalls Haynie. "You could go to other parts of the building and there would be nothing but PCs in some of the financial departments."

It was a job Porter was born to fill and he received the full support of his team, as he was easy to get along with and maintained his humor even under stressful deadlines. "I've got to give him credit, some people transition to the managerial roles and they turn into flaming assholes," says Hedley Davis. "While Porter and I didn't always agree on everything, he was always pretty cool about things."

Porter's collaboration with Henri Rubin was not as promising as the one he had enjoyed with Bucas. "He reported to Henri Rubin and it was sad," laughs Davis.

In many ways, the engineers were now in charge of the products that would be developed at Commodore, with little input at the higher levels. "I was the engineer, I was the marketing guy trying to sell it to the customers. I was living the dream, baby," says Porter. "It was kind of like a billion dollar garage shop. As the head of engineering I got to see it all, whether it was to pick the industrial design, the styling of the case and mechanical design to the PC boards and the FCC approvals. Everything."

CeBIT 1988

As usual, Commodore was the highlight of CeBIT when the doors opened on March 16, 1988. CEO Irving Gould, along with US president Max Toy and COO Henri Rubin in tow, gave a press conference in front of 500 attendees and journalists.

Gould announced the positive financial results from the previous year. The bright spot was that 40% of the revenues were generated by Amiga products. The Amiga 500 and Amiga 2000 were truly taking over revenues from the C64. Gould was also remarkably open, or perhaps undisciplined, and revealed all the upcoming products, including the redesigned PC line, the A2286 bridgeboard, the A2500AT, the A2500UX, the A2620 accelerator, the A2300 Genlock for the Amiga 2000, the Transputer, and even the Amiga 3000 (much to the chagrin of Commodore's engineers).

Commodore Germany's emphasis on PC-compatible products became understandable when Gould revealed Commodore was the leader in the West German microcomputer industry, with a market share of over 50%. In the business marketplace, Commodore ranked second, only behind IBM itself.

Commodore Germany's leadership, including Harald Speyer and Winfried Hoffmann, were ecstatic about the new PC40-III with an ATI graphics card. In fact, a demo running on the PC40 put the non-interlaced scan converter running on the Amiga 500 to shame. (Rubin made Porter turn off the A500 demo in response.) The new PC would also include a Commodore-made 1352 mouse.

Although there was much to be excited for at the show, overall the German Commodore employees were upset that there were no new Amiga computers. In 1987, Porter had intended to have early samples of the new chipset ready by now, and incorporated into an Amiga 3000, but CSG had just missed the deadline for the chips by a few weeks.

The German Commodore marketing team, led by Harald Speyer, proposed telling attendees that the 68020 was on the motherboard rather than as an expansion card, and then later Commodore could design the actual 68020-based A3000, and hopefully attendees would be none the wiser. Porter was able to talk them down from this plan, as it was too early to begin seriously talking about the proposed Amiga 3000 specs.

Instead, he convinced them to promote the expandability of the Amiga 2000, which could effectively create a new, more powerful (and more expensive) computer with the various Zorro cards. In his view, the Germans should have been thankful for this because they could continue marketing the A2000. Unfortunately, when CeBIT rolled around one year later, the situation would not be much improved.

The Unix Group

Following the debut of the Amiga 2500UX Unix machine at CeBIT, it was time to get serious developing the Unix operating system. Up until now, Johann George had created a proof of concept of Commodore's version of Amiga Unix, which he nicknamed Amix. Now he needed to flesh it out.

Johann George was an immaculately dressed programmer who came from the Coherent Unix team. He had worked at Commodore since 1986 as a contractor on an Amiga version of Unix. Now the Unix project required fresh blood. "Johann George came in to run the Commodore Unix group," recalls Bryce Nesbitt. "He had some special relationship with Henri too. They were both from South Africa if I remember right."

Later that year, Henri Rubin began promoting the upcoming Unix machine by defending Unix as an operating system. "English is a complex and illogical language, yet it is still the most widely used," he said, using English as a metaphor for Unix. "Purists take delight in the inconsistencies that frustrate others. Yet if the language is widely used, its technical faults become irrelevant."[3]

"He was constantly saying things that no one really understood but because he was the boss you would nod and smile," says Bryce Nesbitt. "There was a revolving-door at Commodore management, so none of the rest of the company really took management very seriously."

Dave Haynie completed the A2620 accelerator card in early 1988, complete with the 68851 MMU chip, allowing the Unix team to program the operating system on real Amiga hardware. With the core of Amiga Unix complete, George would hire a team to help finish the first release of Commodore's version of Unix 5.3 for the Amiga 2500. On April 27, 1988 he put out the call for experienced Unix programmers.

One of the first members of Commodore's new Unix team was Randall Howard, who had previously worked with George at Mark Williams on the Coherent Operating system Commodore had purchased. The Unix group soon expanded to around four programmers. "There were a lot of those little teams around," says Nesbitt.

Ominously, Commodore's engineering group jumped from 49 engineers in 1987 to 86 engineers in 1988. It was the C900 project all over again, one that had proven costly and helped bring Commodore close to its destruction. "That was definitely a failure of management, one that I didn't fully appreciate at the time, but in retrospect I can see it was just fatal," says Nesbitt.

Commodore was about to move into a new era, which its engineers felt was a golden age while they worked on a dizzying number of different projects for the company. Yet it was also an age in which deadlines were rarely met, and Commodore would notably fall behind the competition.

---

3   *UnixWorld*, December 1988, p. 59. "Apple Conquers The UNIX/68000 PC Market"

Evolving the Amiga 1988

The key to Commodore moving forward with new iterations of the Amiga was an improved chipset with better graphics. Jay Miner's attempt with monochrome hi-res graphics, which he began in 1985, was ready for production in late 1987 but in the eyes of the Commodore engineers it had fallen short and they opted not to produce it. Rather, they would improve upon it slightly by producing a Super HiRes mode with four colors per pixel. They expected to have an enhanced Denise chip by March 1, 1988 with some of the features implemented, called Phase I, so that they could demonstrate it in an Amiga 3000 at the upcoming CeBIT in Hanover.

In January 1988, the engineers began working on an enhanced Fat Agnus chip that would take advantage of the improved Motorola 68020 specs, allowing 1 MB of memory rather than 512 KB of the original Fat Agnus. It would also allow higher resolutions for Denise. They dubbed this chip Obese Agnus (it later went by the name Fat Lady and finally Fatter Agnus).

Unfortunately, the chip engineers at CSG missed the goal and they were unable to debut at CeBIT. The Phase II part of the chip revision would only have the layout done by May 1988, with even more time required to produce the chip.

Amiga 3000 Stalled

After missing CeBIT, it seemed like the engineers did not have the same sense of urgency they had when putting out the Amiga 500 and Amiga 2000 under former CEO and President, Thomas Rattigan. Rattigan had a definite plan of intercompany competition to motivate the engineers. He believed nothing spurred on designers like knowing another team might beat them to the punch. However, under the leadership of Irving Gould and Henri Rubin, there was no such urgency. Both men lacked the experience to get their soldiers moving.

On the A3000 project, those soldiers consisted of George Robbins (and the VLSI team) on the Hi-Res chipset, Bob Welland on the MMU board, and Jeff Boyer (and the VLSI team) on the SCSI hard drive controller. Heading up the group was Dave Haynie on the motherboard, as well as the new 32-bit Zorro III expansion bus. It would be up to him to pull along and cajole the rest of the team to complete their parts of the project.

After Gerard Bucas and Bob Welland left at the end of February, the Amiga 3000 project fell into turmoil. Meanwhile, Dave Haynie completed his 68020-based accelerator card for the Amiga 2000 in early 1988. He then moved to designing another accelerator card based on the recently announced 68030 processor, unveiled by Motorola the prior year on October 30, 1987. The 32-bit Motorola 68030 processor was once again described as a mainframe on a chip, thanks to the inclusion of features like an MMU onboard. Haynie dubbed his new project the A2630.

Despite the urgency of the A3000 project, this new accelerator card would come to dominate Haynie's time in the months ahead. In fact, Haynie still had to bring his A2620 accelerator card to production. And given the delays with the new Amiga chipset, in his mind there wasn't much to do on the A3000 anyway.

By mid-July, Haynie was more or less finished designing the A2630 and had a working prototype. More importantly, the Unix group, headed by Johann George, verified that Amiga Unix (Amix) would run nicely on the new card. Haynie continued working on the project in order to take it to production, but he promised he would begin work on the A3000 in a week or two.

One positive side effect of Haynie's work with the A2630 that affected the A3000 design is that he became intimately familiar with the 68030 processor. Prior to this, the A3000 was to use the 32-bit 68020. But Haynie soon concluded that he preferred the faster processor, with its built in MMU.

All of this meant that, for the short term, Commodore would be unable to demonstrate the Amiga 3000. Instead, for the first part of 1988, the company had to rely on the "Hedley HiRes" in order to showcase any improvement in Amiga graphics.

Hedley Hi-Res Production

Hedley Davis and Dale Luck had successfully previewed the A2024 monitor at the November 1987 COMDEX and subsequent CeBIT, and the reception was positive. Now Davis had to push the A2024 through production. This was no mere formality. Davis had previously encountered significant problems and delays with his 1351 mouse, and Commodore had no experience manufacturing monitors (to this point they had been rebadged monitors from vendors in Asia and Europe).

Davis would rely on Commodore Japan Limited (CJL) to help produce the monitor. A Mr. Kondo from CJL specifically would help find parts vendors for the A2024. For the actual monitor, there were three vendors in the running: Analog Devices, Inc. (ADI), Dotronix, and WYSE. Of these, WYSE had the best monitor but it was expensive, and the company was hard to work with. Davis ended up going with ADI, an American multinational company with offices in Asia. He would use the DM-1550 paper-white (grayscale) 15 inch monitor, which was more than capable of outputting the four colors in the HiRes mode: black, light gray, dark gray, and white.

ADI would charge $180 per monitor, including the case, power supply, and packaging. With the scan converter PCB, cable, disks, and manual, the total bill of goods came to $245.03, meaning Commodore could easily sell the A2024 for $699 and turn a healthy profit.

ADI would also manufacture the entire A2024 for Commodore. Davis' schedule called for production to begin in January 1988 on the first 5000 units, a schedule that would fall apart surprisingly quickly and to an alarming degree. ADI built approximately 15 units to start with. "They built the thing and then we tried to get it through FCC," he recalls. The FCC would check for stray electromagnetic interference (EMI).

By February 20, 1988 the FCC returned with a list of problems with the A2024 monitor. "I didn't know what I was doing in terms of EMI," admits Davis, who was primarily a software engineer. "We fought that thing for probably eight months trying to get it out the door."

The problem resided with the circuit board, which had only two layers in order to save money. "That thing radiated like a son of a bitch. It should have been a four-layer board. It would have been quiet."

Production was put on hold while Davis worked out the necessary design changes. To shield the electromagnetic emissions, he relied on large metal shielding around the electronics and internal power supply. But this proved insufficient, so he resorted to painting the inside of the monitor with copper paint, replacing components and reconfiguring the PCB. "We did all kinds of voodoo shit to try to get it to pass FCC requirements," he says. The total cost of the metallic paint came to $11.50 per monitor, a substantial increase.

Throughout this, Davis continued to push the marketing aspects of the monitor, releasing a preview of Dale Luck's new graphics package that could use the new resolutions and a tutorial for developers.

However, in late April, Davis learned his 390562-01 ASIC chip that was critical to the monitor working was flawed and did not work properly at the specified 4.2V. Commodore would need to redesign the chip and move to revision 2.

In May, Mr. Kondo began to wonder if the project should be cancelled—in light of the slipping time frame. The two engineers approached Gail Wellington to estimate how many A2024 units would likely be ordered for fall 1988. Wellington returned with the numbers and the demand was still strong. The project continued. Production of the first 2000 units was bumped to later in the year, in September.

Hedley Davis Promotion

After Jeff Porter took over as the de facto head of engineering, a role previously occupied by the departed Gerard Bucas, he was in need of a right hand man in the engineering department. Although there were a number of excellent engineers to choose from, Porter needed someone with a special set of skills, specifically good managerial skills and the ability to drive a product to completion.

Back in December 1987, when employees were asked to write their year-end performance appraisal, Hedley Davis had accomplished a lot. He had taken on the challenging 1351 mouse project and succeeded with flying colors. Then he took on a project given to him by Henri Rubin for the A2024 monitor and, within 9 months, displayed the prototype at a major show. And best of all, Davis had hinted in his letter that he was ready to take on managerial duties within Commodore.

Porter began grooming Davis for the role by giving him oversight of small projects, such as the A2232 serial port card. Davis also stepped into the role of Porter's right hand man; someone who could be an enforcer and nag/plead/cajole engineers to get things done. Now Hedley Davis was to Jeff Porter what Porter had been to Gerard Bucas.

In the summer of 1988, Davis began overseeing six employees, who now reported to him directly. These included engineers Greg Berlin, Fred Bowen, Dave Haynie, Scott Hood, Paul Lassa, and Scott Schaeffer.

Davis was well liked, but he could be a bit gruff when handling delicate personnel issues. And he had no patience when it came to incompetence or laziness. In short, he did not suffer fools gladly. At Commodore, there were some engineers but a lot more managers who fell into this category, which meant Davis didn't always get along with management.

New Amiga OS Developers

Commodore had hired a new round of hardware and chip engineers in November of the previous year, in order to revitalize system development. Around the same time, the Amiga software group had added a couple of programmers to the team, including two programmers from the UK: Steve Beats and Paul Higginbottom.

Now, in April 1988, Jeff Porter and Henri Rubin decided it was time to fill out the ranks of software engineers. Commodore needed software developers to manage the very complicated aspects of the Amiga operating system. Among those hired in April 1988 to work for Andy Finkel's group was Bryce Nesbitt. "Essentially I was hired to become part of the kernel of the team in West Chester," he says. "Andy Finkel was a Commodore 64 guy who had somehow ended up being in charge of creating this development group for the Amiga."

Even though the handover of OS development had happened in 1987, full control of the project was still ongoing, with contractors such as Bob "Kodiak" Burns aiding the transition. "Our job, as the West Chester crew, was to learn and take over the Amiga development from Mountain View, transition it with the understanding that the Mountain View group would be closed down soon," says Nesbitt.

Four developers from the original Amiga software team came for an extended stay in West Chester: Bart Whitebook, Dale Luck, Jim Mackraz and Bob "Kodiak" Burns. "All the Mountain View people had open job offers in West Chester as long as they were willing to move," says Nesbitt. "Those guys came out for business trips. One of them Barry [Bart] Whitebook came out for an extended time and took an apartment but he was always going back as soon as this technology transfer was complete."

Compared to the one-man hardware 'team' on the Amiga 2000, the software group was very large. "The thirty people in the software group were all for the operating system," explains Dave Haynie. "That's a lot of work. It wasn't like the C64 where you had two guys doing pretty much the whole thing. There were just countless pieces for this very sophisticated operating system."

In July 1988, all hardware and software engineering work stopped while the employees reconfigured their office spaces. All the recent hires and plans for expanding teams meant the groups needed to relocate so they could work together in the same areas. This meant each team had to figure out where to go, move heavy equipment, change locks, and drag office furniture around. It seemed like Commodore was about to get serious about developing new technology.

Amber Flicker Fixer

By 1988, the Amiga was starting to lose its graphical lead over other computers. Months earlier, in April 1987, VGA was released for the IBM PS/2 computer. This soon became a graphical standard for other PC clones. VGA produced 640×480 screens with 16 colors, and 320×200 with 256 colors. And most importantly, the display was non-interlaced, unlike Amiga's Hi-Res graphics.

"This was a failure of the Amiga's architecture, the core chipset itself, in order to produce the type of video that by that point had become common," remarks Bryce Nesbitt. "The Amiga was a game console that got too big for its britches. TV is interlaced video and it's the right thing if you're just playing on a TV, and it's almost certainly the wrong thing if you are playing on a computer monitor. It's especially the wrong thing for text. When they started out they were going for a game console, they weren't going for a general purpose computer."

Even those within the original Amiga team felt the graphics should have been improved when the Amiga 1000 shifted to the business market. "The people who marketed the Amiga, and the designers too, didn't get how important that was," says Glenn Keller. "Probably, we might have been better off to design it initially to drive something high resolution."

"Everybody said how great the graphics were, and yes, they were, but the thing was that, at the beginning, it was limited to an NTSC monitor," recalls Keller.

By 1987, users wanted to plug the computer into the new IBM multisync monitors, which worked with a variety of resolutions and scanning frequencies. The Amiga refreshed the screen at 50 and 60 Hz for the PAL and NTSC markets, but because of the interlaced display, it meant that every line was only refreshed at 25 and 30 times per second, which was not quite fast enough to be undetectable by the human eye. Working with the Amiga at the higher resolutions caused a noticeable flicker on NTSC and PAL monitors, which also created eye strain for many. Keller recalls, "I remember thinking at the time, 'This doesn't look that good, it flickers. So, how do you deal with that?'"

Commodore made an initial attempt at correcting the flicker with the A2080 monitor, which used high persistence phosphor to retain the image on the screen longer. This worked well for still interlaced images, but users could often detect smearing of moving images, such as a mouse cursor or when text scrolled.

Hedley Davis had already created a "flicker fixer" with his Hedley Hi-Res (while also increasing the screen resolution), by taking the output signal from the Amiga video port, converting it from interlaced video into progressive scan, and outputting it to a monitor.

With the upcoming Hi-Res chipset on the horizon, the engineers began to worry that it did not provide non-interlaced, flicker free displays. Hedley Davis had previously proposed a general de-interlacer card for the A2000 to Henri Rubin, who had noncommittally told Davis that it "may end up being very important."

After his promotion, Davis began wondering how to address the interlaced flicker problem which would otherwise cripple the upcoming A3000, without disrupting the schedule for the Hi-Res chipset. In May 1988 he arrived at the conclusion that the new chipset needed another ASIC chip to take the video signal, deinterlace it, and increase the scanning frequency so it could work with a multisync monitor. This chip could later be integrated with the new chipset.

"On the output from the Amiga chips, it would take this beautiful interlaced output and have a completely separate frame buffer memory that was as big as the screen, in order to store up two frames of video in order to output one frame of video in a progressive fashion," explains Bryce Nesbitt.

Davis interviewed and hired a new engineer, Scott Hood, who would develop the flicker fixer for the A3000, allowing output to the popular NEC MultiSync monitor. Davis called his chip Amber, and he also assigned Hood to work on a video adapter card for the Amiga 2000 called the A2320 flicker fixer.

According to Dale Luck, the new video chip allowed progressive scan, which did not flicker with some images as interlaced scan did. "The next set of chips could drive an NEC MultiSync monitor," he says. "Some guy invented the flicker-fixer which plugged into the Amiga and it regenerated the display for a VGA monitor. You put it in hi-res mode and it could show a 640 x 480 color display."

The A2320 board also contained expensive memory in order to buffer the interlaced images. "That was a lot of memory," says Nesbitt. "In those days the amount of memory that represented one frame of video was significant. That also had to be high speed static RAM."

Nesbitt feels the solution was an expensive hack. "That was a kludge," he says "The proper place to put this was in the chipset and give it the ability to produce progressive video. It's not proper to put an expensive piece of electronics on the output of your chipset in order to fix a problem like this."

The result would increase the cost of the A3000 significantly. "From a company point of view, it was a reflection of a sort of weakness in the silicon group," says Nesbitt. "If you really were on top of making these chips and you were able to make changes to the chips, and you had the original team and you could iterate it, you would have put the progressive scan right on the silicon in version 3.0."

Productivity Mode

Following a week-long "Future of Amiga" meeting in February (and following the departures of Gerard Bucas and Bob Welland the same month) Henri Rubin began calling the shots in engineering. One of his ongoing projects was to bring better business-level graphics to the Amiga. "They were saying, 'Oh, you long-hairs, you made this video game computer and this video toaster stuff. No, no, the real money is in business applications,'" recalls engineer Bryce Nesbitt.

Rubin had also instigated the A2024 "Hedley Hi-Res" monitor in early 1987. Now, with the Hi-Res chipset specs and design finalized, better business-level graphics were on the horizon with 640 by 480 non-interlaced graphics with 4 on-screen colors.

Rubin instructed his Amiga programmers to start implementing these different modes into the next version of AmigaOS, which at the time was called 1.4 (it would later be renamed 2.0). Already Dale Luck had added support for the A2024 monitor. Now the programmers needed to add support for the new non-interlaced modes of the Hi-Res chipset as well.

In July 1988, Rubin decided to coin a new term to describe the new video modes. "Productivity Mode was what management was asking for," says Nesbitt. "So Productivity Mode was the code name for word processing and spreadsheets and something you could sell into an office."

Rubin became an evangelist for Productivity Mode, both within the company and outside it, while ignoring the Amiga game market. "They came up with this crazy idea to create productivity mode and refocus the Amiga on business applications, while ignoring the things that were selling well," says Nesbitt. "Commodore just ignored the things that the computer was good at and under-invested in chasing goals that never happened." He promised to dazzle Irving Gould at an upcoming demonstration of Productivity Mode in September.

The AmigaOS team, principally developers on the West Coast including Dale Luck and Bart Whitebook, succeeded in creating the new graphics libraries, and on September 20, 1988 they were ready to internally release an advance copy to developers. Rather than calling the disk a Kickstart disk, they referred to it as a Jumpstart disk because of the preview nature of the libraries. The West Coast engineers also replaced the despised Amiga checkmark icon with their original Amiga boing ball.

Rubin was able to demonstrate Productivity Mode on both the Hi-Res chipset in an Amiga 2000 computer and using an A2024 monitor. Although Gould liked the flicker free non-interlaced display, he did not approve of the new logo that popped up when the Jumpstart 1.4 disk booted up. Later in the year, Gould began pushing back to get rid of the boing ball and go back to the checkmark.

The new 1.4 disk allowed the Amiga to display Workbench in several high resolution modes from the new Hi-Res chipset, while outputting it to a multisync monitor. The disk would also be included with the new A2024 monitor.

Retargetable Graphics

One subtle problem with the AmigaOS code was that it was tightly programmed around the Original Chip Set (OCS), and that was in turn tightly coupled to TV signal frequencies. The Amiga 2000 had a video slot that theoretically would allow a third party hardware maker to create an Amiga video card, but it was hard to make it work with AmigaOS. "I couldn't solve it at the system level by putting in somebody else's graphics chip or designing my own, because the software didn't permit what we called retargetable graphics," explains Dave Haynie. "We had huge powerful graphics rather than fairly simple graphics, which was a little bit too close to the hardware."

Dale Luck explains the reasons for exposing the hardware to programmers. "There were some decisions made to get the maximum performance out of the machine; to get the best speed and graphics. To do that required that the software not do very much. It had to rely on the hardware to do most of the work and use all the acceleration the hardware could do. That tended to cause the design and the programming to look a lot like the hardware. Initially that was very good because we got a lot of great performance in graphics and games."

Unfortunately, tying the programming of early software to the idiosyncrasies of the early graphics chips was not a very general solution and hindered extensibility. "As we tried to move on to more device independent graphics and higher resolution screens, because so much was tied to the TV screen, it became harder and harder to be able to migrate these old programs without changing them to newer releases of the software. We needed a layer of device independence, which ended up becoming a project at Commodore."

By February 1988, as the team was finalizing the Hi-Res chipset, they realized they would have to address the problem. Now they had the OCS, the new Hi-Res chipset, the A2024 monitor, and soon they would have the Amber flicker fixer for the A2000 and A3000. They even had future plans for a new chipset underway, which would also have to work with the OS.

And of course, Commodore wanted to allow third party hardware developers to make their own video cards that would then work flawlessly with the AmigaOS Workbench. The engineers also wanted the option to use third-party graphics chips in future Amiga computers in case Commodore was unable to keep up with graphics technology. (In fact, Commodore would later manufacture and distribute the A2410 video card in 1991, using the Texas Instruments TSM34010 chipset, which supported a palette of 16 million colors and very high resolutions.)

Now they needed a way for the OS to use all the different hardware consistently. To make the graphics retargetable, the engineers would have to modify the Amiga operating system. "It needed work and work was being done," says Dave Haynie. "The changes that went into OS 2.0 and OS 3.0 were basically the prerequisites you needed to support retargetable graphics."

AAA Chipset

Although Commodore was engaged in the development of the Hi-Res chipset, the company still needed to plan for the chipset that would come after it. The proposed engineer to head the next generation chipset had been Bob Welland. However, when Welland resigned in February 1988, the project stalled as the engineers regrouped. By mid-1988, Hedley Davis seemed the most likely replacement for Welland, as he had been one of three engineers heavily involved in the discussions (and often at odds with Welland), not to mention he had dipped his toes into several video projects with the A2024 and Amber chip.

Jay Miner conceived the original Amiga chipset to allow fast, colorful, detailed graphics while conserving memory. Efficiency was important, because if he had used a full byte to represent each pixel, it would take up more memory than the whole Amiga had in order to display a single screen.

"A one byte lookup table color; that would be more than 128 kilobytes. It would be more than the memory that was available in the system," explains Ron Nicholson, one of the early Amiga chipset designers.

To compensate, he used tricks to conserve RAM. One trick was using only a few bits to represent each pixel in memory (called a bit plane). "To do anything more than six-bit color in full frame resolution was larger than the largest memory in the largest system we were thinking of shipping. So obviously we had to figure out reduced bit planes. That's how we segued our way into a bit plane architecture—mainly due to the extreme memory limitations."

"Basically I was told to design a game graphics engine and so I designed a game graphics engine," says Nicholson. "We ended up with a game graphics engine with enough extensibility so you could stretch it up to be a multimedia personal computer that would last for what we thought was maybe a few years before you'd have to roll it."

However, as memory prices fell, it became possible to allow a full 256 colors per pixel (8-bit color). "Eventually the software people did want to move to 8, 16, 24, 32 bit color," explains Nicholson. Soon the old bit plane architecture became a hindrance. "The fact that we've done a bit plane architecture isn't that extensible once you get to [the amount of] memory that can support software at that level of sophistication."

The original architecture made it difficult for the Commodore engineers to extend the capabilities of the chipset, as the Hi-Res chipset had shown. In December 1987, Bob Welland, a VLSI chip designer named James Redfield, and Hedley Davis began investigating the next generation chipset. The new chipset would not be hardware compatible with the previous Amiga chipset, although programs that used the Amiga software API would theoretically still work. Bob Welland wanted to move away from the Motorola 68000 family and instead use a RISC processor designed by Commodore, or at the very least, a RISC processor from another company.

Then, after Welland left, the next generation chipset plans sat in limbo until around June 1988, when Hedley Davis began discussing them again with other engineers. "Occasionally we'd have meetings and we'd hash out all the details between the systems people and software people and chip designers," says Dave Haynie.

On June 6, Hedley Davis revealed his plan to Henri Rubin. Davis wanted a complete redesign of the Amiga chipset with full backward compatibility and compatibility with the Motorola chip family. He wanted a team of four or five engineers to design the specification for the chipset. His plan first called for a full conversion of the existing chipset to CMOS, and then to extend the chipset to the higher end architecture.

Davis also wanted one of the original Amiga engineers involved. Rubin suggested RJ Mical, whom he had developed a friendly working relationship with, however Davis felt Mical would be inappropriate and instead favored either Jim Mackraz or Dale Luck.

In June 1988, James Redfield began the detailed AAA architecture development, with a new engineer named Bob Schmid joining his efforts in August. They formed a plan to improve the video (Denise), sound (Paula), and blitter (Agnus) chips for the Amiga, which they called the AAA chipset. "AAA stood for Advanced Amiga Architecture," explains Dave Haynie. "AAA was started in 1988. That was the 64-bit chipset."

The team hoped to have the complete specification for the chipset completed within a few months.

19" Moniterm Viking One

Commodore's efforts to improve Amiga video had fallen below expectations for the year. Even the interim solution, the A2024, was running into manufacturing problems. But there was one notable victory that buoyed the morale of the Commodore engineers and programmers.

The A2024 was built around a 14 or 15 inch monitor, but Hedley Davis knew his scan converter would work with any sized monitor. Earlier in 1988, in April, Davis approached a terminal company named Moniterm, located in Minnetonka, Minnesota, and asked if they could supply a large 19 inch or larger monitor with paperwhite phosphor. "Moniterm Corporation, fortunately, was able to build a monitor that worked with this," says Davis.

Moniterm offered him a 19 inch monitor called the Viking-1. Davis subsequently experiment with the monitor and developed a special scan converter card that plugged directly into the video slot. "It was an expansion card that went into the A2000 that would drive this giant monitor," explains Davis.

By September, Gail Wellington negotiated a deal with Moniterm whereby Moniterm would sell the monitors with a scan converter card to interested Amiga owners. Henri Rubin authorized the sale of 500 390562-02 ASIC chips to Moniterm at $50 a piece, which it could use to manufacture its own PCB cards, based on Davis' design.

In turn, Commodore ordered over a dozen Viking-1 monitors from Moniterm which the engineers could use internally. The engineers coveted the huge monitors and they spread like wildfire throughout the company. "The reason it was really super cool is I can remember walking through the halls at Commodore and on every software engineer's desk there was an A2000 and then there was the monochrome monitor," says Davis. "That gave you 1008 by 800 as opposed to the 640 by 480 Amiga running native. Every software engineer wanted one because it actually gave you some real estate to work with. It was very cool."

The morale boost it gave to the Amiga engineers was also realized because now Commodore could truly claim it created its computers *using* its computers. The high resolutions and large monitor size made the Amiga ideal for CAD programs and programming the Amiga OS using a C language compiler.

Moniterm retailed the Viking-1 for $1995 and the scan converter card for an additional $440, plus a "JumpStart" disk containing preview drivers from AmigaOS 1.4. It was an expensive solution that was unlikely to move a lot of product, but it served a niche and improved the reputation of the Amiga. The monitor combo received small articles of glowing praise in publications like *Compute!* and *Infoworld*.

Although it was a luxury product for high-end Amiga users, no other product gave Davis such a sense of accomplishment. "This gets back to what design engineers like. Much like I got a buzz out of seeing the 1351 in the store, I was walking down the hall and seeing all my peers using the systems that I designed. That's a validation of sorts that I'm doing it right. The Hedley Hi-Res was clearly my greatest achievement."

This technological wonder made Hedley Davis a hero among his engineers. Even though 1988 would become another lost year of development towards the next great Amiga, it still had its moments.

CHAPTER 9

Game Machines 1988

By 1988 it was clear to everyone inside and outside of Commodore that Nintendo had successfully taken over the video game market in North America. But Commodore was not ready to concede that ground and began looking for ways to fight back. However, the recent departures of those in top management meant that ideas to counter Nintendo were still lingering from the previous administration, while a variety of Commodore employees had differing ideas on how to counter-punch. This resulted in a lack of focus on a single product, with Commodore jumping from idea to idea, trying to figure out what to do next.

Winter CES

With the success of the Amiga 500 and Amiga 2000, Commodore now had enough money to return to events it had been unable to attend in the past few years. At the Winter 1988 CES, starting January 8, Nintendo dominated the show, along with Sega. It was also the year *Tetris* fever infected the world, and Nintendo would soon capitalize on its success.

Surprisingly, Commodore skipped the Winter CES, perhaps still wanting to appear like a serious business computer maker. Without a presence there, the company continued to lose ground in the video game market.

The only representation of Commodore came by way of software makers for the C64 and Amiga, such as Berkeley Softworks. The company had thrived due to sales of GEOS, and now with former Commodore executive Clive Smith on its board of directors, the company announced a new version of GEOS for Apple II computers. "There were probably 6 or 7 of us in that timeframe when we first started working on GEOS," says Dougherty. "With Commodore and Apple II GEOS, we grew to something like 30-40 engineers working on that."

When word of the new Apple II operating system, built on the back of C64 GEOS, reached Commodore, several engineers and managers felt it was slightly treasonous of Berkeley, as both companies were in a lucrative partnership.

PC compatible computers were also taking off in the consumer market, as noted by *Compute!* magazine. Editor Keith Ferrell noted, "The overwhelming majority of machines on display were IBM compatibles. Commodore and Atari passed on appearing at CES, while IBM and Apple have never been present at the show. That left the field open to the compatibles manufacturers…"[1]

While the big four computer makers, including Commodore, followed Apple's lead and skipped CES and, probably not coincidentally, watched their market share fall in the coming years, others were swooping in to capture the consumer market. By 1988, Nintendo would emerge as the biggest winner, dominating with 70% of the video game market. "Commodore rather kindly gave the game market and much of the home market back again after Jack had left," says former marketing executive Kit Spencer.

Compute! editors Keith Ferrell and Selby Bateman lamented the situation, saying, "While Nintendo and Sega are delightful systems, they may be seizing the lion's share of the game market by default. … We would love to see Atari and Commodore return to both CES shows in the future, if only to continue to remind the industry assembled there just how good their computers are."[2]

Game Machine Pow-Wow

Directly after CES, Commodore's engineering management met with the sales people for the aforementioned "Tech Pow-Wow". Although the high-end systems had garnered most of the attention by Commodore's management, the sales force was extremely interested in what Commodore had planned for the 8-bit games market.

While the rest of the C65 chipset was in development within CSG, Ted Lenthe informed Gerard Bucas (who was still at Commodore at the time) of the new C65 chipset. "Shortly thereafter, Jeff Porter, the manager of the hardware group, got involved as well," says Bill Gardei.

The only official game machine in the works was the C64D, which was effectively a C64 with a built-in 1581 disk drive to use 3.5 inch disks. Jeff Porter was not a fan of the C64D project and did his best to dodge any responsibility for bringing it to fruition. When Henri Rubin presented the C64D to the sales-

---

1   *Compute!* magazine, April 1988, p. 6. "Computers Win Big!"

2   *Compute!* magazine, March 1988, p. 4. "Editor's Notes"

people, they were less than impressed with the concept, thinking it would not be enough to counter Nintendo's hit console.

Porter casually mentioned to Rubin the existence of the C65 project and the latter voiced his approval for it. Support for the C65 among some executives was strong. "I was more a supporter of the C65 because the C128 was expensive relative to the C64," says Gerard Bucas. "It was much more expensive to produce it yet it didn't give you a lot more for your money."

Porter, like Bucas, saw the C65 as a replacement for the C128. "I basically wanted an 80 column C64," says Porter. "The 128 had a lot of duplicate circuitry in it to be a full C64, and it had a whole separate display circuit in there for 80 columns. There were a lot of strange compromises made in that design, and it became pretty expensive because of that and difficult to cost reduce."

Porter had been in favor of attempting to transition C64 users to the 3.5 inch disk format for better storage. But when he found out about the cheaper C65, he instead began to see it as the natural path to introduce a new storage medium into the C64 ecosystem. This in turn could also help to sell more 1581 drives to C64 users. With a sigh of relief, Porter was able to finally cancel the C64D and turn his attention to something more interesting.

German C64g

In 1988, *Computer Chronicles* devoted a full episode to the ongoing popularity of the C64. The hosts noted that C64 software dominated the shelves of Toys "R" Us, and the company continued selling over a million C64s per year worldwide.

At the same time, the software market for the C64 was beginning to decline, with only 475 commercial releases in 1988, down slightly from over 500 the year before.[3] Commodore executives were beginning to feel antsy about letting its number one product fall by the wayside.

Over in Germany, where the C64 was hitting its pinnacle of popularity, Commodore Braunschweig decided to give the C64 a redesign in January 1988. However, rather than looking forward they looked to the past and came up with something dubbed the C64g.

Internally, the C64g was redesigned to make it less expensive to manufacture. The motherboard contained two RAM (Random-Access Memory) chips instead of eight, and one 16 KB ROM (Read-Only Memory) chip. Externally, the keyboard design went back to the "breadbin" style of the orig-

---

3   These figures are from the online games database at Lemon64.com, which focuses on commercial releases and not public domain titles.

inal C64, albeit in white. The German marketing department felt the old keyboard was required because a musical keyboard peripheral no longer fit the newer C64c case.

Commodore Germany relied on Commodore USA to produce the manuals (translated into 9 different languages) as well as application support. Braunschweig wanted six game cartridges to accompany the release of the C64g for the game bundle. In a show of how out of touch Commodore was with the video game market, the applications manager, John Campbell, suggested the first two games as *Jack Attack* (1983) and *International Tennis* (1985), two very obsolete games by 1988, but among the only games which Commodore still held rights. Compared to what Nintendo was doing in the games market, Commodore in 1988 posed no threat. It pointedly demonstrated what a mistake it had been to shut down the internal games development group.

C65 Game Machine

While Commodore fretted over which game machine to back, Commodore's LSI group was hard at work on the chipset to make a worthy sequel. Back in February, while snow was still on the ground, Victor Andrade had completed his design of the 4510 chip, a CMOS sequel to the 6510 chip. He passed it off to CSG to manufacture while Bill Gardei continued working on the more complex VIC-III 4567 display chip.

By early April, the layout of the 4510 was 20% complete and the layout of the 4567 was 45% complete, with samples expected end of May. Gardei had improved the chip to produce screens using 2, 4, or 8 bit planes (4, 16, or 256 colors respectively). Other engineers wanted the chip to have an external video sync, which would allow genlock. And Gardei himself wanted to add a high resolution display.

By June 19, 1988, Gardei finished designing his video chip. The resulting chip exceeded his original plans, able to produce 320 x 200 non-interlaced video with 256 colors, 640 x 400 interlaced video with 16 colors, and 1280 x 400 interlaced video with 4 colors. While the VIC-II had a color palette of just 16 colors, the new chip could choose from a palette of 4,096 colors.

Additionally, the VIC-III could not only output composite video to monitors but also the improved RGB standard. And incredibly, it supported genlock, allowing the video signal to sync up to external video sources for video recording. The new chip would be competitive with the Amiga's Denise chip in almost every way.

Bill Gardei expected to have working samples of the 4567 and 4510 chips completed later in 1988. For now, he wrote a detailed spec of the chipset, including the 4510 and 4567. He then began designing a motherboard for his C65 computer in order to demonstrate the chips, all while contributing to other chip projects for the Amiga.

In July, as Hedley Davis took over the systems software group, Jeff Porter asked him to assign a systems programmer to the C65 project. There was really only one choice. Davis selected Commodore old-timer Fred Bowen, who had been a core part of the C128 team. "Fred was the oldest timer of anybody around," says former Commodore engineer Robert Russell. "He sat there and cut the Rubylith on the floor to make chips."

After the departure of Robert Russell in mid-1986, Bowen inherited the mantle as the standard bearer of the Commodore 64, troubleshooting problems for customers and helping implement new 8-bit devices, such as memory expansions and the recently cancelled C64D. He even held regular online conferences on Quantum Link for C64 and C128 users.

On July 11, 1988 Bowen was brought in and began examining the 4510 and 4567 specs, with input from newcomer Bryce Nesbitt. The specs looked good but he wanted to see the plans for the C65 itself. With some prodding, Gardei delivered a product definition on July 21 that was slightly different from his earlier proposal.

Instead of the planned 7 MHz processor, it would now run at either 1.7 or 3.5 MHz. But it would now come with 128K of RAM and a 32K ROM (slightly larger than the C64's 20K ROM). The keyboard would have 80 keys and include a number pad. Due to the low CMOS power requirements, it would use a small calculator-type transformer.

The connectors included a cassette jack for loading and saving programs, an RS232 port for a modem, a serial port for legacy C64 devices, a cartridge slot, and an expansion slot for a 3.5" disk drive or other devices. The slot was on the right of the computer, and could daisy-chain devices together similar to the Amiga 500. A 512K memory expansion would be available, bringing total memory up to 640K (though up to 1 MB would be possible in the future).

The product definition emphasised that the C65 would not attempt 100% C64 compatibility. Rather, it was aiming for software portability by making it exceptionally easy for software developers to port existing C64 software to the C65.

In the meantime, Gardei continued developing a motherboard for the C65 while Bowen began looking for a cross assembler for the 4510 chip running on either a C128, Amiga, or PC. Once the chip samples arrived, Gardei could insert them into his motherboard, along with Bowen's ROM chips, and demonstrate the C65 to his fellow engineers.

Come to the Bahamas

Back in 1986, after Thomas Rattigan had taken over as president and CEO of Commodore, he held a meeting in order to point the company's engineers towards the same goals. Now CEO Irving Gould would hold a similar meeting, albeit in a style all his own, one where he would try to impress those who worked for him. Officially called "The Bahamas Technology Meeting", dozens of Commodore's most influential would gather on Gould's home turf.

Gould had good reasons for calling the meeting. Since he had taken over, Commodore had been struggling to develop products to succeed the A500 and A2000. The Hi-Res chipset for the new Amiga computers was floundering and plans for the next generation chipset were going nowhere. And since Nintendo's surprise attack on the video game market, Commodore's game machine ideas were all over the place. It was time to turn indecision into practical plans.

As CEO, Gould ran the company from the opulent offices in New York. The *Philadelphia Inquirer* noted, "He rarely visits Commodore's West Chester plant but says keeping his distance is no real problem. 'It's amazing how you can crack the whip over the phone,' he says with a grin."[4]

Front and center at this meeting was Jeff Porter, who began creating some tech demos weeks earlier. He planned to bring a PC laptop designed by Commodore Japan, two PC40-III clones with monochrome and VGA monitors, and the PC10-III with monochrome monitor. He also brought three Amiga 2000 computers demonstrating PAL and NTSC versions of the Hedley Hi-Res monitor, plus one connected to a multisync monitor using the Amber flicker fixer card. It was obvious the business systems were at the center of the show.

Porter found the generational gap between the engineers and his 69 year-old CEO hard to bridge. "Irving Gould is the man who basically owns the company," says Porter. "He could be our grandfather and I was in my 20s."

Most of the engineers saw "Uncle Irv" as something of a rich benefactor who treated his family well. Gould flew both Jeff Porter and PC designer Jeff Frank out to the Bahamas on the Pet Jet, along with all the demonstration computers. The two engineers had the opportunity to meet Gould's wife, a somewhat uncomfortable meeting because it was a well known secret among Commodore employees that Gould maintained other relationships in Japan and Toronto.

Once there, Porter and Frank stayed at the ritzy Lyford Cay Club, Gould's favorite local hangout for rich businessmen. Porter was a little nervous about the meeting and felt the executives were "all out for blood" due to the delays

---

4   *Philadelphia Inquirer*, Aug. 17, 1987. "Commodore Is On A New Course With Gould At Helm"

in getting new projects completed. Porter feared a Commodore consultant named Mehdi Ali in particular, who believed that in order to fix most problems, all he had to do was fire someone.

It would also be an eyeopener for Porter and Frank to see how politics was played at the upper levels. The meeting would be noticeably more political than others had been in the past, due to Gould's control of the purse strings and executives vying for his favor.

On Wednesday, August 10 1988, a very hot and humid Bahamian day, they began plotting its technology for the next few years. For two days, engineers and management would discuss future products at the club.

Attendees included COO Henri Rubin, president of CBM North America Max Toy, Winfried Hoffmann, and Harald Speyer from CBM Germany. Each international region also fielded two attendees, such as Tony Cuffe and Tony Serra from CBM Australia.

Commodore's sole employee in the Bahamas, officially Commodore International Limited's company headquarters, put in a rare appearance to view the prototypes. "Irving asked if I would come up and sit in on some product presentations," says Kit Spencer. "He said, 'I would like you to come along and give me your comments,' which is the sort of thing I still had time for." Normally Spencer wrote the monthly Commodore newsletter out of the third floor of the bright pink Sassoon House in Nassau, so this was a rare chance to make an impact.

Day one of the meeting was dedicated to Amiga technology, while day two was devoted to the PC clone business. The engineers presented a wide range of proposals. "They came along with some very up-market business computers, they talked about [a new] Amiga coming out and a games machine," says Spencer.

The executives were especially keen to see what Commodore's engineers were working on next for the Amiga, but were disappointed to learn there was nothing to show as of yet. All Porter could demonstrate was the old A2000 with different plugin cards. The new Hedley Hi-Res monitor and flicker fixer cards were, however, welcomed as the video output from the Amiga 2000 had been roundly criticized by the press.

Porter presented the A3000 and A800 concepts as adding to the already successful Amiga line of computers. Both would have more memory, faster Motorola processors and the new Hi-Res chipset. However, Motorola had been unable to meet Commodore's goal of $35 for the 68020. This meant the retail price of the A800 would fly closer to $1500, putting it too close to the A2000 price. Executives decided to cancel or rework the product for now.

Porter also presented two variants of the A2000, the A2500UX running Amix (Amiga Unix) and the A2500AT, an A2000 running DOS via a Bridgeboard. The Amiga 2500UX was well received as a potential workstation and samples would be sent worldwide starting in October, but the A2500AT was deemed unnecessary as a standalone product.

Irving Gould made a surprising number of smaller decisions with other Commodore products at the meeting. For example, the 1084S monitor delivered stereo sound, but he decided to save $3 in parts costs by removing the stereo feature of subsequent 1084 monitors, believing video was more important than sound. Canada and Australia were also complaining that they couldn't compete with the Atari ST without a MIDI interface for the Amiga 500. Gould ordered his engineers to make this a priority, even though it was ostensibly a low-level problem.

And with computer networking becoming a big thing in the business world, the gathered executives and engineers wanted a LAN card developed for the Amiga 2000.

Kit Spencer was surprised at the disinterest management had for the low-cost products Commodore built its reputation on. "Nobody was interested in the games machine," he says. "Everybody was interested in going up market."

Jeff Porter elected to not mention the C65, the product most likely to compete against the NES on both price and performance. Although the NES was officially unveiled in 1985, it did not really start its phenomenal run in North America until January 1988, meaning there was still time to respond to the challenge.

Instead of pitching the C65 concept to the assembled executives, Porter presented a new concept for an Amiga-based video game machine. His concept was essentially an Amiga 500 without a keyboard or disk drive, which would accept game cartridges. The total bill of materials for the machine came to $120, which meant it would retail for under $300.

Everyone at the table had a chance to discuss their impressions of the proposals. Spencer said, "Irving, the thing I found most exciting there was the games machine with the Amiga chips in it, because that was what it was originally being developed as, where we have a massive market. The VIC took the games market. The Commodore 64 was a crossover between the computer business and the games market. We wiped Atari out of the business by targeting that market—they used to be number one. In my opinion, we need to keep that going by being our own competitor and coming up with a better games machine to keep other competition away."

Mehdi Ali jumped in with his opinion, saying, "Games is a passing fad. We're in the computer business."

Spencer replied, "Games isn't a passing fad. The type of games will change, but people will always want entertainment. What you have to do is provide the change."

The attitude in the room disappointed Spencer. It was clear Commodore had lost any memory of why they were successful in the first place. "We basically gave the games market away on a plate to Nintendo," he says. "That was a very important strategic decision to miss. At the time we had the market, the distribution, and the name. With the Amiga, we potentially had the next generation product."

Afterward, Porter voiced his disappointment with the lack of understanding about his proposed Amiga game machine. "I am more convinced than ever, after seeing these bozos at this Bahamas meeting, that they lack the ability to envision a product before they can touch it and feel it," he told a fellow employee. "They just don't understand. Their limit is 'Take an A500 and throw away the keyboard and drive.'"

After the meeting, Spencer had a private talk with Gould. "I remember saying to Irving, 'We should get into the game business with Amiga. It's the best game machine ever.' I couldn't understand why the new management couldn't get excited about it. Irving tended to agree with my comment and said, 'I will try to do something.'"

On the second day of the meeting, Gould and the worldwide executives approved of Jeff Frank's work with the PC clones. Specifically they wanted the cost-reduced PC10-III and the Intel 386-based PC40-III to go forward with pilot production in October, although it was agreed to cancel the PC30-III at the meeting.

The executives also approved of a PC50 and PC60 based around the Intel 386 architecture to come after the PC40-III release.

After the sunburned engineers returned to Pennsylvania, Jeff Porter met with his closest engineers, including Jeff Boyer, Andy Finkel, Hedley Davis, and mechanical designer Herb Mosteller, to discuss their new orders. At the insistence of Jeff Frank, the two jointly sent a letter of thanks to Irving Gould for his hospitality. Frank also sent letters to many of the powerful executives he met, including Kit Spencer. While Porter wore his heart on his sleeve, sometimes calling his superiors bozos, it appeared Frank was playing a more patient political game.

As a result of the meeting, there were now five big projects that Commodore was committed to delivering in 1989: an Amiga game machine, the Amiga 3000, the PC50-III, the PC50 laptop, and a new bridgeboard based on the Intel 386 architecture.

A250 Amiga Game Machine

After Kit Spencer's encouragement, Irving Gould became, in the words of Jeff Porter, "hell bent for leather to produce a cheaper A500." For the second time (after the German A2000), Gould took a hands-on approach and tried to make a product happen himself by cracking the whip. Incredibly, Gould asked for the system before Christmas, a mere four months away.

Porter assigned the project to Jeff Boyer, the engineer who was secretly moonlighting for Gerard Bucas at Great Valley Products. Porter asked him to deliver a working mockup by the upcoming January CES. During the previous Monday morning meeting, the engineers had agreed on the specs for the basic Amiga Game Machine as 256K RAM (expandable to 512K), a cartridge port, and two joystick ports. Total cost of parts would come in at $100. Additionally, users could purchase an optional disk drive, keyboard and mouse to transform it into a full Amiga 500.

The difference between Commodore in 1981 and 1988 is interesting. In 1981, the C64 was conceptualized after a two week study in which the designers disassembled all the contemporary game machines and then projected where the technology was going. In contrast, the Amiga game machine was rather hastily thrown together from existing technology without really studying the competition.

Boyer would have no major design challenges with the new system because it was essentially an Amiga 500 board with several unused features removed. The major challenge of the project would be the case and cartridge design.

Porter turned to Yukiya Itoh from Japan to come up with the case design concept. Once complete, it would be up to Herb Mosteller to take the concept sketches and turn them into a manufacturable, mechanically sound design. Henri Rubin asked for a working mockup of the system by October 1, perhaps hoping that if they met that goal they could go into production before Christmas.

The system also required a cartridge design, both at the port on the A250, and an actual PCB design for the cartridges, which would house the ROM chips containing game software. Porter assigned this task to the popular engineer George Robbins, who recently had his Amiga 800 project cancelled.

Robbins was still highly addicted to Usenet newsgroups and continued administering and upgrading the Ultrix operating system on the VAX machine. This did not go unnoticed by management, who felt his talents would be better used designing new systems.

Hoping to get more engineering out of Robbins, Commodore trained another employee, Jim Sloan, to take over administrative duties. This plan was temporarily thwarted when Robbins refused to relinquish his control of the

Ultrix system to Sloan. He obtusely told Sloan that the latter had been cross trained in Ultrix in case Robbins himself was absent, but in the meantime, he would maintain the system.

With management unable to knock Robbins off the VAX machine, they let him get on with it and design the cartridges for the A250. He based the form factor on the cartridges produced for the Plus/4 system, which were rounded like a hockey stick blade. Robbins redesigned the PCB to allow up to 2 MB of memory in ROM chips, which would connect directly to the memory bus on the A250. He ended up gutting some old Plus/4 cartridges and inserting his new PCB.

Meanwhile, by October, Porter was zeroing in on a power supply for the A250. Robbins would continue designing the cartridge and Boyer the main game system, right up until the January 1989 CES.

Remember Me?

As Commodore's system engineering group raced forward with the A250, under Irving Gould's whip, there remained a curious omission. Commodore already had a game machine under development in the CSG group called the C65. On August 23, less than two weeks after the Bahamas Technology Meeting, CSG head Ted Lenthe asked Jeff Porter what this A250 thing was and why Commodore was developing it instead of the C65?

Bill Gardei, the instigator of the C65 project, was also unhappy with Porter that his project was not revealed at the Bahamas meeting. He felt Porter was hiding it from executives in favor of the Amiga game machine and perhaps willfully allowing it to die.

Gardei believed Rubin should be told immediately in order to receive additional resources and backing. Already, the 4510 layout was on hold until the Hi-Res Agnus was completed. Rubin's support could push the C65 project to the front of the line.

In fact, Rubin had been told about the C65 in January but, considering Rubin's age and forgetfulness, Porter suspected he hadn't thought about it since then. Porter assured Gardei that it was better to hold off until he had produced a working prototype to demonstrate the system, otherwise by showing it too early, the always impatient Gould would expect a quick development schedule. The engineers could end up looking bad if any delays occurred.

Porter appeased the suspicious Gardei by telling him that revealing the project too soon would be a bad move. "I am trying to buy you a bit more time, before the natives get restless, and they start pounding the drums for the C65, and start spreading rumors about what a bum this Gardei guy is because he is taking so long to develop the product," Porter explained. "If we get the chips in place, and are able to demo a proto, I have no doubt that Irving will like it."

This was a legitimate concern as the C65 chipset was not yet completed and, when samples arrived in October, unlikely to be bug free. There were other strategic questions too. Should Commodore attempt to do a true NES killer with the C65? Or should they concede this generation of game machines to Nintendo and try to come up with a superior (and costlier) Amiga game machine to overthrow it? Porter believed the best way to find out was to prototype both systems and show them to the engineers to evaluate.

Porter also had some suggestions for Gardei's initial proposal. He feared there could be a lack of software development if they went the same direction as the C128. "Unfortunately, if we tout it as a C64 compatible, we're dead," he said. Worse yet, it could not hope to achieve the same level of C64 compatibility as the C128, making it appear inferior.

Still thinking of the failed C64D, Porter suggested that a 3.5 inch drive be included with the computer in order to establish a standard. Once the drive was established and software started rolling in, he planned to unbundle the drive and sell a low-cost version of the C65 without the disk drive, or perhaps even a cartridge based video game console. And as a bonus, the project already had a case designed by Herb Mosteller for the cancelled C64D.

However, Porter guessed the 3.5 inch drive could be the achilles heel of the system because no form of copy protection had yet been devised for those disks. With piracy so rampant in the C64 community, software makers would have to find other protection schemes—usually revolving around code wheels or game manuals.

After hearing Porter's remarks, Gardei dreaded his simple vision for the C65 would become bogged down by committee discussions. For the most part, he clung to his initial concept.

Jeff Porter was understandably anxious to supply working silicon chips to Bill Gardei for the C65. CSG was getting the hang of manufacturing 2 micron CMOS chips, and was capable of creating up to 500 wafers per month (each wafer could hold approximately 1000 4502 chips, for example). Ted Lenthe predicted in a year CSG would be capable of up to 2000 wafers per month.

The CMOS process used by CSG required 16 layers and was complicated to put together because an error in a single layer would break the chip. This resulted in excess time analyzing the results, more difficulty debugging and checking, and very low yields. However, Lethne expected the 4567 chips to be ready in October.

Fred Bowen was also struggling to get his 4502 assembler working. Gardei was doing his best to help Bowen by creating a special C65 development system based on the 4502 that Bowen could use to test his converted C64 ROM code.

By September 2, 1988, Gardei reported that the 4567 design was 100% complete and 99% debugged. Another LSI engineer had the layout 75% complete, and everyone still expected silicon by October. If all went well, the team could show the concept to Henri Rubin and maybe even demonstrate a C65 prototype at CES in January 1989, with a possible release later in the year. In preparation, Gardei immersed himself in his C65 schematic.

By September 28, Gardei had the schematic complete for the C65 prototype system. He also created the schematic for a 768K RAM expander. And he had completed his disk controller schematic, which could interface up to four 3.5" or 5.25" floppy drives, with single or double sided disks using a fast parallel interface.

Within a few days, C65 boards were being built using Gardei's schematic and a special 512K version was being built for Fred Bowen so he could begin developing the firmware for the project.

However Bowen, ever the grump, asked Porter if the C65 was indeed a real project. Porter decisively dealt with Bowen's concerns, and on October 14, the C65 entered the official "Current Project List" at Commodore, along with the Amiga Game Machine.

Although he should have been happy to see the C65 enter the official project list, Gardei began to feel a little abused because the project lead on the C65 was listed as Hedley Davis. Porter and others felt Gardei's people skills could use a bit of work and other engineers would not want to report to him. "He wasn't ready for management," says Davis. "He wanted to be the boss and somebody else got appointed the boss. There was a big stink about that."

As the October deadline came and went, parts of the 4567 chip were still being tested, the layout was not complete, and there was no timing sheet for the chip. Preparations were being made for testing the chip on the Megatest unit at CSG.

During November, Fred Bowen continued working on an assembler and getting the serial bus to work on Gardei's prototype 4502 board, but he became increasingly concerned about the lack of guidelines, a schedule, or development tools for the project, which so far was being spearheaded by Bill Gardei.

Once he brought up his development board, Bowen copied C64 software from 5.25" disks to 3.5" disks and plugged a 1581 disk drive into the board. None of the commercial software worked. Depressed, Bowen wondered if anything would change Porter's mind about the direction the C65 was going.

To help address Bowen's concerns, the team met at a November 16 LSI review meeting and discussed the setbacks to the 4567 schedule and pushed back the expected release of silicon to early 1989. They also discussed C64 compatibility strategies, and Fred Bowen's favorite topic, a separate mode for the C65 machine—similar to the C128. Victor Andrade would supply a memory map of the new 4510 and VIC-III chip. Satisfied, Bowen continued working on the project.

The task of coming up with a proper assembler for the 4502 was handed off to Bob Norby of CSG. The new cross assembler would run on VAX and IBM PC computers and then upload the compiled code to the C65 prototype for execution. The expected date for the assembler was March 1, 1989.

By December 21, Gardei had made some last minute revisions to his 4567 chip to match C64 timings, which would theoretically make the chip more compatible with C64 software, along with other changes to improve compatibility. He also submitted his final schematics to engineer Mike Nines, who would produce the layout and PCB for the C65 prototype.

With testing of the complicated 4567 chip still ongoing, it was now clear to the team they would not be able to demonstrate the prototype to Rubin any time soon, nor display it at the upcoming CES show.

By the end of 1988, Commodore was holding the line on game machines with its aging stalwarts, the A500 and C64. In addition, three new game machines were in development: C64G (in Germany), C65, and A250. Meanwhile, to the relief of Jeff Porter, the C64D had been shelved. It was a lot of activity for one small company, compared to Nintendo which focused itself on one game machine at a time. Were Commodore's efforts spread too thin to result in even one video game product making it to the marketplace?

Ups and Downs
1988

Through the previous few years, Commodore seemed like it was on the cusp of success if only the marketing team could achieve adequate distribution. After the Amiga acquisition, Commodore's marketing fell apart as the company tried to shift to selling business computers. However, there was one marketing success that resulted in substantial software and hardware development on the Amiga. This group would become "the cat's meow" within Commodore.

CATS

To encourage and aid software development for the Amiga, Commodore had handed out prototype computers to early software developers, such as Electronic Arts and Infocom. The manager behind this initiative was an ex-Brit named Gail Wellington who had previously headed Commodore's software division in Europe. "She was in Europe and it wasn't until the mid-80s she came to the USA to head up the CATS group," says software developer Eric Cotton.

The division was named Commodore Amiga Technical Support, or CATS. Its members worked closely with developers outside of Commodore to develop Amiga games, applications, and hardware. "CATS, as part of their function, was to interact with developers and make software available to developers and documentation and so forth," says Cotton.

RJ Mical has nothing but praise for the CATS initiative. "The whole CATS organization was superb," he says. "That was a technical support group for the Amiga itself, and those guys really had their act together. They were brilliant assistants to aid the development of Amiga software."

Through the years, CATS succeeded in spawning high quality software development for the Amiga. "We had every kind of app that you would want," says Mical. "We had a good spreadsheet program. There were good word processor apps. WordPerfect was a good one but there were a number of other ones that came together as well." With the support of CATS, Amiga software began raining down on users.

The group eventually evolved to support development for other Commodore products as well. In later years, Wellington renamed the group to Commodore Application and Technical Support. The team grew and even recruited one former PET/C64 programmer, Carolyn Scheppner, who became the lead technical specialist of the group.

Under Wellington, the CATS group was also a lot of fun. Wellington herself delighted in calling herself the "manager of cats" and the group named its VAX server Heart of Gold after the starship from *Hitchhiker's Guide to the Galaxy*. "Gail was well liked in the developer community," says Eric Lavitsky. "I think that they were always the victim of having too little resources to accomplish what they needed to accomplish. They were creative people who were passionate about what they were doing, and they made a lot out of the little that they had."

By 1988, Wellington had gained a powerful position in the company because in order for any computer to succeed, it required software. And without the full support of CATS pushing third party developers, software was unlikely to arrive on that machine. "In England she was always a powerhouse and when she came on board here, specifically on CATS, she held significant influence," says Eric Cotton.

As previously mentioned, developers like Hedley Davis often went to her to find out if products they were working on, such as the A2024, were viable in the marketplace. Wellington would contact third party developers or salespeople to gauge the demand. This put her in a position where her word could put an end to products that were liable to go nowhere. In the absence of top-down strategic direction, she would help shape Commodore's output in the years ahead.

Successful Cloning

Another successful marketing effort within the company was the line of PC clones. In 1988, Commodore revamped its PC series with faster processors, including the PC10-III and PC20-III. The engineers also had a new system in the works using an Intel 80286 chip, called the PC-30.

Although Commodore sold modest numbers of PCs in the US, in Europe (and more so Germany) PC sales were strong. "There was always this stigma between Commodore Germany and Commodore UK as to who was doing the best," recalls David Pleasance, who believes the UK made higher revenues than Germany. "Even if there is any doubt, we were at least the second market after Germany."

While Commodore UK was highly successful in mass-market computers, it was less successful in business computers. "The truth of the matter is that the Business Systems Division was notorious in the UK for over forecasting and under delivering," says Pleasance, who was in charge of the consumer division. "Virtually every quarter, without exception, Steve Franklin would come to us and say, 'Hey guys, I need you to help me get out of the shit.'"

Commodore's consumer division would be pressed to work for the business division to push up sales. Pleasance agreed to help, provided his consumer marketing people received commissions and weekend trips with their spouses.

Pleasance also asked Franklin if he could make the PCs more attractive to regular consumers. "I said, 'Let the consumer guys get hold of the PCs to see what we can do with it.'"

His first task was to make the technology more understandable to ordinary customers. "There was a massive amount of confusion and nobody knew about PCs," he says. "They didn't even know how to put one together. People were nervous about them. We had in our range in the UK the PC-10, PC-20, and PC-30."

Pleasance felt he could create bundles for the PC line. "We made a bundle just like we did with our consumer product, but we made it more professional."

To reach the target audience, Pleasance made sure consumers could imagine themselves using the PCs. "We believed that we needed to get to the people that were going to buy this product," he says. "Professional people, business people, and working people. So we decided to have photographs on the outside of the packaging of people in jobs that were easily recognizable. We had an electrician, we had a professor, we had a doctor and photographs of them all incorporated in the packaging." Pleasance himself would pose as the professor. "It was a lot of fun as well as cutting costs. It's the old adage, 'Where needs must.'"

Finally, to simplify understanding, he used color codes on the boxes. "The packaging was identical except for a colored band around all four sides of one end and we had a different color for the PC-10, PC-20, and PC-30.

There was a turquoise, there was a burgundy, and blue. The reason we did that was that we also packaged the peripherals in the same color coding so that you knew that if you bought a PC20 and it had this burgundy colored band on it and you bought something that had a burgundy colored band on it, it was right for your machine. Very simple but very important."

Commodore had previously been criticized for not including sufficient instructions for putting the computer together, so Pleasance thought of a fun solution. "We actually had a VHS video produced and we employed a guy called Tim Brooke-Taylor, who was very well-known UK comedian from a program called *The Goodies*. He played a person in an office and he had a secretary. They got this box and then they followed all the instructions on how to put it together and all the rest of it. It was the very first time ever anybody had approached it in a way that appeals to a consumer to take the confusion out of this."

Although the marketing efforts did not turn Commodore's UK business division around, it was a marked improvement. "We didn't break any records but we did better than we expected of them," says Pleasance.

Commodore would continue to pursue the MS-DOS compatible PC market until the very last days of the company. However, in the late eighties as the PC market continued to grow, competition also became fierce.

Speed Bumps: Round 1

Speed bumps are objects that lie in your path and slow you down. Commodore had both real speed bumps made of asphalt in its parking lots and figurative speed bumps that the engineers encountered at work.

Joe Mecca, the facilities manager at 1200 Wilson Drive, created the real speed bumps. There were strange rivalries between Commodore departments, none stranger than the rivalry between the facilities department and the engineering group. The saga eventually reached the absurd heights of a Stanley Kubrick movie, causing Dave Haynie to dub it, "Dr. Strangemecca or: How I Learned to Stop Worrying and Love Giant Speed Bumps".

The rivalry started off as low-level antagonism towards the facilities department, which was supposed to manage the building and keep the occupants comfortable. However, in the blisteringly hot summer months, for some reason the air conditioning to the engineering department barely worked. For several days each year it was unbearable. "We engineers have a fairly high opinion of ourselves and we thought we were the core of the company," recalls Bryce Nesbitt. "There was this facilities manager just doing annoying things. There was sort of an open war between the engineering group and this facilities manager."

The rivalry began one morning when Mecca observed an Amiga hardware engineer, Joe "Augie" Augenbraun, speeding recklessly in the parking lot as he drove to work. Rather than ask Augenbraun to slow down, Mecca decided to be more inventive and hand out speeding citations.

Needless to say, the engineers were not appreciative of receiving citations from the manager. "He kind of set himself out to control these wild engineers who were allowed to get away with anything," recalls Nesbitt. "One day he went in and he said 'hi' to an engineer who was leaving to go home and sleep. And then that same day the engineer came in as he was leaving for the day. So they had exact opposite schedules. He just viewed us as a bunch of long-haired hippies with no respect for anything, which might have been more or less true, but it escalated into this open tit-for-tat war."

When the speeding citations failed to control the engineers, Mecca upped the ante. In September 1988 he installed asphalt speed bumps in the parking lot. "We didn't like them. We all had sports cars and we wanted to drive 60 or 70 miles per hour in the parking lot and there should be no reason that we couldn't do that," quips Dave Haynie.

Unfortunately, it was Mecca's first experience with speed bumps and they weren't properly constructed. "They laid them on top of the road surface and they didn't adhere well," says Michael Sinz. "They laid macadam on top of macadam, so it sticks a bit but it will get moved by mechanical equipment."

Pennsylvania receives large snowfalls each winter, and this brought out the snow plows to clear the parking lot. Due to the faulty installation of the speed bumps, the snow plows inadvertently ripped them up. "The snowplow basically took the speed bumps away with the snow," says Sinz.

Joe Augenbraun, the original instigator of the confrontation, collected a chunk of asphalt from the parking lot and sent it to a facility manager named Bob Greg through his mail slot, with a note attached saying, "I believe this is yours." The open rivalry had begun.

COMDEX

In 1988 there were even signs that Commodore's US marketing department was having some success. Near the end of the year, the company rolled out advertisements for the Amiga 500 which aired on MTV. The commercials featured a cut-down version of the "Only Amiga" video which had debuted at COMDEX a year earlier. Henri Rubin helped roll out all the different Amiga 2000 variations that he hoped would satisfy the market until the next Amiga was ready.

The PC world was well into the hard-drive phase of computing, where the operating system resided on a hard drive along with installed applications. Rubin unveiled an Amiga 2000 variant, called the A2000HD, which included a 40 MB hard drive with an A2090A SCSI controller. It retailed for $2999.

Another variation, called the A2500, included a hard drive and the A2620 accelerator card with the Motorola 68020 processor running at 14 MHz. The suggested retail price was a whopping $4699.

Existing Amiga 2000 owners could also upgrade their systems by purchasing the expansions separately—the A2090A SCSI controller for $399.95 and the A2620 accelerator board for $1999.

The massive price for the A2620 is explained by the costs of the three coprocessors on the board. Commodore was able to purchase the 68020 from Motorola for $75, the 68881 for $35, and the 68851 for $95. The 16 DRAM chips cost $256 total. Altogether, the A2620 cost Commodore $570 in parts and labor to manufacture. As a result, the A2500 was a product for high-end users only.

Commodore also displayed the A2500UX with its version of Unix System V. No price was given, though the cost would be more expensive than the base A2500 computer. Commodore also debuted a 20 MB hard drive called the A590 for the Amiga 500.

In addition to COMDEX, Commodore hosted dedicated shows just for the Commodore faithful. The same month as COMDEX, Commodore debuted the World of Commodore in Philadelphia for the first time. A month later, it hosted the 6th annual World of Commodore in Toronto, where it received a record 43,300 attendees.

In 1989, there would also be three AMIExpo shows for the Amiga faithful: New York, Chicago, and Los Angeles. Commodore was hitting its stride with publicity. As a result, interest in the Amiga in North America rose to an all time high. Commodore's US marketing department was finally having some success.

Rise of the Shareholders

To Gould, it seemed like he was having a good year. The industry at large was in the throes of a chip famine in early 1988, but Commodore was almost unique in not raising prices in response. "Back in the late eighties there was this huge DRAM shortage all over the world," explains Hedley Davis. "Commodore Japan Limited caught that before it happened and it prebought a bunch of DRAM. So while our competitors were dying for lack of available DRAM to build products, we were just swimming in it. There was not a problem whatsoever."

Unfortunately, Commodore's chief rival, Jack Tramiel, was also thriving amid the DRAM shortages. "I remember he tried to corner the RAM market," recalls Dale Luck. "I don't know if he initially did it on purpose but my belief is that the Atari ST used so much RAM that he started buying up RAM options to ensure that he would have enough dynamic RAM to build the Atari ST. And then there was a DRAM shortage right around that time. So he made a huge amount of money just by holding all these contracts for delivery of DRAM."

The Amiga computers were finally taking off, so much so that Gould began contemplating getting back that corporate status symbol, the Pet Jet, that he sold in 1985 to raise cash for his desperate company.

The Pet Jet played a critical role in Gould's lifestyle. The 70-year-old jetted around the world several times a week. According to *Forbes*, "Gould can only spend on average three days a week in the U.S. before he may be subject to taxation by the Internal Revenue Service." It was a fanatical effort to avoid paying taxes.

"Irving was this wonderful businessman," says Commodore engineer Don Gilbreath. "He figured out how to be a citizen of the world. He was from Toronto, had a home the Bahamas and a beautiful office on Park Avenue. He worked it perfectly where he didn't have a tax burden anywhere, but that meant he was always in New York on Monday and Tuesday, always in Toronto Wednesday and Thursday, and then a three day weekend in the Bahamas. That was his life."

By all accounts, Gould timed his stay in each part of the world down to the minute. "They used to literally sometimes circle around either Toronto or Philadelphia because he wasn't supposed to stay more than 180 days a year in either US, Canada or the Bahamas," says Gerard Bucas. "He was very careful not to spend more than a certain number of days in any one of those countries. So he was a non-resident officially of US and Canada actually. I think he had another business in Canada, a furniture factory or something. He was an interesting character but a strange character."

Since November 1985, Commodore had paid Gould's company, Scientific Packaging, $775,000 to lease the British Aerospace 125-700 jet—approximately $2150 for each hour of flight time. In July 1988, Commodore purchased the Pet Jet back for $2.75 million, well below the estimated market value of over $4 million.[1] The deal would soon come under scrutiny.

After his audit of Thomas Rattigan in 1987, Mehdi Ali continued his consulting role with Commodore. In August 1988, Irving Gould nominated Ali to the Commodore Board of Directors, to be voted on at the upcoming November shareholders' meeting in New York. Unknown to Gould, forces were gathering to oppose his leadership.

Dale Luck was still performing contract work out of the small offices leased by Commodore. He was also operating his own side business called Boing!, selling jackets with the boing ball symbol and a 3-button Boing mouse. The purpose of the products was to raise money while he worked on porting the X Window System (called X-11) to the Amiga from his home in Milpitas, California, 30 minutes from the Commodore-Amiga offices.

Luck, like most of the core West Chester engineers, was a proponent of Unix on the Amiga. He also held strong opinions about Commodore's handling of Amiga. His Usenet Newsgroup signature at the time proclaimed, "Although I do contract work for Amiga-Los Gatos, my opinions probably don't represent those of Commodore or its management or its engineers, but I think the world would be a better place if they did."

By 1988, Luck was deeply dissatisfied with Commodore's stewardship of the Amiga. "A lot of software and hardware developers had invested so much of their money and so much of their time and they knew what it could do, but a lot of people thought Commodore could not get out of its own way," he says. "It was a stressful time. People were thinking the Amiga was going in the wrong direction."

At user meetings within the Amiga community, Luck became known for his outspoken criticism of Commodore. A shareholder and Amiga user named Jim Meyer of New York decided to start a campaign to nominate Luck to Commodore's board of directors, where he could influence decisions. He composed a message saying, "Many of you own stock in Commodore Business Machines, and you will shortly be receiving proxy cards for the upcoming Annual Stockholders Meeting. You may be tempted to discard your proxies, or you may elect to acquiesce to some prearranged assignment of your proxy. I have a better idea."

His impassioned plea, urging shareholders to send their proxy votes to Luck, spread to Quantum Link, Usenet, and bulletin board systems around

---

the country. Soon, proxy votes began arriving in Luck's mailbox at his Milpitas home.

On Tuesday, November 22, 1988 the annual shareholder meeting commenced at the Manufacturers Hanover Trust Co. building in Manhattan. Lasting for more than an hour and with 50 people in attendance, Luck attempted to vote his proxy shares. Unfortunately, his inexperience in corporate matters soon halted his game. "It was a public meeting but the right paperwork wasn't done so I could vote my shares," he says.

Instead of Luck being placed on the ballot for a position on the board, the vote took place only for Mehdi Ali. Most shareholders were institutional shareholders, such as mutual fund managers or retirement funds. Ali won easily. He now took his place as one of six members on Commodore's board of directors and began to enjoy true corporate power.

For his part, Luck had to settle for airing his grievances publicly to the board. His biggest criticism was aimed at the very people in front of him. "There is no one with a significant technical background on the board of directors," Luck told the attendees. "Other companies have someone who has vision or understanding of the basic technologies and can help the board. Even in the high level management of Commodore there really isn't anyone who grasps the technology."

The statement was a direct blow to Gould, who told the audience he was, "ashamed to admit I don't know how to use a computer." However, he countered Luck's proposal with, "This company hires what we think are some very brilliant and capable people. ... Engineers are great, but they also very rarely make good businessmen."

Gould was rattled by the unexpected opposition to his leadership. "They seemed a bit taken aback over things I thought were legitimate questions," Luck later said.

"Luck Trucking" Dale and his proxy shares would have round two at the next shareholder meeting. For his part, Gould decided it might make sense to put someone on the board with technical experience. However, he vowed never to allow Commodore's board of directors to come under public scrutiny again, which would make round two a difficult undertaking.

Amiga 3000 at Last 1989

Commodore's engineers had wanted to start designing the Amiga 3000 back in 1986. When the chipset entered a redesign, they missed debuting the A3000 at the 1988 CeBIT. The chipset belatedly went into production in May 1988. Finally, in late 1988, it looked like CSG would deliver chip samples so the engineers could begin designing the A3000 prototype.

ECS Chip Samples

Although the new chipset had been called the Hi-Res chipset for years, marketing redubbed it ECS when it went to production in 1988. The term stood for Enhanced Chip Set. Soon it went through the usual layout and fabrication process.

Finally, in September 1988, the first chip samples came out of the CSG labs. These chips were put through testing by the Quality Assurance group, a lengthy process in itself that was liable to take until late in the year. The QA group uncovered problems with the sprites and genlock transparency, among other issues.

Meanwhile, Dave Haynie, the engineer responsible for the Amiga 2000, continued working on his A2630 accelerator board. He had his first version running at 25 MHz in July 1988, then a month later he was able to improve the speed to 33 MHz. In September he had his first PCBs of the A2630 produced and stuffed with components. He continued working on this project and had a full 10 accelerator boards ready by the end of January, 1989—although due to heat problems he opted to run them at 25 MHz.

And still, the A3000 project failed to move forward. "For a long time, I looked at the whole thing as a failure, even with all of the technical success we had, because it didn't go on," says Haynie.

During this period, no Amiga 3000 prototypes were created. "At Commodore engineering we weren't really listening to management," says Bryce Nesbitt. "Engineers spent maybe 10% of their time trying to make this business variant of the Amiga and ninety percent of the time doing whatever the hell they wanted. And that's a problem. Commodore had a failure of leadership."

The lack of progress on the A3000 clearly showed the folly of having engineers working on multiple projects concurrently. Many engineers, Dave Haynie included, routinely worked on three things at the same time. Each extra project displaced the time the engineer had to focus on a project, and so the projects were invariably delayed.

By February 1989, CSG was up to revision 2 of the ECS chipset as Haynie began entering pilot production on the A2630 in West Chester. However, Henri Rubin began to worry, rightly so, that Commodore would once again fail to deliver on time.

A New Project Manager

When Henri Rubin found out the engineers would have no Amiga 3000 to demonstrate at the upcoming CeBIT show in March, he decided to put a different lead engineer on the project. Rubin felt that Jeff Boyer, who had been leading the A250 project, was the natural fit.

Jeff Porter had a different idea. Boyer was a respected engineer within Commodore, a fast engineer, and a nice guy by all reports. But at this point in his career he had little management experience, and Porter thought it would be difficult for him to manage a team. And, unknown to engineers at the time, Boyer was also moonlighting on engineering projects for Gerard Bucas at GVP.

Instead, Porter favored Hedley Davis, the fast talking, high strung, straightforward Pennsylvanian. Davis, an avid pilot at the time who was taking lessons from the nearby Brandywine Airport, only truly relaxed when he was soaring among the clouds.

Prior to this, Davis primarily designed the low-level system software called firmware. "And so, because management were the way they were, they always thought the hardware engineer was the guy who was in charge because hardware guys wore the big boy pants in the company and software guys were second class citizens in a lot of ways," says Davis.

Just days earlier, Davis had given a scathing critique of the C65 project to Porter and felt the engineers should be concentrating on the Amiga 3000 instead.

Porter knew Davis was capable of creative engineering solutions and had been grooming him since mid-1988 to take on a management position. "Usually the guy with the best idea at the time got the project lead job," explains Porter. "There were lots of projects happening at the same time so eventually everyone got to have a baby themselves and be the project lead designer."

Davis stood out for his intense drive to steamroll over any obstacles slowing down product development, a trait he learned from C128 designer Bil Herd. "I really think that some of the engineers in the company enjoyed technology and liked to design things but didn't necessarily have an eye towards productization," explains Davis. "Other people had more of an eye towards not only the technology but getting it the hell out the door."

Although both Greg Berlin and Dave Haynie were disappointed they did not get the product lead on the A3000, both felt Davis was the right pick. "Hedley is a very, very intelligent guy," says Berlin. "He was the perfect guy to manage that job, and he did a lot of cool stuff."

There was one problem though. Davis was still struggling to produce even a handful of his A2024 monitors, and they were still under evaluation by the QA group by February 1989. Henri Rubin had promised the product in 1988 and started taking flack from Mehdi Ali when the product failed to appear on store shelves. Rubin expressed his disappointment to Davis for failing to deliver.

However, despite falling out of favor with Rubin, Porter encouraged Davis to prove he could make things happen on the Amiga 3000 project and promised he would pull for Davis "110%" to lead the project. Like many Commodore engineers, Davis tended to hide when Rubin came down the hall, but Porter suggested he should be more visible.

The engineer who had the personality of Dr. Leonard "Bones" McCoy from *Star Trek (1966)* and the willpower to pull everyone else up to his speed was officially put in charge of the Amiga 3000 in March 1989. The waffling and indecision that plagued the A3000 project from 1986 ended immediately and the project began moving forward. "You need somebody to make it their mission in life to make sure this thing is going to happen," says Davis. "At this point in my career, I would not have taken no for an answer. I was going to make it happen, whatever it took. Much in the same way Bil Herd would always say whatever it takes to get it done right now."

A3000 Starts for Real

Compared to the small A500 and A2000-CR teams of one or two engineers, the Amiga 3000 had the largest team ever with six core system engineers: Hedley Davis, Dave Haynie, Greg Berlin, Scott Hood, Jeff Boyer, and Terry Fisher. "Over the years, we were doing the work of entire organizations within the PC industry," says Haynie. "We had maybe 40 people working on all this stuff, versus a company the size of Apple which has 40 people per project."

After an overworked Dave Haynie completed the A2630 accelerator card, which brought the Amiga 2000 up to 25 MHz, he began work on the Amiga 3000. Haynie would focus on creating a new expansion bus, which he called Zorro III. The logic for the bus would reside on a gate array chip he named Super Buster. "There's a lot of stuff I could do at the system level for the high-end because it didn't have to be quite so cheap," he says.

Greg Berlin would end up working on several parts of the system. "I did the some of the motherboard design and some of the chip and gate arrays," he recalls. "I designed the Ramsey chip, and the Fat Gary—which is the overall system controller chip." Ramsey would control the 32-bit fast RAM and provide address generation for the Direct Memory Access Controller (DMAC).

Jeff Boyer had previously created the hard drive controller for the Amiga 500, called the A590. "Jeff Boyer had done the DMA chip for the external hard drive on the A500," says Berlin. Unfortunately the controller had a number of bugs and it took Boyer five revisions before he was able to produce a working chip. "It had issues."

Now Boyer would use what he learned to further the A3000. "The DMA controller was designed by Jeff Boyer," says Berlin. "The DMA controller worked with the hard drive and shuffled data around memory. The floppy drive stuff was all DMA built into the Amiga chips."

Scott Hood, the junior engineer working on the A2320 flicker fixer, would continue developing it not only as a board for the Amiga 2000 to allow the Amiga to use a multisync monitor, but he would also create an ASIC chip called Amber, which would be used onboard the Amiga 3000.

Rounding out the team, as he had for most Commodore projects before, was Terry Fisher, who was responsible for the PCB layout. Fisher, who had been with Commodore since 1983, had done the motherboard layout for the C128, Amiga 2000, and many other systems.

The team planned to have the system completed and released in 1989, and this time, it seemed like it might actually happen. "These guys really were sharp and very capable of handling anything," says Paul Lassa. "Dave [Haynie] is a great example of knowing both the hardware and software side of things, but equal things could be said about Hedley and Greg Berlin. Most of the guys who came into Commodore were just cream of the crop. Very capable engineers that were tapped into what the computer was and where it should go and creative as to how to get there."

Because the lead time for the case design work was longer than other parts of the project, Davis started talking with the designers early. "Herb Mosteller was the mechanical guy," says Davis. "He and his band of guys had a little area. We talked about the basic form factor and where the floppy would be and where the hard drive would be in the motherboard expansion chassis and all that stuff."

Some work had already been done on the A3000 case, which started life as a replacement for the original A2000 case. Many of the engineers detested the A2000 case and wanted to improve upon it. "The A2000 was clunky. It's a big, big box," says Davis. "We decided to put the expansion card sideways in the A3000. We had that so we could lower the overall profile without changing the Zorro form factor."

The form factor would ultimately hinge on the size of the components, principally the power supply, the motherboard, and the disk drives. Davis decided on the specifications of the power supply, then worked with a Japanese company to produce it. "We got our power supply co-produced by Phihong," says Davis. "We had a rep and his name was Ed Raether. This guy would come in and work with us for the power supply specification and Phihong would build the power supplies according to our spec. It was kind of cool."

For the disk drives, Davis turned to another Japanese company named Chinon, whose sales representative had more information on Commodore than the engineers. "This company had a guy named Hama," recalls Davis. "He was a Japanese sales guy and he would come into our company. I remember sitting with him and Jeff [Porter] in Jeff's office and Hama-san would start telling us these stories about stuff going on inside of Commodore that Jeff and I had never gotten a whiff of. We were like, 'No way, that's bullshit. That can't be true.' And Hama-san would go away and we'd sniff around and find out, holy shit, it was true."

Whenever the Commodore engineers wanted to get to the bottom of a rumor, they turned to Hama. "This guy who worked at this other company would come in and talk to us before we knew what was going on and give us these little doses of reality or insight that were hugely amazing."

The Amiga 3000 would also come with a different mouse than the A1000 or A2000, designed in Japan. "Itoh also designed the A3000 mouse," says Jeff Porter. "It was so much better than the original. It was form fitting in the hand and very ergonomic."

The principle change would be improved video output by including the Amber flicker fixer chip. "Hedley came up with a way to include it," says Jeff Porter, referring to the Amber chip. "There was some new RAM technology that had come out that could be used to basically put the flicker fixer type functionality cheaply on the motherboard of the A3000."

The addition of the Amber chip meant the Amiga 3000 could compete with contemporary IBM-PC computers. "We stuck a little 23 pin to VGA adapter [on the motherboard] with the A3000 so that you can get 31 kilohertz instead of 15 kilohertz video coming out of the A3000," says Porter. "So you can get a nice VGA monitor plugged into it and have it look decent instead of the old scan lines you get with a traditional NTSC monitor."

AmigaOS 1.4/2.0

Commodore was not only having problems keeping up with hardware advancements from competitors in the IBM PC and Macintosh world. The operating system itself was becoming more important, and the company had to allocate increasing resources to keep AmigaOS up to date.

Commodore released AmigaOS 1.3 upgrade disks to dealers sometime in late 1988. For $60-$70, Amiga owners received the Kickstart chip, disks, and the installation service. The new Kickstart allowed the system to autoboot from a hard drive, and the AmigaDOS file system was improved with faster hard drive access. As well, the command line interface (CLI) was integrated into the Workbench with a complete text based shell called AmigaShell. Users could finally view and manipulate all files from within Workbench.

With that out of the way, the next version of AmigaOS would be developed for the Amiga 3000 primarily by the Amiga software engineers at Commodore HQ. "Our West Chester group, at the start when I was there, was not strong enough to take control of development," says Bryce Nesbitt. "There was Kickstart 1.3, and eventually we developed Kickstart 2.0, mostly in West Chester, with a lot of help from the West Coast group."

The AmigaOS team had met in February 1988 to discuss the new specifications for the operating system and then dispersed. While the West Chester developers finished off and supported AmigaOS 1.3, the four West Coast programmers made AmigaOS work with the new chipset—primarily difficult items such as Productivity Mode, retargetable graphics, and laser printer issues. They had largely completed this task by September 1988 and had released an alpha version of Kickstart which they called Jumpstart 1.4.

Once the 1.4 alpha was stable enough to work with, and stable samples of the ECS chipset were available to wire into Amiga 2000 systems for experimentation, the east coast software team, under the leadership of Andy Finkel, was ready to begin.

Finkel, an accomplished guitar player in a local Pennsylvanian fiddle band, was mostly well respected. "Andy is a really sharp guy who knew his stuff and he helped me in many ways," says programmer Eric Cotton. "I consider him my mentor in the early days. He's very straightforward and extremely intelligent."

The West Chester Amiga software group had been together since 1985 and had developed a strong bond. "In the early days of the Amiga, each of us had a SUN workstation," recalls Cotton. The computers were assigned networking names. "Each one of them had used *Gilligan's Island* as the theme of our computers. So mine was named Gilligan, Andy's was the Skipper, and someone had Mary-Anne. We actually each had our own little three inch Gilligan's Island figurines that sat in front of the computer."

The team had, for the most part, been around since the early days of the VIC Commandos. Programmers like Eric Cotton and Paul Higginbottom had been working with Finkel since 1980 programming the VIC-20. However, there was some drama within the group as some programmers felt Finkel's C code was ugly, owing to the habits he developed programming assembly language for the 6502 processor.

In August 1988, while the team finalized AmigaOS 1.3, Higginbottom began vying for Finkel's job as head of Amiga software. He felt Finkel was not a strong leader and tended to crush new ideas from his developers rather than nurture them. Higginbottom felt he would make a better group leader than Finkel and shared his concerns with Jeff Porter. Porter chose not to act on the recommendations but gave suggestions to Finkel to better manage his team. When it came time to plan out features for the new OS later that year, Finkel gathered his team together to plot out the future of the Amiga operating system as a group.

Although he was a relatively new hire, Bryce Nesbitt was able to influence the design of the Amiga 3000. "He was a very sharp individual, coming in on the OS side," says Paul Lassa. "They were young guys who were really passionate."

Nesbitt felt that the Amiga should be more flexible with the operating system, rather than being locked into versions that could only be changed via new Kickstarter ROM chips. "Bryce advanced that concept quite a bit and made it a lot more flexible with the Amiga 3000," says Carl Sassenrath. "Later things changed where you could actually select different Kickstarts and things like that."

Nesbitt's new system would, much like the original Amiga, now support disk-based Kickstart as well as ROM based Kickstart. This meant the operating system could easily be upgraded through software only.

Eric Cotton, a longtime Commodore programmer, focused on the Workbench, the GUI part of AmigaOS. "I worked on preferences and some auxiliary software and demos and things like that," he says, referring to the small applications, such as a calculator and clock included with the OS.

Many times, projects were started and never released, such as a simple genlock application. "There was genlock hardware that was designed for the Amiga, so you could do some green screen effects," says Cotton. "One of the tasks that I was given, that I absolutely hated, was to create this software to go with it. It was called Title Graphic and it was basically titling software. It wasn't one of my proudest efforts."

Cotton and his fellow developers also worked on AmigaGuide, a built-in help system for applications and AmigaOS, using a hypertext system with links and a simple help-file browser. And third party applications could now use a standard software installer to install to a hard drive.

New UI Look

On Windows machines, the main OS interface came to be known as a desktop. On AmigaOS, the place with all the tools was of course called the Workbench. The Workbench had not changed very much since 1985 but it was about to get a major upgrade thanks to the efforts of the Amiga team.

Much like the hardware team, the software engineers started projects entirely on their own. "We were all kind of creative people so we always needed our creative outlets to have a little fun or do something different or add our own little footprint to things," says Eric Cotton. "We used our own experience and our own talents and we were even influenced by some of our video game backgrounds."

At the time, graphical user interfaces on the Amiga, Atari ST, and Macintosh looked rather flat. "We were keeping our eyes on what was going on around us," says Cotton. In late 1988, Commodore acquired a curious new computer. "We actually had a NeXT computer that Commodore bought to examine."

The NeXT was the brainchild of Steve Jobs, who had a particular talent for taking existing innovations and wrapping them up into a harmonious whole. Jobs stole the look of his NeXTSTEP operating system from the Silicon Graphics IRIX 3 operating system. The interface looked almost 3D, as though it had depth on the flat screen. Although the NeXT was a commercial failure at $6,500, it influenced other computer makers and operating systems of the time.

It was clear the Amiga's Intuition interface, which looked about the same since 1985, needed a paint job. The NeXT computer became a powerful influence on the West Chester Amiga developers and became a focal point for their plans with the AmigaOS user interface. *Compute!* magazine even ran an article in March 1989 about the upcoming Amiga 3000 titled "NeXT Amigas" which noted the similarities.

The team worked as well as they could with the new chipset through the end of 1988 and into 1989, although as Nesbitt noted, they were initially weak when it came to Amiga development. By late April, the first schedule for the Amiga 3000 was created by Hedley Davis, and the developers were to have AmigaOS 1.4 completed by September 1, 1989, a mere four months away. Most of the team felt the timeline was unrealistic.

In response, Finkel hired several more programmers, including a Pennsylvanian native named Michael Sinz and a Canadian named Peter Cherna. The larger team was an acknowledgement that the OS was becoming more important and complex.

At the time, a longtime "VIC Commando" named Dave Berezowski managed the Workbench application. Another programmer named Steve Beats, who came from Commodore UK, also joined the team. Beats was a programmer going back to the C64 days, where he created a popular sprite editor. He later joined Commodore UK in the shipping department, and then advanced into software development under Gail Wellington of CATS fame. In 1987, he volunteered to rewrite critical parts of AmigaDOS, converting the BCPL code into C. "Steve Beats was probably one of the brightest software guys I ever worked with," says Eric Cotton. "Just an all around brilliant guy."

Berezowski and Beats worked on their Workbench project, somewhat in secret, until they were ready to unveil it to the rest of the team. "We came in one morning, and these two guys looked bedraggled and tired, but smug as all hell," recalls Peter Cherna. "And they wouldn't say why. They said, 'We're not going to show you until the other people are here.'"

Before lunch, enough employees had trickled in and the duo showed them a new version of Workbench. "They had taken Workbench and Intuition and they hacked it overnight," says Cherna. The new GUI looked almost 3D in appearance and much more professional than the old blue and orange Intuition.

The developers created a set of standard gadgets (buttons, text boxes, checkboxes, sliders) for the GUI so that other application developers did not have to write their own. They also created *The Amiga User Interface Style Guide* to explain how applications should be laid out in order to achieve more consistency between different Amiga applications.

The new widgets, which were made accessible to developers in the gadtools library, would give the Amiga an impressive visual upgrade. "Workbench 2.0 was very nicely done. That did help the Amiga quite a bit," says Dale Luck.

With the Amiga 3000 now fully underway, it was only a matter of time before Commodore would release the anticipated system. But would the market react as positively as it had to the Amiga 2000?

C65 Becomes Official 1989

Back in October 1987, engineer Bill Gardei had conceived of a C64 sequel to compete with Nintendo and win back the game market for Commodore. However, since that time his project gained little traction within the company. That was about to change as Commodore's engineers slowly realized they would be unable to drastically cost reduce the Amiga 500.

CES January 7, 1989

For the first time in three and a half years, Commodore attended CES, the biggest consumer event in the world. This was perhaps a sign that Commodore was ready to return to its consumer roots. Meanwhile, rival Atari was nowhere to be seen.

At this Winter CES, held in Las Vegas January 7 to 10, 1989, a burgeoning technology called compact disc was all the rage. The new media format used lasers, invented by Charles H. Townes in 1957 while working at Bell Labs. The idea of using lasers to read and write information was invented a year later, but it took a long time until Dutch electronics giant Philips and MCA released the first commercial product called MCA DiscoVision on December 15, 1978 (this was later rebranded as LaserDisc). The media was used for movies and famously for the video game *Dragon's Lair* in 1983.

By 1982, a smaller version called Compact Disc (CD) started to enter the marketplace, and both Philips and Sony released audio CD players. The format slowly overtook audio tapes as the premier media for music, and by the end of the decade, it seemed like a viable solution for storing large amounts of computer data. CD ROM would soon become a central part of Commodore's strategy.

President and CEO Irving Gould announced Commodore had sold one million Amiga computers since 1985. It had taken nearly four years to reach the one million mark (it took less than a year for the C64 to sell a million). Commodore later announced revenues of $871.1 million for 1988, with a profit of $48.2 million.

In the UK, as the incentives David Pleasance put in place took effect, sales of the Amiga 500 quadrupled to 160,000 units in 1988. And those numbers would continue to rise. The numbers also justified hiring an ad agency to produce and air television commercials in the UK. "Ultimately we went to a company which was Laing Henry," recalls Pleasance. "They did really good work."[1]

But the true star of the show was Nintendo, which announced it had sold over seven million NES consoles in 1988. As a demonstration of its might, the company exhibited its games and hardware in a football-field-sized display in the West Hall called The World of Nintendo.

Gould had little new to show the consumer market at CES. He trotted out new PCs and the Amiga 2500, but those were hardly targeted at consumers. US magazines at the time listed only three companies when discussing video games: Nintendo, Sega, and Atari. If Commodore wanted to remain relevant to the consumer market, it would need a video game console of its own.

The year kicked off numerous articles by *Compute!'s Gazette* noting that sales of NES games were hurting the C64 software market. Month after month, the magazine featured articles comparing the C64 to the NES. Meanwhile, the same monthly magazine was only 92 pages, down from over 200 in its heyday. It was a sure sign the C64 was in strong decline in North America.

To counter this threat, Commodore quietly unveiled its A250 game console behind closed doors to select attendees at CES. Both George Robbins and Jeff Boyer had worked on the machine right into early January, preparing a demonstration. (After the show, a stressed out Robbins would depart for a week of skiing in Salt Lake City.)

The response to the machine was positive but not overwhelming. After all, Amiga graphics had been around since 1985 so there was nothing to blow away expectations. Still, people agreed the machine had superior graphics compared to the 8-bit NES and would likely do well in the marketplace if marketed correctly.

After CES, Gould met with his executives, marketing, and engineering managers and began plotting a course for the new console. One technical challenge that soon became apparent was whether the large, disk-based Amiga games

---

1   The company was so well regarded it was purchased by a leading advertising agency. "In fact, they were ultimately bought out by Saatchi & Saatchi and Jennifer Laing became the chairperson of Saatchi & Saatchi," says Pleasance.

could make the transition to cartridge. After all, each disk was almost one megabyte in size and many games relied on multiple disks. This was a far cry from the 16 kilobyte cartridges for the C64.

The team regrouped on Monday, January 23 to review the plan. At this meeting Gould found out the cost to start cartridge production and console advertising would be $40 million. This immediately spooked him away from the idea of launching a new console.

It would have taken steel resolve and a sense of risk taking to go forward with the idea. "That was probably the key difference between Irving and Jack [Tramiel]," says Kit Spencer. "Irving said, 'Yeah, I think I understand,' but wouldn't drive it through. Jack in that situation would have driven an Amiga game machine version through, I'm absolutely sure."

Now that the Amiga-based game console was dead, Jeff Porter realized it would not be possible to significantly cost reduce the Amiga 500 to get it into the $250 retail price range. But then he hit upon an idea that was brilliant in its use of the technology available to him. Rather than trying to cost reduce the high-end Amiga technology further, Porter would go the other direction and pull up the cheaper technology available.

He would take Bill Gardei's NES killer, the C65, and enhance those features to effectively compete with the A500 features. Rather than being a console to compete directly against Nintendo, the C65 would evolve into an upscale C64. And in doing so, Commodore would finally have a product suited to its core capabilities of mass producing low-cost computer products. If his team executed on the concept properly, the machine could end up replacing the C64 entirely.

Relentlessly Pursuing Commodore

By January 16, 1989 Commodore's LSI group finally had the layout of the VIC-III 4567 chip complete. Fabricating the chip would be an exacting, potentially error-filled exercise, with 16 different layers they would have to apply to the silicon wafer.

With chip delivery imminent, Jeff Porter began to get serious about the C65. The key engineer, currently lacking, would be someone to own the motherboard. At the time, Porter was receiving persistent requests for an interview from a young, inexperienced engineer. He decided to look at his resume.

The engineer's name was Paul Lassa. "Paul was a younger guy, maybe in his early 20s at the time," says Gardei. "He had blonde shoulder length hair as I recall. He was very energetic, but with very little experience."

Lassa was born in 1965, making him the youngest Commodore engineer besides Bryce Nesbitt. He came from a large family. "There were 9 kids in 11 years with no twins or triplets," says Lassa. "We were somewhat of a spectacle.

My mom was virtually an only child except for a younger brother that was eight years younger than her. She always felt like an only child and she longed for having more siblings. So I think the pendulum swung way in the other direction."

Lassa became interested in computers in his early teens and purchased a Timex Sinclair ZX81. "It was maybe $129 and I talked one of my brothers into splitting it with me," he says. He soon took up programming on the pint-sized computer, which led to paid work. "One week I saw that there was a rack with some games from a company named Timeworks. They were little cassettes in shrink wrap packaging. There were a couple of simple productivity applications and one or two games."

Lassa soon realized the software maker was a local company. "This company Timeworks happened to be situated in Deerfield, Illinois which was less than an hour's drive away," he recalls. Lassa made the drive. The company president tested his ZX81 knowledge and soon hired the high school student in 1981. "After my morning classes I'd drive out there and I started doing that for a couple of months."

In January 1983, Timeworks shifted its software development exclusively to a different computer. "My boss was going off to the Consumer Electronics Show in Las Vegas at the time and came back in mid January and he says, 'We're going to drop all this ZX81 stuff. There's this amazing new computer that was announced at the show. We're going to port all our titles to this and write all our future titles for it.' And it was the C64."

Lassa helped port a number of ZX81 titles to the C64 platform. "There was *Robbers of the Lost Tomb*, a take on Indiana Jones. Somewhere in there we got a deal to do the *Evelyn Wood Dynamic Speed Reader* as a license. I was lead programmer on that. There was a push in the industry for doing educational titles, so I did a redo of Robbers of the Lost Tomb with a mathematics theme, and it was called *Dungeon of the Algebra Dragons*. And then the last one I worked on was a port from a much smaller game on the ZX81, it was called *Star Battle*."

In the fall of 1983, Lassa entered the University of Illinois at Urbana-Champaign. "About two years into it, the Amiga was launched," he recalls. "Even though I had been programming for the C64, I was really jazzed about the Amiga." Unfortunately, the Amiga 1000 was priced out of his budget. "At the time I was a struggling college student trying to make the bills for my tuition and so I just had to live vicariously through some of the magazine articles."

When Commodore released the Amiga 500 a few years later, Lassa, along with legions of others in his situation, jumped aboard. "As soon as the Amiga 500 came out, I went and purchased one of those," he says. "And for the most part, it had nearly everything that the Amiga 1000 had in it. I was all set to go, and I was really jazzed about getting that."

In 1988, Lassa received his Bachelor of Electrical & Computer Engineering. "I am nearing the end of college and here I have this background in the Commodore 64, watching Commodore over the years, writing programs, and very excited about it and very excited about the Amiga as well," he says. "I just decided I wanted to go work at Commodore. By this time I wanted to work on the Commodore Amiga because, while I liked the 64 and everything, the Amiga was the next step up in technology capability and really an amazing machine that represented the future of where computing was going."

Commodore was reaping the benefits of having loyal, educated customers eager to join the company. However, if Lassa's experience is any indication, closing the deal was a gruelling process. "I started contacting Commodore and I didn't get much of a response. Not a 'no', not a 'yes', not a 'we're thinking about it.' Just no response. Little did I know that they didn't have much of an HR department and so it was pretty much going into a black hole."

Lassa finally received a break when he attended a meeting of the Champaign-Urbana Commodore Users Group. "Amazingly at one of these monthly users group meetings they had invited a guest speaker, and imagine who it might be among the obvious choices? It was Dave Haynie! He was kind of the rock star of the Amiga community. He'd travel around to the user groups and maybe he'd go to one each month to different parts of the country. It was very gracious of him to go evangelize and just connect up with people in the community."

Lassa tagged along for a dinner with Haynie and several CUCUG members. "Later on at the dinner I said, 'Look I'm finishing up with college and I have an EE degree in computer architecture. I'm really interested in applying at Commodore for a position. Do you guys hire people and are there any openings?' And he goes, 'Well yeah we hire people. I don't know if there are any openings and it's kind of done informally, but I'll give you somebody's name and you can contact them and look into it.' He pointed me in the direction of his boss at the time, the director of engineering, Jeff Porter."

Lassa sent his resume directly to Porter. And heard nothing. "I sent things and it still seemed like it was a black hole," he recalls. The unemployed graduate soon resorted to pestering Porter's secretary. "Most of the time when I'd call she'd say, 'He's not in, he's traveling.' So I wasn't having much success connecting with Jeff Porter. But I was very patient and I'd say, 'Well when can I call him?' or 'Can he call me back?' And I didn't get calls back. I kept asking, 'When might he be in so that I could call and catch him here?' She'd give me various time frames and usually when I called he wasn't around."

It had now been many months since he graduated but Lassa persisted until finally it happened. "At some point I did call at some magic time. She says,

'Oh yeah he's here right now. Let me patch you over to him.' I found out it really wasn't her fighting me off or screening me out or any of that. It was simply that he just wasn't around that much, and even when he was in the building, he was off doing things with other departments and just running around getting a lot of stuff done."

Porter promised to set up an interview. However, Lassa's moment of success proved short lived. "I had this very warm response from him on the phone but then I'd follow up a couple of times and again not get through to him. Any normal, sane individual trying to get a job at Commodore at that time would have given up much earlier than me."

Lassa's devotion to Commodore ran deep and he continued his relentless pursuit. "Eventually I connected up with him again and he was like, 'Oh yeah. I'm sorry this is taking so long. Why don't we get you set up with a plane ticket and a hotel and we'll get you out here for an interview.'"

The interview happened just before Christmas 1988. "Jeff ultimately told me, 'Hey, I've got this new project that we're really excited about getting off the ground. I'd like to get you started on it.' And I'm thinking it's a new Amiga. Once I was hired there, it wasn't the Amiga. It was the C65."

On January 23, 1989, Lassa began working alongside engineers who had built his beloved Amiga 500. "It absolutely was a dream job and it still exists as that in my mind," he says. "I worked there for five years and those were, as I'm sure many people will tell you, some of the best years of my career."

Part of Commodore's secret to releasing low-cost products was the size of its product teams. "Once I was on board, I saw how small this group actually was," recalls Lassa. "We're talking maybe ten engineers and the equivalent over at Apple was probably 50 to 100 at that time. We definitely were dwarfed in who we were competing with, running on a shoestring. But as I came to learn, these guys were very strong and capable technical individuals."

Best of all, Lassa would mentor directly under his favorite Amiga engineer. "Dave [Haynie] was the chief architect in those first couple of years that I was there," says Lassa. "They always had one of the senior guys sort of supervising me."

While mentoring, Lassa worked for Hedley Davis alongside George Robbins for a month. "Paul Lassa was basically a junior engineer we hired during the Amiga years," says Dave Haynie. "He was working for George Robbins for a while on some of the A500 peripherals and he was becoming the senior engineer at that time."

Revealing the C65

After all the trials Paul Lassa had endured to work on the Amiga, it was bitter-sweet to be assigned the sequel of his beloved C64. "I had mixed feelings about it," he recalls. "In any case, I was willing to go and work on the C65 because I thought it was a great idea and a great opportunity for making it available to people at a price point that was much broader reaching than even the low-end Amigas could hit at that time."

Lassa was introduced to his coworkers on the project, Bill Gardei and Fred Bowen, who were two of the most cantankerous engineers at Commodore. Gardei had a well established reputation for not working well with others. "I don't mean this in any negative way but I think somebody like Bill Gardei would be happy off in his little lab completely on his own and not really inter-acting with others that much," says Lassa.

Bowen was the company's resident cynic who had severe doubts about Lassa due to his inexperience. He also had the most experience out of anyone on Commodore's 8-bit line, having worked on them going all the way back to the PET. By late January he was growing increasingly disturbed that his sugges-tions were being ignored by Porter and Gardei.

Porter still wanted to wait until they had a functioning prototype in hand before revealing the project to Henri Rubin. However, with the C65 chipset imminent, he decided to reveal the project to other engineers. "He was great at getting all the hardware, software, and chip people talking with each other," says Lassa.

On February 1, 1989, Porter gathered together a meeting of engineers who could provide input into the project, including Hedley Davis, Dave Haynie, and Bryce Nesbitt. "By the time I knew about it, they were already getting ready to do prototypes," says Dave Haynie. The revelation caused chaos with the system specification.

Nesbitt had known of the C65 chipset since July 1988 when Fred Bowen re-vealed the specs to him. An early software developer for the C64, Nesbitt had watched the years go by as Commodore squandered its chances to introduce a new machine. "It was just the dumbest thing because you could have taken the C64 and added some paged memory and started souping things up within the existing framework, and even had a good old hardware switch where it boots up in one megahertz mode, but then you flip some bit and suddenly it goes four times as fast. That would be awesome!" Nesbitt was immensely curious what his fellow engineers had cooked up.

Porter had the respect of the other engineers, having delivered the Amiga 500 that had saved Commodore, proving that all his instincts for the system had been correct. Now he was about to propose the next C64, a product with even more cache with gamers than the original Amiga ever had. And at a fraction of the price of the Amiga 500, there was every chance it could be the breakout hit Commodore needed.

Porter presented his version of what he wanted in the C65. This included a built-in 3.5 inch floppy disk drive, a serial port allowing users to plug in a 1541 drive to run old software, 128K RAM, and the fantastic C65 chipset. And it would be only marginally backward-compatible with the C64. "It was kind of like a baby A500," says Porter.

Commodore would create a new computer with two modes. The first mode, the C64 mode, would behave like a regular C64 with all the expansions plugged into it: more memory, a fast loader in ROM, an 80-column display, and it would have access to the built in 3.5 inch drive. Hopefully developers would start to release standard C64 software on 3.5 inch disks, resulting in existing C64 owners upgrading to the 1581 drive. He referred to it as C64-zero, or C640 mode. "It wouldn't run any of the standard C64 games, but it was close enough that making the mods to it were trivial," says Porter.

The second mode, C65 mode, would contain all the additional video modes and it would encourage development for the 3.5 inch disk format. Porter planned to produce 50,000 units of the C65D by October of 1989, at a retail price of $300.

Once software developers and users accepted the 3.5 inch disk standard, the software would flood in on those disks. The next year, in June 1990, Commodore would unbundle the disk drive from the computer to release a second version of the C65. This version would sell for only $150 and an initial run of 100,000 units.

The response was a little more contentious than Porter had hoped. There was some resentment by the West Chester engineers, who had been excluded from conversations about the project, especially engineers like Haynie who had helmed Commodore's 8-bit line with the C128 sequels, only to have his proposed C256 rejected.

The engineers grudgingly acknowledged that Gardei had accomplished something amazing in the 4567 VIC-III chip. "He was pretty clever because the C65 had a lot of what we wanted to put into the C128 back in the day," says Haynie.

Andy Finkel felt it was time to give up 8-bit computers and focus on the Amiga. "I'd already moved past the 8-bit stuff. I thought the time of the computers like the C65 had passed, and things like UNIX and the Amiga were just going to get cheaper and we probably should be heading there with as much effort as we can."

Jeff Porter felt Commodore would be leaving money on the table by ignoring the ultra-low-end market it had already established. "I think he saw a dual path for the company because in 1988 from the Amiga we had the capability of doing so much more, but the price point was still a little bit high," explains Lassa. "We now had the ability to do a super enhanced C64 for pretty close to a hundred and fifty bucks."

The most important feature would be the price point. "We wanted to give the customer a lot, but we wanted to target a price point that would set who could actually afford to buy one," says Lassa. "So many more people will make an impulse purchase or a purchase for Christmas when it's under $200, whereas an over $500 is a much bigger family purchase and decision."

Some engineers predicted that, without 100% backward compatibility with C64 software, the C65 would be another Plus/4 and end up wasting company resources. According to Lassa, "Somebody said, 'Why are you doing another C64 spin off when you could be moving forward with things?' There were naysayers saying why rehash it again? It will just fail in the marketplace the same way as the Plus/4 and it will be a waste of engineering effort."

Porter had hoped to win over his two prickly engineers, Bill Gardei and Fred Bowen. Unfortunately neither was satisfied. Gardei had a radically different vision of the system, which was to get it in the stores at the same price as the NES. At first he steadfastly defended his $39 "NES killer" against anyone and everyone. "I had some arguments with him. He argued over little things and some big things," says Andy Finkel, a former game developer on the VIC-20 and C64 computers. "I remember the arguments in the engineering lab with groups of people. We'd be all talking and Bill would be defending his ideas against all comers. He had a very firm concept."

Gardei notes, "The engineers who did most of the arguing were not even on the project."

Eventually Gardei somewhat accepted Porter's concept of including a 3.5 inch drive for the initial release and then unbundling later, but he felt the $99 system would be the best way to start.

Lassa credits Gardei as being the father of the C65, playing a similar role to that of Jay Miner on the Amiga. "When I came in the door, they already had the two main processors under development because those are really multi-year projects," he says. "I think he enjoyed the contest between, 'We'll put a C65 on a desk next to a low-end Amiga and we can be eighty percent as good as that and yet we're half the price.'"

However, he credits Porter with the vision for the computer. "The C65 was Jeff Porter's brainchild," he says. "I would certainly give him credit for it being his baby. He was pretty pivotal in choosing the direction and figuring out what the company was going to do with the computer development and everything."

Afterwards, Fred Bowen would create a summary of the meeting in an attempt to crystalize a product definition. However, he felt the project was still way off base.

Porter would continue to keep the project a secret from Irving Gould, the CEO and President, and even Henri Rubin. Once they had silicon and a C65 prototype, they would reveal it.

SID Chip

One of the most beloved aspects of the original C64 was the SID chip, which revolutionized sound in home computers. Curiously, Gardei had no plans to create a SID-II chip.

One option the engineers considered was to use the Ensoniq ES5503 digital oscillator chip, created by the original SID engineer, Bob Yannes. Unfortunately, the primary goal of making a low-cost computer did not allow it. "Ensoniq supplied chips to both keyboard manufacturers for professional musicians and for higher end sound cards for the PC marketplace," says Lassa. "The chips that they would have had in that time frame might have been too costly."

The engineers also had access to the Amiga Paula chip but decided against it for similar reasons. "The Paula chip is quite a bit more sophisticated," explains Lassa. "You could say, 'Well let's throw a Paula chip into a C65,' but that would've bumped it up significantly in price. A Paula chip wasn't twenty cents more than a SID chip. It was a significant amount."

Furthermore, Paula was engineered as part of a 16-bit chip set, which would have required more complex engineering compared to the 8-bit C65. "You would have had to do a fair amount of design work on the rest of the chipset to support it," says Lassa.

A third option was to moderately improve the SID chip by adding stereo sound output and multiplexing to allow 32 independent voices. This option was not seriously considered as Commodore Semiconductor no longer had an audiophile engineer with the same skills as Bob Yannes. "You would have had to stick one or two more engineers and designers on it," explains Lassa. "That would take another design cycle and there is risk and everything."

The engineers decided to stick with the SID chip. "If you look at the target market for a low-end computer or game machine at that time, everybody was quite thrilled with a blooping beeping thing putting out cool sounds," says Lassa. "Professional musicians weren't your target audience necessarily. Those people could go and get an Amiga 1000 or better."

After the discussions, Jeff Porter decided to include two SID chips to produce stereo sound. At the time, the 8580 SID chip cost only $1.58. "SID was good enough and actually pretty good for the time and it was very cost effective," says Lassa. "We could enjoy the huge economies of scale for using the same chip that was used across a couple of products."

C65 Prototype

After the contentious C65 meeting, Fred Bowen and Paul Lassa created a list of issues raised at the meeting and the team began addressing them. To address Porter's concern of lack of copy protection with the 3.5 inch drive, Gardei quickly formulated a clever strategy to allow copy protection for software vendors.

He came up with a scheme in which the disk drive would be able to read a value, the protection code, from a section of the disk that is readable but not writable by a standard disk drive. Only software vendors or Commodore would be able to write to that section of the disk. This would be verified against another value written to the disk, by the disk hardware. If the values did not match, the software would not load.

They also continued talking with engineers who held five different beliefs for what Commodore should do with the C65. The easiest suggestion was to do nothing and continue to sell the C64 or to use Gardei's CMOS chipset to cost reduce the C64 even further without adding new features.

Then of course there was Porter's vision of the C65 as a dual-mode machine, similar to the C128, except even less compatible with the C64. This drew scorn from engineers Dave Haynie and Fred Bowen. They favored cost reducing the C128 computer rather than letting it die, an unsurprising opinion given that both helped develop the C128.

From Gardei's perspective, his new chipset was not designed with C128 compatibility in mind, but as a C64 successor. "There were not a lot of similarities between the two products," says Gardei. "The C128 was more like a C64 with some extra memory and a high degree of compatibility. The C65 was more of a VGA machine, with better-than-Amiga graphics at that time."

The team was focused on creating a demo unit of the C65 in order to show off the C65 chipset features to Irving Gould. However, the project seemed chaotic to Hedley Davis. He had doubts that Paul Lassa, the engineer Porter handed to him, would be capable of owning the PCB on the project.

It also seemed like Ted Lenthe wanted to ensure his group received the credit when the prototype was presented to Gould, and he was independently making a PCB with Gardei, and even requesting for a smaller redesign of Gardei's initial PCB that was meant for the C64D case. An engineer named Mike Nines would produce the half-sized PCB and he also began creating a purely game system PCB for the C65 chips.

Davis' biggest concern was that Fred Bowen was not onboard the proposal and favored more of a Plus/4 approach the design. Bowen wanted a Plus/4 style machine but with C64 compatibility. Although he proposed this at the meeting, the idea was roundly mocked, and Bowen later admitted it made little sense.

And Bowen was only able to devote about 10% of his time to the project due to work for Commodore's legal team and C64 support commitments. In the meantime, he continued familiarizing himself with the 4502 assembler and porting C64 code over to the 32K ROM, which would go into the upcoming C65 prototype.

Fred Bowen had been an unwilling player in the C65 project since he had found out about it the year prior. By the end of February the situation had come to a head. The biggest problem was that Bowen favored either a C128 or Plus/4 type of computer, something Porter desperately needed to talk him out of. Bowen was also leery of becoming a code slave to the project, implementing whatever others asked of him without any input himself. And finally, his toolset didn't seem very good.

The final point was easy to solve. Bob Norby, a CSG engineer, finally provided a working assembler for the 4502 chipset that would run on VAX or an IBM PC. This was far superior to the hacked together one Bowen had been working with.

Jeff Porter had originally hoped to have C65 chips back from CSG way back in October. This would give his engineers lots of time to prepare a splashy demonstration for Henri Rubin, which he could then reveal to Irving Gould at CeBIT on March 8.

And then it happened. Two weeks before CeBIT was set to commence, on February 20, 1989, Gardei finally received his long awaited 4510 and 4567 chips. Although the 4510 performed admirably, there were problems with the 4567 chip. Gardei would have to work around these problems in order to bring his motherboard to life.

Porter still wanted a 1989 release. If his schedule was to have any hope of surviving, he would have to get both Rubin and Gould to approve the project, at which time he could muster other company resources on the project.

Porter informed Rubin that the chips had been produced and a prototype was imminent. Rubin was overjoyed. "At first, getting support for the project was difficult, save for one Dr. Henri Rubin," says Gardei. "He told me, 'It is fortuitous that someone like yourself is investigating keeping the C64 products alive.' Commodore, after all, needed a cash cow, and this could have very well been one."

Rubin recognized that a large part of the market could not afford an IBM PC clone or even an Amiga or Atari ST. When Rubin found out about Gardei's project, he recognized it as a legitimate attempt at a C64 successor; a product that played to all of Commodore's strengths in mass retail. And it allowed Commodore to leverage CSG to produce a cheap product for the masses.

Rubin promised to tell Irving Gould about the project at the upcoming CeBIT show in Hannover. Once he was on board, the project could receive the support it needed from other areas of Commodore in order to launch later in the year.

CeBIT Hannover

At the annual CeBIT show in Hannover, Germany, held March 8 to 15, 1989, Commodore had lots of products to show. But the only new Amiga system was the A2500UX, a repackaging of the trusty Amiga 2000. Retail pricing and a release date had not yet been determined. Commodore also debuted the PC 30-III, PC 50-III, and PC 60-II.

Henri Rubin unveiled a number of Zorro-II expansion cards, a culmination of his earlier strategy to upgrade the existing A2000. The expansions shown at CeBIT included the A2232 serial interface, A2091 SCSI controller, A2630 processor accelerator card with memory, A2024 Hedley Hi-Res, A2350 frame grabber/genlock/video adapter card, Arcnet Cards, Novell Netware for Amiga, and the Lowell Hi-Res Graphics Card.

One year earlier, Commodore Germany's marketing had been disappointed that no new Amiga 3000 computer had been unveiled. This year, they were doubly so.

As promised, Dr. Rubin revealed the C65 to Irving Gould and others. Gould, who had previously tried and failed to develop the Amiga 250, loved the idea. The C65 would be similar in performance yet with cheaper cartridges due to the smaller game sizes.

In a moment of unrestrained exuberance, Gould revealed to a South German newspaper that Commodore was developing a machine with functionality between the Amiga 500 and Commodore 64. He was of course referring to the C65. Later in the year, *Compute!'s Gazette* described the system and offered a November 1989 release date. Engineers soon began to receive queries from users via Q-Link and Usenet asking about the upcoming system.

Once the project received official backing by Rubin, the perception of the project quickly changed. Gardei recalls, "Soon other groups were asking, 'Can we play too?'"

When the engineers returned from CeBIT, it was clear Irving Gould wanted the system released soon. Henri Rubin called three meetings on his first week back with Porter, Gardei, Bowen, Bryce Nesbitt, and sometimes, Paul Lassa.

In one meeting, Bowen had raised the point that using the 3.5 inch drive in C64 mode would require changes to the C64 ROM, resulting in incompatibilities. The discussion was mainly focused on figuring out if the drive should be an inexpensive "dumb" drive, which would be controlled solely by software, similar to the Apple II drive. This would require Bowen to program an actual disk operating system (DOS) for the new computer. The other option was to include a "smart" drive that had built in DOS commands, similar to the 1581 drive.

With management on board, Paul Lassa and Fred Bowen could now officially spend most of their time on the system. Lassa began studying Gardei's schematics for his prototype board. He would need to design a custom chip to control the internal 3.5 inch drive. Meanwhile, Bowen was told to start working on a new version of DOS for the C65. In two months, new revisions of the 4567 and 4510 were expected to arrive.

Meanwhile, Porter could now approach people in other departments, such as documentation for manuals, marketing and sales, and CATS for communicating with third party software developers. Despite 1988 being something of a lost year for the project, the C65 had just rebounded in a spectacular way.

CHAPTER 13

Mehdi Ali the Second
1989

Irving Gould had remained at the helm of Commodore International as President and CEO for almost two years. During that time there had been no emergencies and Gould had not been seriously tested as the company coasted along from the momentum of Thomas Rattigan's leadership. But then, near the end of 1988, a crisis occurred and suddenly Gould wanted to hand over control to someone else. Time would tell which managers were beneficial and which were merely speed bumps.

Commodore and the Taxman

Commodore had finished an optimistic 1988, but a few days before the annual Winter CES show, the company received some devastating news. Commodore Business Machines International had been incorporated in the Bahamas since 1977. This meant that, on the books, the headquarters was in the Bahamas, and the US operation in West Chester was merely one of many international subsidiaries. This organization allowed Commodore to avoid being taxed by the US government on international revenues.

However, after Commodore had a string of exceptional years from 1981 to 1983, the IRS became interested in collecting taxes from those overseas operations. The federal government launched an investigation in which Commodore was forced to turn over all its internal financial books to the IRS. Shortly after the investigation began, in November 1984, Gould hired former secretary of state Alexander Haig to his executive board and Commodore had been able to keep the IRS at bay.

But 1988 was an election year, and a new administration would soon take over after the November election. In fact, Haig was himself attempting to become the Republican Party's nominee that year.

Throughout August and September, system engineer Fred Bowen had been gathering together archived financial files. As the longest serving engineer within the company, Bowen knew the most about the Tramiel days.

Rather than spending time engineering the C65 system software, Bowen's days were engaged in finding files related to the early days of the C64, straightening them out, indexing them for the IRS, and consulting with Commodore's own legal team headed by Dave Woods. On September 13, 1988, Bowen handed over the files to the IRS and then Commodore collectively held its breath, waiting for the outcome.

Word of the tax problems seeped out, and in November Dale Luck raised the issue at the aforementioned board of directors meeting that Commodore had not properly filed taxes.

Haig was a notorious critic of then vice-president George H. W. Bush, doubting his leadership abilities and publicly calling him a wimp. He had also infamously muddied the succession of leadership after the 1981 assassination attempt on Ronald Reagan, which should have fallen to vice president Bush. When Bush won the presidency in November and took office in January, there was ample opportunity for political payback.

On January 3, as the statute of limitations was about to expire for the tax claim, the IRS presented Commodore with a bill of $74.1 million in back taxes from 1981 through 1983.[1] The staggering amount threatened to destroy the company.

Ron Alexander, Commodore's VP of finance, claimed the IRS was only entitled to Commodore's US revenue and appealed the ruling in tax court. A negative ruling would wipe out Commodore's cash reserves. For the next few years, the possibility of bankruptcy loomed over the company. It was not the start to the new year that Gould had wanted.

President Mehdi Ali II

Irving Gould had been President and CEO of Commodore International since the Thomas Rattigan purge in April 1987. Following that tumultuous event, Gould had wanted Commodore to appear stable to investors. However, the next few months would see major changes within the executive ranks.

Many believed the elderly Gould did not possess the drive or charisma to lead his employees to victory. Jack Tramiel's battle cry had been, "Comput-

---

1   *Philadelphia Inquirer*, January 4, 1989. "IRS Says Commodore Owes $74.1 Million In Back Taxes"

ers for the masses, not the classes." Gould did not have a battle cry. As *Forbes* magazine writer Evan McGlinn remarked, "Maybe the jet-setting Irving Gould should let someone else call the shots."

The financial world had many criticisms of Commodore's chairman. Another Forbes article titled "Lost Opportunity?" blamed Gould for his "absentee-landlord management style." In it, analyst Lee Isgur, who knew Gould for over five years, summed up his management style: "Irving tries to minimize taxes, hates the day-to-day stuff and doesn't like to push the product, so he hires people to do it for him."[2]

By early 1989 Gould felt it was time to let someone else take over. His choices were to hire an outsider, perhaps from a rival computer company, or look for someone internally at Commodore who had demonstrated the required abilities. Gould chose the latter, and he considered three candidates: The first was Harald Speyer, the highly successful GM of Commodore Germany who had recently moved up to GM of Commodore Europe. The second was Mehdi Ali, the investment banker who helped Commodore survive bankruptcy in 1986. And the third was Henri Rubin.

After the IRS Tax situation heated up in September 1988, Irving Gould decided he wanted someone else to run the day to day operations who could deal with the emergencies he didn't want to deal with himself. He was good friends with Mehdi Ali, and soon Ali realized Gould was looking for a new company president of Commodore International.

Ali was only 43 years old in 1989. He also had an impressive resume that began with graduating from one of the oldest Ivy League universities in America, Yale. From there he joined Morgan Guaranty Trust (a banking company founded by J. P. Morgan) in 1969. In 1976 he joined General Motors as a vice president of finance. Then in 1980 he went to Pepsico Inc. as VP of finance where he worked alongside Thomas Rattigan. In 1984 he briefly worked for Dillon, Read & Co. before that job led to his employment with Commodore.

Of the three candidates, Ali was the most astute at waging political battles. In October 1988, a convenient emergency materialized that put both Henri Rubin and Harald Speyer in the crosshairs. Several PC products and the upcoming bridgeboard were late, and Ali began demanding an explanation. Both Jeff Porter and a manager from the European headquarters, Richard Glover, were suddenly caught in the middle of an executive power struggle.

---

2   *Forbes* magazine, "Lost Opportunity?" (November 13, 1989), p. 288.

Ali refused to let the issue drop and demanded to know who was responsible and who should be fired. He even enlisted the help of Winfried Hoffmann to send a fax to Irving Gould explaining the situation. The implication, of course, was that both Commodore Germany and the North American engineering departments were incompetently run.

For his part, Henri Rubin was woefully unequipped to deal with the attacks, and Harald Speyer refused to participate in the charade. This probably did neither man any favors.

Gould had missed the mark completely when he hired his friend Marshall Smith in 1984, and now it looked like he was about to hire another friend in Mehdi Ali. Perhaps Gould no longer wanted polite, professional management and wanted someone more akin to Jack Tramiel. It was true Ali had all the guts and attitude of Tramiel but he lacked the hard-won experience of managing a technology company.

When the smoke cleared, Gould knew who he wanted to promote. "He needed a Jack Tramiel to run his businesses," says Don Gilbreath. "To be a hardass to actually run a business because he was a really soft spoken guy. He loved the idea of technology. He wasn't necessarily great at it, but he loved the idea of it."

Gould felt he needed a Jack Tramiel clone in order to bring back Commodore's past successes. Gould often regaled Ali about Jack Attacks and encouraged the latter to do the same.

In February 1989, Gould appointed Ali to the position of president of Commodore International. In a press release, Gould stated, "Having worked closely with Mr. Ali for the past three years, I believe we are fortunate that he has agreed to expand the role he has been playing in the restructuring of Commodore into a major competitor in the microcomputer industry."

Without a doubt, Gould saw Ali as the person who had saved his ailing company during the financial crisis years earlier. Like Gould, the investment banker came from the world of finance. "They became good friends, for whatever reason, during the whole Prudential[3] thing," says Dave Haynie. "He had been an investment hatchet man or fixit guy, depending on your perspective, for Prudential Investments, and that's where they met. By the time he was put in charge of Commodore, Gould's kids were calling him uncle Mehdi."

---

3   Commodore had received loans from Prudential that allowed it to continue operations.

Ali and Gould decided he would not work from the West Chester head-quarters, unlike past presidents. "Apparently, he fired just about everybody in the New York office and brought in his own people," says Dave Haynie. Working from the Seagram Building in New York would allow Gould tighter control over his president so that no power struggles could surprise him, as had occurred with Thomas Rattigan.

Employees within Commodore soon began to receive missives from Mehdi Ali II, a title he used on business cards, emails and memos. (Ali also had a son, Mehdi Ali III.)

Commodore's employees had misgivings about the new appointment. "Irving brought in a banker to run the company, Mehdi Ali, and that was really bad," says Andy Finkel. "I don't know what his qualifications are as a banker. I assume he was good because he arranged financing for Irving, but in terms of a hands-on guy trying to run the company, it just didn't work for me or a lot of people."

Dave Haynie explains Ali's mindset. "I believe he was a guy who thought every solution was basically a matter of cash flow. If he could cut expenditures then the company would magically become profitable."

It also seemed suspicious to the employees that the man who had helped take down Rattigan was now assuming his former position. "We always thought that was kind of odd that Medhi came in to run things after he was the banker who had done the due diligence in the review," says Andy Finkel.

As president, Ali would be generously compensated. Gould set Ali's salary at $1,380,769. His contract guaranteed at least $5 million in salary and bonuses in his first two years with additional stock options. He also had a "golden parachute" clause such that if he lost his position, he would net a $2 million annual salary and bonus through 1994. As it turned out, 1994 would become a notable year for the company, but for other reasons.

Just prior to the announcement, Harald Speyer, who had been with Commodore since 1977, resigned. He was disappointed he was not promoted to president of Commodore International, but even more, he refused to work under Mehdi Ali as the two had frequently clashed the prior year, and he knew working with him would be impossible. Commodore had lost its most effective international General Manager. However, he would be replaced by the equally impressive Winfried Hoffmann who had founded the Braunschweig factory.

Henri Rubin to the Board

A few months earlier, Dale Luck had memorably urged Irving Gould to place someone with technical ability on the board of directors. Gould took the request seriously, although Luck himself would not be a candidate due to Gould's belief that engineers did not make good business managers. And Luck had seemed somewhat antagonistic to Gould. The last thing he wanted was a board member who might vote him out as CEO.

Dr. Henri Rubin had been with Commodore since early 1986 and was appointed to COO of Commodore International in October of that year. He was also an engineer with technical expertise and loyal to Gould. On March 6, 1989, Gould nominated Rubin to the board of directors, theoretically giving engineering a greater influence at the top strategic levels of the company.

The new appointment was not quite what Luck had hoped for. In fact, Luck himself wanted to become chairman of the board, something he publically told magazines. He was prepared to take his fight all the way to the next shareholder meeting in November, when a confirmation vote of Rubin would occur.

Commodore's engineers had mixed feelings about Rubin. Some felt affection towards him because he was one of the few executives who truly believed in the Amiga, rather than IBM PC clones. "He had to have the fastest, best Amiga that you could get on his desk, and he tried to do everything possible on it," says Dave Haynie. "That made him aware of what was possible and what wasn't. In other words, he was doing exactly what a manager should do."

Rubin regularly came to work with buttons missing from his shirts and habitually wore a bow tie. "He was a little crazy, but other than that he was great," says Haynie.

But most engineers had less respect for him. "He entered the corner office and was more visible than the others," recalls Bryce Nesbitt. "I think his management style was deliberately management by walking around." The term had caught on as a result of a popular business book, *In Search of Excellence (1982)*. In Japan, the practice is known as a Gemba walk. "He would walk around and talk to people and then maybe have an idea about the product they were working on and send them off creating in some other direction from the one that they were doing before he walked in."

Engineers who bumped into Rubin were in danger of having all their plans for the day ruined by a random suggestion, thus the term "Being Henried" was coined. "None of it seemed to have any direction," says Nesbitt. "He wasn't a visionary leader in the sense that people describe Steve Jobs. He was much more random than that. He seemed to think that if he just talked to people and those present, that was enough in order to keep things going. So I would say that, in engineering, we worked around Henri much more than we ever followed Henri."

When Rubin went on one of his Gemba walks, engineers and employees alike scattered hoping to avoid him. "I think he sometimes drove his software people to want to kill him," says Dave Haynie.

This soon became an inside joke that even reached the pages of *Compute!* magazine, which asked, "Is it true, as some Commodore insiders claim, that CBM production managers hide when they see top management coming down the hall with a new product idea?"[4]

Much like Commodore had published a game called Jack Attack in homage to its leader's famous outbursts, the engineers collaborated on a Henri Rubin game. "We once built a little internal video game that had a series of hallways," recalls Nesbitt. "And in it, Henri was walking with his bowtie spinning. He had sort of laser eyes. And you're running around kind of like Pac-Man and if he ever sees you, he'll go boop-boop and run and change your work. You could hide on him if you move in the hallway space correctly, but if you're ever in the same hallway that he is and he can see you then you've lost the game."

Gerard Bucas, whose company GVP rested on the continued success of Commodore, saw the writing on the wall. "Henri Rubin came along and this other guy Mehdi Ali, and that's where the whole thing started falling apart. That was really the beginning of the end. I would say those two guys were the death of Commodore."

Toy Out, Copperman In April 1989

Throughout his first year, beginning in October 1987, Commodore's President of North America, Max Toy, kept a high profile. The aforementioned *Computer Chronicles* episode dedicated to the C64 featured an interview with Toy. He gave a full interview to *Compute!* magazine in its August 1988 issue. A month later, Toy began appearing in print advertisements for Q-Link, the online service Commodore invested in under Thomas Rattigan.[5]

---

4   *Compute!* magazine, March 1989, p. 62. "NeXT Amigas"

5   The president of Commodore US was automatically on the Quantum Link board of directors, due to Commodore's investment in the company.

Unfortunately, Commodore North America was not showing much of an improvement in its profits. In fact, net income only rose slightly from $17.4 million at the end of 1987 to $23.6 million at the end of 1988. This compared to Commodore's worldwide net income rising from $28.6 million to $55.8 million for the same period.

Gould had given him two years to turn things around in North America. Max Toy, like so many executives before him, was on thin ice unless he could stage a miracle in the next few months. By 1989, after less than two years on the job, Irving Gould began losing patience. He was expecting a turnaround in Commodore's flagging US market and instead it continued losing market share compared to Europe. "He didn't last too long," says Dave Haynie.

On April 24, 1989, Gould announced that Max Toy left the company to pursue other interests. On the same day of his resignation, Gould announced the new North American president.

He found a replacement in Harold Copperman, a 42-year-old former vice president and General Manager of Eastern Operations for Apple. Before that, Copperman served for 20 years at IBM. Gould wanted someone who knew marketing and advertising and Copperman seemed a logical choice. Perhaps he believed Copperman could bring IBM marketing and Apple advertising to Commodore.

Copperman lived in Wilton, Connecticut, a small but affluent town located near the east coast. His son was in his final year of high school at the time. Rather than disrupting the school year, Copperman chose to fly his own private plane each week from Wilton to the Brandywine Airport next door to Commodore.

Copperman was one of the few executives to fully understand the relationship between software and hardware, an understanding Mehdi Ali did not possess. "Our objective right from the beginning was to get as many Amigas and C64s in the early days into homes as possible," says David Pleasance. "The moment you get lots of volume going into homes you've got the software companies wanting to write for it because they've got a bigger audience. And then from there, we can develop the software and get more and more serious software. Mehdi would never even have a conversation with any of the people who wrote serious software—serious word processing or accounting packages or anything. He would not even entertain a conversation with them."

In June 1989, Gail Wellington and her CATS group were assigned to Copperman. One of his first tasks was to overhaul the program to encourage software development from major players such as Microsoft. "In terms of Commodore management, Copperman was really the first guy to go that way," says Eric Lavitsky.

Copperman also planned to improve Commodore's North American advertising and try to get Commodore's high end products into government and school markets. The latter seemed unlikely, considering Commodore's track record as a mass-market company.

Employees favorably regarded the relatively young Copperman. "I liked him a lot," says Dave Haynie. "I liked that he was actually planning to organize different sales divisions in the United States."

As president and chief operating officer of Commodore North America, Copperman was given a salary and bonus of at least $500,000; more if he was successful. He was also guaranteed employment until May 1, 1991. If he failed to improve Commodore's US operations by then, Gould would find someone else for the job.

Early Indicators

With Mehdi Ali now in charge of running day to day activities of Commodore International, the employees had their first taste of his leadership. And it wasn't that bad—at first. At the time, he was mainly known as the guy who saved Commodore from financial ruin back in 1986. "He was an investment banker. So great, you know all about big company financing," observes Jeff Porter. "And when you're in the consumer electronics business, that's a big deal."

Porter's biggest worry was that Ali was inexperienced with how an electronics company operated. Ali knew how to finance the operation throughout the year, but he knew less about marketing and sales, including the yearly purchasing schedule, than even Irving Gould. "You float your trial balloons at the January CES, you take your hard orders at the June CES, and you place a whole shitload of money on the table for the Christmas order to have the factories build things in July, August, and September so they show up in the store shelves in October, November, and December for the Christmas quarter," explains Porter. "It's a big risk, big money game. And when you're in that business, you've got to have the right chops to finance that game."

One of Ali's first acts in April 1989 was to close Commodore's Taiwan factory in order to streamline Commodore's operations and reduce costs. The move was not opposed, probably because the Taiwan factory operations were somewhat redundant due to the Hong Kong factory. And with

Commodore late on so many products, the factory was not operating at capacity. In May, Commodore engineers spent almost two months moving production of several products to Hong Kong, including the Amiga 2000, PC30/40, PC10/20, A2058 memory expansion card, A2088XT bridgeboard, A2286AT bridgeboard, and A2090A hard drive controller board.

Already Ali had a reputation for threatening to fire people, but he could also be civil. "He was a very, very strange animal in that regard," says David Pleasance. "He can be really quite charming. I was invited to his home, and I went to dinner with his family and then stayed at his house overnight one time. But it doesn't detract from the fact that he was never really interested in the business as a business."

Six months into Mehdi Ali's leadership, the employees began to notice he was slowly taking over control of the company like someone conquering the board in Risk. He did this by installing a loyal manager between himself and each department, one he could issue orders to, such as Harold Copperman taking over the once independant CATS group. In September George Robbins observed, "Porter and Henri are still on top, but it may not last as Irving has his old buddy/axeman Mehdi Ali gradually taking over everything, though engineering is still independent."

Later in the year, Ali erred when he confused the A2620 accelerator card with the more advanced A2630 card. He inadvertently put A2630 production on hold before restarting it later. Porter noticed a reluctance to openly admit the mistake and correct it in a timely fashion, perhaps fearing it would show weakness. He soon began to wonder if Ali's takeover would extend to the engineering department.

Modems as far as the eye can see

On June 28, 1989, Commodore's stock suddenly dropped 21% on news that the company might not be profitable for the latest quarter. Gould blamed the drop in profits on the strengthening of the US dollar, which hurt Commodore more than other companies since most of its revenue came from Europe. That loss was $8.9 million for the quarter ending in June.[6]

There was also evidence the company was not firing on all cylinders under president Mehdi Ali, who barely had a presence at the company headquarters. "He wasn't around the West Chester office that much," says Dave Haynie. "He spent most of his time up at the New York office."

---

6   *Philadelphia Inquirer*, Sept. 7, 1989. "Commodore Signs An Agreement With Dealer
     That Has 326 Outlets"

As a result, important issues often slipped between the cracks. One example was the overstocked warehouse. "If you went in the back entrance and you walked through the warehouse area, it sort of reminded me of that scene from *Raiders of the Lost Ark*," recalls chip designer Ed Hepler. "Row after row of boxes and shipping crates. If you went through there at night it was dark and spooky."

Much like the movie, the massive warehouse held Commodore's dark secrets from the past. "There were tens of thousands of square feet; these cavernous warehouses full of calculators, literally from the days when Jack Tramiel was head of Commodore," recalls *Amiga World* editor Guy Wright. "There were old PETs in there and tape drives and old crap. It was stuff they couldn't sell but they had it on inventory."

In particular, a product line Jeff Porter had previously engineered had been piling up in the warehouse due to the rapidly falling prices and increasing speeds of generic modems. "We'd go down through the warehouse to go play volleyball, and you would see just row after row of 1200 baud modems at the point when 2400 baud modems were common," recalls Bryce Nesbitt. "Commodore had—pick a number, half a million or a million—1200 baud modems sitting in the warehouse in West Chester. There were a lot of them."

Nesbitt was a habitual problem solver and he saw a problem that needed to be solved. "Here I am, this little engineer, maybe nineteen at this point, and I'm not senior management," he explains. "I didn't become a director of engineering until much later, but I go over to marketing and I say, 'Could we do a bundle where we sell Amiga 500s with a free modem? Wouldn't that be a good idea? Would you buy the Amiga 500 with a free modem?' I thought it was a great bundle."

Unfortunately, the rules created by the SEC for publicly traded companies had led to an odd situation where it made more financial sense for Commodore to not sell the product. "That's when I learned that they didn't want to let those things out because of the book value," explains Nesbitt. "Marketing refused and told me directly that they didn't want to book the loss. It was insanely stupid. Those modems weren't getting any fresher. It had a value as a bundle, but there was basically no chance that you could sell a 1200 baud modem at that point because the 2400 baud modems were already out and they were cheap."

Tragically, sales of the modem bundles could have given a boost to US sales and helped Commodore turn the recent loss into a profit. At this point, Nesbitt began to wonder how profitable Commodore had actually been under Irving Gould's tenure. "The last few quarters of Commodore's rosy financial performance was in part cooked by mechanisms like this," he says.

Speed Bumps: Round 2

Commodore's newest batch of young employees proved to be the most rebellious of the bunch. Over the winter, the loathed speed bumps had been decimated by snow plows, and by spring there were barely any remnants. As soon as the weather allowed, facilities manager Joe Mecca had them re-installed.

After reconstructing them, two speed bumps literally stuck out like half-barrels from the pavement. At first, employees tried to go around the speed bumps by driving on the grass. Unfortunately, there was a swampy area next to the parking lot dubbed "Lake Mecca", and drivers inadvertently became stuck. Going over the speed bumps was almost as difficult, with cars bottoming out on them as metal scraped on rock. Some engineers claimed they had nightmares where they were in hell, forced to drive through the parking lot searching for a parking space for all eternity.

The new speed bumps were so problematic that even management realized they were too extreme. "He put the speed bumps in and screwed up," recalls Bryce Nesbitt. "They put the speed bumps in and there were some technical problems, so they had to take them back out again and then put them back in. And then they were way too high for everybody, so they had to send another crew out with the asphalt and chop them down and put them back in. It was just funny."

The speed bump saga dragged on for months as Commodore's facilities manager struggled to get them just right. Every time a new plan was formulated, Mecca sent out a memo updating the employees of his progress. "It was not cheap, costing Commodore tens of thousands of dollars," says Michael Sinz. "It should not have been a priority."

To make up for the fact that the speed bumps were smaller and less effective, Joe Mecca had them spaced closer together. "It was difficult getting in and out," says Sinz.

The engineers soon found a way to make the whole unpleasant ordeal of parking into a competitive sport. "We had a contest about how fast you could go between them. People were going 55 miles per hour in between them," says Sinz.

The speed bump saga became an ongoing source of friction. Some managers began to tire of the open defiance of their rules. One day, Augenbraun and some engineers were dropping off hardware when they noticed

Joe Mecca and a paving specialist standing beside the parking lot, surveying the situation. Augenbraun began speeding up between each speed bump, from 0 to 55 miles per hour, and then coming to a quick stop before overcoming each bump. The constant revving and screeching caught Mecca's attention, and he stared down the group with arms folded as they unloaded their hardware.

Undaunted, the group returned to the car and departed in the same manner. Mecca was not happy about people mocking his efforts. According to Augenbraun, the next day the speed bumps were four inches higher.

Although the activities of the rebellious engineers were done in fun, underneath the jokes was a genuine protest movement to remove the speed bumps for good. Recent hires such as Michael Sinz, Joe Augenbraun, and Keith Gabryelski were the main rabble rousers, with Bryce Nesbitt the de facto leader of the movement. Nesbitt, who owned a black 1985 Honda CRX-SI, was less concerned with wear and tear, even attempting to gain height off of the speed bumps. "He was always tangling with Commodore security because he would go flying over the speed bumps in the parking lot, and he'd always get citations from Commodore security," recalls Eric Cotton.

Aside from this small group of rebels, many of the engineers and even some in the executive suite agreed there were legitimate gripes with the facilities. Engineers wondered where's the air conditioning? Where's the promised on site showers? And why is all this money available for speed bumps but almost nothing for engineering supplies?

In late June, Nesbitt stuck his protest right in the face of upper management. "Bryce did a very funny memo that caused a problem inside Commodore," recalls Michael Sinz. "Facilities had sent out a memo about taking out speed bumps and putting in permanent ones. Bryce rewrote the memo, instead making it about speed bump practice."

To: All Employees
From: The Facilities Department
Subject: Speed bump rotation plan for early July
Starting on Monday, July 3rd, the facilities department will begin daily reconfiguration and expansion of the important speed bump network at the West Chester facility. Work will be arranged to maximize the disruption and discomfort to all employees. Each day the executive committee will meet to determine pleasing geometric shapes for the day's speed bumps.

The current record for changing the bump network is two hours. This time should drop to under 30 minutes for the planned national championships. Points are gained in the nationals for lowering employee morale, delaying critical engineering projects, and destruction to suspension complements. The Commodore team is expecting stiff competition from a group of former Pennsylvania Department of Transportation pothole diggers.

Committee chairman Robert Greg said that employees have been "laughing at our efforts to strictly enforce the new totalitarian parking lot regulations." and "It is impossible to overemphasize the importance of parking enforcement."[7]

Mr. Greg is on the record with the statement, "If I had my way, there would be ten more speed bumps in the parking lot. Employees attempting to evade the bumps by parking out front will have their tires slashed. A newly designed stealth paint will be used to conceal the location of bumps to prevent naughty employees from slowing down. In August, existing white lines in the front lot will be further widened to reduce available employee parking space and starting in September the death penalty will be used to deter violation of the 15 MPH speed limit.

Nesbitt distributed the memo around Commodore on bulletin boards in the halls and the cafeteria. Small crowds gathered around the memo, causing uproarious laughter. By a strange coincidence, a contractor actually removed and reinstalled a speed bump the next day, causing more ribbing from the engineers and embarrassing Mecca even further. But many in engineering weren't so sure mocking Mecca publicly would produce results.

Soon, a directive came down from Commodore management. "The net result of that memo was a new policy prohibiting the placement of unofficial memos in the building," laughs Nesbitt.

In response, the engineers bought their own bulletin board and placed it next to the official bulletin board. "After this memo came out we weren't allowed to put memos there so I crafted a very official-looking sign. I framed it and made it look just perfect. It said 'Unofficial Notice Board'".

The board was initially used to take pot shots at the facilities manager, although later it turned into something more practical for the engineers. "So the very next day I authored another memo riffing off on that particular theme and posted it all over the building. I don't think it achieved the same legendary status," says Nesbitt. "We would print stuff out or highlight Commodore's stock price or newspaper clippings. Entirely banal, normal stuff."

---

7   The latter was a real quote from the manager.

Inspired by Nesbitt's memo, his coworker Michael Sinz began publishing a semi-weekly newsletter called CBMnews devoted to the speed bump controversy. The newsletter was equal parts satire and real news, written in an urgent tone. For example, "We, at CBMnews, have also learned that there are some high officials that support many of the demands of the engineers. In unconfirmed reports, the president of CBM-USA was heard to say that he was going to do something about the speed bumps."

As the newsletters progressed, the main theme became the eternal struggle between the "Dump-The-Bumps" movement and the "Save the Bumps Foundation", often resulting in teargas-filled protests in "Wilson Square" (a Wilson Drive allusion to the Tiananmen Square protests of 1989). Although the saga was great fun for the young engineers, some managers and employees in the engineering department worried it was spiraling out of control.

Hedley Davis weighed in that, "You are just rubbing salt in the wounds. Our wound because we are stuck with the damn bumps, and their wounds because you both insulted and slandered them." Others like Jeff Porter, Dave Haynie, and Greg Berlin agreed, with the latter weighing in that Lake Mecca would soon have a power-generating dam to power the building.

Even free spirits like George Robbins felt the continued harassment would be unproductive, saying, "Having them removed because we pissed and moaned was doomed from day one. The only real changes have been made when Henri told them to change them or when executive/management types complained to Mecca. The parking thing is probably embarrassing to Mecca, but the various memos have done nothing except piss him off, harden his position, and really brown him off when he had already scheduled height reductions the next day."

The young rebels agreed to drop the outright harassment, although they did continue to have fun with the speed bumps. At the Halloween party that year, Nesbitt dressed up in honor of his favorite bane. "He came to that party dressed as a speed bump," says Eric Cotton.

Deciding Commodore management might respond to outside pressure, Joe Augenbraun leaked a rumor on Q-Link stating that the cause of loose chips in the Amiga 500 was due to shipping trucks bouncing over the giant speed bumps in the Commodore parking lot. "That was a rumor that was intentionally spread, I'm sure," says Dave Haynie. The rumor was completely unfounded. However, much to the delight of Commodore engineers, the press picked it up and it made its way into the pages of *Amiga World* and *.Info* magazine. Augenbraun, the engineer who started the chain of events with his reckless speeding, had the last laugh on everyone.

By the end of the first six months of Mehdi Ali's leadership as President, the engineers suspected a takeover had begun; one that would continue until he held the whole company in his grip. And worse still, the engineers believed Ali knew little about computers or the consumer industry. All of this was unlikely to have a positive effect on the company.

CHAPTER 14

The Other Chipsets 1989

While Hedley Davis and his team worked on the Amiga 3000 with the ECS chipset, parallel work continued on Commodore's other chipset, AAA. Commodore was also relying on Intel for its chips for the PC clone computers. Although the PC clones remained profitable, the long term viability of them came into question in 1989. And before the year was over, Commodore's engineers would embark on a third Amiga chipset—different from ECS and AAA.

AAA Specs

Before the engineers could begin work on the AAA chipset, the team had to clearly define the specification. Not only did the chips have to match VGA standards, they had to have the ability to exceed them. It was hoped the chipset could be used in projects for 4-5 years after it was eventually released in 1990. Therefore, the specs had to be ambitious.

The original Amiga team continued consulting as the specs developed. "Dale [Luck] was consulting on the software," says Dave Haynie. "Jay [Miner] and a couple of other guys were doing chip consulting."

Commodore's James Redfield designed the spec document, with help from a recent hire named Bob Schmid who performed technical studies on the project. By February 1989, Redfield had his spec completed for the four different chips that would comprise the AAA chipset.

The first was a new I/O chip. Glenn Keller, the original designer of Paula, which had 4 voices and 8-bit audio, would design a new I/O chip. Although he was interested in the project, his main motivation was something else. "I worked for Commodore for a number of years, primarily because I met my wife out there at one point, and I wanted to see her," he laughs.

The new I/O chip, called Mary, was a continuation of the "FAT Paula" discussions from 1987. The sound portion of the chip would now support 8 voices and clearer audio fidelity. "I redesigned all of what was Paula," says Keller. "Of course, it had to have 16-bit audio." The chip also included a new floppy disk controller and serial port controller.

The second chip would be a new version of Agnus, called Andrea. This was perhaps the most complex chip in the new chipset. It would have to allow blitter operations with a much larger data size than before to allow for blitting higher resolution graphics.

To keep up with VGA specs, the engineers proposed a successor to Denise. This time, two chips would be designed to handle the graphics: Monica and Linda. Monica would focus on displaying the output to the monitor, while Linda fetched graphics data from memory. Monica was similar to its predecessor, Denise, containing the color lookup table, sprite display, and Hold-And-Modify (HAM) mode.

In 1988, Linda was initially specced for 640 x 480, 800 x 600, and a whopping 1024 x 800 resolution (later reduced to 1024 by 768). These resolutions would keep up with the new SVGA standard.

So far the plan sounded good. Like the original Amiga chipset, AAA was ostensibly designed to scale so it could be built into a variety of devices ranging from video game consoles, arcade machines, low-end computers, and high-end workstations. However, OCS used only one type of RAM: DRAM. This new chipset would need to work with Video RAM, plus less-expensive 32/64 bit DRAM.

The schedule for the AAA chipset was aggressive, to say the least. James Redfield wanted prototypes of Linda ready on July 1, 1989, followed by Monica and Mary prototypes a month later. The most complicated chip, Andrea, would have prototypes ready January 1, 1990. Full production of the entire chipset would be ready for September 1, 1990—at which point the chips would go into a new high-end Amiga computer.

Compared to a company like Apple, which had the advantage of many more engineers, yet did far fewer of its own chip designs, the four chips were a big commitment for Commodore at the time. "We had between 25 and 30 engineers at the West Chester facility, and at least that many at the wafer fab in Norristown," says Bill Gardi.

With the competition closing the technological lead of the Amiga, it was a make or break project for Commodore. Success meant Amiga would take another breathtaking leap forward, capturing the imagination and attention of game and software developers. Failure meant allowing the competition to catch up with the Amiga, or perhaps even leave it behind.

AAA Progress

James Redfield would now lead the development of the four AAA chips. If all went according to his schedule, the team would have working silicon by early 1990. Initially there were six other chip designers working on the chipset: Bob Schmid, Jeff Dean, Paul Anderson, Terry Hudson, Glenn Keller, and Victor Andrade.

In the past, Commodore had required two engineers per chip; one designing and one simulating and testing the designs. With only seven engineers total, another key chip designer was soon added to the team in early 1989 for the most complicated chip of them all. And as it happened, he was perhaps the most knowledgeable engineer among them.

Dr. Ed Hepler was, at the time, an instructor in chip design. "He taught at Villanova [University] back then," says Dave Haynie. "He doesn't like to fly, so he was pretty happy to be with a local company." Hepler taught two graduate courses at the university: Advanced Computer Architecture and Introduction to VLSI Design. However, he longed to put his skills to work in actual silicon and began contacting Commodore.

On August 23, 1988 he emailed Jeff Porter, indicating he was looking for work in the industry. Unfortunately he ran into the same issues Paul Lassa encountered when trying to join Commodore, and his email received no response. He attempted to follow up with a phone call but could not reach Porter. On October 23, he followed up with another email. Jeff Porter, overworked as he was and doing double duty as Commodore's HR department, finally gave him a reply.

On November 11, Hepler showed up for a marathon interview with four different employees: Jim Redfield, Bob Schmid, Ted Lenthe, and Hedley Davis. He was curious what project Commodore would put him to work on. "I think they just needed help in general," he says.

Although Hepler was more interested in RISC chip design at the time, the task of making Amiga's next generation of chips also appealed to him. "There were four chips and there were challenges in all of them," he says.

Redfield and Lenthe were especially impressed by Hepler and decided he was the man to design the most complex chip. "There was a guy there named Jim Redfield who was the lead of the AAA project at the time, and he gave me the responsibility to do the architecture and figure out how to build the Andrea chip," says Hepler. "Andrea was the address generator but with quite a few other features to it. So it was sort of the controller for AAA."

Redfield wanted working silicon ready in 12 to 18 months from the time he hired Hepler, which would put the finish date somewhere in the first half of 1990. The original Amiga chips were 5 micron NMOS, while the new Amiga chips would be 1.25 micron CMOS. With Commodore already having problems producing working 2 micron CMOS chips for the C65 computer, it would be a daunting task with such a small team.

The chips would have to remain backward compatible with the previous Amiga chipset in order to continue supporting the existing library of Amiga titles. The most important person on the team for this aspect was Glenn Keller, due to his experience on the Original Chip Set. "I worked on three chips," says Keller. "I redid some of the blitter stuff, I redid some of the video stuff."

Despite the earlier rivalry between the Amiga group and West Chester, and despite working as a contractor, Keller never felt like an outsider. "The people that I worked with in West Chester were incredibly nice," he says. "They treated me really well, not as an outsider, but really friendly, and inviting me to volleyball games, to do stuff and to be connected to their group. It was a really amazing group of people. I didn't quite get that until sometime later, looking back on it."

As the engineers would discover in the months ahead, the ambitious schedule was not rooted in reality.

Meeting with Mehdi

After Mehdi Ali became President of Commodore International, he had begun taking over other departments within the company but had left engineering alone. In August of 1989 he began to engage with engineering. He asked Jeff Porter and Henri Rubin to present an overview of the engineering department history, showing the total expense by year, number of engineers, and sales from 1984 to 1990.

Porter seized the opportunity to push for a larger budget and more engineers for his department. Commodore typically spent 2% of its sales on Research & Development. In 1989, the engineering department had 101 employees and a total budget of $17.5 million. Estimating $1 billion in sales for 1990, Porter proposed a 3% spend on R&D with a $25.3 million budget and 141 employees. It was a massive increase from the previous year but still well below the $46.5 million budget of 253 engineers under Marshall Smith in 1985.

As Porter would soon find out, Mehdi Ali was a very reasonable president when it came to allocating resources within the company. Ali authorized the budget increase and then some, ultimately exceeding Porter's request by the end of 1990.

Linda, Monica, and Mary were supposed to be done in the summer of 1989, but by September they were not even close. It became clear the AAA chipset was not running on schedule. "It was just very complex," explains Ed Hepler. "Complex chips like that take two or three years to develop and compared to other companies, we had a very limited staff working on things."

Engineer Bob Raible soon noted the project was "slipping at a nice predictable rate of one week per week." AAA was to join the ECS, Amiga 3000 and C65 as yet another project where the deadline was constantly slipping. Something was happening in Commodore. Either all of the management, previously capable, decided all at once to allow their projects to fall hopelessly behind, or there was a root cause.

Most engineers felt they knew the root and the solution. Commodore needed an HR department, and it needed to hire more engineers for the vital project. "The AAA chipset had four chips, and there was really only one person working on each one as far as the main architect," explains Hepler. "I don't have a problem with that, but we could have used some extra support helping to simulate and so forth."

Although Victor Andrade was supposed to have been working on AAA all year, he had instead been working on the 4510 chipset until the middle of October 1989, at which time he began on AAA. By then it was clear they could not meet the early 1990 schedule for working silicon.

With only two engineers per chip (and not dedicated ones at that) it would be impossible to meet the schedule. "There is usually one designer, one circuit designer, and one layout person per chip and that's sort of how things went," says Hepler. "If you look at the way companies build chips these days, there are far more people working on a chip than back then."

Commodore could have made a comparatively minor R&D investment by hiring three new chip engineers, which would cost the company in the neighborhood of $200,000 per year to deliver the chips on time. For some reason, that never happened.

Worse yet, Commodore's secret weapon, CSG (previously known as MOS Technology), was slowly falling behind the times. In July 1989, Ted Lenthe proposed to Henri Rubin an investment in CSG which would allow production of 1 micron chips for AAA, rather than the 2 micron CSG was currently capable of producing. He also wanted to move from 5" to 6" silicon wafers, which produced a superior economy of scale. The investment in CSG would cost an estimated $15 million. Rubin tabled the proposal for now but agreed to review it later when they were closer to actually producing AAA chips.

"That was one of the fascinating things about that period of time," says Bob Welland. "One of the disappointments that one could have about Commodore is that they had such a good core of engineers who understood how to make chips and instead of using that brain trust in interesting ways, ultimately it didn't evolve in as good a way as it could have."

Mehdi Ali also asked Jeff Porter and Henri Rubin to present him with proposals for future products. In September, Porter came to Ali with half a dozen new proposals, most of which Ali would reject. These included another attempt at a low-cost Amiga game console, a high end Amiga Entertainment System, a new low-end Amiga chipset, new PC clones, and a laptop computer.

Porter's Amiga game machine, dubbed the A150, was a resurrection of the cancelled A250 from earlier in the year. He was now able to lower the parts cost for his ultra-cheap Amiga down to $115.55, meaning it would retail for around $300.

Porter's upscale Amiga Entertainment System proposal would look much like a VCR in appearance. The system was cartridge based and would lack even a floppy disk drive. Ali balked at the proposal when he saw the $20-$30 million investment required for marketing and software development of the new system.

Although he cancelled the Amiga game machines outright, Ali would accept (in one form or another) Porter's other proposals: a new Amiga chipset, new PC clones, and a laptop.

Pandora

By late 1989, the 32-bit AAA project was getting bogged down. According to Dave Haynie, several factors allowed the project to slip. "The first reason was that the chip group didn't get enough resources so they couldn't advance the chip technology fast enough," he says. "It really was a matter of not reinvesting enough money in the technology. We had plenty of hard work, which is why we kept up as well as we did."

The second reason was that Commodore was taking on too many projects. James Redfield complained that his staff, especially Victor Andrade, was spending too much time cleaning up problems in the 4510 and ECS

Agnus chips. Andrea development was essentially suspended until those other two chipsets were in production.

While they waited for AAA, the engineers realized it would be an especially long time before the low-end Amigas would get a new chipset. On September 13, 1989, George Robbins wrote a memo proposing a new chipset somewhere between ECS and AAA capabilities.

Ted Lenthe, already overwhelmed with the number of chips in production, was hardly pleased to see one more chipset added to the mix. He wondered if Robbins was opening a Pandora's box by forcing Commodore to work on two Amiga chipsets simultaneously, and thus the name stuck. "It was originally called Pandora," says Dave Haynie. In Greek mythology, Pandora was the first human woman created by the gods.

Robbins ended his memo with a section tellingly titled, "Lessons Learned from ECS Fiasco".

> Make sure of what you want up front, even if it takes a while.
> Make sure it's worth doing by the time it gets done.
> Make sure the project is adequately and continually staffed.
> Make sure management is aware of the benefits expected.
> Make sure there is a program for getting the chips into systems ASAP!!!
> Make sure to minimize software impact/dependencies.

The primary goal of Pandora was to create a video display that was on par with current VGA boards. Robbins was clear that development of the Pandora chipset should not significantly impact the AAA development schedule. He also wanted to avoid software incompatibility in the chipset, and thus he wanted the AmigaOS developers involved in creating the chip specification.

The Amiga engineers were clearly taken aback by the impressive specs of Bill Gardei's C65 chipset. One of Pandora's stated goals was to maintain a clear distinction between the C64/C65 family and Amiga. "I remember getting some flack for the fact that it had more colors on-screen than the A3000 did," recalls Haynie. In other words, it was imperative that the high-end Amiga stay ahead of Commodore's ultra-low-end line of computers.

A minor revision of Agnus would appear in the Pandora chipset to extend the amount of memory it could address. The engineers pulled in Bob Raible, an engineer from the LSI group, to define a chipset spec for an improved version of the display chip that would be a little sister to AAA's Linda, called Lisa.

They planned to include the new graphics chip in an upcoming Amiga computer that would be a generational step above the A2000. It would also include 640 x 480 pixels non-interlaced video, but instead of only 32 colors it could display up to 256 colors. There was also an 800 x 600 interlaced mode. The video chip could also smoothly scroll high resolution images. And then there was Hedley Davis' HAM8 mode, which would be capable of displaying up to 256,000 colors on-screen at once from an available palette of 16.8 million colors with static images up to 1280 x 512 pixels interlaced.

On October 6, George Robbins orchestrated a meeting with Jeff Porter, Hedley Davis, Bryce Nesbitt, himself, and four members of the LSI group: Bob Raible, Ted Lenthe, Jim Redfield, and Dave Anderson. The purpose of the meeting was to obtain management approval for the Lisa display chip and outline the goals, timetable, and required resources.

The team expected the changes in the Agnus design to be completed by October 30, with silicon expected weeks afterwards. The changes in Lisa would take significantly longer, but they hoped those would be ready by early 1990.

Luck commends Dave Haynie and the engineers for spearheading the work on defining the chips. "He was working on the advanced graphics chips. He had to try to come out with a second generation and third generation set of Amiga chips and be backwards compatible, which was a very tough thing to do."

PC Clones

The PC clone division, begun in 1986 under Gerard Bucas, had become one of the cornerstones of Commodore's profits. That trend continued, and now the division, headed by engineer Jeff Frank with some of the German engineers, would remain profitable until at least the end of 1989. "My understanding is that, left over from the PET days, there was a good set of relationships in Europe," explains Joe Augenbraun. "There were corporate accounts that bought Commodore PCs because it was Commodore. It was a fine business. I don't know what the market was worth but there was reasonable volume there."

"They sold PCs for quite a few years, probably four or five years," says Gerard Bucas. "And they were literally one of the leading resellers of PCs in Europe."

While the Amiga division struggled to turn out each new computer, the PC division had no problem churning out one model after another under Jeff Frank. Never mind the fact that each new Amiga required a custom chipset, operating system, and complete redesign while companies like Microsoft and Intel provided much of what went into the PC clones. As a result, Frank's division looked highly competent to Irving Gould and his board of directors.

During 1989, Frank and his team worked on the two latest models in the PC line that contained the Intel 80386 chip, which debuted back in 1985. Frank himself was product manager on the PC-60 tower computer, while the PC-50, a desktop, was in the works.

However, in 1989 things began to change. "That was a time when there was Compaq and then everyone else," says Joe Augenbraun. "Compaq came out with a 386 machine first because they were working directly with Intel. No one else had a 386 machine, not even IBM. And everyone else was scrambling to come out with a 386 machine."

In 1989 Commodore was finally about to match what Compaq had released years earlier. "By the time they came out with a 386 machine, Compaq came out with a 486 machine," says Augenbraun. "So everyone was sort of a generation behind, other than Compaq, including IBM. So Commodore was in with the unwashed masses of being a generation behind, and Commodore was even slightly worse."

Intel had announced the 80486 at the Spring COMDEX in April 1989, with samples of the new chip expected for the third quarter of 1989 and production quantities in the fourth quarter of 1989. And as usual, Compaq was the first to announce a system using the new chip. "Until it got to the 486, Commodore was trying to build the previous generation machine. They were really behind," says Augenbraun.

By September 1989, Frank had the first samples of his 80386-based PC-60 to hand out to other countries. Unfortunately, Mehdi Ali was tired of waiting on the less expensive 386SX PC-50 and decided to go another route in the name of efficiency. "Eventually it was OEMed really from some outside company, mainly because it was difficult to make money in the PC business," says Gerard Bucas. "The last couple of PCs that Commodore really sold were actually OEMed from some company in Taiwan, so there was a mixture. They developed some themselves, they OEMed others."

In September 1989, Ali decided to buy an 80386-based desktop from the Taiwanese company MiTAC. Under the OEM deal, Commodore would supply the case while MiTAC supplied the motherboard. While Ali's OEM strategy would lower Commodore's exposure to risk, in the long term it would be difficult to stand out from other PC companies.

Commodore Laptops

Portable computers remained a niche product throughout the 1980s. Most versions lacked the larger screen sizes that were typical of desktop computers. But perhaps the biggest drawback was a lack of depth in the software library available for portables, since most were not compatible with other operating systems. Those that claimed MS-DOS compatibility often had problems displaying standard software.

Then in 1989 Compaq released the LTE laptop, which became the first commercial success with the laptop form factor. The portable computer worked with most MS-DOS applications and featured a large screen. It sold for $2399 for the basic model with floppy drive only or $2999 for the LTE Model 20 with a 20 MB hard drive.

With laptops becoming all the rage in 1989, Jeff Porter decided to propose his own design to Mehdi Ali. Unlike the powerful Compaq LTE, Porter's laptop would use a CMOS 4510 chip as the CPU with 256 KB of RAM. It would also come with 2 MB of ROM to store the included apps. The LCD display was a respectable 480 x 200 pixels. The power supply was a rechargeable NiCd battery pack and communications came from a built in US Robotics modem.

This design was clearly an evolution of his LCD Portable from 1985.[1] The parts cost came to only $166.69, meaning it would retail for under $500. Porter was clearly aiming for the low-cost laptop market, rather than trying to compete head-on with Compaq and other laptop makers.

Part of Porter's motivation to revisit the LCD laptop concept was due to Eagle-Picher, the LCD manufacturer that still resided inside Commodore's West Chester facility even in 1989. Although no longer owned by Commodore (it rented the space to Eagle-Picher), Porter could keep tabs on the advancements made to LCD displays. Unfortunately the LCD maker was running into trouble.

A few years after its acquisition of Commodore Optoelectronics, Eagle-Picher's investment in industrial insulation products came back to haunt them. "Just about the time we were ready to [produce LCD screens], Eagle-Picher filed for bankruptcy," recalls LCD engineer David Baraff. "What happened with Eagle-Picher is they were a conglomerate. They owned a number of businesses, and one of the businesses that they had bought had been in the asbestos manufacturing industry."

---

1   For the LCD Portable story, see *Commodore: The Amiga Years*, ISBN 978-0-9940310-2-0

In the 1980s a series of asbestos lawsuits took its toll on American business-es. "The big asbestos suits bankrupted a lot of companies. So Eagle-Picher all of a sudden doesn't have any money to continue the project and they shut us down. They ended up selling the facility they had built to a company that did computer hard drives. They needed the clean rooms."

It was a disappointing time for Baraff, who felt confident in the future of LCD and flat screen display technology. "The rest of the guys that were part of that, we tried to raise some money to buy the thing from Eagle-Picher, but we were not able to do that," he says. "By '89 I was pretty much out of the display business."

Commodore had a chance to reacquire the LCD manufacturing facility and enter the laptop market. Unfortunately, it was not the sort of aggressive deal Mehdi Ali was liable to attempt, given his lack of background in tech-nology.[2]

Furthermore, Ali was not interested in Porter's conception of a laptop computer because it would not run MS-DOS software. Porter's design also lacked a floppy disk drive or hard drive, making it difficult to transfer files from desktop computers.

However, Ali remained interested in MS-DOS compatible laptops and would soon use his OEM strategy to acquire laptops made by other manu-facturers.

Shareholder Meeting

At the 1989 COMDEX in Las Vegas, held November 13 through 17, Com-modore had few new products to show. It had the PC-50 and PC-60 clones, but Commodore's PC line was never well received in North America. The company revealed the improved Amiga 2500/30 machine, which included the A2630 accelerator card with a Motorola 68030 chip running at 25 MHz. With no new Amigas to excite consumers, Gould instead announced a 10 to 15% price cut on the A2000 computer line. This meant an Amiga 2000 now cost $1899 while the Amiga 2500/20 cost $3999. (No price had been set for the A2500/30 at COMDEX.)

The company also had a second unprofitable quarter in a row, losing $6.5 million for the period ending September 30. With the upcoming annual shareholder meeting in November, it would be a chance for shareholders to voice their concerns about the company.

---

2   Jack Tramiel and Atari agreed to purchase the facility in 1990 for $5.2 million to make LCDs for the Atari Lynx. He later bailed on the deal.

Dale Luck had given the board of directors a piece of his mind the previous year. In the interim, he did not make himself more popular with Commodore's management.

Earlier in the year, he had inadvertently said too much during an interview with *Info* magazine. "There was a time when some of my thoughts made it out into print in some magazines and that generated some controversy," he recalls.

In the interview, Luck stated, "Commodore's a funny company. It's like they're pretending to be a computer company. When I compare them to any of the major computer manufacturers, there are big differences. The other companies have product lines and product families. They have goals, use long range planning, and have a greater corporate understanding of their goals. They have good management that understands what they're trying to do. Commodore always seems to be trying to catch up."[3]

Luck came to regret the comments and sent an apology to Jeff Porter, explaining that he had meant to talk about his own company's product, the X Window System. He also blamed Info for making his comments seem more damning through editorializing.

The article made Luck a target to some and a hero to others. "Some executives were quite angry with me at Commodore but there were a lot of shareholders who were sending me their proxies to vote their shares," he says.

Luck, a firm believer that Commodore should enter the Unix workstation market, penned a list of grievances to present to the board. "We wanted them to be smarter. They were not doing proper advertising at that time. We didn't feel they were investing in the right technologies. We thought they were spending money very unwisely. And we thought that the Amiga had great potential but the Commodore executives weren't going to allow it to succeed."

The board, including Irving Gould, had felt attacked at the previous shareholder meeting. Some critics and shareholders on Usenet had even given him the moniker Irving Ghoul. This year he decided to move the shareholder meeting from New York all the way to the Bahamas, where it would be much more difficult for shareholders to confront him.

The new venue did not dissuade Luck, who felt an obligation to attend. "They wanted me to go to the stockholders meeting in the Bahamas to see if we could try to change the direction that Commodore was going."

---

3   *Info* magazine, Jul/Aug 1989, p. 22. "Keeping the Faith"

Luck took his responsibility to heart and attempted to follow through with the shareholders' wishes. "I flew to the Bahamas and was there for two days. I paid for a ticket for myself, paid for a hotel room. That was probably around 1989."

Andy Finkel felt sympathy for the Amiga developer. "I would have definitely been on Dale's side and would have loved to be there to see him present it," he says.

When Luck arrived, he found himself locked out of the exclusive Lyford Cay Club on the basis that it was for members only. "They already thought I was a troublemaker so they weren't going to let me in," he says. It seemed he had taken the trip for nothing.

It was soon clear why the board members wanted to keep the meeting away from shareholders. Just prior to the meeting, large raises were given to executives. Gould gave himself a raise from $500,000 in 1988 to $1,250,000 in 1989. This was a lot, considering IBM's more successful chairman received $730,000 in 1989.[4] On top of his current compensation, Mehdi Ali would be given the option to purchase 300,000 shares for one cent each.[5]

Overall, Commodore's top dozen executives were paid $2.8 million for the period ending June 1988, but for the same period recently ended June 30, 1989 they were paid $6 million—a 115% raise in just one year! Considering the Amiga's shaky position in the industry, it was a strange time to give raises to top executives. Things had notably changed since Mehdi Ali had taken a presence on the board.

The board hoped to approve these financial maneuvers without having to worry about being outvoted by Dale Luck and his proxy votes. However, one shareholder—a Philadelphia lawyer named Richard Ash—was able to attend. He stood and suggested the meeting should be adjourned and moved back to New York City, where more shareholders could attend. That motion was immediately denied.

Henri Rubin, who had been nominated earlier in the year, was officially voted in as a member of the board, bringing it to seven board members, including Mehdi Ali, Alexander Haig, Ralph Seligman, Burton Winberg, J. Edward Goff, and Irving Gould.

---

4   *Philadelphia Inquirer*, November 2, 1990. "Pay Went Up As Profits Plunged Proxy Reveals Big Salaries At Commodore"

5   *Philadelphia Inquirer*, November 22, 1989. "At Posh Retreat, Commodore Approves 3 Million New Shares"

The board had no problem voting raises to themselves, and approving three million new shares which they would divide mostly among themselves. They termed the shares part of an employee stock sharing plan. On the plus side, with the board members and executives holding so much stock, they would have little incentive to run the company into the ground.

Although Luck found himself locked out, Gould offered an olive branch. "I did have a meeting with Irving Gould when I was there. He thought it might be a good idea to talk to me so I could express my concerns about what was going on," he says. "I think Irving Gould was a sharp guy. He was getting kind of old, but he had his heart in the right place."

Luck places Commodore's failings on its inability to find the right management. "I think that he had trouble hiring good quality talent to take charge of the company, as is evidenced by the revolving door with Marshal Smith, [Thomas] Rattigan, Mehdi Ali."

Dale Luck had been outmaneuvered again. After his heartfelt talk with Gould, he decided his best chance at influencing the Amiga was to move closer to the company for an extended period. "I went back on a nine month contract to Pennsylvania," he says.

Although 1989 was something of a turnaround year, the decisions made that year regarding the Amiga chipset would have long-term implications for Commodore's continued survival. The decision to limit the staff on the AAA chipset was chief among those concerns. The project really needed four more dedicated engineers (one extra per chip), and the other eight engineers should have been allocated strictly to AAA, rather than helping with other chip projects.

Meanwhile, the decision to start Pandora would have a positive impact on the fortunes of the Amiga, especially at the low-end. But again, Pandora would cut into the development time for AAA. All of these problems would impact the future of this important chipset.

CHAPTER 15

The Baby 1989

From the recent CES in January 1989, it was apparent to everyone who attended that compact discs were going to revolutionize data storage. The Amiga's 3.5 inch disks stored under a megabyte but a single CD-ROM could store over 600 megabytes. With games overflowing onto multiple disks, the CD promised to open up larger games while reducing physical media costs.

The same year, the term "multimedia" came into popular usage and many Commodore executives were surprised to learn that their company had been at the forefront of multimedia computing since 1985. As *Tech Insider* noted in 1989, "The leader in this niche, and a company that may enjoy renewed growth as multimedia computing catches on, is Commodore International Corp."[1]

Compact Disc

Commodore always paid close attention to new technology standards. For example, in late 1988, the head of LSI development Ted Lenthe was already researching HDTV, a technology that would not achieve wide acceptance until more than a decade later. Shortly after CES, in late January 1989, Scott Hood (the engineer responsible for Amber and the A2320 flicker fixer board) began looking at how to use consumer CD players on the Amiga. He was particularly interested in the jack at the back of Philips CD players. Unable to find a spec sheet to describe the digital information coming from the jack, he wrote to Philips directly.

---

1   *Tech Insider*, October 9, 1989. "Special Report"

Back in 1980, Philips and Sony had already developed the *Red Book*, a standard for storing digital audio to CDs. But ROM storage was still being sorted out and the *Yellow Book* defining the CD-ROM standard would not be finalized until 1988.

The person studying CD technology the most at Commodore was Don Gilbreath, who had attended the Microsoft CD-ROM Conference in March 1986, which introduced the CD-ROM standard. "I was tracking CD mechanisms early on," he recalls. "Essentially the Red Book was the first part of defining data CDs. I remember being in an elevator with Bill Gates in Seattle when they were trying to launch what was going to be CD-ROM." One early implementation of the Red Book definition was the High Sierra file format.

At the time, it was a challenge to merely acquire a CD player capable of reading data. "There was no CD equipment for computers at that time at all," he recalls. "It was CD audio basically, but we were starting to work with some of the companies that were making CD-ROM mechanisms, including Sanyo. And it looked like we were starting to see ways to do this."

Back in November 1987, George Robbins began pushing Gerard Bucas and Jeff Porter to acquire CD-ROM drive samples from Chinon, Commodore's favorite disk drive supplier. At the time, Porter was not a supporter of CD-ROM technology and skeptical it would turn into a real product anytime soon. This attitude worried Robbins, who felt that Commodore needed to stay on top of it or else they would be left scrambling to catch up later.

As a point of reference, Apple released a CD-ROM drive called the AppleCD in March 1988 that could read the High Sierra file format. The device was not only for Macintosh computers but also the Apple IIGS. To many, it looked like Commodore's distance from Silicon Valley was causing them to lag behind certain developments.

Once Bucas departed, the West Chester engineers under Jeff Porter did not aggressively pursue the technology, and Don Gilbreath became the primary force pushing CD-ROM within the company.

Don Gilbreath

Don Gilbreath spent most of his 20s working in the shadow of two powerful Commodore executives, Irving Gould and Clive Smith. "There was basically a strategic division headed by a guy named Clive Smith and I was one of his first embeds, if you will, into West Chester," says Gilbreath.

"Someone who reported to him. His role was pretty much trying to develop new sales channels, new products conceptually, and find ways to get them built."

Gilbreath worked for Clive Smith when he brought the Amiga opportunity to Commodore in 1984. "My business card said 'Product and Market Development,'" he says. "It was actually kind of one of these skunk divisions on one side. At that particular time they were just starting to think about digesting the Amiga into the business. They hired a bunch of specialists to get ready for the launch."

In 1984, Commodore executives did not look favorably on their own West Chester engineers (known as the "C128 Animals"), who had released the failed Plus/4 and were working on the C128. "For a while they were trying to separate West Chester engineering from Amiga," says Gilbreath. "There was this whole time of, 'The West Chester guys are incompetent. We just hired a good group of smart guys in California to build the Amiga.'"

Once the Amiga launched, Gilbreath's role was to look for opportunities to leverage the incredible Amiga chip technology. "I knew my way around the company pretty well in terms of some products I worked on and/or software gizmos and things," he begins. "It was really kind of an interesting role where we're getting ready for the Amiga on one side and then starting to build an OEM division for the company where we design our Commodore CPU boards into someone else's products. Vertical market stuff."

With Gilbreath's help, Amiga technology found its way into other products, such as arcade machines. Bally, which had a relationship with Commodore stretching back to the VIC-20 days, used the Amiga motherboards and chips in its arcade machines, such as *Moonquake (1986)*. "There were these funny places to try to place Amigas and other Commodore equipment," explains Gilbreath. "You might find early Amiga 1000 boards ending up in something like Bally's exercise equipment or a pinball machine or whatever."

In the late 1980s a company called American Laser Games was experimenting with Amiga hardware. It would release an arcade game called *Mad Dog McCree* in 1990. "I was the guy that was working to get the boards stable enough to be able to go in those kind of markets," explains Gilbreath. "I already had some credibility from designing computers from other people's products and modifying them enough to do the job."

Gilbreath was also familiar with earlier attempts with LaserDisc entertainment. A company called RDI Video Systems, which had created the immensely popular *Dragon's Lair* video game in 1983, had attempted to use laserdisc technology to create a home video game console called Halcyon. This device actually required a separate laserdisc player and never made it past pilot production before the company went out of business.

Good looking, intelligent, charismatic, and easy going, Gilbreath held a unique position within Commodore. "I built their OEM division at that point. They really gave me a lot of room to be both a technical sales guy and a product development guy."

A fellow smoker, Gilbreath struck up an unusual friendship with the elderly Irving Gould, despite their age gap. "My boss was basically two doors down from Irving, and Irving is always there every Monday and Tuesday," explains Gilbreath. "Because of that, I would go face-to-face with the guy I worked for."

"Irving would be bored and want to have lunch," recalls Gilbreath. "His diet during the week was always tuna fish sandwiches. You'd never see meat; it was always fish related. Other than his smoking, which is probably what took him out, he lived a good life."

Gilbreath became an acquaintance of Gould and learned of his background in the military. "Gould was a Toronto boy. He was a Royal Canadian Air Force pilot."

After leaving the RCAF, Gould worked for his father's shipping business. His father had been one of the earliest businessmen to recognize the importance of CONEX shipping containers. "His real fortune was his dad's container business," says Gilbreath. "Around World War II, if you look at cargo ships, they were still using a lot of netting to put stuff on boats. I think it was his father who had this kind of epiphany. Why don't we use boxes?"

Gilbreath soon found himself with a lot of influence and control over his career. "It kind of led into this funny role where you've got a guy [Gilbreath] who is pretty far down in the food chain, pecking order wise, that has access to hang out and have lunch with Gould! So it gave me facetime to not torch anybody but at least adjust things, and it gave me some room to do stuff."

Gilbreath's arrangement did not sit well with the other West Chester engineers. "Porter and I and the engineering team, we live in this world where we're designing products, and we don't necessarily know what's going on," says Hedley Davis. "But we have got schedules and we plan our programs and we try to meet our schedules. And then there's this other guy named Don Gilbreath. He's running this engineering organization on the side doing wild projects that engineering might have gotten asked to do and then when engineering said it would be too difficult to do or it would take this long to do, they would go ask somebody else. And you know, management being what it was, they run around and ask people until they hear the answer they want to hear and then they say, 'Let's go.' And Don would be quite happy to tell him, 'Yeah, I can do that.'"

Gilbreath also met his future wife at Commodore, Vicki Eubanks, a stunning marketing department manager. "His wife Vicki ran the Commodore booth for CES in 1985," says engineer Bil Herd.

By 1988, at the age of 32, following Clive Smith's departure, Gilbreath worked more and more out of West Chester. He soon became the project leader to develop a network protocol for the upcoming network adapter cards for the Amiga. Taking a cue from Apple's AppleTalk network cards, the engineers internally called the product AmigaTalk.

And then CD-ROM technology came along. "The CD would be a wonderful mass-storage device on an Amiga," says Gilbreath. "Hard drives were still kind of small and not very perky and, to do a lot of great graphics and video stuff, you needed a lot of storage."

Gilbreath was not a superstar engineer in the same league as Dave Haynie or George Robbins, but he knew enough to play with computer hardware. "Don wasn't so much an engineer as kind of a visionary guy," says Eric Cotton. "I mean certainly he was technical."

Although there were not yet any Amiga CD-ROM drives available in 1988, there were expensive PC CD-ROM drives. A few of these entered the offices at Commodore, either connected to Commodore's PC clones, or to the Amiga 2000 bridgeboard. Already at this time, when someone had a technical issue with their CD-ROM, they went to Gilbreath, who was able to quickly troubleshoot problems. Soon he was known in the halls of Commodore as Mr. CD-ROM.

Gilbreath began hacking together an Amiga 500 and his CD-ROM drive. At the time, multimedia PCs could read data from CD-ROMs and also get at the music tracks on the disc. This is described in the Yellow Book as mixed mode. It allowed early CD games to play recorded audio from the CD, as well as reading data from CD-ROM discs. Using this information, Gilbreath began by trying to play a music track through the Amiga's audio channel to the speakers.

He was also able to play and control a music CD through a user interface displayed on the Amiga screen. This was a novel way to play music CDs in 1989. It's important to note that music CDs were the most popular form of compact discs at the time. If users bought a product from Commodore, they would expect it to play their music CDs. But this was only the first step as Gilbreath continued hacking more features onto his CD prototype.

Gilbreath also began talking with Gail Wellington about CD-ROM and the impact it might have on Amiga sales. As the head of CATS, and the person most responsible for bringing software development to the Amiga platform, Wellington became very interested in the new device.

June Amiga DevCon

Commodore had been holding the Amiga Developers Conference every year since 1985, even before the official release of the Amiga 1000. (Apple would copy this format with the Apple Worldwide Developers Conference, first held in 1987.) This year, developers would pay between $200 to $375 to attend the sessions held at the Holiday Inn Golden Gateway in central San Francisco. The sessions, held Wednesday June 14 through the 17th, would mainly focus is on the upcoming AmigaOS 1.4.

Carl Sassenrath, the original programmer of Amiga's multitasking Exec, had since moved over to Apple where he had worked until 1988 as the lead developer of Project Aquarius. This was a planned next-generation object-oriented operating system for a new multi-core CPU being designed at Apple and simulated on a Cray Supercomputer. Since leaving Apple, he wrote a 100 page book called *Guru's Guide to the Commodore Amiga*. He also became an independent contractor and began working on Amiga development tools for the Epyx Handy project (later renamed Atari Lynx) with Dave Needle and RJ Mical. He was also independently developing a Logo programming language for the Amiga.

Sassenrath remained loyal to the Amiga and was particularly interested in the new OS Commodore would unveil. "I still paid attention to the Amiga and went to some of the developer's conferences even after I left," he recalls. "I went to the developer conference in San Francisco in 1989, and I really wanted to push them towards CDs because I thought CD-ROM was just a wonderful way of storing huge amounts of information. I actually stood at the conference and introduced myself, and people recognized me. I said we need the CD."

When Commodore's two CD-ROM supporters heard Sassenrath's exhortations, their ears perked up. "Gail Wellington and Don Gilbreath came up to me and said, 'Hey, we've got something we want to show you up in the hotel room.' So I went up and followed them and they showed me one of their very first mockups. It was like, 'Here we could make this but we really need someone like you to do the software side of it.'"

The mockup was very simple. "There wasn't much to it," describes Sassenrath. "That was not a working system. They didn't have a way to read the CD-ROM. They could play music off of it."

Before Sassenrath could begin programming for Commodore, he needed working hardware connected to a CD-ROM drive. For now, he returned to California and continued working on Logo and his other consulting projects.

In July, Commodore held a meeting of the European subsidiaries in London. All the major executives and marketing managers attended, including Irving Gould. Gilbreath often talked with Gould about the potential of CD-ROM. Now, after noting the hype at the previous CES, he felt strongly that it was time for Commodore to make a firm commitment to the new technology.

At the meeting, Wellington and Gilbreath discussed the current state of CD-ROM, multimedia, and Amiga's standing in both of those areas. Commodore could dip its toes in the new technology by releasing a simple CD-ROM drive for the Amiga 500 and 2000. Instead, the two proposed a whole new device for the living room. They had no defined concept for the device, other than mixing together an Amiga and a CD player. The presentation was met with praise and support.

Afterwards, Gould decided to move forward with this plan, but he wisely limited Gilbreath to exploring CD-ROM technology. He was not yet ready to bet the farm on an unproven product. "He was a go, and I was able to start assembling some other allies in the company to help," says Gilbreath. Although it was not yet an official project, Gilbreath now had license to develop a CD-ROM concept.

Uncle Irv in the Bahamas

With Carl Sassenrath already excited about CDs it was easy for Don Gilbreath to get him involved in the project. "So I signed onto that and the first part of the project was let's fly out and talk to Irving," recalls Sassenrath. The two flew to the Bahamas on the Pet Jet. "Don seemed to be really good friends with Irving Gould."

Since Clive Smith's departure in 1987, Gilbreath had become more familiar with Irving Gould than almost anyone at Commodore. "I was at Irving's house a couple of times," he recalls. "He had a very nice house in the Bahamas and he loved to fish."

Although business titans can have a reputation for aggressive moves and austentatious lifestyles, Gould was a quiet, gentle soul who lived a simple life when in the Bahamas. Despite his millions, Gould's home was relatively modest. "My recollection was it was a rancher style, not multi-story. Of the rooms I saw, I'd estimate it was probably in the 10,000 square foot size, not that over the top," says Gilbreath. "You could literally go off the road to get there, and it wasn't behind any gates. It doesn't look like today's hollywood rock star six million dollar home, but it was very comfortable."

The mansion allowed Gould to arrive by sea from small fishing trips or as far away as the eastern US seaboard. "The home was right on the canal around the water," recalls Gilbreath. "He had two boats there. His fishing guide actually lived on one boat. His captain lived on one of the boats, a Bahamian guy, and there was always a lot of traffic."

Although there were plenty of large mansions on the island, there were also ramshackle homes. "I remember in the evening sometimes strolling around from the house out to some of the local houses where they still did jerk chicken in the backyard that's feeding the locals," recalls Gilbreath. "There was a blend of poverty mixed in along the same street with guys like Gould. It was interesting."

Carl Sassenrath was unsure what kind of reception he would receive from Gould. After all, he had rejected Gould back in early 1986 when the CEO had personally asked him to redo the Amiga file system. Despite being told he could name his price, Sassenrath had rejected the offer—a decision he had later come to regret.

When Gilbreath and Sassenrath arrived, Gould and his wife had a feast ready for them. "His wife was there but they'd have cooks. Lunch for him was like thirty stone crabs," says Gilbreath.

Gould often caught his own fish which he handed off to his cooks. "He had this wonderful boat with a funny name, it was actually kind of a mess," recalls Gilbreath. "Later it was notorious with some other group. It had these twin diesels. In the old days, they could basically go to someplace like Bimini right from his dock and pull out some beautiful fish. He knew how to wear his wealth. He didn't flaunt it but he lived it well."

Gilbreath wanted to sell Gould on the idea of an appliance rather than a computer and a software ecosystem that would provide ongoing revenue. "My whole pitch to the chairman was really how to be part of some recurring business rather than just selling widgets," he says. Gilbreath wanted to licence software development out to developers and collect royalties for every piece of software sold.

But Gilbreath also wanted to see the device in every home in America. "The whole pitch was essentially building something that didn't look like a computer," he says. "It could blend into your stereo system pretty well. And it was kind of meant to bring it into your living room as opposed to keeping it in your office."

Gould had long been worried that, with all the competition among personal computers, the Amiga was being crowded out of the software market by the most successful computer of all, the IBM PC. A living room product could sidestep competition in the PC marketplace altogether. Plus, the Amiga's multimedia chipset was ideally suited for television sets.

Gould loved the idea. "He said, 'Yeah, this is a product that Commodore wants to make. This kind of returns us to being in the living room of the home and the consumer idea of computing and what Commodore had made their success on all those years earlier,'" recalls Carl Sassenrath. "He saw it as being the return to that."

Gilbreath had to assure Gould that he could get the project done without Commodore's West Chester engineers. "When I was first pitching this to Gould, I said, 'I have a good friend in the Tokyo office who also goes back to calculators.' Takashi Tokuda is his name. We go back to the 1979 timeframe. I said, 'I think I can do this with Tokuda in Japan. We can do it completely over there, isolated.' And so that gave him a warm and fuzzy that I had an office group that I could leverage."

Gould saw the new device as a continuation of the Amiga 500. "It wasn't a hard pitch because the Amiga sales at that time were a little bit soft," says Gilbreath. "The Amiga 500 was a cost reduction of the original Amiga 1000, and there weren't a lot of titles for it. It wasn't really big volume so to really try to leverage that huge investment the company made, it wasn't a big stretch to say, 'Yes, let's try it out.' It just wasn't a big stretch at all."

Contrary to Sassenrath's expectations, Gould did not seem upset by his previous rebuff. Instead, Gould seemed to respect him even more highly because he was not swayed entirely by money but was instead moved by the technology. "He was like, 'Any resource you need, you just tell me what you need and it will be done. We'll cut you a check for anything you need,'" recalls Sassenrath.

In order to escape direct competition with the PC market, Apple would later famously come back to life by focusing on new products, such as the iPod and iPhone. Commodore would attempt a similar move first.

Carl Sassenrath's return to Commodore was an unexpected turn, considering he had left in 1986 disillusioned by the company. Now he was on what seemed like a dream project with cutting edge CD-ROM technology that could potentially create a revolution in computer software. And he also knew he could command whatever pay he wanted on the project.

The two engineers returned to West Chester to set up Sassenrath for system development. "We went back to Commodore and spent a few days there while Don Gilbreath and a couple of other guys wire wrapped a board that I could plug into the side of an Amiga 500 and actually access the CD-ROM drive to issue commands," recalls Sassenrath. "I brought that back to California and started working on the drivers for running the CD-ROM."

Tiger Team

Don Gilbreath would not be able to fully engineer a product on his own. Rather, his talents lay somewhere between engineering and marketing. "Don is definitely the wheeler-dealer kind of person," says Carl Sassenrath. "He understands the technology, but he's also really good at talking to people. He's got a lot of charisma and the ability to coordinate with companies and get things done." In many ways he was Commodore's answer to Steve Jobs.

Gilbreath wanted a small team of engineers without much management overhead in order to progress quickly. "It was sort of a tiger team, where he and Gail Wellington put together a small group within Commodore dedicated to just do this concept," says Andy Finkel. "That's actually a Commodore tradition. If you want to get a project done fast you set up a small team and just do it. The Navy used to call them tiger teams. They were separate with their own structure."

By August 1989, Gail Wellington had left the CATS organization in the hands of Harold Copperman and now officially worked for the Special Projects group. She was fully committed to the new CD-ROM device, laying her career on the line if it should fail.

The main purpose of the tiger team at this early stage was to prove the CD-ROM technology could work with an Amiga 500 by building a simple prototype. Although this sounded like a modest goal, CD-ROM technology was in its infancy and difficult to work with, and no one knew for sure if the A500 could operate the CD-ROM drive and retrieve data at sufficient speeds.

Gilbreath began assembling his tiger team. To design the prototype circuitry, he turned to someone he knew. "I hired a hardware friend who was not a Commodore guy, literally from an employment consulting company," he recalls. "There's a guy named Steve Kreckman. He was my first line of defense to help with hardware because there were a lot of details. The quick story there is it was one of those employment consulting companies where you hire them for a week or two and then they go back."

To isolate the project from the rest of the company, Gilbreath and his team temporarily relocated to Japan. "The project really was a skunkworks," recalls Sassenrath. "Don talked alot to Irving and I talked to Irving, but Don was really the main instigator." Once in Japan, Gilbreath recruited Commodore engineer Takashi Tokuda to develop the case and styling.

With time, the project would gain more workers. For now, Gilbreath and Kreckman worked on the prototype PCB board while Wellington developed the marketing and software plan.

Gilbreath also evolved the concept for the machine. As a student of Clive Smith, he was familiar with his mentor's 1986 plans to bring the C64 into the living room with the C64D. Those plans called for a wireless infrared keyboard and joystick, and a computer that would be right at home on the stereo shelf. Some executives, such as Ed Parks, felt the machine should contain an Amiga rather than C64. Now that vision was finally coming to fruition under Gilbreath's hand.

The two engineers developed an adapter card to plug into the expansion port on the Amiga 500, which would allow it to operate a stock CD-ROM drive. For months, the tiger team worked on the product.

While in Japan, Gilbreath noticed how Irving Gould liked to personally use company resources. "I was down there when he had imported from Japan one of the little Toyota two door coupes that wasn't available in North America," he recalls. "All of Commodore Japan spent probably three months translating the manual. And he never drove it, the best I can tell. It sat in one of the garages [in the Bahamas]. There were a few cars there."

In November, Gail Wellington received a phone call from Gilbreath and Kreckman in Japan. Although it was still morning in America, it was the middle of the night in Tokyo. The voice on the other end was ecstatic. "Gail! We've just delivered a 17 pound baby! She worked the first time. There's still a few bugs, but we'll fix them in the morning."

As a result of the call, Wellington soon began referring to the product as "The Baby". With the biggest technological hurdle out of the way, the engineers knew development of the system software could commence. "We got this thing proved," says Gilbreath.

Steve Kreckman had come through, and now Gilbreath decided he would be an invaluable player working for Commodore. "I remember calling Irving one day and I said, 'I think this guy is worth keeping.' And they paid off his employer $50,000 to break his contract. They really were following my lead."

CD-ROM Showdown

By the spring of 1990, Don Gilbreath and his tiger team had a more re-fined prototype of the CD-ROM multimedia device known as "The Baby". Now it was time to come up with a full production schedule. Irving Gould had wanted to spark a competitive spirit into the project to motivate his engineers, but so far there had been no opportunity. Now he saw a window to make it happen.

Gould decided to open up the project to the West Chester engineers, who had real experience bringing hardware to production. He called Jeff Porter, Hedley Davis, and Don Gilbreath to his offices in New York. "I remember getting summoned to Irving's office in New York," says Porter. "Don was there and I was there. There was a concept for this. They said, 'We want to take this Amiga stuff and put it in a black box in the living room, like a stereo component. And it's going to have a CD-ROM in it.'"

The engineers would have a face-off, and the winners would control the project. "They basically said, 'Each of you go to your separate corners in a different office. Come back in an hour and tell us how much it will cost and how long it will take you to develop it,'" recalls Porter.

Gilbreath had a definite advantage. Even though the CD-ROM had only been figured out in November 1989, he had a working prototype by spring 1990, although the software to run applications from CD-ROMs was non existent. "He was able to quickly do something that was smoke and mirrors and demoware," says Hedley Davis.

By now, both Porter and Davis had experience as project leaders and knew that FCC testing and quality assurance could stretch out production timelines. "We worked out the schedule for how long it would take to get this done and we said it would take nine months," says Davis.

"I came back with a number," says Porter. "Unfortunately this was in the spring around March or April. I said, 'I think I can make it for this amount of money. It's going to take me about nine months to do that. You're going to be lucky to be in pilot production by Christmas.'"

Gould always had an unrealistic expectation for timelines going back to the VIC-20 and C64 days. "To Irving and Mehdi and the powers-that-be at that time, missing Christmas was like I might as well commit harakiri," recalls Porter. "Missing Christmas is not good."

In contrast to Porter, Gilbreath had never taken a consumer product through design to mass production. According to Hedley Davis, the esti-mated time was one-third of the schedule they had proposed. "Don Gil-breath says, 'I think I can have a PC board laid out in a couple of weeks.'"

"I give Don credit for being creative and driven and fearless, but when it came to predicting time or cost, well, he just wasn't wired that way," says Davis. "Jeff Porter, on the other hand, he was very solid in that department. He could work out a schedule, plan for the inevitable fuck ups, and usually predict very closely how long and expensive a project would be. Jeff's fault, if there is one, is that he would honestly represent the facts to management to the best of his ability, and sometimes, that isn't what they wanted to hear."

The optimistic schedule for a production PCB was exactly what Irving Gould wanted. According to Davis, "Their eyes lit up. 'Wow Don, you could do that?' 'I could do that, I could have it laid out in a couple of weeks.' 'Wow! You got the job.'"

Kit Spencer blames Irving Gould for not being in touch with the finer details of his company, resulting in unrealistic expectations. "Irving was not a hands-on guy like Jack was," says Spencer. "Jack was very much down and dirty and involved with selling to the retail outlets, and he was strong-minded to push something though. Irving wouldn't have quite the same input and hands on."

Davis felt slightly outraged by the unfounded optimism. "We're like, 'Bullshit, there's no way to do that. That's never going to happen.' But management was like, 'Oh you guys have got your heads up your ass. Don, go!'"

Porter had lost the opportunity to design the product, and it was now out of his hands. "I said, 'Don, I could have a PC board laid out in a couple of weeks, but when are you going to be in pilot production?' He said, 'I don't know, but I can lay out a PC board in a couple of weeks.' I said, 'You're going to be lucky to be in pilot production with all the tooling and with all the shit that goes into building a new product in nine months. It's like making a baby. Putting two men on the job doesn't make the baby come out any sooner.'"

Gilbreath was, for his part, relieved. He knew that if the West Chester engineers were allowed to design the product, he would no longer be the project manager. Now he could deliver his own product independently of Jeff Porter and his engineers. "For me, it was great because it got approved and, as the product manager on this thing, we didn't have to use any resources in the company," he says. "I didn't have to go do Monday morning meetings with engineering. It was in the building. It was like we could set up a group and go do it offline. Go build it in another factory and get it done quickly."

Over the course of the next year, everyone involved would come to realize just how long it would really take to engineer the new CD-ROM product, develop a software library, and put it onto store shelves.

1-1

1-2   4-1

1-1 Main entrance of Commodore West Chester in late February, 1988
(photo courtesy of Gerard Bucas)

1-2 Software manager Andy Finkel coding in his office
(photo courtesy of Bill Koester)

4-1 Demonstrating the Amiga SX-500 Portable prototype

5-2

5-1

7-1

7-2

5-1 Henry Rubin roaming the halls of Commodore (photo courtesy of Bill Koester)

5-2 Commodore's cost reduced PC clone, the PC-I

7-1 Gerard Bucas leaving Commodore on his last day
(photo courtesy of Gerard Bucas)

7-2 Hedley Davis warmly greets a coworker (photo courtesy of Bill Koester)

9-1

11-1   10-1

11-2

9-1 Commodore's PC50-II clone

10-1 Bryce Nesbitt performing his speedbump dance at a Halloween party (photo courtesy of Eric Cotton)

11-1 Hedley Davis' pride and joy, the Amiga 3000

11-2 Greg Berlin at a Commodore Christmas party

11-3   11-4

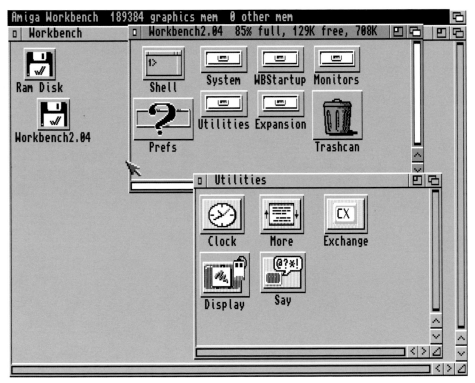

11-5

11-3 Eric Cotton in front of his "Gilligan" Sun Workstation (photo by Bill Koester)

11-4 Workbench manager Dave Berezowski (photo by Bill Koester)

11-5 AmigaOS 2.0x upgraded user interface

13-2

14-1

13-1

13-1 Bryce Nesbitt and Randall Jesup in front of a "Dump the Bumps" ceiling monitor (photo courtesy of Bill Koester)

13-2 Commodore Braunschweig GM Winfried Hoffmann

14-1 Dale Luck working from West Chester, PA (photo courtesy of Bill Koester)

15-1

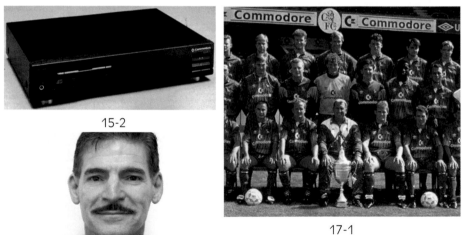

15-2

17-1

18-1

15-1 Vicki Eubanks and Don Gilbreath (photo courtesy of Eric Cotton)

15-2 Early CDTV prototype, named CDA1 at the time

17-1 Chelsea football team sponsorship

18-1 Jeff Boyer, covert engineer

18-2

18-3

19-1

18-2 The only known image of the Hedley Davis Memorial Disk Drive
(captured from *The Deathbed Vigil* by Dave Haynie)

18-3 Dave Haynie showing the A3000 in 1990 (photo courtesy of Dave Haynie)

19-1 Don Gilbreath and Carl Sassenrath posing with the CDTV in Carl's office
(photo courtesy of Carl Sassenrath)

20-1

21-1

22-1

20-1 The final design of the C65 case

21-1 Commodore International president Mehdi Ali and CEO Irving Gould

22-1 A1000 Plus designer Joe Augenbraun doing the limbo

CHAPTER 16

C65 Grows
1989

After the C65 project had been given official project status in early 1989, progress by the engineers Bill Gardei, Paul Lassa, and Fred Bowen was rapid. However, around the same time the project began, Hedley Davis became the Amiga 3000 product manager. This undoubtedly took his attention away from the C65 project he was supposed to be managing. Davis was also doubtful about the C65; he believed the engineers should instead focus on the A3000. With a murky year-end release date and no firm schedule, the engineers would continue toiling away on the project throughout the year.

Paul's PCB

For the C65 team, producing working silicon was proving much harder than it had for the 4502 chip. Back in March 1989, Bill Gardei had devised workarounds for most of the problems within the C65 chipset. It was then up to Fred Bowen to implement those workarounds in his ROM code in order to produce working prototypes while Gardei sorted out the problems in the chips for the next revision.

"The two custom chips were being worked on by Bill [Gardei] and Victor [Andrade]," recalls Paul Lassa. "Those were on the order of say a two-year design cycle and lots of testing and debugging. Even taping out revisions and getting them back was a couple of months cycle. So even if they put in some new capability it would be a couple months before the chips would come back and they were able to test it and move on to the next set of design issues."

Later in the month, Paul Lassa began studying Gardei's prototype C65 schematics and discussing them with Gardei. By early April he was ready to begin his own motherboard. For a junior engineer, the task was daunting. "I owned the PCB and did all the schematics of the board," says Lassa. "I had come in the door to be the hardware engineer for the C65 and develop the PC board and put the sockets for the 4510 and 4567, and the ROMs, and the audio chips, and the expansion ports, and the keyboard interface and all the things that you need on the motherboard. And we put some of the cartridge interface on there to be able to hopefully emulate and play C64 game cartridges that existed out there already as a compatibility mode, because the people who buy this might have 20 or 30 games in their collection."

Dave Haynie and other engineers in his group continued helping Lassa. "They were nudging me and directing me on things as I did them on the C65 and sort of mentoring me," says Lassa.

Unfortunately, the other engineers didn't hold back on their feelings for the C65, which they dubbed "Son of Plus/4". However, Lassa was unphased by the criticisms. "I heard those comments being said and luckily I was not at Commodore during the Plus/4 years. Other than what I had read in the magazines, I didn't have a first-hand appreciation for the failure of the Plus/4, so I was still the optimistic engineer with, 'Hey, the C65 is going to be pretty cool. People will be happy with it and it's got a good set of specs and everything.'"

Paul Lassa came to appreciate the vital role Jeff Porter played within the halls of Commodore. "The whole time he ran around and did so many things. He was a great guy because he tied everybody together," he explains. "We talked and did things with each other, socialized after work and everything. I think that added to what we were able to accomplish." For the inexperienced junior engineer, Porter became his inspiration for how an engineer should act. Even decades later, Lassa's intonation is almost indistinguishable from Porter's.

Lassa's enthusiasm for the project grew as he nurtured the C65. "You make a lot of choices in the early stages of the product design to go for as low as you can without it being a dud of a product," he explains. "There are lots of people out there like me that couldn't have the coolest, fanciest computer on the block. So I really liked that the C65 was targeting the entry-level personal computer and then give them as much bang for their buck as possible."

By Mid-April, most of Lassa's schematic was complete. He submitted it to Mike Nines in the PCB group and he began the layout of the circuit board. Once completed, Lassa waited for the fabrication of his PCBs, along with new revisions of the chipset which were expected in mid-May. He also began training on gate array design in anticipation of creating the custom floppy disk controller chip.

With nothing further to do on the C65 for the time being, he began working with Commodore's mechanical designer, Herb Mosteller, to come up with the casework and keyboard layout. The case would resemble a C128, with a built in 3.5-inch disk drive in the number pad area.

Lassa introduced a fresh idea regarding the location of the 3.5 inch drive. "I believe that it was my idea to have the disk drive sticking out the front of the machine," he says. "We joked that you could set your coffee down on top of it. The thinking was, on an Amiga 500 you had the drive on the side and you had a numeric keypad there. We determined that you weren't going to get a numeric keypad for the C65 because we needed to keep it small. And you needed to put the drive somewhere. I just thought it would be pretty cool to have the drive facing you where you could see the disks and you could guide it in there."

Although the concept worked, placing the eject button proved difficult. "The big problem with that when I first pitched it was, 'Well, where are you going to put the eject button? That's really awkward.' I said, 'Hey maybe we could carve it down here into the edge of the casework and then have kind of a recessed button.' We went and worked with the disk drive vendor supplier to see whether that could mechanically be done. Through various discussions they said, 'Yeah, we can do it.' Then our industrial designer went in and did some mock-ups and sketches. Essentially it was determined that it could be done. It's distinctive and it had utilitarian benefits as well. It was kind of cool."

A trap door on the bottom of the case opened to reveal a memory expansion slot, much like the Amiga 500. "You put eight hi-res photos in there and you've filled up your memory already," explains Lassa. "We added a memory expansion port along with a memory expansion board to the underbelly. It's a way of getting the machine at a lower base price that was accessible to a lot of people. And then for those smaller numbers who wanted or needed more memory onboard, they could add it through an additional purchase."

Bowen's BASIC

Elsewhere, Henri Rubin continued calling meetings with Ted Lenthe, Bill Gardei, Fred Bowen and Rubin's confidante at the time, Andy Finkel. Left out of the discussions were Jeff Porter and Paul Lassa. The team was still trying to define the C65's system software, but Bowen tenaciously held onto his view that it should be C128 compatible. "Fred was our software wizard," says Gardei. "He had dark hair, a dark thick beard. He was friendly and very likable. Fred was a good engineer. He never seemed to figure out the true value of the indirect register addressing mode though."

Everytime the team proposed a feature for the C65 ROM, Bowen replied that it was already in the C128 ROM, so why don't we just use that instead.

Gardei also held his ground, believing that his drive-less C65 planned for next year would crush Nintendo. "Bill was an interesting guy," says Andy Finkel. "He had his own ideas about what was right and how things should work, and no amount of arguing could ever change his opinion."

Finkel did not think Gardei was completely wrong with his vision. "It depends on whether he was right or not," he laughs. "I mean, here is a guy who definitely knew what he wanted. If you liked his C64-like design, then he was right. And if you didn't, then he was still right!"

In any event, Bowen would have to begin developing the ROM code as May was already upon them, leaving little time before the planned release date. To placate Bowen and convert him into a willing participant, Jeff Porter was called in. He alleviated Bowen's concerns that he would be a code-slave by allowing him hire a team of contractors at around $35 per hour to work on the code, managed under Bowen himself.

And finally, to keep Bowen happy, Porter offered him a 256K ROM to work within rather than the originally proposed 32K. Due to the cheap ROM chips CSG could fabricate, it only ended up costing $3 for the 256K chip rather than $2 for the 32K chip. "I let Fred Bowen go wild coming up with the new BASIC," says Porter.

Needless to say, Bowen would become a dedicated supporter of the C65 project from here on in. Unlike on the C128 project, Bowen now had everything he needed for a full C64 backward compatible system with improved graphics: the backward compatible 4567 video chip, the backward compatible 4510 processor, and enough ROM space to emulate the C64 Kernal and BASIC while improving in other areas.

Bowen would start with the BASIC 7 source code, used for the C128, and update it with the hardware features of the C65. The new C65 BASIC would be named BASIC 10. In C64 mode, any BASIC program, even one that used POKE statements, would act the same. "The so called 'Operating System' was the BASIC interpreter," says Bill Gardei. "We had low-level subroutines and drivers accessible in assembly language. But it started up in BASIC and as long as you wrote in BASIC your application would work equally well on any on the C series."

To speed up development, Paul Lassa created a RAM tower to simulate the ROM chips, thus allowing Bowen to quickly upload his code into memory for testing, rather than having to burn EPROMs each time.

In early May, Bowen began hiring software contractors to work on the DOS and graphical library the C65 would require. For DOS, he hired Dennis Jarvis and Jim Springer from a consulting agency. Once they signed the contract, the pair received development equipment, including a modem and access to the Commodore VAX system to upload their code.

To create a graphical library capable of using the improved VIC-III features, Bowen turned to a company called Walrus Software, founded by Lou Wallace, the technical editor for *RUN* magazine who also wrote for *Amiga World*.

Wallace had a history of graphical development. According to Guy Wright, former editor of RUN magazine, "He sent us a complete graphics programming language written for the Commodore 64 that was better than any other language out there for that. It was amazing and I was so impressed that he had done that. Eventually I ended up hiring him to replace me when I went on to Amiga World."

Wallace and his business partner Dave Darus had also created a software package for the C128 called BASIC 8.0. The main impetus for BASIC 8.0 was due to complaints that users could not easily program color graphics for the C128's 80-column mode for RGB monitors from BASIC 7.0, created by Fred Bowen. Now Bowen would hire the same team to make sure users were satisfied with the new BASIC.

Bowen also attempted to contract the actual development of BASIC to Terry Ryan, the former Commodore programmer responsible for BASIC 7.0 in the Commodore 128. Unfortunately that deal fell through and Bowen would take up those duties himself.

Thankfully, when the new 4567R1 chips arrived in the middle of May, Gardei was able to piece together two working prototype computers. If Bowen could manage to get one of them, he could begin developing the ROM and, with a few more prototypes, put his contractors to work.

Clearing the Path to Launch

Jeff Porter still intended to show the C65 by the end of the year, even by the middle of 1989. After all, Commodore had a history of developing its prototype 8-bit computers (the VIC-20 and C64) usually within three months of receiving prototype chips.

During this time, the C65 developers found themselves approached by well meaning Commodore employees who had suggestions for the new system, which usually turned into debates. The situation was wearing thin. Bowen completed a preliminary spec of the system in June and handed out copies to the engineers, including Jeff Porter.

Porter then began pulling in other resources around the company, including a marketing manager named John Campbell. Campbell set someone to work on the C65 manual, although he insisted that the engineers come up with an alternate name for the system that used the C64 brand better. "You walk a fine line, whether you want to leverage the previous name that has lots of mindshare already," says Lassa. "In fact there are cases where if you call it a C65, it's a new product line, but if you call it a C64 then our marketing could lump in all the sales of the Commodore 64 with this and say this is part of the new 64 platform that sold millions of units."

Bowen embarked on a search for appropriate names, settling on 64DX (not to be confused with the unreleased DX-64 portable). "DX was a common marketing thing at that time," says Lassa. "Even the car companies might have a base model and then a DX model. DX was a way of saying that it's the deluxe version."

Porter also handed the C65 spec sheet to Gail Wellington, whom he hoped could use it to entice developers at the upcoming CES. He also suggested hiring a few more CATS employees in order to form a team to work with third party software developers to spur on development for the system. Unfortunately, here he received a dose of Commodore's office politics. Commodore US president Harold Copperman had taken a special interest in CATS, but unfortunately, he was from Apple and favored high end products rather than mass-market consumer products. Copperman refused to hire more CATS employees for the C65 effort.

On the plus side, Porter and Rubin were able to obtain Irving Gould's support, and he promised a big rollout of the C65 at the January 1990 CES show. That would make it harder for Copperman to ignore the product.

Porter had created a bill of materials earlier that resulted in his $300 retail estimate and offered suggestions on where to cut costs. Now it was time for Lassa to create a detailed bill. The result was in line with what Porter estimated at $102.92. The most expensive items were the 3.5" floppy drive at $25, with the 256KB DRAM at $10.84, the keyboard at $7.70, and the case at $5. The cartridge port would use a 50-pin connector similar to that found in the Plus/4, although an adapter would allow C64 cartridges to work.

It was a long way from the $100 NES killer envisioned by Gardei the prior year. However, at half the price of an Amiga 500 it was a good value. Considering a C64 cost an additional $150 with the 1541 disk drive, the C65 with its built-in 3.5" drive was quite a deal.

However, this would not get Commodore products back on the shelves of Kmart, which had switched over to Nintendo, Sega, and Atari video game consoles by 1989. But with Porter's plan to unbundle the disk drive, there was also the possibility to reconfigure the C65 into a video game console; a very competitive one that could get them back into mass market retail. All that remained was to interest software developers in the C65.

With the C64 rapidly falling out of favor in North America, the engineers felt a sense of urgency to complete the project. By 1989, big names in software development such as Lucasfilm games started abandoning the C64, with famous SCUMM games like *Indiana Jones and the Last Crusade* skipping it altogether in favor of the Amiga and PC. Bigger disks, more memory, faster processors, better graphics, and a large C65 user base could sway many of those developers back to Commodore's ultra low end machines.

For some reason, commercial game developers never really embraced the

C128. In anticipation of the upcoming C65 release, Mehdi Ali and Irving Gould decided to retire the C128 line of computers. The C65 would become the next, more powerful C64 instead of the C128. Over its lifetime, Commodore sold an estimated four million units of the 128,[1] making it nearly as successful as the vaunted Apple II line, which sold five million units. Now it would be up to Commodore's engineers to release the C65 on time.

By early July, the C65 chip situation failed to improve. Henri Rubin began visiting the C65 engineers several times a week hoping for good news. Unfortunately the 4510 R0 revision worked better than the R1, which had errors in the fast serial logic added after R0. Now the engineers were waiting for R2, which promised to fix those bugs.

The same month, Jeff Porter required several C65 prototypes for a trip to England in order to entice Commodore UK's sales group and British software developers. But Bowen was not able to create much of a demo due to the software being in such a poor state. Instead, a text-based demonstration of the processor speed was all that he could provide.

The contract developers were well along with C65 DOS because they had working 4510 chips and did not need the 4567 chips. Unfortunately, Lou Wallace was unable to begin his graphics library as only Bill Gardei had working chips in his two prototype motherboards, which Porter needed for his trip. By now the team was 6 weeks behind schedule. Gardei managed to produce another working prototype in mid-July with a patched up 4567R1A chip, and this was sent to Wallace in a C64 case.

Sabotage

Right from the beginning, the C65 had been a contentious project within Commodore, with several engineers upset that it was using company resources that could have gone towards Amiga projects. "I think the main reason that the C65 got done is because Bill Gardei was doing it, and everyone was happy to not be working with him, so they let him do it," says Dave Haynie.

This feeling was all too apparent when accurate reports on the C65 appeared in *Info* magazine and on a local Philadelphia bulletin board system. Both Dave Haynie and Dale Luck had contributed articles to Info magazine. It was clear that whoever had leaked the information had given a very negative report to Info and had hoped to undermine the project publicly.

---

1   This number is from Dave Haynie. He adds, "This info was always hard to get out of Commodore, even when you worked there. We sometimes knew for certain, based on chip deliveries and re-orders."

The article, written by senior editor Mark Brown, lambasted the project and, using language remarkably similar to Commodore's own engineers, predicted it would be another Plus/4. Brown argued that the C64 and C128 were still selling well and software makers would not write new software for the improved C65 mode. "This is marketing 101, guys. Think about it."

Considering Info was founded to support C64 owners, it's surprising the magazine came out against the C65. By 1989, existing C64 owners were desperate for a new upgraded machine, hoping Commodore would finally come out with a system incorporating a VIC-III successor. These customers could afford a $150 to $300 computer more readily than a $600 Amiga 500. It would be worth bringing the C65 to CES and judge the reaction from Commodore's user base, rather than allowing its most popular line of computers to die off.

When Jeff Porter found out about the leak, he wisely chose not to embark on a demoralizing witch hunt that might lead to the loss of one of his talented engineers. Without pointing any fingers, he reminded his engineers not to leak information about unannounced products to the press.

To combat the negative press, Porter and Rubin covertly asked Fred Bowen to speak to Lou Wallace, who had contacts at *Amiga World* and *RUN* magazine. He wanted to start a counter-media campaign to give the C65 a more positive opinion in the press. This included postings to QLink to ensure word got out that the project was not in trouble.

Compute!'s Gazette ran a more positive report about a new 16-bit C64 in September, which they incorrectly dubbed the C64GS. The magazine reported the machine would go on sale in November 1989 in the $300 to $350 range. Unfortunately, the next month, Gazette reported that the machine would never see the light of day, owing to Harold Copperman taking the company in a new direction. However, development continued. But the magazine began assembling a petition to beg Commodore to do more with the 8-bit line of computers. Fred Bowen would later chastise the Gazette editors (along with CompuServ moderators) at the World of Commodore for printing rumors instead of fact.

C65 Backward Compatibility

By the middle of August 1989, the team had four new prototypes assembled using Paul Lassa's new motherboard, stuffed with 4567R1B and 4510R0 chips. One prototype went to the FCC for preliminary testing, one to Fred Bowen, and Lassa kept the third himself.

They could now test the C65 for backward compatibility, a feature that could make or break the success of the computer with existing C64 owners. However, while the C128 had a definite goal of 100% backward compatibility, the

C65 had a more nebulous goal. "We were never sure how compatible we had to be with legacy products," says Bill Gardei. "Obviously, the more, the better."

Porter wanted CATS on board the project, and he gave Gail Wellington a prototype unit for testing purposes. Unfortunately, Wellington had just joined the CD-ROM project and naturally preferred that system over the C65. She tried a number of software titles and reported back that only 15% worked reliably. The results made her even less favorable towards the system than before.

The C65 was capable of two speeds, much like how IBM PC computers had a turbo button which could change speeds to keep compatibility. "The C65 had a turbo bit in a register that selected between 1.05 MHz (the C64 speed) and 3.58 MHz," says Gardei. "I always ran it at the high speed."

If the developers allowed users to run games in C64 mode at the higher speed, many of the latest C64 games would run better. The challenge was to allow the software to take advantage of the new speeds yet remain playable on both old C64 and new C65 hardware. Some of the latest C64 games, such as *Times of Lore* (1988), *John Madden Football* (1989), *Sim City* (1989), *Myth: History in the Making* (1989), and *Project Firestart* (1989) ran slowly. The aging hardware also hosted a new breed of three dimensional polygon games such as *Total Eclipse* (1989), *Mean Streets* (1989), *Space Rogue* (1989), and *Stunt Car Racer* (1989) that could benefit from a faster CPU and graphics hardware. As long as those programmers ensured they used the C64's CIA timing chip properly, those games would run at the proper speed. This was the promise of the 3.5 MHz 4510 chip.

As an avid C64 user himself, Paul Lassa understood the importance of backward compatibility with the C64 software library. "When a machine first ships, there aren't that many software titles out for it because not all the developers have jumped into the new version yet," he says. "That's what put a bigger value on compatibility mode for being able to play your existing software until the new stuff started trickling out."

Backward compatibility was a difficult challenge. "When you go to new hardware, especially when it's faster and has more features, chances are something's going to break in the old software," says Lassa. "An engineering team and a support team have to do a lot of homework up front to provide that."

The biggest problem had to do with game programmers using strange methods to time their code. "Often programmers would write games that had delay loops in them that were based upon how fast instructions were executed," says Lassa. "That's not the best way to do it because that will take a certain amount of time to execute on a 6502. You might emulate the same instruction on a 4502 but if the clock rate was faster on the chip or it was more efficient, then it would execute three 'load zeros' in the time that the earlier processor would have done only one 'load zero.'"

The improvements in efficiency made to the 4510 and 4567 chips wreaked havoc on C64 game titles. "So when game developers would write their programs tied into how many instructions created the delay of an animation moving across the screen, such as a bullet being fired, all of a sudden if you speed up the chip, those things break," explains Lassa. "A bullet is there too early or the animation zips across the screen in a half a second instead of two and a half seconds. You can imagine it can really throw off a game."

Because Gardei's 4502 core was more efficient than the 6502 core, Victor Andrade had to slow down some operations intentionally. "The 4502 core in the 4510 ran up to 40% faster than the 6502 core in the 6510 at the same clock speed," explains Gardei. "This made it very hard to win most of the games. So the 4510 had a logic block that detected when optimized instructions were executed and would insert wait states to make the core look more like the old. It worked, but wasn't perfect."

Unfortunately, dismissing Bob Russell (the original C64 ROM programmer) in 1986 had hurt Commodore badly. "With the loss of so many engineers over the years, many details of the chipset related to timing were lost," says Gardei. "This had a major hit on compatibility."

When Bowen began testing the games using Lassa's motherboard with a 1541 drive plugged into it, the results were not stellar. Most games failed because of the new fastload code Bowen had added to the ROM, causing copy protection schemes employed by software makers to fail. When they loaded properly, there were often graphical glitches and gibberish graphical screens that made the games unplayable.

But there were some successes. Games like *Jumpman, One on One, Jack Attack, Top Gun, Solar Fox,* and *Temple of Apshai* worked flawlessly due to the original programmers' adherence to programming standards. The Infocom games worked as long as Bowen selected a non-1541 drive at the beginning. And many games, such as *Frogger, Battle Through Time,* and *International Soccer* loaded but had small faults that hindered playability.

Out of the 70 disk-based programs attempted, only 22 worked, with the remaining 70% not working. Bowen reported to Rubin that they were unlikely to achieve over 50% compatibility by the time they had corrected timing problems in the chips.

The results did not trouble Porter, as his vision had always been for a system that allowed software developers to easily port their games to the C65. And to get those developers on-board, he had ambitious plans for a slightly revised schedule, which called for 1000 developer units produced by October 15, 1989, followed by production units shipping by December 15. It all hinged on receiving working silicon chips. The second revision of the 4567 was already in layout and expected back by September, which would leave the engineers a month to produce the 1000 developer units.

Given how late Commodore had given developer units to Lou Wallace and the other contractors, it was doubtful the DOS or the graphics library would be completed in time. When Wallace's original prototype burned out due to the power supply, Bowen stole the C65 from Gail Wellington's desk and shipped it to Wallace.

In late August, Bowen finished porting BASIC 7.0 from the C128 over to the C65. Hedley Davis began work on a network interface cartridge for the C65, which he envisioned would be used in a classroom setting. Another engineer, Scott Hood, began work on the C64 cartridge port adaptor and the memory expander.

CSG released new versions of the 4510R3 in late September. This time, only one of the instructions failed. Victor Andrade located the problem in layer 15 and 16 of the chip. He then fixed those layers and CSG quickly produced another run of 4510R3A chips.

Unfortunately, the story with 4567R2 was worse. The new revision barely functioned at all. This was a demoralizing blow for the team, especially Bill Gardei. September came and went without the engineers able to produce any of the 1000 developer systems they hoped to release into the world.

C65 GEOS

In Fred Bowen's earlier compatibility test, GEOS was one of the 70 titles attempted. The program started to load, but unfortunately it crashed. And that seems to be all the thought the C65 team put into getting a worthwhile GUI operating system onto the C65.

By 1989, it was clear that a full graphical operating system was required in order to allow a computer to keep up with the changes in hardware and software. Henri Rubin wanted the C65 to have the ability to use a CD-ROM and even network cards (although Fred Bowen refused to implement the code for these devices). With the GEOS operating system, small drivers could give these devices compatibility. The software drivers that arrived on disk were far more flexible than having to precode hardware compatibility in ROM. It was a new paradigm that Fred Bowen was slow to catch onto.

Clive Smith, the former product manager at Commodore who now worked at GEOS, understood this dynamic going back to 1985. "Clive Smith completely got that," says Brian Dougherty. "Conceivably, you could have had this ever-evolving Commodore 64 line, just like you had with the PC, but at some point it would have stopped being 6502 based and would stop being based on an assembly language operating system and applications just like the PC."

GEOS would have been relatively easy to port to the C65. And compared to the cross-hatched look of the C64 version of GEOS, it would look much better, using 640 x 400 screens with more colors. From a user perspective, the UI could look every bit as good Windows 3.0 at a tiny fraction of the price. And with the improved DOS in the C65, GEOS could allow users to exit the GUI in order to play hardware-intensive games, while productivity software would run within GEOS.[2]

This alone would make the C65 irresistible to a large number of consumers in 1990. In fact, to ship a system in 1990 without a GUI OS seemed positively anachronistic.

Would history have been different if Henry Rubin had given one development system to Berkeley Softworks? What if every C65 included GEOS on disk? Perhaps Berkeley could have integrated GEOS more tightly with the computer, offering suggestions during development, such as allowing an auto-boot feature. Unfortunately Berkeley was not even aware of the C65 project.

Surprisingly, Commodore's hardware-centric engineers were blasé about a GUI OS. "I wouldn't have liked that at the time," says Andy Finkel. "Back then I was really a 'go to the metal whenever possible' kind of software developer, with no operating system to get in the way. I liked the Kernal with useful functions that you may or may not use. At that time I really liked to have everything on the machine under my control."

In retrospect, Finkel sees the importance of a GUI OS. "Nowadays, having a capable operating system is just so much part of software development that it's hard to imagine going back to those days," he says.

DMA Chip Origins

Paul Lassa had little to do as he waited for working silicon. "I finished the PCB, I finished the RAM expansion card. I'd done various other things for the project and I'm now, like the others, patiently waiting for the custom chips to be fabricated and ready to go."

Lassa decided it made more sense to work on something to make the machine better rather than sitting around. "I'm an Amiga user but I came from the C64 and, wherever possible, I'd like to bring some of the Amiga stuff down into the C64 platform where it's economically feasible," says Lassa.

There was a real danger of feature creep on the project that could prevent the machine from ever being released. Paul Lassa felt he maintained the balance well. "You could say, 'Well let's just throw everything that the Amiga has

---

2   This is how Windows 3.x and MS-DOS (as well as GeoWorks) coexisted on IBM PC computers at the time.

into the C65.' If you did that, pretty soon you'd be up to the same price range. We had a mission to greatly enhance the C65, to go as far beyond the Commodore 64 and Commodore 128 as we could, and go as close to some of the capabilities of the Amiga. However, keep the price point down nearer to the C64 and C128."

One thing in particular bothered Lassa about the C65. "I wanted to do some of the Amiga demos of the time," he recalls. "They would put these photos on screen and flip them from one screen to the next to show you a bunch of different high quality photos. I did that on the C65 and had the nice photos and had the nice VIC-III display mode, but when you wanted to flip from one picture to the next it was really slow."

Lassa decided to implement most of the blitter functions that distinguished the Amiga from other computers. "One of the Amiga's chips had a logic block called the blitter," explains Gardei. "This was a buzzword for Block Image Transfer. That was a DMA (Direct Memory Access) block that could move rectangular blocks of memory around. It was primarily used for moving images quickly and drawing lines, but could also be used for just about any DMA application."

Lassa wanted to create a C65 DMA chip, which he dubbed DMAgic. "DMAgic was added to the C65 to give it a blitter function," he recalls. "I said, 'Hey, can I do a gate array of a DMA controller?'"

Lassa pitched his idea to Porter, but was initially refused. "Jeff was the voice of reason saying, 'No. That's a nice idea but, realistically, I don't think we can do it,'" recalls Lassa. "The conventional wisdom was, 'That's why it's the C65. It's going to be cheaper and we don't really have time for that.' And he was right to say that as a manager trying to bring this to market."

Lassa brooded over the idea longer and felt it would be an important addition to the C65. "I was persistent with him and I mustered some support among my colleagues on the team," he recalls.

Lassa convinced Fred Bowen that, rather than sitting on his hands, he should use the time to improve the machine. Given that the team had no hope of releasing the C65 in 1989, Bowen was receptive. At the end of October, Bowen made a plea to the team on behalf of Lassa. He proposed they should start looking at some improved features to make the C65 even more popular.

Both Jeff Porter and Bill Gardei were reluctant, knowing that it was a risky move that could put the schedule farther behind. Hedley Davis felt it made sense, even going so far as to propose an MMU for the machine. In the end, there were three team members in favor and two opposed.

To get Porter on board, Lassa came up with an alternate plan to a gate array. He decided to prototype the chip using ICs, similar to how the original

Amiga team created chips. "I said, 'Let's make a deal. Let me go and prototype a DMA controller. I'll prototype it on a board with random LSI logic.'"

Reluctantly, Porter agreed and in late November Lassa began to piece together a DMA chip using logic chips on a wire-wrapped board. Secretly, he
would go much further than creating just a DMA chip.

The rapid development of the C65 in 1989 was impressive, even though the
team clearly missed the late 1989 release schedule. But the core problem resided in the chip group. Somehow Commodore lacked the institutional processes
to reliably turn out working chips on the first revision. The 4510 and 4567
chips needed engineers to simulate and test the chip designs properly before
they went to production. Once again, this problem could be traced to the reluctance of top management to assign a proper complement of three dedicated engineers per chip.

CHAPTER 17

New Marketing 1989

Commodore's marketing department had been headed by Frank Leonardi since 1985. In those years, its marketing efforts to appeal to the business world had been an unqualified failure. Now the company would change tactics, first by replacing top executives and then by trying a different approach.

Leonardi Out, Mahaffey In

Harold Copperman had become Commodore's US president earlier in the year, and since then he had slowly learned how the company operated. He took over the CATS organization in April and worked closely with the influential Gail Wellington, trying to figure out how to sell more computers to the US market.

In June 1989, Copperman brought in a former Apple executive named Howard Diamond to head up Commodore's education division. Then in mid-July, Copperman replaced Frank Leonardi (the former Apple marketing executive who had little success with Commodore's products in the US) with another Apple executive. "Harry Copperman knew a marketing guy by the name of Lloyd Mahaffey, and he came from Apple," says Jeff Porter.

As vice president of marketing, Mahaffey would work closely with Copperman to increase software development for the Amiga. "When he came he started an initiative to try and really connect with the developers," recalls Amiga developer Eric Lavitsky.

Commodore made visits to smaller conferences throughout the year, such as SIGGRAPH '89 in Boston. "Harry Copperman had a right hand man who was in charge of marketing, Lloyd Mahaffey. They had a little suite at SIGGRAPH and they invited us in to sit down and give them a piece of our minds," recalls Lavitsky. "We talked to them about what we felt was important and what we wanted to see happen. That was the first time somebody at that level at Commodore paid any heed or attention to the developer community."

Copperman and Mahaffey hoped to appeal to government institutions and the education market. One of Copperman's first decisions was closing down *Commodore Magazine*, which had been around in various forms since 1982. "I think that was a strategic mistake," says Kit Spencer. "Our Commodore magazines were making money. This was another important marketing item that I started up in the USA after arriving there, and the circulation had grown very large even by magazine standards."

Although revenues were not extremely high, the marketing value was important for pushing US sales. "In Commodore, we had access to technical information because we are the producer. So we can put in information that is really useful to our users," says Spencer. "Yes, the reader might think we're a little biased, and yes we are probably biased because we are promoting our product, but as long as we do it well and give value for money, users will be happy. Meanwhile it gives us some control over a very important distribution system that keeps in regular contact with many of our users, feeding information to them and promoting our new and existing product lines."

Under Harold Copperman, Commodore US had made some improvements in distribution. His sales team had convinced Electronics Boutique (the forerunner to the mass market EB Games) to begin carrying Amiga 500 computers in its stores. Unfortunately, three months later the chain announced it was dropping the computers, in order to focus on IBM and Macintosh.

However, this was offset by the Copperman team signing a large retail chain named Connecting Point of America. The deal would have the 326-outlet chain selling not only Amiga products but also Commodore's IBM clones.

It was clear to Jeff Porter that Harold Copperman, whom he derisively called "Coppertop", had a distaste for the consumer products such as the C64 and A500, and especially the upcoming C65. These markets were no longer at the top of Commodore North America's priorities. Like many before him, he was more interested in selling expensive products to thousands of consumers rather than low-cost computers to millions. He would try to emulate Apple's success rather than playing to Commodore's strengths.

Amiga 500 Batman Packs

Over in the UK, things were only getting better. In Europe, Commodore had its logo on the major sports franchises of the time, including Chelsea Football Club and Bayern Munich football teams, as well as professional Formula-1 racing teams. Now it was about to leverage the biggest movie franchise for 1989.

It all happened because of the Commodore bundles that David Pleasance had put together. Ocean Software, a major UK game developer, had just made an impressive deal. "We knew that the game that would be huge was *Batman: The Movie*," recalls Pleasance. "Ocean paid a million dollars up front and another million to produce the game."

The marketing manager saw an opportunity to feature the Batman logo prominently on the Amiga 500 box and he wanted it exclusively for Commodore. He called Ocean Software and told them his terms. "I want a bundle that features *Batman: The Movie* software. We'll call it the 'Batman Pack'. Give me that software exclusively for two months before you can sell it over the counter. I want to pay you [next to] nothing for it, and we'll start with 10,000 pieces."

It seemed like the deal was heavily in Commodore's favor. "Ocean had two concerns," recalls Pleasance. "If the dealers can't sell the Batman game, they will be pissed off. And we're not sure we can sell enough through Commodore to become profitable."

Pleasance had thought the deal through beforehand and made sure it would benefit Ocean Software. "First, we worked out how many pieces they had to sell to make their money back," he says. "Second, the dealers won't be pissed because they'll be selling a £400 product, not a £40 product. And third, we will promote your game for you."

The plan was sound and Ocean Software signed the agreement. "I have to give them credit for having the balls to go with it," says Pleasance. In the months leading up to the release of the movie, Commodore put together an irresistible bundle for consumers. It included the standard Amiga 500 computer and TV modulator, Batman: The Movie, plus four popular titles at the time: *New Zealand Story*, *F/A-18 Interceptor*, and *Deluxe Paint 2*. Commodore paid the software companies between £2-3 per unit sold.

The C64c was also included in the deal. "We did the same thing with the C64," says Pleasance, who put together a C64 Batman Pack using Ocean Software's C64 version of the game, among other software titles.

When Batman was released on June 23, 1989, it became a box office smash. The exclusive sales period exceeded everyone's expectations. "I took

186,000 pieces from them in the first two months," recalls Pleasance. "Retailers absolutely demanded the bundles."

Reviews for the game were positive, with *Zzap!* magazine giving the Amiga version a 97% rating and the C64 version 96%. When the 2-month exclusive period ended, Christmas sales of the standalone game went into overdrive. "Their sales were five times greater than they estimated they would be," recalls Pleasance.

Commodore would continue selling its Batman Packs through the holiday season and into 1990. "In October 1989, the A500 dropped its price from £499 to £399 and was bundled with the Batman Pack," recalls Pleasance. "This price drop helped Commodore to sell more than one million Amiga 500s in 1989."

It was the type of marketing strategy that Commodore US was once capable of under Jack Tramiel. But for the former Apple marketing executives in the US, these types of clever marketing ploys were foreign to their way of thinking. Even other parts of Commodore Europe were slow to catch on. "Europe stubbornly refused to adopt our highly successful marketing strategy," says Pleasance. "They were still selling some C64s but nowhere near the volumes the UK achieved."

Lloyd Mahaffey's Ad Strategy

The Amiga was initially second to the Atari ST when it came to game development. When sales of the Amiga 500 began, Atari ST software support soon faded away and the Amiga software market overflowed with games. "They gave it the old college try, but the Amiga won," says RJ Mical.

In the first half of 1989, it was apparent that the Atari ST was dying. Atari earnings fell sharply in the first half of 1989. Unfortunately, Commodore would also have two consecutive quarters with losses, starting in June. Losses continued to mount, despite strong revenues from Europe. It was clear Commodore needed to do something to stop the bleeding.

Back in late 1987, Gould had promised a major television advertising campaign for the Amiga 500, which never materialized, even when Commodore's earning were strong. Now with Commodore's new management headed by Harold Copperman, it was time to act. In September 1989, Gould and his board of directors authorized a major advertising campaign for the Amiga 500, with a $10 to $15 million budget (compared to $1 million the year before).

Lloyd Mahaffey hired advertising agency Messner. Vetere Berger Carey Schmetterer to launch the campaign with Steven Spielberg's Amblin Entertainment producing the commercials. RJ Mical was enthusiastic about the long overdue ad campaign. "A long time later, they finally got around to doing these really cool ads where they invited Spielberg," says Mical. "They did a really cool set of commercials."

According to Dave Haynie, it was a first for Spielberg. "They got Spielberg involved doing his first commercial ad campaign ever because he liked the Amiga so much," he says. "It was just so much more than we were ever expecting."

Amblin hired George Lucas' Industrial Light and Magic (ILM) to produce the special effects. ILM had used the Amiga for *Back to the Future II* (1989). Amblin also contracted a company called Silent Software to produce Amiga animations for the commercials.

The $15 million advertising blitz would feature three commercials directed by Matthew Robbins, who previously directed *Batteries Not Included* (1987) for Amblin. The commercials featured the fictional character Stevie Palmer (played by actor Scott Weinger), a true eighties teenager who used a lot of mousse in his hair. Commodore would air the commercials for the Christmas 1989 season and hope they had not waited too long.

The ads were powerful, but David Pleasance felt there was a missed opportunity for Commodore US to share its ads across national borders. "When we produced the television commercial, it would've been so easy to produce one for every country and just get it dubbed in their own language at the time of production," he says. "We would have saved a fortune. Instead of producing a hundred thousand brochures, you produce a million brochures. You get your price down and it's done in all of the languages and you ship it. The marketing ideas that work in one country generally can work in others."

Although Commodore was underfunding the engineering department during this time, there is no doubt that Gould was addressing one of the key criticisms of Commodore: the lack of advertising. During the Christmas shopping season, Commodore ran its Amblin-produced Stevie commercials. "I thought some of the Stevie commercials were pretty good," says Dale Luck. "Although I wish they would have come out earlier."

The first commercial depicts three girls watching a music awards show. Suddenly the image flickers and next-door neighbor Stevie is on television winning an award. He and his friends are using genlock and a video camera to produce the illusion.

The second commercial, slightly more ambitious, shows Stevie creating a 3D model of his house using a CAD program. "It's just so cool!" says Mical. "The whole house takes off and lifts up off the foundation and goes into the air." Stevie's parents are startled awake as their bed shifts. The commercials, which featured composer Dave Grusin's musical score from *The Goonies* (1985), were far superior to the original 1985 Amiga commercials.[1]

The final commercial shows a procession of celebrities coming to the Palmer residence and asking for Stevie. These include astronauts Buzz Aldrin, Gordon Cooper, and Scott Carpenter, who ask for Stevie's help with a space station. "There's this kid playing in his bedroom and the astronauts come over and he's showing them stuff on the computer and they're all like, 'Ooh-ah,'" recalls Mical. "They are real honest-to-God astronauts in the commercial." Next, the *Pointer Sisters* arrive asking Stevie for some help with a song. Tommy Lasorda of the *Los Angeles Dodgers* arrives for some statistical help. Finally, former house speaker Tip O'Neil comes to the door.

According to Dave Haynie, the commercials aired frequently but not as much as the competition. "Nintendo's first year with the Nintendo 64, they spent more on commercials in the United States than they spent on developing the thing," he recalls. "Commodore never hit that peak, but it was pretty regular. It would be hard to miss it."

The commercials arrived prior to the Christmas 1989 season, two years behind the launch of the Amiga 500 and four years behind the launch of the Amiga 1000. "Is that pathetic or what?" adds Mical.

The agency also produced a series of stylish print ads featuring celebrity Amiga users including Tommy Lasorda, Tip O'Neill, and also blues guitarist B.B. King. The ads appeared in major print publications, including *Time* magazine.

The advertising blitz did not impact sales substantially. For the previous quarter ending September 1989, Commodore lost $6.5 million on sales of $165 million. During the holiday quarter, Commodore had sales of $310.7 million with net income of $11.3 million. Unfortunately, overall sales were down 11% compared to the $349.0 million from the same quarter in the previous year.

Overall for the 1989 year, Commodore had revenues of $939 million, with a healthy profit of $50.1 million.

The less than hoped-for results were likely a result of the poor Commodore dealer network at the time. Running an expensive ad campaign on a

---

1   The Amiga commercial was similar to a 1988 Nintendo commercial which featured two teens playing an NES, followed by the house lifting from the foundations and rocketing into the sky.

two-year old product didn't make much sense. If Commodore could have placed the Amiga 500 into US mass-market retailers by 1989, the commercials would have had more impact. "When I'd see years later they tried an Amiga commercial, it was sad," says Mical. "It was already too late by this time."

January 1990 CES

Irving Gould had promised a splashy introduction for the C65 computer at the upcoming January 1990 CES in Las Vegas, a promise he intended to keep. Unfortunately, the C65 was not even close to ready. Both Paul Lassa and Fred Bowen had managed to place a semi-presentable C65 system together in a finished case for the show in order to display it behind closed doors, but even that plan was cancelled by Jeff Porter, who instead wanted his engineers to be ready for the March 20 CeBIT show in Hanover.

Around the same time, Lassa was reassigned to the Amiga 3000 project temporarily in order to help them finish off the system; a move that promised to set back the C65 project even further. Porter was not looking good in the eyes of management. To make matters worse, he found himself arguing more frequently with Jeff Frank, the project leader on Commodore's profitable line of PC clones.

At the January 1990 CES, Commodore had little to show that would appeal to the mass-market consumer. Instead, software ruled the day, being demonstrated on Amiga 500 machines. The recent Stevie commercials were also prominently shown around the Commodore booth.

Two members of Commodore's Tiger Team, Don Gilbreath and Gail Wellington, brought along their CD-ROM prototype unit. At the time, it was called the CDA-1. The system was shown behind closed doors to Amiga software developers, such as Lucasfilm Games, in the hopes of persuading them to develop CD software.

Perhaps the biggest success story of the previous year was the Batman A500 Pack, which marked a turning point for Amiga sales. "My title was National Accounts Manager Consumer Products, up until the success of the Amiga 500 Batman Pack," recalls David Pleasance. "In January I was promoted to Sales & Marketing Director." The promotion was a fitting birthday present as Pleasance had just turned 40 on December 28th.

The success made Pleasance yearn for a bigger challenge. "For a very long time I kept asking Mehdi to let me loose in America," he says. "I knew that I could change things." For now, Ali turned down his requests and only later, after it was too late, would he acquiesce.

David Pleasance now found himself a popular figure among software publishers due to the Batman Packs. "At the January CES, there were tons of software companies who wanted their game in the pack," he recalls. "We had a meeting with Psygnosis. Steve [Franklin] had to go to the toilet. Suddenly the directors turned to us and said, 'We could give you our game for free.'"

Pleasance was surprised just how desperate the publishers were to partner with Commodore. But he knew the deal was not mutually beneficial and feared Steve Franklin would be angry if he found out Pleasance turned it down. Pleasance replied, "Don't tell Steve this, but we want you around and this deal could break you. If your game is the right one, we will buy it from you. We won't take it for free."

It was a refreshing attitude that someone at Commodore was thinking of long-term business deals. "At the end of the day, business has to be win-win," says Pleasance. "If any one party is not going to win, you should not make the deal."

Amiga 3000 1990

Commodore had started to plan an Amiga 2000 sequel, called the Amiga 3000, as early as 1986. Four years later, in 1990, the company was struggling to complete the new system, but it finally looked like the computer would be released by the end of the year. Would it be a case of too little too late?

Finishing off the A3000

Almost three years had passed since Commodore had released a new computer. With executives starting to wonder if their engineers were still capable of releasing new machines, it would be up to Hedley Davis and his team to finish the next high-end Amiga. "At this point in time, Jeff Porter was in charge of systems engineering, and I was in charge of the A3000," says Hedley Davis. "There's an interesting point of ego versus reality. I identified extremely strongly with the A3000. I worried about that machine in a way that my coworkers didn't really appreciate."

Unlike the C65 project, the A3000 project had been remarkably well managed with realistic timelines and a minimum of feature creep. "This was: push the product out the door and absolutely make it happen," says Davis. The first sample of A3000s had been sent to international countries in December 1989. The production schedule called for all casework, manuals, final software, and ROMs by March 15, 1990, with wide release planned for June.

One of the biggest roadblocks was the operating system. Andy Finkel and his Amiga software developers needed to have AmigaOS 2.0 ready by June. The engineers were dedicated to producing stable software, and in February Bryce Nesbitt even went so far as to create a piece of software to stress test the operating system. "We built a series of tools in order to torture the operating system, and I eventually wrote a tool called Enforcer," he recalls. "We had various memory test utilities and various things in order to deliberately stress the system in order to find failures. We were really focused at that point on making this thing not crash all the time."

The A3000 was a unique project at Commodore because it was a collaboration among many of its top engineers. In fact, no one engineer owned the motherboard design. "The A3000 was my favorite project because we had a real team," says Dave Haynie. "That made for a better result than those systems I did mostly alone."

Back in April 1989, the A3000 with a 16 MHz 68030 chip had a projected bill of materials cost of $805.09. By March 1990, the cost had grown to $998.18. Commodore also had plans for a 25 MHz A3500 with more RAM and placed into a PC-60 tower case, which grew the bill of materials to a whopping $1440.25.

The designer of the DMA controller chip (for SCSI peripherals), called DMAC, departed in the middle of the project in order to work full time at Great Valley Products with Gerard Bucas. When GVP began raking in millions of dollars every year on Amiga peripherals, Jeff Boyer felt it was time to commit to the company. Friday, September 22 was his final day at Commodore.

Greg Berlin, who had developed the 1581 drive for the C64 and then a tape drive controller for the A2500UX, took over DMAC and became a true semiconductor superstar on the A3000. The tall but low-key engineer not only designed Fat Gary, but redesigned several chips designed by other engineers. "Hedley designed the original version of Ramsey, Greg took it over and added burst mode," says Dave Haynie. "Jeff Boyer completed the DMAC before leaving for GVP. There were some issues. Greg looked into that and redesigned it pretty much from scratch. I have no doubts that, if left unchecked, Berlin probably would have redesigned and improved Buster and Amber too, in time."

Hedley Davis, who was passionate at the best of times and hot-headed at the worst, recalls some tension with his engineers. "Haynie and Berlin reported to me, which both pissed them off and pissed me off," says Davis. "I am 100% confident that Mr. Berlin totally resented my ass and Haynie probably did in some ways, although Haynie has a very soft touch and he always tries to keep it positive."

With a tight schedule to meet, the engineers often disagreed on priorities. "I knew that Haynie and Berlin always went out drinking on Friday afternoon," laughs Davis. "I tried to impose a little bit of order and they obviously pushed back. 'You're pissing away 10 percent of your week. Come on man, don't do this!' But they would just go ahead and do it and that's the way it was. So Friday afternoons were totally shot."

Taunting management became somewhat of a sport in the later days of Commodore. "Hedley was a pretty intense guy," says Greg Berlin. "We'd give him general abuse but friendly abuse! I thought so, he may not have. I've got a lot of respect for Hedley. Probably more now than I ever did."

These days, Davis has a more holistic view of the period. "For the period in time we're talking about, I was just a flaming egotistical kid that was highly focused on getting shit out and I called it my own," he recalls. "I never really appreciated the demoralizing factor that may have had on my coworkers or the resentment that may have occurred. And that's something that took a while for me to figure out."

By April 1990, Commodore began production of the first 250 units. These would all become demo units, sent out to dealers. In the end, despite some friction, the team felt Hedley Davis' handling of the A3000 was a highlight of working at Commodore. "I think he did a very good job," says Greg Berlin.

Near the end of product development for the A3000, Hedley Davis ran into what seemed like an insurmountable problem. Davis had submitted his latest revision of the motherboard and then weeks later received almost a dozen motherboards to test. "I've got this motherboard and it's the one that's got to go to production right away. It better be right or you've screwed it up," he explains.

After stuffing the boards with electronic components, he meticulously inserted the Motorola 68030 chip, plugged in the custom chips, plugged in the SCSI hard drive, the floppy drive, the monitor, the keyboard, the mouse, and finally the power supply. "We get this board back and we build it and start testing it and everything is working except for the floppy drive," he recalls.

Davis was now on a bug-hunt. "I'm trying to debug it. It doesn't make any sense! So I'm swapping Agnuses, I'm swapping power supplies and swapping this and that and it just doesn't work. It's to the point that I have to start digging into how the floppy stuff works, even though that's entirely embedded inside of Agnus and Paula; it's embedded entirely in the chips and it's not something that can screw up on the motherboard unless you just have something really dumb going on. And I can't figure it out."

Eventually, as his coworkers started departing for the day, Davis settled in for a long night. He filled his coffee mug, dug out his documentation on the project, and then spent hours analysing the signals from the motherboard using his scope. To his surprise, all the signals looked great, which left him baffled as to why the floppy drive was not working. And then a small light blinked on in his mind. "It's two o'clock in the morning and I'm still in there sweating it," he says. "Finally I go, 'Uh, did I swap the floppy drive?' Okay, so I unplugged this one floppy drive and I plugged in a new floppy drive, and then everything is working perfectly."

The problem was a bad disk drive, perhaps the first thing he should have checked. Davis did what any red-blooded American would do in the same situation. "I'm furious with this floppy drive. It's two o'clock in the morning and there's this giant 55 gallon grey trash can and I just lose it. I grabbed that floppy off the desk, the one that had cost me so much time, and I just start throwing it into this trash can as hard as I can. I'm destroying it because it's just wasted my time and screwed with me and I'm so frustrated."

With his dominance established over the floppy drive, Davis gave it one last reminder. "Simply put, there was no longer room in this universe for both me and that floppy drive," he later recalled. "It was him or me. Sadly, my efforts to propel it into the next universe were interrupted by the wall. I went home."

The next morning, Amiga developer Bryce Nesbitt entered the product development area. The first thing he noticed was the disk drive half-embedded in the drywall. Nesbitt liked what he saw and immortalized the drive with a tasteful frame and a plaque reading, "The Hedley Davis Memorial Disk Drive". "I came along and added the picture frame with Hedley's name on it," recalls Nesbitt. The impromptu art exhibit became a fixture at Commodore for a long time. "I don't think that thing was repaired until after QVC moved in."

The incident has haunted Davis to the present day. "He came up to me and said, 'You know Bryce, you have had a real continual impact on my life. Every time I go to a job interview, the guy who is interviewing me Googles my name and sees a picture of this disk drive embedded in a wall and asks me if I have anger management issues."

On the upside, Davis had been able to confirm that the production design of the Amiga 3000 worked. Now the machine was ready for mass production and a product launch.

A3000 Launch Event

The Amiga 500 and 2000 both had a lackluster launch into the North American market in 1987. Now, in 1990, the new Amiga 3000 would get a proper launch. And even better, RJ Mical believed an anti-Microsoft sentiment at the time could help the computer. "There was a window when the Amiga could have grabbed a lion's share of that market if things had gone right," he says. "People were looking for an alternative to Microsoft and we represented that alternative."

Harold Copperman, president of Commodore US, and his VP of marketing, Lloyd C. Mahaffey, created a splashy event to launch the A3000. Both men came from Apple, and predictably they would do their best to copy Apple's launch events.

Prior to the show, a Commodore engineer had completed an A3640 accelerator board using the new 68040 processor from Motorola. "Scott Schaeffer was developing the original, never released, high-performance 68040 board alongside the A3000 development," says Dave Haynie.

Bryce Nesbitt had hurriedly completed a software demo for the board, as well as a benchmarking app. "The 68040 was the hot new chip, and we had an add-on card for the Amiga 3000 that used the 68040 and ran blazingly fast," says Nesbitt. "It was the fastest personal computer available and the demo was finished."

Motorola had been so impressed by the engineering efforts that, the prior Monday, they couriered the latest revision of the chip, codenamed Queen Bee, to Commodore. "We got the 68040 booting our operating system and we could run benchmarks that blew everybody else away," says Nesbitt. "There wasn't a PC or Mac or Atari or anything that could run that fast and that well. Plus it had a memory management unit. We worked super hard and finished this demo in time to be introduced with the Amiga 3000."

Post-Tramiel Commodore had always tried to link the Amiga to trendy New York venues, this time launching at the Palladium. The 3,000-capacity theater, managed by the owners of the famous Studio 54, was generally used by rock bands. "That was an interesting event," says Eric Lavitsky. "The community itself was this brave conglomeration of creative people and technical people—people who wanted to get things done."

However, at a suggested price of $3,299, the A3000 was clearly not aiming for the mass-market. According to Mahaffey, "The 3000 marks the first step in Commodore's new Amiga product strategy and reinforces our serious bid to capture greater market share within the business, government and higher education markets."

By now, Commodore marketing was fully riding the multimedia wave that was sweeping through the computer industry. *Business Week* covered the event with the headline, "Commodore Plugs into Multimedia". A 12 minute launch video, produced by vocal Amiga champion Keith Nealy, highlighted the multimedia features of the A3000. With computer networks becoming more popular, Copperman also promised "connectivity with ARCnet, Novell NetWare, Ethernet, TCP/IP and NFS standards."

The Commodore engineers in the audience looked forward to delivering their coup with the 68040 board, which would capture the attention of reporters. "We were only the second company on the planet to boot our OS on the '040," recalls Haynie. "We had to get special permission from Motorola to show it; they even hand delivered a 'golden' prototype chip to that event."

Unfortunately, the moment passed and the 68040 board was not revealed. A marketing employee named Keith Masavage decided Commodore had too many unfinished expansion products, namely the A2232, A2410, A2350, and didn't want to announce more vapourware. "Management chickened out at the last moment and left it in a box under the stage," says Nesbitt. "I believe that they didn't want the 68040 board to compete for attention with what they were actually announcing, which was the Amiga 3000."

Once again, the engineers accused Commodore's marketing of shooting itself in the foot.

After the show, Jeff Porter was as busy as ever, doing double duty in marketing. He managed to convince *Byte* magazine of the importance of the A3000. "I personally made sure we got that cover story," he says. Byte ended up putting the A3000 on the front cover of the May 1990 issue, and called it "the most capable multimedia platform you can get in a single box."

Hedley Davis appeared on the venerable PBS show *Computer Chronicles*, hosted by Stewart Cheifet to demonstrate the A3000 on an episode dedicated to the Amiga 3000's multimedia capabilities. Even by 1990, very few television shows covered computer technology. "They called and invited me, and I flew out," he recalls. "They asked preliminary questions before the show. Stuart questioned my tie and the producer said, 'I think it reflects his personality.'"

For the most part, press coverage was positive and all of the reporters emphasised the A3000's multimedia capabilities. Perhaps the biggest complaint was the exceptionally high price (which could run close to $4000 with a monitor) compared to the PC clone market.

The A3000 launch was even better in Europe. The Europeans hosted a developer's conference in Paris, at which Commodore unveiled the new system. "We would have a developer's conference every year in Europe," says Dave Haynie.

Haynie received the ultimate tribute when he met with Jay Miner in Paris. "Jay was invited out to give a talk at the conference," recalls Haynie. "Before then, we crossed paths and never really had anything to say, but when we introduced that in Paris he kind of liked it. I think I actually got a smile or two out of Jay when he saw the Amiga 3000. We had a few dinners together and talked about it."

The Amiga was also winning over a few famous fans, including a popular science fiction novelist. *Amiga World* editor Guy Wright recalls, "I get a letter and I was looking at it and it said, 'something dive shop in Sri Lanka'. I said Sri Lanka? Who the hell? The only person I can think of from Sri Lanka is Arthur C. Clarke. And I open it up and sure enough it was Arthur C. Clarke. He said, 'I've been a subscriber to Amiga World from the very beginning. I have three Amigas. I love your magazine. I think it's great.'"

Video Toaster

On the same episode of *Computer Chronicles* that introduced the Amiga 3000, a true killer app appeared that would cement the Amiga as the leading multimedia platform. After the release of the Amiga in 1985, the concept of a multimedia computer that could play audio and video grew. Incredibly, as all this was happening, the MPEG-1 standard for compressing audio and video was years away. This meant it was difficult to distribute and play videos on a computer. However, something was catching on that allowed users to add computer effects to their tape-based videos.

Third-party developers, along with Commodore itself, had released genlock cards, which plugged into the special video card slot developed by Dave Haynie. However, a company called NewTek was working on the killer app for video editing. Founded by Tim Jenison and Paul Montgomery in Topeka, Kansas, the company had been selling an Amiga video digitizer called Digi View. They later went on to sell the impressive Digi Paint—a program that made extensive use of the Amiga's wide color palette.

In a chance encounter, a friend of Jenison's bumped into an engineer named Brad Carvey, who then introduced Carvey to Jenison. The two talked about making a genlock card for the Amiga that could allow the computer to manipulate real-time images using millions of colors.

Carvey wire-wrapped a prototype board, and the company began developing an application in early 1987. Called the Video Toaster, it allowed users to add wipes, fades, and credits over their existing video.[1] Doing this with video was nothing new, but the price was. What normally cost just under $100,000 could now be accomplished by a video camera, a VCR, an Amiga 2000, and a Video Toaster board for under $5000.

The actual adapter board and software suite was officially launched at the June 1990 CES for $799. When NewTek released the Video Toaster in late 1990, sales of the Amiga 2000 skyrocketed in North America. Finally there was a definite reason for North American users to purchase an Amiga. By chance, the cost of home video recording equipment had also fallen drastically by the end of the 1980s. The product was a hit with small television stations, home video enthusiasts, and companies making corporate videos.

One of these small companies was founded by Jeff Bruette, the ex-Commodore employee who did some of the first genlock effects for Steven Spielberg's *Amazing Stories* in 1986. Like many others, he incorporated the Video Toaster into his productions. "I also did a TV series called *Secrets and Mysteries*," he recalls. "It was a documentary series that covered topics such as the Titanic and aliens and so forth."

The work Bruette performed on the series was a typical case study for Video Toaster users. "Not only did I provide a lot of graphics, but also designed lots of animations that were used for transitions," says Bruette. "Specifically, I would create some unusual animation that started with a black screen that quickly became white. The post production department could use this as a color key, replacing the black with video A and the white with video B. This created a very organic transition appearance that was unique in the industry at that time."

The Video Toaster was capable of producing effects such as the popular 'Star Trek transporter'. The second part of the software package was a full 3D rendering suite (later spun off as LightWave 3D in 1994). This program became popular for modeling, lighting, animating, and rendering everything from professional logos to full movie scenes.

---

1   Brad Carvey is the brother of Dana Carvey from *Saturday Night Live*. It was rumored that Saturday Night Live used the Video Toaster to generate effects for its popular *Wayne's World* skits.

The Amiga 2000 quickly captured the video editing market. "For the longest time, the Amiga was regarded as the machine to do desktop video," says RJ Mical. Major Hollywood pictures used it and its 3D software for special effects. Films such as *Warlock (1989)*, *Back to the Future Part II (1989)*, *Robocop 2 (1990)*, and *Star Trek VI: The Undiscovered Country (1991)* relied on the Video Toaster and LightWave 3D. Science fiction television shows also used the Amiga to render special effects sequences, such as *Babylon 5*, *The X-Files*, *SeaQuest DSV*, and *Star Trek: Voyager*.

The Video Toaster hardware and software bundle was the "killer app" Commodore had been searching for that would allow the Amiga to gain a niche foothold in North America. But ironically, the killer product's hardware would not fit inside the Amiga 3000, meaning customers who wanted to use the Video Toaster would have to purchase an Amiga 2000 or 2500.

A Mysterious Fate: The A2024 Monitor

While Hedley Davis was flying high with the release of his A3000 (and his pilot's license), his previous project continued floundering. The original schedule for the "Hedley HiRes" A2024 monitor called for its release at the end of 1987. But by May 1990, production issues had delayed its release. No one was more disappointed than Dale Luck.

Since 1987, Luck had built up his Boing! company around selling a piece of software called the X Window System for the Amiga Unix operating system (Amix), as well as a three-button Amiga mouse. He had also partnered with Hedley Davis to build the A2024 monitor, which would allow impressively high resolution screens in either AmigaOS or Amix. Commodore had also begun designing network adapter cards for the Amiga in mid-1988, which would be used for networking under Amix or AmigaOS.

It was all coming together beautifully to create a powerful Unix system for a fraction of the price of other Unix machines. And Luck himself had negotiated a deal with Commodore whereby he would include copies of Amix with his X Window System. His X Window sales would also spur sales of the A2024 monitor. The relationship was mutually beneficial but his plans depended on Commodore delivering the products.

However, progress was unusually slow and by early 1989 Luck began feeling frustrated waiting for Commodore to manufacture the A2024 monitor. He told *Info* magazine, "Commodore seems to have learned a few lessons in hardware, but they did make some real mistakes in the past and they continue to have problems. I'm aiming at the workstation market with X Window and many of the machines I'll be in competition with have higher standard screen resolutions than the Amiga. I've been waiting for two years for the A2024 monitor, which has a 1008x800 display. The things that slow up delivery often should have been dealt with at a design or engineering level long before they ever got to manufacturing."

Despite his friendship with Hedley Davis, he obviously blamed the delays on the design of the monitor rather than the manufacturer. "Commodore also has quality control problems which in a proper computer company would be fixed at the engineering level and not patched at the manufacturing level. They don't bite the bullet when they should. They're more into covering their ass than in kicking ass."

Commodore had signed a contract with ADI in 1988 to manufacture 5000 A2024 monitors. However, the problematic design meant that production started and then stopped several times. In May 1990, ADI started again and finally achieved 5000 units later in the year. It also took Commodore until the end of the year to finally produce an updated manual for the A2024 that addressed the new AmigaOS 2.0.

In the end, Commodore chose to manufacture no more than the first 5000 units. As a 14 inch monitor, it was difficult to read the small text at 1008 by 800 resolution, since the AmigaOS did not adjust the font size. "There was this one little problem," says Hedley Davis. "Side by side, the Moniterm implementation was way prettier. It looked great. Everyone wanted that over the smaller A2024 version."

Also, though the image was stable, the text tended to blur when there was movement on screen. "To put a dot on things, the PAL unit sucked," says Davis. "Its refresh rate was really slow, so we used a super long phosphor on the tube to reduce the flicker. It helped a bit, but it was yellow and smeary (mouse trails) and just not that good looking."

And by 1990, the Amiga was becoming known for its color, something the A2024 was not capable of producing. "I think it wasn't really in the mainstream of Commodore's business," says Jeff Porter, referring to gamers. "As a CAD monitor there was no better value for the money. So we all loved it. But the marketing message of the Amiga was 'multimedia'. So that sort of flew in the face of the A2024."

In the end, the few A2024 units that made it into customers' hands were mainly used with A2500 machines and Unix, where a high resolution display was useful for displaying lots of windows.

Amiga Networking Work Group

The other part of Commodore's Unix plan revolved around networking abilities under Amix. In mid-1988, Commodore engineer Ian Kirschemann was finishing off a network adapter for the A500 called the A560, along with a card called the A2060 for the Zorro II port. Jeff Porter had decided to embrace the ARCnet communications protocol over Ethernet, due to the lower cost of ARCnet. In fact, the entire bill of materials for the cards came to only $42, meaning they could sell the cards quite profitably in the $100 or higher range.

By mid-1989, the cards were still evolving with each new board revision. At the same time, a junior engineer named Joe Augenbraun finished off the A590 and A2091 hard drive controllers and was in need of a new project, so Jeff Porter handed him the network cards to finish off. They devised a schedule whereby Commodore would produce and ship 5000 units of the A560 by October 30, 1989. As things turned out, the A560 would finally go into production in early 1991. That was just the way things seemed to work at Commodore.

Amix, which was built upon the Coherent operating system, had no network stack. It was up to Johann George and his group of programmers to implement one. Meanwhile, Andy Finkel and his group would implement a TCP/IP stack to use with AmigaOS, although little more than a network adapter driver came from that effort.

The most coherent effort began with Dale Luck himself, who established the Amiga Networking Work Group at the June 1989 Amiga Developer's Conference in San Francisco. His goal for the group was to make the Amiga a fully functioning partner in a network that included Macintosh, PC, and Unix machines. This included file servers, shared printers, and even an email client.

In the end, Commodore's networking ambitions did not get very far. In 1990, there were not many instances around the world of rooms with lots of Amiga computers. Most Amiga owners had one computer, so the networking abilities would largely be for nothing in the real world. There just weren't enough applications to use the network abilities of the Amiga.

The slowness of getting these products to market affected not only Dale Luck. Henri Rubin had been eager to show this impressive collection of technology to Irving Gould and the board of directors as evidence of his effectiveness. Instead, it looked like Rubin was fumbling many or most projects that he started at Commodore.

The Last Days of Henri Rubin

By 1990, Henri Rubin was beginning to feel pressure from executives, especially from Mehdi Ali. Since he took over from Gerard Bucas, Commodore's ability to complete projects had noticeably diminished. Bucas was able to politely but firmly tell his engineers 'no' when they wanted to add new features, but Rubin allowed feature creep to occur. In fact, he was one of the worst offenders himself.

Some engineers enjoyed working for Rubin, mainly for the freedom it allowed. "[Jeff Porter] and Henri were running [engineering], but Henri was this guy that you had to look after a bit," says Dave Haynie. "He had been an engineer and he understood the engineering process. I was perfectly happy working with him even though he did have his crazy points."

One of the big problems was that the engineers felt demoralized due to the excessive raises given to executives like Rubin.

As an ineffectual leader, Rubin was often the subject of jokes told behind his back. "Whatever top management directed didn't filter down to the level at which things were done," says Bryce Nesbitt. "We were not being led as an engineering team. We as a team disrespected management. Step one in management is that you have to have either respect or control. One of the two! Preferably respect but better ironfisted control than nothing."

An engineer named "Ray" was a particular offender. Many of his coworkers felt he monopolized the NeXT system too much rather than helping them finish AmigaOS 2.0. He even created his own ray tracing program which used the networked Amigas in the office to render animation frames. Impressive as it was, it did not help the other engineers who desperately needed his help. Andy Finkel pleaded with "Ray" to pitch in and help finish off AmigaOS 2.0 when crunch time came.

As the June 18 deadline for the Amiga 3000 ship date neared, Rubin decided to motivate his engineers. Normally, management gave engineers free frozen dinners, soft drinks, and pizza to entice them to stay longer hours. This day Rubin felt they needed spiritual motivation.

According to Director of Software Andy Finkel, Henri called him into his office and said he was going to give the engineers a pep talk. Finkel nervously told his boss, "Henri, I don't think this is a good idea."

Rubin replied, "Andy, I'm glad you agree. Now let's do it!" and marched into the software area. The engineers tore themselves away from their work and assembled around their leader.

For the next fifteen minutes, Rubin gave a rambling motivational speech more suited to a football locker-room, although less coherent. One engineer excerpted part of the talk: "It's always darkest before the dawn, unless you're on the last lap, in which case CD-ROMs are a separate entity, except when they are an add-on to a computer system. But let me make one thing perfectly clear, what I really wanted to say to you…"

According to Finkel, he used every available cliché. "Win one for the gipper. Go for the gold. There is light at the end of the tunnel."

The favorite of the engineers that made it difficult to contain their laughter was, "We need to once again put forth an effort like we've never done before, *again*!"

At the end of his speech, the deflated engineers stood in stunned silence. It was the most uninspiring talk they had ever heard in their lives. After some uncomfortable seconds, Rubin offered his assessment, "I take your silence as a vote of commitment."

Although the engineers departed either puzzled or amused, few realized the situation Rubin faced. Like many executives before him, he felt torn by different demands as his options closed off and Commodore slowly slipped downhill, unable to answer market demands in a timely manner. In desperation, Rubin opted to release Kickstart 2.0 on June 21, 1990, despite only having six hours of QA testing behind it and serious bugs. This decision would spell the end of his career at Commodore.

A Radical New Direction 1990

In the spring of 1990, rumor spread that Commodore was creating a revolutionary new CD-ROM consumer device for the living room, codenamed "The Baby". The potential of the device for mass market popularity suited Commodore because the company excelled at mass-producing consumer goods.

The Baby

The greatest challenge for project manager Don Gilbreath was creating a device that looked less like a computer and more like stereo equipment. Between November 1989 and February 1990, the eventual form factor of the product took shape. "Don Gilbreath was amazing," says Carl Sassenrath. "He coordinated with six or seven Japanese companies that were involved in making different components and parts for the CDTV. And he got it made."

On the outside, the device looked almost exactly like a DVD player, which would not appear until 1995. It was a VCR-sized black box with buttons and a digital clock on the front. Inside, however, it was a regular Amiga 500 motherboard with a CD-ROM drive.

In place of a keyboard and mouse, the system included an infrared remote control that contained audio CD buttons and a flat game controller with two buttons.

During his frequent trips to Japan, Gilbreath became a courier for Gould for something completely unrelated to Commodore. "There were some vitamins that he loved out of Japan, some special herb or some crap," says Gilbreath. "There were times when it's like, 'Hey, while you're there, could you stop by such and such a place and bring back this vitamin?' For a while I felt like I was his drug mule."

When Gilbreath stopped by to pick them up, he saw a window into Gould's complex personal life. "He also seemed to have a whole life and apartment and stuff in Japan as well," says Gilbreath. "She wasn't a spring chicken, but there was a very attractive Japanese woman that was always the source of these vitamins."

Carl Sassenrath, who was programming the system software, collaborated with Gilbreath from California. "I was in charge of the software side of it," he says. "We really had a good time together building CDTV. It turns out that he grew up in a small town that's just south of me and so he knew this area. He'd come out and he'd spend a few days and he'd stay here at the house. We'd work on the CDTV and then he'd fly off to Japan and work with them for a while. He was always flying around but he was definitely an interesting guy. I give him a lot of credit for the creation of the CDTV."

Despite the project taking place outside Commodore's core engineering group, AmigaOS project leader Andy Finkel offered his support, possibly because of his friendship with Gail Wellington. In late 1989 he helped to develop the CD-ROM driver for AmigaOS. "Gail Wellington was there and Andy Finkel got involved in the project really early, helping out from the Commodore side," says Sassenrath.

By early 1990, Finkel had largely finished his part of the project, and the Amiga 500 was able to read CD-ROMs using the "High Sierra" format. Later, developers would built upon this code to implement the ISO 9660 format, which was a more internationally accepted format than High Sierra.

The Baby used AmigaOS 1.3, rather than the most recent 2.0. At its heart was the new file system required to read data from compact discs. Although Sassenrath had known of the project since mid-1989, he only began hands-on coding in March 1990. "The first thing I did when I got on board was I actually had to write the file system for a CD. I wrote the CD file system and really optimized it," he says. "It was a beautiful implementation of the Amiga and it worked quite well."

Sassenrath negotiated his contract with Commodore through Gail Wellington. First and foremost in his mind was that memorable conversation years earlier when Irving Gould asked for his bank account number and said he would deposit any amount in it. Now that Sassenrath was well aware of who was funding the endeavor, he made sure to charge Commodore the full amount for his services.

Sassenrath needed a boot-up screen for his OS and he went to the best in the business. "I had a friend in LA, Werner Randelshofer who had a lot of really talented artists and talented programmers," he says. "They did the user interface for the CD player part of it, the bootstrap screen, and the screensaver. Jim Sachs was one of his friends, so Jim Sachs did the artwork for all of it."

The results of Jim Sachs' work was impressive. Within seconds of turning on the CDTV, it displayed a striking title screen of a laser bouncing off a compact disc. The stylish menu allowed users to choose audio CD tracks or change system settings.

Commodore planned an expansion pack called the CD-1500, which included a black keyboard, a black wireless mouse, a black external floppy disk drive, and Workbench 1.3 boot disks. This would allow users to convert the system into an expensive Amiga 500.

CD Software

Arguably the most important aspect of "The Baby" was the software titles which customers would use in the home living room. Don Gilbreath and Andy Finkel had obtained the hardware needed to write software to CD-ROM discs. "Back then CD-ROMs were really difficult to make," says Sassenrath. "You had to have a $50,000 machine to make a CD-ROM. So he got that all set up and was able to make us CD-ROMs."

Gilbreath had told Gould that Commodore would receive revenue from licensing titles for the platform, similar to Nintendo's arrangement with third-party developers. "We might see somewhere between 25 to 50 cents or more on a per title basis to recoup some of our investment," says Gilbreath. "And maybe there will be an upswing, so we could justify subsidizing the hardware. That was really more the business pitch of this thing. We don't need 4x margins on hardware if we have potentially ongoing revenues."

Commodore would attempt to pioneer an arrangement with software makers that later proved successful for Sony, which relied on a copy protection of sorts. "Commodore wanted to try to pull off this Sony Playstation kind of an arrangement where you had to get certified by Commodore if you wanted to sell your CDTV disks," recalls former *Amiga World* editor-in-chief Guy Wright. "Commodore had the final boot-block proprietary stuff. You had to get that, and the only way to get it was to sign a license agreement with Commodore. That meant if you wanted to mass produce 10,000 copies of your title, Commodore would get a cut."

Wright claims the licensing costs were more than Gilbreath suggests, though not as lucrative as it would be for Sony years later. "You'd have to pay Commodore $5 a piece for those 10,000, whether you sold them or not," Wright says. "Sony had it with the PlayStation. You have to pay Sony a million bucks just to get a license in the first place then you pay them $5 a disc for every PlayStation disc, whether you sell them or not."

Commodore's Gail Wellington, who headed the CATS department, was the key manager to wrangle software developers to the device. "She was really in the developer support team of Commodore, but what was good about that was that she was good at collecting developers who wanted to be part of applications that we needed for the CDTV," says Sassenrath.

Both Wellington and Nolan Bushnell would make an appearance at the June 1990 Amiga Developers Conference in order to beg developers to create multimedia titles. But to acquire software titles from the big companies required individual appeals. "We'd have to get a lot of software titles to make this work," says Gilbreath. "And the only way was to incentivize some of the big guys of the time to even mess around in this media, because they were still using floppy media, which still ruled the world. But there was enough interest in CD media that it didn't take a lot of investments. We literally had contracts with every software group that put a title out with us."

According to Gilbreath, it wasn't difficult to lure companies to CDTV. "If you think about computer titles in that day, a big game might take two or three floppies. There was a lot of stuff to ship," laughs Gilbreath. "So to be able to have a lot of megabytes of data on one disk was very appealing to everybody."

Wellington started her search for CD software developers in February 1990. Given the nature of the Baby, she limited her search to more thoughtful, slower multimedia experiences and skipped over companies that focused on arcade action games. Irving Gould authorized a $5 million budget for development funds to distribute to companies, with Grolier encyclopedia being the big one. The rest of the funds were divided among approximately 35 companies.

Wellington was able to sign contracts with dozens of notable software companies including EA, Broderbund, LucasFilm, Accolade, Bethesda, Interplay, Data East, CinemaWare, Britannica Software (for the encyclopedia), Buena Vista, First Star Software, Aftershock Entertainment, and Argonaut Software—although not all would go on to release software. "Gail Wellington was one of the first inside folks that joined the CDTV team and she knew Trip Hawkins," says Gilbreath. "I remember there was no pushback. Contractually it was a phone call and a piece of paper away."

LucasFilm had released the adventure game *Indiana Jones and the Last Crusade* in 1989 for the North American and UK market. The company was also finishing off a new adventure game called *Loom*. It had plans to release both titles in 1990 for the European market and wanted co-op development funds to release the games as part of a CDTV bundle.

Commodore UK also loved the idea of CDTV and recruited developers in style by wining and dining around 50 developers on May 21 at the Hilton Inn in London. They were able to recruit Animated Pixels, Arcana, SCIT, Next, Music Sales, Multimedia Corp, Mirrorsoft, New Media, Nimbus, Ocean, Virgin Interactive, Format PC, Digita, Psygnosis, Softek, Domark, Mindscape, and US Gold.

Thanks to Wellington, it looked like CDTV would have a healthy stable of launch titles later in the year. However, for the upcoming CES show, there would only be six titles to demonstrate, none of which would be particularly exciting to attendees. This was because the file system was still under development by Carl Sassenrath, leaving little time for developers to get their games in working order.

The Baby Goes Public

By April 1990, Don Gilbreath and his tiger team had several prototypes of the CD-ROM device ready for the summer CES show. Up to that point, Gilbreath's tiger team consisted of a Japanese-based industrial designer named Takashi Tokuda for the case, Steve Kreckman for the hardware design, Carl Sassenrath for system software, and Gail Wellington for developer support.

Now it was time to move the project from Japan back to the USA. All the engineers, with the exception of Tokuda, returned home and moved into the West Chester facility. Gilbreath made sure his group would have a healthy isolation from Commodore's other engineering group within a new division called the Special Projects group. "The special projects section was separate from the rest of Commodore—financially, emotionally, and even physically," says Guy Wright. "We had our own entrance at the very back of the Commodore plant and a small two floor area that had originally been warehouse space."

In order to travel to the cafeteria for lunch, the Special Projects employees had to navigate through the labyrinthine passages of Commodore. "The CDTV group, kind of the skunkworks, was stuffed way in the back," recalls Wright. "We had to walk through all these warehouses and then we had to walk through the factory floor to get to the stairs to climb up to enter into the back of the main building to get to the main offices."

In May, Gail Wellington hired Guy Wright (no longer the editor for *Amiga World*) to create the intro CD for the product. This disk would be included with every system and demonstrate how to use the system so that anyone, even grandparents who had trouble setting the time on a VCR, could use the device. "I ended up in charge of The Welcome Disc project," says Wright. "That was kind of fun and it lasted a long time."

To author multimedia applications, Commodore had its own multimedia suite called AmigaVision, set to be released in early 1990. Unfortunately it did not have CD-ROM support yet. "In order to get The Welcome Disc working, I had to go to a company that had developed their own programming language," says Wright. "It was just one guy and he had written a programming language for the Amiga 2000."

The one-man operation was struggling with the product at the time. "Then he went bankrupt," recalls Wright. "I went to him and said, 'Would you sell it to us? If you can, I need you to modify it to be able to use the infrared remote control, because there were no key traps for different signals coming in.' So he modified the language and I used that to write The Welcome Disc."

Software developers had a hard time adjusting to the new display requirements for CDTV, which would ultimately have to look good on a range of color televisions. "We kind of suspected that there were going to be some problems with it because we first started running into all sorts of problems with the developers themselves," says Guy Wright. "They couldn't really understand the concept. I worked for months with this user interface company. Decades ago I had worked in video on television and there were a lot of rules that we had in television: you can't put yellow letters on an orange background, you can't have more than X number of things on the screen at the same time. You can't do this and you can't do that, because if you're sitting across the living room you can't read it."

Wright came up with his own list of similar protocols to follow with CDTV applications. "We came up with all these guidelines like you can't have drop down menus, you can't have keyboard entries," he explains. "The developers were like, 'What do you mean you can't have keyboard entries?' Because there is no keyboard. I mean they did manufacture a keyboard but nobody was going to have one in their box. So the developers were like, 'Well we'll just have them click on this box.' We'd go, 'Wait, wait, wait. How are they going to click on the box?' They didn't understand the user interface issues because nobody knew exactly whether it was going to be in the living room, or the study, was it going to be a computer? And if it was a computer, they never really did work out how the operating system would be used. How do you save stuff? How do you load files? How do you delete files or edit files? How do you format the damn drive? It was kind of a mishmash."

"Probably the best developers were the British developers," says Wright. "They seemed to pick up on it and to get it."

There were other early additions to the project, including part showman and part marketing expert Nolan Bushnell, the founder of Atari. "He was more of an advisor," explains Andy Finkel. "He was pitching ideas back and forth with Don Gilbreath and Gail."

Not only was Bushnell a well known Silicon Valley legend, he also had experience trying to launch a similar multimedia product in 1985, albeit based on VCR-technology. His system, called the Control Vision, even had two storied games ready that would eventually make their way to CD-ROM: *Night Trap* and *Sewer Shark*. "Nolan was brought in as more of the launch guy," says Don Gilbreath. "They wanted a familiar face."

"Commodore was trying to reinvent themselves," recalls Carl Sassenrath. "They want to be a consumer device in the living room. They want to be back into doing video games mainly and all that fun stuff that was so neat about that kind of market. They were seeing the success of some of the consoles and they needed to have a figurehead to come in who had a reputation for doing that in the past. Who better than the founder of Atari?"

However, Bushnell did not come cheap. "He was paid pretty well for his three or four performances," says Gilbreath. "It was a low seven-figure deal but let's put numbers in perspective. CDTV alone, just tooling and commitments for the first eighty thousand units plus R&D, we were over two million right there. So what's a million for a face in the big picture?"

Aside from the product code name "The Baby", Gail Wellington had come up with the name CDA-1, which stood for Compact Disc Appliance. This name appeared on early prototypes of the system, but the team wanted a final product name before CES. Bushnell hired a company called Fred Meyer Associates to come up with a new name at a cost of $15,000.

In early May, after two days of work, the company presented a new name to Bushnell and Wellington. "We didn't have anything to do with that," says Guy Wright. "One day Gail came in and said, 'Well it's called the CDTV.' All the engineers were looking at each other going, 'What the hell does that mean? Is it color television? Commodore Direct Television?' It's something and it changed with the meaning. It was supposed to be an acronym for something and we didn't have any choice."

Although most people assumed CDTV meant Compact Disc Television, the marketing materials for CES stated it stood for Commodore Dynamic Total Vision. But people started calling it exactly how it sounded: Seedy TV.

Bushnell became the General Manager of Consumer Interactive Products and even visited the developers. "I live in a really small town in northern California and he would come up and visit," recalls Sassenrath. "We'd have some beers and lunches and talk about the design and marketing. He's very marketing oriented. He actually taught me a lot about marketing."

With Bushnell on board, the project began to gain momentum. Later the same month, Gail Wellington and Bushnell hired Tiger Media to produce advertising for CES, along with a PR firm named Rogers and Associates to help acquire mainstream publicity for CDTV. With that in place, on May 8, 1990, Commodore announced it had hired Bushnell.

While development of CDTV took off, the West Chester engineers became discontented. "The engineering team in Commodore were not very happy about the CDTV project," says Sassenrath. "Most of them were upset that it was being done outside of the company. They were not happy that Don had Irving's ear and Mehdi Ali's checkbook and could do whatever he needed to do to get the project done."

CES Summer 1990

At the annual summer CES, held June 1 in Chicago, Commodore lifted the veil of secrecy over the CDTV project. It finally had something exciting to show retailers for the first time since the Amiga 500 had been released in 1987. Lou Wallace, technology editor for *Amiga World*, put it best. "With major technology giants working on some form of consumer interactive CD for years, it is a feather in Commodore's hat that it—and not Sony, Philips or Hitachi—is the first to introduce a product."[1]

Gilbreath had accomplished something the other companies had been struggling with for years. When Commodore had tried to be a follower with Unix, IBM-PC clones, or following Apple into high end systems, it had been a failure. Now it was being a leader once again and in a retail space it was comfortable in. "We were saying look, we're going to be the first to do it," says Gilbreath. "CDTV was pretty much the first integrated CD machine."

---

1   *Amiga World,* July 1990, p. 20. "Exciting Prospects for Amiga CD-ROM"

The effect of the product introduction was more than Irving Gould could have hoped for. Gould, who did not use Commodore's computers, saw the CDTV as his kind of device. He told CES attendees, "It's always been my goal to develop a product that is powerful and exciting but accessible to people like me who find it difficult to use a computer. CDTV is the answer."[2]

The main booth displayed Amiga 500s, IBM PC clones, and even PC notebook computers. Inside a side room, Nolan Bushnell demonstrated CDTV. Unfortunately, most of the software was not quite stable and the CDTV gave three guru errors during one demonstration. "I don't recall it blowing anybody away," says Andy Finkel. "There were some other CD based machines there, like the FM Towns. They all looked somewhat alike, so I don't think it really was a breakout product of the show."

Game designer David Crane had felt that CDTV addressed the largest factor holding back the Amiga as a multimedia device, which was the lack of data storage. "One limiting factor was that the first Amiga system came out with a 3 ½ inch floppy drive, with a capacity of 880 KB," he says. "The Amiga was not really able to shine until it got a CD-ROM. The graphic hardware was ahead of its time. [Amiga 1000] was way ahead of the state of the art of removable media."

Press releases from the show claimed CDTV would launch in November 1990, in time for the lucrative Christmas season. Nolan Bushnell promised over 100 launch titles (a dubious claim). This time Commodore was serious about ensuring software support for its new system.

The press liked what it saw. *Amazing Computing* and *Infoworld*, among others, gave positive coverage. *Compute!* contributor Shay Addams said, "CDTV stands a good chance of finally coaxing the mass market into accepting computers, which hasn't happened so far because 98 percent of the public has trouble setting digital clocks and VCRs. Commodore hopes to achieve that acceptance by getting rid of the keyboard and not calling it a computer."[3]

Unlike prior CES shows, the North American C64 software presence had all but dried up. Most of the 296 commercial C64 games released in 1990 came from Europe, including hits like *Turrican* (1990) and *Creatures* (1990).

---

2   *Amiga Computing*, June 1991, p. 73. "Going for Gould"

3   *Compute!* magazine, "CDTV: The First Wave" (December 1990), p. A-28.

It was the final year of support from long-time North American publishers like Epyx and Activision. Electronic Arts began winding down C64 development and released its final C64 game in early 1991.

Compute!'s Gazette, the mainstay publication for the C64 in North America, was also looking anemic—down to less than 100 pages by 1990. Already at the show, ABC Publishing planned to phase out the magazine later in the year and merge it with the larger *Compute!* magazine.

Irving Gould announced that Commodore has sold 700,000 C64s between June 1989 and June 1990, while selling 550,000 of the more profitable A500s during the same period. It was firm evidence the C64 was in decline and the Amiga was on the rise.

Unfortunately, nothing was shown publicly of the C65. Fred Bowen attended the show and met with Kelly Sumner, David Pleasance, and a delegation of UK developers that included Jez San of Argonaut software, Dave Collier of Ocean Software, and Randy Linden of Readysoft. Sumner was mainly interested in the launch schedule for the C65 and wanted to talk about a new idea for a C64 game system.

CES also marked the final year of Berkeley Softworks' support for C64 GEOS. "We finally stopped distributing it sometime in 1990," says Brian Dougherty. "We sort of technically recognized that we're at the end of the life with what you can do with a 6502 platform. We extended the Commodore 64 life by three years through better software."

Berkeley had a good record of success with the C64. "Between bundling and retail sales, we sold something like 12 million copies of GEOS," says Dougherty, who estimates that he sold two million of those on store shelves and ten million OEM versions bundled with the C64c.

At CES, Berkeley was now focused on PC/GEOS (later renamed GEOWorks Ensemble). The GUI OS found a smaller user base in North America compared to Germany. "PC/GEOS had a big German following and a lot of good German developers," says Dougherty.

Dougherty was going head-to-head with Windows 3.0, which Microsoft released May 22, 1990. Microsoft later released an upgraded Windows 3.1 on April 6, 1992 which dominated the GUI market.

Dougherty also helped Q-Link launch AOL for the IBM PC. "We wrote their original PC client software for them on a private labeled version of our PC/GEOS software," he says. In February 1991, Steve Case would launch AOL for DOS, which used the PC/GEOS interface.

In exchange, Dougherty received AOL stock. "One of my really sad stories was that we at one time owned 3% of the AOL stock which we sold right after they went public because we needed cash at the time. We got a couple of million bucks for what was later worth over a billion."

CES was also a chance to gain more publicity for the Amiga 3000, which was due to arrive in retail stores in July. The most talked about new feature at the show was the built-in progressive scan display to VGA monitors, which reduced eyestrain and produced a clear image. As a result, "We started seeing more productivity software," says Dale Luck.

However, Bryce Nesbitt, regarded as a rising star within Commodore at the time, was disappointed that Commodore again refused to demonstrate the Amiga 3000 running with the CPU accelerator board using the Motorola 68040. "The A3000 had a 68030 and we were peddling, at that point, a 68040 add-on board," he says. "I went as far as I could up the management chain and said we should show this."

Feeling frustrated, Nesbitt laid down a fateful ultimatum. "I said to Jeff Porter that when the decision finally came down the night before and it wasn't going to be shown, I said I'm ok with that, but if we dribble it out in six months or nine months after it's old news, then I think Commodore has lost its edge and I'm leaving." Time would tell if the principled engineer would need to follow through with his ultimatum.

CDTV Delay

By August 1990, Don Gilbreath and his CDTV team continued adding features and defining the CDTV. Nolan Bushnell remained an outside consultant. "Nolan Bushnell was there for a little while, theoretically, but I think I met him three times the whole time he was supposed to be in charge of the project," says Guy Wright. "They basically just hired him because of his name, and I don't think he actually did anything. He sort of showed up, took us out to lunch. Nice guy, then he disappeared and we didn't see him again for another 4 or 5 weeks. He'd show up and ask how it was going. 'Fine, fine.' 'Great, great. Well I've got to get going.'"

In September, Commodore assigned a marketing director to oversee the product launch named Dave Rosen. In an interview to promote the system, he said, "We've taken a Trojan Horse approach by putting computer capabilities into a familiar box."[4]

What would home users do with the CDTV? Not even Commodore seemed certain. Rosen saw it as an advanced audio CD player that could also play multimedia software, educational programs, and of course games. He added, "We don't know what we will be doing with the technology two years from now." Commodore promised it would play videos, once the CD-i (1991) and VCD (1993) standards were finalized.

Even in mid-1990, it was difficult to identify which standards would catch on and which would become dead ends for consumers. In order to hedge their bets, marketing decided to include as many as possible and Gilbreath added a slew of new features to CDTV in August.

Other than the CD-ROM standard by Microsoft, CDTV also supported standard audio CDs. But Gilbreath added a new format called CD+G. The standard was not for video, but rather for still images and audio. "As far as I know, there are only about eight discs that were ever made with CD+G," says Guy Wright. "There's a Jimi Hendrix album that was done in CD+G and a couple others, but it was mainly for karaoke stuff."

The same month, Gilbreath began exploring a digital video format developed by Commodore called CDXL. The format could play short video clips from CD-ROM at resolutions of 160×100 with 4,096 colors at 12 frames per second, including mono audio. "There were a couple of video codecs but they really did suck," says Wright. "We had to jump through all kinds of hoops just to make it appear like it was actually playing video. It wasn't actually playing video, it was playing like animated gifs. That's about all you could do with it."

Gilbreath also started wiring up a prototype PC Card reader. The slot would accept a flash memory board created using Toshiba's new EEPROM chips (electrically erasable programmable read-only memory). In lieu of a disk drive, the flash memory would allow users to save settings and game progress. "In the early days we had an early PCMCIA slot on the front of this thing that was kind of disguised behind a plate," recalls Gilbreath. "For us it was really a game score thing, as opposed to installing games on board like you might have today. Some of the title guys adopted that and used that for highscore things or for bookmarking your favorites."

Gilbreath also asked engineer Scott Hood to begin adapting a genlock adapter for the CDTV. The device would allow users to add credits and simple effects to their videos.

---

4   *Compute!* magazine, "Tomorrow TV" (December 1990), p. 16.

And to round out the multimedia capabilities of the device, Gilbreath added a feature the Atari ST boasted which was missing from the A500. "He wanted MIDI for some reason. I guess he was into music," muses Wright. "That was kind of pointless. I don't think it needed MIDI."

All the additions to CDTV began to make the system more expensive. "The remote control was also kind of expensive because it was custom," says Wright. "Don Gilbreath didn't really care that much about the pricing. He was just sourcing products that he wanted. The memory card reader was an expensive piece and the display was also kind of expensive I gather."

The most costly aspect of the main unit remained the CD mechanism for $137.93 and the elaborate casework, which cost $74.35. At $300, the product would fly off the shelves. At $600, it could be a moderate success. By September, the bill of materials came to $487.62, meaning it would have to sell at retail for around $1200 to remain profitable for Commodore. With such a high retail price, it became questionable whether consumers would spend that much on an unproven product.

As new features were added to CDTV, Commodore's hopes for meeting its aggressive November 5, 1990 release date melted away. At the end of August, the software team met with Henri Rubin to decide what to do. "That was optimistic scheduling," laughs Finkel. "It was an aggressive schedule and sometimes you slip schedules."

Through September and October, CDTV software went through rigorous testing by the QA department. The software had lots of bugs to fix, primarily with developers making incorrect assumptions about user input and display issues.

When the delays started happening, Jeff Porter and Hedley Davis, the two engineers who lost out to Gilbreath earlier due to his optimistic timeline, felt somewhat cheated, especially now that they were supposed to help bring CDTV to production. "There also was some dissension within Commodore, since CDTV was not developed as part of the main engineering group, but by a small separate team," says Gail Wellington. "This resulted in people within the company not giving it their wholehearted support and is, in part, why it was considered a 'crazy younger brother.'"[5]

The engineering groups were physically unable to work together. "They were in a different engineering group and the CDTV was completely separate," says Wright. "I mean we weren't even allowed in the other engineer-

---

5   *Amiga Report International Online Magazine*, May 31, 1997, Issue 5.05. "CDTV Retrospective Update"

ing department. You had to get special permission to go in there. It was company policy and politics."

It is worth noting that the two teams were never hostile to one another. "We were friendly. Everybody knew each other," says Wright. "I knew Porter and everybody. We all ate together in the lunchroom. There was no animosity at all. I knew some of the stuff that they were working on and obviously followed some of the stuff when it was actually shipped."

By November, the plan called for 1500 units to be produced per week, with initial shipments going to Macy's in the US and Dixons in the UK. However, Commodore would ultimately miss the Holiday season for launching CDTV, something which frustrated Irving Gould in particular.

C65: No Direction 1990

The C65 had been proposed in 1987 as an NES killer. For two years it received little high-level support and limited chip development resources. Then when Commodore came to the realization it could not produce a cheaper Amiga 500 in January 1989, the C65 project began to receive management backing as a cheaper A500 replacement. But the new sweetheart project, CDTV, soon captured the imagination of several high-level executives and began to eclipse the low-cost machine.

DMAgic

Back in October 1989, Paul Lassa had convinced his team to allow him to incorporate a simple Direct Memory Access Controller (DMAC) into the C65. When Lassa was pulled away to help finish the Amiga 3000, he wasn't able to dedicate much time to the endeavor. Once his A3000 work was completed, Lassa went back to creating his prototype DMA chip full time.

He also secretly added blitter functions to the chip, unbeknownst to Porter. "I realized that I couldn't replicate the whole Amiga custom chipset but I studied the blitter and its functionality and I determined that I could do maybe seventy percent of what the Amiga blitter did in this very small design as part of my DMA controller."

Lassa made his prototype DMAC, called DMAgic, on a wire-wrapped board with small logic chips. "So I did the initial design of DMAgic on a board like that, and it was around maybe a one-foot square board that would plug into the expansion port on the back of the C65," he says.

Lassa designed a rough schematic for his prototype DMAC by late February and submitted it for PCB layout. By the end of March he had a functioning prototype DMAC on a board. "I was able to work up a demo that showed that it worked. I was able to sell Jeff on the idea of adding DMA channels because it was low risk and sort of a quick design. The key thing being low risk and low cost, low gate count and everything."

The results of his prototype were promising. The DMAC improved performance two to three times, and Bowen expected it would be four times better once he rewrote the kernel code to handle DMA. "We were still waiting on the custom chips, so I got the go-ahead to take my design and tape it out as a gate array," says Lassa.

Paul Lassa was now in a race to complete his gate array before the next batch of 4567 and 4510 chips arrived. As long as his chips were done in time, he would have theoretically not impacted the C65 delivery date.

C65 Game Console

By early 1990, Jeff Porter found his C65 project was in an existential crisis. Commodore UK's David Pleasance had recently been promoted and there was a new VP of marketing. "At that time, the Managing Director of CBM UK Ltd was Steve Franklin, who was successful, and seemingly highly regarded by Mehdi Ali, so I believed that he would not be going anywhere soon," says Pleasance. "I felt it would be better for my career to try to move elsewhere within Commodore."

In January 1990, Pleasance applied for and was appointed General Manager of Commodore International Limited, based in Basel, Switzerland. The division exported Commodore products to 35 countries which had no Commodore regional offices. "This was a perfect position for me, because I am a 'hunter' salesman/marketeer," says Pleasance.

Back in the UK, Pleasance was replaced by a marketing manager named Kelly Sumner. Commodore UK played a vital role on the C65 project because it was its leading supporter. Sumner had decided that what they really needed first and foremost was a C65 game machine to compete with the NES.

Near the end of February. Rubin called Porter into his office and the two tried to see how they could reconfigure the C65 into a game machine. By removing the keyboard and disk drive, Porter was able to bring the manufacturing cost from $100 down to $60. This would allow a retail price of $150. Rubin concluded it was a bad idea to create the game machine because it would not be able to compete head on with the $99 NES. However, they planned to fly to the UK to present the project to Kelly Sumner and discuss strategy.

With the annual CeBIT show approaching on March 13, 1990, Porter instructed his employees to create 10 demo units of the full C65 system with keyboard and disk drive. With Lassa immersed in the development of his DMA controller, it would be a difficult schedule to meet for the week-long CeBIT show.

With only two weeks to go, Fred Bowen began work on some C65 software demos. He also wanted to demonstrate GEOS running on a few of the 10 demo machines and began testing the software. Unfortunately, even though software compatibility was high by now, the GEOS disk copy protection meant that it failed to load. He asked his contractor, Jarvis, to make GEOS compatible with his C65 DOS.

The engineers were also still coming to grips with the latest 4510R3 chip, which worked well and was available by the hundreds. Unfortunately the disk controller chip, a gate array called the F011B, was having problems. With no demo to show, Rubin cancelled the UK trip in order to focus on CeBIT.

As it turned out, Lassa was unable to break away long enough to create the demo units, and Commodore missed the opportunity to showcase the C65 in Europe. However, after CeBIT ended, Sumner continued to push for the C65 game machine and booked a flight to the US for late April to discuss the machine.

Rubin and Porter knew that, with the US region refusing to sell the C65, the UK would play a large role in the success of the C65 and realized they had to keep Sumner happy. On April 19, 1990, Rubin called a meeting with Jeff Porter, Bill Gardei, and Fred Bowen. The team was forced to reluctantly agree that Bill Gardei had been right all along with his original vision for a game system to compete against the NES.

The team discussed ways to create a stripped down C65 game console that could be expandable into a full computer, while minimizing cost and risks. Paul Lassa would be instructed to build a new PCB motherboard for the game console with the ability to accept a plug-in keyboard and disk drive. The DOS and BASIC would come on a cartridge, along with additional RAM. And Lassa would also need to develop a game cartridge board for allowing at least 128 KB of ROM. A Japanese engineer named Itoh Yukiya would be tasked with designing the new casework.

A software strategy was also discussed for the game console. Game developers would be given current C65 machines on which to develop their games, along with 4502 assemblers that could run on C128, Amiga, or DOS machines. The team also discussed ways to sell licenses to game developers for chips that would act as copy protection. And they wanted to improve the console by making cheap Nintendo-like game controllers, and also technology to link two machines together for multi-player games. It was a radical switch to the C65 product definition.

Commodore 64GS

Commodore has famously made decisions that, from the outside, can appear irrational. What is amazing is how rational they can appear when they are viewed within the walls of the company. In late April, Kelly Sumner of Commodore UK visited West Chester to discuss plans for releasing the C65. By the time he left, the engineers would be committed to delivering a highly questionable product.

As the meeting started, Jeff Porter described the new C65 game console they had recently decided upon, and Sumner liked the idea. However, when Porter revealed it would launch in March of 1991, Sumner grew dissatisfied.

He told the engineers that the situation in Commodore UK was urgent. Compared to North America, Commodore UK had an unusually strong relationship with software makers that resulted in a devoted developer community. "Commodore UK, and me in particular, we were the first ever hardware company who joined FAST, which is the Federation Against Software Theft," recalls David Pleasance. "Nobody could believe we paid our subscription and joined them. Why? Because the software companies need to survive and if you encourage pirating and they don't survive, we end up with having machines with no software. It's like having a car with no petrol. It's completely useless."

However, with the rampant software piracy problem on the C64, software makers began abandoning the platform in favor of NES and Sega due to the excellent copy protection of cartridge based games. To keep those developers from abandoning Commodore for the upcoming holiday season, Sumner wanted a new cartridge-based platform this year. In 1990.

Sumner also had to go head to head with Atari, which had released the Atari XE Game System in 1987. The XEGS, based on the old Atari 400/800 chipset, was a moderate success, selling out all 100,000 units in the Christmas 1987 period (it would be discontinued in 1992).

He proposed that Commodore should release a low-cost, keyboardless game system based on the C64. Henri Rubin warmed up to the idea, because unlike the C65, which would cost $150 at retail, a stripped down C64 could undercut the NES in stores. And finally, Commodore could once again have a product that would compete with Atari, Nintendo, and Sega on the shelves of the Kmarts of the world.

Porter and the engineers were less enthusiastic about the product, but they felt they had to appease Sumner since he was one of the few regional supporters of the C65. The key point for Porter was that game developers in the UK should develop the larger 128 KB cartridges so they worked on both the C64GS and the C65. They would be provided with C65 developer units with which to test the new software, although with cartridge backward compatibility already at 100% on the C65, there were no anticipated problems. Then when the C65 computer (with keyboard and disk drive) launched in March 1991, it would have a library of available games.

The plan made perfect sense to those who attended the meeting, to the mass retailers, and to software makers. Unfortunately it made little sense to anyone outside of that circle. "It was a product I openly opposed," says David Pleasance. Why would Commodore go to the trouble of releasing a product in late 1990 only to release an improved product 3 months later? A best case scenario of selling 100,000 units over Christmas was not enough to cause even a blip in software sales. More importantly, what kind of consumer in 1990 would be interested in a system based on outdated C64 technology?

The project showed just how dangerous it was to have an inexperienced marketing manager, Kelly Sumner, calling the shots, who was out-of-touch with the realities of the gaming market. Now Paul Lassa and Fred Bowen would be tasked with bringing the product to market in record time for the upcoming Christmas season. Worst of all, the unnecessary product would further hinder development of the C65.

C65 Prototypes

One year prior, in the middle of 1989, the C65 team had planned to have 1000 developer systems built and shipped by September 1989. Due to multiple chip problems, those 1000 systems did not appear. The team had regrouped and now planned to build the same number and hold developer sessions at the upcoming UK Commodore show September 13-16, 1990. But by mid-1990, it seemed like the team was not much closer to that goal.

True, a lot had been accomplished. Paul Lassa had designed a DMA prototype board, which he was now testing. Many bugs had been worked out of the chipset, although the latest 4567R4 had some minor display issues, such as flickering pixels and sprite display problems on one side of the screen. Backward compatibility with the C64 had skyrocketed so that almost every C64 cartridge tested now worked. Hedley Davis had designed a C65 memory expansion board. And Lassa had designed an external C65 disk drive in matching case, which the engineers named the Commodore 1565.

The fateful decision to add a DMA to the C65 was taking longer than expected, partly because Lassa designed more than Porter had agreed to by adding blitter functions to his circuit board, something he kept hidden. "I put the logic for both into the chip and yet I made the defaults enable just the DMA," says Lassa. "I continued to test out the blitter stuff on my proto board and my simulations, but it was sort of secret."

Lassa felt his blitter additions would be accepted by Porter when he revealed them later. "Time and again, the Amiga engineering group would do things like this of their own initiative," says Lassa. "But for certain things as they neared the shipping date to market, he had to realize that schedule was all important, and you couldn't be messing around with stuff that would jeopardize your overall goal. In this case it wasn't a high-risk maneuver that I did, because I got him to agree to put the socket on the C65 motherboard, but we didn't advertise to anybody that the product needed this. It was simply a significant enhancement that could be ready to go if it worked and if somebody gave it the go-ahead."

After CES, the team felt demoralized for missing yet another chance to show the system. The team desperately wanted Bill Gardei to help Paul Lassa debug and design his DMA gate array, but Gardei, never a team player, said it would make more sense to just redesign the DMA himself. And so he went off and began designing a second DMA chip, which he called ALP (Animation Logic Processor), leaving his teammates wondering how they should react.

With Paul Lassa now learning the gate array design tools, Hedley Davis stepped in and began probing the new revision two C65 boards when they arrived. Because Gardei was uncooperative, Bowen and Davis contemplated pulling in Greg Berlin or Dave Haynie to help put the project back on track. The team felt Gardei was an incredible resource, if only they could get him motivated on the project, and everyone agreed Gardei should be named hardware product leader—except perhaps Gardei himself, who continued his mercurial ways.

Hedley Davis felt the Quality Assurance group should be brought in. But without a DMA chip, it seemed a touch premature. Other executives were indifferent. "Corporate didn't really care, as long as we were getting our other work done," says Gardei.

By early September, Lou Wallace had completed all his graphics code and it was ready to be incorporated into what Fred Bowen now called BA-SIC 10, then burned into ROM chips. The team began preparing demos to show at the World of Commodore show in Europe. Unfortunately, without chips, the demo unit had the unsightly DMA prototype board sticking out the back. The same month, all of the C65 chip developers (with the exception of Bill Gardei) were reassigned to the Pandora and AAA chipsets.

Mehdi Ali wanted the team to interest Commodore Germany in the product, so Jeff Porter brought the demos to them first. The Germans were supportive of the machine but said they wanted developer systems by November with a March 1991 launch date. With Paul Lassa's DMA chip still in development, it was doubtful they could meet that date.

In October, Gardei submitted the 4567R5 chip for production. The 4510R4 was already in production and expected by November, but really 4510R3 was good enough for developer units. All that was missing was the DMA chip and they could have developer units ready in November. Unfortunately, Lassa continued work on his DMA chip, designated F018, and by the end of October the team realized they were going to miss yet another date. Developer units were rescheduled for January.

Feeling despondent as he watched yet another year go by, Gardei became depressed and his work slowed to a crawl. He abandoned his own DMA chip "ALP" and began fixing the long ailing F011B disk controller chip. The team called in Greg Berlin to help with Lassa's DMA chip. Unfortunately, it was the same problem as when they asked Bill Gardei to fix Lassa's chip. The senior engineer said he could only help if he could redesign it from scratch. The team had no choice but to wait for Lassa's chip.

The Gail Problem

Jeff Porter had laid the groundwork for the C65 marketing push, including a plan to attract a large number of launch titles. "That's marketing 101 on how to make the C65 successful," he says. "Get the third party software developers on your side. And how do you do that? By getting the people who work for Commodore on your side to talk to the third party developers."

Porter needed to attract some of the top C64 developers in the US over to the C65 platform. At the time there were many software houses who had made their name on the C64, including EA, Activision, Broderbund, Epyx, Origin, and Access Software. In the latter part of 1990, these companies started embracing the PC world as new video and sound cards made games more exciting. Games such as *Wing Commander* came out that turned the heads of video gamers.

Paul Lassa was excited to see what software developers would create for his new machine. "We've got this dynamite product that's got these great features and everything but it's going to need this support community and especially the developers to develop software and games for it," he explains.

The engineers should have been talking with the marketing department at Commodore to plan a proper product launch. "If you want to create a group effort, you have to have a team that respects each other and works with each other," explains Bryce Nesbitt. "A couple of times I said, 'Let's go coordinate with marketing on that question in the engineering group'. And the answer was, 'It's a waste of time to talk to them.' I don't think you ever want a company where you think it's a waste of time to talk to your own marketing group."

The engineers were more willing to speak to the CATS group, the part of Commodore that communicated with software developers, and Gail Wellington. Unfortunately, Wellington was not supportive of the C65. "I ran into brick wall with Gail Wellington," says Porter. "She was responsible for third-party software encouragement and developers. Gail was on my side 90% of the time when I was at Commodore. That was the 10% of the time that she wasn't."

There were a few reasons Wellington did not support the C65. First, her introduction to the machine in its early stages had been rocky, owing to games failing due to disk protection. "She basically took my C65 prototype, promptly plugged in a 1541, attempted to run every 5¼ inch floppy disk game on it, and said it doesn't work," recalls Porter. "I said, 'No, you missed the point. It's not supposed to work with those damn 5¼ inch floppies. It's supposed to work with 3½ inch floppies. Have your software developers put the games on a 3½ inch floppy and it will work fine. By the way, give them one of the prototypes so they can test it out.' But they didn't do that."

Bill Gardei felt the backward compatibility was acceptable. "Some C64 applications ran well with it, others did not," he says. "It ran about 60% of existing applications flawlessly. About 10% ran acceptably but with noticeable impairments. The rest ran erratically, poorly, or not at all."

Gardei estimates that, overall, his computer achieved 80% compatibility when including BASIC programs. "About 4 out of 5 worked fine. The rest did not," he says.

Paul Lassa speculates that the failure of the 1581 disk drive, and subsequent lack of C64 software on 3½ inch media, hurt the C65. "[The

1581] ending up being something that a user could add in but it didn't have the volume in the marketplace that the earlier 5 ¼ inch software had," he explains. "Amiga caught the wave of 3 ½ inch and a lot of the software library was already at 3 ½. Maybe she perceived the compatibility barrier of the C64 being too entrenched in 5 ¼ inch to overcome."

Wellington also refused to support the C65 because she preferred to back the CDTV project she had co-conceived with Don Gilbreath. "Things at that point were pretty dicey because Commodore was struggling to figure out what the next thing was," explains Porter. "It didn't go very far because the financial situation of the company was not as strong as it used to be. If you don't have the support of the person who is in charge of encouraging third-party software houses, you're screwed."

As a result of Wellington's lack of support, the C65 started to be seen as a second class system compared to the glitzy CDTV. "Full support never really came, especially when there were those who thought we should be putting all our effort into the Amiga line and PC compatibles," says Gardei.

C64GS Released

Throughout the summer of 1990, the C65 engineers worked on the C64 Game System for the UK market. The project was easy to design, providing very little challenge. Fred Bowen made several ROM revisions, including a new display screen if a user turned on the C64GS without a cartridge, and changes to allow 512 KB cartridges.

Because the system lacked a keyboard, the C64GS would come with a two button joystick. This would allow games that required the use of the spacebar or other key to work, once Bowen made changes to the ROM. The joystick chosen was called the Cheetah Annihilator. Unfortunately it was extremely cheap in construction and often broke after mere weeks of use.

In August, Commodore's Braunschweig factory began churning out its first batch of 20,000 C64GS units and would continue making around 20,000 per month for the remainder of the year. With Commodore UK doing so well, having had a 400% increase in revenues since 1987, Kelly Sumner must have felt confident he could move 100,000 units easily that Christmas.

Sumner had been busy. He had corralled over 50 launch titles from publishers including Ocean, US Gold, System 3, Domark, and more. Several notable games were supposed to launch, including *Batman: The Movie, Ultima VI, Space Rogue, Barbarian 3, Turrican 2, California Games, Rick Dangerous 2, Last Ninja 3,* and *Creatures.*

In late September, Commodore UK released the Commodore 64GS. Priced at £99.99, it also included a multi-game cartridge with four titles: *International Soccer, Klax, Flimbo's Quest,* and *Fiendish Freddy's Big Top O'Fun. Zzap!* magazine's preview of the system was largely optimistic about it's prospects against the £80 NES console.

Though it had the same initials as the Apple IIGS, it was decidedly not an improvement over the C64. In fact, it seemed like it was four to eight years too late. Success was not to be, and the console only ended up selling around 20,000 units out of the 80,000 produced.[1]

In a company known for making bizarre decisions, this surely must rank as among the worst decisions it ever made. The biggest error by Kelly Sumner was bypassing input from the consumer marketplace.

Under David Pleasance, UK revenue was up 400% since 1987, yet the flawed launch of an antiquated game system in 1990 would assuredly harm Commodore's reputation.

Still Not Ready!

Bill Gardei had continued working on the C65 chipset revisions throughout the year. "There was never a time after the end of 1987 that I was not working on the C65 chipset," he says. Once the C64GS engineering project was completed in September, the small team was free to continue working on the C65.

In the past, Jack Tramiel assigned 8-bit projects late in the year, with prototypes expected for the January CES. Ominously, Henri Rubin had no apparent deadline for the C65. "I don't think it had a due date," says Gardei.

However, other than the three-man team of Gardei, Lassa, and Bowen, no one else in the company was actively working on the project. Porter calculated he would need an additional six man-months of engineers from within the company to make the C65 production-worthy (above and beyond the existing engineers).

Lassa continued designing the gate array for his F018 chip, which had acquired a new name now that he had added the blitter functions to the chip. "DMAgic started out as the DMA controller and the magic part was the blitter functionality," he says.

---

1   Commodore cannibalized the remaining stock and used the motherboards in standard C64c computers.

In December the DMAgic chip was finally ready for layout. Amazingly, as Christmas 1990 came and went, Commodore did not even show the C65 privately. "The C65 was ready for manufacture several times in my opinion, but we just kept adding stuff to it," says Bill Gardei. "Did we need DMAgic? No. Two SID chips? No. If we had stayed focused on the original product, we probably would have finished it and got it into production."

Bil Herd watched the project sink from afar and wondered what might have been. "I don't mean to sound glib, but I would have handled it correctly," he says. "I don't know sitting here what the correct answer would have been, but I would certainly have figured it out."

Herd's harshest criticism is towards Bill Gardei. "The C65 was doomed to failure," he says. "To begin with, they didn't know what they were doing or how to get there. There was a chip designer [Gardei] who didn't know anything about hardware design. This guy didn't take input and didn't know what he was doing. Freddy [Bowen] tried hard to make it into something and he couldn't push this guy. I've got nothing good to say about the C65."

Part of Herd's frustration stems from his two failed applications to rejoin Commodore and an unrequited desire to take over the project. "I could be accused of being jealous that nobody would let me come back to fix it," he says.

When Jack Tramiel ran Commodore, he gave his engineers deadlines and made sure they followed through. "After Jack left, things were definitely not as good," says Andy Finkel. "Irving really liked toys—computer toys, electronic toys and so on—but he really didn't have Jack's level of understanding of the actual business we were in." Without the force of Tramiel, Commodore's engineers often continued working on and improving their products indefinitely instead of getting them to market. By doing so, they ensured the C65 would become outdated and irrelevant by the time it was done.

Mehdi's Takeover
1990

By early 1990 it became clear to Irving Gould that his good friend Henri Rubin wasn't the best option for advancing Commodore's Amiga products in the marketplace. During his tenure as VP of engineering, Rubin had successfully released expansion cards for the A2000 but scarcely anything else had happened. And the machine they would release any day now, the Amiga 3000, offered only minor improvements in video. Now Amiga's graphics had fallen hopelessly behind the Macintosh and PC clones.

Gould wanted someone with a vision for the future, with the ability to define new technology and execute with authority. He began to look for a replacement for Rubin, and the resulting shakeup would, by the end of the year, leave Mehdi Ali in almost complete control of the company.

Jean-Louis Gassée

In March 1990, Gould spotted a potential candidate for VP of engineering. As was becoming common, he came from a familiar competitor that Gould hoped to emulate. "Jean-Louis Gassée was approached to run Commodore," says Dave Haynie. "He had been the head of technology at Apple."

Gassée had been instrumental in ousting Steve Jobs from Apple by alerting the board of directors about Jobs' attempted coup to depose CEO John Sculley. In the aftermath, Sculley replaced Jobs with Gassée as head of the Macintosh group. In his new role, Gassée wanted to maintain a 55% profit margin on all Apple products, and created a rallying cry of "fifty-five or die" among his employees. He even shut down the Macintosh LC (Low-Cost) project because he favored high-end machines. With his high-priced philosophy, he was a counterintuitive pick for Commodore, where low prices ruled the day.

Gassée both admired and feared Commodore Amiga during his tenure at Apple. "We were really scared of the Amiga," he says. "Fortunately, Irving Gould helped Apple by running Commodore into the ground."[1]

While still at Apple in late 1988, Gassée had joined a consortium of investors interested in acquiring Amiga. "I was involved in one attempt [by] investors to buy Commodore from Irving Gould," says Gassée. The deal involved high-profile investors Mort Meyerson, Bob Kotick (an EA developer who would take over Activision in 1990), and Howard Marks (a billionaire owner of Oaktree Capital Management). With Commodore rebounding due to the success of the A500 and A2000 in 1988, Gould decided not to sell the company.

In 1990 there were rumors of Gassée replacing Sculley as CEO of Apple. Sculley then reportedly attempted to force him out of the company. In March 1990, Gassée announced he would be stepping down from Apple later in the year.[2] According to *USA Today*, Apple employees marched on campus with placards of support for him. Gould saw an opportunity and approached him. "He tried to hire me as VP of R&D in '90 as I was leaving Apple," says Gassée.

According to Dave Haynie, Gassée was enthusiastic about running Commodore. "They wanted him to run engineering," he recalls. "But Gassée knew the history of Gould giving new managers way too little time to effect a real change."

To ensure he had enough time to turn Commodore around, Gassée wanted to run more than just the engineering division. He countered with an intriguing offer to take over as president and CEO of the entire company. "I said no, just let me run the company for 24 to 30 months. We look at the valuation today, we look at the valuation then, we split the difference five ways. You keep four, I get one." If Gassée was successful, both men stood to profit.

There was a high potential to improve Commodore's fortunes because Gassée would be the first person to run the company who had technical knowledge and vision. "A visionary leader has influence throughout the organization. We never had that," says Bryce Nesbitt. "Maybe we would have had a stupid visionary leader who led us astray, but imagine that we have a

---

1   *Amazing Computing*, November 1996, p. 44. "Beware what you say about our beloved Amiga"

2   *The New York Times*, March 3, 1990. "Apple Official Says He Will Leave"

good one and with that amazing team and with our hardware being so far in advance of everything else, we could have done great things."

At Apple, Gassée had regularly gathered together all the employees to share his vision, ensuring everyone worked towards a common goal. This vision was something Commodore had lost by 1990. "There was never a time when we were all herded into an auditorium and given a presentation about the opportunities that are facing the company in the next year or anything like that," says Nesbitt. "None of that happened. We just continued doing our engineering off in our own little vacuum. Even though we loved it, and there were engineering forces that wanted to protect that, it was more like we were building a castle around engineering to prevent management's influence from screwing us up. That's not what a visionary leader does."

But would the Frenchman be a good fit for Commodore? Perhaps he could nurture the high-end systems. And Gassée would be joining other former Apple executives like Harold Copperman and Lloyd Mahaffey, almost making Commodore a second rate Apple. On the surface, this seems like an ill fit. After all, Commodore's strength was in mass market, low cost, high performance computers. Gassée seemed to favor expensive, high-end machines like the $6,500 Macintosh Portable.

Unfortunately, with Gould currently the CEO and Mehdi Ali the company president, Gassée was asking for more control than Gould was willing to relinquish. He just needed a replacement for Henri Rubin in engineering. "Of course, they said no," says Haynie.[3]

But Haynie still favored Gassée over the existing leadership. "It's hard to imagine [Gassée] could have been any worse than having the nineties management team in charge," he says.[4]

Reorganizing

When Irving Gould realized he would not be able to attract Jean-Louis Gassée over to Commodore, he left the hiring decision to company president Mehdi Ali. Since Ali had assumed the title of president, even ordinary engineers such as George Robbins noticed that he was slowly taking control

---

3   Gassée went on to form Be Inc. the same year, in 1990, to make the BeBox. According to Haynie, "[The Commodore talks] got him interested in starting up a computer company and doing in the nineties what Amiga had done in the eighties. That's the catalyst of where Be Incorporated came from."

4   After releasing the BeBox years later, in interviews Gassée nicknamed his computer "Amiga '96".

of the company. For his part, Irving Gould was overjoyed with Ali's leadership and delighted whenever the new president threatened to fire people. Now Ali felt he was ready to make major changes.

One of Ali's persistent observations about Commodore was that the company had lacked an organizational structure since its early days. For example, engineers did not really hold titles and ended up doing a variety of jobs. At any given time, employees like George Robbins could be designing important products like the A500 while also administering the company's VAX machine. Or engineering managers like Jeff Porter could be handling company R&D without really holding the title, while also acting in a quasi-marketing role. Employees just did what they did. Ali was about to change all that.

Some employees doubted Ali knew enough about the company to make structural changes for the better. "You could hire a guy from Pepsi that didn't know anything about the computer business," says Dave Haynie. "A good manager who is hired for that is hired for his management skills. He will come in and learn as much as he possibly can about the business and he will listen to the people who work for him that tell him about what's going on in the business. Well Mehdi Ali thought he knew everything as far as I was able to tell, and the sentiment was reflected by everyone I talked to."

The type of executives and managers Mehdi Ali wanted around him were those who would follow orders. "He didn't really want anyone telling him he was wrong," recalls Haynie. "In fact, you could get fired for telling him he was wrong. He liked people around him who basically did what he told them to do."

The castle Henri Rubin and Jeff Porter had built up around engineering was about to be invaded. The first hint of trouble occurred on Tuesday, May 15 when Mehdi Ali started phoning section heads in engineering and grilling them about the timetables for their future products. He spoke with Ted Lenthe about the new chips, Andy Finkel about the new AmigaOS software, and Hedley Davis about hardware projects.

This was an odd thing to happen at Commodore. Ali had bypassed the normal chain of command, going straight to people below Rubin and Porter. Normally the company's executives did not show an interest in what engineering was doing outside of projects that were ready for release.

Curiously, after Ali was informed of the schedules for each product, he arbitrarily halved the due dates, and informed Copperman that products scheduled for 1991 would be ready in 1990. For example, he claimed the AA chipset would be ready for production by December 1990. The engineers wondered how Ali, someone with no engineering background, had solved the problem of how to deliver products faster.

More alarmingly, Ali told Copperman he should only create marketing plans for products with imminent release dates. The engineers interpreted this to mean that many of their currently planned products could be facing the chopping block. The warning from Harold Copperman alerted the engineers that they could be in trouble, and now they would attempt to hold off Ali's meddling.

Bill Sydnes

Mehdi Ali's background as a company fixer was limited to his understanding of business finances. He believed that to fix Commodore he would need an outsider to enter the organization and examine business practices. Ali had been the outsider who had led to Thomas Rattigan's ousting and now he was running Commodore. But Ali was no engineer. He needed an engineering manager to study the engineering department and discover why products were late and sometimes failing in the marketplace.

One alarming trend for Commodore's PC business was that it was becoming difficult to compete against PC clone makers such as Compaq and Gateway. Irving Gould and Mehdi Ali were anxious to reverse this trend, and decided to bring in some big guns.

In late May 1990, Mehdi Ali hired a former IBM executive, William "Bill" Sydnes, to oversee PC clone development. Sydnes had previously worked for IBM in the battle against the C64 to dominate the home computer market. "Sydnes had been the PCjr guy, which at the time was one of IBM's greatest failures," recalls Dave Haynie.

"He was responsible for the PCjr but he was also on the team responsible for the PC," adds Andy Finkel.

Unfortunately, Ali wasn't aware of his history with the IBM PCjr. "Mehdi hired him to head up PC R&D," says Jeff Porter. "Bill had designed the PCjr but Mehdi didn't know that that computer was a flop. It had a chiclet keyboard. It had incompatible expansion cards and software. Medhi just thought he was the IBM PC guy."

The hiring of Sydnes meant Commodore was taking the PC market even more seriously. "Nobody liked him because he was an IBM compatible guy from the beginning," says Greg Berlin.

On the surface, Sydnes had been brought in to manage the PC division. But unknown to the other engineers, including Jeff Porter and Henri Rubin, Sydnes was actually studying the engineering organization, trying to identify problems. Sydnes was instructed to present Mehdi Ali with a report of his recommendations later in the year. Usually these recommendations would be followed by layoffs while managers were replaced.

Commodore engineer Jeff Frank had headed the PC division but now it was seemingly being taken over by Bill Sydnes. However, the situation would quickly become beneficial for Frank, because Sydnes would come to rely on him to run the PC division. Soon Frank became the newcomer's right hand man, and he was more than happy to reveal engineering's dark secrets, shedding light on what was really going on to slow product development. When it came time to make changes in the organization, Frank might therefore find himself rising to a new position. "Jeff Frank is a very charismatic guy," says Joe Augenbraun. "I like Jeff Frank. But he is absolutely Machiavellian."

In the meantime, as Sydnes studied the engineering group, Henri Rubin and Jeff Porter continued to run it. By the middle of June, Porter wanted to expand his engineering group. He requested 9 programmers for Andy Finkel's Amiga software group, 11 employees for the hardware group, 3 engineers for the chip design group, 3 programmers for the Unix group, 8 employees for QA, plus 3 support employees for engineering services.

Total cost for the 37 new employees would raise the annual budget by $1.635 million, a small drop in the bucket for Commodore's overall expenses, yet it would help Commodore finish products. The employees would require 5,500 square feet of additional office space, and a new catwalk to link QA with engineering. Although the head of the QA department initially approved of the $60,000 catwalk expense, the request was later overturned by Ali while Sydnes evaluated the department.

On June 27, 1990 Bill Sydnes weighed in on an issue with the Amiga 500 network card and support software. Porter sent a message reprimanding Sydnes for his out of line comments, even copying his email to Mehdi Ali, Henri Rubin, and Harold Copperman. Little did he know at the time that Sydnes was being groomed to take over for Henri Rubin.

A day earlier, Sydnes had also surreptitiously requested a full report from Jeff Porter (through Mehdi Ali) of all the products Commodore had in production or in development. He wanted the specification, cost per unit, and dates for pilot production and full product release. It took Porter almost three weeks to compile the report. His final brief, presented to Ali, Gould, and Rubin on July 13, detailed 64 products in active development or production: computers, game machines, mice, disk drives, modems, network cards, expansions, and so on. Porter also listed future plans for products, including a color Amiga LCD laptop.

After reading through the report, it was obvious to Sydnes that Commodore's engineers were developing too many products given the size of the engineering department, and Mehdi Ali had no intention of allowing it to expand. Sydnes recommended giving up the Amiga peripheral market of accelerator cards, memory expansions and networking cards, and leaving it all to third party companies, such as GVP.

He also recommended shutting down the small Lark Avenue Amiga office on the West Coast. He felt Commodore's own internal software engineers were now competent enough to handle changes to the AmigaOS on their own, without help from the original Amiga programmers. On July 20, 1990, Rubin told the remaining original Amiga engineers that they should begin closing down the office. There would be more recommendations to come later in the year.

Laptops

A hot new form factor for PC clones that began emerging in the early 1990s was the laptop computer. Commodore had experimented with a battery-backed LCD laptop in 1985 but had cancelled the project. Now the market seemed ready to embrace the concept.

Bill Sydnes began the Laptop Computer project (LTC) in 1990. However, rather than attempt to design and manufacture his own, Sydnes decided to purchase OEM laptops in volume and rebrand them as Commodore products. He felt this would allow the company to test the emerging market before plunging ahead with actual Commodore manufactured products, while generating extra revenue.

The first LCD laptop would be the Commodore 286LT. The computers were manufactured by Sanyo of Japan in September 1990, the same month the deal was made with Commodore. Underneath the Commodore badge was a Sanyo MBC-17NB laptop. The laptop sold for $2999 at the time. This was followed by the 386SX-LT in April 1991, also produced by Sanyo.

A laptop from this era would not come with a full color LCD display. Instead, it was a mono-display capable of producing blue hues on an off-white background. The display also had a narrow angle of view, which meant the display faded out if you tried to look at it from the top or sides.

Speed Bumps: Round 3

Given all that was happening in 1990, relations between the Commodore engineers and management reached an all time low. Nowhere was this more visible than in the ongoing feud between engineers and site management, the latter of whom performed everything from building maintenance to shipping and security. Since the Speed Bump memo, the feuding became even more heated.

The engineers' request for on-site showers had been denied consistently for years. In the engineering section, the women's restroom was three times larger than the men's, yet there were virtually no women in the department. Porter wanted a renovation to even the size of the restrooms and to create a shower area accessible from both the men's and women's restrooms (lockable of course). This $60,000 renovation request was denied by building manager Joe Mecca.

The final insult to the engineers came when Mecca gave himself his own personalized parking space. According to Speed Bump memo author Bryce Nesbitt, "He had the only reserved parking space in the whole company, and being a modest guy it was spot number one."

The engineers complained to Jeff Porter, who in turn proposed giving numbered parking spaces to 21 of his most important engineers. This was a big request, as not even vice presidents within Commodore had numbered spots—they shared a small VP parking lot out front. Porter's request was denied.

Commodore engineers could not abide the injustice without taking action and they resolved to take away Mecca's prized parking space.

One evening at 2 AM, long after the managers and staff had departed, engineers Bryce Nesbitt, Keith Gabryelski, and Mike Sinz went to work. They removed Joe Mecca's parking sign and replaced it with a handicapped sign they borrowed from a parking lot in the West Chester area. With extreme care, using masking tape, they painted over the orange parking lines with bright blue spray-paint, and even painted a wheelchair icon in the center of the space. It was indistinguishable from the real thing.

The next morning, the engineers positioned themselves strategically so they could witness Mecca pulling into the space. Several could barely contain themselves as the brown Cadillac approached the parking lot, carefully navigating the speed bumps. As he turned into his spot, his car screeched to an abrupt halt.

Mecca swore profusely and began frantically calling departments in Commodore, trying to find out who was responsible. Within hours, a work crew repainted the lines orange, sandblasted the wheelchair icon, and carted off the handicapped sign. The Commodore engineers, who were used to long delays for reducing speed bump sizes, repairing the "Lake Mecca" problem, and installing showers, were amazed at the speed with which Mecca was suddenly able to take care of the situation.

Mecca never found the culprits but he had his suspicions. Among the actual culprits, Bryce Nesbitt had been the most visible with his Speed Bump memo, and Mecca wanted payback for this latest indignity.

At the West Chester headquarters, security was as tight inside the building as it was on the outside—a holdover from how Jack Tramiel had set up operations. "In the Commodore building they would have these black half-domes in the ceiling with frosted glass and there were cameras in all of them," recalls Guy Wright. "There were security doors all over the friggin' place. You had to have your magnetic cards, and some of them would work to go into engineering, some of them wouldn't work."

Under Joe Mecca's management, engineers were not allowed to enter into rooms outside of their own group. In June 1990, the head of security spotted footage of software engineer Bryce Nesbitt in the hardware engineering lab at 2 AM, seemingly unaccompanied.

In a closed and windowless room, Nesbitt was subjected to a two-hour grilling that bordered on physical violence. Although Nesbitt claimed he was accompanied by Jeff Porter, the questioning continued. To Nesbitt, it seemed like intimidation and payback. Although the situation was eventually resolved, Nesbitt, one of Commodore's most dedicated employees, lost his trust in the company.

Top Down Management

Bill Sydnes' report on the engineering department revealed that Commodore had an unusual structure whose setup dated back to its earliest days with Jack Tramiel. Under Tramiel's leadership, the company was very lean, with few middle managers. Tramiel often visited the engineering department and called low-level engineers to his office, where he addressed them directly to keep them on course or motivate them. He was like upper and middle management all rolled into one person.

After he left, Commodore underwent restructuring to hire more middle managers who would guide the different departments, including engineering. But when a financial crisis hit the company in 1986, the middle managers were among the easiest to cut in order to keep the company alive.

Since that time, Henri Rubin had actively repelled management and marketing's influence on his engineers. For all his faults, this was one aspect of Rubin that his engineers appreciated. It had resulted in engineers defining and selecting products from the bottom up. "I think that you hear this from most of the engineers: that management didn't really have an influence on what we did," observes Bryce Nesbitt. "We were unchecked and we were happy to be unchecked, but it's just the wrong thing."

To better understand the existing structure, Sydnes requested an organizational chart from Jeff Porter of everyone in the engineering department. Once again, Porter was unaware that Sydnes was being groomed to replace Henri Rubin, and the request was made through Mehdi Ali.

In the middle of September, Porter presented his organizational chart showing 153 employees in engineering who reported to seven different groups: Engineering Services, Product Development (headed by Hedley Davis and George Robbins), PC Product Development (headed by Bill Sydnes), Amiga Software (headed by Andy Finkel), Manual Development, Product Assurance, and VLSI Development (headed by Ted Lenthe). Unaware of the impending changes to Commodore management, Porter hopefully listed himself at the top of the organization.

To Mehdi Ali, middle managers were loyal people within the organization who reported directly to the president of the company. Their talents lay somewhere between managerial and technologist. It would be their job to work with the employees and make sure they were keeping busy with the projects they were assigned to. They would act as Mehdi Ali's eyes and ears, and sometimes as his whip.

Porter's organizational chart showed no middle management, just practicing engineers as far as the eye could see. Surprisingly, one of the biggest critics of management at the time, the rebellious Bryce Nesbitt, thought managers should have played a more prominent role. "Massive mistakes were made. It was a mistake to let the engineering group run off on its own," says Nesbitt. "There was just a real vacuum in terms of upper management. Either we weren't getting any direction from them, or we didn't listen to it, or it was stupid. None of those three are the things that you want."

The result of four years of this structure was a decided lack of direction or progress. "We weren't iterating on things fast enough," says Nesbitt. "Not every one of Apple's ideas worked out but eventually they started firing on all four cylinders. There was never a visionary leader at Commodore who was in the right position. It wasn't Mehdi Ali. It wasn't Irving Gould. It wasn't Henri. It wasn't whoever came after Henri."

Adding middle managers to the engineering organization was probably necessary to get Commodore back on track. For example, Bill Sydnes had been added to engineering as a manager above Jeff Frank in the PC division. The defining key to whether it would be successful lay with choosing the right managers who were capable, and whether the guy at the top had a true vision to lead the company.

In early October, Henri Rubin was away in Australia promoting the upcoming A3000UX Unix system with Johann George. This meant he was largely out of communication with West Chester engineering and what was happening there. It was the perfect time for Mehdi Ali and Bill Sydnes to begin their takeover of engineering.

Goodbye Henri

Henri Rubin had been brought to Commodore in order to enter the business market. His central plan had been to use the Bridgeboard as a way to sneak Amiga computers into the business world by claiming MS-DOS compatibility. "The stuff that came from management was all really bizarre and most of it didn't really happen," says Bryce Nesbitt.

Rubin also banked on "Productivity Mode" in the new Amiga 3000 as a way to stay current with the VGA capabilities of PC clones. Instead, by mid-November 1990, even Hedley Davis acknowledged to his fellow engineers that the PC and Macintosh had moved far beyond the capabilities of the Amiga line. In a memo to his fellow employees, he wrote, "While the Amiga was first out on the (inexpensive) market with certain interesting capabilities, this lead has rapidly eroded as other vendors have brought the MS-DOS and Mac machines up to and far beyond the capabilities available on Amiga platforms."

He continued, "This situation can be fatal if not remedied. Why would anyone buy an Amiga in the first place? It's not as easy to use as a Mac. There is nowhere near the amount of hardware or software available for the Amiga as on competing platforms. Multitasking is almost impossible to sell. The game markets are largely owned by Nintendo and Sega. Commodore Service is an oxymoron."

The engineers knew they were unlikely to win new business users with the current product offerings. "The Amiga was always a catcher upper, it never succeeded as a business computer," says Nesbitt. "The Amiga never sold in any significant numbers into those markets."

Rubin had also dropped the ball on mass market products. His failure to push C65 developers harder for a timely product release was puzzling. Andy Finkel believes Rubin could have launched the C65 at any time. "No question. Henri was VP of engineering. If Henri had wanted it out, I think it would have been manufactured. It was his call," he says.

Perhaps Rubin was reticent to show the product at CES and promise retailers a delivery date because management did not support the project. "Rubin was always a believer in the C65 but he frequently complained that nobody listened to him," says Bill Gardei. "I know that feeling."

Within Commodore, even executives noticed that Rubin had a mixed reputation among his employees. "He was a doddering old man," says Joe Augenbraun. "A nice guy but a doddering old man."

Employees also circulated several Henri Rubin jokes around Commodore, which reached executive ears. One of his more notorious quotes was, "I don't want a yes man, but I won't take no for an answer."

Marketing aside, Rubin's effectiveness within his own engineering department was questioned. "From my visibility, it didn't appear like he did much of anything," says Joe Augenbraun. "He seemed to have a caretaker personality and things just sort of happened around him. From my perspective, in terms of product direction, it was Jeff Porter."

In November, Gould and his board held the annual shareholder meeting in the Bahamas. The most recent quarterly stock report revealed that Gould had been paid $1.75 million cash for fiscal 1990 and Mehdi Ali had been paid $2,015,949 cash.[5] Despite the hefty raises, this year they felt little opposition from other shareholders because of the difficulty in anyone approaching the board at the private Lyford Cay Club.

By now, Rubin had been briefed on what was happening within the restructuring of executives, so it was no surprise when Rubin was voted off the board of directors at the shareholder meeting.

At the end of November 1990, Mehdi Ali dismissed Rubin as the VP of engineering. However, Rubin was a personal friend of Irving Gould, so it was important it was done amicably. Ali moved him to an inconsequential position in the multimedia division. Some engineers were sorry to see Rubin leave. "He was part of the process and he was a positive factor," says Dave Haynie.

The replacement for Rubin had been preordained since earlier in the year. "He ended up getting Bill Sydnes to come in as like the Nth guy running the company," says Hedley Davis. "This guy is an IBM guy and they put him in charge of everything. If ever there was a guy to find that would believe that the Amiga is not the right thing simply because the IBM PC must be the right thing because 'Oh my God that's what I did,' if ever you could find somebody uniquely qualified to fuck everything up, Sydnes would be your man."

Commodore had a history of executives who did not work out for the company, all hired with Irving Gould's input. To many, Sydnes was perhaps the easiest failure to predict. "Irving Gould did not have any understand-

---

ing of what the business was all about," says David Pleasance. "So they were recruiting people who, on paper, their CV looked good. But they were recruiting them and saying, 'You've got a free hand to do what you want without any direction.' And if you employ people and you don't give them any direction, you have to suffer the consequences, whatever they may be."

Both Gould and Ali probably felt they had hit a home run by securing Sydnes, due to his background with IBM PC computers. Others felt the opposite. "Mehdi recruited the head of engineering, Bill Sydnes, but he didn't know anything about the business," says Pleasance. "And then he recruits a bunch of his mates. What a load of bullshit, it's ridiculous. It's just a great example of the kind of things that were happening."

Sydnes now controlled the engineering projects while Gould and Ali spent their time in New York. "I never saw [Irving Gould] around," says Dave Haynie. "Maybe he came and talked to the bosses and we just weren't involved in that. Mehdi spent a lot of time in New York too and Sydnes was down here doing his dirty work."

On Friday, November 30, 1990, Bill Sydnes took over Commodore's engineering department. Jeff Porter had no choice but to welcome the new relationship, and he passed on his knowledge and plans to Sydnes in the hopes that he might keep some continuity with products.

The same day Sydnes took over, a wave of middle managers entered engineering to head up each of the divisions. A manager named Ned McCook would head up the AmigaOS group. "When Mehdi Ali came in and reorganized, he brought in his own people to head up the top," says Andy Finkel. "Suddenly I got a manager, whereas before I reported directly to the head of engineering."

Most of these managers would be loyal to Mehdi Ali and would follow the direction he set for the company, with one exception. Jeff Porter would become the manager of the Amiga systems group. It was a demotion from his previous title, but hardly one he could complain about. "Jeff had essentially been running engineering for a while," explains Haynie. "Jeff Porter was sort of pushed aside."

Hedley Davis, who had been Porter's right hand man, was also demoted to senior engineer. Those engineers who reported to him now reported to their new middle manager, Jeff Porter.

The restructuring did not happen all at once and would continue into 1991. However, the new layer of middle management loyal to Ali would make the company more political, and those who were not equipped to fight political battles would find themselves on the outs.

The Plus Computers 1990

After Bill Sydnes replaced Henri Rubin in engineering, not all was bad for the engineers. Jeff Porter was now free to concentrate on the Amiga line of computers, and without the distractions of running the engineering group, he would be much more effective. Sydnes brought in his own replacement for the PC division, a well-respected engineer with whom the other Commodore engineers were glad to collaborate. Surprisingly, this new manager would help the team define the new Amiga computers for the next generation.

Lew Eggebrecht

After the shakeup in the middle of 1990, things slowly returned to a new normal. "Eventually Bill became my boss when Henri left," recalls Jeff Porter. "Bill and I never really hit it off but I was polite and did my job."

Another IBM engineer would soon join Commodore who commanded genuine respect from the engineers. In mid-September, just prior to Henri Rubin's demotion, a senior engineer named Lewis Eggebrecht came in to help out the engineers. Eggebrecht, known as Lew, had been the chief architect and design team leader on the original IBM PC, the computer that dominated the business industry. "Lew was brought in as a friend of Bill Sydnes," says Porter. "He was Mehdi's golden boy. I was Henri's golden boy. When Henri left, I was left hanging."

On paper, Eggebrecht was there to give a boost to Commodore's PC clone division. Commodore's board members and executives must have thought their worries about winning the PC marketplace were over. "They mostly OEMed PCs from China and had them rebranded," says Jeff Porter. "Prior to that 'shopping trip' to the far east, Commodore Germany would design PC compatibles and Jeff Frank cost reduced those. Both reported to Bill and Lew, and I was left to do the Amiga."

The difference in respect given to Bill Sydnes and Lew Eggebrecht was stark. "Sydnes came in and I don't think the guy was that smart really, I really don't," says Hedley Davis. "I never saw any evidence other than a guy that he was working with, Lew Eggebrecht, was pretty smart."

Curiously, despite heading the PC division in Commodore, Eggebrecht would remain a consultant, similar to Johann George, who headed the Unix group. Like several others in Commodore, Eggebrecht had a long commute to work every week and only returned home for the weekends. "Lew was like the George Robbins of the IBM PC. He commuted to West Chester each week from Denver," says Porter.

Aside from his duties managing the PC group, Eggebrecht was instructed to help Jeff Porter develop a marketing plan for the Amiga line of computers. He would also study Porter and his engineering group and present his assessment to Bill Sydnes.

Commodore had enjoyed success in the past when its products were closely dependent on the marketplace. Jack Tramiel conducted what he called the "cashbox survey". He would take to CES a prototype, such as a PET or C64, and show it to attendees. Then, incredibly, he would begin taking preorders for the machines even though the product was not ready for production. Because his marketing survey was conducted with real dollars, his survey tended to be a very accurate representation of market demand for his products.

Since that time, Commodore engineering had lost its connection to the market. For the most part, the engineers were making it up as they went along with no cohesive strategy, coming up with machines they would want to use, such as the Unix machines and Amiga variants.

Jeff Porter and Henri Rubin had planned to introduce several Amiga computers in 1991 using the ECS chips and AmigaOS 2.0, including a new version of the A500 in 1990 to replace the aging model, as well as a junior A3000 called the A1500[1] for around $1250 retail. The A1500 was essentially a resurrection of the Super A500/A800 idea that had been spawned in 1987 to fill a product gap between the A500 and A2000.

---

1   Not to be confused with the A1500 by Checkmate which replaced the A500 case with a PC-like case. Nor the A1500 released by Commodore UK which was an A2000 with two disk drives.

They also planned to release a series of updated Amiga computers using the new Pandora chipset, now codenamed AA. The plan called for using the chipset in an A3000 variant, which Porter called the AA3000, for a summer 1991 release. He also wanted the AA chipset in an AA500 by the summer of 1992.

Both Rubin and Gould had been pushing Porter to deliver a cheaper Amiga system since 1988. This goal would continue under Mehdi Ali and Bill Sydnes. Porter was tasked with coming up with an A300, a small Amiga computer in a C65-sized keyboard case that retailed for $300. However, he was having a hard time getting the bill of materials for the Amiga down to the required $120. Instead, he favored the C65 computer, which he felt adequately filled the ultra-low-end computer market.

When Lew Eggebrecht joined the engineers, he was straight with them and tipped them off about the upcoming executive changes. He also warned that they should create a master plan for the Amiga line or else management would do it for them. Hedley Davis gathered the engineers together to try to fend off the upcoming changes from the new management. "Some of us were trying to do management and figure that side of things out," he says. "There was definitely resistance there."

Because Lew Eggebrecht came from IBM, a company renowned for its methodical ways, he wanted to import those practices. Instead of the engineers making prototypes of machines and then showing them to marketing, he proposed something different. He advised Porter to come up with specs for machines and, even before prototyping them, showing the specs to marketing (especially international marketing). They would weigh in on which machines should be built, but not decide on specs necessarily. This approach made sure the engineers decided on the technology while marketing could represent the marketplace.

In November, in preparation for a Commodore International meeting in Frankfurt, Porter developed a company road map for 1991. In it, he laid out plans to create another low-end Amiga 500 to complement or replace the Amiga 500. Porter's initial vision consisted of an improved A500 Plus with the AA chipset for $500, a C65 with keyboard and drive for $250, and a C65 game machine for $150.

While making the roadmap he consulted with Eggebrecht, who offered helpful advice while defining the computers. Eggebrecht felt he should present the regional subsidiaries with a larger variety of low-end Amigas and judge the product based on feedback. "Lew was smart. I'll give him that," says Porter.

Porter agreed that Commodore should sell computers with a wide range of prices for customers with different income levels. He added four low-end Amigas to the list, ranging from a $300 Amiga 200 right up to a $450 Amiga 600.

At the November 9 meeting in Frankfurt, the Germans stated a preference for the A200, the A500 Plus with AA chipset, and the C65. Kelly Sumner of Commodore UK wanted all of the products, although one of his managers felt the cartridge aspect of the A200 would be difficult to pull off. Mehdi Ali felt the A500 Plus should be offered but at the same price as the current A500, rather than dropping the price. He favored the C65 computer over the C65 game machine, and he wanted it released June 1991.

The other indication from the European marketing heads was that they were not interested in the ECS chipset. All they wanted in the new computers, including the new A500 computer, was the AA chipset. And the Europeans insisted that any full-sized Amiga computer, including the cost reduced A1500, should come with a minimum of two Zorro slots.

For the time being, it seemed like Commodore's PC division had received a considerable boost, and with Lew Eggebrecht, Porter now had an experienced mentor to discuss product strategy.

The Plus Computers

After receiving feedback from the European marketing managers, Jeff Porter knew he would have to adjust the specs for his planned Amiga roster. On November 9 he began reconfiguring the existing lineup.

He consolidated the new line of Amiga computers into the "Plus" line of computers, which centered on the upcoming AA chipset, due mid-February 1991. These would include the A500 Plus, the A1000 Plus, and the A3000 Plus. The naming scheme mirrored the previously released Macintosh Plus.

The A500 Plus, due in 1991, would not use the AA chipset. Rather, it would use ECS and the upcoming OS 2.04. Porter had been able to further cost reduce the A500 from just over $200 to only $176. This would allow Commodore to retail the computer for under $500 when it debuted. George Robbins was responsible for the design of the A500 Plus.

Porter also planned to release a sleek computer called the A1000 Plus, which used a faster Motorola 68000 chip, and the upcoming AmigaOS 3.0 with the required changes to handle the AA chipset. He believed it could compete with Apple's low-cost Macintosh LC, which retailed for $2500.

For a while, Porter considered making an A2000 Plus. However, when the A1000 Plus spec changed to include the faster 680EC20 processor, the

A2000 Plus became largely redundant and was cancelled.

The final computer would be an A3000 Plus, which was essentially an A3000 with the new AA chipset and an upgrade to AmigaOS 3.0. This was planned to be the high end Amiga system until the planned A4000 arrived with the AAA chipset, scheduled for release at the end of 1992.

Rounding out the releases would be a cost reduced CDTV and the C65 computer.

All of this sounded good, except for one thing. Commodore was on the hook to release the C65, CDTV, A3000UX, A300, A500 Plus, A1000 Plus, and A3000 Plus all in the same year at about a rate of one new model per month, starting in March. This from a company that had struggled to release a single new system, the A3000, the previous year. As the saying goes, Sydnes had given Porter just enough rope to hang himself.

Auggie

After consulting with Lew Eggebrecht and the European managers in November, Jeff Porter put the A1500 project on hold. He then began to rework it into the aforementioned A1000 Plus, based on the AA chipset. The engineer who had been in charge of the A1500 and would go on to design the A1000 Plus was a young man named Joe Augenbraun.

Augenbraun had a tough start to his career after graduating from the University of Delaware in 1986 with a degree in Computer Engineering. "The year I graduated was just a horrible, horrible year for graduates," he says. "Hardly anyone in my class was getting job offers. It was just terrible and I couldn't get a job."

Given his reckless speeding in the Commodore parking lot, it's no surprise he was also a sports car enthusiast. And at the time, Augenbraun had no choice but to take whatever job he could get. "I always liked Jaguars so I went and got myself a job at a shop that repaired and restored old Jaguars," he recalls. "What else am I going to do? I ended up doing that for a year and for me personally it was an amazing experience."

Working at the garage, lifting hundred-pound motor parts while he repaired engines, toughened the young man in mind and body. Throughout the year, Augenbraun applied for engineering jobs.

In October 1987 he submitted his resume to Commodore. After a while, it happened. "The day that I found out I got the job at Commodore it had just snowed and I was changing oil on a car that day," he recalls. "I messed it up and I had boiling oil on my arm, freezing water dripping on my head and the receptionist said, 'You have a phone call from Commodore.' I found out I got the job. After that, I was thankful every single day I went into work that I didn't have to really work for a living. The level of appreciation I have for people doing blue collar work is high."

From his very first day at Commodore, Augenbraun realized he would be working in a place of chaos. "I had interviewed with everyone except Jeff Boyer. I came in that day and was told I was working for Jeff Boyer," says Augenbraun. Boyer hadn't been informed that Augenbraun would be working for him.

For his first few years at Commodore, Augenbraun worked on side projects under other engineers. "I did the A590 and A2091—the hard drive for the A500 and the hard drive card of the A2000. I did just about every network thing that existed. There was Ethernet, there was AmigaTalk, there were all these weird peripherals I just ended up doing. Bizarrely I actually was responsible for Asian language input internationalization. I don't know how the hell that one happened."

Coming off his difficult previous job, he enjoyed every minute. "The group of people who were at Commodore were the most talented group of people I've ever run across in any company," he says. "I think everyone felt that way. There was a core group of people, including Bryce [Nesbitt], [Dave] Haynie, and George Robbins who were all really involved in keeping things going."

By 1990, "Auggie" as his coworkers called him, was given the A1500 project, an attempt at producing a faster 68000 based Amiga. "No one believed I was ready to do that and I did a demonstration board that showed the double speed processor and how simple it could be," he recalls. "Everyone said, 'That's cool,' and that's when that became a project." Augenbraun even completed several prototypes of his A1500 computer.

As a result, Augenbraun joined the inner circle that ran Commodore prior to Bill Sydnes' ascension. "I didn't perceive myself as a decision maker there but I really was in those late night conversations about what we're going to do for the next product," he recalls. "It was interesting how informal it was. There was no real product manager." That was about to change.

A1000 Plus Design Goals

After Jeff Porter's European meeting, Joe Augenbraun had to convert his 68000 ECS-based A1500 to a new system using the AA chipset. "The idea behind the A1000 Plus was to build something that, functionally, was better than an A2000; it was almost as good as an A3000, but cost just a tiny bit more than an A500," explains Augenbraun. "That's why everyone thought it was an exciting machine."

The new system was true to Commodore's roots of producing high-value electronics for an affordable price. By 1990, the computer-in-a-keyboard design was seen as something of a relic, even for home computers. Users wanted a product that looked like a real computer, with a detachable keyboard, but without the high cost. And with the new AA chipset, it would be superior to the A3000 in graphical capabilities.

Jeff Porter had initially conceived an A1000 Plus in early November 1990 with a $350.42 bill of materials using a 16-bit 14 MHz 68000 processor and two Zoro II slots. However, Augenbraun countered his proposal with a more powerful 32-bit 16 MHz 68EC020 and a single slot for $351.96. "My original concept was it was going to have one expansion card so it was supposed to just have an edge card connector on the end of the board, not the male one that an A500 had where it needed special peripherals," explains Augenbraun. "A female one so it could just take a regular A2000 [Zorro II] card. And it would have a hard drive interface built in."

However, Porter favored two Zorro II slots, based on the feedback he received in Europe. "It was really supposed to have one card but it grew to two cards," says Augenbraun. "Jeff really felt strongly that it needed two cards and I was resistant because of cost. We did a riser card which annoyed me because it was another 20 bucks in cost."

The A1000 Plus would reside in a "pizza box" form factor case, similar to the one used by the original A1000, minus the keyboard garage. The likely inspiration came from the Macintosh LC, which also used the pizza box form factor (which in turn might have been inspired by the Amiga 1000). When Commodore's regional offices heard of the new system, they began waiting in anticipation. "The idea was it was a baby A3000 at a delta price point over an A500," explains Augenbraun. "It was supposed to be a $1000 computer. We were thinking we would ship with a hard drive and everything. My recollection is the higher end ones were $2,000, plus into the $3,000 range. And this was meant to be $1,200, that kind of thing."

Although Commodore placed numerous engineers on its high-end machines, such as the A3000, the money-making low-end machines had barely any engineers assigned to them. The A1000 Plus would have only Augenbraun to design the PCB and gate array chip. "It was me. That's the way Commodore worked," says Augenbraun. "I did the chip for it."

However, Augenbraun was ideally suited to the task. "I am the rare engineer who loves cost reduction," he says. "For me it was all about cost. One of the big battles was if the hard drive should be SCSI or ATA [IDE]. ATA was cheaper, it saves a chip. But there was just this fetish for SCSI. Performance for SCSI is actually lower. But there was sort of a brand with the Amiga at the time on SCSI."

If the AA chips arrived on time, Augenbraun expected to release his A1000 Plus by the end of 1991.

Amiga 3000 Plus Begins

The previously released A3000 had been well received critically by consumers, other than its disappointing graphical improvements from the ECS chipset. Jeff Porter knew he could remedy that deficiency by replacing it with the AA chipset, plus some new features to enhance its multimedia capabilities.

Greg Berlin and Dave Haynie began work on the first system planned for the AA chipset, the Amiga 3000 Plus. "It was an Amiga 3000 with the AA graphics and with the DSP coprocessor," says Haynie.

Haynie even planned to allow a faster 68040 chip running at 25 MHz. "If I had the time and support to get it in there I wanted the 68040 instead of the 68030," he says. "With a few small modifications to the sheet metal, it was going to drop right into the A3000 casework."

Commodore hired the services of a former Bell Labs employee who had helped design the DSP3210 chip that Haynie wanted to place in the A3000 Plus. "Commodore contracted me to work on the integration of that for the next generation Amiga, which ended up becoming the Amiga 3000 Plus," recalls Eric Lavitsky. "My partner at Commodore on the project was Randell Jesup."

The DSP chip would aid in multimedia encoding and decoding, as needed by current and future multimedia digital formats like JPEG and MP3. "There were a lot of people at that time interested in mostly digital audio with the DSP," recalls Lavitsky. "That was of course the big thing that people wanted to do. AT&T internally was part of the working group that was working on all these portable audio standards."

Berlin, Haynie, Jesup, and Lavitsky would continue working on the A3000 Plus throughout the year with an expected late 1991 release date.

Amiga 500 Plus

Back in July 1990, just as the A3000 was going to market, Jeff Porter submitted his proposal for the next generation A500, which he called the A500 Plus. This new system would update the original A500 with the ECS chipset and the new AmigaOS 2.0. Porter estimated this new system would cost $193 per unit if manufactured in West Chester or $212 if manufactured in Braunschweig—about on par with the costs of the original A500.

Porter assigned the project to George Robbins, the caretaker of the low-end Amiga computers. Robbins' design improved on Porter's by adding a full megabyte of memory to the A500 Plus. He also added an onboard real-time clock and battery, something which the original A500 did not include. He retained the original A500 motherboard name, B52/Rock Lobster, for the A500 Plus.

However, Robbins barely advanced the project throughout 1990. By February 1991, Bill Sydnes wanted to know the timeline for the new computer. As it turned out, the project had been delayed waiting for the new R5 Agnus chip, which would be capable of addressing 1 MB of memory.

Initially slated for a January 1991 release, the A500 Plus motherboard finally entered PCB layout on April 24, 1991. The good news was that component prices had fallen by then, and the total bill of materials only came to $191.73. It looked like Robbins might have the A500 Plus ready for launch by September.

Jeff Porter and his engineers had successfully released the A3000 in 1990 and had settled on the three main computers in the Plus line, two of which would use the AA chipset. And this time they had received input from the marketing and sales people who would convey those computers to Commodore's customers. It seemed like the next Amigas were on solid ground, but as history shows, most of the Amiga Plus computers would never make it to production.

CHAPTER 23

Fiasco 1991

While hardware development was finally back on track within the Amiga engineering group, the Amiga software group was about to get a shakeup. A damaging oversight had occurred while developing AmigaOS 2.0, one that lay dormant but was about to reveal itself to Commodore in all its ugliness.

But first, Mehdi Ali had one more change to make to the upper echelons of Commodore before he could have full control of the company.

Advertising

Despite the lackluster results from 1989's massive advertising push with the Steven Spielberg produced Amiga television commercials, the executive board approved Commodore US president Harold Copperman's budget for more advertising in 1990. The push included television ads that were remarkably similar to the ones used against Atari in the early 1980's.

One advertisement shown in 1990 was a play on the Chinese proverb, "Give a man a fish and you feed him for a day. Teach a man to fish and you feed him for a lifetime." It went, "Give a kid a video-game machine and he can shoot down a plane. Give a kid a Commodore Amiga and he not only can shoot down a plane, but pilot one, design one, and write an essay on the history of aviation." It concludes, "There are no scholarships for video games."

The Commodore US team, headed by Copperman, also created CDTV ads. Although the blitz would be unleashed in 1991, they would use them at the upcoming January 1991 CES. The ads were Apple-like in their elegance, featuring music and images and no voice over, stating, "Amiga CDTV. It's nothing short of revolutionary."

Copperman also had a plan to put Commodore back into the software business, something the company had abandoned in 1985. CATS had already lined up three promising software titles for the new software business to launch: a word processor called *AmigaWord*, a presentation program called *MetaSlide*, and a spreadsheet program called *Maxiplan*.

Copperman needed a research specialist to help plan the new business. Mehdi Ali encouraged him to hire John C. Maxwell III[1], a research specialist and VP from Dillon, Read and Co. where Ali formerly worked. In a demonstration of just how much money executives could throw at a project, Maxwell would charge $130,000 for merely writing the business plan, plus an extra $50,000 to add staffing and financing issues, an additional $100,000 to set up the business, and an equity position in the new Commodore software company.

Copperman went against Ali's recommendation and instead hired Barbara Schultz, a former president of Peter Norton Computing, in October 1990. Schultz offered to write the business plan for the relatively bargain price of only $35,000 for one month's work.

It was clear that Copperman was in a rush to establish the new division. His contract would expire in May 1991 and he needed to increase Commodore US's bottom line before then, leaving him little time to enact a turnaround. Irving Gould and his executive board was losing patience once again. In late 1990, Gould laid off six high level executives. The Copperman team was in trouble.

Copperman Gone, Layoffs

In the fiscal year ending June 30, 1990 Commodore US lost $17.7 million on sales of $259 million. By the end of the calendar year the division was heading for a loss of $24.7 million on sales of $192.8 million. While Europe's revenues were going up, Commodore US was going down.

On January 4, 1991, Irving Gould and Mehdi Ali dismissed Harold Copperman as president of Commodore North America, even though his contract was supposed to expire May 1. Under Copperman, the company had learned that spending five times as much money on lavish advertising did not have a positive impact on US sales, seemingly due to a lack of product distribution.

---

1   Not to be confused with the more famous John C. Maxwell, a Christian pastor, author and motivational business speaker.

Gould and Ali also laid off around 90 employees from the 600-person West Chester staff, mostly in manufacturing, the failed education division in marketing, and sales. Copperman's aforementioned Commodore software company never had a chance to get off the ground. As a business analyst noted to the *Philadelphia Inquirer*, "I didn't think they gave Copperman enough of a chance. Every program he started was just coming into fruition. If (Copperman were) given another year, I think things would have changed dramatically."[2]

Dave Haynie feels Gould was too impatient. "Nobody lasted too long," he says. "The job you were given in any of those positions, whether you were head of all of Commodore or head of US operations, was that you had to turn it around in a year. If you didn't do that, Gould was going to fire you and bring in the next guy. But it was a three year job."

Gould also felt that Copperman, who disliked low-end mass market consumer products, would not be right for the year Commodore was about to launch the CDTV and C65. Jeff Porter, who derisively referred to Copperman as "Coppertop", could not have been more happy.

To avoid one year of severance pay for prematurely terminating Copperman, he was "promoted" to the position of vice president of Commodore International, in charge of the multimedia division. "There was this running joke that when you were promoted to be the head of multimedia that meant you were fired but you weren't actually fired," says Haynie. Copperman resigned shortly thereafter.

Gould replaced him with James Dionne, an 11 year Commodore veteran and president of Commodore Canada, one of the company's most successful subsidiaries.

Dionne had his work cut out for him. A sure sign of the dismal state of the Amiga in North America came when *Compute!*, the magazine spawned by Commodore PET users, no longer provided coverage of the Amiga. Instead, the February 1991 issue of *Compute!* coverage fell squarely behind the PC.

When Dionne took over, he instituted new policies that he hoped would improve dealer satisfaction. In March 1991, he introduced on-site warranty service for one year, with optional three year warranty extensions. He also created a 1-800 number called Commodore Express to handle product support calls. And he introduced a leasing program for Commodore's more

---

2   *Philadelphia Inquirer,* January 14, 1991. "Commodore VP Resigns"

expensive Amiga products. Finally, dealers would be informed of upcoming products and price changes in advance. As with most moves by Commodore's executives in this period, it was already too little too late.

January 1991 CES

At the January 1991 CES in Las Vegas, Irving Gould had good news to announce. The C64, which had experienced a decline in sales the previous year, had an uptick and sold 800,000 units in 1990. This unexpected good news was the result of the recent German reunification. East Germans had heard a lot about the C64 but, unable to purchase one, a pent up demand had developed. When the wall fell, those relatively impoverished East Germans rushed out to buy the computers in large numbers.

At the CES show, Commodore debuted Greg Berlin's Amiga 3500, which marketing had renamed to the Amiga 3000T. "There was an A3000T in between [the A3000 and A4000]; the A3000 Tower," says Berlin. "The A3000 version we put into a big monster case with lots of bays and lots of expansion ports. It was a big monster expandable version of the A3000."

The A3000T used the Amiga 3000 motherboard but added a larger 200-megabyte hard drive and 32 megabytes of RAM within a large tower case. Commodore marketed it as a high-end graphics workstation and sold it for just under $5000, in a clear departure from its low-cost consumer origins.

Unfortunately, Commodore found out NewTek, the company that made Video Toaster, was not happy with the Amiga 3000, which had began appearing in quantity in the latter half of 1990. Both Hedley Davis and Jeff Porter spoke to NewTek representatives, who claimed the ECS chipset in the A3000 was "broken". NewTek also claimed their connectors didn't fit, the A3000 power supply was too wimpy, and they had not yet received a CDTV developer unit. Something would have to be done.

Once again, the most exciting Commodore product at CES was CDTV. Both Irving Gould and Nolan Bushnell gave speeches. Gould laid out his vision on the product, while Bushnell touted the technical aspects of CDTV. Afterwards the two, along with Gail Wellington and VP of consumer sales, Bob Larsen, hosted a Q&A session.

The new design included MIDI ports, a memory card reader and a black remote control with a grey trackball in the middle for controlling the mouse pointer. Commodore employees demonstrated CDTV's MIDI capability by creating music with a full sized synthesizer keyboard plugged into the back of CDTV. Commodore even promised the CDTV could play full motion video using the upcoming MPEG standard. "It was a fairly hot product for the time," says Andy Finkel.

At the time, 20% of US homes had computers, while 75% had VCRs. Some investors believed CDTV could capture space in the VCR market. Rumors spread about a possible Commodore takeover by Hewlett-Packard, Apple, Sun, and even Disney. None of these rumors panned out, but they helped the stock price.

Despite CDTV missing the Christmas period, Commodore stock went from a low of $4½ in October 1990 to around $11 by early 1991, the highest since Rattigan departed. "I'm not sure if that's what drove the [stock] price up, but once you showed [CDTV] to somebody it could really get some excitement going," says Finkel.

At a suggested price of "around $1000", the pricing for the CDTV actually seemed reasonable compared to a multimedia PC with video card, CD-ROM drive and sound card, which Bill Gates himself estimated would cost just under $2000.[3]

The 50 launch titles were fewer than the 100 Commodore had promised, but many were impressive. Most were direct Amiga ports by Maxis, Cinemaware, Domark, Accolade, Psygnosis, and Interplay. Disney delivered classic stories and educational titles for children.

To market the CDTV, Commodore produced an infomercial on videotape for distributors. It emphasized reference libraries, like Grolier Encyclopedia, World Atlas, the King James Bible, a dictionary, and the complete works of Shakespeare. It also prominently displayed educational and children's titles. The infomercial even touted genlock capabilities, explaining how CDTV could add titles and screen effects to home movies. It seemed promising to Gould that he might have another hit on his hands.

All was not positive, however, as the new Commodore US president, James Dionne, received an earful from his dealers at the show, who felt the company was not treating them right. "A lot of people were becoming disenchanted with Commodore," says Dale Luck. "I know lots of stories that Commodore did not treat their distributors and dealer networks very well, even after Jack Tramiel left. I had a good friend in Texas who started an Amiga dealer and they would purposely double ship him. He would order four monitors and eight would show up and they would charge him for eight! And he couldn't send them back. They played a lot of games that wouldn't go over real well."

---

3   *Amiga World,* July 1990, p. 6. "Chief Concerns"

Aside from this abuse, dealers complained the company was not keeping them informed of new product release dates or even shipping them product when they asked for it. This particular Christmas season it was difficult to obtain C64 computers because of the unexpected East German demand, and many dealers who had 20 or more backorders didn't have them filled.

Amiga owners also complained that many of their favorite titles were not working with the new AmigaOS 2.0 operating system. During development of the new OS upgrade, Commodore had not done enough testing with software or requested feedback from developers using beta copies of AmigaOS 2.0.

AmigaOS 2.0 Incompatibility

Ever since the release of AmigaOS 2.0 the previous year, there had been an ever increasing flow of reports of incompatible software by customers. By the end of 1990, Commodore's software engineers had tested over 250 Amiga applications, including games. Although most worked well, many did not. "Kickstart 2.0 was a reliability disaster," recalls Bryce Nesbitt. "It was bad. It had compatibility problems and it crashed a lot."

Incredibly, some of the software Commodore planned to bundle with the Amiga 500 did not work with the new system. "One of my early jobs at Commodore was to track down why individual pieces of software, including stuff the marketing department was bundling, didn't work with 2.0," says Nesbitt. "So here we were on the threshold of releasing 2.0 and the Amiga 500 at that point was being bundled with some software in various countries around the world that didn't work with 2.0! That doesn't make sense!"

Amiga developers, some from top software companies, began complaining loudly to Commodore, including Electronic Arts, Accolade, Activision, NewTek, Psygnosis, and Broderbund. Within the company, Amiga OS 2.0 was regarded as a fiasco.

When the scope of the problem became apparent, the new Director of Systems Software, Ned McCook, wanted answers from Andy Finkel. Due to the rush to get the software out the door with the Amiga 3000, the final release version had only received approximately 6 hours with the QA group, resulting in serious bugs. "The 2.0 process didn't have a very good strategy for ensuring backwards compatibility," says Nesbitt.

Nesbitt, a stickler for details, soon replaced Andy Finkel and took charge of creating a new revision of Amiga OS. The entire software group would work with developers to solve the incompatibility problems. "I was the technical lead at that point and focusing largely on reliability," says Nesbitt.

Theoretically, there should have been no software compatibility problems with OS 2.0. Most software worked, including early Amiga titles like *Mindwalker*, so long as programmers used the software library properly. "In each library there was a pointer to the library that was public," explains Nesbitt. "Below that were all of the public methods that you could call to open a window, close a window, and do various system operations. These were all public functions."

Unfortunately, due to an earlier misstep by Commodore-Amiga, software developers cheated by using off-limits methods. "Above this pointer was a data structure that was internal to the library," explains Nesbitt. "The original Amiga team made what in retrospect really was a big mistake. They released the set of internal registers."

This caused many titles to work only with the earlier Amiga operating system. "The older software authors throughout the Amiga community began depending on writing to the internal memory locations of the libraries," says Nesbitt. "People were depending on a data structure that never should have been public. That created a world of hurt for us in terms of trying to move the operating system forward."

One by one, Commodore's software engineers researched the root cause of bugs in each title. "I would go and track down why *Deluxe Paint III* or *Castle Master* or whatever the game was wouldn't work on Operating System 2.0," recalls Nesbitt. "Invariably I discovered it was some stupid bonehead move on the part of the authors of the software rather than something that was the fault of the operating system per se."

However, rather than blame the software makers and drop the issue, Nesbitt wanted Commodore to take responsibility. "I changed the culture from, 'It's their fault' to 'But we deal with it.' So we began to put hacks into the operating system to make old software run, starting with the software that we were actually, as a company, selling," he laughs. "But sometimes we couldn't do it and I ended up being the liaison with lots of companies, saying, 'Hey, we need you guys to produce a new version of this game that fixes this horrible thing that we can't support anymore in Operating System 2.x.'" Nesbitt planned to have the fixes done in time for the release of the Amiga 500 Plus, which would attract mostly games software.

A Teenaged Hacker's Story

Bryce Nesbitt was seen by management as a rising star. He was also fondly regarded by his coworkers—the dependable engineer with a quirky sense of humor who also organized everyone to play volleyball after work. "Bryce had gotten into Commodore as barely a highschool graduate," says fellow programmer Michael Sinz. "He hadn't even started college. He was very bright, somebody who liked getting things done. Sometimes that was working around things you were supposed to be prevented from doing."

At Commodore, Nesbitt worked hard to bring the different groups together. "Commodore was a series of fiefdoms," he says. "I was the weird engineer that said, 'Hey let's go ask marketing that question!' Oh man, was that an unpopular stance. Engineering people said, 'We never talk to the marketing people. Oh my God! Why would you do that? They're complete idiots.' That was the engineering attitude. And I said, 'Well, maybe they're idiots but let's go talk to them. Maybe we can work something out.'"

Under Nesbitt, Commodore's AmigaOS software team gained a reputation in the company. "As good as the hardware team was, I think the software team was even better," says engineer Joe Augenbraun. "The hardware and software guys had a lot of respect for each other."

Bryce Craig Nesbitt was born in Berkeley, California in the summer of 1966. "In the last year or two of high school I fell into computers with the Commodore 64," he says. "I'm pretty sure that's what I could convince my parents to buy me. The Apple II's were a lot more expensive."

The teenaged programmer soon found work with a local company called HesWare, which wanted to port an arcade game called *Rootin' Tootin'* to the C64. "You had a little character that blew musical notes into ghosts," says Nesbitt. "It was extremely derivative of Pac-Man and I was hired to port that to the C64. I went to Hes' offices in downtown Berkeley every day after school and worked on this game. That's the game that taught me programming."

The C64 had a major deficiency, namely a slow disk transfer rate due to a bug in the 6522 chip. "Rather than fix the chip, the people at Commodore went and implemented a data transfer entirely in software and it was just incredibly slow," Nesbitt recalls. He felt he could speed up the transfer rate with a product of his own. "While still in high school, I created a product called *1541 Flash!* for a company called Skyles Electric Works."

The company was founded by Bob Skyles, who had once worked with PET inventor Chuck Peddle at Commodore. "He founded Skyles Electric Works in California down in Mountain View and produced a series of add-ons for the PET and then the C64," says Nesbitt.

Nesbitt's first attempt to speed up disk transfer rates was not very user friendly. "I did the whole thing, the hardware and the software," he says.

"*1541 Flash!* was a hardware modification. You disassembled your drive and you disassembled your computer and you put a new cable between them."

If Nesbitt seemed different from other teenagers, it might be because of a condition he was not aware of at the time. Nesbitt had high functioning autism, the type commonly known as Asperger syndrome.

Sometimes his condition made for awkward social interactions. Working for Skyles, Nesbitt was able to visit CES. There he bumped heads with Bil Herd as he unveiled his C128. Nesbitt was surprisingly blunt in his critique of the new computer, resulting in Herd calling him a "little punk". "In the computer world, when you see a bug in a piece of software, you can fix it," explains Nesbitt. "In the social world, when you see an ill or just somebody doing something wrong, you can't always fix it. You can't always tell them that they're doing their job wrong as I apparently did at a certain CES regarding the Commodore 128. That's an Aspie move. That's a marker that I was exhibiting Asperger's characteristics at the high school age. I just didn't know it."

Nesbitt's quest for perfection and attention to detail eventually drove him to find an easier way to speed up the 1541. "Later I realized that, through a tricky technique, you could actually do this all in software," he says, referring to a ROM chip replacement. "I found a way to do it in software and offered it to Skyles. Skyles turned it down because they didn't want it to cut into their successful *1541 Flash!* business."

Rejected by Skyles, Nesbitt and a fellow high school student named Bruce Hammond formed a company in Gazelle, California. "I went up and worked with StarPoint Software and did a couple of things with them, including an improved software only disk speedup utility, which is how I came to have a falling out with Skyles Electric Works."

The company produced magazine ads for the utility, which he called *Star-DOS*. "We paid this local artist to do this little fire logo thing," he recalls. "I'm pretty sure I did the write-up with Bruce Hammond. We took out an ad in *RUN* magazine."

The irreverent ad showcased Nesbitt's unusual sense of humor. "STARDOS. MAKES GREAT COFFEE! The 1541 is the slowest disk drive on planet earth." After listing all the StarDOS features, it ends, "(Oh, by the way, we lied. STARDOS makes <u>LOUSY COFFEE</u>)"

When Bob Skyles saw the ad for the competing disk loader, he immediately objected. "I released that on my own, precipitating a disagreement over whether I was allowed to do that or not," recalls Nesbitt. "A lawsuit ensued and it was never settled. We had a falling out and I ended up getting stiffed on my royalties for *1541 Flash!*"

Although not a breakout hit, Nesbitt sold thousands of units of Star-DOS for the C64. Then another product caught his eye. "I'm working on StarDOS and the Amiga comes out," he recalls. Soon Nesbitt realized StarPoint Software could undercut Commodore's expensive A1050 memory expansion. "They wanted a lot of money for that and we produced a lower-cost memory expansion for the Amiga 1000. It was half the price of the official one and it worked perfectly. It sold like hotcakes."

Nesbitt's unusual humor was expressed right on the PCB of his memory expansion, which was covered with pictures and writings such as, "I'm schizophrenic and so am I", "Hello hackers", "Kilroy was here", "Humpty Dumpty was pushed!", "Electrons go this way", and "Today's winning lottery number: Pi".

As a developer, Nesbitt filed bug reports directly to Commodore-Amiga through CATS. "Here I am producing a product for the Amiga and I'm filing bug reports with Commodore. That's what attracted their attention to this high school kid," he recalls. "I didn't apply. I just got a physical letter inviting me to a job interview in West Chester, Pennsylvania."

Nesbitt was hired as a software programmer with a salary a little over $40,000. By the time he was tasked with fixing AmigaOS 2.0 his pay had risen to $53,000. And even though he loved the company, he became a critic of Commodore. "We did say at Commodore, very frequently, that before shooting itself in the foot, Commodore would first put its foot in its mouth," he laughs. "It's amazing actually how negative the engineering staff was about the company. We were all fanatically working many hours and very dedicated to our jobs, but the break-room talk about the company was negative all the time. I don't know how that works. Why were we there if we hated the company so much?"

AmigaOS 2.04

After the release of AmigaOS 2.0 on June 20, 1990, the Amiga software developers mainly concentrated on fixing bugs rather than focusing on compatibility issues. These fixes continued all throughout the remainder of 1990, through versions 2.01, 2.02, 2.03, and finally the beta release of 2.04, at which point Nesbitt felt they had addressed all of the outstanding bugs in the operating system. CATS sent this beta release to around 1,500 developers, who were given a cover letter indicating, "Test now or forever hold your peace".

After the January 1991 CES, Commodore felt the full impact of incompatibility issues from users. Nesbitt's technology group began compatibility testing in earnest, booting up hundreds of software packages under the 2.04 beta. The QA testers recorded the failures and attempted to classify the type of incompatibility for each failure. Where possible, the Commodore programmers made changes to the OS to correct the problem.

CATS also contacted the top 25 developers and worked closely with them to resolve problems in the OS. In some cases there was no possible fix for the OS, in which case the developers had to patch their software code instead.

Finally, on March 19, 1991 Nesbitt had a final Beta release of 2.04, which was sent to developers and the different Commodore subsidiaries in Europe. They were given three weeks to thoroughly test their Amiga software with the beta and report and problems to CATS. The team looked at and considered every bug report from developers.

Working on Amiga OS 2.04 became a defining period in Bryce Nesbitt's young career. "I've worked with a lot of other people in a lot of other places and there's good people all over, but the average was higher at Commodore," he says.

Nesbitt was a natural choice to create order within his group. He could identify what was wrong and attempt to address it, regardless of the social implications. "Anyone who's high function [autism] can pass as normal for a long time," he says. "There's problems that come up and you're frustrated because somebody else or some other process isn't working right and you know you can fix it. A normal person is just going to realize the political cost of doing that and the Aspie is going to want to fix it because it's wrong."

Nesbitt managed the OS 2.04 team in an almost bureaucratic way, thinking in terms of policies. Near the end of development of OS 2.04, Nesbitt instituted a lockdown on new code. "We had a new policy called stability period," he recalls. "Several of the Amiga releases were hacked on the night before they were released to the public. Changes were made and sometimes those changes had unintended effects. The idea of the stability period is that if they didn't survive at least two weeks without our needing to make a critical bug fix, it wasn't ready for release to the outside world. The idea was to make less bonehead mistakes in the last days before the thing was released."

Managing via policies also allowed him to control his people and even those in other departments. "We had a quality assurance group. The QA group was in a different portion of the building and they were not drawn from the same high caliber of engineering," he explains. "But they were our QA department. We're working on 2.04 and at one point I go down and talk to them and I say, 'Wait a minute! This computer that you're typing test results into is running the old Kickstart. How come?' And he says, 'Oh, well we found some unreliability problems in the file system and so we were worried about losing data by using the new Kickstart.' This is the QA group!"

Slightly outraged, Nesbitt created a fix. "That's when I instituted a new policy that the QA group was going to eat their own dog food," he says. "If there is a hard drive crash then they could recover it from backups. Basically the hard drive crash should occur to the QA group first, rather than to a customer."

Nesbitt's policy changes resulted in not only a more polished release but lasting changes to the software group. "This was just like somebody on a playground with the big whistle going, 'Tweet! It's time to clean up. Time to stop opening new cans of paint or whatever. Let's put our tools away, let's make everything neat and work.' And it happened. Those specific policies were really helpful but the whole fact that there was a policy tells you what the goal was and everybody got behind the goal. And that was a good thing."

On May 23, after Nesbitt implemented his strict criteria for changes to the code, the final ROM image for Kickstart 2.04 was created. Now the team would only attempt bug fixes to Workbench until close to the release of AmigaOS 2.04.

Ned McCook, the manager of the Amiga software group, recognized Nesbitt had put in an extraordinary effort. He also knew Nesbitt was seriously underpaid and requested a pay raise to $60,000, retroactive to January. He also requested a bonus for one of Nesbitt's programmers, Peter Cherna, for $3,500. It was becoming clear to McCook that Nesbitt was a shining light within his group.

NewTek Fiasco

After Hedley Davis and Jeff Porter had a conversation with NewTek's Tim Jenison at the most recent CES, they began to realize the company founder was not happy with Commodore, despite the success of his Video Toaster product for the Amiga 2000. "The Video Toaster was an add-on video processing device and it was selling really, really, really well and it was causing a significant fraction of the Amiga sales," recalls Bryce Nesbitt. "But Video Toaster did not work with OS 2.0. NewTek announced they would not support 2.0. This was a crisis."

Commodore desperately wanted the Video Toaster for the Amiga 3000 (which only used OS 2.0) and would lose sales if it did not work. Jeff Porter, Hedley Davis, and Bryce Nesbitt began communicating with New-Tek's management and engineering staff to work out the problems. Nesbitt mailed out new revisions of Kickstart and Workbench to NewTek. However, the company still seemed perpetually disgruntled at Commodore even through March, complaining about problems such as the physical difficulty of making the card fit into the A3000 with its smaller backplate.

By April, with no support yet for the A3000 and sales of Video Toaster skyrocketing, the situation became dire. Porter decided NewTek needed hands-on support. "I was flown to Topeka, Kansas in order to sit in New-Tek's offices to get the Video Toaster to work on 2.0," says Nesbitt. "My official mission was to be the engineering liaison and go there and grind through all the problems."

Once there, Nesbitt realized the problems with the A3000 were not really technical in nature. NewTek was like any other company and needed to be able to reliably plan out what it would work on every year. However, Commodore had sprung the Amiga 3000 on developers without giving them time to develop for it. "Companies like NewTek felt unsupported and unloved," he says. "The reason that they refused to support Operating System 2.0 was much more a social thing than a technical thing. It was just they weren't getting the level of attention from Commodore corporate that they felt they should, given the number of Amigas that they were selling."

With Video Toaster so vital to Commodore's success in North America, Nesbitt was determined to do anything to make the relationship work. "Eventually we had to come to an agreement to provide whatever grease necessary to get it to happen," he says. "I solved it and I had a good rapport with the engineers there and Tim Jenison."

NewTek was finally happy, but Jenison saw the value of having a Commodore engineer on his team and tried to lure the young programmer to stay. "They took me to a strip club and tried to hire me," says Nesbitt. "That was certainly my first strip club at that point." Nesbitt politely declined the job offer and returned to West Chester, with NewTek ready to attempt Video Toaster for the A3000 (although it never released the product).

Quelling Small Rebellions

Although Nesbitt's policy changes were largely followed by those in the company, a fellow programmer named "Ray"[4] rebelled against the change. "Ray wouldn't upgrade to the new operating system," explains Nesbitt. "I was in charge at that point of quality for the operating system and the project was actually in trouble. It was not stable and my job was hell bent on making it stable enough to actually release. If we weren't ready to run it on our own desktops, it wasn't ready to be released to the world. And Ray was a holdout. He'd locked his office and he said that he wasn't going to upgrade."

Nesbitt knew he would have to make Ray eat his "dog food", otherwise he would lose the respect of his employees. "He didn't want to run 2.0 because he didn't like some of the things that we did in 2.0 to support backwards compatibility," explains fellow programmer Michael Sinz. "So he still ran the 1.3 system on his machines."

The employee was smart and creative but inflexible to the point that it bothered those around him. "He had his way of doing things and he was very against doing backwards compatibility work for it," says Sinz. "It had to work his way or not at all."

Predictably, the attitude that everything had to be done his way made him unpopular. "Ray was not universally liked among the engineering staff," says Nesbitt. "He was a prima donna."

Nesbitt felt it didn't set a good example to allow employees to decide which policies they would follow. "So Bryce, Peter, and I said, 'Well we've got to get him onto this,'" recalls Sinz. "So Peter hacked together a version of Intuition in 2.0 that looked just like 1.3. When it booted, you'd swear it was 1.3, until you looked at a few things which were obviously features that didn't exist in 1.3. But otherwise it was running just the look and feel of 1.3 with all of the code of 2.0 and we built the ROMs for all his different machines."

The side project became a team effort. "We all got involved," says Nesbitt. "Every one of the software engineers and a couple of the hardware engineers contributed a piece to this. The Amiga team in Los Gatos contributed some code. Jim Mackraz was involved because he was the UI guy. Everyone was in on it but Ray. It was awesome."

---

4   The name "Ray" is used throughout this book to preserve his anonymity.

The engineers were of course intensely curious as to how long it would take Ray to discover the deception. "This was so evil that there was a betting pool in the office with a substantial amount of money in it," recalls Nesbitt. "I would say just about everybody put money in it."

With the fake OS complete, the next challenge was to install everything on Ray's computers, a difficult problem due to the engineer's high level of mistrust of his coworkers. "Ray locked his office and booby trapped it," says Nesbitt. "He also booby trapped his computer so that he would know if anybody touched it. And more than anything, this is what caused him to be a target. If he had just been sort of a refusenik and an asshole, it wouldn't have been half as much fun to bypass all of his locks, enter his cubicle through the ceiling, disassemble his computer, reverse engineer all of his locks, change his ROMs, boot it up, and then exit. That's why we did it."

The day after the covert operation, the engineer returned from a short vacation. "We must have had a mouse cable not quite in the right position because he came in and he said, 'Somebody's been in my office.' He closed the door and looked around on his computer," laughs Sinz. "He couldn't quite tell what was up but it wasn't quite exactly the way he expected it to behave, which is true because 2.0 was different. He thought that somebody may have done something to him. So he went and wiped his machine and started restoring from backup. Of course that didn't solve the problem because the OS was still the same."

"Dave Haynie and I were having a discussion about the new CPU architecture and we were standing by the coffee machine," recalls Sinz. "He was drinking coffee, I'm drinking water and talking about this. All of a sudden we hear this yell out of Ray's office and he runs out, slams the door shut, and leaves the building without talking to any of us."

It turned out Haynie had won the betting pool. "Dave Haynie was so casual too," laughs Nesbitt. "We were all hanging around the notice board and we hear the scream and Dave Haynie doesn't miss a beat. He casually lifts his wrist, speaks the time and says that he's won the pot."

Although Amiga OS 2.04 was well tested and ready for release by the end of May, due to Commodore management, it would take a surprising number of months before the software would be released to users.

Amiga 3000
1991

George Robbins was the engineer of Commodore's most profitable computer, the Amiga 500. He was also preoccupied with administering the company's VAX machines. In early 1991 his life was about to become a lot busier. Unfortunately, progress would be slow due to some intriguing distractions.

A300 Project Begins

Ever since late 1988, Commodore had toyed with different ideas for an ultra-low-end Amiga computer, even cheaper than the A500. For a while, George Robbins worked on an A250 game system, expected to cost $250 at retail, but it was cancelled when management realized the marketing and cartridge manufacturing costs were too high.

In late 1989, facing pressure from executives, Jeff Porter made another attempt at a full Amiga, again called the A250, this time with keyboard, mouse, and floppy drive. To reduce the cost, he was forced to cripple the abilities of the system by including only 256KB of RAM. The projected cost came to $162.83, meaning it would retail for around $400. However, because most games required 512KB, Commodore's engineers realized users would be unhappy with the result.

Then when Bill Sydnes took over engineering, Porter again began feeling pressure to develop a lower cost Amiga. The instincts from Commodore's executives were probably correct. Much like the C64, the A500 had launched around $600. But C64 sales really went into overdrive when Commodore lowered the price to $300. "There's some magic price points in consumer electronics," explains Porter. "And if you can get it down to $299 you can sell twice as many as the $499 price point. You've got to hit the magic price point."

The problem with the A500 was that it already was cost reduced. The A1000 started around $1295. Looked at proportionately, it seemed like the most Porter could hope for was something in the $400 range. And the Amiga packed in a lot more computer compared to the C64, with 512KB memory, a built in floppy drive, a mouse, and a very sophisticated operating system. The task was formidable to say the least.

Even though Porter was in charge of the engineering group, he remained Commodore's best engineer at cost reduction. He gamely took on the task, searching for even miniscule cost savings that might add up to something significant. After all, when it came to cost reduction, Commodore was among the best in the industry. "At Apple, I looked at the competitive analysis of the Amiga 500," recalls former A500 engineer Bob Welland. "What struck me was how far off they were. They were off by close to an order of magnitude. It cost us $14 for all three chips and they thought it was a hundred something dollars. They thought we couldn't make money at the price we sold it at."

By December 1990, Porter felt the answer to cost reduce the A300 was to shrink everything. He decided to removing the numeric keypad on the keyboard, reducing the total keys from 96 to 76.

Porter also had to decide how expandable to make the A300. The original A500 had a Zorro interface that allowed a large degree of expansion through sidecar products. This allowed third party companies, such as Great Valley Products, to create expansion devices for the A500.

Porter wanted something a little sleeker to fit the smaller A300 motherboard, which would allow software makers to supply games on a cartridge. He found a new standard called PC Card developed by the Personal Computer Memory Card International Association (PCMCIA). IBM, Microsoft, and Intel were already members of the association.

PC Card (known then only as PCMCIA) used a thin slot for credit card sized expansion devices. The primary use for the interface was for ROM cards, SRAM cards, and Flash ROM cards, although other devices like Ethernet cards could also be connected.

The PC Card slot was a natural fit for the A300's goal of reducing the motherboard size, replacing the large and unwieldy expansion port on the A500. In early April of 1991, George Robbins began researching and implementing PCMCIA into the A300.

Due to the lack of an expansion port, the computer could use a smaller low-cost power supply. Porter also reduced the size of some of the connectors, allowing a further reduction in size of the motherboard.

But there was one other thing he could do to make the PCB smaller. All of Commodore's computers up to this point had used the standard through-hole resistors, transistors, and capacitors. These parts were inserted through holes in the PCB. Now he would explore a radical new technology that Commodore had no prior experience with. This new technology allowed parts to be soldered directly to the surface of the PCB without holes. It was called Surface-Mount Technology, or SMT.

SMT components had a smaller footprint than through-hole components, which meant the A300 could have a much smaller (and cheaper) PCB. All these changes meant the casework for the A300 would also be smaller and therefore cheaper. And it would not compromise on performance, with the A300 using the same ECS chipset as the recently released A3000.

Porter initially estimated the A300 bill of materials would be $40 less than the A500, coming in at around $150. This would allow a retail price of around $400. Now all Porter had to do was hand off the project to George Robbins.

George and the Internet

The A300 project initially had one engineer assigned to it, or more accurately, half an engineer because he was also assigned the A500 Plus. "George Robbins was working on a cheaper computer, which we were calling the A300," says Dave Haynie. Robbins named his A300 circuit board June Bug, after the B-52's song, *Junebug* (1989).

Porter had an aggressive schedule. He estimated samples of the A300 could be ready by July, ready for testing and debugging, with mass shipments to customers following in September 1991.

With veteran Robbins at the helm, the project had a good chance of succeeding, provided he could tear Robbins away from his other obsession. Robbins spent a lot of his time administering the VAX systems within Commodore. "George got very interested in system administration and we were a huge node on UUCP (Unix-to-Unix CoPy) relaying news," recalls Joe Augenbraun. "Commodore was a really important node because George put a lot of effort into it and that's where he spent most of his time. He had done the A500 and then he didn't do much for Amigas. He was just sort of doing system administration stuff, keeping the VAX running and keeping us connected, which at that time was kind of a hard thing to do."

Eric Lavitsky, who was helping Dave Haynie on the A3000 Plus, grew accustomed to seeing Robbins in the computer room. "He practically lived at Commodore," recalls Lavitsky. "The lights were always off, it was completely dark, and the air conditioning was so loud. I think they were blasting music over some speakers just to try and make it sound a little bit more normal. It didn't matter what time of day or night you went to Commodore, George Robbins was always there."

There was one very important technology emerging that, surprisingly, Commodore was slow to adopt. "In the world at that time, we weren't connected to the Internet directly," recalls Augenbraun. "I had an account on an Internet machine back when I was in college and it was hard to get one. There weren't many machines on the Internet back then. So actually to me, Commodore's setup was a step backwards."

Throughout the eighties, people referred to the Internet as "The ARPA Internet". The culture of the Internet was much different then, with a strict policy against anything of a commercial nature.

Back in December 1989, Robbins began researching methods to connect to the Internet, which ranged from hooking into the regional Pennsylvania Internet connection to using a dialup modem.

In order to gain access to the Internet, Commodore would need an Internet Protocol (IP) address assigned by the DDN/ARPANET Network Information Center located in Menlo Park, California. First Robbins had to convince them Commodore belonged on the network, something that was easy for companies with government contracts. However, Commodore had very few government contracts to speak of. Instead, Robbins applied on the basis that Commodore sold Unix machines and needed Internet access to help develop those machines. It worked, and in January 1990 he received an IP address and registered the Commodore.com domain name.

Robbins then began trying to drum up management support for a permanent connection to the Internet. He wanted to provide Internet access to every one of Commodore's 175 machines on the Ethernet network, plus the smaller ARCNET network. Robbins partnered up with Johann George in the Unix group and received a favorable response from management. They authorized him to purchase a router from Wellfleet, an early competitor of the dominant router maker, Cisco.

Now all he needed was a line to connect Commodore to the Internet. Unfortunately, this is where he ran into a brick wall. None of the managers wanted to dedicate a portion of their budgets to leasing a line that would be used by the rest of the company. Robbins considered creating a fake outage to the Newsgroups, knowing that managers also used the service, and then blaming the outage on the lack of an Internet connection. He quickly abandoned this plan. Then Johann George attempted to add the cost for a 19.2 kbit/s or 56 kbit/s line to his budget. Unfortunately the request was denied.

All was not lost, however. Even though real-time access was denied, Robbins was able to establish access to that killer Internet app called email. He could receive emails sent to grr@commodore.com. "It's strange that Commodore didn't just get on the Internet," says Augenbraun. "I guess it was because George could just make UUCP happen. We could email to the Internet and the Internet could email to the UUCP."

The best Robbins could arrange was a dialup connection to a service called Tymnet, through a lousy 1200 baud modem. This meant Internet access was only directly available from select machines within Commodore. In late 1989, Bryce Nesbitt wrote to Tymnet, a San Jose, California based company, to upgrade the local Pennsylvanian node to 2400 baud, giving the connection a lot more speed.

By March 1991, as the A300 project was ready to begin, Robbins was attempting to have management approve of a $2500/month T1 line connected to a service called Alternet. Unfortunately, all of this meant Robbins was almost too busy to bother with the A300 project.

Auggie to the Rescue

George Robbins was understandably distracted by his attempts to get Commodore onto perhaps the most societally-changing piece of technology ever to come along in his lifetime. "When the A300 came around, he was sort of half-assed on it," says Joe Augenbraun. "My recollection is Jeff Porter was working to get George engaged in it. Jeff was the one who came to me and he said, 'Look, we need some mass behind it so it gets some momentum. I'd like you to work with George and do whatever needs to be done. Just keep this project rolling.'"

Augenbraun was waiting for samples of the AA chipset to complete his A1000 Plus prototype. With little else to do, he accepted. "I said, 'Okay, I can do that.' So for me, it was sort of like taking one for the team because at that point I was running a major project by myself," he says.

Robbins' life at Commodore was an eye opener to the young engineer. "You want to talk about an odd bird," laughs Augenbraun. "George lived in the office. He had what a lot of people called the front porch, which was the office part of his office. The back one was the nest where he lived, which was a double office next to my office. You couldn't walk in there. It had a bunch of junk and it had a sleeping roll, and that's where he slept. This was his home."

However, Robbins still occasionally returned to the other place he called home. "He had lost his driver's license and he lived like an hour drive away. He would bike back to his house once every few weeks, but that was something like 40 miles away."

Robbins' house, filled with old mainframes and server equipment, was equally eccentric. "He bought an old train station," recalls Augenbraun. "It was way out in the sticks. We were asking the question, 'If you stood out there with baggage, would the train stop and pick you up?' And he thought it was probably true."

To fuel his hacking exploits with the early Internet and news servers, Robbins relied on a daily supply of Dr. Pepper, cupcakes, and other nourishing substances which he picked up from a local deli. During his long bike rides,

Robbins took an interest in the New Garden Airport, which was close to where he lived. He realized he could cut his trip shorter by flying from there into the airport right next to Commodore's headquarters. After talking with Hedley Davis, Robbins soon obtained his pilot's license and began weekly flights.

In order to stay in shape and improve his locomotion around Commodore's vast halls, Robbins adopted a new hobby. "He decided he wanted to learn how to roller skate so for a couple months he was just on roller skates," explains Augenbraun. "At first he was unsteady on roller skates. You would see George in the lab and he would roller skate to his office and roller skate back."

Robbins was committed to his new sport and even posted messages to roller skating newsgroups in an effort to improve. He also attended different roller skating rinks in the Philadelphia area three to five times per week, usually for the public skating, but sometimes roller dance and freestyle. Other employees, including Eric Cotton, also picked up the sport of roller skating through Commodore's halls.

Robbins had few issues with Commodore's previous management, but when the former IBM executives took over engineering, there were some cultural clashes. "Basically it was all just like, 'Well that George Robbins guy is a slovenly engineer. What the hell? Clearly based upon your dress, you people don't know what you're doing,'" recalls Hedley Davis. "It was bad."

Augenbraun had to subtly pull Robbins along on the A300 project. "I was George's junior sidekick on this thing and I took it very seriously," explains Augenbraun. "It was absolutely a subservient role. Basically my job was to do the chip verification. George was doing this chip and I saw I could back-lead by doing the verification on the chip. I could be George's customer and force him to his timeline by saying, 'Hey I need to test this part of the chip, when can you deliver it to me? I've got test vectors all written for this piece. I'm ready to go, can I have it by Tuesday?' That kind of thing. I was just doing test vectors. It was just horrible but it was about a six month project."

The SMT Struggle

By early April 1991, Jeff Porter had received a more accurate list of SMT part costs and realized his $150 estimate on the A300 had been too optimistic. The cost of SMT parts was slightly higher than through-hole parts in 1991 (though prices would drop below through-hole with time). "One of the goals was to do surface-mount, which is so bizarre because everyone knew at that time that surface-mount was more expensive," recalls Joe Augenbraun. "The only reason you would do surface-mount was to make something smaller. It was clearly a price premium. Yet it was supposed to be a cost reduction at the same time."

This brought the costs up to $161.64, just over $10 less than the A500 Plus bill of materials. As a result, Porter was forced to report to Mehdi Ali that his cost reduction was not as impressive as first believed which resulted in a Mehdi Attack. "Mehdi loved giving people a hard time, especially me," says Porter. "He was a real asshole."

Commodore not only needed SMT motherboards and SMT components, but also custom SMT chips from Commodore Semiconductor Group. By the end of April, CSG had produced 200 each of the ECS Amiga chipset in SMT packaging. Robbins' preliminary schematic for the A300 was expected by month end. Meanwhile, Porter worked on getting the keyboard and case designed.

Another challenge was teaching engineers how to use the new surface-mount technology. "The bigger issue was the lab guys went and got an SMT training course," says Augenbraun. "They brought people in, and there was this big SMT rework station that was bought with a little vacuum wand and paste. Everyone was just kind of trying to figure it out. And the lab guys got to the point where they could really do it but all of us engineers, we were kind of struggling."

To stuff the circuit boards with components became an arduous task. "None of us knew how to do this so we ended up getting stencils made for laying down the solder paste," recalls Augenbraun. "You'd put down the stencil where the chip or whatever was supposed to go and you would have this little squeegee thing to push the solder paste around. Then you'd stick your chip on top. Then you had this hot air wand that you would wave around it. That all seemed to work pretty okay but you had to know the tricks."

In order to produce the boards, Porter had to obtain a "pick and place" machine to populate the A300's SMT boards with components. Even though engineering produced a relatively good return on investment compared to other divisions, such as marketing, Mehdi Ali seemed overly concerned about engineering costs and denied the request for an expensive Universal pick and place machine.

Instead, Porter and his engineers had to come up with a bargain basement solution. "It was Commodore's first big surface-mount technology board," says Porter. "I remember buying a really low cost 'SMT pick and place machine' from a Russian dude in New Jersey, controlled by a simple IBM PC back then. We had a little wave solder machine from the West Chester factory floor so we could prototype everything without spending mega bucks for a production SMT machine."

Porter also connected a Moniterm monitor with the Hedley-Hires to display CAD images. "Hedley wrote some awesome software to take the CAD drawings to magically control this pick and place machine," says Porter. "And we borrowed a baby wave flow solder machine from the West Chester factory that wasn't using that any more. We did that for a fraction of the price of a standard pick and place from companies like Universal."

Although the final cost of fabricating the PCB's would be cheaper, it was costly to obtain the prototype motherboards. "Something I always found interesting at Commodore was how much we spent on prototype boards," recalls Augenbraun. "We were constantly wasting time and then trying to make up for it at the end. At that time we used to spend ten, twenty, thirty thousand dollars to get prototype boards. The quote would be, 'Alright, you can have these for $10,000 in seven days, $50,000 in three days or $150,000 in one day. What do you want?' And I would go to Jeff and say, 'What do you want to do?' He'd say, 'Get it in one day!' Really? We spent so much money on boards just because we're getting them quick. We regularly spent $50,000 to get three prototype boards."

Once the motherboards came back, the pick and place machine stuffed them with the chips and other electronic components. "The prototype boards were built in West Chester. After they wave-soldered the boards they literally put them into home consumer dishwashers," laughs Augenbraun. "They used a water-soluble rosin. They put in consumer dishwashers, like a regular built in dishwasher except sitting in the middle of a factory floor. It was funny that they used consumer dishwashers. No sides, like they were ready to be installed under a kitchen counter. They put in racks of boards instead of racks of dishes and ran them through a wash cycle. They might do a thousand boards in there."

Things seemed to be progressing well on the A300 project, but that would soon come crashing down when Commodore's upper management decided to make even more changes to the engineering organization.

CDTV Unleashed 1991

In March 1991, CDTV would go into production and then start arriving on store shelves. But even before then, Mehdi Ali had identified the high cost of production as a major obstacle and he initiated a new project to produce a cost reduced CDTV. A contest between two rival engineering groups would determine who would win the new project.

Winter CES Redux

Rewind back to the January 1991 CES in Las Vegas, where Commodore would show off a more complete version of CDTV. Irving Gould and Nolan Bushnell presented speeches to the attendees at the opening banquet. This was followed by a Q&A session with the two, along with Gail Wellington and Bob Larsen, VP of consumer sales. The speeches and subsequent questions also revealed Commodore's marketing plan was full of holes.

Irving Gould, who had been integral to launching the project, sounded like a proud father at CES. He had high expectations for CDTV, saying, "My personal vision is that CDTV, like VCR a decade earlier, will profoundly transform the way we are informed."

Since becoming involved with Commodore in 1966, he had longed for a product he could understand and use. "Over the past 25 years it has been my goal to develop a product that is powerful and exciting yet is accessible to those of us who find working on a computer a trying experience," he said. "I'm pleased to report that CDTV has achieved this simple, but all important, technical requirement."

Nolan Bushnell, leagues ahead of Gould when it came to charisma, gave a talk more technology and marketing focused that also happened to be inspiring. Bushnell felt CDTV could pull in the legions of people who had still not purchased a computer. "To some people who are afraid of the computer revolution, this will be a Trojan Horse that will allow them to ease into the computer revolution without actually having to confront a qwerty keyboard until they're really ready to," he explained.

However, parts of his speech hinted that the Special Projects group had still not solved the marketing conundrum of CDTV. "People have asked us, 'Who buys this? Is it the audio buyer?' The reality is that this is a new category and we don't care who buys it."

Bushnell was acutely aware that the software titles for CDTV would either make or break the product. "I believe that we can make our education entertaining, and I think we can make our entertainment educational. And I think that's a wonderful dream," he said.

During the Q&A session, Bushnell stated they wanted CDTV to support the JPEG image standard, but, more importantly, the MPEG video standard.

He also indicated sales would begin in the first quarter of 1991, and Gail Wellington mentioned they would be ready with large quantities for Christmas. Bob Larsen began taking CDTV preorders at the show with units expected on store shelves later in the year.

At the same January 1991 CES, Philips announced the CD-i would retail for around $700 ($300 less than CDTV) which would make the CDTV uncompetitive. The design by Don Gilbreath and his team was expensive with a bill of materials of $487.62 per unit, meaning that at the retail price of $1000 Commodore would likely lose money. "Looking at it from the Commodore perspective, Commodore now has this product called CDTV and it's a little expensive to make, so the profit margins aren't great on it," explains Carl Sassenrath. "They really do believe it's the future, so Irving and Mehdi decided you need to make a cost reduced version of this."

Mehdi Ali went to Jeff Porter and told him to begin researching how to cost reduce the CDTV. "Mehdi is really the key person on this," says Sassenrath. To reduce the retail cost by the required $300, the bill of materials would need to be cut by $100. "Mehdi says, 'Okay you've got to make this for $100 less or whatever it was.' Jeff really felt that was achievable."

Back in September 1990, Porter had started researching the cost reduction on his own. He was almost immediately able to shave the cost down to $435.94 by using a 2-layer board and using regular ROM chips instead of flash memory for the OS. However, to go further he would need to find ways to cost reduce the most expensive component, the CD-ROM laser mechanism itself, which cost $137.93. By November 1990 he had found a supplier of a $100 mechanism which, along with other cost reductions to the case, now brought the cost down to $360. The CDTV would at least be profitable now if it sold for $1000 retail, but Ali wanted to lower the retail cost.

Porter also wanted his version of CDTV, dubbed CDTV-CR, to play full screen video, much like a VCR. In early September 1990, he sent Hedley Davis to attend a meeting with the ISO MPEG group in San Jose. The main focus of the MPEG group was to develop a standard for compressing and decompressing video, allowing longer playing times of video on CD-ROM media. It seemed like Porter's vision of CDTV was evolving into something resembling a DVD player—albeit with compact discs.

CD-ROM Odyssey

After receiving the go ahead, Jeff Porter felt motivated more than ever to create a CD-ROM machine. His CDTV-CR project was an opportunity to steal back CDTV development from the Special Projects group and shine the limelight back on the West Chester engineering group.

At the time, CD-ROM engineers were concerned the fragile CD-ROM discs could be scratched, so discs were first loaded into a protective "caddy" before going into the CD player. "The original CDTV had a caddy that you put this CD in and you shoved the caddy in this slot," explains Jeff Porter. "It was a SCSI based CD-ROM drive that cost about $400 [retail] just for the CD-ROM drive. And I said, 'Well that ain't going to work. I'm going to go find a consumer CD mechanism that's in an audio CD player for cheap. And I'm going to make a CD-ROM out of that."

On January 16, Porter and Hedley Davis began a journey to the heart of CD-ROM manufacturing on a fact finding mission. "I went on a big tour of Japan, Korea, and the Netherlands to talk to all the folks about our concept of making a cost reduced CD-ROM," recalls Porter. "It wasn't going to be SCSI, it was going to be IDE, which later was a popular standard for hard drives and CD-ROM drives for PC based computers."

Porter and Davis met with Philips, Ricoh, Sanyo, Sony, Mitsumi, MKE, and Chinon, as well as Commodore Japan Limited. Everyone thought Porter's concept for a cheap CD-ROM was crazy. "All the traditional guys that built CD-ROM drives said, 'You're going to do what? Are you kidding me? No way that'll ever work.' I said, 'Watch me. We're going to make it work.'"

Although Philips and later Sony had pioneered CD players, Porter really hoped to find a cheaper knockoff that could do the job. "After touring the world to see who has the best technology for CD mechanisms, it came down to Sony and Philips," he recalls. "They were the only two. Everyone else really did a bad job of copying Sony and Philips."

Ultimately Porter found a solution from Sony that cost a fraction of the CD-ROM device used by Don Gilbreath. "I bought a CD mechanism for $15 that had a push-button auto eject tray, which was awesome," he says. "I said, 'Okay, I want the tray that pops out with a little motor drive.'"

Although he found a suitable CD mechanism, he still needed the electronics to drive the unit. "I needed some help from somebody to be able to put that together because Sony wasn't going to do it," he says. "They would supply the components but they wouldn't help me do the rest of the thing."

He turned to the company that had supplied low-cost 3.5 inch floppy drives for the Amiga 500. "We had a pretty good relationship with Chinon Industries which made a bunch of the 1541's and they made a bunch of the floppy drives for the Amiga. I knew all the principals over there in Japan pretty well," says Porter. "I went to them and I said, 'Can you help me take all these components from Sony and wrap them together a little bit so I've got a cheap CD-ROM drive? Hedley's working on the chip and the software to be able to talk to this interface.' They said yes."

Porter and Davis reported back to Bill Sydnes in February with the results. Davis estimated the total cost of the CD-ROM drive at $60, down from $137.93 in the original CDTV. The team prepared a report, which would be presented to Mehdi Ali in New York in April. The trio, including Bill Sydnes, didn't want to lose the project to Don Gilbreath's Special Projects Tiger Team.

Porter had a plan, now all he had to do was convince Mehdi Ali he could do it. He invited Hedley Davis, Ned McComb, and Ted Lenthe to help make a presentation to Ali. The night before the presentation, the four engineers delivered a warm-up presentation in front Bill Sydnes to make sure it was flawless.

CDTV Contest Part II

Jeff Porter travelled with Hedley Davis to the Seagram Building in New York on April 18, 1991. According to Porter, "It was almost a year to the day later, I get called up to New York again. 'Jeff, the CDTV is great but it costs too fucking much and we didn't sell any.' There was a *Groundhog Day* (1993) replay of the previous year going on in my brain. I said, 'I think I can cost-reduce that pretty significantly and I can get it in at this price point.'"

Carl Sassenrath felt it was the right move to pull in Commodore's West Chester engineering team. "Don and I were kind of the skunk works but now it's time to really bring it into the lab, get more engineers on it, really try to knock the price down to make it for a lot less," he says. "And Porter does it in a much more engineering-friendly way."

Porter and his team gave a comprehensive summary of the CDTV-CR project and the incredible cost savings, which reduced the bill of materials from $487.62 to $325. This meant the CDTV could now profitably sell for something in the range of $800 to $1000.

Sassenrath felt that a fresh pair of eyes on the project could result in some serious cost savings. "It made a lot of sense to actually have another group being involved with cost reduction more than the group that does the first one because there was a little bit of ownership of, 'I really wish I had those five connectors and this pinout or whatever.' It was over-built."

Ali liked the pitch, but both Porter and Davis were concerned they might lose the project again due to the timeline. Ali wanted the CDTV-CR for a summer 1991 release, in time for the holiday season. Porter knew no one could meet that goal, so he took a page from Gilbreath's winning pitch in 1989. According to Porter, he told Ali, "'And I think I can lay out a board in a couple of weeks.' 'You can! Oh, that's awesome. You got the job.' But I didn't tell them I was going to be lucky to be in pilot production by the following Christmas."

Although he was denied the project the previous year, Porter now had license to create the next CDTV. His success would depend on the plan he had conceived to substantially reduce the cost. And like the A300 project, Porter was determined to shrink the size of the motherboard by using SMT. "I paved the way for that as well," says Porter.

However, Porter also knew the project came with an estimated release date in April 1992, long past the summer 1991 release date Ali wanted. And this timeline totally missed the holiday season, the period where Commodore would expect to move the most units. Ali would be furious when he learned of the true release date, and he was not the forgiving type.

CDTV Production

While Jeff Porter worked on the CDTV-CR, Don Gilbreath and his Tiger team finished off the production design of CDTV. By the time it was fully designed, it contained a lot of features. "We probably had more gizmos and accessory possibilities than we ever could leverage," laughs Gilbreath, referring to the MIDI ports, the PCMCIA card reader, and various I/O ports. "It was a little over-built. But at least we got it delivered."

The tiger team celebrated by included in a hidden easter egg in the CDTV preferences screen that listed everyone involved, from Takashi Tokuda to Irving Gould himself.

By March 1991, mass production of the CDTV began, but this time it would be manufactured in Japan. Commodore's production engineer was Takashi Tokuda, a veteran of Commodore. "The whole Commodore Tokyo office really became the extension office of CDTV logistics," says Don Gilbreath. "All of the other vendor relationships, all the stuff that finally went down, was a lot of heavy lifting."

Interestingly, the CDTV would be built in the same place as its rival. "Guess where the CD-i player was also being manufactured? One of the Panasonic factories," says Gilbreath. "CD-i and CDTV were literally being assembled almost by the same guys. If you look at where the magic at that time was needed, it was in the CD mechanisms. They were already building CD mechanisms and we had them customized for our particular use."

Gilbreath also had a line of external devices ready for sale along with the CDTV, on par with what customers expected from a personal computer. "By the time we launched it, we had more remote controls than you can imagine," laughs Gilbreath. "Not just the one that was bundled but multiple joysticks and roller balls and various things that would sort of make this where you can put this thing into your Hi-Fi rack at home. Potentially you could throw modem on it. You could do a lot of other things for genlock. We had a lot of accessories at launch." These included an infrared keyboard, an infrared mouse, an infrared trackball-remote control, a floppy disk drive, a joystick, the 1084S monitor, and a genlock card.

Compared to Hong Kong, Japan was the premium location to manufacture electronics, and the results would be high quality. "When it came to actually producing the product, it took quite a lot of time and at the end of the day the product was very expensive," says Hedley Davis.

Although the costs had been high and the schedule overrun by several months, Gilbreath had achieved an impressive feat. Yes, it took him a year to produce the machine from Spring 1990 when the project was given the official go ahead, but one year was not that bad compared to other Commodore products that also fell behind schedule. And most importantly, he had beaten Philips to the finish line. Whatever happened from here, Gilbreath had a lot to be proud of.

Even though the hardware was finalized and in development, the software proved to be a bigger challenge. Gould had hired Ali to crack the whip and make projects happen, and when the pressure was on to deliver the CDTV in time, Ali took a hands on approach. Those working for him didn't see it as benevolence, however. "Mehdi Ali was a complete asshole and he was a horror to work for, or work with or anywhere near," says Guy Wright.

Guy Wright's *Welcome Disc* had just under an hour of audio and visual information, presented interactively, making it a formidable challenge to produce. "He wanted to launch the CDTV on a certain date and they were having trouble in engineering but I was also having trouble with the Welcome Disc," says Wright. "He called me and a bunch of the engineers and Gail and everybody into this conference room and said, 'Okay we need that Welcome Disc finished by next week.' And I said, 'That's impossible, it can't be done.' And he said, 'I don't care what it costs.' I said, 'It doesn't matter, it can't be done.' And he goes, 'If you need to fly to England tonight, we will do it. If you need me to fly engineers from Germany back over here, I'll do it.' I said, 'It doesn't matter. I can't do it. It can't be done. It's not possible to do it.' And he started screaming at me. He's like, 'You little bastard. You get it done next week or you are out of here.' I said, 'Fine. I can't do it. Nobody can do it.' 'We'll turn it over to somebody else. I'll get somebody else to do it.' I said, 'Fine, but they can't do it either. I'm sorry, it just can't be done. You're not believing me. I'm the one building this stupid thing. I know it cannot be done. You're not listening to me.' He just got even angrier. People in the room were shrinking back in their seats. I wasn't going to back down. I don't think I was irate or anything. I just kept saying, 'It doesn't matter what you say. It doesn't matter how much money you spend. It doesn't matter who you bring in. It can not be done.'"

Commodore was also under pressure to deliver 100 titles at the launch of the CDTV. Mehdi Ali took a trip to the UK to ensure the software developers were onboard for the release schedule. "Mehdi had a meeting with a software developer in the UK," recalls Andy Finkel. "Mehdi was unhappy with the way the program worked, the pace of the program, and so on. There was a software meeting and Mehdi started really yelling at this guy, who was a Canadian software developer for the Amiga. And in the middle of Mehdi's tirade in front of other software developers, the guy calmly stands up and says, 'Mehdi, I don't work for you. You can't yell at me like that.'"

June 1991 CES

Commodore attended the annual summer CES in Chicago beginning Saturday, June 1, 1991. This year, Irving Gould and Mehdi Ali had some good news to report. The fiscal year ending that month had generated revenue of $1,047,200,000 and a profit of $48.2 million. This compared to $887.3 million and a paltry $1.5 million profit the prior year. Gould must have felt exceedingly satisfied with his choice of company president. For his part, Mehdi Ali expected sales of $1.2 billion for the next year, generated mainly by the upcoming CDTV and C65 products.

However, those who looked closer at the annual report noted that Commodore's expenditure in R&D was exceedingly low for a billion dollar company, spending only 3% of its revenues, or $31.4 million, on engineering. All this while the company spent $174.3 million, or 16.6%, on Sales and Marketing. This put Commodore at the bottom of computer companies, including Apple and Atari, in R&D expenditures.

At the summer CES, Philips planned to launch its long awaited CD-i player. "Philips was knee-deep in their CD-i product which was probably the closest thing to what a CDTV was in terms of a CD playing multimedia device," says Don Gilbreath. "It had its own set of operating system requirements and standards for the software guys to write against."

In order to compete against CD-i, Gilbreath felt the CDTV would have an advantage because of the underlying Amiga hardware. "The only way for CDTV to even have a chance was that it had a software following around the planet, people that were writing applications on their own for the Amiga architecture. They knew the Amiga operating system."

Both Philips and Commodore implemented CD-G, but Philips planned to unveil compatibility with Photo CD, the Kodak standard for digital photography, at the show. Unbeknownst to them, Commodore had beat them to the punch. "One of my favorite moments was at a CES," recalls Gilbreath. "We had implemented Photo CD, where you could take a Kodak photo CD disc and the CDTV could play it."

Although Commodore was competing directly with Philips, it also relied on Philips to supply a good portion of its monitors. "We do $10 million a quarter with those guys," laughs Gilbreath.

Gilbreath helped set up the CDTV stations at the Commodore booth and noticed a conflict with Philips. "At this CES, Philips got a booth not on the main floor, somewhere farther away from the main congestion of the CES floor," recalls Gilbreath. "They're also thinking of essentially introducing Kodak Photo CD to the world as a title-type for the CD-i player.

And here we are on the main floor, our signage also shows we are doing exactly the same thing."

Commodore's marketing executives immediately came under fire. "We were totally cutting into their splashy launch of Photo CD," says Gilbreath. "I remember the Philips general manager coming into the booth, recognizing one of the marketing guys, Dave Rosen, who was the launch guy for CDTV, who also worked at Philips at one point, and they almost got into a fist fight about taking down the signage."

Uncertain what to do next, and leery of angering such an important partner, Gilbreath consulted with CEO Irving Gould. "I'm nervous Philips is going trash our show," he recalls. "I went over to the Chairman and said, 'What should we do?' And he says, 'Fuck 'em.' And we're doing $10 million a quarter with Philips on monitors. 'Fuck 'em.' That's all he said. 'Leave the sign up, fuck 'em.' It was great."

This was also the CES where Nintendo finally announced its upcoming 16-bit console, the Super Nintendo. The system had been available in Asia since November the prior year, but now it would be appearing on retail shelves on August 23, and in Europe in 1992.

The Super NES was based on a 16-bit version of the 6502 chip, designed by 6502 co-designer Bill Mensch, called the 65816 chip. "I was not surprised that Nintendo used the '816 because they just wanted to make money," says Mensch.

Surprisingly, even though the 65816 was compatible with the 6502 in the original NES, the SNES was not backwards compatible. "They did not stay loyal with the game cartridges of the NES when creating the Super Nintendo with the '816," says Mensch.

If there had been a window for Commodore to launch the C65 in North America, that window had now been slammed shut. The C65 was originally an answer to the NES and now Nintendo had leapfrogged the company. Commodore would have no hope of capturing market share from the dominant video game competitor, especially since the system was 16-bit.

Commodore would now have to rely on 16 and 32-bit Amiga technology to compete in the games market. One advantage Commodore had over the competition was the large library of video games already available for the Amiga, and a legion of third party developers. Hit Amiga games showcased at CES included *The Secret of Monkey Island, Turrican II, Lemmings, Out of this World, Formula One Grand Prix, Eye of the Beholder, Populous II*, and the open world 3D polygon game *Hunter*.

Anatomy of a Massacre

Back in January, it was apparent Commodore did not understand the market for CDTV. By the time it launched the product, they still had no idea. In an interview with *Amiga Computing*, when asked who would buy the product, Gould replied, "The consumer!" When asked how he saw the CDTV developing, Gould shrugged his shoulders.[1]

Even though the CDTV was essentially an Amiga 500 with a CD-ROM drive, Commodore had much different plans for selling it. "We didn't really want to sell it as a computer, even though it was a computer," says Guy Wright.

Nolan Bushnell's strategy, devised in early 1990 at great expense from Dillon, Read and Co., called for displaying the CDTV at least 25 feet away from the computer section. "It was really about how to bring this into a consumer play," says Don Gilbreath. "It was expensive but it was like where the C64 could've gone, if you will. It's like the next generation of friendly computing, for lack of a better way to describe it. It's really an appliance, something that tucks into your Hi-Fi gear."

And that meant CDTV would never reference the Amiga name. "They wanted to try and differentiate it from the A500 but it wasn't any different," says Guy Wright. "It was going to be a set-top box like an Xbox. It was going to be an entertainment system. There really wasn't enough content to sell it as a game machine and it was a little pricey for the time."

"It had all this weird stuff in it and MIDI built in and it had all this sound stuff built in. But was it going to be an audio device? Was it going to be a game device? They didn't really know," says Wright.

The strategy best describing Commodore's US release of CDTV was, "Build a better mousetrap and the world will beat a path to your door." Commodore hoped the strength of CDTV alone would draw in both consumers and distributors because Commodore's distribution by 1991 was very limited.

The president of Commodore US, Jim Dionne, hoped to have the machine on sale in select regions on April 19 in Chicago, Los Angeles, San Francisco, Sacramento, and San Jose. The larger nationwide launch would occur by the end of June in at least 25 of the nation's major markets. In Canada, the machines were sold in Canadian Tire stores, in the sporting

---

1   *Amiga Computing*, June 1991, p. 73. "Going for Gould"

goods section of all places.

The first US chain to accept the CDTV was Macy's. "From approval to seeing it in a Macy's store in San Francisco was 15 months," claims Gilbreath. "It was awesome to see the whole cycle from 'That's a good idea' to literally seeing it launched in Macy's."

Macy's had a hard time figuring out where to put the CDTV. "We said, 'Look, this is an early infotainment piece of gear. It's not a game machine.' The Internet wasn't there. Compuserve was there but it wasn't really a net play, there wasn't a comm side," explains Gilbreath. "So literally Macy's had to put it in three different departments: the music department, where the game machines were, as well as in the hi-fi area. They didn't know either. No one really knew."

Gould had hoped his CDTV would be a revolutionary new product as the VCR had been. However, the VCR could do a lot of things CDTV could not. For starters, in 1984 it had been declared legal in the US to record television shows. VCR owners could set a timer and record their favorite shows on tape while they were away, then watch them later (with the added bonus of fast forwarding past commercials).

There were also thousands of VCR tapes available for purchase or rental. CDTV did not even have the capability to play MPEG movies yet, and the quality of video that could be compressed to CD-ROM disks was poor.

Commodore's marketing department predicted they would start off selling 20,000 units per month. The most pessimistic prediction from engineers was 10,000 per month. They should have been more pessimistic.

Incredibly, Commodore did not seem to test the waters with the product to predict the demand. They obviously had no idea who the market was, with Gould intoning that stay-at-home moms might be a key demographic, or people scared of regular computers. It seemed like high fantasy that a soccer mom would stumble into the stereo equipment section and lay down $1,000 for an unproven product.

The other problem was that Commodore would not use its established dealer network for CDTV. Instead they would rely on Macy's, Montgomery Ward, Video Concepts, Software Etc. and McDuff for the launch.

The early sales of CDTV surprised Commodore executives, but not in a good way. By May 1, the company had sold 80 units in the United States. Nolan Bushnell commented, "I felt that I could sell a hundred thousand of something that costs $800 standing on my head. I thought that it would be a no-brainer. And I can tell you that the number of units that we sold in the US at $800 you could put in your eye and not draw tears."[2]

Bushnell would eventually help push the product into Sears, a chain he had dealt with early in his career at Atari. Sears put its trust in Commodore, a risky move that not a lot of mass market retailers were willing to take at this point in time. Sears would later learn if its trust in Commodore would reward them or cost them dearly.

Gould also approved of a large advertising budget for the new system. "One of the biggest failures was when it finally did start shipping," recalls Wright. "Our marketing guy, Kurt, took out this two page ad in the *New York Times*—full two-page spreads promoting the Commodore CDTV. They got something like a hundred and fifty orders based on that ad. And at lunch, he was joking in a miserable way. He said we could have delivered these things by hand, to each and every one of those 150 people and given it away for free and it wouldn't have cost us as much money as those two pages of the New York Times."

CDTV received coverage in computer-focused magazines such as *Amiga World* but it also received non-traditional coverage by *Popular Science*. The killer app for CDTV was the Grolier Encyclopedia. But in February 1991, a UK company called Psygnosis released *Lemmings*, both for the Amiga and CDTV, and it proved a popular yet accessible title for families.

In the UK, the system sold for £699. A £200 expansion kit called the CD-1500 Professional Pack turned CDTV into a fully functional Amiga, complete with a keyboard, mouse, floppy drive, and Workbench disks.

Advertising was stronger in Europe. Commodore UK hired an advertising firm to create commercials for CDTV. "Steve Franklin the boss at Commodore UK was a bull of a man who had come up through sales," says John Griffiths, who helped create the ad campaign. "He reputedly fired the bottom performing 25% of his sales force every quarter. To encourage the others."

Commodore sold 25,800 CDTVs in Germany, under 30,000 in the UK, and a small number in the US. Commodore UK's Kelly Sumner reflected on the failure. "We got the basics wrong. Wrong price, wrong spec, no support. It came out with Workbench 1.3 when we were launching Workbench 2.0 so the operating system was out of date. It could have done with a bit more RAM and I think it should have come with a built-in 3.5" floppy disk drive."

---

2   *Next Generation*, April 1995, p. 9. "What the hell has Nolan Bushnell started?"

In a follow-up meeting with Commodore UK's advertising firm, Steve Franklin was not happy. "Christmas came and went. The CDTV did not launch well," says Griffiths. "I was ushered into a tense meeting to present the campaign results. I had barely got to my third slide when Steve Franklin lost his temper. 'This is all bullshit,' he raged. Pointing at one of the founders he said, 'In Grouchos last September he promised me that we would sell 15,000 units. You sold only 3,000. Do any of your slides tell me why?'"

"I was on my own. It was time for truth telling. 'You never had any chance of hitting that target. The CDTV was a brand new product and you sold it to gamers without recruiting the developer community. You didn't have enough gaming titles to support it.' There was a long silence. I waited for the floor to open up. 'I agree with you,' he said. 'Move on.' So we did!"

One of the reasons for the failure was the content did not inspire people to purchase the machine. Thus there was no real reason to own it, other than perhaps that encyclopedia. "We didn't think people would see it and say, 'Oh I really need that in my Hi-Fi.' Or, 'That's a great looking game machine,'" says Don Gilbreath. "But we believed because the titles showed enough diversity and that the encyclopedias were kind of like the Internet (although) the data may be stale now… The games are pretty good. With the CD music we tried to make the thing friendly to use. It was just an interesting twist."

Sassenrath was disappointed to learn that many of the launch titles were slow to load from disc. "Unfortunately they isolated those developers a little bit too much from me and a lot of those guys didn't follow the right rules for doing CD," he explains. "I wrote a lot of the documentation for the CD-ROM developer manuals but they weren't following the rules. With a lot of those titles, you would put them in and they would just crank. You could hear the CD laser going back and forth trying to get the thing to start up and it would take several minutes before the game started. There's no reason the games couldn't start within seconds if they had done things properly. That was just bad coordination."

Current owners of the Amiga 500 also had little reason to buy a CDTV. For around $500, customers could buy an A500 with keyboard, mouse, disk drive, and a massive software library. The $1,000 CDTV could have a keyboard (for $149.95), disk drive (for $199), and mouse (for $129.95), but those cost extra. Informed consumers wouldn't touch the machine.

The failure of CDTV hurt Commodore badly. They had spent in the neighborhood of $90 million designing, marketing, and manufacturing the risky machine and it did not pay off. It was a catastrophe to equal the Plus/4 fiasco, which had nearly bankrupted Commodore.

Commodore, like Philips, was too early.[3] "CDTV was really kind of a disappointment in terms of its acceptance in the marketplace," says Carl Sassenrath. "It was just way too far ahead of its time."

---

3   Philips CD-i players lasted until June 1999. By that time, the DVD player had supplanted CD-i. Philips lost an estimated $1 billion on the venture.

The Final Takeover 1991

In 1990, Mehdi Ali had significantly restructured Commodore, adding a layer of loyal middle managers in order to exert his control across the company. In 1991 he made one final move to attain absolute control of the products Commodore would build. The year marked the lowest point for Commodore's engineers, who were well on their way to delivering the Amiga Plus line in 1991.

"Things went from 'not great, but we're making do' to 'this sucks' sometime after the A3000, around the spring of 1991," says Dave Haynie. "That's when [Mehdi] Ali grabbed the ropes, and one-by-one, group by group, starting making the company his."

Rattigan Lawsuit Result

Former CEO and president Thomas Rattigan's $9 million lawsuit over his premature dismissal had slowly made its way through the court system since 1987. Both Rattigan and Commodore made their claims to the US District Court, Southern District of New York. "There had been a series of depositions that were taken on both sides," says Rattigan. "I think they had me in for deposition for five days."

Back when Rattigan had showed up to work as usual after his termination and was subsequently escorted off the premises, it was not delusional behavior but rather a strategy insisted upon by Rattigan's lawyer to deliberately show he was not vacating his position voluntarily. Rattigan knew he would not be allowed to stay (although he was legitimately surprised he could not even enter his office to collect his personal belongings). This established without a doubt that his resignation was involuntary, triggering the escape clauses in his contract.

Commodore lawyers dragged the lawsuit out as long as possible. "In that four year period, there was movement of paper back and forth and a few things like that," says Rattigan. "That's a pretty typical strategy."

Rattigan's lawyers initially attempted to receive a summary judgement for the case, which would allow a judge to determine the outcome based on the merits of the case without presenting detailed evidence or testimony. This was done in order to attempt a speedy resolution. District Judge Michael Mukasey[1] denied this motion on May 5, 1988, meaning the case would go to court.

Commodore filed a motion that it was not responsible for paying some conditional damages listed in the contract with Rattigan in the event of involuntary resignation. Gould's lawyers wanted these damages removed. On June 5, 1990, Judge Mukasey denied this motion in favor of Rattigan, meaning the case was now clear to proceed to court.

In early 1991, witnesses testified and evidence was presented before the US District Court in Southern New York. "Court appearances didn't take place until 1991," says Rattigan. "[Nigel Shepherd] turned out to be an unbelievably helpful witness in the trial."

In February 1991 judge Mukasey ruled in Rattigan's favor, while dismissing Commodore's $24 million countersuit. Surprisingly, after the judge took a recess to calculate the value to be awarded, Commodore's lawyers approached Rattigan's lawyers to settle the case out of court.[2] Commodore agreed to pay Rattigan $9.2 million, which probably saved them the legal fees that Rattigan may have been awarded.

It was a harsh lesson for Gould that would undoubtedly hamper Commodore's cash flow at a time when it needed every dollar to continue development and marketing operations. After the settlement, Mehdi Ali began looking for ways to cut costs across the company in order to ensure the next quarterly report would still appear profitable.

AAA Chipset Scrutinized

When Bill Sydnes had been hired, one of his tasks was to figure out why Amiga chipset development was always falling behind schedule. Dave Haynie felt the reason was simple. "The chip designs were just taking too

---

1   Mukasey later became the 81st Attorney General of the United States.

2   *Philadelphia Inquirer*, April 23, 1991. "Legal Settlement Cuts Commodore's Profit By $9.2 Million In Quarter"

long because they weren't funding it at the level they should have been," he says.

However, with 15 people working 100% on the AAA chipset alone, it seemed like Commodore had been willing to invest a lot into the project. Other system engineers felt the chip people were not as dedicated as the core system engineers. "Everyone thought that they [chip designers] were probably really good but they weren't part of the [core engineering] group," says Joe Augenbraun. "They all had families and they went home at 5 o'clock and didn't feel like they had the fire in their belly like the other people."

One of the key problems of the AAA chipset was the breadth of the spec, which required it to work with a variety of disparate computer systems. It was designed for the high-end Unix workstation market using VRAM, high end multimedia Amiga computers using fast DRAM, and low-cost Amiga 500 level systems using DRAM. It was also designed to work with Reduced Instruction Set Computing (RISC) processors, 16-bit and 32-bit Motorola 680xx chips. It was designed for backward compatibility with existing Amiga graphics modes using bitplane graphics architectures. It was also designed to produce 8-bit, 16-bit, and 32-bit graphics modes similar to VGA computers (known as chunky modes).

When Jay Miner had absolute authority over the original Amiga chipset, he kept the goals simple and focused. Unfortunately, the AAA chipset had all the hallmarks of design by committee.

Sydnes sought proposals from his engineers for the short, medium, and long term for Commodore Semiconductor Group. The short term plan called for minor enhancements to the Paula chip. The long term plan, written by Ed Hepler, called for a RISC based chipset, called Hombre, that would be incompatible with the current Amiga computers.

The medium term proposal, written primarily by Lew Eggebrecht, was a proposal for an Enhanced Amiga Architecture to replace AAA. Ted Lenthe circulated the memo to the core Amiga engineers, including Jim Redfield, Dave Haynie, Hedley Davis, Greg Berlin and of course Jeff Porter. Eggebrecht's proposal was met with disdain.

Hepler, Redfield, Haynie, and Davis all wrote responses largely deriding the naivete of the author, who sounded uninformed regarding the Amiga. "These guys were getting paid just obscene amounts of money, didn't understand what they were doing, and didn't take the time to learn about why, and came in with the preconception that everything we did was fucked up," says Davis. "They didn't bother trying to figure it out, they didn't try to understand it. 'All right, what do you have that we can take advantage of? Is there any good here?'"

However, the memo indicated to the engineers what was on the minds of Sydnes and Eggebrecht and it didn't look good for the current crop of Amiga computers. Sydnes and Eggebrecht regrouped after the responses from the systems engineers. Regardless, they would continue trying to fix the problematic development of the Pandora and AAA chipsets.

AA First Prototypes

Back in September 1989, George Robbins proposed an intermediate level Amiga chipset, called Pandora, to bridge the gap until AAA appeared. The chipset, consisting of a graphics chip called Lisa and an improved Agnus called Alice, was supposed to be ready in early 1990. Rubin had given the go ahead and six chip engineers had been working full time under the project leader, Bob Raible.

The Pandora code-name was soon changed. "Then it was called AA," says Dave Haynie. The new name took its meaning from baseball, where AAA (triple-A) was the top tier league and AA was the next tier down. "There was AAA and this was a little bit less than AAA, so it was two A's, which didn't really stand for anything."

As work progressed on the graphics chip, Lisa, it became clear that the timeline was too ambitious. Jeff Porter set a more realistic expectation of late 1990. As Porter predicted, CSG produced the first prototype chips by late November 1990 and testing began.

By early December, the team felt the Lisa chip would be delivered ahead of schedule. All but the color table was working, a problem Raible felt he could overcome with a hack.

The lowered ambitions of AA had allowed a rapid development cycle. "AA was hybrid 16/32-bit," says Dave Haynie. As a result of the 16-bit operations, some modes such as Super HAM were still only fast enough to display static images rather than fast animation.

The AA chips continued to be revised and tested through early 1991 until they were good enough to use in the A1000 Plus and A3000 Plus prototypes. Dave Haynie managed to boot up his A3000 Plus with AmigaOS and the AA chipset in February 1991.

In an interview given to *Amiga Computing* magazine, Irving Gould revealed, "As a matter of fact, there is a new chip set for the Amiga we've been working on now, I guess, for almost two years that should be ready this fall."[3] The reason Gould was unsure of the release date was because the engineers were considering some improvements for the chipset.

By March 27, when the tested AA chips were ready, the list of stable features was impressive. AA could display 256 colors from a pallet of 16 million colors. It could theoretically play 24-bit digital video (although presently it could only display 8-bit video) due to a four times increase in bandwidth (and using the digital-to-analog converter chip in the A3000 Plus). It could use 64 bit sprites, which could now be controlled in the border areas. It had the aforementioned new 8-bit HAM mode, called Super HAM. And finally, the scan doubling and deinterlacing hardware, formerly on Amber, was now handled right on the chip.

There were also nine features the engineers discussed in October 1989 which had not yet been implemented, including: 16-bit processor support, 8 MB chip RAM, 16 and 24 bit color modes, faster HAM modes, and a simple integrated digital-to-analog converter (for the low-end Amigas).

They also had a list of 10 other features they wanted to add to the AA chipset, primarily in Paula, including: high density floppy support, 16 bit sound, audio input support, and designing the chipset in CMOS for laptops.

On Thursday, March 28 at 9 AM, Jeff Porter, Greg Berlin, Dave Haynie, George Robbins, and Hedley Davis met to decide what they wanted to do with the AA chipset spec. They chose which features to add and which they could live without. This change to the spec would cause the chipset to slip behind schedule and Porter estimated that AA systems such as the A1000 Plus would be pushed back to April 1992.

Sydnes relied on his right hand man, Lew Eggebrecht, to provide him with an assessment of Commodore's engineering department. As Eggebrecht later noted, the Commodore engineers sometimes had problems finishing products. "We have some very free thinking engineers in both hardware and software—very very creative," said Eggebrecht. "And if you don't give them specific goals they'll just continue to develop and develop. The process of converting a design to a product is something Commodore has always had difficulty with. We're stopping all that."

Once upper management found out about the proposed changes, they decided they needed to make some changes of their own. Lew Eggebrecht had a vision to streamline the chip development process that would result in delivering new technology quicker than in the past. Secondly, Commodore

---

needed to ramp up the technology in order to remain cutting edge with other companies. And third, Commodore would contract other companies where appropriate to develop and fabricate chips.

Eggebrecht knew chip development well and would work tirelessly to refine the processes the engineers used to produce the chips by importing processes he learned at IBM. These changes had the potential to slow down chip delivery in the short term as the engineers grew accustomed to new processes, but once learned, Commodore's chip development problems would be a thing of the past.

The GVP Problem

By 1991, Great Valley Products had become a great success with the help of one of the original C64 engineers, Dave Ziembicki. "We designed our first hard disk controller, a SCSI hard disk controller, and we needed to manufacture it," explains Gerard Bucas. "Dave Ziembicki had a small assembly. He could assemble PCBs and that type of thing, not far from where Commodore was."

GVP soon became profitable selling Amiga devices. "The first year we were already close to two million dollars and we were profitable," says Bucas. "This was one of the most exciting things I've done."

By 1991, GVP earned over $20 million in revenue. "We were the largest third party add-on supplier in the Amiga market. Eventually we outgrew him [Ziembicki], " says Bucas. "He gave up on his own little factory because he wasn't making any money. Probably, GVP was squeezing him too hard in the first place. Then he became our VP of Operations. He handled all the production for GVP. We mostly outsourced it to other places."

As GVP began to gain more market share, its sales took away from Commodore's own Amiga expansion products. At this point, Commodore management became confused as to whether GVP was an ally or a competitor. Mehdi Ali figured the revenues made by GVP were lost revenues that Commodore otherwise would have earned, which amounted to almost the entire engineering budget at Commodore. "They sort of felt we took away all their peripheral sales," says Bucas. "We were reaping all the profit and they were getting all the low margin CPU sales." Mehdi Ali wanted to do something to deal with GVP.

Although GVP hoped for Commodore's long term success (after all, the company was dependent on Commodore's computer products), the same sentiment was not returned by upper management. "Believe it or not, Commodore started telling their employees, especially engineering, no one was allowed to talk to us," recalls Bucas. "Basically we were the arch enemy at that time."

On June 11, Ali ordered everyone in the CATS department to cease communications with GVP. The memo sent to employees read, "Effective Immediately, no-one in Developer Support is to communicate with any employees of Great Valley Products (GVP). This policy has been set by Mehdi Ali, our President. ... Please be advised that violations of this policy will result in termination." Ali also discouraged his employees from socializing with GVP employees after hours.

As word spread, the decision had third party developers in an uproar. Many wondered if they too would end up in the crosshairs. The policy only lasted until June 26, at which time a manager Jeff Scherb was able to reverse Ali's decision. Sherb instructed his employees to give GVP the same level of support as others, but warned, "Inappropriate disclosure of any confidential information may result in termination, per Mehdi Ali."

Commodore also gave up on making its own peripheral devices soon after this confrontation. "I did some hard drives and things that they never really marketed because there were a lot of third party companies making a lot of stuff," says Greg Berlin. "The company decided we don't need to make a lot of these peripherals because they are not big money makers. So they let some of the other companies do those peripherals."

GVP had won this round against Mehdi Ali, who would remain committed to eliminating GVP from the Amiga market.

Dethroned

Mehdi Ali's changes to the Commodore organization came to a head in the summer of 1991. "Irving Gould had a company and he had some guy named Medhi Ali running the company," says Hedley Davis. "You will find a lot of universal hatred for Mehdi."

Though Gould resisted Rattigan's power grab in 1987, he now allowed Ali to do the same by installing loyal managers in every department. "It's ironic that [Rattigan] got tossed out of Commodore for trying to basically take over real leadership of Commodore, which is exactly what Mehdi Ali did a few years later," says Dave Haynie. "Ali was just more shrewd about it and he became good pals with Uncle Irving before making the attempt. When Rattigan tried that it caused big friction."

Most of Ali's managers came from IBM, and they attempted to import parts of the IBM culture. This included a desire for employees to dress professionally at work. Employees noted a sudden emphasis on making

George Robbins presentable. Robbins would have none of it. "He could see through a lot of BS," says Eric Lavetzky.

Employees all over the company felt pressure to conform their appearance. "He [Bill Sydnes] didn't like the fact that I would only shave twice a week," says Bill Gardei. "We weren't the best-groomed bunch."

Other changes also came. Prior to Ali's takeover, Commodore had an open company culture among engineers. Now suddenly dozens of company memos were marked confidential and threats were made about revealing too much proprietary information to other companies.

On June 6, 1991, Bill Sydnes, Lew Eggebrecht, and Jeff Porter flew to Frankfurt to host a large meeting of regional Commodore heads. The purpose of the meeting was to show the upcoming computers and set product strategy. Originally, Commodore had planned to introduce the C65, A300, A500 Plus, A1000 Plus, and A3000 Plus in 1991 (along with the delayed CDTV and A3000UX). However, with the AA chipset not ready for production, only the first three low-end computers could be ready.

Mehdi Ali was not happy to find out about the delays with the AA chipset. Furthermore, Ali had learned of the schedule for the CDTV-CR, which had a release date of April 1992. With his shield, Henri Rubin, long since departed, Porter now faced repercussions from executives.

Bill Sydnes himself told Ali he could do a better job with the Amiga technology if it was under his direct control. "He eventually convinced Mehdi to let him have the entire Amiga development team," says Porter.

To accomplish this, Sydnes would need to place his own loyal people into leadership positions. "Sydnes was a PC guy, so he immediately promoted PC guys," recalls Dave Haynie.

Jeff Frank saw the pieces being moved around on the chessboard. "Jeff Frank was running the PC group and Jeff Porter was running the Amiga group and Jeff Frank was pretty Machiavellian," recalls Joe Augenbraun. "He was very ambitious and he wanted to run both groups; he wanted to move up one level in the organization. And of course Jeff Porter didn't want that to happen. But in that political battle Jeff Frank won."

Frank put himself forward with a proposal to cut back on the cost of Amiga computers while bringing them out in a timely fashion. "When Bill Sydnes came in, there was a bit of a power struggle and Jeff [Porter] wasn't built to fight a power struggle," explains Augenbraun. "Jeff is a hell of a nice guy. Probably too much of a nice guy for corporate politics."

On June 20, 1991, Jeff Frank took over the entire Amiga group, leaving Porter in the cold. Even the C65 project would now be managed by Frank.

The handoff occurred right while Porter was in the midst of sending the final A500 Plus PCB artwork to Hong Kong for manufacturing. It was a nightmare for Porter, who had now lost his dream job to someone he had personally hired.

In order to make his takeover go smoother, Frank attempted to send Porter to a PCMCIA conference. Porter would have none of it, and suggested Lew Eggebrecht should attend instead. Frank continued his demands for four days, with Porter declining each time. Porter still held onto the hope that he could retain his position and did not want to allow himself to be undermined.

A few days later, Porter was left out of the Monday morning engineering meeting and was soon notified he was no longer allowed to park his car in the VP parking lot, although he continued attempting to. Relations between Porter and Frank soon became heated. Porter wore his heart on his sleeve and taunted Frank whenever he had a chance, resulting in the two verbally sparring when they met.

In early July, managers were instructed not to invite Jeff Porter to meetings (except for CDTV) unless Jeff Frank requested the invite. Porter was now only left with the CDTV-CR project in the multimedia division—the same place Henri Rubin and Harold Copperman had been demoted to before him. "That was a real crime," says Joe Augenbraun. However, Porter would make the most of his new lot in life.

CHAPTER 27

Killing Projects 1991

After Mehdi Ali and Bill Sydnes had taken over the engineering department, they began to look for projects to cut. "Sydnes' main job for six months was to kill every on-going project, lest anyone start to suspect that maybe Henri's administration had really been running things perfectly well," muses Dave Haynie. In the process of cutting projects, several critical engineers would lose their jobs.

A3000UX Released

Commodore had planned to release the A3000UX machine in September 1990. However, the first units arrived to dealers in January 1991 and Commodore began gearing up for the launch. A few months later, in March 1991, they were available for purchase in the US.

During its development, Henri Rubin and Johann George had demonstrated it at shows. Despite the impressive accomplishment of running Unix on Amiga hardware, the computer did not appeal to Commodore's core audience, who preferred AmigaOS to run common applications and play games. Tech journalists and attendees found the A3000UX an interesting curiosity. Meanwhile the existing Unix community tended to look down on Commodore's Unix offerings.

Amiga users might feel good knowing that, if they wanted, their Amiga could become a powerhouse Unix machine—with a multi-thousand dollar investment. But overall, a very small subset of users planned to use Amix.

There were several variants of the A3000UX available. Most systems came with AT&T Unix System V Release 4 operating system, a three button mouse, (and usually) the A3070 tape backup unit, the A2410 graphics card, and the A2065 Ethernet card. The A2410 graphics card was an expensive card developed at the University of Lowell.

The A3000UX was not well received by the press. *Unix World* magazine reviewed the system in depth and found that, although it had outstanding graphics and sound compared to competing Unix workstations, it was no bargain at $6998, excluding monitor and tape drive. The reviewer found fault mainly with the outdated 68030 chip (which had been superseded by the 68040) and the sparse software available. Around 100 of the most popular Unix programs had been compiled to Amix by Commodore, and most of those did not use the Amiga's remarkable sound and graphics capabilities.

It's difficult to say if Commodore could have found success with its Unix machines. The original vision by Bob Welland seemed plausible enough, by using low-cost Amiga technology to release Unix workstations that even a student could afford. Somehow in the ensuing years since Welland had departed, the Unix machine's price rose to over $4000 at minimum and was now targeted at educational institutions. Lacking the ability to market to education, the Unix machines never really took off for Commodore.

Sunk Cost Fallacy

The "sunk cost fallacy" is a well known phenomenon by economists. It describes a situation where an organization continues spending money on a project that no longer has a viable economic return. The fallacy happens because an organization has spent so much on the project already that it seems reasonable to spend a comparatively small amount complete it. This phenomenon is usually present among the engineers who have pored an effort into the project and thus wish to see it through to the end. Mehdi Ali, trained in economics, had no such misgivings and had little hesitation in cutting projects that were not economically feasible.

Commodore had made a major investment in the Amiga Unix machines. Johann George had been working with Commodore since around 1986 on Commodore's version of the Unix operating system. He had a team of between 7 to 9 engineers working for him, and had completed the latest version, Unix System V Release 4, earlier in the year.

The well-dressed engineer was well respected by his coworkers, who liked to have fun with him. "Unlike us ratty engineers who came in with flip-flops and slept under our desks, Johann always wore an immaculately pressed suit," recalls Bryce Nesbitt. The engineers came up with a contest called "dress better than Johann day" where, as the name suggested, "We all tried to dress better than Johann."

Outside the Unix group, many engineers, such as Hedley Davis and Bryce Nesbitt, felt apathetic towards the Unix group. Everyone loved the Unix operating system, they just didn't feel Commodore could make a dent in the marketplace, and recent sales of the A3000UX supported that.

In an attempt to salvage what Commodore had created, Johann George and members of his team had approached Sun Microsystems and set up a potentially lucrative deal. "Sun wanted to use Amiga's version of Unix for Sun's low-end Unix solution," recalls Bryce Nesbitt.

The deal was hammered out and all that was left was for Mehdi Ali to come in and sign the deal with Sun. However, when Ali entered the room with Sun's executives, he felt compelled to wring more money out of the deal. "There was a lot of ego involved," says Dave Haynie.

"Medhi Ali and his team sabotaged the deal twice by demanding a fortune in licensing fees," says Nesbitt. "Sun eventually gave up and Amiga's chances to expand into the Unix market dried up forever."

As the third annual Dress Better than Johann day approached on June 25, George was caught up in the recent changes taking place to reshape the company. Mehdi Ali and Bill Sydnes finally put a stop to the dubious Unix division. According to Commodore employees, Mehdi told them, "Stop it, drop it, fuck it. We are no Unix company."

The decision was supported by many of Commodore's engineers. "The Unix group was another total distraction that didn't go anywhere," says Nesbitt.

Layoffs

For the past few years, Commodore's engineers had felt overworked and understaffed. Jeff Porter had pushed for and succeeded in increasing their ranks, though they were still not up to levels comparable to Atari or Apple. Then in mid-1991 Mehdi Ali sought to reduce Commodore's engineering department, a risky move considering how thin the ranks were already. Those cuts would include some of Commodore's most skilled and seasoned engineers, along with engineers who had been underperforming.

Johann George and his entire Unix group (except for one engineer to support Commodore's existing Amix user base) were laid off by Ned Mc-Cook. This was predictable and understandable given the results of the Unix group.

Mehdi Ali also decided he could find cheaper manufacturing outside of the United States and shut down the production lines at West Chester. "They had a large manufacturing facility there," says Guy Wright. "One day instead of two hundred factory workers there were only 50. And then a week later only ten. And a week later the assembly-lines weren't running any more. Then a week after that, they started tearing apart the assembly lines. And a week after that there was nothing. It was just another open empty warehouse area now."

It's hard to argue with this decision, as Ali had been able to study and analyze the costs of manufacturing Commodore's products. He was merely following the same logic that had led numerous US companies to rely on offshore manufacturing in order to reduce prices.

There were also non-political layoffs that occurred purely because management felt they were needed. "Engineering decided it was a good time to get rid of some people that needed to be gotten rid of," says Michael Sinz. "Since it was a layoff, you have some cover and you don't have to go through the long process of proving that you need to fire somebody."

This included engineers who either were not competent or had in some way alienated their fellow engineers. One individual was the aforementioned engineer who refused to upgrade to AmigaOS 2.04. Although not known for his warmth to his coworkers, the engineer was extremely bright and creative. "He spent a lot of his time building this ray tracer, which is sort of funny that his name was Ray," explains Sinz. "It would run distributed at night. You just start up his little agent on your Amiga and he would, through our network, do distributed ray tracing across 30 Amigas. It was nice that he did that and we didn't really stop him from doing it because it proved out some stuff that we were testing. But he spent a lot of time on that."

It seemed clear that the software engineer should have been working at a graphics company, rather than working on an OS at Commodore. Even after Andy Finkel had to plead with the engineer to help with the urgent work needed for the OS, and he had refused to help fix bugs.

A fanatic for the burgeoning field of computer rendered imagery, the engineer paid his own way to SIGGRAPH that year. "Since he was at SIGGRAPH, we realized that Fedex was when you absolutely positively need to lay off somebody overnight," quips Sinz. "He got his pink slip sent to him while he was at SIGGRAPH."

Layoffs like this were probably for the best, both for Commodore and for engineers who might not have been working in a field they were excited about.

When Ned McCook had been hired in November 1990 and became Andy Finkel's boss, Finkel had remained to allow McCook to learn the job from him. "He brought in a guy of his own to be head of software in engineering and I was superfluous," says Finkel. "So it was more a matter of him wanting to have his own team in place rather than anything else."

McCook became known to programmers as a NOP, the assembly language instruction for No Operation. 'Ned McCook forced him to be let go," says Michael Sinz. "He was stupid, a blight on any engineering organization. He brought in someone less confrontational and almost had a full revolt of the engineering team."

A month after Jeff Porter was demoted, McCook was planning changes in the software engineering department. "Andy Finkel was my boss and Andy was being fired," says Bryce Nesbitt. "I was told the night before. I was asked to walk him out and basically deliver his termination message and process him through human resources."

However, Nesbitt thought it was wrong for Commodore to dismiss the talented engineer. "I refused to do this," recalls Nesbitt. "I said instead, 'Andy is a great engineer and he has the most history of anybody here. I think there's another place in the company for him.' I spent that night rapidly trying to find another position for him within the company, but they were insistent on firing him."

Finkel had also been by Henri Rubin's side for all of his management career, which tainted him with the new management who wanted to erase Rubin's legacy. "I guess I lost the political battle that I didn't really know I was fighting," he says. "I wasn't aligned to the right group of people. I was considered part of the old guard who had worked for the previous head of engineering. And now that the new one was in, I guess I was viewed as too loyal to him."

Sydnes wanted his own team leading development. "I had no particular loyalty, except I worked for Commodore," says Finkel. "I just wasn't part of the Bill Sydnes team."

With barely any time to search, Nesbitt was unable to find a suitable position in any of Commodore's departments. "They fired him the next morning," he says. "It's ridiculous. It was poor management on the part of the people who wanted to fire him."

Finkel and hundreds of his coworkers were called to a meeting in the company cafeteria on July 31, 1991. "It was the usual Commodore mass meeting where you bring everybody who is going to be let go into the cafeteria and you tell them all at once," recalls Finkel. "It's pretty quiet. Some people are surprised, some people are not. It caught me completely by surprise, otherwise I would have arranged to switch to the CDTV group or to another part of the company beforehand. It was sad."

Commodore also held another meeting of employees to prevent people from guessing ahead of time what was afoot. "At the same time as they are having the layoff announcement with everybody who is being laid off, Commodore also has the meeting of the survivors in a different larger area," says Finkel.

Mehdi Ali's reshaping of Commodore was now complete. From then on, the company was run by executives and managers he had chosen, all under his control. Unsurprisingly, after 1991, Ali also became the biggest speed bump in the eyes of the engineers.

Killing the High End Amigas

Mehdi Ali, Bill Sydnes, and Lew Eggebrecht were faced with the challenge of restructuring Commodore. Earlier in the year Eggebrecht had performed some initial investigations regarding the AA and AAA chipsets. One thing that had become increasingly clear since then was that the A3000, Commodore's current high-end Amiga, was not selling well.

The A2000 had sold 124,500 units in Germany and was considered a great success due to the high profitability of the A2000-CR. In contrast, the A3000 would go on to sell 8,300 units in Germany, with the A3000T selling around 6,000 units. Much of the failure of these computers had to do with the aforementioned AmigaOS 2.0 fiasco and the negligible improvements of the ECS chipset, although the high price was probably the biggest barrier to entry.

Ali and Sydnes were ready to change Commodore's path. The two had to decide whether Commodore should even continue with the high-end Amiga products, or instead concentrate on IBM PC clones and low-cost, mass-market computers such as the A500 and C65.

Bill Sydnes decided to cancel the A3000 Plus computer, which would have been Commodore's answer to all the criticisms in the A3000. "He was the kind of guy who came in saying, 'I'm gonna do everything my way.' He started to basically put every single project at Commodore on hold," says Eric Lavitsky, who had helped with the A3000 Plus. "Basically the A3000 Plus got put on the back burner. We continued to work on it a little bit as we could. Dave Haynie was working on the hardware."

Cancelling and putting the projects on hold was a big blow to the morale of the remaining Commodore engineers. "What's really sad is that you've got all of these brilliant engineers, they're coming up with incredible product ideas and they're being told, 'Okay, proceed with that.' And then six months into it they're told, 'stop that project, we want something else now,'" says David Pleasance.

The current plans for the high-end computers rested on the AAA chipset. Unfortunately, Ted Lenthe predicted the chipset would cost $120 per system in low volumes or $60 in high volumes, a far cry from the $15 cost of the OCS developed by Jay Miner. The high cost of AAA made it almost inconceivable to use in the low-end systems.

Lenthe also predicted the first R0 versions of AAA would be fabricated by June 1992, followed by R1 versions by December 1992, with the first 1000 production chips ready in February 1993. Even Lenthe, the head of the LSI group, was doubtful of Commodore's ability to produce a new chipset.

At first, the new management regime allowed Jeff Porter to attend meetings dealing with Amiga issues, owing to his experience and knowledge of the product line. Porter estimated the parts cost of an A500 using AAA at a whopping $339, resulting in a retail price of over $1000, excluding a hard drive. He preferred to see AAA used in a machine similar to the A1000 Plus, called the A2000 Plus, that would retail for $1500 without hard drive.

Lew Eggebrecht believed that Commodore engineers were reinventing the wheel, and he felt they should be using more "off the shelf" parts in the Amiga computers. Porter strongly disagreed that Commodore should use standard parts, feeling that would give up Commodore's only advantage. The one area in which Porter and Eggebrecht agreed was that today's high-end will eventually become tomorrow's low-end. But with Porter estimating AAA would be available in large quantities in August 1993, it would be a long time before AAA could appear in low-end systems.

In August 1991, Eggebrecht presented his findings on whether Commodore should continue pursuing the high-end Amiga market. He believed the Motorola 68000 architecture was no longer feasible and noted that competitors were increasingly using RISC processors. He also believed AmigaOS could not compete with Unix, the upcoming Windows NT, or IBM OS/2. And he felt Commodore would not be able to attract name brand, state of the art software developers to the Amiga platform.

Surprisingly, Eggebrecht believed Commodore's marketing department could support the high-end market, provided they were properly staffed and managed. He was highly critical of Commodore's habit of assigning only two engineers per system, feeling it should be at least six. And he was somewhat critical of Commodore's hardware and software engineers, feeling they were "hardware hackers" and unprofessional. In contrast, he found the VSLI (semiconductor) division more professional but lacking direction, which came from the system engineers.

His recommendations were even more startling. Although Eggebrecht felt Commodore should pursue the high-end market, he felt the Amiga was not the appropriate architecture. He wanted to develop a new chipset for the low to mid range Amigas for the near future. At the high end, he felt Commodore should strip out backward compatibility from the AAA chipset, and support VRAM and RISC processors only. But if AAA development interfered with low-end chip development, Commodore should kill the AAA project. And to reduce the engineering effort required for the first RISC system, he proposed acquiring an OEM system instead of making their own product. Finally, he felt the systems engineering staff needed to be upgraded.

A few days later, Bill Sydnes handed the report to Jeff Porter over dinner together. When Porter saw the report, he was understandably concerned. His first priority was his engineers, who he felt had been limited by the headcount management would allow in the past. He made an impassioned plea that replacing Commodore's systems engineers would be a mistake. Although he agreed with many of Eggebrecht's comments on the high-end Amigas, he felt AmigaOS could survive in the low to medium end computers. He also felt it would be easier to maintain Amiga backward compatibility in AAA, which was already implemented and working, rather than trying to remove it.

Porter's impassioned critique was seen by Sydnes as opposing the new direction of management. As a result, he was mostly cut out of future strategy discussions, which he complained about to Sydnes. In the meantime, Mehdi Ali would attempt to get Porter under control. "I got called into the executive conference room once, with an audience," recalls Porter. "And he just started screaming and swearing at me for doing something he didn't like. It seems like Bill Sydnes was complaining to Mehdi about me instead of telling me what he didn't like."

There were a few differences between a Jack Attack and a Mehdi Attack. The first was that Tramiel only rebuked an employee when there was a definite mistake that had been made. His personal critiques, though heated, were specific and at the end he wanted to know if the employee understood what he had done wrong. The second difference was that a Jack Attack was never given on the spot, but rather the employee—or more likely manager—was called to Tramiel's office for a private rebuke, away from embarrassment in front of others except the secretary and maybe a few executives down the hall.

Ali's rebukes seemed undefined and worse, they always happened in front of coworkers. Porter was understandably embarrassed but unsure why he was being rebuked. "I responded, 'Mehdi, is there anything specific or am I just a general asshole?' He didn't have an answer, so yes, I was just a general asshole. I now know who the asshole was."

The Fate of A1000 Plus

The other AA product under review by Bill Sydnes and Mehdi Ali, the mid-tier A1000 Plus, was highly anticipated by Commodore International sales managers, especially in the UK and Germany. Commodore engineers had every reason to believe it could even sell more units than the highly successful A2000.

However, Ali wanted a new system soon and did not want to wait for the AA chipset. To meet this timeline, Eggebrecht recommended reconfiguring the A1000 Plus using the ECS chipset, which would have pushed it back to being similar to the previous A1500 Augenbraun had prototyped.

To attempt to combat this move, Jeff Porter wrote a small report on the A1000 Plus. He emphasised that using ECS would be an embarrassment for Commodore, saying, "We desperately need AA to be moved as quickly across as many platforms as possible. Making a new ECS model sends the wrong message to our customers."

Other engineers also chimed in, with Randell Jesup writing to his boss Ned McCook, "My opinion is that if AA is dropped from the A1000 Plus design, you might as well not even bother doing the machine. ... If I were an Amiga developer (which I used to be), and saw Commodore's 'new' machine not having AA (i.e. not being even close to competitive with cheap VGA PC clones in video or processor), I would probably wrap up any projects near completion, and start developing for PC's. I'm not exaggerating; as a third party I would truly feel that Commodore would never catch up to (let alone pass by) the PC clones."

Dave Haynie echos the enthusiasm of the engineers towards the A1000 Plus. "More than anything, I think that machine, done the way it was being done in early 1991, could have kept Commodore around, given the times."

The proposed change to ECS was also accompanied by a physical change. Joe Augenbraun had long ago chosen a "pizza box" form factor. "The mechanical tooling was at least a minimum of nine months," explains Paul Lassa. "In the first couple of months, our industrial designers would do artistic mock-ups that they would carve out of wood or something. Those would be shown in front of the senior management saying, 'Which shape do you like? What do you want the product to look like? What do you want the bezel to look like? Where do you want this or that?'"

After all that work designing the A1000 Plus case, Jeff Frank made a proposal to lower development costs. According to Joe Augenbraun, "One of the first things that he did was he said, 'It's stupid that we're making metal boxes for PCs and making metal boxes for Amigas. It's stupid. We're doing two different metal boxes. We should reconcile those two product lines. All the Amigas should be redesigned to fit into PC cases.'"

The problem was, Joe Augenbraun already had an A1000 Plus case designed by Herb Mosteller. "The guy who ran the group was a real nine to five guy," says Joe Augenbraun. "Herb Mosteller was his name. It was not like this is his dream to work on the Amiga. It was just a job to him. He had a young guy working for him, Chuck, who was ambitious and good and fast. Chuck actually did most of the real work."

Jeff Frank's larger metal PC styled case even came with a panel that could be locked, preventing unauthorized users from turning on the computer or inserting disks. Unfortunately, the change meant Augenbraun would have to totally redesign the motherboard around the new size of the case, slowing down the project further.

Things came to a head in early August with a run-in in the engineering labs involving Jeff Porter, Joe Augenbraun, Jeff Frank, and Bill Sydnes. Augenbraun came close to insubordination in Frank's eyes, but Frank was able to get him in line and he remained in the company.

Although the year began with engineers believing in the Plus computers, by the end of the year it looked like any future projects would be determined by a group of former IBM managers with no particular fondness for Commodore's unique Amiga computers.

23-1

25-1

26-1

28-1

23-1 NewTek booth at CES

25-1 Gail Wellington dressed as a Lemming at DevCon (photo by Steve Tibbett)

26-1 Ian Kirschemann and Jeff Frank (with the gun) (photo by Bill Koester)

28-1 Peter Cherna and Paul Lassa at the Commodore Christmas dinner the same month as the C65 project was cancelled (photo courtesy of Peter Cherna)

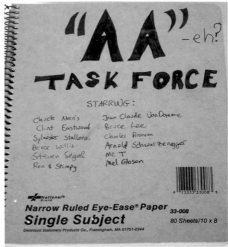

29-1

29-2

29-3

29-4

29-1 Passing through the front gate of Commodore's HQ (photo by Gerard Bucas)

29-2 Dave Haynie's AA Task Force notebook (photo by Dave Haynie)

29-3 Carl Sassenrath with a bottle of his wine at "Sassenranch"
(photo courtesy of Carl Sassenrath)

29-4 The Amiga 500 Plus

30-1   30-2

30-3

30-4

30-1 Outside the fairgrounds of CeBIT 1991 (photo courtesy of John Schilling)

30-2 Commodore's CeBIT booth (photo courtesy of John Schilling)

30-3 View of the upstairs dining area (photo courtesy of John Schilling)

30-4 Bill Sidney's Amiga 600

33-1

34-1

34-2

34-3

33-2 Commodore's team at the 1992 Corporate Cup (from the back) Greg Berlin, Sandra Roshong, Bill O'Donnell, Dave Schwendeman, Paul Lassa, Rhonda O'Donnell (photo courtesy of Sandra Fisher née Roshong)

34-1 Commodore UK's VP of finance Colin Proudfoot

34-2 Commodore UK's GM Steve Franklin

34-3 Commodore Holland's GM Bernard van Tienan

36-1

36-2

36-3

36-1 Commodore Hong Kong's assembly line

36-2 A testing technician from Commodore Hong Kong

36-3 Commodore Hong Kong's parts aquisition office (photos by John Schilling)

36-4

36-5

36-6

36-4 Commodore's Philippines factory with helipad logo

36-5 Testing motherboards at the Philippines factory

36-6 Inside the Philippines factory (photos courtesy of John Schilling)

36-7

37-1

38-1

36-7 A typical CD32 prototype mounted on a plywood base

37-1 George Robbins in the 1990s

38-1 The final CD32 "Spellbound" SMT motherboard produced by Terry Fisher
 (photo courtesy of Terry Fisher)

38-2

38-3

38-4

38-5

39-1

38-2 David Pleasance's ad outside Sega headquarters UK

38-3 Commodore's CD32 video game console

38-4 A CD32 print ad aimed at Sega

38-5 David Pleasance with host Chris Evans at CD32 launch event

39-1 Father of the unproduced Hombre chipset, Dr. Ed Hepler

The Fate of the C65
1991

Although most of Commodore was focused on Amiga based products by 1991, some engineers and managers hoped to continue the legacy of the company's most successful product to date, the C64. The marketing department estimated sales of the upcoming C65 would be at least 50,000 units per month. They also predicted C64 sales would drop 60% one year after the launch of the C65, but that total sales of both computers would exceed current sales of the C64. These figures indicated there was a definite financial incentive for Commodore to pursue the C65 market, especially in light of the bungled A3000 launch.

The main barrier against C65 support was the perception that the 8-bit line of computers was over. To combat this problem, LSI head Ted Lenthe gave a demonstration of a prototype unit in December 1990 to Commodore's engineers and management. The prototype showed off the VIC-III chip's admirable graphics capability, along with DMAgic's abilities. The engineers were impressed by the demo, with everyone conceding it blew the A500 away. This demo won over the old guard of engineers and managers alike and cleared the way for C65 production. Unfortunately, when the major reorganization of July 1991 occurred, the C65 would have to contend with new management.

C65 Pilot Production

For the first half of 1991, Jeff Porter anticipated a summer release of the C65. The quality assurance group tested the system and reported any bugs they found to the C65 team for Fred Bowen to fix in code. A manual was in the works. Preparations were underway for large scale manufacturing, with the first 10,000 units produced in May 1991. It looked like at long last, the C65 would be introduced to the world.

Problems in the chipset still haunted the project, however. The fifth revision of the VIC-III chip, 4567R5, had intermittent failures of sprite 7. The engineers considered releasing this version for production, but after a meeting decided to use R5 only for pilot production. They would instead use the upcoming 4567R6 for production. Failures like this were understandable, given that the AA project had 6 full time engineers, and AAA had 14 engineers. Contrast this to the one full-time engineer working on the C65 chipset, which was actually competitive with the Amiga chipset, and the delays start to make sense.

For his part, Bill Gardei was understandably a little grumpy, as was Fred Bowen. Both believed the computer could have a considerable impact on Commodore's fortunes, yet the project was given hardly any support. It was a thankless job and the two engineers, stressed by the sheer workload, sometimes fought like an old married couple.

In February, C65 designer Paul Lassa finished his chip. He chose this moment to reveal to Jeff Porter that he had also incorporated a blitter into his chipset, which he would use to animate large objects. "I kind of kept that secret but once I tested out the chip, it actually did work and then I said, 'Oh by the way I put this extra stuff in there and if we enable it, it's here.'"

Lassa travelled to Hong Kong in February to help produce 300 PCB motherboards, once the controller chips were ready. "The two controllers came back, the DMAgic controller was solid as far as working correctly," says Lassa. "We went and did a pilot production run. I went over to Hong Kong and assisted in that. We made a couple of hundred units."

The young engineer was impressed by the sheer output of the factory. "Commodore had at least one manufacturing facility in Hong Kong that I went to and they had assembly lines for stamping out C64s and C128s and 1541 disk drives and monitors and this and that," he says.

Commodore's factory was in the northern location containing about half of the population of the country. "The main factory was out in the New Territories in Hong Kong," says Joe Augenbraun. "There's Hong Kong island, there's Kowloon Peninsula, and then there's something called the New Territories—new as of 1880. It was the less developed part of Hong Kong."

Joe Augenbraun was also able to visit the factory as the A1000 Plus took shape. Prior to his visit, Augenbraun had felt slightly guilty using a fork in Chinese restaurants in the USA. "It was about seven stories tall, and it changed my life forever after visiting the factory," laughs Augenbraun. "I saw that in the cafeteria, the Chinese people were serving Chinese lunch to Chinese factory workers and they all used a fork and not chopsticks. So from then on, whenever I went to a Chinese restaurant, it was okay to use a fork."

By month's end, Commodore Hong Kong had produced over 300 C65 motherboards. Of these, 60 units were shipped to developers in the UK, Germany, and Italy (but none for North American software developers). Approximately 30% of the motherboards did not work due to the floppy disk controller, but this was easily solvable with the newer version of the chipset.

Many of these units also came to West Chester for testing. By 1991, Commodore had at least 205 pilot production C65 machines. "We had a room full of them at one point," says Gardei. "If you counted all the variants, 205 would not be an unreasonable guess."

By April, CSG had fabricated working DMAgic chips. "So the chip came back and the two custom chips weren't done yet," says Lassa. "We enabled the DMA functionality and it allowed for this much faster copying that was good for flipping pictures on a screen for a demo."

Jeff Porter wanted to take the C65 on a road-show in June, in both North America and Europe, in order to get Commodore marketing interested in the new system. To this end, Lassa wanted to showcase the blitter, which turned the 8-bit system into something of a pocket battleship. "I started to do a couple of demos to use it and it worked out pretty well," he says. "It was not a full clone of the Amiga, but it was a good seventy percent of the blitter functionality that was in the Amiga. It would have enabled some very cool advanced graphics on the C65 platform that you simply didn't have on the C64 or the C128 and that you could have really done a number of things that, at that time, were only possible on the Amiga."

By May, the 4510R5 and 4567R7 chips were coming out of CSG. Initially the systems with the new chips could not run for more than 5 minutes without crashing. However, a small revision to one of the layers produced the 4567R7A. This chip had a minor problem the engineers dubbed "sprite glint", but other than that, the chip was solid. It seemed the time had come to mass produce the C65.

Porter and Bowen brought the C65 to the aforementioned regional meeting in Frankfurt on June 6, 1991 to show to the sales people. The demo he played demonstrated the fantastic graphical capabilities of the system. It even included a GUI WorkBench demo, modeled on the Amiga Workbench, written by Dave Haynie. A version of DPaint also demonstrated some impressive graphical artwork.

In Jeff Porter's mind, the C65 was a product for both North America and Europe, and the engineers worked on NTSC and PAL versions simultaneously. However, whenever Porter inadvertently mentioned the NTSC chip in front of executives, Mehdi Ali rebuked him, loudly proclaiming the product was for Germany only.

Although parts of Europe were receptive towards the C65, Commodore's VP of engineering disapproved. "Its days were numbered when Commodore hired Bill Sydnes out of IBM," recalls Gardei. "He said, 'If I was here when this project was started, it wouldn't have been started.' He would have never let the C65 out the door."

By June the final C65 manual, mostly written by Fred Bowen, was complete. In it, he acknowledged Commodore was now targeting the C65 to the international market—in other words, anywhere but the United States. It was an acknowledgement they had missed their opportunity to compete against Nintendo. And indeed, by 1991, the C64 received no support from major North American game developers. Most of the 206 releases that year came from Europe or small publishers. With little enthusiasm remaining for the C64, it would be a difficult environment to launch the C65.

Most Commodore employees felt time had run out for a C64 sequel. "There really wasn't much of a place for an enhanced C64-class machine in the early 1990s," says Dave Haynie. Commodore could not realistically release the C65 in 1991 and expect success without a marketing miracle.

After Sydnes' damning words, plans continued for C65 production, with 100 to 200 German PAL units expected to be assembled by the end of July. "We still carried on and had meetings like it was still an active project," says Gardei.

Project Review

In June, all the C65 chips were shipped en masse to Hong Kong where full scale production of the C65 would begin. Unfortunately, Mount Pinatubo in the Philippines erupted and the shipment was delayed as worldwide flights were grounded. Meanwhile, Jeff Porter was about to send the final PCB artwork to Hong Kong when he lost his position in engineering.

After Jeff Porter's demotion, Jeff Frank took over responsibility for the C65 project. At the time, Fred Bowen believed the chipset was good enough for production because all of the chip bugs were adequately handled by workarounds in the ROM software. The only problem that could not be handled in software was the aforementioned "glint", a slight flashing of some sprites in 80-column mode. Since most games would run in 40 column mode, the problem was not deemed serious enough to halt production.

Jeff Frank brought Greg Berlin onto the project to help specify the chip timings, something Gardei had been asked to do but repeatedly failed to provide, and to adjust the timings to make the chips more reliable.

Greg Berlin attempted to work with Gardei regarding the timing issues, but the discussions did not go well, with both engineers trading differing opinions about the 4567 chip. In the end, Berlin concluded the timing was stable in conjunction with the 4510 and DMAgic chips but could pose problems if the chips were used in other systems with different timings. It looked like the C65 could be cleared for mass production.

On July 9, Frank became concerned about heating issues with the chip. After running some heating tests overnight with the sample chips in ceramic packaging, the preliminary results were favorable. However, tests on the plastic packaging would be necessary.

It soon became clear Bill Sydnes wanted to halt the C65 and just needed to find a way to do it. "It wasn't his idea and he didn't want it," says Bill Gardei. "Commodore could have been up there with Nintendo, Sega, or Sony. But they didn't want the image of being a toymaker. They forgot why they were in business: to make money."

Sydnes instead favored releasing his cost-reduced Amiga 300. "I think that Commodore as a whole wasn't really behind the C65, and they didn't think it was the right product for the market at that time," says Andy Finkel. "It was competing against things like the A500, given the time frame. I would imagine something like the C65 would be a hard sell."

In many ways, Sydnes saw the C65 as a direct competitor to the A300 project, which he had taken over. "Upper management said, 'We can't really launch two big products in the same time window and especially at such a close price point and maybe even the same target audience," says Paul Lassa. "It might be interpreted as either a mixed message or not a clear focused message. I think that there was supposed to be a big gap between the C65 and an Amiga 300."

Sydnes knew Irving Gould had a soft spot for the low end 8-bit line and wanted to recapture and continue the C64 market. And the two most powerful European marketing departments, the UK and Germany, also wanted the project. He would need to present a better case to cancel the machine. In the meantime, he had the power to delay the product.

In mid-July, Frank, Sydnes, and Eggebrecht began discussing what to do about the C65 project, with Frank pushing for an immediate management decision. Frank requested a detailed post-mortem of the project from Ted Lenthe, with an emphasis on what went wrong. Lenthe replied with what everyone knew was wrong. There had been a lack of full, top-level support for the project, inadequate resources given to testing the chips (especially timing specs and rigorous system timing analysis). He also mentioned problems within the team, such as a lack of a unified view of the final system specs and alleging Bill Gardei had alienated all of the system design engineers.

A few days after the report was presented to Bill Sydnes, Jeff Porter wrote a counter-report fighting for the C65. He argued that the latest chip results were favorable and that Greg Berlin, initially a skeptic of the C65, was now indicating the system was ready for production.

Despite his pleas, Bill Sydnes and Jeff Frank felt the C65 project might steal company resources from other Amiga projects. "I could see just from my experience in other jobs I've had where some projects stopped or failed or were cancelled because an engineering team was struggling to complete one project and another project was begging for resources, even a small amount of resources," says Paul Lassa. "They simply said, 'We don't have the people, we don't have the expertise. The only way we could give you a bunch of people is if we take people from this other project.' If the company at the top level said, 'Well we can damage the Amiga's development path to peel off a few people and give them to the C65,' upper management might take the low-risk path and say, 'No, let's not do that. You guys stay on your path because we don't want to jeopardize Amiga's future as the main path of the company.'"

Getting Rid of Bill Gardei

As Ted Lenthe's report had stated, Bill Gardei had alienated most of the C65 development team, including the most recent newcomer to the C65 project, Greg Berlin. Dave Haynie discovered a tense atmosphere in the group when he ran some chip simulations. "I never really worked with Gardei but I ran into him at one point," he recalls. "It seems that there was a simulation package that ran on one of the VAX [systems] that everybody used for chip design. However, whenever he got pissed off at somebody, you would lose access to that."

Haynie accidentally took away Gardei's source of control. "I didn't know any of this," he recalls. "I played with the terminal and thought, 'This is way too slow. I'm going to fix it.' At the same time, I was writing a magazine article for *Amiga World* on the new SAS C++ compiler. So I combined these two jobs and wrote my own viewer using the new C++ compiler."

Haynie's program simultaneously improved on the old VAX program and freed his chip designers from Gardei's grip. "Apparently Bill Gardei did not like that too much," says Haynie. "I built this display program that solved an issue I didn't know existed in this little power struggle that was going on in the chip department."

Bill Gardei was the key to the C65 project, but after the postmortem report, and in light of the round of layoffs occurring at the same time, he found a target on his back. "Commodore was looking to cut costs any way it could," says Gardei. "With the A3000 launch a failure, there would be none of the anticipated revenue from that product. They didn't have the cash and needed to downsize."

At the end of July, along with dozens of other employees, he was dismissed from Commodore in the middle of a worldwide recession. "I'm just glad I wasn't part of the final layoffs, because when I left there were still jobs in southeastern Pennsylvania," he says.

Although Bill Gardei was no longer working at Commodore, work on the C65 continued. "My chips were finished and my job was done," says Gardei. "I don't know of a time when work ever stopped, at least until well after I left."

After Gardei's departure, management decreed that there would be no further revisions on the 4567 and no replacement for Gardei. If any major bugs were found in the chipset now, it would spell the end for the project. Fred Bowen wondered how the project could continue without Gardei.

After Gardei's departure, Jeff Frank continued disparaging the project and Gardei's chip work, perhaps attempting to build the political will to kill the project completely. Frank said he wanted to "deep six" the project and no longer had any faith in the C65, even though there were no major problems with the timing parameters. Surprisingly, engineers such as Hedley Davis stood up for Gardei and his chip work, even though he was no longer with the company.

Chip Characterization

In late July, Ted Lenthe wrote a proposal for an exhaustive set of chip tests on the 4510 and 4567. The purpose of the tests was to figure out timing issues and verify they could be manufactured en masse and remain cost effective. Engineers would subject the chips to different voltages and temperatures to see what extremes made them fail. They would also be tested by the huge multi-million dollar chip tester, the MegaOne.

The tests, called chip characterization, would be conducted by a CSG employee named Ben Rappaport and would take 13 weeks at a material cost of $17,200. Mehdi Ali okayed the tests in August, and the results were expected in early November.

The tests were sure to find problems with the chips. The irony, of course, was that the chip designer was no longer employed at Commodore, and it would be difficult or impossible to correct the problems when they were found.

The final characterization report, whatever the results, was largely moot by the time it was presented in November 1991. Commodore had already missed the Christmas season and launching in 1992 was far too late. "It was a cute little product but it was just five years too late," says Hedley Davis.

Wrapping Up the C65

Anticipation for the C65 was strong, with GM Kelly Sumner eagerly awaiting the system. *Zzap!* magazine in the UK had been running a monthly column in late 1991 posting comments from readers about the new bedroom computer. The general response from readers was one of anticipation, noting the C65 sounded like what the C128 and C64GS should have been. Then in December, the magazine reported it was highly unlikely the machine would ever see the light of day.

Although the C65 had won many backers within the company, others preferred to concentrate on the Amiga. "I for one was very pleased [about the cancellation]," says David Pleasance. "I had been very vocal to head office about not having a market for it in the UK. We had very little marketing budget compared to Nintendo and Sega, who were making all their profit from the sales of the games, not the hardware."

Pleasance thought Commodore lacked the infrastructure or ability to copy Nintendo's marketing plan. "I was unhappy that we did not (and I believed could not) have a satisfactory licensing arrangement with the software publishers, who we had an exceptionally strong relationship with," says Pleasance. "And probably more importantly, we had no credible means to administer such a scheme."

On December 9, 1991, Lassa was ordered to archive all his C65 work and remove the project from Commodore's server. Bill Sydnes transferred the C65 employees over to the A300 project. Paul Lassa asked Jeff Porter why it was cancelled. "There were probably a couple of contributing factors, but one of the things that he told me is that Commodore was obviously at least in the beginnings of, if not well into, financial difficulties," says Lassa. "To launch a product was a significant ramping expense."

So how did the once promising C65 project become a failure? The answer probably goes back to late 1985 when Bill Gardei began work on the 4502 chip. Assuming the chip was meant to target a faster C64 successor, Commodore should have had a coherent plan to develop improved sound and video chips. Development on the VIC-III should have begun in 1985, as well as a possible SID-II chip with stereo and multiplexed voices.

But back in 1985, Commodore had just released the C128, and most of the industry believed video games were dead. They felt they needed to concentrate on the business market. When they realized the C64 was still alive in early 1986 after record Christmas sales, they should have begun planning not to extend the life of the current C64 model but to create a more advanced model.

Instead, one guy (Bill Gardei) was left to develop multiple chips, one after another, which inevitably stretched out the development time of the whole project. These chips had to contend with improvements with each new revision, along with new bugs. But started early enough, the C65 could have emerged in 1988 when it would have been not just relevant but timed precisely as the C64 began to die off. Instead, work began on the VIC-III in October 1987; and as history shows, that was a three-year project given Commodore's minimal resources.

For software makers invested in the success of the C64, it was a disappointment. Perhaps no one was more disappointed than GEOS creator Brian Dougherty. The GEOS operating system would have benefited the most from faster processor speeds, better resolutions, and more memory. Unfortunately, the failure to upgrade the C64 line meant that GEOS would be left behind with the antiquated C64 hardware.

Brian Dougherty would have been prepared to evolve GEOS along with improved versions of the C64. "If we'd have been a part of that, probably the first step while we were still on the 6502 architecture would be faster 6502 variants that came out. You could have added more memory and had a full color bitmap high-resolution version. But at some point you would have then switched over to a linear 32 bit C-based operating system."

Bill Gardei would have also been prepared to follow up the C65 with a more sophisticated processor. "Would we go 16 bit? Yes, if we had survived," he says.

With PC compatibles already dominating, Brian Dougherty feels an 8-bit computer was not enough for the time. "Maybe a better generation Commodore 64 successor product could have extended it a little longer," he says. "You could have squeezed another couple of years out of that architecture on the 8-bit platform, but that wouldn't be a long-term success for Commodore."

Gardei believes he could have released the C65 if management had pushed for it. "We can always blame management," he says. "The C65 was not a technical failure. The product was not ready, and management did not have the will to finish it."

Dave Haynie wonders if the 8-bit C65 would have been viable. "I don't think there was any real demand for any 8-bit machine in those days, sorry to say, other than nostalgic purposes," he says.

The Sydnes Era 1991

Now that Henri Rubin had been deposed from his position atop Commodore engineering, a new era would begin; one that would be better in some ways and worse in others. First, the new VP of engineering, Bill Sydnes, would try to realign Commodore to concentrate on the company's most profitable products.

A300 Continues

Mehdi Ali had recently placed his own people in positions of power, and now Bill Sydnes took control of product development. "They got there and between the two of them they decided that nobody needed Amigas. They wanted PCs," says Dave Haynie. "They spent the first six months pretty much deciding that they should get out of the Amiga business, so they weren't doing anything but the Amiga 300."

With Jeff Porter out of the way, Sydnes was free to steer the A300 project himself. "Whenever you have a successful product, there's always the next regime coming in to say, 'You know, we've got to cost reduce it,'" says Porter. "He relieved me of all my Amiga duties because he wanted to do it. He said, 'I can cost reduce the A300.' And I said, 'Oh yeah? Do you actually know who designed the A500? Just try it asshole.'"

Sydnes was confident he would be able to shave more from Jeff Porter's bill of materials. "Sydnes came in and said, 'We're going to cut $50 off the price of the A500 and come out with this new computer,'" recalls Dave Haynie.

The A300 already had the relatively expensive 16-bit Type II PCMCIA slot, similar to the one in the CDTV. However, after meeting with managers in Commodore Europe, Sydnes felt it needed something more. "The Germans said, 'We won't sell anything without a hard drive,'" recalls UK marketing manager David Pleasance.

As a result, the A300 motherboard would have to undergo revisions to include a 44-pin ATA controller to support a hard drive. "They bring in this guy and he starts doing some just major dumb shit," says Hedley Davis. "He's like, 'I'm in charge. I'm doing the management shit. We're going to build this and we're going to build that.' And he starts moving the features around and comes up with this product that does less than what the A500 does and cost more to build."

The changes would ultimately push back the release date from November 1991 into 1992, while adding to the cost of the bill of materials. "The project was codenamed the A300, because it was supposed to cost that much less. It ended up costing more," says Jeff Porter.

Joe Augenbraun had helped Robbins design the A300 but when Sydnes came aboard, he was glad to be off the project. "I did that for six months. I didn't step on his toes at all. I was the perfect assistant," says Augenbraun. "It was funny because at the end of it, George was like, 'Wow it was really great working with you. Let's do another one!' I'm like, 'Nope.' I wanted to get it done as quickly as possible because it was so uninteresting."

Robbins soldiered on with the design under Sydnes but was apathetic, adding whatever new technology to the A300 that his boss requested. "George and the other engineers couldn't (for the most part) care less what it costs," says Porter. "They were just having fun designing cool new stuff."

Jeff Frank, overseeing Robbins, ultimately saw the project through to completion as ordered by his boss, Bill Sydnes. They would continue working on the A300 for the remainder of 1991 and into early 1992. "There were just enough people sucking up to his ass that the thing went through," says Hedley Davis. "That's the sad truth of it."

Jeff Porter's Comeback

After Bill Sydnes pushed Jeff Porter out of the Amiga hardware group, the latter had wisely fought to stay in West Chester, rather than follow Jeff Frank's order to attend a conference. This gave him the ability to make the most of a bad situation, instead of allowing decisions to be thrust upon him. Porter was able to convince Sydnes of his usefulness due to his knowledge of Amiga technology. He asked that he be allowed to remain in research, and Sydnes even announced in writing and verbally that Porter would contribute to advanced technology, specifically on the AA and AAA chipset direction.

In return, Porter agreed he would focus on the CDTV-CR project in the multimedia division and not interfere with Sydnes' leadership. "He said, 'Why don't you go play on that CDTV thing. Have a ball,'" recalls Porter. "He gave me the CDTV-CR and a small team to deal with that including Hedley. I went off to go do my own thing."

As previously mentioned, the engineers had a joke that the multimedia division was where managers go to die. Both Harold Copperman and Henri Rubin had both been assigned to the group and then departed when they realized they held no influence there. But for Porter, the division held a special significance because he had previously lost out on the potentially game-changing CDTV product to Don Gilbreath.

Still steaming from being relieved of his management role of the Amiga group, he was determined to beat the A300 with his own version of the Amiga, the CDTV-CR. "I said I can build CDTVs to kill every Amiga that was ever built," explains Porter. "I can build a CDTV that will replace the Amiga. I can build a whole new product line in CDTV land that you won't have to worry about the A500 or the A600 or all these other things. I'll just do everything in this new shape and size of CDTV."

In many ways, Porter welcomed his comeback to hands-on engineering. After all, the management decisions were now relieved from his shoulders and he would be largely left alone to create. "It was a fun project," he says.

Initially a skeptic of CD-ROM, Porter had became passionate about the technology and was determined to improve on the previous CDTV, while adding new features—occasionally to the detriment of the "CR" aspect. "The only thing that we didn't cost reduce on the CDTV-CR was the vacuum fluorescent display on the front panel," says Porter. "We had the most awesome vacuum fluorescent display. When the disc was spinning, you had a little spinning disc. We had VU meters that bounced up and down with the right and left audio channel. It was sex on a stick. It was great."

Hedley Davis designed the artwork for the display and decided to play a prank on rival CD-i. "I had a couple extra electrodes that were left over that I could put whatever I wanted," he explains. "When I made the display, I put a CD-i logo directly in the display. I knew sooner or later these guys are going to get one of these and take it apart and see CD-i on there. It was just totally to mess with them. I had fun with that project."

Porter also wanted his CDTV to play video from the disc—a precursor to DVD movies. In order to retrieve data fast enough, he also proposed including a double speed CD-ROM drive.

By August, Porter knew the cost of his design came to $284.30 for parts and labor, meaning the product could sell for approximately $750 at retail, competitive with the Philips CD-i. He estimated he could have pilot production by December 1991 and full production by April 1992.

Porter proposed a team of eight full time engineers for the project, which Porter estimated would cost $1.63 million to complete. Unfortunately, Mehdi Ali had instituted a hiring freeze, so engineers would either be pulled from other projects or hired on a contract basis.

Porter was a little hesitant to re-hire Carl Sassenrath for the job, partly because he would only work out of California, and partly cost. "Carl in particular was a serial offender," says Bryce Nesbitt. "Carl kept raising his hourly rate. He was eventually $250 an hour and we still hired him! And they were working 60 and 80 hour weeks writing code." At up to $15,000 per week, Sassenrath could quickly drain the project's budget.

Porter wanted to upgrade his CDTV to AmigaOS 2.04, which would require a skilled and experienced AmigaOS programmer. It was fortuitous timing that Andy Finkel had been laid off at the same time, because Finkel knew more about 2.04 than even Sassenrath. "At that point I was laid off by Commodore, but they hired me as a consultant," says Finkel. "I worked in the CDTV group but I was not a Commodore employee anymore. I became the software guy down there."

Finkel knew CD-ROM technology had great potential. "At the time, it was kind of interesting and unique that you could actually look at a CD-ROM as a distribution medium for software, which really opened up a lot of possibilities that you just couldn't do before," he says. "For me, that was the game changing thing about CDTV. Finally you weren't limited to loading a game on 200 floppies or an encyclopedia that had almost no information, because trying to load that kind of thing on floppies was incredibly painful. Having a CD on every unit was a big change, and it would really change the kind of software you could do."

As a contractor, Finkel received even greater pay than he had at Commodore. "Andy was a great engineer who thrived after his firing from his position at Commodore," says Bryce Nesbitt. "He did great work on CDTV. And CDTV itself I thought was a another product that had promise."

Hedley Davis would help design two chips for CDTV-CR. "We had a couple of gate arrays in there called Grace and Beauty, and they were the system glue," explains Davis.

The central task of the project was to cost-reduce the CD-ROM drive. The two chips would eliminate a lot of internal circuitry from the original CDTV. "He did the whole inexpensive interface for the low-cost CD-ROM drive, which was really an audio mechanism for a cheap CD player," says Jeff Porter. "Then we had to come up with the right firmware on the CD-ROM drive. We worked with the guys at Chinon to do that to optimize the algorithms for seek times and all this other stuff. It was pretty cool to use incredibly low-cost technology to make a CD-ROM drive which everyone said could not be done."

During this time, Davis began to experience employee fatigue and demoralization for a number of reasons. Earlier in July, he had met in New York with the CDTV-CR team to discuss the project with Mehdi Ali and Bill Sydnes. At the meeting, Sydnes had verbally denigrated the previous two years worth of efforts from the previous engineering team. Before he realized what he was doing, Davis began talking back to the high ranking executive. He bit his tongue before too much damage was done, but he worried his prospects for career advancement had been cut short due to the outburst.

At the same meeting, Mehdi Ali had made clear the importance of the CDTV-CR project to save Commodore from hemorrhaging more money on Gould's favored project. He asked Davis to put in 16 hour days on the two chips while Bill Sydnes promised more support for the team. That support never came—Steve Kreckman was supposed to replace the recently departed Scott Hood, but he had no loyalty to the new CDTV project and proved unhelpful. Despite this, Davis worked diligently on his two chips throughout August and early September, turning in regular 12 to 15 hour work days (not quite the 16 hour days Ali had asked for).

Davis voiced his concerns to Porter, wondering if he would ever be in line for another raise or promotion for his efforts. Porter was able to temporarily mollify his concerns, but it was clear Davis' allegiance to Commodore was beginning to fade, as it was with other longtime engineers.

Davis finished his two chips in a surprisingly quick fashion. Unlike other chips of late, the CDTV-CR chips worked on the first revision. "An engineer named Chris Coley designed those and integrated those new chips and it was a pretty slick thing," says Davis. "We did system simulations of the whole thing front to back; and when we built it, it fricking worked. That was pretty cool."

Don Gilbreath had remained on the Special Projects group since he lost his bid to design the CDTV-CR. In the meantime, he had created the A690, a CD-ROM drive that would allow the A500 to play CDTV discs. It was an interesting project that would allow scores of A500 owners to join the CD-ROM craze.

Hedley Davis still felt Gilbreath was overestimating how quickly he could complete projects. "Now Don, whom I like, who rightly deserves to be called the father of that program, would talk shit like nobody's business," he says. "He would explain how something could be done in X months no problem. After a while, of course, we stopped believing him. This drove him nuts as he would try to explain how we were wrong."

During development of the A690, Davis decided to prove just how off base his estimates were. "Well, it got so bad that one day I wrote on the top of my white board in my office the date and what he said would happen," explains Davis. "He was right there and agreed that was his point. This happened a few times. I had maybe five, 'Don said on this date' things up there. And then when he would come into my office on his latest tirade, I would point at the board and say, 'Yeah, but this didn't happen when you said.'"

When Mehdi Ali called a September 1991 meeting in New York to update him on the progress of the CDTV-CR, Gilbreath attempted to grab his CDTV project back from Porter. "To me, CDTV was my baby," says Gilbreath.

Gilbreath informed Ali about the slow seek times of Porter's cost reduced CD-ROM drive. He also created his own alternate concept for a CDTV which he called CDTV Phase 2. His proposal would be delivered quicker, because it used mainly the same technology in CDTV, including AmigaOS 1.3, but with an improved CD-ROM drive with faster seek times.

Luckily Porter had enough time to prepare a demo and show that his double-speed drive actually booted up faster than the one Gilbreath proposed. "There were a lot of Doubting-Thomas' on the design of the CDTV-CR where I was using a cheapo audio CD player mechanism with a motorized drawer," recalls Porter. "Most folks thought I was completely nuts. But we did it."

In the end, Porter succeeded in massively cost-reducing the CD-ROM drive. With a final parts cost of $73.27, resulting in a retail savings of over $200 compared to the CD-ROM drive in CDTV Phase 2. "We kind of put low-cost CD ROMs on the map because of that," he says.

Porter soon found support in surprising places. "Carl Sassenrath sent a letter to Irving Gould telling him that he was actually shocked at the performance on that CD mechanism," says Porter. "As good as any on the market at that time. That meant a lot from a top Los Gatos software guy who was always quite critical."

Bryce Nesbitt Resigns

Throughout 1991, Bryce Nesbitt worked to develop and release AmigaOS 2.04. Once it was verified stable, he sent out disks and ROM chips to developers so they could ensure their software worked with the new operating system, which would appear first on the Amiga 500 Plus.

During his time heading the Amiga software group, Nesbitt was able to foster not only a culture of reliability and stability, but also set up methods for users to report bugs. Users could send an email directly to Commodore's "suggestions" email address, or send bug reports through the online service BIX.

But Nesbitt was never able to establish better relations among engineering and marketing. "I did my best to coordinate and cultivate friendships and connections across the company," he says. "I was able to do things with those connections at a stealth level. So yes, I did go to talk to them but no I never really had the support of the engineering management group to do that. I didn't really have a deep influence."

Although upper management now held a tighter grip on engineering, Nesbitt felt they did not appreciate the importance of the OS and didn't help to guide its development. "That's the failure of management. It's not a failure to coordinate, its failure to lead or inspire. It's a failure to have influence deep enough down into the organization," he says. "If the influence didn't get to my level as the head of the operating system group, it definitely didn't get far enough down, because I was making decisions about what features we would be adding to the operating system and where we would be spending our engineering resources, and my choices as a young kid weren't coordinated with what the rest of the company was doing except by osmosis. It wasn't like we were all reading from a plan and doing it."

After Jeff Porter was demoted and Bill Sydnes took over, Nesbitt saw that Commodore was unlikely to improve.

Nesbitt was also tiring of the clashes with site management. At the front of Commodore headquarters was a security booth with a boom gate that raised and lowered to allow employees and visitors onto the premises. "They had guards at the front gate and you couldn't take equipment in or out," explains Guy Wright. "You had to have special slips and stuff. It was all from Jack Tramiel in the early days of Commodore. They were all afraid that Atari was going to steal their stuff or something. Mattel or somebody. So they were really big on corporate spying and stuff. They were very paranoid."

Nesbitt's fellow programmer, Michael Sinz was a member of the "speed bump resistance". In July 1991, as he returned from lunch, he passed through the gate when it "accidentally" came down and landed on his car, damaging the paint and body. It seemed like security might be trying to get back those engineers who had been mocking them.

That, coupled with the weirdness of having the security guards rob music CDs from his office, and the ongoing battle with building management, meant Nesbitt no longer felt at home in Commodore.

June 1991 marked a turning point for Bryce Nesbitt's career at Commodore. He had previously taken a stand that if Commodore failed to announce the A3640 board in a timely fashion, he would resign from the company. "We had it! It worked! It was fast. It was the latest processor and we were the first ones to have it, but the thing that was revolutionary about it was the memory management unit."

Commodore had failed to publicize the board at CES that summer and Nesbitt felt he had no choice. "That in fact precipitated my leaving Commodore," he says. Although he did not immediately resign, he began telling coworkers his disappointment in the company after CES.

With OS 2.04 on its way, Bryce Nesbitt's final day was August 30. Pranks were a part of the hacker culture at Commodore and an email was sent from Jeff Frank's account inviting everyone in Commodore to his place for a send-off party for Nesbitt. Frank, of course, had not sent the email and was unaware of the party. However, someone tipped him off about the party and it never materialized.

The departure of Nesbitt was a loss for Commodore. Other engineers now saw that respected engineers were leaving. "It's the most interesting group of people I've worked with ever," says Nesbitt. "I enjoyed the time strongly. We didn't respect the company that we were working for, but we respected each other and it could have been much greater than it was."

Nesbitt fully expected Commodore to release an upgrade kit for AmigaOS 2.04 after he departed, but with the new management headed by Mehdi Ali and Bill Sydnes, it did not look like it would happen. "Basically, marketing had decided they weren't going to release AmigaOS 2.04 as an upgrade, but instead were going to force everyone to just buy new hardware to get the new OS," says Denny Atkin, a full time editor at *Compute!* magazine. "Engineering was of course aghast."

The Amiga software team wanted Commodore US, run by Jim Dionne, to release an upgrade kit for existing Amiga owners. Commodore's engineers had a history of leaking information to magazines in an attempt to pressure management. AmigaOS developer Mike Sinz reached out to the Compute! editor to attempt to exert pressure. "I knew Mike from the BIX online service and he got in touch with me and told me anonymously," says Atkin.

"I knew people in the computer press," says Sinz. "Denny Atkin and I were talking. I told him, 'You can't quote me but Commodore is saying they won't make the 2.04 upgrade kit for existing systems. We think it's a horrible idea because we need people to upgrade, otherwise we can't make forward progress. At some point 1.3 won't be compatible at all.'"

Atkin went to work, not only covering the story but also posting online messages to places like Usenet about the decision. He pleaded with Amiga users to generate a letter writing campaign aimed at Jim Dionne. "Denny leaked the information without making it traceable to me," says Sinz. "There was immediate public backlash and corporate had to make the 2.04 upgrade kit. It was extremely subversive."

AA Task Force

Earlier in the year, Irving Gould had expected the AA chipset to be done by the fall, with the release of the A1000 Plus computer to follow shortly after. The first revisions of the chip had even been produced earlier in the year. But by early October, the chip was not ready for release. "AA was sort of languishing," says Lew Eggebrecht. "The design was done but there were a lot of bugs."[1]

Bill Sydnes needed to deliver a computer soon. Rather that wait on the AA chipset, he altered the specs for the A1000 Plus by replacing the AA chipset with ECS, something Jeff Porter had previously warned would be a terrible mistake.

The A3000 Plus was now demoted to becoming a test vehicle for the AA chipset, but not necessarily a production system. "By the second revision of the board I was ordered to not make it into a product," says Dave Haynie.

Commodore sold the 50 existing Amiga 3000 Plus machines they had built as development systems for programmers. "I had been forced to take out some of the features just to get the thing out the door," says Haynie.

Sydnes habit of disparaging and shutting down existing projects rankled the West Chester engineers. "His first mission was to destroy the appearance that the former administration, Henri Rubin and Jeff Porter, were as organized and far along as they were," claims Haynie.

Eggebrecht, Sydnes, and Jeff Frank eventually restarted AA development in October. They created a group, called the AA Task Force, led by AA project leader Bob Raible to deal with the problematic chipset. Thirteen engineers including Ted Lenthe, George Robbins, and Dave Haynie attended the weekly meetings, starting October 3, 1991.

Dave Haynie felt the meetings were mostly pointless, or worse, slowed down development of AA. "Basically, in order to slow down the advance of the AA chipset, the new management formed the AA Task Force, which met something like once a week to report on the chips and basically just say stuff still worked," says Haynie. "There had been a couple of chipset bugs I found, but I was able to fix them externally."

Whether or not the task force helped, it was sure to make the new engineering management appear responsible for the inevitable success of the chipset, as though they had rescued it from disaster.

Haynie brought a notebook with him and wrote down the name of a 1980s action star on his cover every week. "At every meeting I added one more member to my personal task force, the one that in my imagination was going to come in all action-hero like and obliterate any evidence there had ever been

---

1   *Amiga User International.* June 1988. "The AUI Interview"

an Ali or a Sydnes," he recalls. The notebook started with Chuck Norris and soon added Clint Eastwood and Sylvester Stallone. Even though the weekly meetings were supposed to speed up AA development, Haynie's roster of action stars would grow to include a dozen members—which meant the release of the AA chipset was dragged out until early 1992.

1991 Shareholder Meeting

In late November, the annual shareholder meeting was once again held in Nassau, Bahamas for the third year in a row. Less than a dozen shareholders showed up to hear Commodore's annual report from the board of directors. This year, Dale Luck was a no-show because Commodore ended his contract with the company and Luck sold off his company shares.

As it turned out, he sold at just the right time. Commodore's stock performance in 1991 had made Irving Gould exceedingly happy. The share price had been around $5 in September 1990. By March 1991, just prior to the launch of CDTV, the stock had risen to $17.5 on the hype around multimedia. "Their stock jumped 10 points or something," recalls Guy Wright.

Gould was also quite satisfied at the results of the previous fiscal year, which ended June 30, 1991. Commodore reported sales of $1.05 billion, the first time the company had exceeded a billion dollars since 1984. Furthermore, due to Mehdi Ali's cuts, the company posted a profit of $48.2 million.

Sales of the Amiga line had increased by 20%, C64 sales increased 30%, and PC clone sales rose 35%. However, the stock fell from $13.25 to $11.875 after the report emerged due to the lower than expected revenues. Analysts predicted revenue for the 4th quarter at $246 million, and they came in at $216.5 million.[2] Worse still, Commodore US was barely generating any revenue, with 85% of those profits coming from Europe.

Despite the lower than expected revenues, Irving Gould and Mehdi Ali received substantial compensation for the year. The previous year, Gould had received $1,750,000 in salary and compensation. His total stock ownership, which fluctuated wildly based on how well Commodore traded on the New York stock exchange, made his shares worth almost $100 million.

His second in command, Mehdi Ali, had been guaranteed $5 million in his first two years with Commodore. By 1991 he had received $2,015,949 in salary and compensation, owned $6,089,730 in stock, and had accumulated around $9,000,000 in stock options in the last three years.

One shareholder, Philadelphia lawyer Richard Ash, had persistently dogged Irving Gould through the years. He attended the Bahamian meeting. Before

---

2   *Wall Street Journal,* August 7, 1991, p. B3.

official proceedings began, he accused those present, saying, "You're holding it in Nassau because you don't want shareholders to come."[3]

Ron Alexander, Commodore's chief financial officer, asked Ash to make his comments in the question period afterwards. Instead, Ash continued his tirade, "No one is able to attend the meeting in the middle of nowhere."

Gould claimed it was proper to meet in the Bahamas, saying, "Are we a Bahamian company?"

When Ash would not back down, he was asked to leave or be physically ejected. Choosing the latter option, two security guards entered the room and escorted him out. Later in the meeting, Gould apologized to shareholders for "what happened earlier." Other than this one small rebellion, no one seriously challenged Irving Gould's leadership at the meeting.

Trading Stock

During his time with Commodore, Mehdi Ali had accumulated a lot of stock. "He got one of those deals when he came on," says Guy Wright. "He's making like a million dollars a year, but they gave him like 10 million dollars worth of stock."

It would have been a tempting time for anyone who owned Commodore stock to sell, but a lock-up period on trading would have restricted Ali from selling his shares until that period ended. The stock price subsequently fell to $11, following the debut of CDTV; but then by November, it had again risen to $17. "I was in the legal office one day when I was working on CDTV," recalls Wright. "Mehdi Ali's secretary came in and asked the legal secretary if she could get copies of some paperwork that said when the dates were when Mehdi Ali could start selling his shares of stock in Commodore."

After this momentary boost of the stock price, it began slowly dropping again. Commodore, and of course Irving Gould, were becoming more aware by the day of the failure of CDTV, the very product that had provided a boost to the stock. It is around this time that he probably saw the writing on the wall and began to lose hope for Commodore.

Gould had steadfastly held onto his 17.9% share of Commodore for an admirably long time. He even forbid Commodore from holding a stock offering to raise money for marketing and development for fear that it would dilute his own shares. However, he would soon join others in a desire to sell off those shares.

---

3   *Philadelphia Inquirer*, Nov. 26, 1991. "Commodore Shareholder Meeting in Bahamas"

On March 25, 1992 Commodore had good news to report. The IRS lawsuit against the company, which had hung over Commodore since January 1989, was finally resolved. According to the *Philadelphia Inquirer*, "...it had settled the major issues involving its tax litigation with the IRS. Under the settlement, Commodore is to pay the government about $2 million in interest. The IRS originally had sought $109 million in taxes for the years 1981 through 1986."[4] This news resulted in a 9.5 percent climb in the stock price that day.

The next day, in what can only be described as suspicious timing, a New York based reporter from CNBC and *Money Magazine*, Dan Dorfman, reported that Nintendo was interested in buying Commodore. Normally Commodore shares averaged 418,000 trades per day, but volumes on March 26 exceeded 1.9 million shares. Commodore's stock price rose an additional 9.6% that day based on the rumor.

Dorfman attributed the rumor to an analyst with Standard & Poor's Corp. named Lawrence Freitag. Freitag had previously described Commodore's stock as "the single best value in the computer industry" and predicted the shares would reach $25 in 12 months.

Nintendo was swift to deny the rumor, calling it "totally unfounded". A few years later, Dorfman was unmasked as a stock manipulator and fired from CNBC and *Money Magazine* for ethics violations.

Premature Release

Due to the AA Task Force, Commodore did not release the A1000 Plus in time for the 1991 holiday season. The engineers felt this computer, more than any other, could help Commodore's fortunes. "Changing the casework probably set it back nine months. It missed Christmas because of the case," says Joe Augenbraun. "And once it missed Christmas, the company started rolling downhill. At a $1000 price point, that would have been a high-volume product. That would have done really well for the company.

Although Commodore had planned to release several new products in 1991, the company only introduced the failed CDTV and A3000UX. Surprisingly, these failures were offset by the rising popularity of the A500. For example, in the UK the A500 sold 160,000 units between July 1988 and June 1989. By 1992, Commodore UK sold over 300,000 units for the same 1 year period.

But not all was well. Manufacturing on the A500 had been stopped when production on the A500 Plus began in late 1991. Commodore did not plan to ship any Amiga 500 Plus computers to the USA and sent all of them to Europe. But they had underestimated demand for the original A500 and ran out of stock sometime in October 1991, before the holiday buying season had even started. As a result of halting production on the A500, a desperate Commodore Germany, which ran Commodore International's distribution, began putting A500 Plus computers in ordinary A500 packaging and shipping them out. These ECS Amigas appeared in the "Cartoon Classics" bundle, which included *Lemmings, Simpsons, Captain Planet,* and *Deluxe Paint III*.

As *Amiga Format Magazine* reported, "Why had the new machine appeared with no announcement from Commodore? At first Commodore claimed that "only two or three thousand" A500 Pluses had gone into circulation, but it soon emerged that this was not the case. It became evident that the Plus was intended to be launched after Christmas and huge demand for A500 packs had led Commodore UK to take shipment of whatever Amiga 500s they could get their hands on."[5]

On the surface, those owners who opened up their A500 box and found an A500 Plus should have been overjoyed to have been given a free upgrade that no one else had. The problem was the A500 Plus was incompatible with about 30% of Amiga games. Many of them ended up replacing the Kickstart 2.04 chip with a Kickstart 1.3 chip in order to retain backward compatibility.

Amiga Power magazine later listed the "Top Six crap things done by Commodore." Number one on the list was, "Bringing out the A500 Plus and then denying responsibility for incompatibility problems and not doing anything to help, thereby alienating and annoying loads of loyal customers."[6]

Winter CES

At the January 1992 CES in Las Vegas, held January 9 through 12th, Commodore had some excellent news to announce. The company had sold three million Amiga computers since 1985, with one million sold in the prior year alone.

Irving Gould was probably feeling good about the recent management changes. After all, the company had surpassed a billion dollars in sales for the year ending June 1991, and now for the past six months the company had revenue of $575.7 million and a profit of $45.4 million.

Gould gave credit to Mehdi Ali for keeping Commodore profitable while awaiting new products. Even in the face of the CDTV failure, Ali had still managed to turn a decent profit. To Gould, it was a testament to his financial skills.

---

5   *Amiga Format*, Dec. 1991, p. 9. "New Amiga surprises everyone including Commodore"

6   *Amiga Power*, Dec. 1993, p. 71. "Top Six crap things done by Commodore."

There was equally good news out of Europe. According to market research firm International Data Corp., Commodore controlled 12.4 percent of the European personal computer market, slightly behind IBM with 12.7 percent. This put Commodore ahead of Apple, at 5.2 percent, and Compaq with 4.6 percent.

As for the CES show itself, Jim Dionne chose to promote the CDTV front and center, along with new CDTV titles, including an improved version of *Defender of the Crown*. Commodore also demonstrated the A592 CD-ROM drive (the renamed A690 product, so as not to confuse it with an Amiga 600 device) that transformed an Amiga 500 into a CDTV.

Surprisingly, there was no demonstration of the upcoming A600, nor the "credit card" games that were destined for the PCMCIA slot in the A600. Commodore also did little to highlight the upcoming release of the Amiga 500 Plus, perhaps indicating already that Jim Dionne was planning to put more emphasis on the new A600 from Bill Sydnes.

As it turned out, 1991 would also be the final year for the products developed under Henri Rubin and Jeff Porter. The A500 Plus, largely built under Porter, would make its official debut in 1992. However, the momentum built up by that team would draw to a close in 1992. From here on, it was the new Sydnes/Eggebrecht/Frank team in charge. Now it remained to be seen what the new team was capable of achieving.

Amiga 600
1992

Commodore's greatest failure, the Plus/4 computer released in 1984, had started life as a low-cost $99 computer to compete with the Sinclair ZX Spectrum. An influx of new management and marketing people caused its features to bloat and it was eventually released at $299 US—three times its target price. As a result, the Plus/4 bombed in the marketplace and Commodore almost went out of business. With the ongoing replacement of management in the years since, there was every chance the company had lost its corporate memory of the event. Would history repeat itself now that new management was in place?

A300 Becomes A600

As George Robbins finished off the A300 design, it became clear the cost reduction goal for the system could not be met, largely because of the SMT form factor. "I think George probably did a pretty good job and the surface mount screwed him," says Joe Augenbraun.

Bill Sydnes had set out to have two Amiga computers at two different price points: the A500 Plus and the less expensive A300. Instead, the opposite happened. "They took over what George [Robbins] was working on and said, 'We have to change this.' They wanted new features, but the A600 didn't give anybody any new features that anybody would consider useful," says Dave Haynie. "It didn't work with the Amiga 500 peripherals. It took away the keypad. The result cost $50 more than the A500. There was this whole list of things that were wrong with it."

The resulting product would appeal to almost no one. "Bill was out of his depth when it came to the Amiga," says Jeff Porter. "The A300 was started because he promised Mehdi he could cost reduce the A500. It cost more.

That'll teach you to try to out cost-reduce Porter. No one could touch me on that topic!"

Porter believes the project manager should have monitored the development of the computer more closely and have been prepared to abandon ideas. "Surface mount parts cost more. Four layer PCB costs more," he says. "No one was watching the costs."

By all accounts, Robbins was apathetic during the A300 development, having to be pulled along by coworkers and even Jeff Frank. It probably would have made more sense to allow Robbins to concentrate on the A500 Plus while handing off the A300 to a more motivated engineer who embraced cost reduction and wanted to prove himself. "If I had been given the project to cost reduce the A500, I think I probably could've gotten $100 off of it, maybe $150," says Joe Augenbraun. "It wasn't that cost reduced. The keyboard was a pretty nice keyboard. There's money to take out there. There's a lot of shielding. There was a lot of plastic. There were extra components on the board. The board was bigger than it needed to be."

Augenbraun concedes he would have had to abandon SMT. "It was absolutely clear that SMT was more expensive," he says. "It was just totally obvious. I can see my way to getting some money out of that thing but I wouldn't have been able to do it going to surface mount."

The PCMCIA slot was also expensive. "That added some cost from a circuitry point of view because they were changing a little bit the architecture," says Gerard Bucas of GVP. "The bottom line is, manufacturing cost was higher than the A500, I think, like thirty, forty dollars and of course that made it impossible."

To get out of this conundrum, Sydnes renamed the A300 the A600 on January 2, 1992, in order to give the impression that it was a step up from the A500. The plan would require Commodore's customers to overlook the obvious. "Did it have new features? They sold it as if it did, but I don't think it did," says Augenbraun. "It was not a good product."

This left marketing in a difficult position, with two products at almost the same price point; the A500 Plus and the A600. Sydnes began to ponder the unthinkable. He began contemplating the elimination of Commodore's best selling product line, the A500.

By April, the A600 was ready for production. However, the A300 PCB boards had already been manufactured in large numbers and had the A300 name engraved on the board, potentially revealing Sydnes' ruse to curious owners who ventured inside the computer case.

Attacking GVP

Commodore had attempted to deny technical support to Great Valley Products (GVP) the prior year at Mehdi Ali's request. Within a month, Ali was forced to reverse his decision, but GVP had continued growing since then and surpassed Commodore in 1992. "I wasn't anymore at Commodore and GVP is, let's say, doing all the profitable part of the Amiga. We were at about thirty five million dollars per year eventually, which wasn't that big compared to the size that Commodore was," says Gerard Bucas. "But believe it or not, that is still more than Commodore's peripheral sales."

One of GVP's most profitable and popular peripherals relied on the Amiga 500 and 2000's CPU expansion capabilities. "It's all made possible because the A500 and the A2000 had the CPU expansion slot," explains Bucas. "That implies that you can literally disable the CPU on the motherboard and plug in another board. Now it's as if you have a much faster motherboard, which was totally an incredible architecture in the PC world."

In 1992, GVP released a CPU accelerator called the A530 Turbo. Amazingly, it boosted the A500's 7 MHz speed up to 40 MHz using a Motorola 68EC030 processor. "In A500 we had a box that you plug in the side slot because it also had the CPU expansion board," says Bucas. "Bottom line, that's why GVP could do all those CPU accelerator products which were super successful. We made tonnes and tonnes of money on those."

Mehdi Ali and Bill Sydnes continued looking for ways to hurt GVP's dominance of the Amiga peripherals aftermarket. "Basically a number of people at Commodore felt that GVP was growing too large," recalls Bucas. "So finally Commodore management decided that, 'Listen, on the so called A300 (which eventually was A600), we're going to make no expandability. We're going to screw GVP.' That was the mantra inside. 'We want to make sure they can make no money on this.'"

The A600 would allow no expansion, other than devices that could plug into the PCMCIA port. "The bottom line is, they took away the expansion port," says Bucas. "On top of that, the A300 or the A600 didn't have a faster CPU than the A500. Really what they designed was a product which is supposed to slot in below the A500 and instead of the CPU expansion port they put in a so called PCMCIA slot. You could add peripherals and a few other things but you could not add a CPU accelerator. They said, 'We don't want to make it compatible. Let's screw all these third party manufacturers. We are going to add these PCMCIA slots.'"

In order for this plan to work, Commodore would have to discontinue the highly popular Amiga 500 line, which was still growing in sales year after year. When Commodore had released the Plus/4 in 1984, at least the company continued to sell the popular C64. Would Commodore really end its most popular product and try to force the A600 onto the marketplace?

A1000 Plus Becomes A2200

A month or two after Bill Sydnes renamed the A300 to the A600, he also chose to rename the A1000 Plus to the A2200 for similar reasons. This new A2200 now resided in a metal PC-style case rather than the sleek pizza-box originally envisioned by Joe Augenbraun. As a result, the motherboard designed for the pizza-box no longer fit the new casework, requiring a complete redesign. "There was a lot of work," says Augenbraun.

Mehdi Ali issued a priority on the A2200 and wanted it released in the middle of 1992, alongside the A600. In order to make this ambitious schedule, Bill Sydnes tapped the fastest and most reliable engineer among Commodore's experienced engineers, Greg Berlin. By 1992 Berlin was familiar with all aspects of Amiga development, and he was also intensely focused when given a project. Sydnes named him project manager of the A2200 with Joe Augenbraun working under him, designing the motherboard.

Originally envisioned as an AA computer, Sydnes reverted the graphics chipset back to ECS after it became clear AA would not be ready in 1991. "The PCB had to be redesigned," says Augenbraun. "With the product cycle at Commodore, it was very difficult to get a product out."

The A2200 also lost the ability to handle Dave Haynie's Zorro III bus for expansion cards. "They did the backplanes 2-layer, and when I pointed out that Zorro III didn't run on a 2-layer backplane, they disabled Zorro III mode," explains Dave Haynie. "These were Zorro II only."

The engineers derided the machine by calling it Amiga 1000jr, which was meant to annoy Bill Sydnes. Even Greg Berlin and Joe Augenbraun were in on the joke.

By the time the project was completed, about the only part of the system Augenbraun felt pride for was the custom gate array chip inside, which worked the first time it was manufactured. "All of my chips were one rev," he says. "You should never have to rev your chips. You're spending six-months doing verifications before you tape out. It better work!"

On the bright side, Augenbraun brought the product in at the proper cost. Originally, when conceived in 1990, there was the option for a floppy-only version at $800 retail. By 1992, however, the hard drive was no longer an option. "It was $1000 because it was never going to ship without a hard drive," says Augenbraun. "The cost of a HD was between $100 and $200."

By the end of April 1992, Greg Berlin began getting ready for the pilot production run of the A2200. But before then, Commodore would show off the system to its European sales managers to evaluate their reactions.

A1200 Origins

Mehdi Ali had received criticism from Commodore engineers over the years, but that's not to say that everything he did was wrong. He was perhaps more astute than his charge Bill Sydnes when it came to product selection. Ali knew how vital the low-end Amiga computers were to the survival of Commodore. By 1992, the major video game developers were programming primarily VGA games and not bothering to develop ports of those games for the sub-VGA Amiga. This was because the developers could not easily reuse the same artwork in the Amiga version and would have to recreate each piece of art for the Amiga. By using the AA chipset in a low-end Amiga it would be much easier to port those VGA games.

In February 1992, Ali told Sydnes he wanted a "full court press" to produce an A500 class machine using the upcoming AA chipset by September 1992. He wanted it completed even before the AA chipset had finished beta testing and months before the A600 launch in May.

On February 26, Bill Sydnes asked his subordinate Jeff Frank how he could meet the aggressive September schedule. To expedite the project development time, Frank proposed building the new system starting with the A600 design, with modifications to the custom gate array chips to accommodate the AA chipset.

Frank had a freer hand with this new AA system than he had with the A300/600 and was allowed a higher bill of materials cost. "That project was not as cost sensitive," says Jeff Porter. "I thought it was pretty good." As a result, the product definition for the AA600 (as Sydnes called it then) improved markedly over the A500 specs. The AA600 would use a 32-bit Motorola 68EC020 processor running at 14Mhz (a considerable speed-boost over the A500/A600). It would also come with 2 MB of memory—double the RAM of the A500 Plus. The 68EC020 processor could also address up to 16 MB of memory. The system could also accommodate an internal IDE hard drive. And of course, the AA600 would have notably better graphics on par with VGA standards.

The AA600 would retain many key features of the A600, such as PCM-CIA slots, allowing the Amiga to share in the same ecosystem of PC laptop peripherals. This included SRAM cards, CD-ROM controllers, SCSI controllers, network cards, sound samplers, and video capture devices. However, it still seemed strange for a desktop to use expensive laptop peripherals.

The AA600 would also have the same ports as the A600, including a standard RS-232 serial port and a Centronics parallel port. Unlike the Amiga 500, neither the A600 nor the AA600 would include a Zorro II bus. This once more excluded the AA600 from the Amiga 500 ecosystem of peripherals, leaving a big hole for A500 users.

The AA600 would include a 32-bit CPU/RAM expansion slot, a feature that made Gerard Bucas of GVP happy. "Expendability was back," he says. "The CPU speed was twice what it was on the A500. It was a great computer."

Once again, George Robbins would own the design of the AA600 motherboard. "It was the same crew as the A300. There were a lot of folks," says Jeff Porter. "George and Hedley and all the guys that were on the A500 project. I was put out to pasture, so to speak, so Sydnes could do his thing." Jeff Frank was now the project manager of the AA600.

Robbins would develop the new AA600 motherboard schematic as he built his prototype. In keeping with the previous Amiga code names for motherboards, he decided to name it after the B-52's single *Channel Z*, from their 1989 album *Cosmic Thing*.

Although Robbins liked the B-52's and used their titles due to the link with the A500 codename B-52, by the early nineties Gothic Rock would fuel his engineering of the AA600. He blared *Siouxsie and The Banshees* through the speakers in the Mentor workstation room, creating a truly otherworldly atmosphere for those who visited.

The AA600 would require a special AA version of the Gayle chip used in the A600. It would also need a budget version of Bridgette, the chip in development for the A1000 Plus. The development of these two custom gate array chips would be the most time-sensitive tasks in order to meet the deadline. After the product description for the AA600 was set, Robbins immediately began working on them. "There was a scramble to do an A1200 which turned out to be a great machine," says Gerard Bucas.

On March 19, Robbins finished the design requirements and pinouts for Budgie (a budget version of the Bridgette chip for the AA600) and AA Gayle. He named Budgie after The Creatures guitarist Budgie AKA Peter Edward Clarke. He would design the Budgie gate array himself.

By May 18, 1992, Robbins had all the schematics completed for the gate array chips and his motherboard. Unlike previous Amiga computers, the gate arrays would not be manufactured by Commodore. Ted Lenthe began looking for a company to fabricate the Budgie chip, offering bids to NCR, TI, Motorola, SGS-Thomson, and VLSI Technology, with the latter winning the bid.

By now, Jeff Frank had pushed back the release date of the AA600 to October 1992, but given the stability of the AA chipset, he was confident the team could meet the target for full production.

The situation now was very similar to the 1986 time period when Commodore was under severe financial pressure to deliver a hit product. Commodore often did its best work when under time and money constraints, producing minimal designs with lots of value for the dollar. The AA600, along with the next two products Commodore conceived, would be, from a design and marketing perspective, some of the best work the company had ever produced.

CeBIT A500 Plus

At the annual CeBIT in Hanover, March 16 to 20, the Commodore booth was once again the center of attention for the 600,000 attendees that year. With Eastern Europe freed from Communism, the region began growing in importance and Irving Gould announced he was opening a new sales office in Warsaw, Poland.

Of those attendees, many of them were Amiga hackers belonging to popular cracking groups. Known as "Amiga freaks", they roamed the halls of CeBIT by the hundreds, exchanging cracked software and BBS phone numbers. The Amiga Freaks covered a wall next to the Commodore booth with stickers and graffiti with addresses to meet at in order to exchange their wares. Commodore responded by painting over the wall on the evening after the opening day.

At the center of Commodore's massive booth were the PC clones, which were still important to the German market. Gould announced Commodore was the second most popular seller of PC clones in Europe.

The prior holiday season, as *Amiga Format* magazine noted, the A500 Plus was "not launched, it just appeared."[1] Now at CeBIT Commodore officially launched the A500 Plus. While the extra memory, AmigaOS 2.04, and flicker-free productivity mode were well received, it was somewhat offset by a large number of incompatible games. Amiga Format estimated some

---

1   *Amiga Format,* Jan. 1992, p. 26. "The year of the Amiga"

30% of older game titles did not work with the new OS. Though this fault was easy to overlook with the high-end Amigas, it was more concerning to low-end users who primarily used the A500 for video games.

Confusingly, as the A500 Plus made its official debut, Commodore also showed off the upcoming A600, which was set to replace the A500 series only six months later.

Additionally, in the US, Jim Dionne had decided against releasing the A500 Plus to North America. Dealers and developers there were asked not to make mention of the A500 Plus in documentation. Effectively, the A500 Plus would be a well kept secret on the continent.

The Amiga was still a popular platform for game development in Europe, with 1992 debuting a number of strong games, including *Monkey Island 2: LeChuck's Revenge, Civilization, Pinball Dreams, Eye of the Beholder II, Dune, Sensible Soccer*, and *Black Crypt*.

The year also marked a recovery for the PC market. Many people remember the PC clones as having a non-stop growth rate throughout this period, but actually PC clone sales peaked at 17.5 million units in 1989 before falling to 16.8 million in 1990 and 14.4 million in 1991.[2] This while competing machines from Apple and Commodore were on the rise.

The Amiga had historically dominated IBM PC clones in the game market, but by 1992 PC graphics and sound cards allowed the clones to surpass the Amiga. Furthermore, with clone prices falling, PCs began to look very tempting as home computer/game machines. Game developers began to concentrate on the PC game market, excluding computers from Commodore, Apple, Atari, and other companies.

The year 1992 also coincided with the first wave of games to usher in the 3D game revolution. The first was the technologically impressive *Ultima Underworld: The Stygian Abyss*, released in March 1992.

Then on May 5, 1992, a monumental killer app appeared when id Software released its shareware game, *Wolfenstein 3D*. This game alone made up the minds of many computer buyers. The release of Wolfenstein 3D came at a critical juncture and game players shifted to the PC en masse. This had a devastating impact on the low-end Amiga market, which did not receive a port of Wolfenstein 3D.

---

2 *Ars Technica*, Dec. 14, 2005 "Total share: 30 years of personal computer market share figures."

Later in the year, other classic 3D games such as the atmospheric *Alone in the Dark* (October 1992) by Infogrames would showcase 3D graphics and Sound Blaster audio samples. The release was even more painful for Amiga owners because Infogrames had been a prolific developer of Amiga games up until 1992. The new title signalled the French developer was pulling out of the Amiga market.

In 1992, Commodore's longtime rival, Atari, began to see staggering losses, which spelled the end for the company.[3] The Amiga and Atari ST had been running neck and neck from 1985 to 1987, but since 1988, Amiga dominated the Atari ST. The turning point in sales came in 1991 when the Atari ST faded into oblivion.

Atari and Jack Tramiel made one last ditch effort by going back to its roots with a game console, called the Jaguar. Although the machine was dutifully covered by the gaming press, it failed to compete with Nintendo, Sega, and 3DO and would spell the end for Atari.

It was gratifying for Commodore veterans to see their nemesis fall. Several ex-Atari employees also joined Commodore, including the new GM of Commodore Germany, Alwin Stumpf. However, there was also the feeling that Atari could be the canary in the coal mine.

Retreat of the Clones

Commodore was one of several clone makers, while IBM continued competing with its IBM PC line of computers. It also held hundreds of patents and would often use those against competing clone makers. This made Commodore executives increasingly nervous about costly lawsuits. "I spent a year with our lawyers on and off as a technical adviser on an IBM lawsuit," says Dave Haynie. "IBM had this habit of coming after every computer company individually, slapping a big stack of patents on them, and getting cross licensing and royalties back from them because they had about 20 or so PC patents."

According to Haynie, much of IBM's actions were preemptive. "IBM, being extremely big at that time, was very nervous that somebody was go-

---

3   The end of the Atari ST was also the end for the GEM operating system from Digital Research. Gary Kildall, CP/M inventor and television co-host of *Computer Chronicles*, had to contend with a lawsuit by Apple against the supposed similarities of GEM to MacOS. It was a slap in the face to Kildall, who invented the personal computer operating system. Kildall quit Digital Research in 1991. In July 1994, the ex-Navy man had a fight at the Franklin Street Bar and Grill in Monterey, California. Three days later, he died of head injuries at the age of 52.

ing to get a patent on them that they didn't have a license for," he says. "So one of the main reasons they did this was to get a cross license with you." With cross licensing, if IBM unintentionally violated a patent, they would not be liable for lawsuits or back royalties.

All IBM wanted was protection from Commodore-Amiga patents that might overlap with their IBM PC designs. "There was this whole argument about the Amiga," says Haynie. "We knew they wanted a license on the Amiga patents to keep them out of trouble if we came after a patent on them and wanted royalties on several million machines made that year. It was just one of those general-purpose 'cover your ass and get some money out of everyone else in the business' deals"

Haynie believes IBM lawyers sometimes used its patents to generate revenue. "We went down to their office. Their legal department in Boca Raton, Florida was actually larger than the engineering part of Commodore's building," says Haynie. "They ran it as a profit center. They had some engineer lawyers there who were whoring themselves defending some of the worst patents you have ever seen."

Rather than fight IBM, most companies agreed to the cross licensing agreement and royalties or settled out of court. "They have ridiculous amounts of patents they can go against you with," says Haynie. "When you've got a stack of 20 and you know IBM will come after you with 20 more after that and 20 more after that, you settle. They came after Commodore and said, 'You make PCs, which is pretty straight forward. You're not going to win. You're going to pay us a royalty for PCs.'"

Bill Sydnes had originally been brought in to rescue Commodore's PC clone business, which had become unprofitable. In the process, he ramped up the number of engineers working in his division. "When I went to the States in January of '93 and I went into the engineering department, there were seven Amiga engineers and 40 PC Engineers," says David Pleasance. "That was Bill Sydnes, he had been recruited as head of engineering and he brought all these mates of his with him from the company he came from."

Tucked away in secret, the other engineers rarely rubbed elbows with the PC clone group. "That's funny because, for all that, I had plenty of contact with Jeff Frank; I didn't know any of the PC engineers," says Joe Augenbraun. The only thing the two groups shared was the mechanical group who came up with the case designs.

Onc markcting challenge Commodore faced was that its PC clones were no different from those of other companies. "The problem in those days is the whole world, including Commodore's marketing, felt that the only way to really be successful longer term is to really be PC compatible, which of course is partially true," explains Gerard Bucas. "But the reality of it is, it was very competitive and difficult to differentiate. Eventually you just become another one of the many people doing the same thing."

Pleasance believed they should have distributed OEM PCs at low risk rather than engineering and manufacturing their own. "It was complete and utter nonsense. What a waste of money! Who needs them when they are reinventing the wheel? They should have rebadged the PCs."

For the past few years, Commodore had manufactured too many of its low-end PC clones and built up too much stock. When the PC market took a dip in 1990 and 1991, Commodore ran into a major problem. "At that point in time the market for the PC had fallen kind of flat," says Carl Sassenrath. "They were left with huge amounts of inventory that were just going to be sold for junk basically."

As the PC clone market became more competitive and the components more commoditized, Commodore had a hard time finding ways to remain profitable. Furthermore, Commodore was unable to cut prices as far as other clone makers had.

In February 1992, Bill Sydnes began negotiating with two different companies, Twinhead and Mitac, to deliver the next laptop. Commodore ended up going with the Taiwanese Mitac laptop and released the pinnacle of its laptop line, the 486SX-LTC. The company would send several shipments of these computers to Europe, Canada and the US.

In March 1992, right after the CeBIT show, Commodore discontinued its low-end MS-DOS machines. Customers were no longer buying the 8088 and 286 based PC clones. "It was bad because they made a side bet on the IBM PC clones that really bankrupted the company," says Sassenrath."They had way over-purchased their inventory and committed to way too many PC clones."

Commodore's PC clone engineers also came up with unique prototypes for portable computing. The PC engineers, headed by Ian Kirschemann, designed a palmtop computer. "In fairness they did show me once a 486 in a tiny little notepad," says Pleasance. "But nothing ever came of that anyway." Mehdi Ali cancelled the Commodore Palmtop in October 1992.

However, Commodore would remain in the high-end PC clone and laptop markets. The company decided to try a new strategy by using motherboards developed by other companies. "At one stage they were all developed by Commodore in-house. Then later on, it was sort of partially developed, casework only and motherboard somewhere else," says Bucas.

A600 Released

Commodore Hong Kong began manufacturing A600 SMT motherboards in February 1992 and had shipped almost 50,000 of them to Germany by March, where they would undergo final assembly and boxing. By April 1992 the A600 was in full mass production and set to launch in May.

However, many of Commodore's old guard had worries about the release. "One question many of us had was why the A600, a lesser form of the A500, was favored by management over the A500 and marketed at a higher price," says Hedley Davis.

In fact, engineers began hearing that the A500, Commodore's most successful product to date, which continued selling in higher volumes every year since its release, would be cancelled prior to the A600 launch. "Sydnes, the supposed inventor of the IBM PC, was involved," says Davis.

The move was meant to ensure demand for Sydnes' A600 while hurting GVP. "The Amiga 500 was still popular," says Dave Haynie. "They cancelled the Amiga 500 and put out the Amiga 600."

Soon A600 systems began arriving in the UK, which came as a shock to most of the marketing there. "They asked, 'Can we make a low cost Amiga and get more products into homes?' That was the A300 idea," says David Pleasance. "It's not rocket science. The next thing you know, A600s begin to arrive in the warehouse. What the hell is an A600? There were also models that had a hard drive, which we never asked for."

Pleasance feels it was a mistake for Sydnes to push the product on Commodore UK without first consulting them. "In my opinion, the problem of Commodore has always been that they never ever had a plan of any kind," he says. "Sometimes we would just be sent something that was this fait accompli. It's done, it will be in your warehouse in two weeks time without any discussion about what was needed. I don't think anybody ever asked anybody anywhere in the world what we actually needed. It seems really bizarre."

Under the Tramiel system, Commodore regions had the freedom to order whatever machines they wanted. "It was natural selection," says Dave Haynie. Now Commodore told their subsidiaries what to order. "That's the only time I know that they circumvented that, and the results of course were disastrous."

The A600 was priced at £399, compared to the A500 Plus which had been selling for around £299. The aforementioned A600 HD with a 20 MB hard drive retailed for even more. "We were totally behind the development of the A300, and the initial boards all came out marked A300 because that is what is was supposed to be," says Colin Proudfoot. "But when they did the analysis on the final costing and they couldn't get the cost down to make the price point right, or the price below the A500 because there wasn't really any product management in Commodore that I can think of. So if you design by committee, you get a camel. There was too much functionality in the A600 to be the A300. What was most important was hitting the price point and they didn't do that. So we launched the A600."

Commodore Germany refused to replace the A500 Plus with the A600, probably because they controlled the Braunschweig factory which produced Amiga 500 Pluses. "The UK boys saluted smartly and charged up the hill and they said, 'Okay, we're selling the A600 now instead of the A500,'" recalls Porter. "The Germans thought the A600 was a piece of shit, and they wanted to sell the A500. The powers that be at the time let them sell that, so you have a really strange thing in the marketplace that one country was saying that the A500 was king and that the A600 is a piece of shit. And another country is saying the A600 is it, the A500 is a piece of shit. So it's like, 'Oh my God! What a terrible thing.' No one was sorting that out. We did not have a clear voice when the A600 came out."

Commodore UK could do nothing because the A600 was forced upon them. "We were told the A500s weren't available," says Proudfoot. "Basically all the A500s were going to Germany so we had to sell the A600 or sell nothing."

While Commodore UK had been able to sell over 300,000 Amiga 500 systems the previous year (an average of 25,000 per month), they only sold 65,000 A600s from May to August—about 16,000 per month. And it only got worse once the reviews started coming in and people slowly realized the A600 was not a step up from the A500 Plus.

Critical reception of the A600 was, as expected, not very good. "The magazines at the time and all the pundits really slammed them," says Gerard Bucas. "Here was an A600 which did not run faster than an A500 and, on top of that, was less expandable."

Amiga World gave a preview of the Amiga 600. Unlike prior releases of new Amigas, the write-up was unusually short at only two pages. Chief editor Doug Barney wrote, "But is the bright white A600 worthy of assuming the low-end mantle? The answer for Amiga users is yes and no."[4] He criticized the lack of expandability, the slow 7 MHz processor, and the bulky power brick.

According to Colin Proudfoot, "When people started reviewing it and it had less functionality than the A500, you go, 'Why would I buy an A600 when the A500 is a perfectly good machine?' It bombed and we didn't want to sell it."

AmigaOS 2.1 was a slight improvement over AmigaOS 2.04. At the time, Commodore was trying to make its interface customizable by language and country, through something called localization. "The Amiga was trying to appeal to a world market so there were things like that we had to do," says Eric Cotton, who implemented localization.

As noted by *Amiga Format* magazine, neither software nor hardware makers made use of the PCMCIA slot. "In time-honoured fashion, Commodore have largely chosen to just spring the A600 on the software industry. … The ROM card slot on the A600 is likely to be used for little more than storing coinage."[5]

Gerard Bucas feels the poor reviews were well deserved. "They cancelled production of A500 which was a top selling product. Totally stupid," he says. "People like Mehdi didn't realize that in a computer market you can't come up with a new model that's not faster and better. Anyone knows that."

The UK magazine *Amiga Power*, in its list of "Top Six crap things done by Commodore" listed as number two, "Bringing out the A600 as soon as the A500 Plus had established itself as the Number One Amiga, thereby alienating and annoying loads of loyal customers."

Gerard Bucas predicted the machine would bomb in the marketplace. "That's why Commodore died eventually, and it was all because of the A600," he says. Mehdi Ali would not have definitive sales results of the A600 until after the holiday season of 1992. Until then, he left his head engineer, Bill Sydnes, to continue product development.

---

4   *Amiga World*, Oct. 1992, p. 44. "Small Talk: The New Amiga 600 Revealed"

5   *Amiga Format*, June 1992, p. 9. "A600 smart cards: an end to piracy?"

Sales & Marketing Makeover 1992

Mehdi Ali had received a mandate from Irving Gould to fix Commodore, which was arguably quite broken when he took over. Through Bill Sydnes and Lew Eggebrecht, many improvements had been made to engineering. But Ali had a larger task in front of him of fixing Commodore's poor sales and marketing in the United States. It had always been a mystery why Commodore's US marketing was such a failure compared to the European subsidiaries. In 1992, one of the UK's most successful executives was about to find out why.

Hunting in International Waters

David Pleasance had been working in Basel, Switzerland since late 1990 as Commodore's GM of Commodore International Limited (CIL). In this position, he sold computers to any region of the world lacking a local Commodore office. There were 35 countries in CIL, including Greece, Finland, Turkey, Israel, Cyprus, Jordan, Saudi Arabia, Lebanon, Morocco, and South Africa. "In Africa we sold maybe 1000 units per month," says Colin Proudfoot. "Scandinavia was strong and there were no subsidiaries there."

Major political changes at the time allowed Pleasance to expand CIL. After the Soviet Union collapsed and Poland revolted against its Communist government, Pleasance acted swiftly and established Commodore as a major force. He pushed the low cost computers, including the Plus/4, which were a good fit for the fledgling economy. Decades later these computers are still remembered fondly there.

Meanwhile India's socialist government finally collapsed the economy in 1991 and the country lifted its protectionist policies, allowing Commodore entry into a market with over a billion people. For someone who regarded himself as a hunter, David Pleasance had a lot of target opportunities. But there was one target he valued above all others.

He had, for a long time, been aware of Commodore's pathetic US sales compared to the rest of world and wanted to show what he could do in the biggest market on earth at the time. "I used to beg Commodore to let me get into the consumer business in the US," he recalls. "I told them, 'I'll sort it out.'" Unfortunately, when Commodore US needed it most, he was denied the promotion.

Pleasance had always wondered why Commodore did not try to bring some of the UK sales magic to the US, especially with sales executives being fired so frequently. "I mean these guys were just not around very long," he says. "They lasted about a year, most of them."

Rather than continually hiring poor marketing and sales managers, Pleasance thought Commodore should have pulled proven employees from Europe to repair the US market, as Jack Tramiel had done when he launched the VIC-20. "I'm just shocked that nobody ever came in and said, 'Let's analyze what it is you are doing right.' If you're going to look at the numbers of machines that we sold, we got it right," he says. "So why not try and replicate that as best you can around the world. To me it just seems like the most logical thing to do."

This was about to change, but perhaps a little too late to enact a major turnaround.

One on One

In May 1992, David Pleasance attended a general meeting among the various Commodore subsidiaries. "I went to a meeting in Frankfurt," he recalls. Pleasance would represent CIL, the international subsidiary.

Throughout Commodore's existence, the company hosted an annual gathering of upper management from all the international subsidiaries. Mehdi Ali continued the tradition in his own way when he called together a meeting in May 1992. "He would call a meeting and the management team—basically the CEO and the finance guy of each country—would show up at whatever location he was holding the meeting," says Colin Proudfoot. "It usually rotated between Holland, Germany and the UK."

During the Tramiel years, attendees at the annual meeting came together to discuss product strategy. However, in the 1990s the meetings revolved around one-on-one sessions with Mehdi Ali. "We'd all show up at eight o'clock in the morning and would sit around and wait," says Proudfoot. "We would sit there all day waiting to get into the meeting and have between ten minutes and an hour with Mehdi in the meeting and then go home. We'd get called into the meeting individually whenever he got around to whatever he wanted to talk to each one of us about."

It was a far cry from the lively collaborations that occurred during Commodore's heyday. "He didn't want to be argued with when he made a decision. He just wanted you to implement his decision," says Proudfoot. "We would get an opportunity for some input but it was not really a discussion. He would talk to people and say, 'What do you think?' And then later he says, 'This is what we're doing.' It was probably something totally different from what you told him."

It seemed like a waste of company resources to gather the top executives in the company together in one place and not use the opportunity to hash out corporate strategy. "I remember the day that the guys from Australia flew in," says Proudfoot. "They got 10 minutes and flew home."

The strange inconsistency with Ali was that he wanted to cut costs, especially in engineering, yet he seemed to spend lavishly in his own circle of influence. "So the question is, why?" asks a bemused Proudfoot. "Why don't you have a set agenda? Why don't you have a time table? Why don't we, as different countries, discuss ideas and find common solutions to common problems? But nope. It was divide-and-conquer. We were supposed to compete with each other rather than to cooperate."

While Ali often denied small requisitions for his engineers, he also spent lavishly on his own hotels, meals, and airfare—all at Commodore's expense. To the engineers, the inconsistencies were infuriating.

Near the end of the meeting, Ali pulled Pleasance aside to announce some life changing news. "It wrapped up around 1:00 in the afternoon, and as everyone was leaving Mehdi said, 'Hang on Pleasance.' He finally conceded to my wishes and allowed me to head up US consumer sales. At the time, Jim Dionne was the head of the consumer division."

Incredibly, Ali didn't want him to start next week or later in the week. In fact, he didn't want to waste a single minute. "Mehdi booked a 7:00 PM flight out of London that night," recalls Pleasance. "He booked my flight on the Concorde for the first time in my life. It was quite a treat."

Adventures in the USA

After Pleasance arrived in West Chester as VP of consumer sales, he resolved to find out the exact reason for Commodore's US marketing woes. At the time, the consumer division sold product to major retailers throughout the USA, including Sears, CompUSA, Best Buy, Circuit City, and Good

Guys. There was also Commodore's former rival, Tandy, which operated hundreds of retail stores under different names, collectively referred to as the Tandy Name Brand Retail Group. These stores included McDuff Electronics, VideoConcepts, The Edge in Electronics, Incredible Universe, and Computer City, among others.

Then Pleasance found out a startling piece of information. "Commodore had a team of people in place. They were nice, good people," he says. "But I wanted the truth and to find out what was going on. So I organized a meeting off site where people could speak freely. And I heard these stories that we have all these retail accounts but nobody is paying their bills."

Major organizations such as Sears had received product from Commodore yet failed to pay the bill for those products. Pleasance decided to talk directly to someone from Sears to find out what had happened. "I visited the VP of a US sales company," he recalls. "I told him I wanted honesty so that I could see what the situation was, then I can see what I can do. Basically to find out why our retailers are not paying their bills. And he told me they were waiting for Commodore to take back excess stock."

Pleasance now had some idea of what had been going on. He arranged a larger meeting with Sears to work out a deal and resolve the situation. "I told them, 'Let's sort it out.' We held a meeting with 20 Sears executives and me and my rep because, frankly, we were a bit concerned about the retail market. And they told me that Commodore had been selling them a shedload of CDTV's into Sears. They told me, 'We were snookered.' He had stuffed them to gunnels with CDTV's and he knew nobody could sell it. We all knew that."

It seemed somehow a log jam had occurred, which prevented retailers from accepting more Commodore products. Worse yet, Commodore had promised Sears that they could sell the CDTVs or return them, but when Sears tried to return them, Commodore would not accept them. "It was sale or return," explains Pleasance. "I never expected that but I told them, 'I'm working here now and I will honor it, even though I wasn't here when the deal was made.'"

However, it would be disastrous for Commodore to just take back the CDTV en-masse, no strings attached, so Pleasance found a win-win solution for everyone. "At the time, we were selling the Amiga 500 hand over fist," he explains. "I said, 'Can I ask a favor? Would you give me an order for A500s for the same value as the CDTVs we're taking back? They are selling like hotcakes. Would you do it? In return, I will create a bundle for Sears exclusively.'"

It was the type of deal that required an experienced and engaged sales-person to figure out. And it worked. Pleasance produced a special Sears-on-ly package. "I got in touch with my UK pack designers, and we printed it in West Chester. That got us trading again with Sears," he says.

Over the rest of the year, Pleasance would work to clear out log jams from the remaining retailers. Usually his plan succeeded, but not always. "There was one company that reneged, even though they had agreed to the deal that I would take their stock back and then give them replacement stock of the same value of A500," recalls Pleasance. "Only one company reneged on that, and that was Tandy Name Brand. That was a guy named Hank, and he said he would do it. I took all his stock back and then he wouldn't give me an order for anything else. Some people are like that. Some people are not honorable."

Pleasance feels the ultimate responsibility for the fiasco lay with Commodore's president of Commodore US. "Jim Dionne hadn't told Mehdi Ali a thing about it," says Pleasance. "That was a fundamental problem. As an international company, they didn't run it properly. Commodore should have had random audits."

Dionne had been somewhat lucky that he began running Commodore US at the same time the Video Toaster caused a surge in demand for the Amiga. The recent CDTV fiasco, once the news reached Ali, would un-doubtedly leave him with some explaining to do. In the meantime, his or-ganization could once again begin selling products. "They were all trad-ing and they were all selling Commodore-Amiga products and doing okay with it," says Pleasance. "I don't think they were setting any records but they were doing okay." Ultimately, even Commodore UK's star salesperson would have a hard time rescuing the US market for Commodore.

Stuffing the Channels

One of the big mysteries for Commodore employees was why, at certain times of the year, large numbers of trailers sat out in the parking lot load-ed with merchandise, sometimes for months at a time, without going any-where. "In West Chester there was a chain-link fence around a pretty big section of the parking lot," recalls Bryce Nesbitt. "There was a back park-ing lot that was never full, over by the volleyball courts, and a section of that was roped off. Periodically, oddly enough on quarterly boundaries, it would fill up with semi trailers full of products that had shipped that quarter."

This happened in both the US and European divisions. The answer to this mystery lies in a quirky side-effect of quarterly reporting requirements for publicly traded companies. Employees suspected the reason for the semi trailers was a scheme to cook the books. "I can't say I know that from an accounting point of view, but everyone in the building thought that," says Nesbitt. "It was common knowledge at the water cooler or the unofficial notice board that that's what those trucks were about. Why would they do that around reporting time every quarter?"

Commodore's fiscal year ended on June 30th, 1992, at which time the finance group put together a tally of all the sales for the previous quarter. Theoretically, they stop recording sales for the current fiscal year at that point. This was a big deal for sales people because it determined their yearly bonus. If they could cram in more sales before June 30th, Commodore would reward them with a larger bonus. Sometimes a salesperson required just a few more sales to surpass a higher bonus tier. "We shipped huge volumes of product on the last day of the fiscal year, June the 30th," says Colin Proudfoot.

With most sales made in the second half of the year, this made it tempting for salespeople to secure orders for the holiday season. "We convinced the channel to take Christmas product in June when we know they're not going to sell it until October and November," says Proudfoot. "We give them discounts and incentives to do that but they are genuine orders and they pay for the goods. But you're incentivising people to maximize for the year end."

This led to conflict with the auditors about which sales qualified for the current fiscal year, because sometimes product wasn't delivered until October or November, along with the actual payment for the goods.

Colin Proudfoot, who was investigating corruption at Commodore UK, also kept the financial books. He noticed in the past five years, Commodore UK's yearly reports did not pass cleanly. "I know in the UK, before I got there, there were always issues with the audit," says Proudfoot. "Every company usually has some issues. If it is a major issue then that's reportable."

An audit that included qualifications reflected poorly on a company and often meant there were financial shenanigans occurring. Proudfoot wanted a clean audit with no qualifications, which meant he would need to have no issues with the year end cutoff for reporting sales.

Proudfoot approached Commodore's auditing firm to sort out the problems that prevented a clean audit. "The finance guys negotiate with auditors all the time to determine the rules. It's what we do," he says. "It was Coopers & Lybrand, a major UK auditing firm. You're talking about major players and it's all arms-length."

Proudfoot attempted to define what criteria would be acccptable for sales to count for the current fiscal year. "In the UK, I sat down with the auditors in the first year I was there and said I want a clean cutoff," he recalls. "I knew the orders we were getting were good orders. So I said to the auditors, 'Let's agree to the cutoff rules.' Because when we make a sale to Dixon's, we take the order and then they give us a delivery window. They say, 'We will take title to the goods on June 30th but we want you to deliver it on August 15th at nine o'clock.' So I'm saying, 'They are not my goods; Dixons bought them.' And the auditor said, 'Well they can't be in the warehouse. To claim revenue you have to have shipped them.' So I get it, they are going to be in transit for two weeks. That's fine. We will fix that."

As Proudfoot understood it, goods counted as "in transit" as long as they were aboard trailers. "I worked with the distribution folks and said, 'Everything is going to be on trailers by midnight, June the 30th, no exceptions. If it's not in a trailer it doesn't count.'"

Unfortunately, the auditors did not agree with Proudfoot's view of the world. "The auditors phoned me up at nine o'clock on July the 1st and say, 'There are 53 trailers full of goods in your parking lot!' I said, 'Yes I know.' They said, 'You can't do that!' I said, 'We came to an agreement. The agreement we had, and it was documented, was as long as I had valid sales on the trailers before midnight on the 30th we can count it as revenue.' 'But they're still on your premises.' I said, 'Well if you told me they couldn't be on my premises, I would have rented the yard across the road and parked them there. Come on, we've got a definition.' So they said, 'Okay well we're going to monitor your receivables very closely and if they are not all paid for by October we're qualifying your accounts.'"

It had seemed like the 1992 audit could be in trouble, but Proudfoot's proactive approach worked out in the end. "Come October, all the goods were received at the right time by the right customers and they had all been paid for," he says. "So we got a clean audit for the first time in 5 years."

Although it might seem like a lot of hassle for the salespeople to preload their sales each year, it's worth keeping in mind the high turnover rate among salespeople and the shaky financial ground Commodore was on at the time. "You are always trying to meet or beat whatever forecasts or expectations Wall Street has for your business," says Proudfoot. "People get incentives and bonuses to hit targets, especially at the end of the fiscal year. The question is, when is it legal and when is it not legal?"

Yet the inefficiency of renting trailers, storing them, giving discounts to retailers, and the general hassle probably could have been avoided by moving the fiscal year to December 31. "Say you're the head of a public company. You're only as good as your last quarter. If you miss a quarter, you can get fired," says Proudfoot. "Wall Street expectations drive it. The whole industry is doing it and customers are now expecting it. So if I want to buy a computer, if I'm a major company, I know I'm going to wait till the last week of the quarter and start negotiating, because I'll get the best deal."

Although this cut into profits, it was cheaper than allowing product to build up in the warehouse. "Stocking up is expensive, especially on a product with a limited life cycle like a computer," explains Proudfoot. "The thing about the computer industry is costs continue to fall and products get obsolete really fast."

The Expensive World of Mehdi Ali

Mehdi Ali had been hired by Irving Gould as a specialist to reverse the company's fortunes. "There is a precedent for turnaround specialists being brought in to run companies," says Colin Proudfoot. "If you get the nuts and bolts in the finance right then the company will succeed where it's failed in the past. If people are too close to the product or too close to the market, they do things that don't make financial sense. You need financial discipline."

In the interim, Ali's friendship with Gould had blossomed to the point where they both now lived on the same street in Nassau, Bahamas. "Later he and Mehdi had moved to some gated spot. I never went down to that one," says Don Gilbreath.

Proudfoot felt the management style of Ali resembled the hands-on approach taken by Jack Tramiel. "Financially, Commodore had been in trouble, and it was being kept afloat," says Proudfoot. "What it needed was strong management under Mehdi."

Ali had made several, arguably difficult decisions, such as closing down manufacturing in West Chester and outsourcing production. This move was being made by many corporations at the time, including Apple, in order to become profitable and keep consumer prices down. Ali had also shut down the unprofitable PC clone and Unix divisions.

However, Proudfoot felt Ali should have split his powers up rather than attempt to take it all on himself. "There was no controllership. The finance function wasn't strong. The marketing function wasn't strong and it wasn't coordinated. The development function wasn't strong. The ability to market in the US was absent."

Working as financial controller of Commodore UK, Proudfoot reported directly to Ali, as did many in Europe. "Commodore didn't have any checks and balances. The financial function totally answered to Mehdi," says Proudfoot. "He managed people directly, so there was no European office. I think he had something like seventy direct reports."

Proudfoot remarks on something other employees had noticed working under Ali, which was a propensity to fly people around the world for almost no reason. "I found his management style to be totally chaotic. It was very inefficient," says Proudfoot. "I would often get calls on Saturday afternoon saying, 'Be in my office 9 o'clock Monday morning.' So Sunday I get on the plane, fly to New York, go see him, get 10 to 15 minutes and fly home."

Meetings like this often perplexed employees because, with Ali watching every dollar so closely, these short meetings could have been handled easily on the phone. "I think he liked to look people eye to eye when he was talking to them," says Proudfoot. "Certainly the company was run for his convenience."

Ali also kept his offices far from the rest of the company, which had side effects, such as disrupting the days of employees who had to travel to New York to meet with him. "Mehdi had his office on Park Avenue when the company is being run out of West Chester," says Proudfoot. "Mehdi liked being in New York. That's where he was used to living. He lived in Connecticut and didn't want to relocate." This led to Ali not always knowing what was going on within the company he ran.

Likewise, his indulgence when it came to travelling irked many of Commodore UK's managers. "He always flew Concorde to get to the UK and then he'd stay in the Dorchester in a suite, which was a big hotel," says Colin Proudfoot. "When he landed in the UK, he would have a car, a driver, and a phone waiting for him at the airport. The driver was there 24 hours. Once he got in the car, he was always on the phone and we used to get the bill. It was about seven thousand dollars a day for the phone bill plus the car and the driver. They would bill us in the UK and we would rebill West Chester."

Proudfoot, always watching his budget, couldn't stand for the inefficiency any longer. "The deal I did with him was, we will provide you with a car, a driver and a phone whenever you are in the UK and charge you half of what you're currently paying," explains Proudfoot. "We leased a car, hired a part-time driver, got a cell phone with an international plan, which was a tiny fraction of what he was being charged by the car company to use the phone internationally. We saved him fifty percent of the money."

As a bonus, since Ali only stayed for a few days, Commodore UK management got to indulge a little themselves. "We had the car and the driver 28 days of the month when Mehdi wasn't there," explains Proudfoot.

Many employees felt there was something dark at the core of Ali's personality. "He was mad at the world," says Proudfoot.

Employees were often at the receiving end of his aggressive management style. "He basically felt he could either berate people or pay people or if you threw enough money at it you could solve any problem in any time period," says Guy Wright.

Although Ali had been making some decent big-picture changes to the company structure, it seemed like he should have stepped aside once he made those changes, in order to allow someone with technology and consumer experience to take over.

Returning Home

David Pleasance had been in the USA for six months and had reopened the sales channels that had previously ground to a halt. Unfortunately, because Commodore had accepted CDTV returns in exchange for the same amount of Amiga 500s, his efforts did not result in positive revenue growth for the North American operation. "I don't think what I did actually gained them very much in terms of revenue because I had to take back all those bloody CDTVs at their value that they were sold at," says Pleasance. "We didn't have a negative on the books with the current products. So I don't think I added to their revenues but certainly we got trading again with all the major companies, including Sears."

When Commodore reported its financials for the quarter ending September 1992, revenue had fallen from $204.1 million (the previous year's quarter) to $158.6 million. Most of this drop was due to cancelling the low-end PC clones. And instead of a profit, the company reported a loss of $18.8 million.[1]

Surprisingly, David Pleasance felt he had done all he could for the US operation. "I went to Mehdi in New York and said, 'Look, my job here is done.' And he said, 'What are you talking about? You've got lots of more work to do.' And I said, 'No, I've filled all the channels with Amiga 500s, which they are all selling and they are all doing ok with it. But I do not want to stuff them up because you and I both know we have the A1200

---

1   *Philadelphia Inquirer*, Nov. 6, 1992. "Commodore Posts a Loss in Quarter"

coming any minute, and I want them to sell out of A500s before we release the A1200.' I knew if I had gone back and sold them more A500 products then it would have been another nightmare when the A1200 came out and I didn't want that. Which made sense, and he reluctantly agreed. He didn't like it because he's like all of these people that don't know anything about the business. They just want to sell, sell, sell and screw the consequences without any thought for the long-term business."

Ali had hoped David Pleasance would grow the US market rather than just resuscitating it. "When I left there in November of 1992, Mehdi was shocked," recalls Pleasance. "The truth of the matter was there was nothing more I could do. I'd cleaned up the channels and I'd taken back all those bloody CDTVs that Jim Dionne sold on sale or return. And God knows whatever happened to them [the CDTV stock]. It's not my responsibility to get rid of stuff that nobody wants."

Clearly if Commodore wanted to regain the market it once had, it would need to do another deal with a major retailer to distribute its low-end products.

Kmart had begun faltering by November 1990, pushed into the second place spot as a rising up-and-comer named Walmart came to dominance in North America. A furious expansion of Walmart began in the early 1990s. It would have been the perfect "Kmart deal" to put Commodore back on the map in the US. In many ways, Walmart and Commodore were simpatico, with both obsessed with cutting prices. Walmart also had a "made in the USA" policy at the time. Gaining Walmart distribution would have been the perfect move to leapfrog both Apple and the PC clone makers.

In order to entice Walmart, Commodore would have needed a low-cost product to offer, such as the C65. And then the company would have to pull out all the stops, doing anything and everything to secure a distribution deal. Executives and managers like Jim Dionne and David Pleasance would need to formulate a plan to win over Walmart and ultimately show them how much profit they could reap from Commodore products. Unfortunately, at this moment in time, Commodore US did not seem to have the same level of dedication and creativeness as it had during the Jack Tramiel period, and so no Walmart deal was attempted.

International Redundancy Department

When David Pleasance returned from the USA to England, he wanted to enact some changes to the way the European subsidiaries operated. He wanted to model Commodore on how major international corporations behaved. "I said to Mehdi, 'You know, we are supposed to be an international company but everybody gets treated like a national company. That's ridiculous. You're wasting money."

Ali was intrigued by the thought of saving money. "I said, 'I'll give you an example, Mehdi. Last week I went to Málaga on holiday. When I went to Heathrow airport there was a great big poster sign from Sony with a message and when I landed in Málaga they had the same sign with the same message, but in Spanish. That's what I'm talking about with international branding. It costs you a lot less money to do that than it does with every person doing their individual thing."

Pleasance wanted to reduce the redundancy in marketing and advertising materials. "I said, 'You know we really should be doing international marketing. Just imagine that we produce a television commercial. Let's produce it and have it overdubbed in all the languages at the same time. It just costs them more for the language. The film and everything costs the same money. When we produce brochures, let's do them bilingual. Instead of producing half a million brochures, let's print a million and then ship them to every country. It will cost you a lot less money.'"

Ali liked the idea and decided to enact it within Commodore, though not quite how Pleasance imagined. "One day I got a phone call from Mehdi saying, 'Oh, Pleasance I've listened to you. I just appointed an international marketing guy and he's good.' He appointed a guy for consumer and a guy for business. I said, 'Good, that's a good step in the right direction.' I was pleased."

Unfortunately, the actual implementation was anything but cost efficient. "The next thing you know, these guys turn up in the UK," recalls Pleasance. "The first thing they do is they don't come and use our offices, even though we've got space. We could easily fit them in and it would cost bugger all. They took a very expensive central London office because we were outside of London in Maidenhead. The next thing you know, the guy whose name is Peter who was recruited as the main man for international marketing, spent £170,000 having a suite of office furniture custom made for himself in his office."[2]

Although Pleasance respected Ali for trying different things to fix the company, his execution was lacking. Ali just didn't seem like he was in it for the right reasons. "I was always going to Mehdi to [get him to] wake up and

---

2   When Commodore UK was later liquidated, the suite sold for £600.

smell the coffee," says Pleasance. "But he wanted to collect his $3 million and manipulate the share price so he could sell it or buy it."

A few months later, in March 1993, Pleasance could no longer bottle the feelings he had regarding Ali's leadership. "Every time I went to New York or whenever Irving came over to CeBIT in Hanover, I would say, 'Look I need to talk to you about what's going on.' I'd try to tell him about some of the things that were costing the company a fortune. And he said, 'I don't want to know. Look, David, I put Mehdi in charge. Whatever he says goes.' And he would never listen.'"

Gould, who by this time appeared apathetic about Commodore's fate, most likely wanted an exit strategy from Commodore after seeing his CDTV product fail miserably in the marketplace. "I don't have a great deal of empathy for Irving Gould," says Pleasance. "He just didn't want to know. I do not speak ill of the dead but the truth of the matter is that he's only got himself to blame because he had loads of opportunities to be informed about what was happening and he did not want to know. He chose not to know. Sad isn't it?"[3]

---

3   David Pleasance released a memoir in 2018 of his time at Commodore titled, *Commodore The Inside Story: The Untold Tale of a Computer Giant.* ISBN 9781782817819

Changing of the Bozos 1992

Bill Sydnes had taken over as VP of engineering in November 1990. Since then, his reputation within the company had degraded to the point that Mehdi Ali began to notice. All of Sydnes' initiatives would come to fruition in 1992, and none of them would be successful.

Acutiator

Dave Haynie had been on the A2000-CR project and the A3000, the latter of which was not highly successful in the marketplace. "I've always been a harsh self-critic," he says. "By the time a new Amiga was done, I had been living with it every day for a year or more, and I could mostly just see the flaws, or all the better stuff I wanted for the next one."

In late 1991, while he sat on the AA Task Force awaiting the first AA chips, he began putting together all the ideas he had for an improved architecture for the next generation Amiga. Haynie wanted to address the problem of overly expensive Amiga CPU accelerator cards. The previous accelerator cards duplicated much of the circuitry already in the Amiga, which added to the final cost for users. Instead, he wanted a motherboard architecture that would allow users to plug in a new CPU right onto the motherboard without additional circuitry.

On December 20, 1991, Dave Haynie and Greg Berlin finished their proposed spec for a fourth generation Amiga system architecture. They called the proposal Acutiator, which was a medieval term for a sharpener of weapons. They wrote, "One of the main design goals of the Acutiator architecture is to separate functions into modular pieces. This gives us the flexibility to design low-cost systems which make use of some subset of these components, or to use them all to create a 'feature enriched' machine for those customers willing to pay the additional cost."

The engineers wanted to allow the then-new Motorola 68040 processor to work with the next generation of Amigas. And of course, the architecture would work with the upcoming AAA chipset, as well as the more imminent AA. And because AAA was designed to work with different processor families, Haynie wanted his Acutiator motherboard to also handle different processors. Specifically, there were at least three major RISC processor families at that time and he wanted Acutiator to accept these RISC chips.

Their architecture required three custom chips: Epic, Amos, and Sail. In cost comparisons, Haynie calculated that the Acutiator architecture would add approximately $125 to a system (including the cost of a 68EC040 chip), resulting in a $300 retail price increase. This was a bargain, considering the user received a significant processor upgrade. Haynie proposed that Commodore should assign Scott Shaeffer, Paul Lassa, and himself to each create the three required gate array chips. He expected prototypes in 7 to 9 months, with the first systems shipping in 1992.

AA Chipset Done

In early 1992, the AA Task Force was winding down, having found and eliminated dozens of bugs in the chipset. On March 11 the chipset entered beta testing. As Lew Eggebrecht describes it, "We put together a little task force, did a final run of the chips, and got everything right and the products came out. The engineers were happy to have a project to work on so that lack of direction really was overcome."[1]

Eggebrecht also believes his involvement speeded up completion of the project. "...we used to do 4 or 5 revisions of a chip but now it's 1 or 2 at the most," he says. "We like to get it right first time and we now have a lot of powerful in-house tools and simulations of chips to help us do that. We're also using a lot more industry-standard chips rather than unique things—if you leave engineers alone they'll re-invent the wheel every time and we can't afford to do that."

His belief that his new techniques speeded up development is at odds with the perceptions of some of Commodore's engineers. Normally the engineers worked on the chips until they worked well enough and relied on software and hardware fixes to get the computers out in a timely fashion.

---

[1]   *Amiga User International.* June 1988. "The AUI Interview"

The first AA chips had appeared early in 1991, with plans for AA systems later in the year. According to engineers like Dave Haynie and Joe Augenbraun, that would have happened if the AA Task Force had not delayed chip production.

In April, 1992, CSG began producing the AA chipset in volume. The company was now ready to use the chips in an actual computer, which most engineers believed would be for the low-end to mid-level line of computers. However, those engineers would be surprised by which computer would be the first to use the chipset.

A2200, Sydnes in Trouble

The A1000 Plus with an AA chipset and elegant pizza-box case had been teased to European and North American marketing managers and was highly anticipated. However, when Bill Sydnes and his team placed it in a PC case, used the ECS chipset, and renamed it the A2200, the anticipation evaporated. They attempted to release it in April 1992.

Product manager Greg Berlin was not happy about having to neuter the A1000 Plus by removing the AA chipset. "I heard about the decisions coming out of there because I kept in touch with Greg Berlin," says former Commodore engineer Bil Herd. "Greg was talking about how he had worked on his next rev and made it cheaper and more powerful, and he got told to take the thing out that made it more powerful. He said, 'So here I am going to market with a machine that sucks worse than the old one and costs more.' He used to get pissed."

When Commodore unveiled the A2200 to European marketing managers, they firmly rejected it. Their biggest beef was that is still used the ECS chipset. The managers explained to Ali that they needed the AA chipset, which could compete with VGA. As a result, the Europeans did not place any orders for the A2200, which was slated to begin mass production soon.

Sydnes now had another resounding failure on his hands. "From time to time, taunting management was a sport that you played with great joy inside of Commodore," says Hedley Davis. "Some management you agreed with and some management made sense; it seemed like they had a clue. And then you had these other guys that we're just trying to tell you what to do who didn't know what the fuck they were doing. It's like I'm not even going to put up with you."

Sydnes was now in full-on panic mode, racing desperately to come up with something to save his troubled career at Commodore. Dave Haynie describes Sydnes in engineering terminology as a "human bus error".

"Sydnes didn't have the chops to run a computer, much less a computer design department," he says. "The software people had the expression, 'human no-op'. In programming it's 'No Operation'; it's an instruction you stick in there that does nothing. So a person who sits around and does nothing is a human no-op, but a person who causes problems everywhere they go must be a human bus error."

Amiga 3200 Started

Ever since Bill Sydnes had risen to power within Commodore, he had appeared indecisive about what, if anything, he wanted to do for the high end Amiga line. About the only thing they knew for sure was that they did not want to release the Amiga 3000 Plus. "The Amiga 3000 Plus never saw the light of day," recalls Eric Lavitsky. "We would have certainly been ready in '92 to finalize and get the thing out into production, but it was unfortunately just a little bit too late down the curve in terms of management at Commodore."

Sydnes' reluctance to release a new high-end Amiga had some logic behind it. By 1992, even die-hard Amiga fans were beginning to falter in their support of the computer in the face of improving PC technology. "I basically stopped at the A3000," says Guy Wright, founding editor of *Amiga World*. "The A3000 had taken it about as far as it could have been taken. They could have obviously gotten faster and faster processors and stuff but there were other constraints that kind of limited it. I don't think that they could have grown the market much beyond where it was."

The European view of Commodore was, of course, a different story. "They were very popular in Europe and the UK especially. Germany as well," continues Wright. Pressure from the European operations for a replacement eventually forced Bill Sydnes and Mehdi Ali to commit to a high-end Amiga replacement for the A3000. And the only available chipset was AA.

On April 30, during a weekly product conference call with Mehdi Ali in New York, a new Amiga named the A3200 began under project leader Greg Berlin. Sydnes also told Berlin that the A2200 he was working on with Joe Augenbraun, the unwanted ECS version of the A1000 Plus nicknamed the A1000jr, would be delayed or cancelled. Ali wisely decided it was better to give the Europeans what they wanted rather than trying to force a product on them. Ali also began taking control away from Sydnes and overriding his decisions.

A few days later, on May 4, Sydnes made a public announcement to the Usenet newsgroups. He began, "I have noticed some comments on the network over the past few weeks questioning Commodore's commitment to the Amiga. ... We have plans to release a number of other new Amiga models this year. While I can't reveal the details of these machines at this point, I would like to say that we plan to provide significantly better capability and value for the user in these new systems."

Normally Sydnes did not bother addressing users directly, and the tone of the release revealed some insecurity. It seemed as though he was reasserting that he was the one in charge. Reading between the lines, Sydnes was no longer sure of his position as head of engineering.

In May 1992, he went to Greg Berlin to begin a new Amiga computer— the Amiga 3200. "It was the next logical succession to the A3000. I was in charge of the hardware design of what we called the high-end systems," explains Berlin. "That was the expandable stuff which was along the lines of the A2000. I was in charge of the group that was doing all of those, and that was Paul Lassa, Fred Bowen, Dave Haynie, and me."

Both Lassa and Bowen had worked with Berlin on the C65 and now luckily found themselves in critical engineering roles despite the C65's failure. "When I became available, I went on to the Amiga 4000 [as it later became known] team and began by testing and validating the design with different peripherals—just proving out that the new features they were adding worked," says Lassa. "In doing all that, I got to know how all the chips worked with each other."

However, Mehdi Ali wanted the impossible. He gave project leader Greg Berlin less than five months to produce the machine, which he wanted to ship in September 1992. Naturally it would be a rush job. Berlin and the others were now faced with no vacations for the entire summer. If Berlin met the schedule, this would be a record development time for a system from start to finish.

Unfortunately, none of the ideas from the Acutiator could be implemented in Berlin's new system. Ali wanted the system out quickly, and the three custom chips required by Acutiator were months away. As Lew Eggebrecht recalled, "We had a chipset that was fully functional, very cost effective and 32-bit... so we started converting our entire product line."[2]

---

2   *Amiga CD Format* (special) 1993, p. 5. "Tech Talk"

The A3200 would borrow technology from previous Amiga machines, including the A3000 Plus and A1200. "All of the motherboard chips we used—the Ramsey, DMAC, and Gary—were the same as the A3000," says Berlin. "To be honest with you, a lot of it was based on the A3000."

In fact, the development of the new A3200 would be remarkably similar to the pattern set by another hit Amiga product, the A2000-CR. "The A3000 had the same circuitry as the A500 but had this flicker fixer stuff built in," recalls Jeff Porter. "The A4000 was the AA version so that had the same circuitry as the A1200 [then known as the AA600]."

Even though the A3000 Plus was cancelled, parts of its motherboard design were incorporated into the new computer. "I know that Dave would often help fix things or improve things," recalls Eric Lavitsky. "Certainly some of the work that he did coming up with the A3000 Plus found its way into the A4000 in terms of things that he learned."

With so little time for development, the engineers would not seek to add many new features. In fact, one wonders why Sydnes didn't just go forward and release the A3000 Plus. "The A4000 is mostly the A3000 Plus but no SCSI, no DSP, and the really bad Parallel ATA bus we all loathed," recalls Dave Haynie.

Interestingly, the A3200 motherboard would not include the Motorola CPU. Instead, the CPU would be on a separate processor card, which plugged into the motherboard. "Scott Schaeffer did the 030 and 040 plug-in cards," says Berlin. "The plug-in cards for the 68030 and 68040 actually consisted of several small programmable PLDs (Programmable Logic Device) on it. There was not one custom gate array to do the 68040 stuff. Part of the problem was that the gate arrays that we were doing in-house were too slow. That had some discrete PLD logic on it that was able to be much faster, which added some cost to it. In-house capability for gate array stuff was kind of limited in speed."

Without enough time to develop a new case, Jeff Frank stuck with his plan of using PC-like cases for the Amiga line by using the A2200 case for the A3200. The move was unpopular among the engineers. "It ended up somehow the Amiga 4000 came to be in a very horrible PC-like case," says Lavitsky.

It would be up to the PCB layout designers to make the motherboard fit in the case, using SMT components but even smaller than Commodore had previously used with the A600. "We had a bunch of PCB layout guys, Terry Fisher and Mike Nines," says Lavitsky. In order to ensure the motherboard fit, the team decided to use the smaller 0805 SMD size, as they had with the AA600.

With such a limited schedule, the team had barely a few months to produce the first working prototype in order to leave enough time for quality assurance testing, FCC certification, and setting up production.

AA+

With AA chipset production underway, Commodore needed something to supercede the AA chipset for the low-end computers. After all, even though A1200 systems were largely used for gaming, gamers still expected better graphics every year. "AA+ will be a more profitable version of AA with all the things we wished we'd got in but didn't have time," said Lew Eggebrecht. "AA+ is an extension, not radically new architecture. We're doing the best that we can, taking advantage of advances in technology, significantly reducing the cost and that's the goal."

George Robbins had been the first Commodore engineer to broach the topic of an AA successor back in December 1991. Some of the features he wanted for AA+ included: 16/24-bit true color, direct video, recycling sprites, hi-res monochrome (1280*1024, 2 bitplane support), enhanced HAM replacement, and CD-i level video decompression for full motion video.

Robbins' proposal was met with enthusiasm and on Monday, January 13, 1992 Bill Sydnes and the core team of Lew Eggebrecht, Jeff Frank, Jeff Porter, Ned McCook, Hedley Davis, Bob Raible, James Redfield, George Robbins, and Ted Lenthe gathered at the West Chester Inn. After the customary coffee and pastry, the engineers got to work planning the next chipset for the rest of the day.

After the talks, Bob Raible began working on a detailed spec for the new chipset. On April 22, 1992, Sydnes held a meeting of the core engineers to discuss the AA+ roadmap. Those discussions continued on and off through informal company talks until May 14, when Raible finished the first spec for the AA+ chipset.

Primarily, the AA+ chipset would try to move from bit-plane graphics to 8-bit and 16-bit color graphics (found in VGA) which they called 'chunky graphics'. "We have a list of all the problems we currently have at the low end," said Eggebrecht. "The serial port, we can't read high density floppies, there isn't enough bandwidth to do 72 Hz screens plus there are no chunky pixel modes for rendering. We listed all those and said, 'OK let's go out and fix them as quickly as we can.'"

AA+ would be capable of displaying 800 x 600 non-interlaced at 72 Hz in 256 colors, or even 1024 x 768 interlaced screens. The 16-bit chunky

mode could display 65536 colors, though it was limited to 640 x 480 resolution.

In July, after discussions involving Jeff Porter and others, work formally
began on the AA+ chipset. There would be three chips: Ariel, Belle, and
Debi. The chips were expected to take 10 weeks to design and would enter
layout and fabrication in October, but engineers did not expect to release a
product using AA+ in 1992 as testing and chip refinements would continue
into 1993.

Sydnes Canned

After the Europeans rejected his A2200, Bill Sydnes' position within Commodore became increasingly tenuous. Mehdi Ali had begun taking over
product development decisions since February. Once the A600 hit the
shelves and sales began bombing, it became increasingly clear to everyone
that Sydnes had been a dud. "They should have just said, 'Can it, thank
you very much,' and focus on the A1200," says Gerard Bucas. "There were
other factors in there but bottom line is that the A600 should never have
seen the light of day. They spent a fortune on it, built too much inventory,
and eventually had no cash."

Commodore would now only concentrate on machines with the AA
chipset going forward. The engineers were excited by this prospect, but
also disappointed with how late AA was, with most feeling it should have
been out in 1990 in order to make a splash in the marketplace. Sydnes had
wasted almost six months of development time with the ECS A2200 and
now the engineers would have to race to catch up.

The other big mistake that occurred under Sydnes was the over production of low-end PC clones, which resulted in the company having to write
off inventory.

Then Commodore received more bad press on July 12, 1992 when the
San Jose Mercury News, known locally as The Merc, published an article in
the computing section titled, "Commodore Lets Amiga Die Slow Death".
In it, writer Phillip Robinson, a former Amiga supporter, wrote, "The Amiga is dead. It's sad but true. But we shouldn't be surprised. The poor Amiga has been at death's door for several years. It managed to live because
of its potent basic design and thousands of rabid Amiga fans who would
rather switch to a typewriter than a PC or Mac. The Amiga died because
Commodore denied it growth, support or even respect. And I watched this
eight-year-long execution, hoping a reprieve would come and marveling at
how much abuse the computer with the cute, friendly name could take."

It was a public relations nightmare launched in the heart of Silicon Valley. Robinson received the most feedback he ever had in the eight years writing his column, including threats of violence. A few weeks later, on July 27, Commodore sent out a request to online users asking for help in replying to Robinson and urging them to write to newspapers.

The next day, on July 28, Mehdi Ali terminated Sydnes' employment. Ali and Gould realized Sydnes was not the right person to run Commodore engineering. "Sydnes was fired shortly after that," says Dave Haynie. "I think he had been there for about a year at that point."

The shakeup had little impact on the engineers designing the A1200 and A4000. George Robbins remained unphased, calling the recent shakeup the "changing of the bozos".

"It was like a revolving door," says Greg Berlin. "I just stopped paying attention. After a while we just did our thing and did what we thought was right."

Amiga 4000
1992

After taking control of the engineering group in 1991, Bill Sydnes and Mehdi Ali discontinued development of high-end Amigas in favor of mid-level (A2200) to low-end (A300/600) Amigas. This included halting development on the AAA chipset. But in 1992, Ali reversed that decision and instructed his engineers to create a new high-end Amiga.

Lew Eggebrecht in Charge

After Mehdi Ali dismissed Bill Sydnes, he needed a new VP of engineering. The choice was obvious to everyone. "Commodore needed somebody who could run R&D correctly," says Colin Proudfoot. "When I talked to the engineers, nobody thought very much of Bill Sydnes but Lew Eggebrecht was a breath of fresh air."

Unfortunately, rescuing Commodore would be a difficult proposition for Eggebrecht given the hole Sydnes had dug for the company. "He was starting to put the company on the right path; starting to bring more discipline into the development process and bring the right products to market," says Proudfoot.

No one doubted Eggebrecht would easily surpass Henri Rubin's and Bill Sydnes' tenures. "I asked Dave Haynie what was Lew like," recalls Proudfoot. "He said, 'Well he wasn't really there long enough to do much, but he supported seven of my skunk projects and brought them out in the open so I guess he was a good guy.'"

Eggebrecht had a huge challenge ahead of him. He had to get the A1200 and A4000 out by Christmas because the A600 had bombed. Without the A1200, sales would be dismal. And this would probably be one of the first years where the C64 would have almost no impact on sales. Despite the obstacles, Eggebrecht would soon prove he had the ability to reverse Commodore's fortunes, provided he had enough time.

AmigaOS 3.0

AmigaOS 1.x supported OCS while AmigaOS 2.x supported ECS. Once the AA chipset was ready, it was time to modify AmigaOS again. Even before the Budgie and AA Gayle chips were complete, Commodore's new Director of Software Development, Allan Havemose, was able to start his team working on the new operating system.

Back in the middle of 1991, before Mehdi Ali and Bill Sydnes took over engineering, the AmigaOS developers had a schedule to complete AmigaOS 3.0 by Jan 17, 1992 for the A1000 Plus and A3000 Plus. When those projects were put on hold, development for the new OS also ground to a halt.

Then in November 1991, the software engineers restarted development on AmigaOS 3.0 by putting together a list of features they wanted for the new OS. Havemose, who replaced Bryce Nesbitt, drew comparisons to Windows 3.0, which at that time was the darling of the PC world. He wrote, "Even though I like Workbench and Intuition, it is obvious to me that Windows 3.0 is far superior from a functionality point of view to our UI. It's easy to see the research and thought that has gone into Windows 3.0, and it's not surprising that Windows is a big success."

Throughout November and December 1991, the core members of the team (Randell Jesup, Michael Sinz, and Peter Cherna) honed the feature set as they waited for hardware. When AA chips finally appeared, they were able to test their new code in prototype A3000 Plus machines.

By late February 1992, the OS was running on AA hardware and most of the new features had been implemented. Havemose requested beta testers, which included former employees like Bryce Nesbitt and large software companies like Electronic Arts. The team would allow bug reports until July 1992, with the final OS release slated for August 28.

Michael Sinz, who was responsible for changes to the Exec and other core system features, felt joy working with the original AmigaOS code. "It was an honor to build on top of their work," he says. "Sometimes it meant throwing out their work, but it was the first cut of things. They always talk about you always throw away the first waffle. Not that everything needed to be thrown away but their first piece of work there set a tone that we really wanted to continue and expand upon. The actual mechanics sometimes required significant rework and sometimes just needed appropriate tweaking. The core tone and intent was there and that was wonderful."

One challenge of AmigaOS 3.0 was the limited ROM size of only 512K for Kickstart. The memory had been almost all used up since the AmigaOS 2.0 release, and programmers were forced to write very efficient code in order to fit new features into the memory space.

On top of better color remapping for high-color display modes required to support the AA chipset, the new version of AmigaOS 3.0 added a universal data system, known as DataTypes, that allowed programs to load pictures, sound, text, and other content through the use of standard plugs. And the Workbench desktop had further visual improvements.

During this period, Sinz began to notice hints that Commodore's financial situation was not doing very well. When Sinz attempted to requisition more RAM for development computers, he was denied. "We couldn't buy $30 in RAM chips. That was just not possible," he laments. "We couldn't even get the mouse pads that marketing gave out to customers."

The extreme frugality by Mehdi Ali mystified Sinz. "I guess Commodore wasn't that tight on money because I mean Irving and Mehdi were only getting two million dollars a year in cash," he says. Knowing Commodore was headed for trouble, the engineers felt additional motivation to meet their deadlines.

AmigaOS 3.0 signified a huge leap for Commodore, but it still lacked a few key items: a built-in network API to allow Amigas to join a network effortlessly, along with built-in printer and file sharing on a network. They would have to wait until AmigaOS 3.1 to include those features.

On June 16, 1992, Mehdi Ali renamed the A3200 to the A4000 and simultaneously renamed the AA600 to A1200. This new name change would hopefully signal to the marketplace that the A4000 was not merely an evolution of the A3000 but a more powerful computer in a whole new class—even if this wasn't entirely true.

A4000 Release

Compared to many projects at Commodore that had dragged on in the past, the A4000 project under Greg Berlin was completed in record time. Having a solid chipset to work with no doubt helped. Commodore stopped production of the A3000 in 1992 shortly before releasing the A4000.

When the AA chipset had been temporarily suspended and the Task Force formed, the engineers had lost six months of development time, but since then development had been precise and without problems. AA chipset fabrication was rolling smoothly by August 1992, and CSG released Alice, Paula, and Lisa in volume just in time for the A4000.

One big letdown in the chipset was the failure of the new Paula chip, which the engineers had dubbed Super Paula. "Glenn Keller designed Portia, then Paula, and then went on to design Super Paula," explains Carl Sassenrath. "That was just incredible. I remember talking to him about the capabilities of that chip, in terms of its advancements in sound and it was just amazing."

Unfortunately, Super Paula never made it out the door. "Where they failed, and it was actually a really fundamental failure of Commodore, was that they weren't aggressive enough in the making of the new expanded capability chips," says Sassenrath.

With the rushed schedule, the engineers were not able to complete Super Paula in time. As a result, the new A4000 would use the old Paula chip. This meant that in order to support the new 2 MB floppy disks, the engineers had to slow down the disk drive speed to match the original Paula, giving the A4000 one of the slowest disk access speeds on the market.

On August 28, the test engineers were wrapping up the last loose ends on the project. No one was more surprised than Commodore's management. "We were too conservative in trying to put it into a product and flesh things out so we decided we wanted a AA product by Christmas '92, and we achieved that," says Lew Eggebrecht. "We put more focus on doing things quicker and better."

The project had taken a toll on Greg Berlin, and he came to appreciate the pressures that had been on Hedley Davis, his previous boss. "Berlin had really fucking resented me," laughs Davis. "He did the A4000 and then many years later he came back to me and said, 'Dude, I had no idea you did all that work.' Because once he had to manage the A4000, all of a sudden he had to deal with all these things he had never dealt with before."

On September 12, 1992, Commodore lifted the non-disclosure and publicly unveiled the A4000, right on schedule. At the same time, the company renamed the AA chipset to AGA. "AGA stood for Advanced Graphics Architecture," says Dave Haynie. "The marketing department wanted to make it sound something like VGA."

Owing to the cost reductions of the A1200 on which much of the technology was based, the A4000/040 had a total parts cost of $903.25. Going by a conservative three times multiplier, the product could have comfortably retailed for around $2700.

But Mehdi Ali was looking for ways to maximize Commodore's revenue. Incredibly, Commodore would use a four times multiplier and issued a suggested retail price of $3699, meaning the company would take a larger profit margin than usual from the machine, more in line with what Apple made on its systems.

As far as manufacturing the systems, rather than use Commodore's in-house Asian factories, a company called SCI would manufacture the machines. "That one was actually built in Scotland of all places," says Greg Berlin. "I remember taking a trip there. It seemed like an odd place at the time, but that's what they picked."

In addition to the standard 68040 version, Scott Schaeffer had also developed a processor card for the A4000 with the Motorola 68EC030, which reduced the total parts cost of the A4000/030 to $621.73. However, this card would not be produced and released until April 1993.

Commodore's marketing department even showed signs of life as they prepared for the A4000 release. The company put on a contest in September to name "4000 reasons to use Amiga." The winner with the best entry would receive an A4000.

By October 1992, A4000 systems began appearing on store shelves in Europe and North America. The A4000 received a full preview in the November issue of *Amiga World* (which appeared on shelves in October). This timely press was all because the prototype systems had been available at least four months earlier, in July.

With the A4000 out in good time before Christmas, and under budget, it appeared as though Commodore could have an excellent Christmas season—if the launch of the accompanying A1200 was handled properly.

World of Commodore-Amiga

To launch the A4000 in North America, Commodore would continue using targeted advertising (magazines and conferences with no TV) because they lacked the distribution to warrant a major advertising campaign. Still, the company needed a venue to launch the computer.

The World of Commodore was created by Commodore Canada and hosted its first show in 1983, with over 38,000 users in attendance. The show gained popularity and was a success throughout the 1980s. In 1988, Commodore began hosting the event in multiple locations, including the United States.

With Jim Dionne, formerly of Commodore Canada, now president of Commodore US, he decided to launch the A4000 at the World of Commodore. Held in early September, 1992 in Pasadena, California, the theme of the show was "4000 reasons to own an Amiga."

The show had a steady crowd, with approximately 20,000 attending. Most people seemed interested in the A4000 but there was not much interest in the A600. Although users appreciated the improved specs of the A4000, the universal opinion of the machine was that it was ugly. Major developers were planning a cross-platform approach, supporting the PC first with a "wait-and-see" view of Commodore.

Along with the four A4000 demo machines, Commodore also showed off five A600s, an A3000UX, an A3000T, seven plain A3000s, nine CDT-Vs, and two A500s. They were also showing off the new A570 CD-ROM reader. To get rid of excess inventory, Commodore announced a program where users received a free CDTV with the purchase of an A3000.

At the show, Commodore presented Amiga pioneer Jay Miner with one of the first production models of the A4000. Curiously, at the same show, a mail order distributor named Creative Computers began taking orders for the new machine for less than $3000 even though the recommended price was $3699.

Commodore rolled out the same launch events at the World of Commodore in Germany, held November 26-29, 1992 at the Frankfurt Fairgrounds with over 100,000 attending. The A4000 was also shown at the original World of Commodore in Toronto in December, with over 40,000 attending. Lew Eggebrecht attended all three events, speaking about the A4000 and future plans for Amiga.

A4000T Begins

Paul Lassa, the engineer who overcame months of rejection to work for Commodore, had initially met with skepticism of his ability to handle the C65 board design. Since then he had proved himself to be a goldmine of talent and was assigned a secondary role on the A4000, but by September 1992 he was ready to take on a solo project. "While those guys were all still finishing the design and support of the A4000, I peeled off and started doing the A4000T," says Lassa. "One of the goals was to put it in a tower case."

With the Video Toaster leading Amiga sales in North America, it was important to satisfy that market. "We expected that people using the Video Toaster would want a tower case because at that time the Video Toaster was also growing in size," says Lassa. "It was already kind of a sandwich board and they were packing ever more stuff onto it and it needed more power, more space inside the case. The tower would go beside your desk on the floor and you wanted enough space in there and fans and air movement to take a Video Toaster and whatever other five cards you wanted to throw in there."

At the time, NewTek was working on a sequel to its popular product called the Video Toaster 4000, specifically for the A4000. Interestingly, the actor who played ensign Wesley Crusher on *Star Trek: The Next Generation*, Wil Wheaton, had left the show after season four of the series and moved from Hollywood to Kansas to work for the company.

The actor had a start in computing with an Atari 400. He even entered programs from *Compute!* magazine into his computer. "That led to my love of computers, my love of technology, and my love of programming," he later recalled. "When I worked for NewTek and worked on the Video Toaster 4000, I didn't do any of the actual programing. I did a ton of product testing and quality control, and worked in the marketing department and then I was sort of one of their technology evangelists."[1]

Commodore's management emphasised fast development time done cheaply for the A4000T. "We wanted to do two things: faster time-to-market and leverage some of the infrastructure that was out there," explains Lassa. "A key decision on the A4000T was to say, 'Okay make an Amiga 4000 and design it to fit in an off-the-shelf tower case that you could go buy.' Because as long as some of the chips took to design, when you design a custom case and you have to do all the tooling for it and everything, that is a very long process and it's very expensive."

Designing a motherboard around the case was a new approach for Commodore. "An Amiga 4000 did not naturally fit into a PC brand tower case. It just did not," recalls Lassa. "There wasn't an easy way to do that because PC towers would have added graphics cards and add-in audio cards that were perpendicular to the motherboard."

The task seemed impossible to do at first, but Lassa persisted. "I put as many of the chips on the flat motherboard as I could and where it all made sense," he says. "This wasn't rocket science necessarily. It was being industrious. First off you say, 'Oh this definitely won't fit. We can't do it. Things don't line up and it's going to be too much of a hassle.' But if you say, 'Look we're either going to do this or we're not,' then you find a way to do it. It was kind of an exercise in packaging and creative layout of things."

---

1   *Geeks of Doom* (website), May 29, 2008. "Conversations with GoD: Wil Wheaton"

The A4000T offered a feature that was in high demand at the time. "The one other thing that we put in the A4000T that was not in the A4000 was an integrated SCSI controller," says Lassa. "And in this tower case, we had a couple of Amiga Zorro expansion slots but we also put in the PC expansion bus so that technically you could throw in additional PC format expansion cards."

Lassa would continue working on the A4000T motherboard into 1993, with a planned debut at the June CES and eventual release later in the year.

AAA Progress

Commodore had begun planning the AAA chipset in December 1987 with Jim Redfield, Hedley Davis, and Bob Welland, with detailed AAA architecture design started in the summer of 1988 by Redfield. At the time, it was optimistically expected to debut in 1989. Now, almost five years since the project began, the chipset was not yet complete.

During Bill Sydnes' reign at Commodore, Amiga development had all but stopped. "Then they came to the realization that Commodore couldn't make PCs for less than anybody else," says Dave Haynie. "All of a sudden the Amiga was on again but they had been dragging their feet on the whole AAA and AA stuff."

After Mehdi Ali asked for the A4000 computer, signalling a return to high-end Amiga computers, work on the AAA chipset resumed. The engineers began to get serious about finishing Linda, Andrea, Monica, and Mary in time for a system to be released in late 1993. "We worked on it from an architectural point of view for a long time but it's only been serious for about a year," said Lew Eggebrecht in 1993. "It was obvious that AAA was not going to meet our cost targets for the mid to low end systems. ... It would have been nice to have AAA at the same time as AA but we just couldn't get there."[2]

It would not be an easy task. Compared to the AGA chipset, which had around 80,000 transistors in total, AAA had 750,000 transistors spread among the four chips. (Two other chips were required for the chipset to operate in the 64 bit configuration, bringing the total to a million transistors.) It was a complex ordeal.

Unlike the OCS, ECS, and AGA chipsets, which were used on both the low-end and high-end Amiga systems, this chipset would be for the high end only. This made the eventual payoff worth that much less.

---

2 *Amiga User International*. June 1988. "The AUI Interview"

By the 1990s, Commodore Semiconductor Group no longer designed chips by hand, as they had in the past. Now almost everything was designed on computers.

Ed Hepler, the designer of Andrea, used a variety of tools to take his design to layout. "We had some tools from a company called Silicon Compiler Systems," says Hepler "They made tools that you could do something called procedural layout. Instead of sitting in front of a monitor and drawing out the outlines of diffusion and polysilicon and metal and making transistors and contacts and so forth, you could use scripts to describe the structures and do layout like that."

The most computer-intensive procedure was called logic synthesis, in which the abstract design of the chipset is turned into an actual implementation of logic gates. By this time, the CSG designers used computers for layout, based on a rule set by the layout designer. "They came out with a synthesizer called AutoLogic that we used for the synthesis," says Hepler. "Then for the standard cells, I wrote procedural layout routines that produced the standard cell library that we used for all the 'random logic'. So all the control logic was done using the standard cells that I did using this procedural layout language."

The industry as a whole had not yet settled on the language of Verilog to design chips. "We wrote in a high-level language called M, which is no longer used," says Hepler. "Verilog and VHDL were in their infancy."

Hepler actually designed his chip in a simulator by Silicon Compiler Systems, which allowed him to test the circuitry as he designed the chip. "We were using a fantastic simulator called LSim," he says. "It had a behavior language called M. M was basically a superset of C, that gave you all the things you can do in C but then it also had extra stuff that allowed you to model any kind of device and figure out how to interconnect devices."

Although much of the layout was automated, the designers still had to manually lay out some of the data paths. "It was built using something we called structured custom," says Hepler. "All the data paths were done using manually laid out circuitry, and all the control logic was synthesized."

Hepler had worked on Andrea and the AAA chipset constantly since he was hired in 1989. The company expected the layouts for all four chips to be completed by November 1992, after which time chip characterization would begin. Now Commodore was working towards a 1993 release. And if all went well, the chipset would still be viable after such a long development time.

The Motivator Board

With the AA+ chipset a long way from release, it seemed like Commodore was destined to lag behind VGA graphics for the immediate future. "The chip guys were working on a new chipset but it was going to be a couple years before it was done and everyone recognized there was a gap to fill," says Joe Augenbraun. The rebellious engineer who fought with site management, who fought with Jeff Frank, and who had his A1000 Plus cancelled, decided to fight for Commodore and help save the company from its chip predicament.

AGA was only able to do 800x600 interlaced, which caused flicker. "I had no idea that the Amiga had a problem," says Augenbraun. "The Amiga was lower resolution than the PC. PCs were super VGA at that point, doing 1024 by 768, and the Amiga was stuck at 640 by 480 [640x400 NTSC] and we couldn't even do 800 by 600."

The only thing that could do better on the Amiga was the Hedley Hi-Res monitor. "The Hedley monitor was a monochrome monitor that took four images and married them together," recalls Augenbraun. "It was a real product but things would tear when you moved windows around and stuff."

Inspired by the basic premise of the Hedley Hi-Res, Augenbraun planned to improve what it could do, but with much better color. "I had this idea," he says. "How flexible are the chips that we have? Can they do a slower scan rate with a higher resolution? Is the limitation the pixel frequently coming out? And the answer was yes it was."

Augenbraun planned to harness the existing AA chipset but have it draw more pixels by updating the screen less frequently. "I said, 'Okay, why don't we build a scan rate converter. We'll program this thing to do a slow scan rate—30Hz, 20Hz whatever it is—in a much higher resolution and do a scan rate converter buffer where it then spits it out at 70 Hz or whatever it is you want to spit it out at.'"

The product would truly be a successor to the work Hedley Davis had pioneered. "This was sort of a dramatically more advanced version of flicker fixer," says Augenbraun. "It used the AA chipset. It was just a scan converter."

Augenbraun asked his manager if he could go ahead and develop the product. "And Commodore wouldn't," he says. "It wasn't an approved project and didn't get approved. They said this was too good an idea."

Undeterred, Augenbraun formed a team of rebels within the company to work when everyone else had gone home. "Over Thanksgiving break me,

Chris Coley, and Spence [Spencer Shanson] went and built this thing. We built it in four to five days, whatever the Thanksgiving break was."

Augenbraun did his best to keep his partners in crime motivated, and in the process came up with a codename for the project. "Chris and Spence said, 'Why are we doing this? It's not approved.' I said, 'Once they see it, they'll be motivated.' So it became the Motivator."

Without any budget, the team used whatever they could find to build the Motivator. "We couldn't even order parts for it so we had parts we scrounged in the lab," says Augenbraun. "They were too slow and you had to spray it with freeze spray. It would work for 10 or 20 seconds because it sped up the parts when they were cold."

The parts the team used to build the video card were purely to demonstrate the product. Once the concept was proven, they would find cheaper ways to make the board. "I used PALs, programmable logic chips, but for production I probably would have just done an ASIC," says Augenbraun. "It would have been a three to six-month effort to do an ASIC for something like that. Not a big deal compared to a custom chip. In fact, for that kind of thing, the verification is dramatically easier because if there is a bug, it goes away a sixtieth of a second later. You don't have to be that bug free."

When Commodore's managers returned from vacation, they were surprised to find a new product awaiting them. "It was totally cheap but it could do 1280 by 1024 resolution. It was perfect. So that was the Motivator. It hooked up to a PC monitor and had VGA output," says Augenbraun. "Everyone was interested. First it was Jeff [Frank] but that's a case where Lew jumps in and everyone was really excited about it."

Eggebrecht approved full development of the project and the team began designing a gate array for the board called Darcie. "Doing something complex in a chip is all about figuring out how to verify it," says Augenbraun. "It's all about figuring out how to organize it so that you can do unit tests on the subsystems and make sure they work so that when it goes together it will work."

This burst of creativity would be Augenbraun's swan song at Commodore. The young engineer had been looking for another job since March of that year, after the delay of his A1000 Plus due to the new case work and subsequent cancellation. "It would've been the volume product, and it was going to make it miss Christmas. That's why I left the company actually," he says. "I said, 'I just can't work for a company that could do something so stupid. You know, miss Christmas for the case.'"

He left in late 1992 before the project was complete, leaving it to his team-mate. "Chris Coley is an amazing engineer. Chris is really down to earth," says Augenbraun. "Chris was supposed to take that forward after I left but I think somehow it just kind of petered out. It's a shame. It was really needed, and it was an elegant solution to the problem." By December, 1992, changes were made to Kickstart 3.0 in order to accommodate the Motivator card. Prototypes of the card were nearing completion and were to be shown at the January 1993 Devcon in Orlando, Florida. Unfortunately the project was officially cancelled in early 1993 in favor of the AA+ chipset.

CHAPTER 34

Rooting Out the Rot
1992

One of the benefits of Mehdi Ali's restructuring of Commodore was the addition of financial control mechanisms to the company. Commodore had once been run with Jack Tramiel as a de facto company financial controller. After he left, Commodore never really installed a proper accounting mechanism. Now Mehdi Ali would put in controls that made sure the company was operating properly. What he found was unexpected to say the least.

The Investigator

When Mehdi Ali first took control of Commodore as President, he was alarmed by the poor corporate structure of the company. "They didn't take stock of the whole accounting procedure of Commodore worldwide," explains David Pleasance. "They didn't have a team of independent auditors to drop in on all of the subsidiaries and check all their books. They never did that so how could they know what financial position we were really in? They never knew!" The lack of independent auditors would eventually lead to some alarming consequences.

Due to the lack of controls, Commodore was often moving from one problem to another, putting out fires before the next flame popped up. Ali had his work cut out for him in order to get Commodore back under control. He decided to hire a number of accountants who could track down problems with the company and offer suggestions for restructuring.

One of the big problems with Commodore Germany was the inventory management system, which wreaked havoc with its manufacturing ability. "They couldn't track inventory and the inventory records were inaccurate so production kept halting for lack of parts," says accountant Colin Proudfoot. "They didn't know why."

Ali went to Commodore UK's Finance Director Andrew George-Kelso to find someone appropriate for the job of fixing the inventory system. George-Kelso had previously worked with an accountant named Colin Proudfoot at Wang and brought him to Ali's attention. "He and I went way back," says Proudfoot. "I was consulting and doing some recruiting. Basically self-employed. He called me up and said, 'Would you be interested in going to Germany on an assignment to help Commodore?' I said sure. Then I didn't hear anything for a couple of months and he called me up one afternoon and said, 'Can you meet me and Mehdi Ali at a hotel by Heathrow Airport tomorrow morning at seven o'clock?' So I said sure."

Proudfoot arrived and found Mehdi Ali to be direct and to the point. "Mehdi and Andrew and I have breakfast and Mehdi asks some questions about my background, which is essentially financial analysis. I had worked with inventory so then he said, 'Okay, that's enough time. Andrew knows that if you don't work out he's getting fired and he's vouching for you, so that's good enough for me. Be in Amsterdam tomorrow morning at eight o'clock.'"

Proudfoot's first impression of Ali stuck with him. "He was charming, he was articulate, he was direct, and he asked good questions," says Proudfoot. "The big question mark in my mind was when he said, 'You screw up and Andrew gets fired.' I thought, 'That's kind of an interesting management style.'"

Proudfoot started his new job the very next day to examine the $40 million of inventory at the German factory. "I showed up to Amsterdam the following morning at eight o'clock and he gave me a three-month assignment to work on inventory in the Braunschweig plant, which was a mess," he says. "One of the things I found out by looking at the industry reports and the usage reports that they had on the system, was that there were clearly a lot of data entry errors."

Next he went to the actual factory, accompanied by the local Braunschweig inventory controller, to see with his own eyes what was going on. "I went to the warehouse just to look around and I noticed that all the bins had sheets of paper with numbers on them," he recalls. "I asked the inventory controller what they were and he had no idea because I don't think he'd actually been to the warehouse. So we asked the warehouse foreman what they were and he said, 'Well that's how we keep track of what we have.'"

This was strange because Commodore had a computer-based inventory system, which should have made paper unnecessary. "The inventory controller was aghast and said, 'But we have a computer system.' The guy said,

'Yes, we record the transactions and a girl comes in every Friday afternoon and enters them into the computer.'"

The redundant, inefficient, and error prone system explained why the factory often believed it had parts when they had actually run out already. "I said to them, 'Then what that means is that for four and a half days a week your inventory on the system is totally inaccurate because you're not entering the transactions real-time. If you don't post them real-time, nobody's going to rely on them so nobody will look at the system.' They had no idea what to do."

Proudfoot then stumbled onto a major problem which could have landed Commodore in serious legal trouble. "I noticed there were some odd location codes on the inventory reports and asked what they were," he recalls. "I found out that there were extra warehouses where all the old junk was stored, kept on the books at full value. We were hiring these warehouses to store them."

This was a problem because publicly traded companies are supposed to accurately report the value of their assets. All companies of course want to show a higher book value which will cause the stock to trade higher. But Commodore Germany had old, overvalued assets that were not worth as much as they were reported in the books. "As I dug more and more and looked at the usage reports, I found out that there was a vast amount of inventory on the books at full value which hadn't been used in years," he says. "If you are holding inventory on your books at value which it does not have, then that is illegal because you are overvaluing your assets. Now what the hell the German auditors were doing I don't know because they should have found that and flagged that as an issue."

Several warehouses housed old parts from past devices that were no longer marketable, such as PET, Plus/4, and VIC-20 computers. For example, Commodore had only assembled 20,000 C64GS systems but had manufactured 60,000 cases. They had reworked the C64GS motherboards into regular C64 computers but were now stuck with all those cases. "There was a C64 game console project which basically you took a C64 and you put it in a different case, which came without the keyboard," explains Proudfoot. "Somebody thought that was a good idea. They built all the cases and there was a warehouse full of parts."

To remain compliant with the rules for public companies, Proudfoot realized Commodore would have to write down the value of those warehoused parts. He prepared a report for Mehdi Ali. "The German management were aghast that I was going to tell him all this stuff," says Proudfoot. "He had a reputation for firing people who gave him bad news. I said, 'Well I've got my three month assignment. I'm guaranteed money so I don't care if he fires me. That's ok.'"

Ali was not amused by the findings. "I told Mehdi the true value of the German inventory was a fraction of what they had on the books," recalls Proudfoot. "For the number of years it had been going on, it's very poor management if they're not aware of it. We just went through the report and Mehdi exploded. I had answers to all his questions because I had done my homework. But he fired three or four of the German management after I had left the meeting because it was a mess. It was a big write-down."

Ali was impressed by Proudfoot's speedy resolution of the inventory problem and his discovery of the overvalued inventory. As a result, Ali would later hire him to address an even more serious issue. "Ever since then Mehdi and I got on, because I wasn't hiding anything from him," says Proudfoot. "I just gave him honest answers and I knew what I was doing."

Resignation Letter

In late January 1992, Tony Ricci, Commodore's corporate controller in West Chester, Pennsylvania, received a letter of resignation from Commodore UK's financial director, Andrew George-Kelso. Kelso, a reliable family man, had been trying to bring financial discipline to the UK. "Andrew had left Germany to take over as head of finance for the UK and he was sorting out some of their accounting issues," explains Colin Proudfoot.

Kelso was an intelligent man with an attention to detail who took his responsibility very seriously. As Ricci read through the six-page resignation letter, he could sense something was not right. The word intimidation kept cropping up. "...intimidatory influences could make the development of healthy and logical processes for pack build, inventory control and especially warranty and repair management an almost impossible one." "Meetings are infrequent and tend to consist of intimidatory monologues." "...the ongoing approach of unilateralism and intimidation continues to create unmeasured proposals and decisions which are not always in the interests of the company."

Many of the points seemed aimed at Commodore US and Mehdi Ali's autocratic management style. "He talked mostly about the UK and the people in the UK but he dropped some hints about his view about what's going on in the US," says Colin Proudfoot.

There were also hints of something afoot with Commodore UK's maintenance group, FMG, which provided technical support and repairs for Amiga computers. "Serious innuendo relating to major trading relationships between Commodore and third party companies (especially FMG, Evans Hunt & Scott, Quentin Bell, and others)" "...offers of employment not reviewed adequately..." "'Steve agreed...' is probably the most commonly used phrase in the company." "...resignation effective immediately..."

The letter was all kinds of confusing to Ricci, especially since Commodore UK had hired Kelso scarcely eight months earlier. "It gives an insight to the way Commodore operations were being run, and I don't think any other subsidiaries were in much better shape," says Proudfoot. "Commodore business practices and controls were questionable at best. The environment that he describes in the UK was exactly the same as what was going on in Holland and was going on in Germany."

After Kelso and Proudfoot had finished cleaning up Germany's inventory problems, Kelso decided he wanted to clean up possible financial mismanagement in the UK. "He believed that the maintenance company that Commodore UK was dealing with was charging an awful lot of money and it seemed to him to be very expensive," says Proudfoot. "He wanted that investigated so he convinced Mehdi that that was a bigger problem than what was going on in Germany."

Colin Proudfoot, who was working in Germany with Kelso, was also brought in to help. "By that time, Mehdi liked me so they offered me a position as commercial controller of Commodore UK. That was December 1991," says Proudfoot. "So I came back to the UK and started looking into the maintenance company."

By January, Kelso had done much to improve Commodore UK's financial operations. But now, he decided he no longer wanted to work for the company, and he recommended his friend Colin Proudfoot as his successor. "Andrew decided ethically he wasn't comfortable with the things that were happening at Commodore, plus there was a lot more suspicion about corruption," says Proudfoot. "Basically I could deal with the greyness that was Commodore better than he could. He just hated it and all the things that were going on."

Ali had seen Proudfoot sort out the problems with Commodore Germany and wanted him to investigate the UK subsidiary. "When Mehdi appointed me, the conversation I had with Mehdi is, 'There are all these allegations. From what I've seen so far, this stinks. There's a lot of stuff going on. If I find evidence, are you going to act on the evidence?'" Had Proudfoot known of Ali's reputation for firing people, he wouldn't have asked. Ali replied, "I give you my word."

Proudfoot had experience helping companies such as Xerox and Wang improve their controls in the areas of finances, inventory, and employee hiring. However, what he saw at Commodore was worse than anything he encountered before. "Commodore's troubles ran far deeper and took more cleaning up," he says. In fact, they swirled around the man at the top, Steve Franklin, the general manager of Commodore UK.

The Money Detective

In February 1992, Colin Proudfoot took his position as Commodore UK's financial director. Proudfoot was born March 17, 1955 in Essex county, England. He had an unusual surname, used by J.R.R. Tolkien for hobbits and sounding vaguely American Indian in origin. "The Proudfoot name is from medieval times," he says. "Very old medieval."

Proudfoot soon grew more acquainted with his boss Mehdi Ali and felt he could work with him. "Personally Mehdi can be charming. He can be very good company," says Proudfoot. "We always ate in great restaurants, had great food. He could be generous if he liked you. If he didn't like you, you were in trouble."

Ali approved several safeguards to ensure Proudfoot's investigation could not be derailed. "Mehdi made sure that I was on the board of directors officially so I had equal standing [with Steve Franklin]," says Proudfoot. "That gave me status to investigate Steve so he couldn't bully me around."

Proudfoot, a cautious man by nature, also made sure that if things went bad, it would be difficult for anyone to inflict repercussions on him. "Some of these people are not nice," he says "So I went ex-directory, which in the UK means you are delisted from all public records. In the UK back in the day, you were in the phone book unless you opt out. I had recently moved and the company did not have my real home address anywhere in its records."

Proudfoot started his investigation of his boss Steve Franklin and FMG, the maintenance company. As Proudfoot knew, FMG and Franklin had a cosy relationship going back over a decade. "I knew the guys that were running the maintenance company and Steve Franklin, because they were all sales managers at Xerox when I was at Xerox in 1979," says Proudfoot. "I knew that they knew each other, so I knew it wasn't an arms-length relationship. Quite how close it was only emerged later but it never smelled right."

Despite having worked with Franklin before, no one suspected Proudfoot would go easy on him. "He's a 100% straight guy which is one of the reasons I love him so much," says co-worker David Pleasance.

Steve Franklin had been hired during a low point at Commodore UK in June 1987, when the C64 was fading and the Amiga 500 had not yet been introduced. He had sacked the entire sales division, save David Pleasance. Ironically, he had reeled off integrity and honesty in Pleasance's interview. As the managing director of the subsidiary, he oversaw gains from £20 million to £170 million in four years, primarily due to the explosive growth of the Amiga 500. With Commodore UK now pulling in hundreds of millions of dollars per year, and no independent auditors reviewing the books, there were many opportunities for revenue to fall through the cracks.

Proudfoot began looking into the personal life of the 45 year old, recently divorced executive. The most visible signs of corruption were the lavish houses he and his ex-wife lived in and the fancy cars. "I came to the UK and very quickly established that something was going on," he says.

Proudfoot needed hard evidence, however, so he hired a corporate investigation firm named Kroll Incorporated. "They're a global consultancy. It's scary what they can do and what they can find out about people," says Proudfoot. "Names, addresses, contacts, copies of bank statements, copies of financial records, copies of investments, everything they own, everything they do."

As with most investigations, there were gray areas that had to be traversed in order to produce results. "One of the first questions they ask is, 'How far do you want us to go? Do you care what we do? Do you care about the results or do you care about how we get the results?'"

Kroll's investigations produced some interesting documents for Proudfoot to mull over. He soon identified how Franklin was receiving kickbacks from the companies that Commodore overpaid. "We called in Kroll, the investigators, and they started digging into these people and their connections," says Proudfoot. "At the same time we started investigating, Steve Franklin had gotten divorced and was living in a house owned by the maintenance company. He was driving a Jaguar which was a $200,000 car and it was held by our advertising agency. His wife was driving a Porsche which he bought from one of the software vendors and hadn't got round to paying for yet."

Proudfoot now had to investigate the service companies that worked for Commodore, including the maintenance supplier. "The maintenance supplier is the company that repairs Amigas," he explains. "They are hired by the commercial controller, with various contract relationships."

By examining the service companies, with help from Kroll, Proudfoot hoped to determine how Franklin extracted money from Commodore. "I knew the two guys who ran the maintenance company from Xerox," says Proudfoot. "The maintenance company was specifically set up for Commodore business. They supported no other business. And Commodore was paying three times per machine over what they should have."

However, the scheme didn't end with just overcharging. By combing through past statements, Proudfoot noticed phantom customers where Commodore received charges for repairs, but no shipping receipt was found for mailing the system back. "We worked out that there were missing machines," says Proudfoot. "They took in more Amigas than were sent back to customers."

Proudfoot also relied on asking questions of coworkers and even Franklin himself, which he knew could raise suspicions. As a precaution, he made sure his phone lines and office space were clean. "We had Kroll in there," he says. "I had my office swept every week. We never found a bug but I always suspected."

Early in the investigation, Proudfoot and Kroll felt they knew the basics of the swindle. Franklin extracted money from Commodore by overpaying to service companies owned by his friends. They in turn paid Franklin back through property or even loans that would never be paid back. However, Proudfoot could not move in yet. "I knew I was clean. I knew Steve wasn't clean, and I had to decide on everybody else in the company because the assumption was he couldn't be doing it entirely by himself," he explains.

Proudfoot also knew he might just be scratching the surface, with other schemes yet to uncover. He would secretly work throughout the year to unravel the whole sordid mess.

Promotion

By the summer of 1992, Colin Proudfoot had done enough investigating to know that Steve Franklin was the central figure of corruption within Commodore UK. However, he still did not know who else was corrupt. "Every conversation I had, I didn't know who I was talking to," says Proudfoot.

What he did know, he passed on to Mehdi Ali, who then prepared to remove Steve Franklin from his post as GM of Commodore UK. Proudfoot was still building his case against Franklin however, so Franklin would be demoted to the multimedia division for the time being.

At the same time, David Pleasance received a call from Ali for one of his infamous 10 minute meetings. "I got summoned to New York," says Pleasance. "Basically it had transpired that Steve had financial involvement with some of the companies that we were giving business to as an organization, which of course is completely illegal. Even if it's not illegal, it's certainly not above board."

The corruption in the UK called everyone under suspicion, even David Pleasance. Ali knew Pleasance had, prior to moving to Switzerland, worked with Franklin for many years. "Because I had a very close relationship with Steve, I think they took the opinion that perhaps I knew all about it," recalls Pleasance. However, Pleasance had been in Basel for well over a year by then. "By complete fortuitous chance I did not know about it. So I was questioned by Mehdi. 'Be honest, what do you know about this service company? What do you know about this hospitality company?' And for similar things. Of course, I knew all about them, although I really didn't even know anything about the service companies because they literally had just been appointed before I left. I didn't even know any of the people that were there. Thankfully I was genuinely unaware of these things and Mehdi accepted that as true."

Pleasance had barely moved his family from Switzerland to the US when Ali suggested yet another move. "I was then told that [Steve] Franklin had been dismissed and was asked by Mehdi to take over as MD back in the UK," recalls Pleasance. "I turned it down because I am a hunter, not a farmer. As such, I was totally delighted with my new role."

It was obvious Pleasance had been Ali's number one choice for the role. He then wanted to know more about his number two pick. "So then Mehdi asked me what I thought of Kelly Sumner," says Pleasance, referring to the sales manager who had been central to the C64GS product. "I told him he's a good guy. He's a guy who applies himself and he can probably do the job. He has an ego a mile high. If he gets into trouble, he will not ask you for help. But everything else is fine."

And with that, Mehdi Ali appointed Sumner the new GM of Commodore UK. At 31 years of age, Sumner was remarkably young among Commodore's general managers. He had left home at the age of 16 and promptly landed a job at Commodore on June 11, 1979. Initially, Commodore provided Sumner with engineer training to repair watches, calculators, and chess games. He then moved on to provide service and support repairs on the VIC-20 and C64. When Commodore launched the Amiga 1000, Sumner moved up into sales, which led him to take a key role at Commodore UK.

Sumner could bring a new era of prosperity to Commodore UK, if he could survive under Mehdi Ali long enough.

J'accuse!

By September 1992, Colin Proudfoot was almost done his investigation into Steve Franklin and other Commodore UK employees. As a final task, the corporate investigators (Kroll) went to the courts in order to move on the evidence. "We brought them in as consultants and they got enough information about the maintenance guys that we got Miranda orders on them," says Proudfoot.

Gradually, the evidence revealed how Steve Franklin received his cut of the corrupt proceeds. "There was some inventory that had gone missing that we knew about," says Proudfoot. "There were stories of thousands of pounds in brown paper bags passing hands. People would tell me about that. There were a couple of other independent retailers who were involved, who had furnished the house that Steve was living in. There were just lots of improper relationships."

Franklin even pulled his family into his scheme to receive illicit proceeds. "We found things like Steve Franklin's mother was being paid $10,000 a month by these guys [FMG]," says Proudfoot. Finally it was time to move in and confront Franklin with the allegations. The reason for his mother's expense was laughable. "He claimed that was because she was providing house cleaning services to them."

Proudfoot asked Franklin about suspicious deposits into his account. "And then there were sums like $50,000 coming from them into his account," recalls Proudfoot. Franklin's replies were unconvincing. "'That was a loan.' 'What was the loan for?' 'Can't remember.' 'Did you pay it back?' 'Not sure. He's a friend, that's what you do for friends.'"

Even the sponsorship with the Chelsea football team was suspected. "The entertainment people, who were also buddies of Steve, were involved in negotiating the contract between Commodore and Chelsea," explains Proudfoot. "That had already taken place, and I'm quite sure that they got some commission on that. Where that money went, I don't know."

As for how deep the corruption went, Proudfoot was unsure until the final month. "I couldn't believe one guy, who I really liked, was involved," he says. "I found out he definitely was involved. Funny enough, I was at his house chatting with him when the FMG guys called him. His wife came into the meeting and said so and so is on the phone. I didn't know he knew them! He looked at me and I looked at him, and we knew. We both knew. I went, 'Damn!' I so hoped he was one of the good guys, but he wasn't."

Conversely, Commodore employees under strong suspicion turned out to be innocent. "There was another guy who I was convinced was a bad guy but never found anything on him, so I have to conclude he was a good guy," says Proudfoot. "I ended up with five people that were definitely involved alongside Steve."

Earlier in the year, Mehdi Ali had promised Proudfoot that he would act on whatever he uncovered. "If I found evidence on Steve, he would fire Steve." Now Ali proved he was good to his word. On October 19, 1992, Steve Franklin and his five accomplices were summarily terminated from Commodore. "I worked for Steve so technically I got to fire my boss," says Proudfoot.

The same month, FMG, the service company Commodore hired to repair Amigas at the National Repair Center, had its assets frozen by the British court. This resulted in FMG no longer being able to operate and it quickly shut down. Commodore UK instead hired Wang to provide service warranty for the Amiga 600 and other computers.

It had been a stressful, uncomfortable year for both Colin Proudfoot and Kelly Sumner. Luckily, the previous caretakers of Commodore UK had arranged the perfect antidote to all the stress by booking a lavish retreat aboard the famous Maxim's de Mer ship. "It was for the top three distributors and the top retailers," explains Proudfoot. "Maxim's de Mer is a boat that was a minesweeper in the Second World War. Pierre Cardin converted it for Jean-Paul Gaultier as a floating replica of Maxim's restaurant in Paris. It was used by Prince Rainier III for his holidays. Princess Stéphanie used it for her honeymoon. There is a crew of 35 for 24 guests. Each cabin has a minimum half a million dollars worth of artwork in it. In the salon, the walls are all lacquered and the ceiling is mirrored. It is an amazing boat."

Proudfoot found it was too late to cancel the trip, so he and Sumner had no choice but to use it. "It had been booked and scheduled," he says. "Steve Franklin had booked it with his buddies and we were told the contract was too tight to cancel, so we didn't waste the money. We took it. That was unbelievable."

Commodore International and Holland

There's an old saying in business, "When the cat's away, the mice will play." Nowhere did it apply more than in Commodore's European division. Years of no accountability had led to a number of irregularities that originated right at the top of some of Commodore's subsidiaries.

After his stint in the USA, David Pleasance returned to Commodore International. "In November-December of '92, when I sorted all the mess out with the CDTVs and all the distribution channels in the USA and got them all selling A500 packs, I went to Mehdi and said, 'My job here is done. Until we bring out the A1200 I don't want to sell them anything else.' To which he ultimately reluctantly agreed."

In the meantime, the former headquarters of Commodore International had been moved closer to home. "I came back to do the International job that I'd been doing because, when I left Switzerland to go to America, they gave some of my countries to the UK office and some to the Dutch office, and between them they kind of screwed them up actually," he says. "They hadn't done a very good job at all. So I went back to do that role for a while but I was based out of London, not Switzerland, because they moved everything from Switzerland to Holland and London."

Due to the split with Holland, Pleasance was exposed to the GM of Commodore Holland, Bernard Van Tienen. He immediately began to receive hints that there might be corruption rampant throughout the Commodore subsidiary. "This was a company in complete disarray," says Pleasance. "They would employ someone because of his CV and assumed he knew what he was doing. No instructions were given to them, nothing."

In the absence of any monitoring, the GM of Commodore Holland invented ways to achieve his quarterly bonuses. "The head of the Dutch sales company, Bernard Van Tienen, used to boast that at the end of every quarter, if he had not reached forecast target, he would invent invoices and put products onto lorries to record sales, get his commission, and then take them back again," says Pleasance. "That was happening on a regular basis. He boasted about it!"

Commodore Holland had been renting out its headquarters when Van Tienen suggested a potential investment. "Commodore was renting that building that they had been in for quite some time and the building came up for sale. As I understand it, Bernard contacted Mehdi and said, 'The building is up for sale. Why don't we buy it?' Mehdi said, 'We're not in the business of property management.' Which I think was nonsense. We were paying so much dead money on rent."

Once his proposition was turned down, Van Tienen found an inventive way he could personally benefit. "The next thing you know, Bernard Van Tienen bought it himself," says Pleasance. "He ultimately bought the building that Commodore Holland was renting. So he is landlord to himself! And again, there is something very fishy about that. That cannot be right."

Later, an auditor was able to examine some of the expenses Van Tienen had claimed. "He showed us a piece of paper and it was expenses claimed by Bernard Van Tienen," recalls Pleasance. "It was invoices and receipts to the tune of 250,000 US dollars that he had spent on expenses in the most high profile brothel in Amsterdam, a place called Yab Yum."

The brashness of claiming the expenses in print showed just how much the Commodore subsidiaries could get away with. "Well how else could he get it paid for it? He had to put something in the books," says Pleasance.

The corruption that happened in Commodore Holland, Commodore UK, and even Commodore Germany was preventable. David Pleasance lays the blame for the corruption in Europe on one simple and boring reason: lack of yearly audits. "One of the biggest failings of Commodore International is that they never did any auditing," he says.

Executives like Bernard Van Tienen and Steve Franklin were basically normal executives who would have been kept in line by regular audits. Both of these individuals did many beneficial things to help Commodore, but the lack of audits gave them too much power, and power eventually corrupts.

Amigo 1992

Jeff Porter and Hedley Davis had succeeded in radically cost-reducing Commodore's CD-ROM mechanism. They worked full-time on the CDTV-CR well into 1992, even researching MPEG capability. But the continuation of their project hinged on the success of the original CDTV and it was not going well.

CD-500

Although Jeff Porter was focused on the cost reduction aspect of CDTV, he did not shy away from looking into potential new features to his machine. One piece of technology was of particular interest to him. "Philips CD-i had an MPEG board, so I was in a 'me too' mode," he says. "I wanted it for CDTV-CR."

Porter created a new bill of materials for a proposed CDTV using the AA chipset and an MPEG decoder. The decoder itself would add $75 to the bill of materials. "I looked at a ton of suppliers for the decoder chips for that," he says. "Motorola, SGS-Thomson, and others, but I settled on C-Cube, a Silicon Valley Startup." Along with 2 megabytes of memory and a 68020 processor, the total bill of materials for the new AA system came to $517.30—even more costly than the original CDTV.

The vision of this video multimedia game machine was more in line with systems released in the 2000's. "The Xbox One is a modern equivalent," says Commodore engineer Michael Sinz. "The tech back then wasn't able to do everything but that was clearly on the same path that CDTV was on. ... We were part of the original MPEG standard committees. We were pioneers."

For the week of January 27, Porter traveled to Boca Raton, Florida for an ANSI MPEG meeting, which was currently developing the MPEG standard. "I was the Commodore representative to that ANSI/ISO group that established the MPEG standards," he says. "It was sort of like the UN for technology. Sony and Philips were big players there. But I was the 'yin' on CDTV to Philips' 'yang' for CD-i."

The MPEG version was just a plan for the third generation of CDTV, however. Porter and his team spent January 1992 preparing to produce 200 second generation CDTV-CR machines, which Commodore would hand out to software developers, retailers, and Commodore personnel. Porter even had one specifically earmarked for Irving Gould.

Although the CDTV-CR was supposed to be cost-reduced, it was decked out with even more features than the original CDTV. The unit had ports for PC-Card, MIDI, stereo audio, parallel, serial, floppy disk, composite video, RGB, S-video, RF, and infrared. Due to the space saving SMD motherboard, there was also room for an internal hard drive and a 3.5 inch floppy disk. The CD-500 model name, chosen in April 1992, reflected the computer-like status it shared with its sister product, the Amiga 500.

Unfortunately, the final cost of the CDTV-CR came in higher than Mehdi Ali had anticipated. Porter had hoped for under $300 as his low-ball estimate, but the final cost was $351.19. "What ended up happening is after it gets built, it's a really nice machine and it's really slick and they've also incorporated the potential for doing MPEG decoding, so it can play movies and that kind of thing," says Carl Sassenrath. "And it ends up not meeting the cost estimates. So it was a little more expensive."

Ali called Porter and his CDTV team for a meeting in order to regroup. "I remember sitting in a meeting with Jeff Porter and Don [Gilbreath] and Mehdi Ali and we went through every single component of the design," says Sassenrath. "Jeff had to justify the cost of all those different components. It didn't save an adequate amount for Mehdi Ali so Mehdi was pretty upset about it."

Ali and Gould were staking the future of Commodore on a miracle product that could infiltrate the living room instead of the home office. When those plans fell through, Ali took his frustrations out on Porter—who he saw as contributing to the failure—in some strange ways. "I remember going to a trip to France to meet with SGS-Thomson Semiconductor to discuss their MPEG decoder chips," recalls Porter. "Mehdi called me back. 'Get your ass on the first plane back here.' And so I did. But when I arrived there was 'nothing special' he wanted."

Ali also severely curtailed Porter's pilot production run to just 60 units—barely enough to supply Commodore International with demo units. Porter proceeded and SCI began producing the 60 motherboards on February 5th, sending those to Commodore Hong Kong for final assembly.

Hedley Davis, the system software developer on the CDTV-CR, was also having bad experiences with his manager. "I had resorted to playing tricks on management, which is something that I don't like," he says. "In the CDTV-CR there's a bitplane-to-pixel converter. I was told, 'No, you can't do that,' by this guy who wanted to be the boss."

Davis wanted it so badly, he decided to trick his boss. "He wanted a list of all the features that we're putting in the CDTV-CR design so that this is what we agreed to do," says Davis. "I write a list of these nine features that we were putting in the CDTV-CR and I hand it to him and he takes it. I know he's not going to fucking read it or pay attention to it or really think about it. He's just bossing me around and just being the boss."

One of those features was the forbidden bitplane-to-pixel converter, disguised slightly. "The CDTV-CR comes out and lo and behold there is this bitplane-to-pixel converter thing in it," recalls Davis. "He's like, 'I can't believe you did that, it wasn't on the list. We had an agreement and you're going to be fired.'"

Davis insisted the item was on the list. "He's like, 'It wasn't on the list.' I said get the list out. It was at like number eight and I worded it so I never used the nouns 'bitplane to pixel converter' but rather came up with some obtuse wording about allowing better graphics processing by minimizing processor overhead for conversion between bitplane or whatever. It was in there but I tricked him by putting it in such a way because I knew he wouldn't read it."

Understandably, Davis' relationship with his boss soured to the point that Davis refused to go to his boss' office when called. "He wanted my head and he couldn't get it," says Davis. "I got called by someone a couple of management levels up, asking, 'Why are you doing this and why don't you even go into the guy's office?' He's calling me into his office because he wants to have the home turf so he can try to win the argument based upon home turf, and I'm just not doing it."

Soon, Davis began to feel uncomfortable working at Commodore. "The threat level was just insane," he says. "We're playing these stupid games. We aren't really doing the right stuff."

CDTV Program Faltering

According to Don Gilbreath's original business proposal, the high cost of the CDTV was supposed to be offset by Commodore receiving royalties from software publishers. But without high sales, the whole program was in jeopardy.

Guy Wright, one of the CDTV system developers, had attempted to start his own business called Wright Works III by releasing content for the CDTV. His story is emblematic of the problems working with Commodore. "I actually started another company that produced two or three different discs for it," he recalls. "One was called *Dinosaurs for Hire*. I went out and licensed a bunch of old comic books from an independent comic company for next to nothing because they were just rotting in a warehouse someplace."

Wright turned the decidedly plain comics into multimedia extravaganzas complete with sound effects, music, and voice actors. "I scanned all the images and then we took out the word balloons. We hired a bunch of college student acting majors to do voice overs. You could play the entire comic book on your CDTV."

The product was not a hit, partly because Wright feels Commodore was supposed to market the product for him, which they never did. "I got my license agreement and then three months later I got a bill from Commodore for $20,000," he says. "They were supposed to be selling them for me. They were supposed to be the distributor. It was kind of a mess there."

Like several other CDTV software licensees, Wright did not pay the bill as he felt Commodore did not uphold its end of the bargain.

Meanwhile, Commodore was having problems clearing out the original CDTV inventory, which acted as a roadblock to launching the CDTV-CR. "Mehdi refused to launch it until all of the stock of the overbuilt expensive CDTV was sold, so he effectively killed the product," says Colin Proudfoot.

An engineer on the CDTV named Bill Richard proposed to Ali a way to get rid of the stock by sending all the CDTVs to the education market, similar to how Apple conquered education. "Give it away to schools to get great publicity, bring a generation of kids up on Amiga technology like Apple is doing, and then put the product out that is going to make you money," recalls Proudfoot. "As opposed to hope you can sell them, leave them sitting in a warehouse rotting. That gives you a write off and then that brings the stock down."

Ali rejected the idea, which led to excess North American inventory. "The problem we had with the CDTV was it was a new market space, with

CD-based processes," says Colin Proudfoot. "Mehdi said, 'I'm not touching that until we sell the inventory we've got. We have too many CDTVs in inventory to launch a new product.'"

In Europe, things were no better. *The Times*, a prestigious newspaper in London, reported that the CDTV was a commercial failure. In June 1992, Commodore formed a plan to sell off the original CDTVs as "black Amigas" in Germany and the UK. These bundles would each include a keyboard, mouse, and disk drive—along with a price drop from $799 to $599. It was a great deal, considering that adding a CD-ROM to the A500 would be relatively expensive.

The End of CDTV

The obvious difficulty Commodore had selling its CDTV units gave Mehdi Ali cold feet. He knew that if he continued the project, he would be guilty of perpetuating a sunk cost fallacy. He was also aware that the CDTV was a favorite of his good friend, CEO Irving Gould. The decision would be a hard one to make.

On July 6, 1992, he ordered Jeff Porter not to order any parts for the manufacture of more CDTV units, promising that they would revisit the issue in August once Porter found the required cost reductions. "We never really made any more than a few of those so that was unfortunate," says Porter. "It got to pilot production but that's it."

Porter was able to cost reduce his CDTV-CR to $281.29. With AA Amiga products on the horizon, he also produced a cost estimate for an AA version for $325.99 called the CDTV-2. "They were going to do the CDTV-2 which was slightly different," says Guy Wright. "It was an upgrade from CDTV-CR. The CDTV-2 has different chips that never appeared in any other Commodore product up to that point. They really did improve the Agnus and Daphne and what not. They made some other modifications to it."

On Monday, August 3, 1992 Porter met with Ali and presented his plans. The basic CDTV-CR without MPEG ability was deemed inferior to the Philips CD-i while the AA version was too costly. "And he canceled the project," says Proudfoot. Ali laid off the CDTV staff, including Gail Wellington and Ben Phister, a CDTV supporter from France. Wellington had been a strong force for not only CDTV but also the Amiga and the C64. Later in the month she would join Philips on the CD-i project as a marketing manager.

Jeff Scherb, the head of CATS, was also laid off, along with many employees of CATS. "It was hard," says Guy Wright. "At the same time, that was when the marketing department was being shut down. Everything was being shut down. There was no support, nothing."

For their part, Commodore's engineers were sorry to see the cancellation of CDTV. "I don't know if it was cost prohibitive but that was a pretty good product," says Greg Berlin. "I wish that had seen the light of day, but things weren't going so well at that point. And it cost money to get that product into production. As I recall, that was the key issue."

Other engineers felt it was wrong to have Mehdi Ali determining which products Commodore went forward with. "I don't think he understood a thing about engineering, and I don't think he understood a thing about the computer business," says Dave Haynie. "He was actually quoted, asking, 'Why in the world is it important for computers to talk to televisions?' This was a guy who didn't watch television and didn't use computers."

Porter himself felt ashamed to have misled Commodore's parts supplier, Chinon, into thinking it would receive large orders from Commodore. "When the CDTV-CR project was cancelled I had one last trip to Japan," he says. "I apologized to the President of Chinon. They had spent a lot of time working with us on this project to make that low-cost CD-ROM drive happen."

Surprisingly, the president replied, "Jeff, no need to apologize to me. On the contrary, I need to thank you. Our guys would have never thought of this without you forcing us to do it. We now have the know-how to make low cost CD-ROM drives."

Although CDTV-CR never came into being, Porter and Davis' work on cost reducing the CD-ROM mechanism would have a wide-ranging effect on the CD-ROM market. "Our whirlwind tour of all CD-ROM makers got them all on our train of thought," says Porter. "The CDTV-CR was the 'landmark product' that paved the road for all future low-cost CD-ROM drives for all platforms. The low-cost interface that Hedley and I designed for the Sony Audio Mechanism was the key to reducing the $400 SCSI CD-ROM with caddy and making CDTV-CR possible. An industry first. We don't get much credit for that but I know it."

Years later, most Commodore engineers look back on CDTV as a missed opportunity, given the success of entertainment consoles based on optical media. "It was a beautiful idea to do an interactive home entertainment system," says Michael Sinz. "It was a great idea a bit ahead of its time. CD-i was hokey and not so great a system. Both of us failed and we died in the process. But then there was the Sony Playstation and every smart TV with Internet connectivity. CDTV was before the web, but it had modem connectivity if you wanted it. It had interactive content. Movie playback was just one component of the whole thing."

Video compression schemes that could compress an entire movie onto one CD-ROM disc, such as Advanced Video Coding/h.264, would only arrive later in the early 2000s. With this technology, it's possible that CD-ROM-based video players could have had as much success as DVD players. "The limiting factor was that CDs didn't have enough data for full length video," says Michael Sinz. "Tape was better. Two or three CDs were not as big, and you had to change disks."

CD-i ended up dominating over CDTV, largely due to its movie playing abilities. CD-i also had two killer-app games released in 1993: *7th Guest* and *Myst*. However, it only sold around one million units and was considered a commercial failure, losing Philips approximately a billion dollars in the process.

In light of that result, perhaps Mehdi Ali made a wise decision to cancel the product. But Commodore was not yet done with CD-ROM technology. The engineers would significantly change the product definition for a CD-ROM device and try again.

Amigo

At the exact same time as Mehdi Ali closed down the CDTV division, another CD-ROM product rose from the ashes. This time, the company would make sure the product made sense commercially right from the start. "Clearly we will continue with the living-room type of box," said Lew Eggebrecht. "We learned a lot of things from CDTV—where our best price point is, how important the quality of the software is, and the fact that running Amiga software is important. Most of our sales come from applications where it is sold as a computer—not a CDTV."[1]

Commodore had learned that consumers did not particularly want the CD-ROM device for the stereo rack. Furthermore, the product Commodore had designed did not even use the AA chipset. It was also not great for gaming due to the poor controllers. And most of all, it had been too costly!

Commodore needed to correct those problems and return to its strengths in retail. "Finally, we said, 'What are we going to do about this CDTV

---

1   *Amiga User International.* June 1988. "The AUI Interview"

product?' It was doing well against CD-i, but that wasn't saying a lot," says Eggebrecht. "We concluded that we wanted to build a games console which would play games and also be an interactive multimedia player."[2]

Already by early 1992 there were several companies developing a new type of device using CD-ROM and the engineers were aware of them all. Principle in their minds was SMSG, the new company headed by Electronics Arts founder Trip Hawkins, along with ex-Amiga employees Dave Morse, RJ Mical, Dale Luck, and Dave Needle.

The Sega Genesis also received an accessory called the Sega CD, which was due in North America in October 1992. Even Microsoft was designing a CD game console (predating the XBox by over a decade) codenamed Haiku and later Gryphon, which would be built by Tandy for an eventual release in 1992. And of course Commodore's nemesis, Atari, was designing a game console, although without CD-ROM, called the Jaguar.

When it became clear Commodore was not going to have a hit with the CDTV, the executives did something Commodore UK's David Pleasance thought they should have done long ago. They asked the UK's Kelly Sumner what product the UK developers wanted. "So, in mid to late summer, we began to talk to several of the key [games] developers in the UK, saying 'We have this technology, what do you want?' The consensus came back—stick with games, it's gotta be CD-based, it's gotta be 32-bit, but the key point was the price. We had to have a price that was competitive with 16-bit technology today," says Lew Eggebrecht.

Commodore also hoped to regain US market share with the new product. US dealers had virtually dried up for Amiga computers by 1992. Now, Commodore US hoped to enter retail stores such as Kmart, a market that Commodore was historically more comfortable with. In many ways, the new machine was a last ditch effort to survive in the US. "The CD32 [the eventual name for the system] happened when Commodore main engineering got its hands on the CDTV and were told to cost reduce it and make it better," explains Andy Finkel. "The CD32 was basically one of those efforts."

On June 27, 1992, at the behest of Jeff Frank, Jeff Porter made a first attempt to cost out a stripped-down CD Game System, which he called CD Stripper (pronounced "seedy stripper"). The new system would have no keyboard, no disk drive, and limited expansion. This first proposal also in-

---

cluded a whopping 8 MB of RAM, a lot of memory at the time for a game system. The total bill of materials for the AGA system came to $232.67.

By mid-August, real planning for the CDGS as it became known was underway. Hedley Davis and Jeff Porter travelled to Japan to negotiate for a CD mechanism. This time, on the advice of George Robbins, they were looking at a small, top loading double speed CD player meant for the Walkman market. Because it did not have a motorized drawer, the item offered another significant cost savings.

They settled with Chinon, the same company that had produced the prototype CD-ROM mechanisms for the CDTV-CR. "Probably the most interesting cost reduction of the whole CDTV-CR, which found its way onto the CD32, was the CD-ROM drive," says Porter.

On September 4, Jeff Porter began writing a formal product overview for the system, which he dubbed the Amigo. Once again, just like the CDTV, Porter promised the machine could expand into a full Amiga computer with keyboard and mouse. "We then went back and wrote a design specification in late September, and also established that we could achieve the price point," says Lew Eggebrecht.

In order to speed up development on the system, much of the technology in the Amiga would be inherited from George Robbins' A1200. "The chief engineer on each project had a lot of discretion to build what made sense," says Porter. "So for the CD32, we took an even cheaper CD mechanism without a motorized drawer (both Sony and Philips models) and wrapped an A1200 circuit around it. Again using surface mount technology to get the size down."

Amigo used the Motorola 68EC020 32-bit processor running at 14.28 megahertz. It was the first true 32-bit console. It also used the AGA chipset, providing incredible graphics. "At the time, it was not really competitive with some machines in some ways, but in other ways it was pretty good," says Dave Haynie.

With the preliminary spec ready, Porter and software engineer Allan Havemose travelled to Commodore UK on October 7 to meet with UK game developers and show them the Amigo specification. They met with three of the UK's leading game houses: Ocean, Psygnosis, and Gremlin. "This was an interesting project from the standpoint that it's probably the first time that we went to the developers and end users and we really tried to find out what they wanted with respect to development environment and respect to the product specifications," says Eggebrecht.[3]

When Porter returned from the trip, he had a good idea what developers wanted from the new system. "We learned that the price point of CDTV was much too high for consumer environments, we learned that we needed more performance, and we learned that people really wanted entertainment on these kinds of products," says Eggebrecht. "Education type titles, reference material titles—they're all really nice, but people really like to play games."

One of the biggest changes came from the expensive RAM. Porter had previously proposed a machine with 8 MB of memory, which added over $20 to the bill of materials. When the developers found out it added over $50 to the retail price, they settled for 2 MB.

Commodore's software engineers set the software strategy for the Amigo. They wanted all CD games and apps to work across all Amiga platforms with CD-ROM. New Amiga CD titles were not expected to work with the old CDTV, but Andy Finkel would attempt to achieve compatibility of existing CDTV titles with the Amigo. Furthermore, Amigo titles would also work with any AGA Amiga (A1200 or A4000) with a CD-ROM.

The Amiga system software engineers would also concentrate on backward compatibility. "We really brought on a few more of the software people from the Amiga team to evolve the software and make it bridge the path to having more Amiga-oriented games be able to go on the system," says Paul Lassa.

After all this, the team was ready to go. "By late October, we were off and running," says Eggebrecht.

Engineering efforts towards a prototype motherboard began, and Jeff Porter delivered the final draft of his spec on November 2, 1992. He considered the Amigo to be a super-cost-reduced CDTV that resembled a fat Walkman. The device would have connectors for two joysticks, a television, and a proprietary expansion connector similar to that of the Amiga 500. Each unit would cost Commodore $226 to manufacture.

By now, Don Gilbreath had been completely cut out of development on CD-ROM products. "There was a CDTV cost reduction and ultimately there was a CD32, and both of those efforts came out of the traditional engineering side of the company," says Gilbreath.

---

3   *Genie Viewport Magazine*, Sept. 28, 1993. "The Eggebrecht Tapes"

The Amigo team was composed of the same members as the A1200 team, which was in development at the same time. George Robbins would own the Amigo motherboard, which was essentially a stripped down A1200 board.

Hedley Davis and an engineer named Chris Coley would work on the Akiko chip design (called Arizona early in development). "The most challenging part was developing the gate array called Arizona, which would collect all of the various signals and take over the functions of many of the chips on earlier Amigas," says Lew Eggebrecht.

Jeff Porter was still intensely interested in playing video using the new MPEG video standard. "I spent some time developing MPEG video support," he says. "The intent of the slot on CDTV-CR was to add an MPEG card, but I got the rug pulled out from under me by Bill Sydnes and the CD32 got the adapter instead."

For his part, Mehdi Ali continued giving Porter a hard time, figuratively yanking his chain by calling him back from important engineering trips. "He did that to me one time when I went to the Commodore factory in Hong Kong," says Porter. "I don't think I even spent 24 hours there before turning around. I eventually got wise to Mehdi jerking people around."

The new project was everything Dave Morse had hoped to create for a video game console using the Amiga chipset back in 1985 (although Morse now worked at rival 3DO). "Quite honestly, they could have made a video game version if they wanted to [circa 1984], just like they did later with the CDTV and CD32," says Dave Haynie. With a $399 retail price target, the Amiga had come full circle.

CHAPTER 36

Amiga 1200 1992

Although Bill Sydnes had departed, his A600 product had left behind a serious flaw in the Amiga product line when it came time for the A1200 release. It was a problem that was not immediately obvious to Mehdi Ali, who was inexperienced in the electronics industry. A disaster was building at Commodore that nobody would notice until it was too late.

A1200 vs Mount Pinatubo

Commodore had a plan to manufacture and sell the A600 for most of 1992 and then switch manufacturing and sales to the A1200 by the end of the year. But there was a potential problem. Throughout 1992, Commodore had slowly moved from a production model of manufacturing its own products within its own factories to outsourcing. This transition would begin with the A600 and then intensify with the A1200. If the transition did not happen smoothly, it could result in disastrous supply problems.

The A600 motherboards had been manufactured primarily in Commodore's Hong Kong factory and then sent to Commodore's Braunschweig factory for final assembly. In June 1992, Commodore began transitioning manufacturing to SCI-UK, which had received major investment from the UK government. "Amigas were made in Hong Kong. Amigas were made in the Philippines. Amigas were made in Scotland by SCI," says Colin Proudfoot. "Some A500s were being made in Braunschweig and they also made C64s."

Mehdi Ali planned to phase out Commodore's Braunschweig production lines gradually. "We used outside contract manufacturers," says Greg Berlin. "We had one factory that we actually owned that was in Hong Kong, but at some point they sold that. I guess the one in Germany—in Braunschweig—was owned by Commodore as well, but most of the factories were third parties."

Ali was a worldly person and he began to worry about a situation in Hong Kong that could influence production. "Mehdi decided that Hong Kong was politically unstable because in '95 it was going from British to Chinese rule," recalls Colin Proudfoot. "So in 1990 he announced to the staff in Hong Kong that they were relocating manufacturing to the Philippines. The next day none of the supervisors showed up for work because they had all gone to find other jobs. They wanted jobs with international companies so that they could get out of Hong Kong."

Ali worried that the Communist Chinese government might decide to nationalize the Hong Kong factory—essentially stealing the facility from Commodore. In making the move, he may have been too smart for his own good. Although he held an informed big picture of the situation, his execution of the details left something to be desired. Ali settled on the Philippines as the cheapest place for Commodore to manufacture its products. He struck a deal with the government, which began manufacturing a new facility in 1991. The factory was slated to open in early 1992.

The Philippines had several problems that made it politically unstable at the time. Although it had achieved democracy five years earlier, in 1986, the government had problems with national debt, corruption, coup attempts, a Communist insurgency, and military conflicts with separatists. "That to me was another example of 'brilliant' decision making," says Proudfoot.

Then in 1991 Mount Pinatubo, a still active volcano, erupted. The event, which was the second largest volcanic eruption in the 20th century, had the effect of dropping a couple of nuclear bombs on the country, causing worldwide disruptions to weather and airlines. The timing of the event couldn't have come at a worse time for Commodore. "They built another plant in the Philippines and a volcano goes off and it delays completion for six months," says Proudfoot.

Meanwhile, Commodore Semiconductor Group played less of a role in the fabrication of the Amiga's famed chipset. It would fabricate the Alice and AGA-Gayle chips for the A1200, but the Lisa chip would be fabricated by Hewlett-Packard, while the Budgie chip would be fabricated by VLSI Technology.

In June 1992, George Robbins began gathering components together in order to start hand-building A1200 prototype units for the Amiga OS developers. On June 22, eight mechanical cases arrived from Commodore Hong Kong, ready to be fitted with prototype motherboards.

Because the Budgie chips were not yet fabricated, Robbins used FPGA chips to simulate Budgie. These chips were too slow to perfectly simulate some parts of Budgie, therefore Robbins ran the 68020 at half speed. This would allow the software developers to test AmigaOS 3.0 on the A1200. He was also able to simulate Gayle by using the old chip, along with two additional LSI chips.

In a testament to the effectiveness of the new engineering department under Lew Eggebrecht, Robbins had his A1200 prototype, with FPGA Budgie chip, working perfectly by July 10, 1992. It could boot up and run the new OS and run the famous Robocity demo. FCC compliance testing began when the chips arrived in August 1992. This left only quality assurance testing and debugging, packaging materials, and preparation for a pilot production run. Commodore was able to hand out A1200 prototypes to developers. However, this time the prototypes were crudely fastened to pieces of plywood, since the finished cases were not yet ready.

Robbins worked tirelessly, sometimes working as late as 3:00 in the morning or overnight before retiring to his office for a well deserved rest. In late August, he took a small respite by attending the Philadelphia Folk Festival—the only vacation he was allowed for the entire summer.

Unfortunately, when it came time to manufacture the machines, poor planning had resulted in a shortage of crucial chips. "I recall one mistake towards the end of Commodore where they did not order the correct chips for the A1200, the AGA chips," recalls Dale Luck. "People wanted the new graphics of the A1200 and the A4000, but they didn't order enough of the chips from Hewlett-Packard to actually make a half-million of the new Amigas."

Because there were not enough AGA chips to manufacture the A1200, Ali went to his backup plan of manufacturing A600 systems instead. In early September, SCI-UK began producing A600 computers for the Christmas season. This was an odd move, because Commodore should have been trying to clear out its inventory of A600 systems in anticipation of the A1200 launch.

As a result, Ali's team manufactured too many A600 computers for the market to absorb. "There were some mistakes made with buying a million A600s and then having to write them off," says Dale Luck. "They just said, 'Well let's just make the same ones we did a year ago.' But nobody wanted them. So they spent millions of dollars making a product nobody wanted, thinking they could make people buy it."

The delays in opening the Philippines factory also meant the factory was not ready to manufacture the A1200 on time. "Manufacturing in Hong Kong had basically shut down," recalls Colin Proudfoot. "Manufacturing was coming out of the Philippines which opened up six months late because of the volcano. And then we found out in September that the Philippines Manila Airport doesn't have the air freight capacity to ship all the product we needed. There were two routes: one through India and one through Tokyo out of Manila, and we just couldn't get space on planes to bring the product over in time for the retailers. So we missed the shipping window."

All of the preorders lined up by Commodore's sales people would be for nothing if the factory could not deliver the shipments on time. "Commodore was a very cyclical season-oriented company," says chip designer Ed Hepler. "We designed stuff and built it and had to make sure all our parts and raw materials had been purchased so that by October the warehouses were full."

With all the manufacturing delays, Ali chose an alternate factory to supplement A1200 production. He soon committed vast resources to a production run of A1200 systems at SCI-UK in Irvine, Scotland.

The week of October 12, SCI began a small run of 200 PAL A1200 systems. Of the first few days worth of systems, 22 passed while 45 failed the automated tests. Although this sounded bad, most of the failures were attributable to incorrect, missing, and reversed parts, unsoldered connections, shorts, and damage to the PCB. In other words, the design was fine; it was just a matter of calibrating the production line and workers gaining more experience with the assembly line processes.

SCI engineers David Rees and Cameron Radford gave the go ahead to start producing 1000 units for shipping in the next week. By November 1 they would ship 4,200 units. They planned to ramp up to a peak capacity of 11,000 units per week by November 16, and by December 15 SCI would have produced the full 70,000 units as specified in the contract with Commodore.

To make up for some of the delay and get A1200s on store shelves more quickly, Ali made an additional expenditure. "He would airfreight shit in at Christmas time," recalls Jeff Porter. "When you do that, you're putting $100 bills in each box instead of $5 bills in each box to ship it from China on a boat. But it takes a month to get here versus a week to get here, and if someone thinks that's worth it they may decide to do that."

Still, to Commodore's engineers, it seemed like too little too late.

The Osborne Effect

As long as all the money that flowed out for production flowed back in by the end of the year, Commodore would have a nice balance sheet to show the world in January. "Hopefully by Thanksgiving or December the warehouses were empty, and hopefully we made enough profit to cover all the costs incurred in the prior 12 months," says Ed Hepler. "Hopefully by the end of the fiscal year we brought in more money than goes out, and therefore we had a profit."

The Osborne Effect, named after computer pioneer Adam Osborne, is when a company prematurely announces a product while the previous iteration is still in inventory. "You know, you tell that to a Mehdi and he doesn't know what that means," says Jeff Porter. "You shouldn't be calling the shots if you don't know what Osborne syndrome is."

Word got out about the A1200 while Commodore had not even a marginal number of A1200s in Europe, and NTSC A1200 production was not slated to begin until December. "The story that I heard was that Mehdi Ali had basically spilled the beans at a conference he went to," says Ed Hepler.

On October 25, 1992 a New Zealand dealer named Mark Stuart received the specs for the A1200 in advance of the actual release. For some reason he was not asked to sign a nondisclosure agreement, and he posted a full description of the A1200 online. The cat was out of the bag.

On October 27, Commodore released a position statement for the US launch of the A1200, even though the plan had been to announce it at the upcoming Comdex. In part it read, "This machine has already been announced in several European countries and will be officially announced in the U.S. at COMDEX, November 16 in Las Vegas. It is currently expected to be available in the United States before Christmas, 1992."

Ready or not, the computer world found out about the A1200 in magazine previews in Europe while there were still tens of thousands of A600 systems in production or in inventory. "In October that year they announced the A1200, which was too late to get in stores for Christmas but it killed the A600," explains Colin Proudfoot. "The market heard and said, 'We'll just wait for the A1200 to come out rather than buy the A600.' And all the Amiga magazines were telling people don't buy the A600 because the A1200 is going to be great, based on the specifications that we'd announced on the A1200."

Commodore would go on to launch the product in Las Vegas in November. "The only thing bad about the A1200 was that it was introduced at the wrong time of year," says Jeff Porter. "It was introduced the day after

Thanksgiving for $100 more than the A500. It's like really? Why would you do that? Your factory is full of A500s. You can't make enough A1200s to meet your Christmas demand because they didn't decide early enough that they wanted to do that. I'll be lucky if I'm in pilot production by Christmas again."

Demand for the A600 nosedived, leaving Commodore with a situation eerily similar to the Plus/4. "He was introducing new products that were not in his warehouse," laments Jeff Porter. "He introduced the A1200 when the warehouse was chock-a-block full of A500s and A600s."

On December 2, SCI-UK began manufacturing the first 250 units of the NTSC A1200. There were problems, such as the floppy drives not fitting in the case properly. By December 14, at the World of Commodore in Toronto, Commodore Canada didn't even have a demo A1200 to show.

With the A1200 barely rolling out of production in Europe, the premature announcements killed the demand for the A600s. "They maybe had a few thousand A1200s for the world and everybody wanted an A1200 and they couldn't get it," says Porter. "So they sucked wind on the Christmas quarter and when you're a consumer electronics company that sucks wind in the Christmas quarter you're screwed. That's when they Osborned themselves."

Joe Augenbraun feels most of the computer industry was still learning. "To be fair to Commodore, nowadays there is a formula for how you do these things. At the time there really wasn't. People didn't understand how to do this. They didn't understand products with a shelf life—neither consumers nor companies."

Porter feels Ali should have waited until the new year to even talk about the A1200. "He wanted a new product. He wished he had his A1200 sooner. But he didn't have it sooner so what he needed to do was pick one: A500 or A600, please not both. Pick one. Tell the world that's what they're selling at Christmas and wait until the start of the next year to start selling the A1200 so you don't screw your Christmas quarter. It's consumer electronics 101."

Commodore had released a flood of money towards A600 production—money that should have flowed back to the company in larger waves. "No one bought it [A600] and basically Commodore died because of too much inventory," says Gerard Bucas. "They couldn't sell it; that killed them from a cash flow point of view."

Now it was as though that cash flow was dammed behind a brick wall. "Companies like Commodore would borrow money to go out and buy all the stuff they needed and then pay those loans off after they sold every-thing," says Hepler. "That year they couldn't pay those loans off and that started the death spiral. What do they say about loose lips sink ships? I think we sank a ship."

Red Christmas

The holiday season was typically the high point of the year for Commo-dore's sales. However, a perfect storm of events had aligned that would make this year particularly gruesome. The aforementioned *Wolfenstein 3D* turned into a juggernaut killer app for PC gaming, along with a slew of other 3D games. And finally, Microsoft released Windows 3.1 in 1992, and analysts agreed this version finally got it right. As a result, even diehard Amiga fans began giving up on the Amiga.

Nothing summarized the mood more than a December 8, 1992 Usenet post by a former Amiga user named Andy Patrizio titled, *Why my Amiga is gone*: "Not one major hardware chain carries the Amiga. Not even Intelli-gent Electronics, a 1700-store chain founded by a former CBM Exec. VP, Richard Sanford, carries Amiga," the screed said. "Commodore has prov-en itself ineffectual at any kind of advertising, promotion, or grabbing and holding market share."

Like many, Patrizio blamed CEO Irving Gould, saying, "...under his ef-fete, inept, impotent management, Commodore fires or boots aside its most promising people..." The post was widely read within Commodore.

In technical terms, multitasking and Genlock were really the only defin-itive advantages the Amiga had over PCs and Macintosh. But multitask-ing really hadn't come into its own yet. In the early 1990s, most users just wanted a computer that could play games, dial BBS numbers, and perform word processing. As it turned out, the advantages of multitasking would be-come apparent during the upcoming Internet era, with users downloading and unpacking files while playing MP3 music in the background. With the Internet not yet available to the masses, it made multitasking a hard sell.

On top of that, major US game companies like EA, Activision, Sierra, SSI, Origin, and LucasArts abandoned or were in the process of aban-doning the Amiga platform. No major software stores in North America carried Amiga software because there was little money in it.

Given this climate, it's no surprise that Amiga 4000 sales would not be in the same league as past sales numbers for the Amiga 2000 or even the Amiga 3000. All this despite the successful conception and timing for the A4000 marketing debut. Commodore even ended sales of the successful

A2000 just in time for the A4000 to take over (and after cancelling the A3000 earlier).

There were the usual problems releasing a new system, such as air cooling fans being installed backwards. But overall, it was bittersweet to have engineering executing so well, only to be met by a soft Amiga market.

Things were much worse for Commodore's low-end systems, which were traditionally the products that generated the bulk of Commodore's revenue. The absence of large sales from the C64, and the absence of its replacement the C65, was definitely felt, leaving a gaping hole in revenues. "The C64 was an absolute dead duck," says David Pleasance.

Commodore really needed C64 revenue to remain a billion dollar company, yet in 1992 they lacked a modern sub-$300 product. In the current fiscal year, Commodore would only sell less than 200,000 C64s compared to the prior year of 650,000. And the margins were low. "IBM were making $300 bucks off each one. Apple was making $600 bucks off each Mac they sold. Commodore was making nothing on these things," says Guy Wright.

The low-end Amiga market was particularly confusing for buyers throughout 1992. "We got all these A600s and it killed all sales of the A500," says David Pleasance. "Then people realized it was not better than the A500. That was one crisis they created. Even the motherboard has A300 printed on the circuit board. They were creating their own fire and then having to put it out."

Pleasance, who was no fan of the A600, had attempted to get more A500 Plus systems to retailers but it did not go over as well as he had hoped. "Prior to them launching the A1200, the A500 Plus was some attempt to get us back to the A500 market which didn't really work," says Pleasance. "We sold a few Plusses but once we killed the goose that laid the golden egg, until we got the A1200 we were kind of in limbo land."

Even in Europe, the facade of Commodore as a leading computer company was beginning to crack. Commodore UK released what should have been a dynamite bundle containing the hit game *Lemmings* with *Deluxe Paint II. Amiga Format* magazine reported that dealers were getting 10 calls for the A500 Plus for every call for the A600. In response, Commodore slashed the A600 price by £100 to counter the sluggish sales, releasing the "Wild, Weird and Wicked" bundle containing *Formula One Grand Prix, Pushover, Putty* and *Deluxe Paint III*, all for £349.

Adding to the confusion of the A500 versus the A600 was the CD-ROM add-on, called the A570. The device would allow a low-end Amiga to run all CDTV software, as well as read regular CD-ROM discs. There was one big problem, however. It could only connect to the recently discontinued A500 because the A600 lacked the required expansion port.

Originally meant for release alongside the CDTV, the product development dragged on throughout 1992. It was announced in March 1992 under the name A690 in the UK, then quickly renamed A570 when it was realized it would not be A600 compatible. It was also supposed to sell for £269 but by the time of the release in September 1992, the retail price had risen to £349. Needless to say, among all the confusion, the product bombed and was put on fire sale prices the next year to clear out the remaining stock.

Jeff Porter blames the debacle squarely on Mehdi Ali and his inexperience in the computer industry. "What did Mehdi know about manufacturing? Zero. Engineering? Zero. Marketing? Zero. Sales? Zero. Anything but finance, he was shooting blanks."

Porter claims he warned Ali of the possible Osborne Effect he was setting up, but to no avail. "There are certain things you don't do in sales and marketing that he didn't have a clue about, but he was calling the shots," says Porter. "He messed up Christmas royally. I tried to tell him but I was a young kid then. What the heck did I know? In the end, Commodore's downfall was because Mehdi was calling the shots."

All of these missteps in 1992 would, unfortunately, be reflected in the upcoming quarterly financial report. And when the analysts saw the numbers, financial support for the company—its very lifeblood—would begin to wither.

January 1993 CES

Despite the recent financial problems that resulted in poor cash flow, Commodore hosted a booth at the January 7, 1993 CES in Las Vegas, right next door to a large IBM booth. This time, the stars of the show were cellular phones, wide screen TV, and satellite TV. New games like *Alone in the Dark* and the CD-ROM hit *7th Guest* were also on display.

The massive Commodore booth hosted six third-party developers, including pseudo-rival Great Valley Products, which demonstrated its new genlock adapter, G-Lock.

Commodore sent engineers and marketing people, including Jeff Porter, who brought along a prototype of his Amiga 4000 MPEG adapter playing a Bon Jovi video. The demonstration was impressive for the time. He even had a chance to demonstrate digital video to an actor and former spokesman for Atari computers. "We did a prototype card that fit into an A4000," says Porter. "I remember demoing this to Alan Alda of M*A*S*H fame."

But the real breakout star of the show was a company called 3DO and a prototype of its new video game system, engineered by former Amiga engineers Dave Needle, RJ Mical (who both appeared on stage running the demos), and Dale Luck, among others. Perhaps most interesting was that CEO Trip Hawkins believed the machine could be a marketing success at the incredible price of "under $700".

It was Jeff Porter's first look at the main competition against his CD Game System (Amigo) he had in the works. Porter was relieved that 3DO had settled on the same 2 MB of RAM that he had with his Amigo spec and even more relieved Commodore would undercut 3DO's price by such a wide margin.

Unnervingly, there was a lack of Amiga games at CES, a stark contrast to previous years where many companies used to bring games to the Amiga first, even before the PC. Most of the Amiga games were also on the PC, including *Dune II: The Battle for Arrakis* (Westwood Studios), *Syndicate* (EA), and *Indiana Jones and the Fate of Atlantis* (LucasArts). These games were also joined in 1993 by a number of strong titles from Europe that included *The Settlers, Cannon Fodder, Flashback, Simon the Sorcerer* (AGA), *The Chaos Engine, Pinball Fantasies* (AGA), *Ambermoon, Lemmings 2: The Tribes, Frontier: Elite II, Waxworks, and Lionheart.*

Normally, CEO Irving Gould gave a speech in order to preview the previous year's financial situation. This year he gave no such speech, due to the crisis resulting from much lower revenues. Owing to the many poor decisions in 1992, Commodore ended the year with $731.6 million in revenue, a monumental 30% drop from $1.04 billion the previous year.

Much of this was explained by the cancellation of the low-end PC clones, which, even though they were losing money, had helped to prop up the revenue column on the financial reports. "There was also a big decline in PC sales. The market wanted the 486, and we didn't have one," says Colin Proudfoot.

Worse still, despite budget cuts, Commodore was unprofitable, losing $76.7 million over the holiday season, which should have been its most profitable quarter. Commodore's stock—which began January trading at 7½—would gradually tumble through the remainder of 1993. "Commodore is going down baby," laughs Jeff Porter.

As a show of solidarity, executives sometimes take a pay cut when performance has not been good. Not this time. "Even when Commodore was losing boatloads of money, a lot of the executives continued to get paid a whole lot of money," observes Dale Luck.

The *Philadelphia Inquirer* reported, "Commodore International Ltd. stumbled through the first half of its fiscal year, reporting sharp declines in sales and a hefty loss on the bottom line. The company, whose North American operation, Commodore Business Machines Inc., is based in West Chester, blamed currency exchange rates, restructuring costs, and price cuts that were designed to stimulate sales to key customers."[1]

Gould was quoted by the Inquirer giving his frank assessment of his company's performance. "We are extremely disappointed with our results for the first six months of the fiscal year. We have taken and will continue to take aggressive steps to reduce costs."

His words signalled to Commodore's employees what they could expect for 1993: more budget cuts and layoffs.

Legacy of the A1200

The A1200 was a much more definitive successor to the A500 legacy than the A600. Unfortunately, the poor timing meant it came out too late in 1992, especially to the North American market.

One sign of just how poorly Commodore's marketing had timed the A1200 launch, the very first preview of the system appeared in North America in the January 1993 issue of *Amiga World*. After Christmas, many users discovered the A1200 was incompatible with at least 60 A500 and A600 games, including popular titles like *Zak McKracken, 3D Pool, New Zealand Story, R-Type, PowerMonger, Jimmy White's Whirlwind Snooker, RoboCop, Defender of the Crown, Sidewinder, Rainbow Islands,* and *Grand Prix Circuit*.

Despite the poorly timed launch, the A1200 was eventually recognized as a worthy successor to the A500 and a success, especially in Europe, where it began to rejuvenate the Amiga market. The system launched in the US for $599 and in the UK for £399. "My understanding is that they did do quite well with it," says David Pleasance.

"The A1200 was the perfect product to succeed the A500," says Gerard Bucas. "That was very sad because I think that the A1200 was a phenomenal machine both from a price point and a features point of view. It was good but by that time Commodore had no cash."

---

1   *Philadelphia Inquirer*, Feb. 5, 1993. "Commodore Posts Loss, Lower Sales"

Commodore and Apple had been in a steady race since the Amiga launched in 1985. Throughout that time, Amigas consistently sold approximately half of the number of Macintosh computers sold by Apple. But in 1992, Commodore's numbers took a nosedive. Apple sold 2.5 million Macintosh computers versus only 390,000 Amiga computers. It was apparent something had radically changed in 1992.

Despite the heroic efforts from Commodore engineers, they had conceded the North American market. Though customers could still purchase Amiga computers, IBM PC compatibles and Macintosh systems overshadowed them. "Commodore was in a death spiral at that point," says Bil Herd.

CHAPTER 37

Management by Fire Extinguisher 1993

Commodore had a reputation for jumping from one disaster to another as it went along. Under Mehdi Ali, this was supposed to stop. But once Commodore posted a loss for 1992, money was in short supply, which meant it became even more difficult for the company to stay on top of problems. Ali spent much of 1993 putting out fires before they spread too far.

Internet!

By early 1993, the Internet was almost ready to explode into mass acceptance. Already, it had a host of popular applications: FTP, a method to store and download digital files. Telnet, a method to access remote computers. IRC, a method to talk with multiple users in real time. There was even a rising star called Gopher, a text-based, menu-driven system to present information to users. And of course, the ever popular Usenet News and email were the stars of the show.

Surprisingly, big computer companies like Apple and Microsoft were slow to notice the potential of the Internet. Commodore was among those companies that did not yet realize a revolution was taking place. But within Commodore there were engineers who knew of its importance.

George Robbins was still Commodore's main network and mainframe administrator, on top of designing most of Commodore's mass-market computer systems. It was an odd situation for a computer company, but Robbins stubbornly refused to defer tasks such as setting up new users, providing support to employees, and managing the ever changing networking technology.

Robbins had been attempting to secure a permanent Internet line for Commodore since 1989 but management would not make room for it in the budget. The best Robbins could do was set up email and Usenet News through an intermittent dial up to other nodes on the UUCP network. Those other fabulous real-time Internet applications were not possible without a dedicated connection, blocking Robbins and others from exploring the nascent Internet.

Back in August 1992, Robbins had finally realized how to crack through the managerial barrier preventing Internet access at Commodore. He and an employee named Greg Rettew put together a case that the ongoing long-distance dialing costs of maintaining the UUCP node were actually higher than if Commodore had a dedicated Internet connection.

His plan worked, and by January 1993, Robbins had acquired a dedicated 56 kbit/s line from Internet provider PSI of Reston, Virginia. Robbins likely knew the speed would not be enough to keep up with all of Commodore's employees. Instead, he was counting on management becoming hooked on the Internet, then desiring faster speeds. He and Reston spent most of January migrating the email and Usenet News servers from the previous modem connection to the dedicated Internet connection.

After dropping Commodore as a UUCP node, Robbins had to find a way to connect every personal computer in the building to the shared Internet connection. This would prove difficult, especially considering operating systems like AmigaOS did not come with integrated Internet connectivity.

Then the World Wide Web arrived. On January 23, 1993, Marc Andreessen (a former Commodore 64 owner) released an Internet browser called Mosaic for the X Window System. The Web Browser, as it would be known, became the first killer app for the Internet. Soon, websites started springing up. These pages contained not only text but images and sounds, bringing multimedia to the Internet. And most importantly, each page linked to other pages on the Internet, creating the aforementioned World Wide Web. People began creating homepages for themselves, providing a sense of permanence. Soon the World Wide Web began to experience exponential growth.

Andreessen released Mosaic ports to both Microsoft Windows and Macintosh in September 1993, with the Amiga following in October. In 1994, he released the Netscape browser, which quickly became the de facto standard. Many early adopters saw Netscape as the Internet. Because the PC had Netscape and other computers did not, another stampede occurred towards PC clones. Even within Commodore, longtime employees like CATS director John Campbell had purchased a machine to run Windows, calling it a "career investment".

On the upside, a result of Robbins' efforts to connect Commodore to the Internet meant that Amiga software engineers understood the demand and potential of the Internet, and they began looking for ways to develop a TCP/IP stack for Amiga OS. Unfortunately, there was always a lag for new developments to appear on the Amiga and Macintosh, giving the perception that they were always playing catch-up with the Windows/MS-DOS world.

Epson Amiga Distribution Deal

As president of Commodore International, Mehdi Ali found it difficult to turn around Commodore's failing fortunes. As many noted, his resemblances to Commodore's founder were mostly superficial. "Mehdi was nothing like Jack Tramiel, other than he had a temper and raised his voice," says Don Gilbreath. "He really had no clue about the computer industry. Here was a guy who was just out of his league, but the closest thing to a Tramiel in attitude."

It was his job to finalize deals on behalf of Commodore. In early 1993, Commodore had a chance to bring the Amiga to Japan. "There were many, many deals that were screwed up by Mehdi Ali," says Dave Haynie. "Epson wanted to deal with Commodore. They wanted to sell Amigas in Japan. At the time, the PC really didn't have the stronghold it had in the US because it was split between PCs and NEC machines."

The PC-9800 series by NEC dominated Japan, with over 50% market share. These machines were similar to MS-DOS machines but not fully IBM PC compatible. By 1993, the Macintosh had climbed to the number two spot with 8% market penetration.

While Commodore released every new model of Amiga in Japan, the installed base was less than 10,000 compared to over 500,000 Macintosh computers. This was in large part because the Amiga could not use proper Kanji characters. If a major Japanese company like Epson handled the Amiga, market share would increase dramatically.

Engineers and managers worked to make the deal happen. "The deal had been put together," recalls Haynie. "All the underlings had drawn up all the agreements and they were going to be putting Amigas into Japan. We had already been working on Asian character sets for the Amiga."

The Japanese Front End Processor (FEP), as it was called, had been discussed at Commodore since late 1991 and at one time was a project assigned to Don Gilbreath. However, the Epson deal in 1993 moved it to the highest priority. Commodore's VP of software, Allan Havemose, hired

Andy Finkel for a three month contract on March 24, 1993 to develop the FEP. Commodore acquired a C language based FEP from a company called Ergosoft, which they would port to the Amiga. This would be integrated into the latest version of AmigaOS, which they called 3.1J.

Epson wanted the Japanese version of the product ready to market in October 1993. Commodore would have to develop a special Japanese keyboard, documentation, and packaging.

But in early July, things went bad when Mehdi Ali entered the picture. "The story is that there was a final handshake kind of thing at dinner," explains Haynie. "It was a very Japanese sort of thing where the bosses meet. Mehdi Ali came into that and started demanding that they change things and just being his old ballsy self. That was a huge slap in the face based on their culture, so the guy said no."

Short and stocky, Ali was like Jack Tramiel but without the success. It looked like the deal was dead, but Commodore received a reprieve. "Apparently, whatever manager that was in Epson left," recalls Haynie. "His replacement came in, looked over the agreement, looked over all the paperwork, learned about the Amiga and said, 'This is a crazy thing to have lost. We need to go back and get this deal signed.' So they did and the same damn thing happened again! They called up and said they wanted the deal. [Ali] apparently met with them to finalize it and screwed it up again. There was no deal with Epson and no Amigas in Japan."

CADtrak

As if there wasn't enough going wrong in 1993, Commodore's US operations came to an abrupt halt due to a questionable lawsuit. It started in the early eighties when the US Patent Office could not decide which software patents were legitimate. One fundamental concept of patent law says a patent must be a real invention, and more specifically, something 'not obvious to one skilled in the art'. Back then, the US patent office did not have any patent officers with software engineering skills, so they were unable to determine if a software patent application was obvious or not.

This led to outrageous situations, such as IBM receiving a patent for programs that cut and pasted text between two buffers, which UNIX had been doing since the late 1970s. The patent office granted software patents as long as a patent search turned up no similar patents.

Meanwhile, a company called CADtrak received a patent for a programming technique called the XOR cursor in 1978. This small piece of code used a very basic logical operation to display a cursor over top of other graphics on the screen. Programmers usually discovered the algorithm on their own when they begin programming, but the patent office considered it a new invention. "Fred Bowen was working on that," says Haynie. "They had a patent on exclusive-OR. As Fred said, 'Damn, I should have patented AND, OR, and NOR.'"

CADtrak produced hardware but soon realized it was more lucrative to sue other companies over its perceived invention. The company cut personnel to almost zero and effectively became a litigation company. "CADtrak was just lawyers," says Dave Haynie. CADtrak's rampage began pulling in millions of dollars, mostly through settlements with other companies. Commodore decided to fight and the lawsuit dragged out into the 1990s.

CADtrak had been pestering Commodore about the C128 even before the Amiga acquisition. By 1990, the company eventually went after the Amiga chipset, claiming it infringed three times: once in the blitter, plus the split-screen and panning capabilities of the Copper.

By July 1990, CADtrak filed the lawsuit and Commodore's lawyers began frantically looking for evidence to nullify the baseless claims. Fred Bowen, Randell Jesup, Andy Finkel, Allan Havemose and other engineers coached the lawyers, looking for key evidence and explaining the XOR function. Most notably, the lawyers wanted to find code showing pre-1974 use of XOR to show motion on a display. If this code could be found, the entire patent would be invalidated. Unfortunately, 20 years had passed and Commodore was unable to find the code from that earlier era.

On April 6, 1993 the jury trial began at 9:30 a.m. at the California Northern District Court in front of Judge Vaughn R. Walker. Several of Commodore's engineers attended in order to explain concepts to the jury.

CADtrak's lawyers knew what they were doing. While the jury and judge knew little about technology, they understood simple pictures the prosecution held up. "The tactics seemed to be to request a jury trial—their constitutional right—even though this was a very technical issue which would be very difficult to explain to most jury pools," explains Ed Hepler. "Then a large poster board listing all the companies which have licensed their patent is shown. These include large companies which would rather simply pay a licensing fee than contest—the clear implication being that these big companies, with large R&D departments, felt it necessary to license their technology."

CADtrak's lawyers also showed a convincing side by side demonstration. "Then a computer using the technology is shown panning and compared to an Amiga panning," says Hepler. "The clear implication is that panning looks like panning and that the Amiga must be violating the patent if the result is the same. The non-technical jury is basically being asked to make a judgement based on the results, not on the technique used to create the results."

Commodore's lawyers now had the task of rebutting the argument. "This requires the defense to make the technical arguments to the jury, which is a difficult task, showing the technique which was patented and the one used by the Amiga," explains Hepler. "If you lose, you have to pay damages and end up licensing. If you simply license, you pay the license fee, even though you aren't using it. Either way, your name will probably end up on the poster of licensees used in the next suit."

The trial never reached a verdict. After days of Commodore trying to explain the concepts and largely fumbling, the lawyers decided to settle. On April 12, Commodore agreed to award the plaintiff $2,700,000 in damages. Judge Walker dismissed the case and thanked the jurors before excusing them. In the end, it was clear Commodore would have done better just to settle the case out of court. With Commodore short on cash as it was, this made it impossible for Commodore to continue normal operations.

Pleasance and Proudfoot

Commodore UK's managing director, Kelly Sumner, had led the subsidiary since the summer of 1992. But the young executive had a difficult time working for Commodore's president. "After Steve left, Kelly Sumner was appointed," says Colin Proudfoot. "Now Kelly was very young and not very experienced. He held strong opinions and Mehdi doesn't like people with strong opinions that aren't the same as his. They clashed."

Sumner's biggest clashes with Ali happened when he was asked to foolishly launch the A1200 at the same time as Commodore was filling up its warehouse with A600 computers. Sumner knew it was a recipe for disaster. "He was incredibly frustrated with the A600 coming out, which was crazy, and the launch date of the A1200, which was equally crazy," says Proudfoot. "It was announced in October. We couldn't get any of those for Christmas. Nobody bought A600s."

After the dismal holiday season and financial numbers started coming in, Sumner could no longer keep his feelings bottled and he subsequently resigned in April 1993.

Ali had to find a replacement and he knew just who he wanted. Ali had previously asked David Pleasance to take on the role in 1992, but Pleasance had been in a hunting mood. Since then, he had taken over Commodore's

International Subsidiaries. "I happened to be in Greece," recalls Pleasance. "I had just been out the night before trying to appoint a new distributor for Greece and then at five in the morning Mehdi rang me up and he said, 'Right, I want you in London today. No excuses. Meet me there.'"

Pleasance had no idea what the meeting would be about, but he was used to Ali's summons and booked a flight. "I went over to London and that's when he said, 'Right, I don't want any more excuses. As of today you are MD of the UK company. You built it, it is your business. You know it better than anybody. You are in charge.'"

After the dismal previous year, Ali laid all his cards on the table. "He said, 'The reason I'm saying that is to be candid. The international company is in big trouble. We need as much cash flow as we can possibly get. Our strongest company is the UK and you are responsible for it. I'm relying on you.'"

Despite working in the computer industry, Pleasance had no idea how to perform financial calculations on a spreadsheet. "This is probably going to shock you when I tell you, but I never used computers while I was at Commodore," he says. "I never even switched one on. Isn't that bizarre? I'm not very proud of that, I have to say, but it just happens to be true."

Pleasance knew he could not say no to Ali this time, but he had his reservations. "I said to him, 'Well look Mehdi, I'm happy to do it under the circumstances but I'm not a financial person. I can read a spreadsheet, I can do all those things but finance is not my bag. I'm sales and marketing and you're going to need me to concentrate on that. How about you giving Colin Proudfoot, the financial director, joint MD with me. He'll look after the finances and I look after sales and marketing. In between us, we'll make a good team.'"

Ali saw no reason to turn down a good offer. "That's what he agreed to do," says Pleasance. "That's why I became joint MD. And that was absolutely the best thing I did. Concentrate on your strengths."

The split in duties worked for both Pleasance and Proudfoot. "I was already running pretty much everything apart from sales and marketing," says Colin Proudfoot. "David's focus was on the product offering and the relationship with the software makers, which is key. Building a bundle, working out what's going to go into the bundle, making sure the developers are developing the right games. Talking to West Chester on their product development. Putting input into what we wanted to see and what we didn't want to see. We both used to sit down and talk with Lew Eggebrecht when he came over."

David Pleasance also knew he had to help repair Commodore UK's reputation after the scandal and bad press it had received at the end of 1992. "One of the things I felt was wrong with Commodore was that we were this faceless company that nobody knew anything about," says Pleasance. "I said, 'Right, I'm going to approach the magazines and see if I can address their public.' I ended up getting columns in four of their magazines where I answered questions. It was really successful. All of a sudden Commodore become this friendly face—I have a pretty ugly face—but friendly nevertheless."

Even though the recent scandal had resulted in the firing of Steve Franklin, there were still issues to resolve. "Once I was appointed as managing director of the UK company, we faced the situation knowing that Steve Franklin had been involved in these things," explains David Pleasance. "Did we, as a UK Limited company, want to proceed with action against him to try to get some money back?"

Pleasance had personal reasons that made such a decision difficult. "I was faced with the very, very awkward situation of what do I do," says Pleasance. "He's my friend, he has been very good to me but on the other hand, I'm representing the UK company—all the staff and all the creditors. I ended up making the decision, 'Yeah, I think we should prosecute because there is a chance we can get some money back and that money belongs to the creditors.'"

The lawsuit was complex because Commodore would have to retrieve the money from multiple parties. "Our managing director of Commodore was getting remuneration back from the service companies," explains Pleasance. "What we were trying to do is to retrieve monies that had been paid him from monies paid to these service companies."

Colin Proudfoot also wanted compensation for Commodore's fees to investigate Steve Franklin since the beginning of 1992. "We spent two and a half million dollars on legal fees investigating Steve and the other two guys," says Proudfoot "We got a miranda order on the guys in the maintenance company to freeze their worldwide assets. The biggest asset was the company headquarters, worth something like $2.5 million."

The court case would drag on for years, as these proceedings usually did. "Proving fraud is difficult," says Proudfoot. "The fraud squad never successfully prosecuted white collar crime. After two years, Franklin and his partners settled out of court. They paid legal bills of $2.5 million. The bank foreclosed on their headquarters and seized their property."

As part of the settlement, Franklin and FMG would go free. "They paid our legal bill without prejudice because we settled and they denied wrong-doing," says Proudfoot. "That was the settlement."

Summer 1993 Layoffs

Shortly after Thomas Rattigan had saved Commodore from bankruptcy in 1987, he remarked, "We didn't fall off the edge. We may have gotten close, but we didn't fall."[1] Since the departure of Rattigan, Commodore had wandered dangerously close to the edge again. This time, they were starting to fall.

After the stunning losses at the end of 1992, Commodore reported an-other significant loss for the quarter ending March 31, 1993 of $177.6 million. Revenues were to blame. It was Commodore's lowest third-quarter re-sult since 1982. Revenues for the past three quarters totaled $512.2 million, down from $770.3 for the first three quarters of fiscal year 1992.

Commodore's share price plummeted to $2.875 on the New York Stock Exchange. Following this loss, Mehdi Ali laid off around a dozen sales em-ployees on Friday, April 23rd. He also closed offices in Reston Virginia and California. With no more sales people in the field, all US sales would be made from West Chester by telephone. This was only the start.

Although Commodore had just lost an enormous amount of money, it still had cash flow from ongoing sales of its inventory. The most pressing issue was a $33 million loan by Prudential Insurance of Newark, New Jer-sey. Commodore's cash flow was not enough to keep up with repayments, resulting in a default on the loan in May.

Mehdi Ali was forced to appear before the lenders and beg them to give him an extension. He promised them the company would have a better holiday quarter than it had in 1992. As Commodore's chief financial offi-cer, Ronald B. Alexander, told the Philadelphia Inquirer, "If Christmas is another bad season in Europe, this company's going to be hard-pressed to continue." Alexander retired from Commodore shortly after. The banks gave Commodore until July 31 to restructure the company enough to put together a suitable schedule for repayment.

As had occurred before, the two principal ways to restructure Commo-dore were selling off properties and reducing staff. Commodore was already at minimal staff levels. In fact, it could be said that minimal staff was a

---

1   *Commodore* magazine, "What Next for Commodore?" (May 1987), p. 76.

key part of Commodore's business model, allowing the company to offer cheaper products. But to cut into Commodore's employees now would curtail chances for future success.

In the summer of 1993, Commodore went through a series of massive layoffs. The building at West Chester, which once housed thousands of employees, was about to become almost vacant. The layoffs meant Commodore could pay salaries and continue to operate, but with less staff, there was little chance for a rebound.

On June 11, Commodore cut over 80 employees from its payroll, leaving under 200 workers in the entire West Chester facility. The cuts came from all divisions, including engineering, manufacturing, tech support, and marketing.[2] Of these cuts, 29 were laid off from engineering. CATS was most severely hit, dropping from 17 to 7 employees.

The AmigaOS group was hit hard too, with department head Ned McCook departing. One of his key developers, Michael Sinz, asked to be let go because he didn't want to be part of a slow, agonizing collapse. "I told Commodore to lay me off in 1993," he says. "Steve Beats said he was going back to England. My fiancee was laid off. I said, 'Take me out.' I thought it was horrible."

Like many employees, Sinz would find a way to continue working with Amiga technology at a new company called Scala. "I had lined up a position as director of engineering at Scala in the US," he says.

Commodore also warned 14 additional employees would be let go the following month. This included upper management, such as facilities manager Joe Mecca and Commodore US president Jim Dionne, who was replaced by Commodore's VP of sales, Geoff Stilley—a former fighter pilot.

Due to the overproduction of A600 computers and low-end PC clones at the end of 1992, and subsequent inability to sell them, Mehdi Ali was forced to take a $65 million dollar write off on the computers, which sat in a warehouse decreasing in value. Rather than take responsibility for the fiasco, Commodore blamed the poor sales from the previous holiday season on the recession in Europe.

Ali's cuts would have a temporary, short-term effect on the financial books that would look positive to investors. "They were having problems with the banks, the refinancing," says Guy Wright. "Essentially what they did was shut down manufacturing, they shut down marketing, they shut down cus-

---

2   *Philadelphia Inquirer*, Jun 12, 1993. "80 Lose Jobs At Chesco Concern 29 Engineers Were Among Those Sacked By Commodore. That Could Be A Bleak Signal."

tomer support, they shut down distribution, and then they wrote off all of the crap that was sitting in their warehouses. They were going to shut down the R&D department and if you're shutting down your R&D department then you aren't going to come out with any new stuff. There's no hope."

Curiously, Mehdi Ali, the man who had presided over Commodore's worst year in a long time, was allowed to remain, even though his contract expired in June 1993. Irving Gould had gone through a number of perfectly good Presidents and CEO's over the years. The best of them, Jack Tramiel and Thomas Rattigan, had been fired at the height of their success. Surprisingly, even in the face of disaster, Gould remained satisfied with Ali.

Just after the layoffs, Dave Haynie hosted his fifth annual Commodore employee summer party. Along with swimming, barbecuing, and ample drinking, the attendees indulged in torturing effigies of their favorite executives, bobbing for A600 computers (the participants preferred to let them sink) and a game dubbed the "The Chapter 7 Game." According to the invitation, "You play Commodore as you sit on a battleship grey float in the middle of the pool. Everyone else in the water gets to play one of the many enemies of Commodore: *The Wall Street Journal*, Ackers, *InfoWorld*, Sculley, Tramiel, Barrett, Sydnes, or one of the many others, including any number of the hundreds of Commodore's creditors. They attack! How long can you stay afloat?"

Commodore also closed its remaining manufacturing facilities in favor of outsourced manufacturing in the Philippines and UK. Genie's *Viewport* magazine reported, "Among the changes have been significant reductions in staff, an overhaul of distribution (instead of shipping to 180 direct dealers, Commodore will use 5 distributors), and a new, more efficient manufacturing facility in the Philippines which replaces facilities in the US, Taiwan, and Germany."

When Irving Gould and Mehdi Ali met with their creditors, Prudential Insurance in New Jersey on July 31, they had three definite goals. The first was to impress upon them that they had successfully restructured Commodore and the company could become profitable with its future products. The second was to secure additional loans to continue operations. And the third, and most important goal, was to prevent Prudential from foreclosing on the loan, which would mean immediate bankruptcy proceedings for Commodore.

Of these goals, the first two goals were definitely not achieved. Prudential did not want to risk throwing good money after bad—no new loans were extended. This forced Irving Gould to ante up the financing himself to convince Prudential that they could pay off the original loan if Commodore had more time. Gould used his other companies to extend a loan to Commodore for $7.5 million in order to continue operations. As a result, the third goal was achieved and Prudential extended the foreclosure deadline to January 1994.[3] By risking his own money, it was clear Irving Gould was still hopeful for long term success.

Ending PC Clones

Commodore had entered the PC clone market in 1985 and profited quite well for many years. Then in 1992 things started to go bad when competition became more intense and the low-end products were no longer profitable. However, as a percentage of revenue, PC clone sales were important to Commodore. For fiscal 1992, the high end MS-DOS PC compatibles accounted for 24% of sales, while in fiscal 1993 (July 1992 - June 1993), those sales rose to 37% of revenue.

At the same time, the PC division did not produce very much of a profit due to increasing competition at the high end. "They really screwed up because this is a time when we were going through this period where Intel used to eat its own young," says David Pleasance. "It was going through a stage where it would release a new chip and then, before that chip was exploited, they would announce another chip which was faster and cheaper."

New improved PCs with faster processors and more memory appeared in rapid succession, resulting in a shorter lifetime for the product. "CPUs change all the time, so motherboards change all the time," explains Gerard Bucas. "The problem is, just as you finish a new motherboard design and take it into production, yet another new chip is available from Intel which means you've got to scramble and make yet another new motherboard."

The shorter product life span was not a business model Commodore was set up to compete in. "From Commodore's point of view, volume wise, it certainly wasn't in the millions of PCs," says Bucas. "You could never optimize it because before you get into very high volume production, you have to have another motherboard. It took a long time and a lot of engineering effort."

This meant Commodore was always slightly behind the curve. "It went on and on and on and everybody was so nervous about what they were

---

3   *Philadelphia Inquirer*, Mar. 26, 1994. "Computer Company's Decline Continues Commodore Lost $8.2 Million In Its Second Quarter. This Follows A $77.2 Million Loss Last Year."

going to buy," says Pleasance. "It kind of stopped us for a very long time because people are really reticent to buy if they know that, if they just wait, another chip which has better performance and costs less money will come."

Mehdi Ali found himself in a difficult position. If he continued the PC clone division, Commodore was likely to lose a lot of money. However, the division accounted for 37% of Commodore's revenues. To stop it now and remove all that revenue would look bad on financial reports.

In June 1993, Ali made the decision to abandon the PC clone business altogether. He sold the PC division to the Taiwanese clone maker Acer. The loss of this division meant Commodore Germany would no longer play as large a role in Commodore International's revenue. Now Commodore UK was the single strongest subsidiary in the company.

Commodore's original decision to sell PC compatible computers back in 1985 mystified C64 engineer Robert Yannes. "They lost their vision," he says. "They really didn't know who they were as a company and what people expected from them. They had made a name for themselves doing home computers. For them to go into the PC compatible business with a PC compatible that really had no advantage over any other PC compatible just didn't make sense."

Yannes believes executives should have concentrated their energy on the Amiga. "They could have been doing things like the Macintosh and multimedia machines," he says. "The Amiga really was the first multimedia computer, and they really had no idea what to do with it or where to go with it."

Yannes believes it would have been difficult for Commodore to survive in the PC clone market. "There aren't that many [companies] that are doing great profits," he says. "If you are a Compaq or an HP, you are so tied to the bottom line all the time you can't do anything. The margins are terrible and at any given moment you are either one-month away from being a major success or out of business."

Not Going Down with the Ship

Although Mehdi Ali worried about Commodore's finances, he never seemed particularly worried about all the people working under him. In fact, some people felt he worried more about himself. He made sure he had the best Concorde flights, the best meals, and the best hotels no matter what the cost. "We had executives who I think were just looking to line their own pockets," says longtime Commodore employee Eric Cotton.

Irving Gould, with his jet-setting ways, didn't set a very good example for Ali, whom he worked with on Park Avenue in New York. "The executive offices in Manhattan were very opulent," says Eric Lavitsky. "I remember going to the bathroom there and it had black marble and gold in it. It was kind of ridiculous. I remember going into the reception area. There were just a couple of offices, probably for a couple of Commodore executives, so Irving Gould and Mehdi and whoever could have an office there to show people."

Within the company, the engineers felt no love for the decisions made by their company president. "We had very little respect for our executive staff, the Mehdi Alis and whatnot," says Eric Cotton. "I don't want to slander anybody or anything but the pervasive feeling amongst us with the boots on the ground was that they were just looking to make a buck for themselves. They didn't really care about Commodore like we did and I was very disillusioned."

Normally Commodore released its annual shareholder report in August of every year. Investors had been expecting the report for fiscal 1993, which ended June 30 1993, to be presented on schedule. But this year the report was inexplicably delayed. To outsiders it looked like a child hiding a bad report card from his parents.

Meanwhile, since July of that year, the Commodore Shareholders Movement had been gaining steam. A software developer named Mike Levin had organized the movement online and announced his intentions in *Amiga World* that he was seeking to oust chairman Irving Gould.[4] The plan had a good chance of succeeding because the three-year terms of both Gould and Alexander Haig were up for reelection in November. The possibility of his ouster was very real because Gould only owned 19% of Commodore's shares. If the Commodore Shareholders Movement could collect enough proxy votes, Gould would be out.

August passed without a shareholder report, then September and October. It seemed increasingly clear to outsiders that Commodore had something to hide. Finally, on Friday November 12 at 5:48 pm (after the stock market closed), Commodore released its annual report. As expected, the news was not good.

For the year ending June 30, 1993, Commodore had lost $365 million— an average of one million dollars per day. To put that in perspective, on

---

4   *Amiga World*, Oct. 1993, p. 4. "Editor's Drawer"

June 30, 1992, Commodore had a net worth, on the books, of $325 million. That meant shareholders' equity was valued at negative $53.2 million. This had happened all within the space of a single year.

Commodore had held off the results until November when they could release the July to September results, hoping to show an improvement in finances. And indeed, the quarterly report showed a marked improvement. When Ali had shut down production and marketing over the summer, it gave a temporary boost to Commodore's financial books. "What that did was, even though they were in the red, it gave a spike to the profits because they were no longer paying for manufacturing," says Guy Wright. "They were only selling inventory that was out in the field. So their stock jumped. This was I think November or December the year before they folded." On November 5, 1993, on rumors of the upcoming report, the stock spiked to $4⅝ with over 1.7 million shares trading that day.

The engineers who loved the company blamed the captain of the ship, their company president. "Mehdi Ali was to us the devil," says Eric Cotton. "We saw him as the person who was going to drive Commodore into the ground. In retrospect, I don't know if he was explicitly responsible for it, but it does seem like he was partially responsible for it. I mean we really got to the point where we didn't really feel like the executive staff cared anymore. They were just looking to make a buck or maybe even make a few bucks until it went under."

For the third calendar-year period, Commodore had another loss of $9.7 million. This was considered good news, because for the same quarter a year ago the company had lost $18.8 million. "We have made progress in reducing the net loss," said Gould in the report. "Having largely completed our operational restructuring, we are now planning to undertake a restructuring of our debts to allow the company to continue normal operations." Gould and Ali were unavailable for comment at the time.

As for the upcoming shareholder meeting, Gould planned to avoid squaring off against the Commodore Shareholders Movement. In previous years Gould had been able to outmaneuver attempts to criticize or replace him, usually by closing off the meeting as best he could. This year, Gould used his most audacious move ever by postponing the meeting indefinitely, thus delaying a possible vote of confidence against his leadership.

CD32
1993

Despite the worsening disaster of 1993, Commodore had one more ace up its sleeve to play. After taking over from Henri Rubin and Jeff Porter, the Bill Sydnes/Lew Eggebrecht/Mehdi Ali trio had decided to cut out high-end Amigas including the A3000 Plus and focus on low-end Amigas, such as the A600 and A1200. They also focused on the PC clone market, while cutting out the low-end PC clones. And they cut the low-end video game machine, the C65.

Since then, the executives had reversed course and restarted the high-end Amiga line with the A4000, as well as starting a low-end video game machine, the CD32. In other words, they were now back to the same product categories they had previously abandoned. The project with the most urgency for the company was indisputably the CD32.

CD32 Prototypes

After the disastrous 1992 Christmas season, Mehdi Ali placed extra emphasis on completing the "CD Game System", known internally as Amigo. Executives hoped this long-shot product would continue retail success where the C64 left off.

Since October 1992, Commodore engineers George Robbins, Chris Coley, Bill Richard, and Hedley Davis had been working on the gate array chip for the system, known as Akiko (and sometimes Arizona). On January 13, 1993, Davis put Akiko in lockdown mode: no new features, just finish it off so it would be production ready. "We had the first prototype chip of this running in the first week of January," says Lew Eggebrecht.[1]

---

1 *Amiga CD Format* (special) 1993, p. 5. "Tech Talk"

The Akiko chip performed an incredibly useful function aimed squarely at PC game developers. Akiko allowed "chunky to planar" graphics conversion (or the reverse). This feature would allow PC games using up to 24-bit graphics to be easily ported to the Amigo. It was a brilliantly conceived feature to deal with a persistent marketing issue.

By February 1993, the engineers were nearing completion on their design of the Amigo video game console. Commodore knew the machine needed high quality games in order to give customers a reason to buy it. Hoping to spur software development, they assembled 15 prototype units destined for game developers.

For his part, George Robbins, fuelled by goth-rock, hurriedly finished off the shielding required for his motherboard design just in time for the first working Akiko chips. Since the plastic case for the game system wasn't completed, the engineer put together prototype units attached to plywood.

In keeping with naming his motherboards after the songs that accompanied the development of each system, Robbins named his motherboard *Spellbound*, after the song by the English goth-rock band Siouxsie and the Banshees.

Commodore's marketing department renamed the device just before handing out the prototypes. The new name was elegant in its simplicity. It would be called CD32, a name that told customers everything they needed to know about the system—CD-based with a 32-bit processor. "By the end of February we had 15 prototypes of the CD32 which went to developers," says Lew Eggebrecht.

Carl Sassenrath received one of those prototypes with the hope that he could test it and contribute code to the project. "I remember when I got the first prototype of it; it was on a piece of wood, and they said 'check this thing out,'" he recalls. "It was like wow, this is awesome. Go team go!"

Given that the AGA chipset was already designed and tested, perhaps the most important addition to the console would be the game controllers. For years, the playability of Amiga games had been limited by the one-button joystick that the Amiga supported. Now there was a chance to break free from that crippling limitation.

Back in late October 1992, the designer of the A500 case, Yukiya Itoh, began work on a new game controller for the CD32. "I had a favorite guy in Japan that did all the Industrial designing for products that I worked on," says Jeff Porter. "Itoh-san was amazing. The pictures that he would draw of what the computer would look like looked like photographs. It was just stunning."

Instead of a joystick, Itoh based his design on the Hudson Super Joycard controller for the Nintendo Super Famicon, including a D-pad controller. In fact, Commodore would have had to pay for a license from Nintendo in order to use the D-pad form. Instead, the company planned to include a rubber adhesive D-pad to stick onto the round controller in order to avoid licensing fees for using a true D-pad.

Itoh also added a total of four action buttons, two shoulder buttons, and a start/pause button to the controller. The overall "flattened U" shape of the controller was distinct among other game consoles, providing a more ergonomic shape than the NES controllers. "Itoh's designs were works of art," says Porter.

Once George Robbins completed his motherboard design, it was time for the case design to begin. The case designer was Don Kaminsky, who had been hired by Bill Sydnes to design the A600 and A1200 cases, along with the A4000 front bezel. "They brought in some rank amateur in the US that could barely draw straight lines to do the other computers after I got pushed to the side," says Jeff Porter. "What a hack."

Herb Mosteller would design the sheet metal chassis for the prototype design. On January 13, 1993, Kaminsky travelled to Tokyo to work on the tooling for all of the case parts, which would eventually be manufactured in the Philippines. The tooling for 10 different parts, including the controller, would cost Commodore $62,600. It would be complete by May 1993.

The outward appearance of CD32 was radically different from CDTV, even if the functionality was similar. While CDTV resembled a VCR, the new CD32 was a pure game console. It was compact with round molded plastic, a top-ejecting CD player, and colorful hand controllers. "It looked just like a Sega or something," says Dave Haynie.

Kaminsky designed the shape around the top-loading CD that was based on low-end portable CD players, rather than the high-end sliding motorized tray of the CDTV. Porter was unimpressed. "They were nowhere near as pretty as Itoh-san's creations," he says. "The CD32 was probably one of the ugliest computers out there. It had this flip-top lid. Remember those old record players? You basically lifted the lid, lay the CD on the spindle and closed the lid. That was it. It wasn't very sexy."

Having just come off the CDTV-CR project, Porter was understandably underwhelmed by the cost effective CD32 design. Others also agreed with Porter. "It was ugly in the sense that it wasn't the sleek, stereo looking box that the CDTV was, with the metal cabinet sitting next to your stereo," says Carl Sassenrath. "It was slick looking but it was much more like a console. Like a Nintendo or something."

Jeff Porter was responsible mainly for the separately released MPEG video decoder card, allowing the CD32 to play digital videos from CD. This allowed CD32 to play the popular Video CD format (VCD). Engineers also snuck in the ability to play CD-i digital movies, which included late eighties and early nineties CD-i films like *Black Rain* and *Hunt for Red October*.

Andy Finkel had since departed Commodore for good after the Japanese Kanji project was cancelled and now worked at Commodore's competitor, 3DO. Hence the Amiga software team led by Allan Havemose developed the CD32 system software.

Jim Sachs supplied the artwork for all the menus and launch screens. He even began work on a possible launch title for the console, which Commodore had agreed to distribute. Now they were ready to unveil the system at the next CES.

June 1993 CES

Commodore's engineers had produced samples of the CD32, with controllers and cases, in time for the Summer CES in Chicago, held June 3 to 6. Rumors were swirling in the tech community that Commodore would unveil a CD-ROM game console with AGA graphics, with a retail launch later in the year.

And then the unthinkable happened. Just days prior to CES, on Friday, May 28 at 6:30 pm, less than two hours after the stock exchange closed, Commodore announced the aforementioned loss of $177.6 million. Due to the devastating financial results, Commodore simply did not have the money to attend CES with a large booth.

Instead, the company set up a very small portable office to take orders from interested retailers on the show floor. As the *Philadelphia Inquirer* described it, "The West Chester computer-maker's presence at the important trade show was little more than an office in a box, only slightly bigger than a kitchen pantry and hidden behind the glitzy displays set up by its personal-computer and multimedia competitors."[2] This was an impossible situation, since CES was the prime venue to launch a new game console for the consumer market.

Lew Eggebrecht and Jeff Porter would provide demonstrations of the CD32 and other products in Irving Gould's rented suite, with Gould, Mehdi Ali, and president of Commodore US, Jim Dionne. These demonstrations were to convince financial institutions, such as Prudential Insurance, that the CD32 had potential.

With hardly any companies showing Amiga software at CES, it was up to NewTek to represent the Amiga. Thankfully, it was a good year for the company. Major TV shows and movies were using the Amiga to bring along a new wave of digital special effects in 1993. These included *Babylon 5*, *seaQuest DSV*,

---

2   *Philadelphia Inquirer,* July 19, 1993. "Video Toaster Warms Commodore's Future An Electronic Amigo For The Amiga."

and the most anticipated movie of the summer, *Jurassic Park*. The latter relied on NewTek's LightWave 3D for previsualization of scenes.

In contrast, Commodore's big competition for the CD-ROM console, 3DO, was "the hottest company at the show" according to *Dow Jones News*. The company claimed it had licenses signed with 302 software developers, including Electronic Arts, Interplay Productions, MicroProse, Psygnosis, Spectrum Holobyte, Trilobyte (makers of *The 7th Guest*), and Virgin Games. The 3DO company had gone public the month prior at $15 per share, and at CES it was trading at $37¼.

The 3DO company also succeeded in luring several Commodore engineers. Due to the grim future of Commodore, along with his upcoming wedding on June 19, Hedley Davis started looking around for new employment. He didn't think it would be a good idea to be unemployed at the start of a new marriage.

Dale Luck of 3DO contacted Davis in April, owing to his CD-ROM expertise, and lured him to California by the end of May. "There were a lot of politics that started developing around the company, and that's ultimately why I left," says Hedley Davis. "It wasn't making any sense, you know? There was nothing good happening. It was just this infighting and arguing."

It was the another indication that Commodore was losing even diehard believers.

AAA Fabrication

Commodore's chip engineers had worked on the AAA chipset on and off since 1989. Years later, in the summer of 1993, they were nearing completion and layout began. "I remember laying that out with one of the guys," says Glenn Keller. "And being really impressed by his ability to lay things out in a structured manner, and all of that stuff. That was very cool."

Because Commodore was using 1 micron technology, the chips Andrea, Monica, Linda, and Mary would be fabricated by Hewlett-Packard. Tape out is the final result of the design cycle for integrated circuits or printed circuit boards—the point at which the artwork for the photomask of a circuit is sent for manufacture. "From tape out to getting the part back, that's measured in weeks and months," says Andrea designer Ed Hepler. "It's not like you send something off to Shutterfly and then a week later you get your pictures. It takes a long time."

Commodore would not use CSG because the small micron chips required by 1993 had surpassed them. "They didn't have the technology," says Hepler. "Those were being fabbed by HP for us. The original Amiga chips that they were building were 5 micron NMOS. The AAA was 1.25 micron CMOS. They couldn't do 1.25 micron."

Finally, by August 1993, Commodore's engineers received the first samples of the AAA chipset. "If I remember correctly there were just one or two other very minor things wrong," says Hepler. "There was one signal that was inverted or something, so we had to throw an extra inverter on the board instead of having the wire driven directly, but that was minor."

Mehdi Ali approved the budget to proceed with monthly runs of revised AAA chips. Meanwhile, Dave Haynie had been working on a motherboard since late 1992 called Nyx to test the AAA chipset. By August 20, 1993, Nyx was able to display true-color 24-bit screens, a first for Commodore. "Dave Haynie made a board that took the chips and we were able to run code on them and make them work," says Hepler. "The Andrea chip for example had something like 16-bit planes and what they called chunky pixels which are normal pixels of today."

Chunky pixels was a term used by engineers to describe the style of graphics displayed on IBM PC machines. "The Amiga had bit-plane graphics where you could put together multiple single bits to get a pixel that had more than two colors (black and white) that you would get from a single bit plane," explains Hepler. "Most computers these days don't do that sort of thing; they have 8-bit or 16-bit or 24-bit pixels where R,G, and B each have 8-bits. That's what we were calling chunky pixels back then. So Andrea could do chunky pixels and it could do bitplane pixels."

The chips improved performance over AGA by 10 to 20 times. Lew Eggebrecht expected fully working chips by early 1994 and new Amiga systems ready mid-year.

A5000

Dave Haynie's Nyx board (for testing AAA) was based on A3000 technology and would not be used for production. Instead, he and Greg Berlin had plans for a full high-end Amiga based on the Acutiator testbed they had previously developed, which would allow a high degree of modularity with the system.

In August 1993, Lew Eggebrecht tasked Greg Berlin with designing the motherboard for the next generation Amiga, the A5000. Berlin dusted off the Acutiator spec and began creating a spec for the new A5000. At the core of Acutiator was Dave Haynie's Amiga Modular Interconnect (AMI) bus. However, the PC world had released the PCI bus in June 1992, and it fulfilled the same function as AMI. Lew Eggebrecht encouraged Berlin to adopt PCI instead.

Berlin scratched out the AMI bus in his plans and replaced it with the PCI bus. He continued working on a proposal for the A5000 through September, and by October it was done—including a block diagram of the system. Curiously, rumors of the new system hit *Amiga Format* magazine in the UK almost real-time, with the September issue discussing the new project.

Berlin and his engineers began working on the motherboard design and hoped to have samples ready in early 1994, at which time the AAA chipset would be a few more revisions better and fully tested. Amazingly, Commodore was putting a lot of effort into high-end machines this late in the game. It showed a deep commitment by the engineers to continue the Commodore-Amiga legacy.

SCI Financial Deal

One year earlier, Commodore had asked SCI UK of Scotland to mass produce Amiga 600 and 1200 machines. Unfortunately, most of those A600 machines did not sell. "Commodore in '92 used SCI to manufacture Amigas offshore," recalls Colin Proudfoot. "They got shipped but Commodore didn't pay the debt. Commodore owed SCI about $20 million."

By mid-1993, Commodore had run out of A1200 systems and needed more for the holiday season. Mehdi Ali called up Gene Sapp, the CEO of SCI UK, and negotiated a very unfavorable (for Commodore) deal to tempt them to continue production. As Colin Proudfoot recalls, "Mehdi went to SCI and said, 'We want you to build Amigas again for us. For every Amiga we buy, we will pay you $50 off the old debt. We'll set up a trust account in the UK and for every Amiga we sell we'll give you 69% of the proceeds.'"

The crux of this agreement was that Commodore UK would directly deposit money into an account from its sales of Amiga machines. Commodore UK's general manager Colin Proudfoot found the agreement troubling. "I get sent a copy of this agreement and I go, 'Holy cow, this is crazy.' I had been trading profitably in the UK, and I was making sure we stayed solvent and stayed profitable."

In November 1993, SCI opened a trust account with Citibank for the deposits. Soon A1200 computers began flowing to Commodore UK's headquarters from SCI. "I'm buying them from Commodore Switzerland, who's buying them from Commodore Hong Kong, who's buying them from Commodore Antilles, who's buying them from SCI," explains Proudfoot. "So I pay Commodore Switzerland the transfer price of the machines and put the money into the trust account."

Ali had successfully restarted the manufacturing of Commodore's machines. But there was a risk that the terms of the deal were not financially favorable, with Commodore essentially giving up $50 for every machine it sold. Time would tell if the deal would pan out for SCI UK.

CD32 Manufacturing

For the 1993 holiday season, Commodore hoped to launch the CD32 game console in Europe and North America. Manufacturing took place in a Philippines government-owned factory. Back in July 1993, George Robbins travelled to Manila to help the production line.

By August, the plant was operating at full capacity and plans were to turn out 10,000 units per week that same month, 15,000 units per week for the first three weeks of September, then 25,000 units per week thereafter. 90,000 units for October, 90,000 units for November, and 40,000 units in December. By the end of the year, the Philippines factory would have shipped 330,000 units. Along with the NTSC units, it would theoretically be enough to save Commodore financially.

Three of the production lines in the Philippines would produce CD32 systems, while the fourth production line was dedicated to producing A4000 computers. (And as mentioned earlier, Scotland's SCI UK would produce the A1200.)

But Commodore had difficulties paying their parts suppliers to stock the factory. When too much money went unpaid, the vendors stopped sending parts. "The problem was, Commodore at that point owed so many people so much money, they were having to pay cash for everything," explains Dave Haynie. "And they just didn't have that much cash."

Irving Gould extended another loan of $9.9 million in order to keep the parts supply flowing.[3] Most of the money went towards the cost-reduced CD-ROM mechanism. "I think the issue with the CD32 was the actual CD drive mechanism itself, which was a custom mechanism," says Colin Proudfoot. "Why we didn't get a market standard mechanism I have no idea, but we decided to design and build a custom mechanism and that was in short supply."

Many of Commodore's parts suppliers instigated lawsuits against Commodore for unpaid parts. The parts shortage had devastating consequences. Commodore could only purchase enough parts to make approximately 100,000 CD32 units. "By the time the fall of 1993 rolled around, and the CD32 was coming out, they couldn't make enough CD32s because they didn't have enough money," says Dave Haynie.

Haynie estimates Commodore needed to build about 400,000 to survive. "They could make something like 125,000, but they had potential orders for double that," he says.

---

3   *Philadelphia Inquirer*, March 26, 1994. "Computer Company's Decline Continues Commodore Lost $8.2 Million In Its Second Quarter. This Follows A $77.2 Million Loss Last Year."

Ultimately, all this was for nothing when the CADtrak lawsuit came back to haunt Commodore. Due to a lack of cash, Commodore stopped payments to CADtrak. On July 23, CADtrak filed an injunction on Commodore due to a breach of the settlement agreement. Judge Vaughn R. Walker sided with CADtrak and placed injunctions on Commodore which limited how it could operate.

As a result, when October rolled around, the US government prevented Commodore from importing product into the country. The CD32 units from the Philippines could not make it past customs. Commodore was relegated to selling the NTSC CD32 units in Canada only, with a limited number of units then making their way across the border into the US.

According to Haynie, the customs problems would not have hurt Commodore anyway. "There was so much demand for them they probably could have sold them in Europe," he says.

CD32 Launch Parties

When it came time to launch the CD32, Commodore was in unknown territory. The company had never dominated the game console market and had never really released a full-blown game console. They were comfortable in the low-end computer market. This made the new CD32 launch potentially risky, given the low odds they would be able to one-up industry leaders Nintendo and Sega.

Commodore planned to launch the CD32 in the US in October at $399, a launch that would not occur in 1993 due to the CADtrak situation. As the *Philadelphia Inquirer* noted, "It could go either way for the CD32 because Commodore can't or won't spend more than pocket change in the high-stakes business of consumer electronics to promote the device."[4]

The long-suffering *Amiga World* magazine, still gamely promoting the Amiga despite its near absence from North America, also announced the launch. "According to Commodore, CD32 will initially be available in 'limited quantities' and sold at 'strategic areas' in the US before the national push slated for CES in January."[5]

In September of 1993, Commodore announced the CD32 in North America at the World of Commodore-Amiga, held in Pasadena, California. It was

---

4   *Philadelphia Inquirer*, Oct. 4, 1993. "New Item Runs Into An Old Problem Commodore Will Be Introducing A Cd Player. The Troubled Company Will Not Be Spending A Lot To Promote It, Though."

5   *Amiga World*, Dec. 1993, p. 27. "Games Engine Par Excellence!"

a faint shadow of what the announcement would have been, had it happened earlier at the Summer CES in Chicago.

President of Commodore US, Jim Dionne, gave a lengthy talk describing the North American plans for the CD32. He also described problems manufacturing A1200 and A4000s (due to poor finances) and promised they would begin manufacturing more soon. Lew Eggebrecht gave an impressive technical talk about the CD32 and then went on to describe the progress of the AAA chipset, much to the delight of audiences there. John Campbell of CATS demonstrated the CD32, including a flight simulator, the CD32 demo disc (featuring artwork by Jim Sachs), and a *Jurassic Park* demo. But the demo that brought the house down was Jeff Porter's Bon Jovi video clip playing at 30 FPS with stereo sound—an incredible feat for 1993.

Although the technology was impressive as usual from Commodore, a ghost was hanging over the show. As GEnie's Jim Meyer noted, "This year, more than a few exhibitors talked about going to WoCA for 'one last party.' And more than a few exhibitors stayed home, too. Expectations were low, and I suspect that many attendees went with the feeling that this would be the last World of Commodore-Amiga show, ever."

Commodore UK's launch of the CD32 was a different story. It's worth taking in the technological achievement accomplished by Commodore's engineers. As *Amiga Format* noted, "Commodore have beaten Nintendo, Sega, Atari, and 3DO to the milestone of the first 32-bit console. Not only that, but it's also the first 32-bit CD console, and the first standalone CD console to go on sale in Europe."[6]

It seemed Commodore might have found a good product fit for the company at last. "They realized CD was the future and that then was the birth of the CD32, which was even more incredible in terms of being something for the market," says Carl Sassenrath. "It was nice compared to other consoles of the time."

Commodore had succeeded in the past by offering technologically superior hardware for less than its competitors. With the CD32, it had the same factors in its favor. As David Pleasance explained at the time, "The Amiga CD32 simply wipes out the opposition. It is considerably more powerful, has better software support and, best of all, it costs less."

David Pleasance did not want to launch the CD32 so early, without much time to prepare and line up software titles. But due to Commodore's rocky financial situation, he was forced to launch on July 16, 1993. As usual for Com-

---

6   *Amiga Format*, Sept. 1993, p. 16. "Mega CD beater"

modore UK, the company was able to make a splash with the product. "I booked the Science Museum in London to launch the CD32," recalls Pleasance.

Much like the VIC-20 launch, Pleasance was able to secure a noteworthy entertainer to promote the new system. "We launched it with Chris Evans, who is still a TV and radio personality in the UK," says Colin Proudfoot. "It was early in his career and it was a big launch."

Crush Sega

Although Nintendo ruled America, it was Sega who dominated Europe when it came to video game consoles. The rise of the Sega Mega Drive in Europe (known as Sega Genesis in the US) spelled the end for low-end video game computers like the Amiga 1200. But the CD32 was tailor made to fight against the Mega Drive.

Sega had thrived on running edgy ads and making fun of Nintendo, which sometimes resulted in Nintendo threatening to sue Sega. Now Commodore's David Pleasance was looking for a way to undermine Sega's lead. "About three weeks before the launch of the CD32 there was an article released in one of the PC magazines by Tom Kalinske who was the worldwide president of Sega," recalls David Pleasance. "In the article the interviewer asked, 'What about 32-bit games technology? What's your take on that?'"

Kalinsky replied, "We could bring a 32-bit console out tomorrow... but the problem is the price and I don't think that problem will be solved this year or next year."

Pleasance now had all the ammunition he needed. "I just said, 'Thank you, there is a God!' Obviously I utilized that opportunity."

During the CD32 launch at the Science Museum in London, Pleasance gave a test drive of his idea. "When we actually held the launch, it was absolutely full of retailers, software companies, magazines, and everybody who would possibly be involved," he recalls. "We did a mock voice of Tom Kalinske saying what he said in the magazine. He said it! It was absolutely true and he couldn't deny it. That was the most beautiful thing. We could use it without any fear of discussion about whether he did or didn't."

After the July launch, Pleasance formulated a campaign with a very specific focus. "We did a 'Crush Sega Campaign'", recalls Colin Proudfoot. "At that time, Sega did a campaign, 'To be this good will take ages', and then they switched 'Ages' around to form 'Sega'."

Although Sega did not yet match the CD32's 32-bit processor, they were about to enter the CD-ROM market in Europe with the Mega CD add-on (known as Sega CD in the US). "They were the major competitor in the CD-based games console space," says Colin Proudfoot. "At that time in the marketplace, Sega and us were vying for the maximum market share. Philips had a machine that was comparable but they weren't really seen as major players in the game space. We're really talking about the gaming industry. And the key—certainly coming up to Christmas—is to get share of mind, share of shelf space. We wanted the major retailers to put us in prime position on the shelves rather than Sega."

Whereas Commodore US did virtually no marketing, Commodore UK was very focused with its marketing effort. "Over the summer we focused on pointing out that 32-bit technology was the future and that the CD32 was way better than the Sega game console, which would be a thing of the past as the market got to see what the CD32 could do," says Proudfoot. "At that time Nintendo was still an 8-bit, so they were behind where we were and Sega was. Of course that was pre-Sony."

Commodore's aggressive war against Sega reached new heights in late-summer. "About two weeks later I got a phone call from a guy and this guy said, 'David, you probably don't remember me but I've done some business with you before. We have big poster sites all over the UK. I've got a deal for you,'" recalls Pleasance. "I said, 'Okay, what's that?' And he said, 'We have three major, large 96 sheet poster sites in central London that somebody booked and paid 50% deposit on ages ago, and they've just pulled out. So I'm going to offer them to you at 50% price, because I've already got half the money. But the best thing is that one of them is right outside Sega's head office.'"

Pleasance saw a chance to attack Sega right where they lived. "Needless to say I said, 'Yes, we will take them.' So I put a 96 sheet billboard poster outside Sega for the CD32 saying, 'To be this good will takes Sega ages.' It got worldwide applause. I can't believe how many people responded to that. It was phenomenal."

The advertisements showed that, despite Commodore's well-known financial difficulties, the company still had some fight left. "About a week later we had our annual Christmas industry dinner at the Grosvenor Hotel," recalls Pleasance. "Nick Alexander, who was the MD of Sega UK, walks up to us. We had about three tables and he said, 'Mr. Pleasance, it's a bit close to home. A bit close to home.' I just said, 'Look Nick, where needs must, where needs must.' No other words were said but they were obviously fuming and they couldn't do anything about it. It was great."

Sega had pulled itself to the number one spot in Europe through a series of bold television and print ads known for being edgy and offbeat. By the time Pleasance arrived to take over as the shared MD of Commodore UK, the advertising campaign had already been created and signed. "The very last advert they did, I actually inherited it," says Pleasance. "It had already been commissioned before I got back and I inherited the advertisement for the CD32."

The one-minute television commercial was very cinematic in nature. It shows a future laboratory where a scientist unleashes a giant robot brain to playtest the CD32 console. All seems to be going well until the robot is overwhelmed by the games and begins to short circuit, eventually exploding in a shower of smoke and sparks.

Ignoring for a moment the association of the CD32 with faulty hardware, the ad is memorable. "I personally thought it was bloody awful but I couldn't do anything about it," says Pleasance. "It had been commissioned and it had been costed in, and it was virtually finished when I got back."

An ad agency, Laing Henry, had created the ad campaign, as well as worked on the aggressive Crush Sega Campaign. "They were the ones that actually produced the artwork and stuff," says Pleasance. "Another one of theirs was, 'After Sega's new baby, Amiga bring you the mother,' which is quite good as well."

Retail stores selling the CD32 also received a large vacuum-formed wall display of the brain featured in the commercial. The advertising campaign was leagues ahead of anything Commodore US had mustered.

CD32 Released

One thing the Amiga did not lack was magazine coverage. "We had 13 independently published Amiga dedicated magazines—for which we never got a penny's royalties by the way, which is something I would have addressed," says David Pleasance. "They had a monthly audited and guaranteed circulation of six hundred and thirty thousand magazines every month between thirteen of them, and it was estimated that there were 2.2 readers per household. That's 1.2 plus million readers every month. Sony would have killed for that. It was absolutely huge."

Commodore could generally expect favorable coverage from those magazines, but by the end of 1993 there was evidence even dedicated magazines were growing tired of Commodore's antics. In December, *Amiga Power* wrote an article titled, 'Top Six crap things done by Commodore'. Items included bringing out the A500 Plus with software incompatibility, releasing the A600 just as the A500 Plus became the number one Amiga, the CDTV, dropping the price on the A1200 so quickly, and releasing the CD32 without sufficient software.

Despite the odd grumble, reviews were expectedly favorable from *Amiga Computing Magazine*, *Amiga World*, *Amiga Power*, and *Amiga Format*. "All the reviews we got on the CD32, because we were competing with Sega who were doing a

16 bit machine, were great," says Colin Proudfoot. "Everybody loved the machine, and I got magazine articles comparing the competition with us, Philips, and Sega; the CD32 was by far the best machine, the best value at the price point."

Across the Atlantic, the main competitor to the CD32 was the 3DO. There, most people felt the 3DO was superior to the CD32, although it came at a cost. Reviewers also felt the 3DO game library took better advantage of the CD-ROM itself.

Central to the success of any game console is the selection of games available at launch. In this regard, CD32 had both an advantage over other consoles and a hinderance. The advantage was that the A1200 was almost identical to the CD32, meaning there was a steady staple of games and developers ready to work on the CD32. But there was another problem. "When we launched the CD32, we had probably twenty software companies that were writing for us," says David Pleasance. "We had actually given the machines to them and they were sworn to secrecy. But because of the financial circumstances of Commodore International, we were forced to bring the launch of the CD32 forward. Therefore the games weren't actually ready so we had to use ports from the A1200 machine, which obviously weren't really showing the 32-bit machine to its full potential."

The launch lineup of games showed off the AGA chipset adequately. "The games were incredible that they were putting on it," says Carl Sassenrath. "It had a new graphics chip in it so it could do better colors and some of the games were really nice. I think they were right there where they needed to be."

The main problem was that the A1200 games did not make much use of the massive CD-ROM capacity. "The issue we had in the first year of the first Christmas was there weren't any games written for the CD32 available on the market. What we had were ports to the CD32," says Colin Proudfoot. "The games didn't take advantage of the technology that was there. So the games weren't that great but the machine certainly had an awful lot of potential."

Pleasance promised 70 games by end of year. In truth, only 26 games were released for the CD32 in 1993 (plus about 60% of the 110 CDTV titles that were CD32 compatible). Some of the key games being promoted included *MicroCosm*, *Chaos Engine*, *Dangerous Streets*, *Oscar*, *Wing Commander*, and *Diggers*.

Jim Sachs, who had worked on the CD32 title screens, also created a game of his own for the system: *Defender of the Crown II*. "When Cinemaware went bankrupt, I took control of all my graphics, added about 50% more, and replaced the only scene that Rob Landeros had done (Robin Hood)," says Sachs. "I spoke with Gail Wellington about Commodore funding a reboot for CDTV/CD32 and she sent me $10,000 to get started (that's all I ever got)."

The one-man production team finished the game with a record budget. "I changed the object of the game to be money-oriented like the other hit game I worked on, *Ports of Call*," says Sachs. "Then I rewrote every line of code in a language called 'The Director' from The Right Answers Group. I also wrote a symphonic musical score using an Amiga 2500 with a Studio 16 sound board supplied by Anthony Wood's Sunrize Industries. I hired voice actors and translators to record the narration for the game in 5 languages." Sachs planned to launch his game in early 1994.

In total, over the lifetime of the CD32, there were 134 commercial releases. Most of the games were released in 1994 and 1995 before the market trailed off. However, even US developers such as MicroProse, Mindscape, Interplay, Electronic Arts, and Time Warner all made games for it.

Christmas Sales

With Commodore in such a financial mess, the holiday season of 1993 could either make or break the entire company. All eyes were on the performance of Commodore Germany and the UK. Surprisingly, sales of Commodore's low-end A1200 had been slow, with Commodore UK reporting they had only sold 100,000 since the previous year. The computer-in-a-keyboard concept was starting to be seen as hopelessly outdated. As a result, David Pleasance of Commodore UK cut the price by £100 to £299 in an effort to reach a 1993 goal of 250,000 units. He also cut the price on the A600 to £199. Reports at the time say this cut doubled or tripled sales in most cases.

Going into the holiday season, David Pleasance had a UK sales target of selling 200,000 CD32 units by end of the year. The results were a mixed bag. CD32 dominated the early CD-ROM market in the UK, with CD32 games beating PC CD-ROM sales. Commodore UK ended up selling 87,000 units by December 31, 1993.

Over in Commodore Germany, customers purchased 25,000 Amiga CD32 systems—the entire quantity that was allocated to the German market. The subsidiary also managed to sell 95,500 of the Amiga 1200, which was now available in mass quantities. The high-end Amiga 4000 also sold 11,300 in the two available units, the original A4000/040 and a discount A4000/030 version.

Commodore CD32 sold 46,000 in the rest of Europe (particularly in the Scandinavian countries), 12,000 units in North America, and 21,000 in the rest of the world, for a worldwide total of 166,000. This was considered a failure, largely because Commodore would have needed to sell 400,000 units to survive. The main problem was not demand for the CD32, which was strong, but rather a lack of production capacity.

Needless to say, the C64 was not a major contributor to Commodore's bottom line. Even in the UK and Germany, sales of the C64 were slow. There were only 73 commercial titles released for the C64 in 1993.

There were also other indicators that Commodore UK's retailing prowess was not what it used to be. Tottenham Court Road in London had long been known for selling electronics, similar to Akihabara in Tokyo. Normally, a stroll through the electronics stores would reveal only a few stores not selling Amigas. This year, only a few stores sold the CD32.

Would sales of CD32 and A4000, along with the substantial number of A1200s sold in the UK due to the price drop, be enough to sustain Commodore into the next year? If not, Commodore would soon be out of business.

CHAPTER 39

The Last Hurrah 1994

Although Mehdi Ali had made some costly mistakes, it was doubtful Commodore could have maintained the low-end Amiga market if he had executed perfectly. Even with drastic price cuts to the A600 and A1200, the systems were being dominated by cheap PC clones. Recent developments in the PC world seemed a lot more interesting to users than what was happening on other computers, including the Amiga and Macintosh. However, there was a sliver of hope for Commodore in the video game console market. If Commodore could produce a better video game system than its competitors at a better price, the console could possibly come to dominate Europe. But first, Commodore required an entirely new chipset.

Three Revolutions

Although much of Commodore had been gutted by early 1994, its LSI semiconductor design division remained mostly intact. Under Lew Eggebrecht's guidance, the engineers continued to devise a new chipset that would be at the heart of Commodore's future products. There were three important trends that Eggebrecht could not ignore with his technology strategy.

Commodore was on top of the CD-ROM revolution, having already released two dedicated CD-ROM systems and several more CD-ROM products. But CD-ROMs had not received wide acceptance early on.

But in 1993, the CD-ROM drive finally became standard in PCs. The first killer CD apps appeared with visually stunning best-sellers like *Myst* and *7th Guest*. These titles set new standards in software sales and consumers purchased CD-ROM drives just to play them.

To software developers, it was clear that games and software would soon be delivered to computers exclusively on optical discs, which not only held more data than floppies but were also cheaper to manufacture. Any post-1993 computer simply required a CD-ROM drive.

Video compression, then known commercially as Full Motion Video (FMV), was a part of the CD-ROM revolution, and Commodore had the necessary technology to play FMV.

Another obvious revolution in computing was the 3D revolution, and nobody knew where it would go in 1994. Virtual Reality was becoming a common buzzword and Amiga hardware became the center of many VR systems. A company called *Virtuality* created an Amiga 3000-based VR system that appeared in arcades and shopping malls in 1991, along with the game *Dactyl Nightmare*. However, Virtual Reality was ahead of what technology was able to accomplish for the time.

Yet 3D gaming was undergoing a revolution. There had been modest stabs at 3D gaming in the past, including groundbreaking titles such as *Elite* (1984) and the Freescape series of games, starting with *Driller* (1987).

But it was really Id Software's *Wolfenstein 3D* in 1992 followed by *Doom* on December 10, 1993 that brought 3D gaming to the mainstream. Unfortunately, these games skipped the Amiga. Id Software's chief programmer, John Carmack, had no plans to port Doom to the Amiga, saying, "The Amiga is not powerful enough to run Doom. It takes the full speed of a 68040 to play the game properly even if you have a chunky pixel mode in hardware. Having to convert to bit planes would kill it even on the fastest Amiga hardware, not to mention the effect it would have on the majority of the Amiga base."[1]

Doom and other games established the PC as the gaming platform of choice, leaving the Amiga and (mostly) Macintosh behind. "As PCs began to play videogames and as Macs started to play videogames, that took away the 80% of unit sales that was the [Amiga] video game market," says Dave Haynie.

A seminal game released on March 27, 1994 was *Wing Commander III: Heart of the Tiger*. Not only was it on CD, but it used 3D polygon graphics. It was also the most expensive game produced to date, with a $4 million budget. The game was developed by Chris Roberts, a former UK developer and programmer of *Times of Lore* for the C64.

Europe remained strong enough to keep Commodore alive, especially in the UK and Germany. However, Amiga game development began to slow

---

1   *Amiga Report International Online Magazine*, Sept. 14, 1994. "A Letter to ID Software"

down towards the end of 1993. Even Electronic Arts and LucasArts, long time supporters of Commodore computers, ended support for the Amiga. Without games, the low-end Amiga market could not survive.

Recognizing the shifting sands, Lew Eggebrecht wanted the next chipset to make it extremely easy to port existing PC games to the new platform. The third revolution was not as obvious as the first two, but in engineering circles it was seen as the inevitable future of computing.

RISC

Ever since the late eighties, when A500 co-designer Bob Welland was still working for Commodore, the company had been investigating RISC processor technology, often in relation to developing its Unix machines.

RISC (Reduced Instruction Set Computing) is a CPU design philosophy that stands in contrast to the CISC (Complex Instruction Set Computing) philosophy of the Intel x86 and Motorola 68000 series of chipsets. With CISC, semiconductor companies added more and more features to their chips in the form of larger instruction sets. This meant CISC chips required more circuitry, resulting in a larger footprint, thus producing less chips from each silicon wafer. This of course made them more expensive to fabricate.

Commodore's engineers wanted to design computers around RISC. Using RISC chips, the processor could theoretically operate faster with the most common opcodes in an instruction set. It would be up to the programmers to use this reduced instruction set to create more complex instructions, in software. RISC also didn't require as much electricity, resulting in smaller power requirements and cooler operating temperatures.

The other factor pushing the engineers towards RISC was that even Motorola was abandoning the 68000 line of processors in favor of RISC. Motorola released the final chip in the 68000 family, the 68060, in 1994. The 68060 was not well adopted by the industry, due to most manufacturers wanting to move onto RISC—although Commodore engineer Paul Lassa briefly considered using the 68060 in a variation of his A4000T.

Commodore's Ted Lenthe began looking into RISC chips with the AAA chipset back in the summer of 1989, specifically the Motorola 88000. But the engineers always balked at concrete plans due to the incompatibility problems a new processor would cause. For his part, Ed Hepler favored creating his own RISC CPU on the basis that Commodore could produce it much cheaper than buying the 88000 from Motorola.

In late 1990, Hepler began writing a formal design for a new chipset dubbed Hombre, which would use a RISC processor. However, department heads Ted Lenthe and Ned McCook tried their best to keep him focused on AAA.

By 1992, Dave Haynie and Greg Berlin began designing the aforementioned CPU-agnostic Acutiator specification, which allowed for a RISC based processor. Haynie himself considered the Motorola 88110 the most likely RISC chip to adopt.

Eventually Motorola gave up on its 88000 RISC line. "They agreed to abandon that when they made the grand alliance with IBM and Apple to do the PowerPC," recalls Ed Hepler. "I think the only one that really even went forward with that was IBM. They did a little bit with it. Motorola continued on with it, but it became an embedded controller instead of a mainstream processor."

By 1993, Ed Hepler began favoring the PA-RISC chip (Precision Architecture) from Hewlett-Packard, the same company that fabricated many of Amiga's custom chips. "What we were looking for was something that we could integrate right into our design," says Hepler, who had temporarily given up his dream of designing his own CPU. "Obviously we weren't going to build a 68000 chip at that point."

The PA-RISC chip allowed Commodore's semiconductor engineers to implement a graphics chip on the same chip as the PA-RISC CPU core. "You could buy cores from some folks. Most of the time the cores were rectangular in shape," explains Hepler. "If you put the core down on a chip, all you had left was a periphery around the edge where you could put your own logic—an L shaped thing was all that was left because typically chips are made to be rectangular and you want to make them as close to square as possible because they're stronger that way. If you make something that's a long thin rectangle, they'll break sometimes."

The big question from Commodore's customers was whether this architecture could run the existing Amiga software library. On this point, even Commodore was loathe to give a straight answer. "We thought that we could emulate a 68000, if we needed to, very efficiently using a PA-RISC," says Hepler. "It just seemed like a pretty good fit."

Curiously, Lew Eggebrecht favored the MIPS and PowerPC RISC chips because they were likely to run an "industry standard" operating system, such as Unix and the upcoming Windows NT. "A lot of Amiga people don't like to hear this, but we also had some guidelines from our management that said that whatever we picked had to be able to run Windows NT," recalls Hepler. "Obviously for game kinds of systems, people wanted something like an Amiga. But if we were going to get third party software, it was pretty important to have an operating system that you could get things like MS Office—productivity packages as they were called back then."

One of the key reasons management was taking a serious look at Windows NT is because Commodore lacked enough employees to continue to adequately update AmigaOS. Another reason is because Windows NT was a processor-independent operating system, meaning it was not programmed specifically for Intel x86 chips. Although as it turns out, Windows NT was not ported to the PA-RISC chip, it was ported to PowerPC, DEC Alpha, MIPS, and SPARC processors among others—all of them RISC— as well as Intel x86.

Privately, the engineers did not support the plan for Windows NT. As one engineer expressed it, "The Windows NT Amiga thing was never more than a pipe dream of misters Eggebrecht and [David] Pleasance. None of the engineers ever believed it. Nor was it ever even proposed as a real project." Most engineers thought it was included in specs to make any potential sale of Commodore's assets more appealing.

A RISC chip would essentially cause a break with the old Amiga computers. "I think we would have come up with some emulators, but it would not have run natively," says Hepler. "It would not have taken object code for an Amiga that was running 68000 and run it directly on the hardware. There would have been an emulation package."

The engineer's reluctance to commit to full hardware backward compatibility had to do with previous efforts at retaining compatibility in the AAA chipset. "There were a number of reasons for that. In doing AAA we had to be backwards compatible and that came at a pretty high price," explains Hepler. "The folks that did the original Amiga did an amazing job but all of the registers and addresses were 16-bit addresses. Later on, to expand things in the AGA chipset, we added some address extensions. However the registers came in two parts, so you'd write the lower-order 16-bits in one place and the high-order 4-bits someplace else. That made for very unclean software."

Ed Hepler feels the emulator would have been effective at running legacy software. "With the instruction set of the PA-RISC and the addressing modes and things like that, it would have been pretty efficient to run a 68000 emulator on a PA-RISC," says Hepler.

Ed Hepler

Ed Hepler, the engineer who dreamed of designing his own processor, was 42 years old when he officially began work on the Hombre project. Hepler grew up in a small city in rural Pennsylvania with a population of over 25,000—though in the years since the population had significantly dwindled. "I was born in a place called New Kensington, Pennsylvania in 1952. It was a suburb of Pittsburgh," he recalls. "I grew up in New Kensington, then went to college in Drexel, Philadelphia across the state."

At Drexel, Hepler took a remarkably accelerated path towards receiving his PhD. "I did my undergraduate and master's degree in a program they had called the honors program," he explains. "Drexel's normally a five-year undergrad but they had a program where you get a Bachelor of Science and Master of Science in five years. I did that, stayed on and became a PhD candidate."

Hepler, always in a hurry to get to the next big thing, couldn't wait to enter the workforce. "In order to make more money, I decided to go [for my PhD] in absentia," he says. "I got a job with Bell Labs in Naperville, Illinois. That's where they design all their electronic switching systems, including the computers that drive them."

Like many engineers encountered in this book, Bell Labs was his introduction to computer engineering. "I was involved in this small processor laboratory as it was called," he says. "We designed the processors that drove the electronic switching systems. We had gate array technology inside Bell Labs. I started doing that and started seeing the power that could be unleashed when you design your own chips. Amazing things can happen when you control all the gates."

His days designing gate arrays came to an end due to the historic breakup of AT&T. "Later on, right before Bell was broken up, we were designing what we hoped would become commercial machines. It was at that point that I left for GE and returned to the Philadelphia area."

In 1982, Hepler applied to Commodore. "I had actually interviewed with Commodore when it was still being run by Jack Tramiel," he recalls. "They were still looking at using Z8000s and that sort of thing. I didn't get that job for one reason or another."

Hepler then joined what he believed would be a cutting edge technology division. "I went to General Electric Space Systems division [GE Aerospace] in Valley Forge, Pennsylvania," he recalls. "That was a culture shock because I went from a pretty high-powered R&D organization into what I thought was going to be a high-tech environment. And it was high-tech, but GE was making satellites that went into geosynchronous orbits. They didn't want to use anything new because the spacecraft were going to be out in the geosynchronous orbit, which is twenty thousand miles out into space, and you can't send a repair truck out there to fix it. So they only wanted to use technology that had been around for 10 years or so and was well grounded."

The work at GE mainly consisted of boring government contracts that offered very little freedom. "We were responding to RFQ's [Request for Quotations] from the government, not looking forward to more consumer oriented kinds of things," says Hepler. "When you respond to a government request for quotes, you basically have to do exactly what they're asking for and say how you're going to do it versus being a little bit more creative and trying to think how best you would move a product or an idea forward on your own."

Hepler longed for something a little more cutting edge. He also had a severe aversion to flying and wanted a job requiring less travel. "So I started looking around," he says. "One friend in particular I'd known from my days at Drexel was working at Commodore and said, 'Hey give me your resume.' He took my resume in and I took the job."

Commodore was a very different company from the one he had applied for in 1982 under Jack Tramiel. "There was a whole new cast of characters running the place at that point," he says.

Upon seeing that Commodore too had adopted gate array technology, Hepler knew he had found his new home. "It was more like what I'd been doing near the end of my Bell Labs career," he says. "We were building personal computers—effectively game machines. That was a whole lot of fun. It was a lot more easy-going than working at GE, where we were doing government contracts, and much more."

Hepler started in January 1989 and was soon a rising star within the company. By 1994, he was practically the sole person working on Commodore's next generation chipset.

Hombre

Back in October 1993, as the engineers were working out bugs in the AAA chipset, a new chipset was beginning to take shape. "There was a follow-on to AAA called Hombre," says Dave Haynie. The name was in keeping with the Amiga name and meant a particularly tough man in Spanish. Ed Hepler had been talking up his chipset since late 1989.

On October 8, 1993, Hepler was putting the finishing touches on a document called, "Hombre: Beyond Amiga". The five part, 145 page document even contained several appendices detailing each instruction in the complete instruction set.

It is clear from the document that Hepler primarily intended the chipset for a video game console to succeed the CD32, but with better specs than anything on the market. And the chipset would also work for any personal computer, much as the original Amiga chipset could support a wide range of platforms.

Hepler proposed two chips in the Hombre chipset, which would be fabricated at 0.6 microns (versus 5 microns for the original Amiga chipset). "That had its own RISC processor built into the graphics chip, which was the Agnus replacement chip," says Haynie. "There were only two chips in that chipset and that could give you an entire game machine or you could use the graphics processor in a regular computer."

The chipset included "Nathaniel", the PA-RISC CPU core with a blitter, copper, audio, bus controllers, MMU, and cache. And then there was "Nathalie", the video chip. These two chips would rely on fast VRAM, a ROM chip, and an optional peripheral chip to provide UART (serial communications), floppy disk, keyboard, and other computer related functions if they chose to use Hombre in a personal computer.

The proposal was met with enthusiasm by Lew Eggebrecht, and he gave Hepler the go ahead to begin preliminary work on the next chipset. But before real work could begin on the chipset, the engineers needed to finish off the AAA chipset.

January 1994 CES

Commodore had quietly announced the CD32 to the US market at the World of Commodore-Amiga in September 1993. But this was not even close to the type of launch a major game console would require, especially since Commodore had skipped launching it at the two previous CES shows—shows where 3DO, Sega, and Nintendo had a large presence.

When the CD32 launch was delayed in the US due to CADtrack litigation, Geoff Stilley, the new President of Commodore US, decided to host a product launch at the Winter CES in Las Vegas, held January 6 to 9, 1994. Stilley was able to brag about the CD32 outpacing sales of other CD-ROM consoles, such as 3DO, by 3 to 1. This was likely accurate, considering the CD32 sold over 166,000 units in 1993, while the 3DO had reportedly only shipped (not sold) 60,000 units in its first four months, causing *Electronic Gaming Monthly* to award 3DO with Worst Console Launch of 1993.

Although Nintendo's primary console at the time, the Super Nintendo, was outclassed by the CD32, it showed an impressive demonstration of the technology in its next console, which was codenamed Project Reality. This preview sported 3D texture mapped objects moving around with an impressive frame rate, including a 3D city which the user could drive through. Although this console would only emerge more than two years later as the Nintendo 64, it showed Commodore they had work to do if it wanted to remain relevant in the console wars.

The CES event was largely organized by Kieron Sumner, brother of former GM of Commodore UK Kelly Sumner. Commodore hosted a moderately large booth with enough space for 18 display stations. Six of those were reserved for CD32 developers, such as Grandslam Entertainment, Ocean, Mindscape, and others. Jeff Porter showed off the MPEG player for the CD32, which would retail for $250. The remaining stations, manned by Carolyn Schoeppner and her CATS team, showed off A1200, A4000, and other Commodore products. Unfortunately, the booth was not on the main floor but upstairs, far from the other major video game companies.

Geoff Stilley promised Commodore would launch the CD32 in US retail stores in March, 1994. He also debuted 30 and 45 second commercials, adapted from the European commercials produced by Commodore UK featuring the cybernetic brain. One questionable piece of his strategy relied on a $10 to $15 million budget for the US CD32 launch. This was highly doubted by the press, considering Commodore's finances.

Instead, the press was confident that Commodore's lack of marketing would quickly relegate the CD32 to insignificance in the US. "This wasn't the market for them because we didn't have established relationships with dealers and distributors here for any sort of product really," says Dave Haynie. "Commodore had burnt the bridges with the small retailers, and then they basically stopped selling the computers that play in Kmart."

Although Stilley said the launch would be in retail stores, most of Commodore's dealers felt that approach would fail. In fact, dealers wanted to sell the CD32 themselves, something Commodore's John DiLullo, head of marketing, forbid, claiming it would foul his retail marketing plans. Even more troubling, DiLullo reportedly told a dealer from Bloomington, Indiana, "the fanatical Amiga owners are an embarrassment to Commodore."

Although the CD32 was a hit in Europe, not a single dedicated game magazine bothered to mention the CD32. To be fair, Commodore wasn't exactly being generous with its advertising money, giving the magazines very little reason to offer the company free publicity. *GamePro US* contained sections for Sega Genesis, Super NES, 3DO, CD-i, and the Atari Jaguar. There just wasn't room for the CD32, even though it sold the same or better than the Atari Jaguar and 3DO. Even in the UK, gaming magazines such as *Computer and Video Games* and *Edge* failed to mention the CD32 altogether. It was not a good sign.

Massive Losses

Irving Gould, Mehdi Ali, and other top executives generally found out how well Commodore performed for the holiday season in January of the following year. This year they were banking on the CD32 and price cuts to the A600 and A1200 to sell large quantities of product. Because suppliers knew of Commodore's financial position, they would only accept cash up front to supply parts or manufacture computers. This led to production problems and limited how much Commodore could sell in 1993.

By late January, all the receipts were in from the international subsidiaries. The previous holiday season, Commodore had generated $237.7 million in revenue. This holiday season, the company generated $70.1 million. Furthermore, the October-December quarter usually did almost double the revenue of the July-September quarter. However, this time revenue actually fell from $82.6 million in the previous quarter.

Even considering that customers were abandoning the company and moving to other platforms with more potential, the drop seemed unusually precipitous. Engineers blamed Commodore's executives for failing to properly navigate manufacturing difficulties during the financial crisis. "You can't screw up the Christmas quarter," says Jeff Porter. "Mehdi did that two Christmases in a row. Most companies can't survive one Christmas."

Commodore's engineers believed the CD32 was the right product for the holidays, but executives failed to manufacture larger volumes which hampered its success. "You place a lot of money on the line and you hope to hell you have the Tickle Me Elmo," says Porter, referring to the Christmas hit by Tyco Toys in 1996. "You get really good knowing whether what you're building is the Tickle Me Elmo or not. And if you don't know what you are doing in that game then you shouldn't be in that game. That's what happened to Commodore."

With Commodore so reliant on the Holiday season, the company needed seasoned executives who understood the market. "You've got to start early if Christmas is your key quarter," explains Porter. "You need to be thinking the previous Christmas what you're going to do for that next Christmas in order to have enough time to develop it, get it to production, and have it be on the store shelves for the following Christmas. Making a baby takes nine months so if you screw up the timing on the Christmas quarter and you don't have the right products and you try to will it into existence, which basically is impossible, your revenues will take a nosedive."

With such low revenues, losses continued to mount. Expensive failures like CDTV, the Amiga 600, Unix machines, and the PC line had devastated Commodore's financial outlook. It was obvious the company could not continue operations much longer.

AAA Suspended

After the dismal financial results, Lew Eggebrecht reevaluated Commodore's current projects, including AAA. "I think there were a lot of other things involved," says Ed Hepler. "AAA took a lot longer than anyone expected and we wanted to move on and do some other things. I think there were questions on what priority to do various other things. They filled the gap using the AA+ and the question was, do you go and finish AAA or do you move on and do other things?"

Although the AAA chipset was complete and going through testing and revisions, Eggebrecht did not believe the project was vital to the company's long term success. Commodore just didn't have the money to indulge in projects without an immediate benefit to the company, and the A5000 was still a long way off. Furthermore, in the past, Amiga chipsets could be used in both high-end and low-end systems. AAA was the first chipset that, at over $100 to fabricate, would only ever be used in the high-end systems. As Eggebrecht stated, "It was obvious that AAA was not going to meet our cost targets for the mid to low-end systems."

Ed Hepler was somewhat relieved to abandon AAA, despite having worked on it for 5 years. "There were things like the line drawing algorithm," he begins. "When I was doing AAA I had to make sure that the line drawing algorithm worked exactly like it did in the old chips. That presented a number of problems. First of all, I had to follow their algorithm exactly like they did it in order that the same pixels would be lit up when you drew a line. The problem with that was that there were some developers out there that found that if you didn't program the registers the way that they were supposed to be used, you could get some pretty interesting effects. Things like explosions and whatever sometimes used the line drawing algorithm in a way that it was never intended to be used. While I'm sure the people that used those facts really thought that was pretty cool, it made producing a next-generation system extremely difficult when it had to be backwards compatible."

One other factor that Eggebrecht had to juggle was the lack of employees. He needed to begin work on a project for Commodore's low-end, something it historically excelled at. After all the layoffs in 1993, there were too few people to finish off AAA and work on the next generation chipset.

And finally, the graphical specs of AAA were not as good as SVGA by 1994. AAA could output 1280x1024 in 8 or 16 bit color. It could also do 1024x768 with 24 bit color. But by 1994, SVGA could display up to 1600 x 1200 with 24-bit color using the VESA standard. Plus, graphics cards were on the horizon which allowed 3D hardware acceleration. "With the AAA chipset, they were too late on that," says Carl Sassenrath. "They needed to have that kind of extra color and they needed to be committed to making those chips because as soon as they could make them and put them into mass production, the price of the chips would come down. They could make computers with even greater capabilities than the original Amigas. If they had done that there would have been a much greater likelihood they could have survived in the marketplace, and they would have been competitive to every game machine out there. It would have blown them away."

On January 6, 1994, Ed Hepler estimated Hombre could be fabricated at only $22.40 for the entire chipset, plus it would be vastly superior to AAA. "I preferred to see us go on and just do what I had started with the Hombre because it was a leap forward," he says. "I think that, had AAA come out on time, it would have been very good, but they needed to come out sooner if they really wanted high-volume and not just the niche and game market."

By January 26, as the financial results rolled in, Eggebrecht decided to suspend work on AAA indefinitely. "AAA never got to production," says Dave Haynie.

Hedley Davis, who had moved on to 3DO by now, feels Commodore had doomed the Amiga chipset in the late eighties. "We failed to innovate," he says. "We took the design and kind of moved some gates around then did some stuff. But when it came to really doing long-term hardcore development and moving the design forward—in spite of the fact that Haynie and the chip guys got that AA chipset kind of done and got the AAA chipset kind of done—it was too late by then."

Ultimately, the moderately well funded LSI department may have been stretched too thin on too many projects. "I believe that the people responsible for our LSI design just failed to come out of the gate running," says Davis. "They did a lot of cost reduction, we made a lot of projects, we did a bunch of stuff. But at the end of the day when it came down to really moving the product forward, we didn't. The Amiga had a huge head start on everybody else, and we failed to maintain that lead. That's the sad truth of it."

Commodore now lacked the funds for future product development. "I'm an engineer so I'm going to point at management, and management will point back at us," laughs Davis. "I don't know why but we didn't move it forward and that's what ultimately caused things to fold. There's lots of blame to go around on that one! I don't think you can lay it at the feet of any one individual."

Hombre Spec

Ed Hepler's proposal was discussed by the engineers and modified through the later part of 1993 as they tested and refined the AAA chipset. But in January 1994, when AAA was cancelled, Hombre work began at a frantic pace.

Engineers held meetings throughout the early part of the year, and by March 3, 1994 a preliminary spec for the Natalie chip emerged from Ed Helper. The new chip would display at resolutions up to 1280 x 1024. It could also display four different playfields, including HAM, to create layered backgrounds. Natalie would also allow 16-bit and 24-bit true color modes. It was clear, however, that Hombre was not a continuation of the Amiga chipset, even though it supported some ideas from it, such as HAM.

Although Hepler originally estimated a chipset cost of $22.40 in January 1994, he now set a revised target of "less than $40". "That would've been pretty inexpensive for that class of machine," he says.

As with so many things in life, success often begins after a failure. In this case, Hepler had learned a lot during the failed AAA design. Now he believed he knew how to make an unqualified success. "When you're moving forward you like to make things faster and cleaner," he explains. "AAA actually had two line drawing modes. There was a mode where they did things exactly the way they were done before but then it had a newer line drawing mode that went much, much faster, but it didn't have all those backward compatible hooks in it. In AAA we put both of those things in."

Hepler would now drop compatibility in favor of performance. "When we went to Hombre we said, 'Let's make a clean break. Let's define some of these registers so in order to write an address we don't have to write two or three locations where some of the bits are in register one, some of the bits are in register two, and some of the bits are in register three. Let's write the complete address and be done with it.' We attempted to clean up things like that."

These changes would undoubtedly cause incompatibility issues with current Amiga software. When asked about this by *Amiga Format*, David

Pleasance replied, "Lew Eggebrecht, our vice president of engineering, has stated categorically that Commodore are committed to being downward compatible. By this he means that software and so on purchased now will work on all future generations of the Amiga, so long as they are OS legal."

Of course, the big question was whether the engineers had enough time left to complete the project, or were they merely building castles in the sky? For their part, the remaining engineers believed that Commodore would pull through as it had in the past, giving them at least two more years to develop the technology.

Allan Havemose and OpenGL

The person within Commodore who would push the company to begin taking 3D graphics seriously was the head of software development at West Chester, Dr. Allan Havemose. Havemose was similar to other Commodore engineers hired in the late eighties, such as Bryce Nesbitt and Paul Lassa, who grew up with Commodore computers, graduated from computer sciences in university, and then pushed hard to work for Commodore.

Born in Denmark in 1962, Havemose was 27 years old when Commodore hired him—slightly older for a fresh recruit, due to pursuing a Master of Science in Electrical Engineering and a PhD in Communication Theory from the Technical University of Denmark. In fact, he was hired just as he was completing his PhD on August 1, 1989.

Much like Bryce Nesbitt, Havemose developed products for the Amiga and was a registered professional Amiga developer. He developed an Amiga package called CAD-Line, which was distributed by Commodore Denmark; he attended the yearly Amiga Developers Conferences and CeBIT, becoming well known to Commodore employees.

So it would be fairly accurate to call Havemose the European Bryce Nesbitt—albeit with impressive education credentials. As an outside developer, Havemose also had a keen eye for what Commodore needed to do better. And much like Nesbitt, once he was hired, he attempted to instigate change within the company.

Initially, Havemose was hired by Commodore Germany in Frankfurt to perform Amiga technical support with the European version of CATS, called ESCO (European Support & Coordination Office). However, he wasted no time in attempting to influence engineering decisions. He tried several times in 1989 and 1990 to put together a meeting with veteran engineers like George Robbins and Dave Haynie, only to have the latter wonder who this person from Europe was who kept booking them for meetings.

Despite several unsuccessful attempts, Havemose persisted and eventually began a dialog through the intercompany email system to discuss his ideas with engineers in West Chester. Soon he was taken seriously, and by January 1991 Ned McCook and Andy Finkel felt it would be in Commodore's best interests to promote him to software development in order to lead the effort for retargetable graphics. Havemose relocated from Germany to West Chester and began his career as a product engineer.

Havemose soon pushed for a separate group to deal with user interface improvements, noting that AmigaOS's interface had not changed much despite the improved AGA graphics chip. He felt that, to keep up with Windows, AmigaOS needed a specific focus on the user interface.

In the past, Commodore's system engineers had driven chip development. By November 5, 1993, the software developers in the AmigaOS group were finally given a voice. Havemose, now the head of the Commodore Software Group (replacing the recently departed Ned McCook), along with nine other engineers including veteran Eric Cotton, created a document called, "Future Product Options: A Software Perspective". In it, the group pushed for retargetable graphics in AmigaOS 4.0, which would allow the computer to use a variety of graphics cards, much like Windows was capable of using graphics cards from different hardware manufacturers.

The software group also proposed creating a new operating system specifically for the game console, projected for a 1995 release, which they dubbed the CD3D—the successor to the CD32. They called this gaming-centric operating system "RISC/3D OS 1.0".

Havemose also pushed for Commodore to make the AmigaOS compatible with OpenGL, a new industry standard graphics library released by SGI (home to many ex-Commodore employees at the time).

The benefits of OpenGL were overwhelming. Most games were programmed in C or C++, making them highly portable to other computers. By using an industry standard 3D software library, those 3D games would be even easier to port from the PC world.

Hombre included 3D instructions such as hardware-accelerated texture mapping and Gouraud shading. Havemose merely needed to develop OpenGL drivers to support the Hombre chipset. According to Hepler, "It would have been competitive with any of the game consoles currently available [in 1994]."

Lew Eggebrecht supported Hombre's 3D rendering instructions, going as far as learning about OpenGL in technical detail. "I remember a dinner where he explained to me how Hombre 3D rendering works and to me that's a genius," says Colin Proudfoot. "I'm non-technical, and a guy that can explain really complicated technology in real simple terms that even I can understand is amazing."

Together, Dr. Hepler and Dr. Havemose worked on the Hombre's 3D graphics routines. "He was doing the software architecture," recalls Ed Hepler. "He and I worked together to try to determine the best hardware acceleration for the kinds of 3D graphics objects that we wanted to support."

Havemose created an impressive simulation of the texture-mapping algorithm, which wrapped an angelfish picture around a rotating cylinder. "He had done a couple of simulations," says Hepler. "I remember a texture mapping demo where he had taken a photograph and wrapped it around a cylinder. That was all done in software. We wanted to be able to support doing things like that in hardware."

Most 3D graphics are done using millions of triangles to create 3D objects. Havemose used trapezoids—four sided polygons. "There were hardware accelerators to deal with texture mapping and trapezoidal shading," says Hepler. "What you want to do is break all the images down into very small trapezoids and then you shade them properly and that makes things look like they're three-dimensional."

According to Hepler, the unusual trapezoid-focused chip would have been more robust than triangle-based 3D chips. "A triangle is just a trapezoid where the two points at the top are the same point," says Hepler. "That's sort of how we viewed things. If those two angular sidelines happened to meet at the top then you end up with a triangle. If you want a triangle, you can make a triangle."

Hepler would take the basic algorithms created by Allan Havemose and convert those algorithms into his Hombre hardware instruction set. "We look at the algorithms that are being performed and figure out what algorithms are needed," says Hepler. "Then he would make sure those algorithms worked by writing software that implemented those. Then we would make sure that those algorithms could be implemented in hardware as well. Many times you do things very differently in hardware than you would do in software but the result is the same."

The Hombre chipset would have output 3D graphics with far more polygons than other 3D games of the time. "He put together a presentation on how many thousands of trapezoids per second we could do," recalls Hepler. "I remember they were based on our simulations and we were extremely competitive, especially considering that everything was going to be on a chip."

Hombre: The Last Hope

Ed Hepler's Hombre paper mentions at least six products that could be built using the chipset: a CD based game machine, a cable TV set-top box, a dedicated MPEG player, a home computer, a PCI graphics accelerator card (for any computer), and a desktop/tower PC. "A lot of time, money, and effort goes into building a chipset," explains Hepler. "You don't want it to be limited to just one product. It was my aim, when I did the architecture for that, to make sure that it could be used in a standalone sense for a game console or as a peripheral for a larger machine."

Of all these systems, Mehdi Ali and Lew Eggebrecht favored the CD32 replacement, which they referred to as alternately CD3D or CD64. They had a rigid timeline for the new product. "We wanted to have parts in systems for Christmas of 95," says Hepler. "Commodore was very much a seasonal company. Everything was sold for Christmas gifts basically and so that was our target. You work backwards from when you wanted to have things on the shelves."

The schedule also called for Hewlett-Packard to produce the first Hombre chips in late 1994. As development continued, money became a problem for Commodore. In the early eighties, MOS Technology lacked the funding to design a 16-bit successor to the 6502. Now, even a video chip was becoming a difficult burden. "You could see the same thing happening again in the nineties with the graphic chip," says Dave Haynie. "Commodore certainly had the engineering talent, but we didn't have enough people and enough money to apply that talent in a timely fashion."

The release of another game console so soon after debuting the CD32 was also questionable. After all, game consoles have traditionally had life cycles of 5 to 10 years. Introducing a successor so soon after the CD32 release did not give the latter much time to mature before a replacement came along. Plus, why would Commodore management think they had a chance of better success with the CD64 when they had so badly fumbled the CD32 release in the US? The answer would soon become apparent to the engineers at Commodore.

The Fall of Commodore 1994

Good things don't last forever. Commodore's executives knew the company was on a precipice, ready to fall over the edge. What they did not expect was the speed with which its traditional customers would abandon the company in the face of growing competition from the Windows-PC market. Within Commodore's halls, a gallows humor took over the traditional company culture.

Shareholder Meeting

Irving Gould had delayed his shareholder meeting since November 1993, but by early 1994 he could put it off no longer. On March 2, the shareholder meeting once again took place at the exclusive Lyford Cay Club in Nassau, Bahamas.

Both Gould and Mehdi Ali had long been criticized by shareholders for their exorbitant salaries compared to other computer companies. However, for the previous fiscal year, the pair had received no bonus, owing to Commodore's poor performance. This year, the board members voted to reduce Gould's salary to $250,000 and Ali's to $750,000.[1] To outside observers, it seemed like too little too late.

This year, Michael Levin and Marc Rifkin of the Commodore Shareholder Movement (CSM) attended. Also attending was a disgruntled Commodore dealer named Jeffrey Moscow. Their goal, presented to the media in 1993, remained the same: to oust chairman Gould. Would the CSM succeed where others had tried in the past? Most were skeptical, considering they were

---

1   *Philadelphia Inquirer*, May 8, 1994. "The Decline And Fall Of Commodore Intl. It Was A Failure Of Marketing, Not Technology."

playing a game against Gould and his lawyers, all seasoned professionals, on Gould's home turf.

Gould had a mixed record as Commodore's chairman. To outsiders, they saw an incredible company emerge in the late 1970s then suddenly fade from dominance after the departure of Tramiel in 1984. In 1987, they saw Commodore reemerge with the Amiga 500 and again fade away to nothing after Gould dismissed Rattigan. Each time Gould had exerted his control over the company, Commodore faded a little more.

"Irving was a very good chairman but he wasn't a good General," says Kit Spencer. "He and Jack were a good combination together. They complimented one another very well."

Sitting in on board meetings, Thomas Rattigan had seen the real, uncensored Irving Gould. "His favorite expression about people he didn't like was, 'He wanted to live long enough to urinate on the guy's grave.'" As Atari posed the largest threat to Commodore at the time, Gould was likely talking about Jack Tramiel.

After the big advertising push in 1989, Amiga advertising in North America all but stopped. It was even difficult to find print ads in Commodore magazines. In 1990, not even a single Amiga advertisement appeared in the official *Commodore Magazine*.[2]

While he did not use computers himself, Gould should have been well aware of his target market. Between 1988 and 1991, his son Jason Gould ran a bulletin board system from his home in Toronto, called the Star Trek BBS. Jason, who briefly worked for Commodore Canada in 1992, was representative of the typical Amiga 500 user.[3]

Dave Haynie believes Irving Gould's key weakness was a lack of patience with his executives. "He would hire someone, expect a miracle, then fire them long before any chance of such a miracle working could have happened," he says. "Problems take time to solve and Uncle Irv apparently didn't understand this. They had some potentially good guys in the power seats at Commodore International and Commodore Business Machines, but they didn't get their chance to prove it."

As of late, Gould had been remarkably patient with Mehdi Ali, despite the chaos he had brought to Commodore. At the shareholder meeting, Jeffrey Moscow appealed to Alexander Haig to help remove Irving Gould from his post. Haig had famously convinced Richard Nixon to resign as president of the

---

2   *Commodore Magazine* had merged with *RUN* magazine by 1990.

3   Jason Gould was an illegitimate son and did not live with Gould's wife in The Bahamas.

United States, and now Moscow dramatically pleaded with Haig to convince Gould to do the same.

The Commodore Shareholder Group also urged the board of directors to pursue the emerging interactive television market, something Jeff Porter had already been exploring on behalf of Commodore.

Rifkin, head of the CSG, felt the confrontation had been a success, noting, "We don't think our warning fell on deaf ears; we now have an open line to Irving Gould, and he seems willing to listen. That is the critical first step." As events would soon demonstrate, it was more like the final step.

CeBIT

At the weeklong CeBIT show in Hannover, starting March 16, 1994, it was business as usual for Commodore Germany despite the financial problems of its parent company. Commodore unveiled the A4000T, designed by former C65 system engineer Paul Lassa.

They also debuted some questionable products. In a desperate attempt to generate revenue, Commodore Germany had licensed out the Commodore name to third-party companies which produced a multitude of products including telephones, fax machines, paper shredders, and typewriters.

GM Alwin Stumpf reported that for the 1992/1993 calendar year, Commodore had generated £407 million in revenue, of which £187 million came from Germany. This proved, he stated, that Germany was the most important market for Commodore. In the past year, Commodore Germany had sold 15,000 A4000s, 115,000 A1200s, and a somewhat disappointing 25,000 CD32s.

Since moving all of Commodore's production to the Philippines and closing down the Braunschweig factory, Commodore Germany's payroll had shrunk from over 500 employees to around 50. Stumpf also announced the upcoming discontinuation of the C64, which had been in production since 1982. He stated the reason was due to the 1541 disk drive being too expensive to produce.

Stumpf was unusually candid about past company missteps. Regarding Commodore's efforts from 1983 until 1992 to produce a Unix based machine, he said, "Unix has cost this company dearly and we are, for now, cured from this virus."

And perhaps the biggest revelation came regarding Commodore's PC clone business. For the first time ever, Commodore publicly admitted that its PC business had not generated a profit as of late. It appeared the PC sales had been used to pump up Commodore's revenue figure. Stumpf said the recent losses were mainly from the PC division and lamented the fact that the Amiga had carried the PC division for too long.

Commodore Germany also unveiled the CD-ROM for the A1200, unofficially dubbed the CD1200. The externally connected device resembled the CD32 case almost exactly, down to the top-loading mechanism, although it was white in color to match the A1200.

Since its inception, the CD1200 had become a controversial product within Commodore, mainly because it could not be used with Jeff Porter's MPEG decoder. Commodore UK's David Pleasance was especially vocal about his opposition to the product, publicly saying, "I do not think it makes any sense to launch a CD drive which does not support Full Motion Video."[4]

At the European Computer Trade Show in the UK, held April 10, Pleasance virtually ignored the CD1200, displaying it in the corner of the room all alone on a table, unloved. However, he did promise—out of duty more than anything—a September 1994 release date.

CD32 US Launch

President of Commodore US Geoff Stilley planned a fairly modest launch for the CD32 with a $10 to $15 million advertising budget (compared to Sega and Sony, which launched with $50 million advertising budgets). Stilley's sales target for the US market was 300,000 to 500,000 CD32s by the end of 1994. He and his head of marketing, John DiLullo, would launch the machine in late March 1994 at a price of $399, though he hoped to drive the price down to $299 within a few months as game royalties started flowing in.

In order to allow the CD32 to pass customs, Commodore reinstated regular payments to CADtrak and requested to have the injunction against imports lifted. But after the financial results for the latest quarter, Mehdi Ali had no choice but to deny Stilley his advertising budget for the CD32. As a result, Stilley quit Commodore in the first week of February. Now there was no one left to launch the machine on US soil.

By April, advertisements for the CD32 began appearing in US game magazines such as *EGM* (Electronic Gaming Monthly), *GamePro*, and *Electronic Entertainment*. The ads read, "The game machine that took Europe by storm, now available in the US." The only problem was the machine was not available in stores. It could, however, be ordered by dialing an 800 phone number.

Jim Sachs, who had invested both his heart and his money into *Defender of the Crown II*, was just about to release it for the CD32. "It's a shame almost no one ever got to play the game, as I was rather proud of it," he says.

And such was the launch of the CD32 in the United States. The CD32 was fated to be the last consumer product released by Commodore. In the end,

---

4   *Amiga Format*, Mar. 1994, p. 177. "The Man at the Top"

the *Sony PlayStation*, released in the US in September 1995, succeeded where Commodore hoped to dominate.

Many engineers and managers felt the CD32 could have made a greater impact on the fifth generation of video game consoles. "It's too bad," says Carl Sassenrath. "A little bit more of a startup vision and they would have realized what they had in CD32 was really going to hit big if they just stuck with it."

Set-Top Boxes

Although Commodore did not have the funds to develop a new product, much less manufacture and market one, the company could still license out its technology to other companies. This of course would give Commodore some much needed cash flow.

Due to his work with modems, MPEG, and CDTV, Jeff Porter was in a unique position to recognize the potential for a low-cost device whose sole purpose was to receive and display digital content on a television. The device came to be known as a set top cable box.

At the same time, several ex-Commodore employees, including programmers Mike Sinz and Peter Cherna, were working for a Norwegian company named Scala, which had recently opened offices in Malvern, Pennsylvania. Scala had a few Amiga software products, similar to Microsoft PowerPoint, which displayed multimedia presentations on televisions—often in hotel rooms and lobbies.

Scala began talking with Porter in late 1993, and soon Porter proposed a set-top box that would run on Amiga hardware using Scala's software. "I was pushing to have the Amiga chipset built into cable and satellite TV set-top boxes as the next big thing," he recalls. "I grabbed the Scala founder, Jon Bøhmer, and we went on a tour of STB (set-top box) companies."

Porter, loyal to Commodore right to the end, saw an opportunity to rescue his ailing company. His plan was to jointly develop a set-top box product with Scala and sell it to a larger company with the funds to market it properly. "We started with Zenith in Chicago," he recalls. "I told Jon, 'If we screw this up, it won't matter since they only have 10% market share.' Then we headed for Scientific Atlanta. They had 30% market share. Finally, we ended up with General Instrument, with a 60% market share."

Porter's pitch won over GI, but success was denied to Commodore. "Scala got a seven figure contract out of the deal to port their stuff to the GI platform, but Commodore got left at the altar since GI already had their own hardware," says Porter. "In spite of the fact that the Amiga hardware was the key to getting third party software support for future apps. It was a 'not invented here' problem."

Although Commodore's deal with GI did not happen, engineers and Commodore watchers were sure something good could come out of the Amiga hardware when applied to digital entertainment and television.

Presentations

Irving Gould had always felt like the belle of the ball in past years, with companies and private consortiums making offers to purchase Commodore. But there was always the implication that Commodore needed real leadership and management, a slight dig at Gould. And he had always turned them down. Now on the precipice of destruction, Gould was desperate to sell.

Throughout 1994, Lew Eggebrecht, Ed Hepler, and Allan Havemose began giving presentations to dozens of companies, hoping to garner a sale. "I think everybody saw the writing on the wall," says Hepler. "A lot of people had either left on their own, or there had been a big layoff and people had gone away."

Of those, Hewlett-Packard, Samsung, and Philips expressed strong interest in making a deal. Hewlett-Packard was in the process of developing a new product and needed a video chip. "We had some meetings with some of their folks," recalls Hepler. "HP had been considering using the Amiga chips in their set-top box. They were looking at possibly entering the set-top box arena and one of the things that they were considering was using the Amiga chipset as the foundation for the set-top box itself. In fact, they had shown an HP set-top box at a video show. They had a set-top box there that effectively had HP on the front, and coming out of the back of it was a cable that went to a box behind the curtain that was really an Amiga for the prototype."

HP's set-top box was full-featured for the time, making use of genlock. "The thing I liked about it was the fact that they could connect a cable modem to it and pump video through, but then all of the TV Guide kind of stuff they could do on an Amiga and put the graphics on top," says Hepler. "There was also some thought of being able to play games on it, using the cable to distribute games or play interactively. There were lots of interesting ideas."

Due to Commodore's existing relationship with Hewlett-Packard to fabricate Amiga chips, things became serious. "One of the thoughts was, 'Gee, they have this processor. We are working with them anyway. The PA-RISC architecture is a very nice architecture.'" Although there was interest, nothing ever came of the HP-Commodore alliance.

One of the last presentations the trio gave was to Philips, Commodore's competitor for the CDTV market. On April 15, 1994, Eggebrecht, Hepler and Havemose all attended a 9:00 AM meeting with Philips executives. They hoped to interest the company in the CD64, something they might be hungry for after the expensive CD-i had failed to make significant inroads into homes. The meeting lasted until 3:00 PM that day, but as with HP, nothing concrete came of it.

As it turned out, Commodore was running out of time. "We ran out of cash and ran out of runway," says Colin Proudfoot. Gould needed someone to take over the whole company, just as Jack Tramiel had taken over a bleeding Atari from Warner, in order to fend off the creditors. The computer world was about to lose the most colorful company in the business.

The End is Near

On March 25, Commodore released a written statement of its financial situation saying there was, "no assurance that the company can attract additional financial resources and complete a successful restructuring. In the absence of additional resources and a restructuring, the company may become subject to reorganization or other liquidation proceedings."[5]

Those final words would undoubtedly send a shock through Commodore's shareholders. The bleak statement continued, "The company's inadequate financial resources continue to restrict its supply of products which will significantly reduce sales during the quarter ending March 31. The company is attempting to negotiate a restructuring plan with its creditors, including suppliers who have restricted the company's credit and instituted legal action against the company, and lenders who have indicated that they may accelerate their loans to the company."

Unfortunately, none of Commodore's creditors were willing to extend more credit to the company. "They had to go back to the banks and the banks refused to extend their loans because they had no new products in the pipeline, they had no products in the inventory, they weren't manufacturing new products," says Guy Wright. "Why would they bother to loan more money to this sinking ship?"

With debt in excess of $116.5 million (most of it to random suppliers, including some $350,000 to Marriott Hotels who had hosted the previous Amiga Developer Conference) it was clear Prudential Insurance, the primary lender of $33 million, had run out of patience and now wanted liquidation proceedings to begin before the company lost even more money. Commodore's share price, which had been at $3 at the time of the announcement,

---

5   *Philadelphia Inquirer*, Mar. 26, 1994. "Computer Company's Decline Continues Commodore Lost $8.2 Million In Its Second Quarter. This Follows A $77.2 Million Loss Last Year"

collapsed to $0.35 by early April before rebounding to around $1.00 by April 15 on rumors of an impending buyout.

Hopes for a buyout faded when it became obvious Commodore was no longer an attractive acquisition. Debts were too large and the technology was not as cutting edge as it had been. In 1994, the same year one of the last commercial titles for the C64 appeared, *Lemmings*, Commodore walked over a cliff. Employees saw there would be no miracle.

Throughout April, work was at a standstill. Approximately 80 people remained in the huge West Chester building. The massive, now quiet spaces seemed to mock the remaining employees. It was eerie to walk through the once bustling corridors.

On Friday, April 22, Commodore quietly laid off 47 employees—about half from West Chester and half from the Commodore Semiconductor Group in Norristown. Each employee received an exit interview in the near empty cafeteria by the personnel director. The interviews were more out of tradition than necessity. When asked what they disliked most about Commodore, employees invariably mentioned Mehdi Ali.

The things that bothered most of the former Commodore engineers was that, while they suffered, Ali had profited greatly. "I'm sure Mehdi Ali, if you asked him, was like, 'Okay, they gave me a $1,000,000 signing bonus, I get a million dollars a year, three years later I sell 10 million shares of stock and get fifteen million more dollars. So I've just made 24 million dollars in the course of three years. That's a pretty good deal. I may have put 1000 people out of work and bankrupt a perfectly viable company," laughs Guy Wright.

On Wednesday, April 27, 1994, Dave Haynie drove to the West Chester facility as usual. Today, there were only about 30 people remaining in the whole building. It was surreal. As he drove up, he noticed the US flag on the front lawn flying at half-mast.

Eggebrecht laid off even more engineers the same day. At noon, 50 employees and former employees headed to Margarita's Evergreen Inn for the customary layoff-lunch. Margarita's was almost an extension of Commodore by this time. Back in 1983, it had been a run-down biker bar. After ten years of constant patronage by Commodore employees for lunches, parties, retirements, and layoffs it had prospered.

Though it was a somber occasion, the mood was one of giddy defeat with plenty of gallows humor. When engineer Dave Haynie came around with his video camera, employees let out their pent-up feelings. Haynie pointed the camera at Jeff Frank, who summed it up saying, "We're fucked!" Employees singled out Mehdi Ali as the cause of Commodore's early demise. The lunch extended until well into late evening.

A few days later, Irving Gould called it quits. "To the bitter end, it was Irving's company. He was truly in charge," says RJ Mical. On Friday, April 29, 1994, Commodore International Limited filed for liquidation in the Bahamas Supreme Court. Within hours, the company released its remaining employees and locked the doors.

Word reached Commodore's US headquarters before the day was out. Suddenly, managers began racing up and down the halls trying to tie up loose ends before the creditors vacated them. Others in management hurried to the bank to secure cash for the employees before Commodore's accounts were frozen. The remaining employees would at least get their last week's pay—in cash.

Meanwhile, Commodore's Philippines factory had manufactured products with no one to pay for them. In response, the government seized thousands of unshipped CD32 units and A4000s as payment for the use of its factory.

On April 30, 1994, the *Philadelphia Inquirer* broke the story that would have seemed unthinkable ten years earlier. The headline proclaimed, 'Commodore Goes Out of Business'. Under Mehdi Ali's leadership, the company had lost $374 million in the past 18 months alone.

What Happened?

The announcement caught RJ Mical by surprise. "I guess they just couldn't get it together enough to get Amiga sales up high enough to cover the cash flow of the corporation," he speculates. "I didn't think they would go all the way down the way they did. I was shocked they went completely belly up like that."

C128 designer Bil Herd was not shocked. "It took them eight years to die. I recognize that what had been driven under Jack Tramiel got a little worse without Jack," he says. "Commodore was in search of a CEO, but none of them understood the marketplace. The failure of Commodore was not a surprise to any single one of us who worked there."

Although most engineers saw the end coming, most had a hard time pinning down exactly what went wrong. Or asked another way, what could Commodore have done to survive? By the time Windows 3.1 and *Doom* were out, and with Windows 95 on the horizon, the answer seems to be nothing. Atari, Commodore, and Apple all faced the same challenges. (Only Apple was saved by Steve Jobs' return in 1996, along with a $150 million investment by Bill Gates.)

Another question is whether proprietary hardware could survive beside the open hardware of IBM clones. (The answer seems to be yes, given Apple's long term success with the Macintosh). But could a proprietary hardware platform dominate?

Software engineer Neil Harris believes it was inevitable that an open-architecture system like the IBM PC would dominate. "Looking back on it, there were some core philosophical issues with Commodore that made it more challenging for Commodore to succeed as the market got bigger. The closed system model was not the right model for the industry as it expanded. Those lessons could have been learned."

Harris also believes the biggest mistake was firing Jack Tramiel. "There just wasn't a way to keep the ship moving forward. I don't think you can blame Jack for that, the way a lot of the Amiga people might. But it wasn't the engineers' fault, it wasn't Jack's fault, I think it was the fault of the business managers that were brought in after Jack. Frankly, it was a hell of a tough act to follow. Look at what happened when Steve Jobs left Apple for many years. It was all the same company except for the one guy, and it really lost its way until he came back. And Jack never came back. It was unfortunate."

One of the longest serving employees of Commodore, Eric Cotton, believes Commodore had a window to dominate, if they had done things properly. "Another thing that people miss out on is the Amiga was all well and good but I think even at that time [in 1985] Commodore's downward spiral had already begun," he says. "We put on a good face but every six months it seemed like they were having layoffs. Every now and then people talk about the Amiga this and the Amiga that but quite frankly it was the C64 that made Commodore. And when Commodore didn't really have a good response to the C64, I think that's when things took a nosedive."

Along the same lines, Bill Mensch, the 6502 codesigner, focuses on the microprocessor. He believes the company needed a 16-bit C64 sequel rather than the C128. "The spectacular rise of Commodore probably had more to do with market timing with a good processor," he says. "The spectacular fall had more to do with bad attitudes and even poorer decision making. Not using and working with me on the '816 and '832 probably doomed Commodore as much as anything."

But could the Amiga have survived as a niche platform, much as the Macintosh did? "I always think back on it. Could Commodore be here today where Apple is now if things had been different?" asks Cotton. "The Amiga really was an extraordinary machine in its time, but it was totally mismanaged. They didn't really understand what they had and basically torpedoed the company."

"Whatever it was that they tried to do, it just didn't work," says RJ Mical. "I don't believe it was because of the technology."

Dave Haynie clearly believes the premature failure of Commodore was a result of poor management decisions. "You have to actually have a business that's viable, and when you don't understand the business it's hard to run it the right way," he says. "You had some of the hardest working people and some of the smartest people in the industry, but that doesn't get you 100% of the way there alone."

The US operation's failure was perhaps the largest factor, along with taking too long to update Amiga technology. "If they could have sold a lot more in the United States, they might have made it," says Haynie. "It really turned out to be the low-end machines sold in Europe and the high-end machines sold here for video purposes, but that wasn't going to last forever if we didn't advance the technology."

Bryce Nesbitt feels Commodore went wrong when they started chasing the business market rather than playing to their strengths in low-cost, high value retail computers. "Commodore was never comfortable with what it was," he says.

C65 designer Bill Gardei agrees. "Irving Gould did not like the idea that Commodore was seen as a toy manufacturer," he says. "They didn't listen to customers. The fact is, the majority of PCs are used for entertainment. If corporations could remember that they are in business to make money, maybe they would be less focused on their public image, and Commodore, like Nintendo, would still be around."

In opposition to this theory, Dale Luck thinks Commodore could have achieved lasting success with high-end Amiga computers. "I think they should have left a lot of the development in California and continued to work towards the high-end," he says. "And go as quickly as possible to device independent graphics to ensure longevity for the hardware. Better commercials. I knew some of the guys who were involved in making the commercials. They spent a lot of money making the commercials. The Pointer Sisters, B. B. King. They were trying to go into creative markets like music and stuff like that. I think Commodore ran into the whole issue with economic tough times as well. It could have turned out so much different."

GEOS developer Brian Dougherty believes Commodore failed to work with software developers properly, especially early on before CATS hit its stride. "The Amiga never had the right OS software and developer support behind it. They never really quite got behind the Amiga in the right way, and the Amiga never became the volume success that the Commodore 64 was."

Andy Finkel sees success as well as failures as part of Commodore's legacy. "Commodore did a lot of good things but also squandered a lot of opportunities. I wish things had been a little different and there'd be Amigas everywhere instead of PCs. But it was a pretty impressive thing for what's basically a small operation since Commodore was always very lean."

VIC-20 product manager Michael Tomczyk, who later worked 18 years for the Wharton School of business, puts most of the blame for Commodore's failure on CEO Irving Gould. "The minute Jack left, that strategy died because we lost the momentum and the impetus from the top. Innovation requires commitment and impetus from the CEO level. The minute you lose that, you lose the innovation culture. That's what happened to Commodore. We were selling IBM clones in Europe. We were trying to look more like Apples and IBMs than the Commodores. We were trying to make the Amiga into something it was not. It was a nice graphics machine and a media machine. It could have gone places there, but we didn't exploit that properly, so basically we lost all of that."

A Party at Randell's

Coincidental with the liquidation of Commodore was the wedding of two former Commodore employees, Michael Sinz and Theresa Zurbach on April 29th. As a result, a large group of ex-Commodore employees gathered in Pennsylvania on the weekend of Commodore's demise. "Mike Sinz got married and it was at Randell Jesup's house," recalls Bryce Nesbitt. "I was staying at Randell's house as a houseguest and his party came. And then news of the bankruptcy started to go around and the party just started to swell."

On Friday evening, Jesup held a party he named the "deathbed vigil" as everyone felt as though they were at the bedside of a dying patient, the company they once worked for. About 50 former employees attended. "We came up with this idea that the party was now the deathbed vigil," says Nesbitt. "We decided to make a commemorative t-shirt. Dave Haynie had his video camera out and he was doing on-camera interviews with people.[6] None of that was planned. It was just magical."

The purpose of the party/wake was to remember Commodore. Flowers arrived from Amiga engineers Dale Luck and RJ Mical, who were now at 3DO. Technician Mike Rivers added to the funereal mood by providing peaceful background music with his harp. Like any wake, there was plenty of drinking.

Once the sun dipped below the horizon, the engineers vented their frustrations on a pile of PC keyboards. They swung the keyboards by their cables, pounded them with hammers, and one particularly frustrated engineer resorted to head butting a keyboard. Finally, an engineer backed his car over the whole pile.

Engineer Mike Colligan produced a small effigy with a name-tag on it. At first glance, it looked like the name-tag read 'I.B.M.' in commemoration of the company that drove all others into the ground. A second look revealed that it read L.B.M.—Little Brown Man.

Mike Rivers switched over from the harp to electric guitar and played the Star Spangled Banner while Colligan set the effigy alight. As the little figure

---

6   Haynie compiled his footage of the last days of Commodore and released a DVD called *The Deathbed Vigil*. Appropriately, he edited the material and added effects using his one-of-a-kind Amiga 3000 Plus.

burned, CATS manager Gail Wellington commented, "This is about the only warmth we ever got out of the man." With five years of pent-up frustrations purged, the former employees got on with the task of celebrating Commodore.

Mike Rivers performed an improvised song he called 'Chicken Lips Blues', along with Keith Gabryelski on harmonica. The rambling, nonsensical song went as follows:

I got the Chicken Lips Blues, I got a computer I can no longer use.
I got the Chicken Lips Blues, I got a computer I can no longer use.
(Except for those of you who already know how to do something with it.)
Well, in the last days of Commodore, with their creditors roaming the halls.
And in the last days of Commodore, they got creditors roaming the halls.
They got accountants all over Commodore, and the taxmen and the creditors roaming the halls.
(I'm ad-libbing here folks, thank-you.)
And help me Jesus, there's a rock lobster I got me attached to the walls. No, attached to my balls.
Well, where the heck am I gonna go? I guess I'll go call 3DO.
Where the heck am I gonna go? I guess I'll go call 3DO.
But you know, I just don't know how they're going to pay their CEO.
Well, a billion to nothing in just about three. That's a strange kind of genius, that Mehdi Ali.
I said they got the Chicken Lips Blues, I got that computer that's got no use.
(Except for those of you who know how to use it.)
Well, what do I do when my 8520s blow?
Well, what do I do now, now that my 8520s are blown?
Well, oh God, I got to buy a PC! Oh, no.

Afterwards, employees gathered around the fire, telling their favorite Commodore stories. They recalled the speed bump saga, a Lemmings skit put on by the CATS team, and the trials of property passes. For those who had been with the company, it was magic to hear the firsthand stories that had only been rumors.

It was hard for the former employees to leave Randell's party that night. Many, such as Dave Haynie, joined Commodore as teenagers and learned their most important lessons while working there. Commodore was the only life they knew. Sometime in the early morning, the former employees began dispersing one by one. A few remaining engineers found it too hard to leave and wanted one last adventure. They decided to go back to Commodore headquarters.

Bryce Nesbitt, Keith Gabryelski, and Dave Haynie arrived in the Commodore parking lot in darkness. The creditors had already locked and chained the doors to the West Chester facility to prevent ex-employees from walking away with company property.

The trio pulled out a few cans of spray paint and masking tape. Carefully, they masked out the names of infamous managers from Commodore's past. Appropriately, they spray painted their names onto speed bumps. Among the names were Mehdi, McCook, Toy, Sydnes, Archie (director of US sales Dave

Archambault), and Irving. Mehdi appeared on the largest speed bump. Not satisfied, they spray painted his name on a second one.

Their work done, the three stood in silence before the building that had been their home for so many years. The building that was once Commodore stood vacant. It seemed like it deserved a better fate. Eventually, the three went home. It was over.[7]

---

7   The bankrupcy proceedings and sale of Commodore's assets are detailed in David
    Pleasance's 2018 memoir, *Commodore The Inside Story: The Untold Tale of a Computer
    Giant.* ISBN 9781782817819

Special Thanks

The Group of 128

Kevan Harriman
Stephan Ricken
Marcin Kozinski
Daniel Mackey
Petter Nilsen
Johan Larsson
Yves Grethen
Arild Kvalbein
Jan Borsodi
Kai Engelbrecht
Peter Bourauel
Darren Webber
Lee Huggett
Graham Thomson
Per Zetterlund
Andre Bergei
Chand Svare Ghei
Steven Croucher
Steven Saunders
Dirk Vael
Simon Hardy
Héctor Juan López
Filippo Santellocco
Tim Jenness
Trevor Dickinson
Eero Rantanen
Sebastian Gavilán Gurvitsch
Dennis Trace
Gianluca Clos
Jeroen Knoester
Chris Van Graas
Alexander Kaasjager
Eric Slight
Seppo Seppälä
Andrew Fisher
Will Green
Dennis Woodruff
Keith Monahan
Richard Ohnemus
Wayne Booker
Wei-ju Wu
Paul Gasselstorfer
Andreas Johansson

Jean-Francois Reynes
Steven Solie
Justin Cooney
Todd Vierling
Jeremy Hoel
Andreas Falkenhahn
Kenneth Rath
Kevin Rutten
Richard Horne
Jon Rushton
Sarmad Gilani
Greg Soravilla
Tony D'Addario
Gene Johannsen
Gary Wolfe
Severin Stefan Kittl
Randell Jesup
Rob Clarke
Hugo van der Aa
Stefan Holmes
Ryan Barry
Henrik Ripa
Balazs Szaszak
Armas Rautio
Kevin Wong
Steven Innell
Paul Newport
Gary Akins
Marc Rifkin
Ian Fordham
Randy Epstein
Carl Scarlett
Kevin McKinnon
Detlef Koehlers
Chris Luke
Panagiotis Athanasiou
Knut Kraushaar
Tero Mäyränen
Andrew Chilton
Tuomo Notkola
Joergen Schumacher
Derek Chandler
Tapio Koivuniemi

Manuel Haj-Saleh Ramirez
Ernst Gunnar Gran
Jan Dwornizky
Roberto Pacioni
Lasse Lambrecht
David Thomas
Andrea Gini
Sigurbjörn Lárusson
Roy Eltham
Tomas Kristiansen
Ronny Wagener
Giacomo Amoroso
Dallas Hodgson
Sami Karhulahti
Demetrios Kouzios
Terrence Crossley
Claudio Rodrigues
Jarkko Kytölä
Kay Bensberg
Mark Burton
Richard Beno
Simon Stokes
Ferdy Hanssen
Robert Mattin
Jarkko Lehtola
Mauro Tarantino
Christopher Chapman
Ed Finkler
Christian Liendo
Sebastian Stuetz
Mark Scholmann
Leif Oppermann
Daniele Balestrieri
Simo Koivukoski
Jonathan Schmidt
John Gruver
Anthony Becker
Steven Toth
Peter Tilcock
Thilo-Walther Finger
Carsten Bärmann

Defender of Commodore - Jan Hering

The Commodore Series

Index

516